D1605322

LEARNING SALES LAW

Carol L. Chomsky

Professor of Law
University of Minnesota School of Law

Christina L. Kunz

Professor Emerita
Mitchell Hamline School of Law

Jennifer S. Martin

Professor of Law
St. Thomas University School of Law (Florida)

Elizabeth R. Schiltz

Professor of Law
University of St. Thomas School of Law (Minnesota)

LEARNING SERIES

WEST
ACADEMIC
PUBLISHING

© 2016 LEG, Inc. d/b/a West Academic
    444 Cedar Street, Suite 700
    St. Paul, MN 55101
    1-877-888-1330

West, West Academic Publishing, and West Academic are trademarks of West Publishing Corporation, used under license.

Printed in the United States of America

ISBN: 978-1-63459-681-7

Preface to Students

The Uniform Commercial Code (UCC) is one of the classic codes in American law. This book's primary subject is Article 2 of the UCC, a pivotal portion of the Code that provides many of the rules of law governing sales of goods. You will be introduced, as well, to other portions of the UCC that interact with Article 2 and to several significant sources of commercial law that provide additional context for problem-solving related to sales of goods.

To teach this body of law governed primarily by statute, the book focuses your attention on close textual analysis of Article 2, while supplementing your understanding of the text with a wealth of information about how the courts have understood and applied it. You will learn how the Code works by first parsing the statutory language and exploring its interpretation, guided by questions designed to help you read the text effectively. After helping you make sense of the statutory words in a section or sections of the Code, the book presents examples of court application of those sections, drawn primarily from recent cases, so you can see the statute in action. Finally, you will be able to assess your understanding of the statute using the problems at the end of each assignment, also often based on recent cases. Because the statute itself is the source of authority, judicial opinions, the bulk of most casebooks, are included only when a court's explanation of its reasoning is important or particularly helpful to your understanding of a piece of the Code. The book thus focuses on two essential skills for any attorney: reading statutory text critically and determining how to apply it to facts. Although you may already have had some experience reading and applying statutes, this book will help you strengthen and extend those skills and knit them together into a comprehensive ability to use code-based rules to solve complex problems. As you learn the specifics of Article 2, you will also learn how to approach and master any statute.

We hope you enjoy this hands-on approach to learning and applying the Code, developed based on our insights from years of teaching. We have worked hard to craft a book that enables you to master this subject and its skills, so that you truly can "own the Code."

> Carol L. Chomsky, Christina L. Kunz,
> Jennifer S. Martin, Elizabeth R. Schiltz
>
> June 2016

Acknowledgments

We appreciate the assistance that our respective law schools have given this project. Special thanks to Deans David Wippman, Alfredo Garcia, and Robert Vischer, for providing the space, time, and support we needed to complete the lengthy process of creating a textbook of such breadth.

We relied on the excellent research assistance of Jessica Cutrone, Janelle Vega, Joshua Harrison, and Damini Sharma in tracking down lines of cases and checking the finer points of sales law.

This book represents a truly collaborative effort, as we wrote, discussed, edited, taught, and rewrote the materials. We early adopted the practice of meeting weekly by video conference to share our thoughts and our experiences in teaching the evolving material. The book is much richer from the sometimes obsessive attention we all lavished on the project and from the tolerance we each had for what may have occasionally seemed like unending instances of "one more edit I think we should make."

We thank our families and friends, who suffered through our devotion of many hours to the project and learned to live with our unexplainable enthusiasm about Article 2. And finally we thank our students, who confirmed the value of our approach by heartily embracing the materials and by learning the Code well enough to challenge our own understandings.

We acknowledge the late Robert Hudec, professor from the University of Minnesota Law School, whose insightful student handout on the parol evidence rule was the source on which Example F in Assignment 8 was based.

Our thanks to West Academic Publishing, which created the "Learning Series" and invited us to contribute to this innovative approach to course materials. This is an almost entirely new book, but it grows out of a previous book on Article 2 (Chomsky & Kunz, *Sale of Goods: Reading and Applying the Code* (2d ed. West Academic Publishing 2004)), which began our exploration of active learning of Article 2. The new series has allowed the four of us to expand the active-learning techniques pioneered by two of us in the earlier book and create an even more effective platform for student learning. Our special thanks to Pamela Siege, Louis Higgins, and Staci Herr, who believed in the project, and to Carol Logie and Greg Olson, who provided terrific technical support, tolerated our long lists of formatting suggestions, and cheerfully incorporated our detailed line-by-line edits.

Cases and related trial documents are reprinted from Westlaw with permission of Thomson Reuters. In Assignment 27, the CLOUT case summaries appear with the permission of UNCITRAL.

Summary of Contents

Table of Contents

Table of Cases

Table of Statutes and Treaties

Uniform Electronic Transactions Act

Electronic Signatures in Global and National Commerce Act (15 U.S.C. §§ 7001 et. seq.)

Florida Statutes

Official Code of Georgia

Hawaii Revised Statutes

Table of Authorities

LEARNING
SALES LAW

Chapter 1
Introduction and Overview:
The Uniform Commercial Code, Article 2, and How to Learn the Code

Key Concepts

- The Uniform Commercial Code as a source of law
- Overall structure of Article 2
- Interpretative guidelines for construing the Code
- Active learning and the Uniform Commercial Code

This book explores the law of sales as established in Article 2 of the Uniform Commercial Code (UCC or the Code) and in a few related enactments. In this initial Chapter, we provide an essential orientation for your study of Article 2. Sections A and B discuss the nature of the UCC as a source of law and introduce you to the overall structure and content of Article 2 and its relationship to the rest of the UCC. By reviewing the UCC and Article 2 charts below and returning to them as the course progresses, you will gain a context for understanding the individual provisions you will study and how they relate to each other. Section C continues your orientation by outlining the organization and content of this book, identifying the subject of each chapter and the sub-topics that appear in the collection of "assignments" in each chapter. Although the charts of the UCC, Article 2, and the book may initially appear to be just a list of section and chapter numbers and titles, you will find that reviewing them will allow you to step back periodically from the "trees" (the detail of the UCC section-by-section analysis) and see the "forest" (the way the sections fit together to form a comprehensive code).

Section D shifts from an overview of the course content to an introduction to the pedagogical methods reflected in the book's selection and presentation of materials. As you will see, this book demands your active engagement with the material and most importantly with the Code itself. Section D offers suggestions about how to make effective use of the features of the book and how to read and study the Code sections successfully.

The Chapter concludes with Assignment 1, which introduces you to foundational UCC Article 1 provisions that guide interpretation of the UCC, which you will use throughout your study of Article 2.

A. The Uniform Commercial Code as a Source of Law

The primary subject of this book is Article 2 of the UCC. The UCC, first published in 1952, is a model law offered to the states to help create a consistent body of law across the United States to govern a broad range of commercial transactions. The UCC is one of a set of uniform laws promulgated by the American Law Institute (ALI) and the Uniform Law Commission (ULC, formerly known as the National Conference of Commissioners on Uniform State Laws, NCCUSL).

The UCC is comprised of "Articles," each addressing a different aspect of commercial transactions. Knowing the overall structure and content of the UCC will help place your study of Article 2 in context. The Code covers:

Article of the UCC	Subject Matter
1	General Provisions and Definitions
2	Sale of Goods
2A	Leases of Goods
3	Negotiable Instruments
4	Bank Deposits and Collections
4A	Funds Transfers
5	Letters of Credit
6	Bulk Transfers
7	Documents of Title
8	Investment Securities
9	Secured Transactions

In addition to Article 2, this book will introduce you to related aspects of Articles 1, 2A, and 7. Articles 3, 4, and 4A are typically addressed in a course on Payments or Commercial Paper. Article 9 is typically addressed in a course on Secured Transactions or Creditors' Remedies.

Like other uniform codes, the UCC is a model code that has no authority by itself, but becomes law when adopted by a state legislature. The UCC has been adopted in whole or in part in all 50 states, as well as in the District of Columbia, Puerto Rico, and the U.S. Virgin Islands, implementing the ALI and ULC vision of a common commercial code. States can and do adopt variations on uniform laws, but the UCC variations have been mostly confined to a handful of provisions, so knowing the uniform version used in this book will give you a foundation for understanding the provisions enacted in particular states and construed in particular cases. One exception, particularly relevant for this course, is that Louisiana has retained its civil law tradition in contracts and has not adopted Articles 2 or 2A, though it has enacted the other parts of the UCC.

The UCC is not static, however. Articles and provisions within Articles are revised or amended by the ALI and ULC as part of their ongoing efforts to update and modernize the Code. Such changes may (or may not) be adopted by the states and territories, and even when the changes become universal, it takes time for the 50+ state and territorial legislatures to act, producing additional state-by-state variation. For example, Article 1 was revised in 2001; by 2010, three-quarters of the jurisdictions had adopted the revised version, and by July 2015 only 2 jurisdictions continued to rely on the unrevised version.

Not all revisions or amendments are successful, however. The 2001 revision of Article 1 contained a substantially changed choice-of-law provision (§ 1-301) that was not adopted by numerous states otherwise enacting the revised Article 1; in 2008, the ALI and ULC amended § 1-301 to return it to language "substantively identical" to the pre-revision version.[1] Similarly, the ALI and ULC adopted substantial amendments to Article 2 in 2003, but after several years of unsuccessful attempts to have the changes enacted in the states, they withdrew the proposed amendments in 2011. The official text of the UCC included those amendments between 2003 and 2011 and thus differed significantly from the state-enacted versions, but the ALI and ULC removed the amendments in 2011. You can find out more about the history and adoption of the UCC and other uniform acts at www.uniformlaws.org, the official website of the ULC.

---

[1]   *See* 1-301 Official Comment—Changes from former law.

Because of the possibility of variations, whether because a particular state legislature modified the "uniform" language before adoption or because the provision in state law or in a court opinion reflects an older version of the provision, you should always be aware of the possibility that a case you are reading may be relying on a non-uniform version of a provision. You should check the particular state's statutory provision when dealing with a problem in practice.

B. The Structure of Article 2

Article 2 parallels in many respects the subject matter of your first year Contracts course (formation of contracts, determining performance responsibilities, ascertaining if a breach has occurred, and applying remedies). Article 2 is divided into seven "Parts," each dealing with a different aspect of the law relating to sales of goods. The title of each Part is a general guide to the contents, as shown in the chart below. Your understanding of each Part will increase as you learn about the sections within each one. Progressing from Part 1 through Part 7 roughly approximates the chronological analysis of a possible contract for sale of goods:

- Is this a transaction within the scope of Article 2? (Part 1)

- Was an enforceable contract created? (Part 2)

- What are the rights and obligations created by the contract? (Parts 3 and 4)

- Did the parties perform their obligations? (Part 5)

- What are the parties' rights and responsibilities in the absence of full performance? (Parts 6 and 7)

Here is a more detailed description of the Parts:

Part #	Sections	Title	Contents
1	2-101 to 2-107	**Short Title, General Construction and Subject Matter**	Laying the foundation: scope of Article 2, definitions
2	2-201 to 2-210	**Form, Formation and Readjustment of Contract**	Creating an enforceable obligation: formation and modification of contract, statute of frauds, parol evidence, assignment and delegation to third parties

Part #	Sections	Title	Contents
3	2-301 to 2-328	**General Obligation and Construction of Contract**	Determining the parties' obligations: default terms, warranties, meaning of certain contract terms, unconscionability limitation
4	2-401 to 2-403	**Title, Creditors and Good Faith Purchasers**	Passing title to the goods: when title passes, what kind of title passes, rights of third-party purchasers
5	2-501 to 2-515	**Performance**	Defining parties' performance obligations: seller's delivery of goods, buyer's delivery of payment, risk of loss of goods in transit
6	2-601 to 2-616	**Breach, Repudiation and Excuse**	Understanding parties' actions during performance phase: buyer's acceptance, rejection or revocation of goods; anticipatory repudiation; right to adequate assurance of performance; impossibility and impracticability
7	2-701 to 2-725	**Remedies**	Remedies for failure of performance: claiming or reclaiming goods, liability for damages, specific performance, statute of limitations

The divisions described here are not precise; that is, cross-references, definitions, and interlocking provisions will keep you flipping back and forth among the Parts. Nevertheless, the rough organization outlined here should be a helpful guide for situating your study of the individual statutory provisions.

C. Overview of the Book

The book is organized into nine chapters, each of which focuses on an aspect of the Code as it applies to sales contracting, followed by a tenth chapter that compares UCC Article 2 to Article 2A (governing leases of goods) and to the United Nations Convention on Contracts for the International Sale of Goods (CISG). The subjects of the chapters are broad conceptual areas such as scope of the statute, contract formation, warranties, and performance issues. The chapters are divided into separate "assignments," each of which addresses a particular subset of topics and sections within that broad conceptual area. Each assignment is designed to be studied in one or two class sessions. Reviewing the organization of the chapters as you begin and end each set of assignments will help you see and remember the overall trajectory of the course and how each piece of the UCC you study fits into the whole Code.

Chapter	Title	Contents
1	Introduction and Overview: The Uniform Commercial Code, Article 2, and How to Learn the Code	Assignment 1: Interpreting the UCC
2	Scope of Article 2 and Special Obligations of Merchants	Assignment 2: Article 2 Definition of Scope Assignment 3: Mixed Transactions and Article 2 Assignment 4: Definition of Merchant
3	Contract Formation and Content of the Contract	Assignment 5: Contract Formation by Offer and Acceptance or by Conduct Assignment 6: Express, Implied, and Default Terms Assignment 7: Determining the Content When Offer and Acceptance Differ: Battle of Forms Assignment 8: Parol Evidence Rule
4	Contract Enforceability: Statute of Frauds	Assignment 9: Statute of Frauds
5	Warranties	Assignment 10: Creation of Implied Warranties Assignment 11: Creation of Express Warranties Assignment 12: Warranty Disclaimers and Conflicts Assignment 13: Extending Warranties to Third Party Beneficiaries
6	Sales Contracts in the 21st Century	Assignment 14: Electronic Contracting, Statute of Frauds, and Contract Formation Assignment 15: Terms in the Box

Chapter	Title	Contents
7	**Performance Issues (Living in the Contract, Escaping from the Contract)**	Assignment 16: Identification, Tender of Delivery, Risk of Loss, Passage of Title Assignment 17: Buyer's Rights after Tender: Inspection, Rejection, Cure Assignment 18: Buyer's Rights after Tender: Acceptance, Revocation of Acceptance, Risk of Loss after Breach Assignment 19: Insecurity, Repudiation, Retraction, and Excuse
8	**Engaging with Third Parties in Complex Sales Transactions**	Assignment 20: Documents of Title Assignment 21: Power to Transfer Title
9	**Remedies**	Assignment 22: Buyer's Remedies for Seller's Breach Assignment 23: Seller's Remedies for Buyer's Breach Assignment 24: Modification or Limitation of Remedies Assignment 25: Statute of Limitations
10	**Comparing UCC Article 2 to Article 2A and to the Convention on Contracts for the International Sale of Goods (CISG)**	Assignment 26: UCC Article 2A: Contracts for Leases of Goods Assignment 27: The Convention on Contracts for the International Sale of Goods (CISG)

D. Engaging with the Material and Learning Article 2

This book is designed not simply to present the subject matter (the law of sales in the UCC) but to help you learn that subject matter through active engagement and transparent pedagogy. It starts by identifying at the beginning of each chapter a list of **Key Concepts** that will be addressed, giving you a checklist of what you should understand by the end of that chapter. When you first encounter the list it will simply be a set of undefined terms, providing a partial roadmap of what is to come. By the end of the chapter, you should be able to return to the list and articulate what you learned about each concept.

Understanding concepts is only the first step, however. The goal of this book is for you to be able to use the Code in problem-solving. To help focus your study on that goal, each Assignment begins with a list of **Learning Outcomes and Objectives**, identifying what you should be able to *do* (rather than just what you should *know*) when you have mastered the material in the Assignment. To illustrate, here is a set of Learning Outcomes and Objectives for the book's coverage of sales of goods:

LEARNING OUTCOMES AND OBJECTIVES

If you take advantage of the opportunities offered to read and apply the Code throughout the book, by the end of your studies you should be able to

- find in Article 2 the appropriate provision to apply to a fact situation you encounter;
- use a variety of techniques to represent the content of statutory provisions to aid in analysis and understanding of Article 2 and of any statute; and
- address complex fact situations involving sales of goods, identify which Code provisions are implicated, and articulate how they interact to provide arguments regarding the validity and operation of a contract for sale of goods.

Learning to read and understand a statute, particularly a code with interwoven provisions, is both a skill and an art, and it is different in many ways from reading and understanding cases. Court opinions are written to address the particular circumstances of an individual case, while statutes are written as general rules to address all future cases. A court's statement of the legal rule it follows or declares may be rearticulated and reinterpreted by creative legal analysts and future judges, while statutes change only if the legislature amends them. The meaning of a legal rule is not tied permanently to the way any one judge articulates that rule, while the meaning of a statute is always grounded in the particular words in the statute. Though paraphrasing and re-articulating a statutory rule may sometimes assist your analysis and explanation, you must return to the precise words of the statute in order to find your authority. Every word in a statute is operative and therefore meaningful; there are no *dicta*.

This does not mean that statutes are somehow clear on their face and require no interpretation. Because they are drafted as general rules, even well drafted statutory provisions require analysis and interpretation in order to determine how to apply them to real circumstances. Perhaps because a statute represents an effort to establish broad but precise rules, statutory language is also often more difficult, more convoluted, or more awkward than ordinary writing. Ambiguities, vagueness, internal contradiction—any or all of these may complicate your task. You may need to draw on your understanding of the purpose of the statute, on legislative history, and on public policy to help understand the words. Moreover, statutory meanings sometimes change over time based on judicial interpretation, though all such interpretations must still be tied to the text itself.

This book is premised on the idea that the best way to learn the Code—indeed, to learn any statute—is to rely primarily on the statute itself rather than on court opinions telling you what the statute means, and to practice (and practice and practice) the skill of reading and applying the statutory provisions. The structure and content of the book is designed to help you effectively learn both the substance of the relevant law and the skill of working with statutory language in general and the UCC in particular.

To that end, each provision or set of provisions is introduced using a **Reading the Code** box that directs you to read the specified Code section(s) and asks questions designed to guide your reading and understanding. At the "reading" stage, we suggest the following methodology to help you understand the statutory language:

(1)   As you read a provision—and especially as you read a group of provisions—make a "jot" list of the general subject matter to help give you an overview. Paraphrasing rather than simply repeating the title may help you understand and remember the contents better.

(2)   Read the provision closely (probably more than once), identifying defined words (use the definitional cross-references listed at the end of the Official Comment, but be aware that there may be defined words not listed there), and noting the grammatical structure of the sentences (e.g., finding the subjects and verbs—not always obvious—and noting qualifying clauses and the words they modify).

(3)   Consider—and answer—the questions posed about the provision in the Reading the Code box. Make notes about and highlight language that

you find confusing or ambiguous or vague or about which you think you need more information.

(4)   Rewrite the statutory rule in some fashion, e.g., through paraphrase, creating a bullet list of points, writing the pieces as an if/then statement, creating a table, or drawing a flowchart or diagram. This is a critical exercise for learning and remembering the provision; rewriting will force you to go beyond a simple repetition of the language of the provision and figure out how the pieces of the provision fit together. If rewriting uncovers additional ambiguities or other lack of clarity, add to your notes and highlighting.

(5)   Read the Official Comments accompanying the provision, written by the drafters and included in the published UCC; they can help you understand what the drafters intended by the statutory text and may add substantive content to the statutory rule. Check the cross-references at the end of the Official Comment, as they may provide additional clues to connections between statutory sections.

(6)   And then read the statutory provision again. You will find that you already understand the words of the provision better and can better see where interpretative issues may arise.

As you progress through the course, learning the contents of individual sections, you will also need to expand your vision periodically to include multiple sections, diagramming a "big picture" representation of the connections.

Once you have parsed and analyzed the statutory language itself, the next step will be to think about its application to the circumstances of sale of goods contracts. To help you develop your ability to apply the statutes, the book provides **Examples and Analysis** drawn from decided cases, giving you the opportunity to learn how courts have construed and applied the provisions. The **Analysis** discussion often includes questions about the arguments for and against the court's outcome, inviting you to explore the issues from both sides and to benefit from as well as critique the court's conclusion. You will find it useful to annotate your copy of the Code with ideas gleaned from your review of those examples to help you remember the additional understanding gained from seeing the way the courts have used the provisions.

From time to time, the book includes cases that offer an in-depth analysis of particular Code sections. Each case is preceded by a set of questions intended to focus your reading of the case on the most salient facts or aspects of the court's analysis. Review these questions before reading the case, and try to answer them as you read the case.

Finally, the book includes many problems appearing in **Applying the Code** sections, which will allow you to solidify and practice your understanding of the Code sections. Problems sometimes will test only the sections just introduced and sometimes will also require application of earlier materials to help you weave parts of the Code together. As you solve the problems, be sure to note the particular statutory language that applies so that you can more effectively explain your reasoning and demonstrate your understanding of and ability to use the statute.

As a result of completing the active exercises, which require repeated reading of, remembering, and analyzing the Code language, you will most effectively learn the meaning of the provisions and how to apply them.[2] In the process, you will also become accustomed to and more proficient at working with statutory language, a skill that will be useful throughout your legal education and career.

A Note About Case Presentations

When presenting cases, we indicate where text is omitted, but, to avoid cluttering the text, we occasionally omit citations within a case without special marking. When important for clarity, we have also occasionally added section headings or paragraph breaks where those markings were not included by the court.

---

[2]   *See* Brown et al., Make It Stick 43-44 (2014) ("*Effortful retrieval*" makes for stronger learning and retention. . . . *Repeated retrieval* not only makes memories more durable but produces knowledge that can be retrieved more readily, in more varied settings, and applied to a wider variety of problems"; self-testing adds to retention).

Assignment 1
Interpreting the UCC
§§ 1-103, 1-107, 1-302, 1-303, 1-201

In this Assignment, you will be introduced to provisions in Article 1 that help guide interpretation of all parts of the UCC. Some explicitly address interpretation; others provide general principles that must be understood in order to apply sections of Article 2 appropriately.

As you work through the materials, in this and future Assignments, you will be asked first to study the text of the relevant UCC sections, and in most instances will be asked as well to read and understand the Official Comments. As noted in the Chapter 1 overview, the Official Comments are drafted as part of the development of UCC provisions, written by the drafting committees of the Uniform Law Commission (ULC) as those committees write and edit proposed amendments. The comments generally accompany the text when the amendments are considered by the ULC and the American Law Institute, so they are reliable explanations of the meanings attributed by those bodies. When state legislatures enact a UCC article, however, the comments may or may not be considered by the legislature, and often only the statutory provisions, not the comments, are enacted. Because of their role in the adoption processes, the Official Comments do not have the authority of the statutory text itself, but they are well respected by judges and commentators as providing insight into the meaning of the Code, especially when the text is ambiguous or unclear, so it is important that you learn to understand and rely upon them as you learn to use the Code.

LEARNING OUTCOMES AND OBJECTIVES

At the completion of this Assignment, you should be able to

- use the purposes of the UCC to advocate for particular interpretations of Code language;
- articulate the nature and limits of parties' freedom of contract under the UCC;
- identify provisions that establish mandatory and default rules for sale of goods contracts; and

> • understand the components of a contract for sale of goods and how the pieces fit together.

A. General Principles of Interpretation

**Reading the Code:
§§ 1-103(a), 1-107**

Read 1-103(a), which describes the "underlying purposes and policies" of the UCC and provides general guidance on how to construe its provisions.

Question 1. Do the articulated purposes of the UCC increase or decrease the weight that one jurisdiction should give to other jurisdictions' rulings that interpret and apply UCC provisions? Does 1-103(a) suggest construing the statutory provisions broadly or narrowly?

Read Comment 1 to 1-103.

Question 2. After reading the Comment, are your answers to Question 1 the same or different than after reading only the statutory language?

Read 1-107.

Question 3. Karl Llewellyn (the primary drafter and proponent of the UCC in its formative years) described two common (and somewhat conflicting) rules on statutory interpretation this way: "Titles do not control meaning; . . . section headings do not change language" and "The title may be consulted as a guide when there is doubt or obscurity in the body; . . section headings may be looked upon as part of the statute itself."[1] How does the rule in 1-107 compare with Llewellyn's formulations?

---

[1]   Remarks on the Theory of Appellate Decision and the Rules or Canons About How Statutes are to be Construed, 3 VAND. L. REV. 395 (1950).

Reading the Code:
Mandatory vs. Default Provisions
§ 1-302

Read 1-302, 1-302 Comments 1 to 3, and 1-201(b)(20).

Question 4. What do 1-302 and the Comments say about the parties' ability to modify the effect of the provisions of the UCC? What limits exist on that freedom?

Question 5. How can you tell the difference between mandatory provisions (those that the parties cannot change) and default provisions (those that become part of the contract if the parties do not agree otherwise)?

Question 6. Read the following provisions, create a jot list (note the general subject matter), and decide whether each provision is mandatory or default or a mix of the two.

(a) 1-103(a)

(b) 1-103(b)

(c) 1-304

(d) 2-302

(e) 2-306(1)

(f) 2-306(2)

(g) 2-307

(h) 2-308

(i) 2-309

(j) 2-725(1)

B. Commercial Context: Course of Dealing, Course of Performance, Usage of Trade

Reading the Code: § 1-303

Read 1-303 and its Comments.

Question 7. What must a party show to establish a "course of performance"? Give an example of something that would constitute a course of performance.

Question 8. What must a party show to establish a "course of dealing"? Give an example of something that would constitute a course of dealing.

Question 9. What must a party show to establish a "usage of trade"? Give an example of something that would constitute a usage of trade.

EXAMPLES AND ANALYSIS

Example A: *Enpro Systems, Ltd. v. Namasco Corp.*[2]

On July 19, 2001, Enpro Systems, Ltd. placed an order for a quantity of steel plates with Namasco Corp. Defects were found in one of the plates while Enpro was using it to fabricate a pressure vessel section for a refinery. The reverse side of the delivery ticket accompanying the shipment of the steel plates to Enpro disclaimed express and implied warranties, disallowed claims for consequential damages, limited remedies to repair and replacement of or credit for defective items, and specified a ten-day claims limitations period commencing with the date of billing. Namasco used the same delivery ticket in 34 previous sales to Enpro beginning in 2000.

---

2   382 F. Supp. 2d 874 (S.D. Texas 2005).

When Enpro sued to collect damages for breach of warranty, Namasco moved for summary judgment, relying on its disclaimer of warranties and limitation of remedies on the delivery ticket in this and many previous sales. The court first found that the terms on the delivery ticket delivered with the steel plate ordered on July 19, 2001, did not become part of the parties' contract because Namasco had accepted Enpro's offer to purchase before the delivery ticket arrived with additional terms. The court then considered Namasco's claim that use of the ticket without objection from Enpro in 34 prior purchases constituted a course of dealing between the parties that meant the term was part of the July 19 contract and that there was an applicable trade usage for sellers to limit liability as it had on its delivery ticket.

Analysis: Applying the Texas enactment of 1-303, the court concluded that the use of the same disclaimers in the series of transactions between the parties did not create a course of dealing. It contrasted the situation with that occurring in another Texas case (*Preston Farm & Ranch Supply*) where "a buyer's continued purchases and payment of all charges for over a year, despite monthly statements conspicuously showing that a service charge was being imposed, was a course of conduct that gave rise to an implied agreement to pay the charge." The court declined to follow a 9th Circuit case (*NNR Aircargo Service, Inc.*) that applied the California enactment of 1-303 to conclude that a course of dealing was created by receipt on 47 prior occasions of identical invoices "from which knowledge of the terms could be presumed." Although the Enpro court did not mention it, the front of each NNR invoice stated: "NNR handles shipments subject to the terms and conditions set forth on the reverse side of this invoice", and the reverse side began with the bold caption: "TERMS AND CONDITIONS OF SERVICE (Please Read Carefully)" and included a clause that limited liability on large shipments of goods to $50 unless the buyer paid the seller to take on additional liability.

To support its assertion of a trade usage, Namasco cited the sworn statement of its branch manager that, on the basis of his "extensive experience in the steel industry" it is the "custom and practice" in industry sales transactions to disclaim warranties, exclude consequential damages, and limit liability. Namasco's sales supervisor asserted the same custom and practice in his affidavit, and the company pointed to similar terms and conditions of several other steel suppliers. In response, Enpro provided the sworn declaration of its president and CEO that he understood industry attempts to disclaim liability were "limited to situations where defects in the delivered products were detectable upon delivery" and he cited instances in which Enpro requested and received compensation from vendors for damages beyond replacement of the purchased material. Enpro also noted that Namasco's branch manager acknowledged in his deposition that he had never encountered a situation in which defects were discovered only after use in fabrication. The court concluded that it could not resolve the trade usage claim at the summary judgment stage.

With respect to course of dealing, what language in 1-303 supports the outcome in the Enpro case? Why might the court have distinguished *Preston*? *NNR Aircargo Service, Inc.*? How would you support finding a course of dealing in *Enpro*? No course of dealing in *Preston* and *NNR Aircargo Service*?

With respect to usage of trade, was the court correct in refusing to resolve the issue in summary judgment? What facts offered support a finding that a trade usage exists? What facts support the opposite result? What language in 1-303 establishes the standard against which to judge the evidence? What else would you do, and what questions would you ask of the parties, to collect evidence for the trial or hearing on the trade usage issue?

C. Components of a Contract

Reading the Code:
§ 1-201(b)(3), (12), (40)

Read 1-201(b)(3), (12), and (40) and the associated Comments.

Question 10. Construct an equation or set of equations (e.g., $A+B+C=D$) or a diagram that represents the relationships among the following:

Agreement	Course of performance	Mandatory rules
Contract	Default rules	Term
Course of dealing	Language in contract document	Usage of trade

Question 11. List the following in hierarchical order, indicating which prevails over another (or others) in the event of a conflict, and explain why:

Course of dealing	Default rules	Mandatory rules
Course of performance	Language in contract document	Usage of trade

Question 12. A waiver may occur if a party's conduct demonstrates an intentional relinquishment of a known right or privilege. A contract modification may occur if the parties' communications or actions show mutual agreement to a change (and under 2-209 no consideration is required for a modification to be binding). Do those statements lead you to change anything about your answer to Question 11?

D. Applying Commercial Context

Nanakuli Paving and Rock Company v. Shell Oil Company, which follows, demonstrates the power of course of dealing, course of performance, and usage of trade to affect the meaning of contract terms. It also illustrates how a course of dealing, course of performance, or usage of trade may arise and what facts a party may use to try to prove their existence. The excerpt is lengthy to provide sufficient background for you to understand these critical concepts and how to work with them in interpreting contracts.

As you read the case, consider the following questions to help guide your analysis:

(1)   What did the express terms of the contract say about price?

(2)   What evidence did Nanakuli offer to demonstrate course of dealing, course of performance, and usage of trade with respect to pricing?

(3)   What arguments did Shell Oil Company make that Nanakuli's evidence was insufficient to establish the existence of course of dealing, course of performance, and usage of trade?

(4)   How did the court apply § 1-303(e) with respect to reading all the pricing evidence together? Do you agree with the court's conclusion?

(5)   How did the court apply § 1-303(f) with respect to the showing of waiver? Do you agree with the court's conclusion?

A note about the statutory text: The *Nanakuli* opinion is from 1981, before the Code revision creating § 1-303 from the then-current versions of §§ 1-205 and 2-208. See the Source note and "Changes from former law" in the Official Comments to § 1-303. The text of § 1-303 reflects only slight modifications of the substance of §§ 1-205 and 2-208, so you can use § 1-303 to answer the questions posed here, but you should watch for differences in the statutory text as you read the opinion. You can find the former text of § 2-208 in Article 2 in a section now marked as [Reserved]. The former text of § 1-205 is available in an Appendix in many statutory supplements used in Sales courses. Comment 3 to former § 2-208, on which the court relies in its opinion, does not appear in the Comments to § 1-303.

NANAKULI PAVING & ROCK CO. V. SHELL OIL CO.

664 F.2d 772 (9th Cir. 1981)

HOFFMAN, DISTRICT JUDGE.

Appellant Nanakuli Paving and Rock Company (Nanakuli) initially filed this breach of contract action against appellee Shell Oil Company (Shell) in Hawaiian State Court in February, 1976. Nanakuli, the second largest asphaltic paving contractor in Hawaii, had bought all its asphalt requirements from 1963 to 1974 from Shell under two long-term supply contracts; its suit charged Shell with breach of the later 1969 contract. The jury returned a verdict of $220,800 for Nanakuli on its first claim, which is that Shell breached the 1969 contract in January, 1974, by failing to price protect Nanakuli on 7200 tons of asphalt at the time Shell raised the price for asphalt from $44 to $76. Nanakuli's theory is that price-protection, as a usage of the asphaltic paving trade in Hawaii, was incorporated into the 1969 agreement between the parties, as demonstrated by the routine use of price protection by suppliers to that trade, and reinforced by the way in which Shell actually performed the 1969 contract up until 1974. Price protection, appellant claims, required that Shell hold the price on the tonnage Nanakuli had already committed because Nanakuli had incorporated that price into bids put out to or contracts awarded by general contractors and government agencies. The District Judge set aside the verdict and granted Shell's motion for judgment n.o.v., which decision we vacate. We reinstate the jury verdict because we find that, viewing the evidence as a whole, there was substantial evidence to support a finding by reasonable jurors that Shell breached its contract by failing to provide protection for Nanakuli in 1974. *Quichocho v. Kelvinator Corp.*, 546 F.2d 812, 813 (9th Cir. 1976). We do not believe the evidence in this case was such that, giving Nanakuli the benefit of all inferences fairly supported by the evidence and without weighing the credibility of the witnesses, only one reasonable conclusion could have been reached by the jury. *Cockrum v. Whitney*, 479 F.2d 84, 85-86 (9th Cir. 1973).

[Nanakuli argues that] all material suppliers to the asphaltic paving trade in Hawaii followed the trade usage of price protection and thus it should be assumed, under the U.C.C., that the parties intended to incorporate price protection into their 1969 agreement. This is so, Nanakuli continues, even though the written contract provided for price to be "Shell's Posted Price at time of delivery," F.O.B. Honolulu. Its proof of a usage that was incorporated into the contract is reinforced by evidence of the commercial context, which under the U.C.C. should form the background for viewing a particular contract. The full agreement must be examined in light of the close, almost symbiotic relations between Shell and Nanakuli on the island of Oahu, whereby the expansion of Shell on the island was intimately connected to the business growth of Nanakuli. The U.C.C. looks to the actual performance of a contract as the best indication of what the parties intended those terms to mean. Nanakuli points out that Shell had price protected it on the two occasions of price increases under the 1969 contract other than the 1974 increase. In 1970 and 1971 Shell extended the old price for four and three months, respectively, after an announced increase. This was done, in the words of Shell's agent in Hawaii, in order to permit Nanakuli's to "chew up" tonnage already committed at Shell's old price. FN4

FN4. Price protection was practiced in the asphaltic paving trade by either extending the old price for a period of time after a new one went into effect or charging the old price for a specified tonnage, which represented work committed at the old price. In addition, several months' advance notice was given of price increases.

. . . .

Shell presents three arguments for upholding the judgment n.o.v. or, on cross appeal, urging that the District Judge erred in admitting certain evidence. First, it says, the District Court should not have denied Shell's motion *in limine* to define trade, for purposes of trade usage evidence, as the sale and purchase of asphalt in Hawaii, rather than expanding the definition of trade to include other suppliers of materials to the asphaltic paving trade. Asphalt, its argument runs, was the subject matter of the disputed contract and the only product Shell supplied to the asphaltic paving trade.[FN5] Shell protests that the judge, by expanding the definition of trade to include the other major suppliers to the asphaltic paving trade, allowed the admission of highly prejudicial evidence of routine price protection by all suppliers of aggregate.[FN6] Asphaltic concrete paving is formed by mixing paving asphalt with crushed rock, or aggregate, in a "hot-mix" plant and then pouring the mixture onto the surface to be paved. Shell's second complaint is that the two prior occasions on which it price protected Nanakuli, although representing the only other instances of price increases under the 1969 contract, constituted mere waivers of the contract's price term, not a course of performance of the contract. A course of performance of the contract, in contrast to a waiver, demonstrates how the parties understand the terms of their agreement. Shell cites two U.C.C. Comments in support of that argument: (1) that, when the meaning of acts is ambiguous, the preference is for the waiver interpretation, and (2) that one act alone does not constitute a relevant course of performance. Shell's final argument is that, even assuming its prior price protection constituted a course of performance and that the broad trade definition was correct and evidence of trade usages by aggregate suppliers was admissible, price protection could not be construed as reasonably consistent with the express price term in the contract, in which case the Code provides that the express term controls.

FN5. Shell's argument would, in effect, eliminate all trade usage evidence. First, it argues that its own acts were irrelevant as mere waivers, not acts in the course of the performance of the contract. Second, it contends that all acts of price protection by the only other asphalt supplier in Hawaii, Chevron, the marketing division of Standard Oil Company, were irrelevant to prove trade usage because Chevron at one time owned all or part of the paving company it supplied and routinely price protected Hawaiian Bitumuls (H.B.). The court correctly refused to bar that evidence since the one-time relationship between the two went to the weight, not the admissibility, of the evidence. Nanakuli was given permission to offer evidence in rebuttal that Chevron price protected other customers in California with whom it had no such relationship in the event Shell tried to impeach that evidence.

FN6. The judge excluded evidence of price protection usage by suppliers of cement because cement was too infrequently used in the production of asphaltic paving and, when used, formed too small a percentage of the finished product.

We hold that the judge did not abuse his discretion in defining the applicable trade, for purposes of trade usages, as the asphaltic paving trade in Hawaii. . . . We base our holding on the reading of the Code Comments as defining trade more broadly than transaction and as binding parties not only to usages of their particular trade but also to usages of trade in general in a given locality. This latter seems an equitable application of usage evidence where the usage is almost universally practiced in a small market such as was Oahu in the 1960's before Shell signed its 1969 contract with Nanakuli. Additionally, we hold that, under the facts of this case, a jury could reasonably have found that Shell's acts on two occasions to price protect Nanakuli were not ambiguous and therefore indicated Shell's understanding of the terms of the agreement with Nanakuli rather than being a waiver by Shell of those terms. [FN8]

[FN8]. In addition, Shell's Bohner volunteered on direct for Shell that Shell price protected Nanakuli again after 1974 on the only two occasions of later price increases in 1977 and 1978. Although not constituting a course of performance, since the occasions took place under different contracts, these two additional instances of price protection could have reinforced the jury's impression that Shell's earlier actions were a carrying out of the price term.

Lastly we hold that, although the express price terms of Shell's posted price of delivery may seem, at first glance, inconsistent with a trade usage of price protection at time of increases in price, a closer reading shows that the jury could have reasonably construed price protection as consistent with the express term. We reach this holding for several reasons. First, we are persuaded by a careful reading of the U.C.C., one of whose underlying purposes is to promote flexibility in the expansion of commercial practices and which rather drastically overhauls this particular area of the law. The Code would have us look beyond the printed pages of the contract to usages and the entire commercial context of the agreement in order to reach the "true understanding" of the parties. Second, decisions of other courts in similar situations have managed to reconcile such trade usages with seemingly contradictory express terms where the prior course of dealings between the parties, trade usages, and the actual performance of the contract by the parties showed a clear intent by the parties to incorporate those usages into the agreement or to give to the express term the particular meaning provided by those usages, even at times varying the apparent meaning of the express terms. Third, the delineation by thoughtful commentators of the degree of consistency demanded between express terms and usage is that a usage should be allowed to modify the apparent agreement, as seen in the written terms, as long as it does not totally negate it. We believe the usage here falls within the limits set forth by commentators and generally followed in the better reasoned decisions. The manner in which price protection was actually practiced in Hawaii was that it only came into play at times of price increases and only for work committed prior to those increases on non-escalating contracts. Thus, it formed an exception to, rather than a total negation of, the express price term of "Shell's Posted Price at time of delivery." Our decision is reinforced by the overwhelming nature of the evidence that price protection was routinely practiced by all suppliers in the small Oahu market of the asphaltic paving trade and therefore was known to Shell; that it was a realistic necessity to operate in that market and thus vital to Nanakuli's ability to get large government contracts and to Shell's continued business growth on Oahu; and that it therefore constituted an intended part of the agreement, as that term is broadly defined by the Code, between Shell and Nanakuli.

I. History Of Nanakuli-Shell Relations Before 1973

Nanakuli, a division of Grace Brothers, Ltd., a Hawaiian corporation, is the smaller of the two major paving contractors on the island of Oahu, the larger of the two being Hawaiian Bitumuls (H.B.). Nanakuli first entered the paving business on Oahu in 1948, but it only began to move into the largest Oahu market, Honolulu, in the mid-1950's. Until 1964 or so, Nanakuli only got small paving jobs, such as service stations, driveways, and small subdivision streets; it was not in a position to compete with H.B. for government contracts for major roads, airports, and other large jobs. In the early sixties Nanakuli owner Walter Grace began to negotiate a mutually advantageous arrangement with Shell whereby Shell, which had a small market percentage and no asphalt terminals in Hawaii, would sign a long-term supply contract with Nanakuli that would commit Nanakuli to buy its asphalt requirements from Shell. On the other hand, Nanakuli would be helped to expand its paving business on Oahu through a guaranteed supply and a discount on its asphalt prices. Nanakuli's growth would expand the market for Shell's asphalt on the island, which would justify Shell's capital investment of a half a million dollars on Oahu, to which asphalt would be brought in heated tankers from Shell's refinery in Martinez, California.

. . . .

[Lennox became president of Nanakuli in 1965.] Lennox's testimony . . . was that Shell's agreement with Nanakuli in 1969 included a commitment by Shell never to charge Nanakuli more than Chevron charged H.B., in order to carry out the underlying purpose of the agreement to make Nanakuli competitive with H.B. and thus expand its and Shell's respective businesses on Oahu. . . .

. . . He said Nanakuli understood the price term to mean that Shell would not increase prices without advance notice and would hold the price on work bid for enough time to allow Nanakuli to use up the tonnage bid at the old price. Smith's testimony backed up that of Lennox: the price was to be "posted price as bid as was understood between the parties," further explaining that it was to be Shell's price at time and place of delivery, except for price increases, at which point the price was time and place of bid for a period of time or a specified tonnage.

. . . .

II. Trade Usage Before and After 1969

The key to price protection being so prevalent in 1969 that both parties would intend to incorporate it into their contract is found in one reality of the Oahu asphaltic paving market: the largest paving contracts were let by government agencies and none of the three levels of government—local, state, or federal—allowed escalation clauses for paving materials. If a paver bid at one price and another went into effect before the award was made, the paving company would lose a great deal of money, since it could not pass on increases to any government agency or to most general contractors. Extensive evidence was presented that, as a consequence, aggregate suppliers routinely price protected paving contractors in the 1960's and 1970's, as did the largest asphaltic supplier in Oahu, Chevron. Nanakuli presented documentary evidence of routine price protection by aggregate suppliers as well as two witnesses: Grosjean, Vice-President for Marketing of Ameron H.C. & D., and Nihei, Division Manager of Lone Star Industries for Pacific Cement and Aggregate (P.C. & A.). Both testified that price protection to their knowledge had always been practiced: at H.C. & D. for many years prior to Grosjean's arrival in 1962 and at P.C. & A. routinely since Nihei's arrival in 1960. Such protection consisted of advance notices of increases, coupled with charging the old price for work committed at that price or for enough time to order the tonnage committed. The smallness of the Oahu market led to complete trust among suppliers and pavers. H.C. & D. did not demand that Nanakuli or other pavers issue purchase orders or sign contracts for aggregate before incorporating its aggregate prices into bids. Nanakuli would merely give H.C. & D. a list of projects it had bid at the time H.C. & D. raised its prices, without documentation. "Their word and letter is good enough for us," Grosjean testified. Nihei said P.C. & A. at the time of price increases would get a list of either particular projects bid by a paver or simply total tonnage bid at the old price. "We take either one. We take their word for it." None of the aggregate companies had a contract with Nanakuli expressly stating price protection would be given; Nanakuli's contract with P.C. & A. merely set out that P.C. & A. would not charge Nanakuli more than it charged its other customers.

The evidence about Chevron's practice of price protection came in the form of an affidavit by Bery Jameyson, Chevron's Division Manager-Asphalt in California. He stated that Chevron had routinely price protected H.B. on work bid for many years, the last occasion prior to the signing of the 1969 contracts between Nanakuli and Shell being a price increase put into effect on March 7, 1969, with the understanding that H.B. would be protected on work bid, which amounted to 12,000 tons. In answer to Shell's protest that such evidence was not relevant without the contract itself, Nanakuli introduced the contract into evidence. Much like the contract at issue here, it provided that the price to H.B. would be a given percentage of the price Chevron set for a specified crude oil in California. No mention was made of price protection in the written contract between H.B. and Chevron.

In addition to evidence of trade usages existing in 1969 when the contract at issue was signed, the District Judge let in evidence of the continuation of that trade usage after 1969, over Shell's protest. He stated that, giving a liberal reading to Section 1-205, he felt that later evidence was relevant to show that the expectation of the parties that a given usage would be observed was justified. The basis for incorporating a trade usage into a contract under the U.C.C. is the justifiable expectation of the parties that it will be observed. That later evidence consisted here of more price protection by the aggregate companies on Oahu, as well as continued asphalt price protection. Chevron after 1969 continued price protecting H.B. on Oahu and, on raising prices in 1979, price protected Nanakuli on the island of Molokai, where Nanakuli purchased its asphalt from Chevron. Additionally, Shell price protected Nanakuli in 1977 and 1978 on Oahu.

III. Shell's Course Of Performance of the 1969 Contract

The Code considers actual performance of a contract as the most relevant evidence of how the parties interpreted the terms of that contract. In 1970 and 1971, the only points at which Shell raised prices between 1969 and 1974, it price protected Nanakuli by holding its old price for four and three months, respectively, after announcing a price increase.

. . . .

IV. Shell-Nanakuli Relations, 1973-74

Two important factors form the backdrop for the 1974 failure by Shell to price protect Nanakuli: the Arab oil embargo and a complete change of command and policy in Shell's asphalt management. The jury was read a page or so from the World Book about the events and effect of the partial oil embargo, which shortened supplies and increased the price of petroleum, of which asphalt is a byproduct. The federal government imposed direct price controls on petroleum, but not on asphalt. Despite the international importance of those events, the jury may have viewed the second factor as of more direct significance to this case. The structural changes at Shell offered a possible explanation for why Shell in 1974 acted out of step with, not only the trade usage and commercially reasonable practices of all suppliers to the asphaltic paving trade on Oahu, but also with its previous agreement with, or at least treatment of, Nanakuli.

. . . .

We conclude that the decision to deny Nanakuli price protection was made by new Houston management without a full understanding of Shell's 1969 agreement with Nanakuli or any knowledge of its past pricing practices toward Nanakuli. If Shell did commit itself in 1969 to price protect Nanakuli, the Shell officials who made the decisions affecting Nanakuli in 1974 knew nothing about that commitment. Nor did they make any effective effort to find out. They acted instead solely in reliance on the 1969 contract's express price term, devoid of the commercial context that the Code says is necessary to an understanding of the meaning of the written word. Whatever the legal enforceability of Nanakuli's right, Nanakuli officials seem to have acted in good faith reliance on its right, as they understood it, to price protection and rightfully felt betrayed by Shell's failure to act with any understanding of its past practices toward Nanakuli.

V. Scope of Trade Usage

The validity of the jury verdict in this case depends on four legal questions. First, how broad was the trade to whose usages Shell was bound under its 1969 agreement with Nanakuli: did it extend to the Hawaiian asphaltic paving trade or was it limited merely to the purchase and sale of asphalt, which would only include evidence of practices by Shell and Chevron? Second, were the two instances of price protection of Nanakuli by Shell in 1970 and 1971 waivers of the 1969 contract as a matter of law or was the jury entitled to find that they constituted a course of performance of the contract? Third, could the jury have construed an express contract term of Shell's posted price at delivery as reasonably consistent with a trade usage and Shell's course of performance of the 1969 contract of price protection, which consisted of charging the old price at times of price increases, either for a period of time or for specific tonnage committed at a fixed price in non- escalating contracts? Fourth, could the jury have found that good faith obliged Shell to at least give advance notice of a $32 increase in 1974, that is, could they have found that the commercially reasonable standards of fair dealing in the trade in Hawaii in 1974 were to give some form of price protection?

We approach the first issue in this case mindful that an underlying purpose of the U.C.C. as enacted in Hawaii is to allow for liberal interpretation of commercial usages. The Code provides, "This Chapter shall be liberally construed and applied to promote its underlying purposes and policies." Haw. Rev.Stat. § 490:1-102(1). Only three purposes are listed, one of which is " (t)o permit the continued expansion of commercial practices through custom, usage and agreement of the parties; . . . ." *Id.* § 490:1-102(2)(b). The drafters of the Code explain:

> This Act is drawn to provide *flexibility* so that, since it is intended to be a semi-permanent piece of legislation, it will provide its own machinery *for expansion of commercial practices*. It is intended to make it possible for the law embodied in this Act to be *developed* by the courts in the light of *unforeseen and new circumstances and practices.* . . .
>
> . . . The text of each section should be *read in the light of the purpose and policy* of the rule or principle in question, as also of the Act as a whole, and the application of the language should be *construed nar-*

rowly or broadly, as the case may be, in *conformity with the purposes and policies* involved.

. . . [t])he Code seeks to *avoid . . . interference with evolutionary growth*. . . .

This principle of *freedom of contract is subject to specific exceptions* found elsewhere in the Act. . . . (An example being the bar on contractual exclusion of the requirement of good faith, although the parties can set out standards for same.) . . . *In this connection*, Section 1-205 incorporating into the agreement *prior course of dealing and usages of trade is of particular importance.*

Id., Comments 1 & 2 (emphasis supplied). We read that to mean that courts should not stand in the way of new commercial practices and usages by insisting on maintaining the narrow and inflexible old rules of interpretation. We seek the definition of trade usage not only in the express language of the Code but also in its underlying purposes, defining it liberally to fit the facts of the particular commercial context here.

The Code defines usage of trade as "any practice or method of dealing having such regularity of observance in a *place, vocation or trade* as to justify an expectation that it will be observed with respect to the transaction in question." *Id.* § 490:1-205(2) (emphasis supplied). We understand the use of the word "or" to mean that parties can be bound by a usage common to the place they are in business, even if it is not the usage of their particular vocation or trade. That reading is borne out by the repetition of the disjunctive "or" in subsection 3, which provides that usages "in the vocation or trade in which they are engaged or of which they are or should be aware give particular meaning to and supplement or qualify terms of an agreement." *Id.* § 490:1-205(3). The drafters' Comments say that trade usage is to be used to reach the " . . . commercial meaning of the agreement. . . ." by interpreting the language "as meaning what it may fairly be expected to mean to parties involved in the particular transaction *in a given locality or* in a given *vocation or trade.*" *Id.*, Comment 4 (emphasis supplied). The inference of the two subsections and the Comment, read together, is that a usage need not necessarily be one practiced by members of the party's own trade or vocation to be binding if it is so commonly practiced in a locality that a party should be aware of it. Subsection 5 also shows the importance of the place where the usage is practiced: "An applicable usage of trade in the place where any part of performance is to occur shall be used in interpreting the agreement as to that part of the performance." The validity of this interpretation is additionally demonstrated by the Comment of the drafters: "Subsection (3), giving the prescribed effect to usages of which the parties 'are or should be aware', reinforces the provision of subsection (2) requiring not universality but only the described 'regularity of observance' of the practice or method. This subsection also reinforces the point of subsection (2) that such usages may be either *general to trade or particular to a special branch of trade.*" *Id.*, Comment 7 (emphasis supplied). This language indicates that Shell would be bound not only by usages of sellers of asphalt but by more general usages on Oahu, as long as those usages were so regular in their observance that Shell should have been aware of them. This reading of the Code, in our opinion, achieves an equitable result. A party is always held to conduct generally observed by members of his chosen trade because the other party is justified in so assuming unless he indicates otherwise. He is held to more general business practices to the extent of his actual knowledge of those practices or to the degree his ignorance of those practices is not excusable: they were so generally practiced he should have been aware of them.

. . . .

Shell argued not only that the definition of trade was too broad, but also that the practice itself was not sufficiently regular to reach the level of a usage and that Nanakuli failed to show with enough precision how the usage was carried out in order for a jury to calculate damages. The extent of a usage is ultimately a jury question. The Code provides, "The existence and scope of such a usage are to be proved as facts." Haw.Rev.Stat. § 490:1-205(2). The practice must have "such regularity of observance . . . as to justify an expectation that it will be observed. . . ." *Id.* The Comment explains:

> The ancient English tests for "custom" are abandoned in this connection. Therefore, it is not required that a usage of trade be "ancient or immemorial," "universal" or the like. . . . (F)ull recognition is thus available for new usages and for usages currently observed by the great majority of decent dealers, even though dissidents ready to cut corners do not agree.

Id., Comment 5. The Comment's demand that "not universality but only the described 'regularity of observance'" is required reinforces the provision only giving "effect to usages of which the parties 'are or should be aware'. . . ." *Id.*, Comment 7. A "regularly observed" practice of protection, of which Shell "should have been aware," was enough to constitute a usage that Nanakuli had reason to believe was incorporated into the agreement.

. . . .

VI. Waiver or Course Of Performance

Course of performance under the Code is the action of the parties in carrying out the contract at issue, whereas course of dealing consists of relations between the parties prior to signing that contract. Evidence of the latter was excluded by the District Judge; evidence of the former consisted of Shell's price protection of Nanakuli in 1970 and 1971. Shell protested that the jury could not have found that those two instances of price protection amounted to a course of performance of its 1969 contract, relying on two Code comments. First, one instance does not constitute a course of performance. "A single occasion of conduct does not fall within the language of this section. . . ." Haw.Rev.Stat. § 490:2-208, Comment 4. Although the Comment rules out one instance, it does not further delineate how many acts are needed to form a course of performance. The prior occasions here were only two, but they constituted the only occasions before 1974 that would call for such conduct.

. . . .

Shell's second defense is that the Comment expresses a preference for an interpretation of waiver.

> 3. Where it is difficult to determine whether a particular act merely sheds light on the meaning of the agreement or represents a waiver of a term of the agreement, the preference is in favor of "waiver" whenever such construction, plus the application of the provisions on the reinstatement of rights waived . . . , is needed to preserve the flexible character of commercial contracts and to prevent surprise or other hardship.

Id., Comment 3.[3] The preference for waiver only applies, however, where acts are ambiguous. It was within the province of the jury to determine whether those acts were ambiguous, and if not, whether they constituted waivers or a course of performance of the contract. The jury's interpretation of those acts

---

[3] Note that Comment 3 was not incorporated in the Comments to 1-303 when 2-208 was removed as part of the Article 1 revision in 2001. See the note preceding *Nanakuli*.

as a course of performance was bolstered by evidence offered by Shell that it again price protected Nanakuli on the only two occasions of post-1974 price increases, in 1977 and 1978.

VII. Express Terms As Reasonably Consistent With Usage In Course of Performance

Perhaps one of the most fundamental departures of the Code from prior contract law is found in the parol evidence rule and the definition of an agreement between two parties. Under the U.C.C., an agreement goes beyond the written words on a piece of paper. "'Agreement' means the bargain of the parties in fact as found in their language or by implication from other circumstances including course of dealing or usage of trade or course of performance as provided in this Chapter (sections 490:1-205 and 490:2-208)." *Id.* § 490:1-201(3). Express terms, then, do not constitute the entire agreement, which must be sought also in evidence of usages, dealings, and performance of the contract itself. The purpose of evidence of usages, which are defined in the previous section, is to help to understand the entire agreement.

> [Usages are] a factor in reaching the commercial meaning of the agreement which the parties have made. The language used is to be interpreted as meaning what it may fairly be expected to mean to parties involved in the particular commercial transaction in a given locality or in a given vocation or trade. . . . Part of the agreement of the parties . . . is to be sought for in the usages of trade which furnish the background and give particular meaning to the language used, and are the framework of common understanding controlling any general rules of law which hold only when there is no such understanding.

Id. § 490:1-205, Comment 4. Course of dealings is more important than usages of the trade, being specific usages between the two parties to the contract. "[C]ourse of dealing controls usage of trade." *Id.* § 490:1-205(4). It "is a sequence of previous conduct between the parties to a particular transaction which is fairly to be regarded as establishing a common basis of understanding for interpreting their expressions and other conduct." *Id.* § 490:1-205(1). Much of the evidence of prior dealings between Shell and Nanakuli in negotiating the 1963 contract and in carrying out similar earlier contracts was excluded by the court.

A commercial agreement, then, is broader than the written paper and its meaning is to be determined not just by the language used by them in the written contract but "by their action, read and interpreted in the light of commercial practices and other surrounding circumstances. The measure and background for interpretation are set by the commercial context, which may explain and supplement even the language of a formal or final writing." *Id.*, Comment 1. Performance, usages, and prior dealings are important enough to be admitted always, even for a final and complete agreement; only if they cannot be reasonably reconciled with the express terms of the contract are they not binding on the parties. "The express terms of an agreement and an applicable course of dealing or usage of trade shall be construed wherever reasonable as consistent with each other; but when such construction is unreasonable express terms control both course of dealing and usage of trade and course of dealing controls usage of trade." *Id.* § 490:1-205(4).

Of these three, then, the most important evidence of the agreement of the parties is their actual performance of the contract. *Id.* The operative definition of course of performance is as follows: "Where the contract for sale involves repeated occasions for performance by either party with knowledge of the nature of the performance and opportunity for objection to it by the other, any course of performance accepted or acquiesced in without objection shall be relevant to determine the meaning of the agreement." *Id.* § 490:2-208(1). "Course of dealing . . . is restricted, literally, to a sequence of conduct between the parties previous to the agreement. However, the provisions of the Act on course of performance make it clear that a sequence of conduct after or under the agreement may have equivalent meaning (Section 2-208)." *Id.* 490:1-205, Comment 2. The importance of evidence of course of performance is explained: "The parties themselves know best what they have meant by their words of agreement and their action under that agreement is the best indication of what that meaning was. This section thus rounds out the set of factors which determines the meaning of the 'agreement'. . . ." *Id.* § 490:2-208, Comment 1. "Under this section a course of performance is always relevant to determine the meaning of the agreement." *Id.*, Comment 2.

Our study of the Code provisions and Comments, then, form the first basis of our holding that a trade usage to price protect pavers at times of price increases for work committed on nonescalating contracts could reasonably be construed as consistent with an express term of seller's posted price at delivery. Since the agreement of the parties is broader than the express terms and includes usages, which may even add terms to the agreement, FN34 and since the commercial background provided by those usages is vital to an understanding of the agreement, we follow the Code's mandate to proceed on the assumption that the parties have included those usages unless they cannot reasonably be construed as consistent with the express terms.

FN34. "The agreement of the parties includes that part of their bargain found in course of dealing, usage of trade, or course of performance. These sources are relevant not only to the interpretation of express contract terms, but may themselves constitute contract terms." White & Summers, *supra*, § 3-3 at 84.

Federal courts usually have been lenient in not ruling out consistent additional terms or trade usage for apparent inconsistency with express terms. The leading case on the subject is *Columbia Nitrogen Corp. v. Royster Co.*, 451 F.2d 3 (4th Cir. 1971). Columbia, the buyer, had in the past primarily produced and sold nitrogen to Royster. When Royster opened a new plant that produced more phosphate than it needed, the parties reversed roles and signed a sales contract for Royster to sell excess phosphate to Columbia. The contract terms set out the price that would be charged by Royster and the amount to be sold. It provided for the price to go up if certain events occurred but did not provide for price declines. When the price of nitrogen fell precipitously, Columbia refused to accept the full amount of nitrogen specified in the contract after Royster refused to renegotiate the contract price. The District Judge's exclusion of usage of the trade and course of dealing to explain the express quantity term in the contract was reversed. Columbia had offered to prove that the quantity set out in the contract was a mere projection to be adjusted according to market forces. Ambiguity was not necessary for the admission of evidence of usage and prior dealings. FN35 Even though the lengthy contract was the result of long and careful negotiations and apparently covered every contingency, the appellate court ruled that "the test of admissibility is not whether the contract appears on its face to be complete in every detail, but whether the proffered evidence of course of dealing and trade usage reasonably can be construed as consistent with the express terms of the agreement." *Id.* at 9. The express quantity term could be reasonably construed as consistent with a usage that such terms would be mere projections for several reasons: FN36 (1) the contract did not expressly state that usage and dealings evidence would be excluded; (2) the contract was silent on the adjustment of price or quantities in a declining market; (3) the minimum tonnage was expressed in the contract as Products Supplied, not

Products Purchased; (4) the default clause of the contract did not state a penalty for failure to take delivery; and (5) apparently most important in the court's view, the parties had deviated from similar express terms in earlier contracts in times of declining market. *Id.* at 9-10. As here, the contract's merger clause said that there were no oral agreements. The court explained that its ruling "reflects the reality of the marketplace and avoids the overly legalistic interpretations which the Code seeks to abolish." *Id.* at 10. The Code assigns dealing and usage evidence "unique and important roles" and therefore "overly simplistic and overly legalistic interpretation of a contract should be shunned." *Id.* at 11.

FN35. As discussed earlier, the District Judge here mistakenly equated ambiguity with admissibility. He said, "I think this is a close case. On the face of the contract it would seem to be unambiguous," although acknowledging that liberal commentators on the Code would let in evidence of usage and performance even without ambiguity. He only let in usage evidence because Shell's answer to interrogatory 11 provided some ambiguity, *see* note 16 *supra*, saying "I think if these can be consistently used to explain the apparently unambiguous terms, they should be allowed in." In fact, this court has ruled that ambiguity is not necessary to admit usage evidence. Board of Trade of San Francisco v. Swiss Credit Bank, 597 F.2d 146, 148 (9th Cir. 1979).

FN36. State court cases have interpreted express quantity as mere projections in similar circumstances. E.g., Campbell v. Hofstetter Farms, Inc., 251 Pa.Super. 232, 380 A.2d 463, 466-67 (1977). (Express agreement to sell a specified number of bushels of corn, wheat, and soy beans was not, as a matter of law, inconsistent with a usage of the trade that amounts specified in contracts are only estimates of a seller-farmer's farms); Loeb & Co. v. Martin, 295 Ala. 262, 327 So.2d 711, 714-15 (Ala. 1976) (It was a jury question whether, in light of trade usage, "all cotton produced on 400 acres" called for all cotton seller produced on 400 acres or for 400 acres of cotton.); Heggblade-Marguleas-Tenneco, Inc. v. Sunshine Biscuit, Inc., 59 Cal.App.3d 948, 131 Cal. Rptr. 183, 188-89 (1976) (Usage in the potato-processing trade that the amount specified in the contract was merely an estimate of buyer's requirements was admissible); Paymaster Oil Mill Co. v. Mitchell, 319 So.2d 652, 657-58 (Miss.1975) (Additional term that the seller was not obliged to deliver the full 4000 bushels of soy beans called for in the contract was admissible).

. . . .

Numerous state courts have interpreted their own state's versions of the Code in line with the weight of federal authority on the U.C.C. to admit freely evidence of additional terms, usages, and prior dealings and harmonize them in most instances with apparently contradictory express terms.

. . . .

The district judge, "in his refusal to bar evidence of the circumstances surrounding the transaction, was applying this modern principle," which was the "same view adopted" in a law review article cited by the court:

> As between immediate parties, however, all evidence whether written or oral, whether of conditions precedent or subsequent, should be admitted to determine what the parties understood the true contractual relationship to be. Any inherent improbability, such as a contradiction between what allegedly was agreed upon and what was signed will naturally affect the weight to be accorded such evidence, but procedural wrangles can be avoided by allowing the fact finder to hear all the evidence which either party wishes to bring to bear.

Id. at 396 (citing E. R. Jordan, "Just Sign Here-It's Only a Formality": Parol Evidence in the Law of Commercial Paper, 13 Ga.L.Rev. 53, 95 (1978)).

. . . .

[The court rejects as misreadings of the Code the results in "the two leading cases that have rejected usage evidence as inconsistent with express terms. . . ." One of the courts held] that only consistent usages are admissible, which is an incorrect reading of the Code. Usage is always admissible, even though the express term controls in the event of inconsistency, which is a jury question.

. . . .

Some guidelines can be offered as to how usage evidence can be allowed to modify a contract.[FN44] First, the court must allow a check on usage evidence by demanding that it be sufficiently definite and widespread to prevent unilateral post-hoc revision of contract terms by one party. The Code's intent is to put usage evidence on an objective basis. J. H. Levie, Trade Usage and Custom Under the Common Law and the Uniform Commercial Code, 40 N.Y.U.L.Rev. 1101 (1965), states:

> When trade usage adds new terms to cover matters on which the agreement is silent the court is really making a contract for the parties, even though it says it only consulted trade usage to find the parties' probable intent. There is nothing wrong or even unusual about this practice, which really is no different from reading constructive conditions into a contract. Nevertheless the court does create new obligations, and

perhaps that is why the courts often say that usage . . . must be proved by clear and convincing evidence.

. . . .

Id. at 1102. Although the Code abandoned the traditional common law test of nonconsensual custom and views usage as a way of determining the parties' probable intent, *Id.* at 1106-07, thus abolishing the requirement that common law custom be universally practiced, trade usages still must be well settled, *Id.* at 1113.

FN44. White and Summers write that usage and dealings evidence "may not only supplement or qualify express terms, but in appropriate circumstances may even override express terms." White & Summers, *supra*, § 3-3 at 84. "(T)he provision that express terms control inconsistent course of dealing and (usages and performance evidence) really cannot be taken at face value." *Id.* at 86. That reading, although at odds with the actual wording of the Code, is a realistic reading of what some of the cases allow. A better formulation of the Code's mandate is offered by R. W. Kirst, Usage of Trade and Course of Dealing: Subversion of the UCC Theory, 1977 Law Forum 811:

> The need to determine whether the parties intended a usage . . . to be part of the contract does not end if the court finds that the commercial practice is inconsistent with or contradicts the express language of the writing. If an inconsistency exists, the intention of the parties remains unclear. The parties may have intended either to include or exclude the practice. Determining the intent of the parties requires that the court attempt to construe the written term consistently with the commercial practice, if that is reasonable. If consistent construction is unreasonable the Code directs that the written term be taken as expressing the parties' intent. Before concluding that a jury could not reasonably find a consistent construction, the judge must understand the commercial background of the dispute.

Id. at 824.

. . . .

Levie, *supra*, at 1112, writes, "Astonishing as it will seem to most practicing attorneys, under the Code it will be possible in some cases to use custom to contradict the written agreement. . . . Therefore usage may be used to 'qualify' the agreement, which presumably means to 'cut down' express terms although not to negate them entirely." Here, the express price term was "Shell's Posted Price at time of delivery." A total negation of that term would be that the buyer was to set the price. It is a less than complete negation of the term that an unstated exception exists at times of price increases, at which times the old price is to be charged, for a certain period or for a specified tonnage, on work already committed at the lower price on nonescalating contracts. Such a usage forms a broad and important exception to the express term, but does not swallow it entirely. Therefore, we hold that, under these particular facts, a reasonable jury could have found that price protection was incorporated into the 1969 agreement between Nanakuli and Shell and that price protection was reasonably consistent with the express term of seller's posted price at delivery.

. . . .

Because the jury could have found for Nanakuli on its price protection claim . . . , we reverse the judgment of the District Court and reinstate the jury verdict for Nanakuli in the amount of $220,800, plus interest according to law.

Reversed and remanded with directions to enter final judgment.

APPLYING THE CODE

Problem 1-1.

Amplicon is a lease financing business; it assists companies in need of goods by purchasing those goods from a supplier and leasing them to the company. Amplicon does not purchase materials for its own use or inventory; rather, Amplicon seeks to condition its purchases on a successful lease to the interested third party. On April 20, 1989, Amplicon issued a purchase order to Radiation Systems, Inc. (RSI) for 200 antenna installations, which were to be delivered to United Press International (UPI). The purchase order was a preprinted form prepared by Amplicon which included the following language:

> Please enter our [Amplicon's] order for the above-described property, herein called the "Equipment", subject to the following terms and conditions:
>
>> 1. If the Lessee [UPI] does not accept the Equipment or any part thereof for any reason, by executing our [Amplicon's] Delivery and Acceptance Certificate within 90 days of the date hereof [April 20, 1989], or if the Lessee [UPI] does not execute any other required lease documents for any reason, we shall have no obligation hereunder.

. . . .

> 7. We [Amplicon] shall pay the total price of the Equipment within 30 days after receipt of your [RSI] invoice and written acceptance of the Equipment by the Lessee [UPI] by execution and delivery of our [Amplicon's] Delivery and Acceptance Certificate. No payments shall be made for partial shipments other than the last partial shipment, unless otherwise agreed by you [RSI] and us [Amplicon].

Beginning September 28, 1989, RSI delivered partial shipments to UPI over a 10-month period, through July 31, 1990. RSI provided Amplicon with installation certificates signed by UPI, but the certifications did not use Amplicon's "Delivery and Acceptance Certification." Amplicon paid RSI for some of the partial shipments, but did not pay 53 of the invoices totaling $70,365.04. RSI brought suit against Amplicon for payment of the outstanding invoices. Amplicon has moved for summary judgment on the grounds that (1) RSI failed to satisfy the contract's express condition that it deliver executed "Delivery and Acceptance" certificates to trigger Amplicon's obligation to pay and (2) RSI failed to execute the proper documents or complete performance within the 90-day time frame set by paragraph 1 of the contract.

Using 1-303, what arguments should RSI make to try to defeat Amplicon's motion for summary judgment? How should the court rule?

Chapter 2

Scope of Article 2 and
Special Obligations for Merchants

Key Concepts

- "Transaction in goods" (§ 2-102)
- "Goods" and "goods to be severed from realty" (§§ 2-105, 2-107)
- "Contract for sale" (§ 2-106)
- Article 2 coverage for mixed contracts (sale and non-sale, goods and non-goods)
- Who is, and is not, a merchant (§ 2-104)

This Chapter addresses two fundamental questions related to Article 2. First, which contracts are covered by Article 2? Assignment 2 begins the inquiry by considering the meaning of § 2-102, which declares the scope of Article 2. But whether a contract is governed by Article 2 is not as simple as applying § 2-102. Many contracts are "mixed transactions," combining aspects that fall within the § 2-102 definition with aspects that fall outside that definition. Assignment 3 considers how to handle such mixed transactions.

Second, although Article 2 applies to contracts entered by both merchants and non-merchants, some provisions impose additional obligations on parties who *are* merchants. Assignment 4 considers the Article 2 definition of merchant, found in § 2-104.

Assignment 2
Article 2 Definition of Scope
§§ 2-102, 2-105, 2-106, 2-107

LEARNING OUTCOMES AND OBJECTIVES

At the conclusion of this Assignment, you should be able to

- identify which contracts are within the Article 2 statement of the scope of the Article;
- determine whether a transaction is a "contract for sale," a "present sale," or a "contract to sell"; and
- determine whether the subject of a sale is "goods."

A. Article 2 Scope: "Transactions in Goods"

Each Article of the UCC includes a provision that defines the scope or applicability of that portion of the Code. The scope provision of Article 1 (§ 1-102) says that Article 1 "applies to a transaction to the extent that it is governed by another article of" the UCC, so the definitions, legal rules, and principles of interpretation contained in Article 1 apply to all transactions within the scope of Article 2.

The scope provision of Article 2 (§ 2-102) directs that Article 2 applies to "*transactions* in goods." Many words used in Article 2 are defined, either in Article 2 itself or in Article 1. Yet, "transactions" is not defined, although it is used hundreds of times in the Code and the Official Comments. So what does "transaction" mean? In common understanding, "transaction" suggests some variety of business dealing. A look at dictionary definitions of the word confirms that understanding (e.g., Black's Law Dictionary says a transaction is "the act or an instance of conducting business or other dealings; especially, the formation, performance, or discharge of a contract"). But some definitions of "transaction" are broader, e.g., "an exchange or transfer of goods, services, or funds"[1] and "agreement, contract, exchange,

---

[1]   http://www.merriam-webster.com/dictionary/transaction.

understanding, or transfer of cash or property that occurs between two or more parties and establishes a legal obligation."[2] So we start with the idea that Article 2 covers any kind of business dealings related to "goods," though it may also include non-business transactions (any kind of transfer).

But section 2-101 indicates that Article 2 should be known as "Uniform Commercial Code—Sales" and "sales" seems like a particular kind of business dealing, one that is less comprehensive than "transactions." Section 2-106(1) gives another indication of a more limited coverage: It says that in Article 2, "unless the context otherwise requires", the words "contract" and "agreement" are understood as "limited to those relating to *the present or future sale of goods*" (emphasis supplied). Because many Article 2 provisions use the words "contract" or "agreement" or other such limiting words (e.g., seller, buyer, contract to sell, sales), the result is that most of Article 2 is, indeed, limited in effect to "sales" transactions, despite the breadth of the scope provision itself. But you should remain attentive to instances in which a broader meaning is warranted or made explicit, as a few Article 2 provisions apply to non-sales transactions.

B. Scope and "Sale" of Goods

Because section 2-106(1) tells us that most provisions of Article 2 are understood as applying only to "the present or future sale of goods," the next step in understanding the scope of Article 2 is to explore the meaning of those words. Sections 2-106 and 2-102 also refer to "sale," "contract to sell," "contract for sale," "future sale," and "present sale," so we will need to look at those as well.

Reading the Code:
§ 2-106(1)

Read 2-106(1).

Question 1. The first sentence of 2-106(1) limits "contracts" and "agreements" under Article 2 to contracts and agreements relating to "*the present or future sale of goods.*" The next 3 sentences contain the definitions of "*sale,*" "*present*

---

2   http://www.businessdictionary.com/definition/transaction.html.

sale," and "*contract for sale*." Section 2-106 also refers to a "*future sale of goods*" and "*a contract to sell goods at a future time*." What is the relationship between all those concepts? Which is the broadest? Which is the narrowest? Try diagramming or drawing a picture. Where would a transaction in goods fit into your diagram? What about a lease of goods? A gift of goods? A sale of services or real estate?

APPLYING THE CODE

Problem 2-1.

At the grocery store, Jennifer fills a bag with 5 apples, takes them to the checkout counter, pays, and brings the bag to her car. Is this a sale? A present sale? A future sale?

Problem 2-2.

Florist promises to create and deliver floral centerpieces for an upcoming gala dinner. Organization promises to pay $26.00 for each centerpiece, with the number of tables (and centerpieces) to be specified when dinner reservations are complete. At the conclusion of the dinner, Organization suggests someone at each table take the centerpiece home. Guest takes the arrangement from his table. Is the transaction between Florist and Organization a sale? A present sale? A future sale? Is the transaction between Organization and Guest a sale? A present sale? A future sale?

Problem 2-3.

Taiesha agrees to loan Crosby her bicycle so he can get across town while his car is in the shop being fixed. Is this a sale? A present sale? A future sale?

Problem 2-4.

Tom orders a fancy latte at the coffee shop, pays, and moves to the spot where the drinks are delivered to customers. Is this a sale? A present sale? A future sale?

Problem 2-5.

In *Dahl v. Atritech, Inc.*,[3] the plaintiff agreed to participate in a clinical trial of an experimental medical device to be placed in his heart by a surgeon working for the device manufacturer. He signed a document prepared by the manufacturer that said the device was provided "at no cost" and that he would not be compensated for participating in the research. The document stated that study participants must return for follow-up exams to check on the operation of the device and that the costs of implantation and follow-up care would be the patient's responsibility.

After suffering injury from complications that arose during implantation of the device, the plaintiff sued the manufacturer of the device, claiming breach of warranties (promises about the quality of goods) and negligence. The manufacturer moved for summary judgment, asserting that there was no "sale."

How would you rule, and why? Read 2-304(1) as you consider your answer.

C. Scope and Sale of "Goods"

You will recall that § 2-102 defines Article 2 as applying to "transactions in goods." We have explored the meaning of "transactions" and the subset of transactions encompassed by "contracts for sale" of goods. Now we turn attention to the other part of the scope definition: "goods." "Goods" is defined in §§ 2-105 and 2-107.

**Reading the Code:
§ 2-105**

Read 2-105(1) and (2) and Comments 1 and 5.

Question 2. From the first sentence of 2-105(1), create a bullet list of what is "goods" and what is not "goods."

Question 3. What is not "movable" but is still bought and sold regularly?

---

[3]   66 UCC Rep. Serv. 2d 770 (D. Minn. 2008).

Question 4. What do you think "at the time of identification to the contract for sale" means? Read the first sentence of 2-501 for additional information on what "identification" means.

Question 5. What do you think "things in action" means?

Question 6. What are "future goods"? Can "future goods" be the subject of a "sale"?

EXAMPLES AND ANALYSIS

Do the following transactions involve goods?

Example A. Brenda engages a brick mason to tuck-point the bricks on her chimney, which involves digging out the old crumbly mortar and replacing it with fresh mortar.

Analysis: The contract involves goods: the mortar, which is a thing movable at the time of identification to the contract. The contract also involves services (the work of replacing old mortar with new). Whether such a mixed transaction is considered a "contract for sale of goods" for the purposes of Article 2 is considered in Assignment 3.

Example B. Bonita sells half of her thousand-acre farm to her neighbor.

Analysis: The contract involves only the sale of real estate, not the sale of goods.

Example C. Stacy sells her customers' past-due debts to a collection agency. The agency pays Stacy 50 cents on the dollar and then pursues the customers for payment of what they owed Stacy's business.

Analysis: This transaction involves only the sale of intangibles (the right to collect on the debt), not goods.

Example D. In *Duff v. U.S. Gold & Silver Invs., Inc.,*[4] plaintiffs agreed to pay defendants $84,950 for the purchase of nine bags of "face-value pre-1965 U.S. silver coins." When the defendants failed to deliver the coins, the plaintiffs sued, claiming liability under Article 2.

Analysis: The court ruled that the purchase was within the scope of Article 2, citing the Comment, which states the definition of "goods" is "intended to cover the sale of money when money is being treated as a commodity," rather than simply as the medium of payment.

APPLYING THE CODE

Problem 2-6.

Emmanuel sells his dry-cleaning business to Sue, including his equipment, his customer list, the business name, and transfer of the remainder of the lease term for the retail shop. Does the transaction involve a sale of goods? If so, which part is "goods"? What else does the transaction involve?

Problem 2-7.

PerfectFit Tailors agrees to make a custom-fitted suit for Yang. Does this transaction involve a sale of goods? If so, which part is "goods"? What else does the transaction involve?

Reading the Code:
Goods to be Severed from Realty
§ 2-107

Read 2-107(1) and Comment 1.

Question 7. What is included in the definition of "goods" in this subsection? What is the meaning of the phrase starting "but until . . . " and why would the drafters have included it?

---

[4]   2011 WL 4738246 (D. Or. 2011).

Read 2-107(2) and Comment 2.

Question 8. What is included in the definition of "goods" in this subsection? (There are multiple clauses and modifying phrases in the subsection; take care in parsing the sentence.)

APPLYING THE CODE

Problem 2-8.

Which of the following contracts involves "goods," at least in part? Which "goods" definition is applicable (2-105, 2-107(1), or 2-107(2))?

(a) In June, Fred Farmer sells to BigAgra at a specified price per bushel his entire crop of wheat, which he will harvest at the end of the current growing season. Would your answer be different if the sale occurred in December, before Fred planted his wheat?

(b) North Slope Oil contracts to sell 100,000 barrels of crude oil to Petro Refinery, which North Slope will pump from its oilfields in Alaska.

(c) Roscoe Rancher's property has oil deposits below the surface. He contracts with Olin Oil Company for OOC to sink a test well and buy any oil it pumps to the surface for a two-year period.

(d) Rehab, Inc. agrees to buy from Homeowner a historic building located on Homeowner's land. Rehab will move the building to another site for renovation; Homeowner intends to build a new house on the vacated site.

(e) Gretchen serves as her own general contractor in building a new house, hiring subcontractors to do various tasks in the construction. One subcontractor is Wall Systems, which sells a webbed frame made out of polystyrene into which concrete is poured to create the exterior walls. Fifteen months after her new house is completed, Gretchen discovers cracking in the walls, parallel to the location of the webbed framing.

(f) Tyesha agrees to sell her house to Buyer. The sales agreement identifies the following items as included in the sale: track lighting fixtures, gas stove, built-in kitchen appliances, speakers attached to in-wall wires for sound system, free-standing entertainment unit with shelves at appropriate height for sound system wires. The agreement specifically excludes two antique chandeliers. Tyesha sells the chandeliers separately to Architectural Antiques, which removes the chandeliers from the ceiling, leaving behind a few neatly capped wires hanging out of an electrical junction box where each chandelier had hung.

Assignment 3
Mixed Transactions and Article 2

We have seen that the process of determining whether a transaction is within Article 2 starts with asking whether the transaction involves a "contract for sale" of "goods" under § 2-102, but the task often does not end there. Many transactions that involve a contract for sale of goods also include a non-sale-of-goods aspect, most often an agreement to provide services. For example, a purchase of carpeting often includes installation; servicing of a car often includes the cost of an itemized list of parts. Other kinds of mixed transactions are possible (e.g., combining a sale of goods with a sale of real estate, or a sale of goods with a lease of goods or property), but the combination of goods and services is by far the most common.

> ## Article 2 Coverage: Why Does it Matter?
>
> Article 2 provisions parallel common law contract doctrine in many instances, but some aspects differ dramatically. The most important differences are with respect to the existence and disclaimer of warranties, the standards for rejecting performance, the statute of limitations, and the rules for finding agreement in the presence of differing terms in offer and acceptance.

LEARNING OUTCOMES AND OBJECTIVES

In this Assignment, you will learn the factors generally considered to determine whether a mixed transaction is within the scope of Article 2. At the completion of this Assignment, you should be able to

- identify a mixed transaction;
- make effective arguments about whether a mixed transaction falls within the scope of Article 2; and
- predict the likely outcome of "easy" cases.

A. Preliminary Question: Is the Contract Divisible?

Sometimes a mixed transaction is comprised of two or more separate contracts. Whether any particular contract is "divisible" into multiple contracts is a question of law (decided by the judge), though the answer depends on a factual analysis (whether the parties intended such a separation of the contract parts). In reaching its decision, a court would typically consider (i) whether the parties gave a single assent to the whole transaction or instead assented separately to several transactions, and (ii) whether a unified price was paid for the whole transaction or instead separate consideration was given for different performances. If dividing the transaction into its separate parts results in a sale-of-goods part and a non-sale-of-goods part, the court then applies the proper body of law to each part of the contract. Whether a transaction is or might be understood as divisible should be asked at the outset, as the outcome affects how and whether to conduct the next steps in the analysis of Article 2 coverage. Note, however, that most mixed transactions are not divisible because the facts do not establish that two separate contracts were entered.

B. Predominant Purpose Analysis of Non-Divisible Mixed Contracts

If a mixed contract is not divisible, courts almost uniformly rely upon a "predominant purpose" analysis to determine whether Article 2 applies to the transaction. Under this analysis, the test for including the entire transaction within the scope of Article 2 "is not whether [the contracts] are mixed, but granting that they are mixed, whether their predominant factor, their thrust, their purpose, reasonably stated, is the rendition of services, with goods incidentally involved (e.g., contract with an artist for a painting) or is a transaction of sale, with labor incidentally involved (e.g., installation of a water heater in a bathroom)."[1]

Applying this test "requires consideration of both the contractual language and extrinsic evidence, such as the circumstances surrounding the contract formation and the parties' performance of the contract." *Action Group, Inc. v. Nanostatics Corp.*, 82 UCC Rep. Serv. 2d 305 (Ohio App. 2013). The question whether goods or services predominates in a hybrid contract is one of fact, but a court may decide the question as a matter of law if there is no genuine issue of material fact. In *Insul-Mark Midwest, Inc. v. Modern Materials, Inc.*, 612 N.E.2d 550, 555 (Ind. 1993), the court described aspects of the contractual circumstances that may be considered to determine if the predominant purpose of the mixed transaction is a sale of goods:

---

[1]   Bonebrake v. Cox, 499 F.2d 951 (8th Cir. 1974).

To determine whether the predominant thrust of a mixed contract is to provide services or goods, one first looks to the language of the contract in light of the situation of the parties and the surrounding circumstances. Specifically one looks to the terms describing the performance of the parties, and the words used to describe the relationship between the parties.

Beyond the contractual terms themselves, one looks to the circumstances of the parties, and the primary reason they entered into the contract. One also considers the final product the purchaser bargained to receive, and whether it may be described as a good or a service.

Finally, one examines the costs involved for the goods and services, and whether the purchaser was charged only for a good, or a price based on both goods and services. If the cost of the goods is but a small portion of the overall contract price, such fact would increase the likelihood that the services portion predominates.

The factors listed above and the examples below should help you articulate a rationale for calling a contract primarily one for goods or for services. That said, a party may use any relevant circumstance to persuade the judge.

EXAMPLES AND ANALYSIS

From the discussion above, you should create a list of relevant facts and factors to use in arguing predominant purpose. As you read each example, supplement that list with additional items you glean from the case descriptions.

Example A: *Pass v. Shelby Aviation, Inc.*[2]

As part of an annual inspection and servicing of a small plane, an aviation company replaced both rear wing attach-point brackets on the plane. After the plane crashed, the estate of the decedents sued the aviation company, relying on Article 2. The plaintiff alleged that (1) the brackets sold and installed by the aviation company were defective because they lacked the bolts necessary to secure them to the airplane; and (2) the company's employees failed to install the necessary bolts.

---

[2]   2000 WL 388775 (Tenn. Ct. App. 2000).

The lawsuit complaint said that Shelby Aviation was "in the business of maintenance, service, storage, and upkeep of aircraft." The invoice prepared by Shelby Aviation contained a handwritten description of repairs performed and parts used, with a preprinted paragraph authorizing "the following repair work to be done along with the necessary material." The invoice checked a box indicating performance of the "annual 100 hour periodic inspection," noted the parts used and the amount charged for each and the service performed with its cost, and called for signature of the plane's owner acknowledging "acceptance of repaired plane." The plaintiff argued that 75% of the final bill was parts-related; the parts themselves were 37% of the bill, with an additional 38% to install them.

Analysis: The court concluded that the transaction was not predominantly a sale of goods and thus not within Article 2. What facts would you cite to support the court's conclusion? What facts would you cite and what arguments would you make on behalf of the plaintiff to support a conclusion that the contract is within Article 2? If you were the judge, which way would you rule?

Example B: *Action Group, Inc. v. NanoStatics Corp.*[3]

NanoStatics is a company that creates nanofibers (fibers with diameters of less than 100 nanometers) for commercial use. Action Group is a company that specializes in product development and manufacturing. NanoStatics approached Action Group seeking its services in developing and manufacturing a "head" for use in NanoStatics' nanofiber production process. The contract was created when the president of NanoStatics signed a letter from Action Group that said Action Group looked forward to "working with NanoStatics and servicing your needs in the initial research and development stage along with the production stage of your products." The letter specified hourly rates for labor during the development phase and a cost-plus-30% rate for billing on production "of your items." Using specifications provided by NanoStatics, Action Group created a "head," but Nano-Statics rejected delivery because it claimed the product had severe defects and was unusable. Action Group filed a complaint, seeking payment for "manufactured goods as requested by and delivered to'" NanoStatics.

---

[3]   82 UCC Rep.Serv. 2d 305 (Ohio Ct. App. 2013).

Analysis: The court concluded that the contract was predominantly a sale of goods and, thus, within Article 2. What facts would you cite to support the court's conclusion? What facts would you cite and what arguments would you make to support a conclusion that the contract is not within Article 2? If you were the judge, which way would you rule?

Example C. *Distributorship Contracts*

A distributorship contract typically involves both services (creating sales opportunities for the manufacturer's goods) and sale of the goods themselves (the distributor buys goods from the manufacturer and resells them to third parties). Whether such a mixed transaction is within the scope of Article 2 depends on an analysis of the relative importance of sales and service.

In *Buttorff v. United Electronic Laboratories, Inc.*,[4] the plaintiff was hired to develop a market for the sale of a camera manufactured by the defendant and used primarily for security purposes by banks and other money-handling institutions. The defendant agreed to sell the product to the plaintiff at a net price of $440 per camera and for the plaintiff to resell the product to his customers at a price of $985 plus installation cost. The orders for the cameras were always forwarded directly to the defendant, which then shipped the purchased product to the customer and billed the customer directly. After the customer paid, the plaintiff would receive the difference in the established prices. The plaintiff also alleged an agreement for him to operate as the exclusive agent to sell or distribute the camera and to receive a commission on the sale of all cameras and also film for the cameras, whether he sold the particular items or not.

In *Leibel v. Raynor Manufacturing Co.*,[5] the parties entered an oral agreement for the plaintiff to have an exclusive dealer-distributorship for the defendant's garage doors in a 50-mile radius territory. The defendant agreed to sell and deliver its garage doors to the plaintiff at the factory distributor price, and the plaintiff agreed to sell, install, and service the defendant's products exclusively. The plaintiff borrowed substantial sums of money to make capital expenditures, purchase an inventory, and provide working capital for starting the business, including rental of storage and office space, employment of personnel, and purchase of a service truck, tools, and equipment.

---

[4]   459 S.W.2d 581 (Ky. 1970).

[5]   571 S.W.2d 640 (Ky. Ct. App. 1978).

Analysis: *Buttorf* and *Leibel* were decided in the same jurisdiction by the same court (Kentucky Court of Appeals). The *Buttorf* opinion noted that "isolated expressions in the instrument indicating whether it is [a sales or an agency contract] are not necessarily controlling; on the contrary, the courts will ignore apparently inconsistent language used, and look to the real nature of the agreement between the parties, what its real purpose was, and what, from the nature of the transaction, must have been in the minds of the parties." It concluded that the camera distributorship agreement was predominantly a services, not sale of goods, contract. In the later *Leibel* case, in contrast, the court concluded that the contract was a sale of goods contract.

What facts would you cite to support the court's conclusions in the two cases? What facts would you cite and what arguments would you make to support a different determination? If you were the judge, which way would you rule in the two cases?

Additional Examples:

Cases finding primarily a contract for sale of goods and therefore Article 2 coverage include

- *Pittsley v. Houser,* 875 P.2d 232 (Idaho Ct. App. 1994) (contract for $4319.50 for sale and installation of carpet and removal of old carpet, where the choice of carpet of a certain quality and color appeared more important than who would provide or install it, and the part of the price attributable to installation was $700);

- *Neibarger v. Universal Cooperatives, Inc.,* 486 N.W.2d 612 (Mich. 1992) (contract for sale of milking system, where the buyer testified that he "'bought the system complete' and hoped 'just to go to the barn and turn it on and everything worked,'" demonstrating that the "thrust or purpose" of the contract was to acquire a milking system that incidentally required design and installation services); and

- *Meyers v. Henderson Const. Co.,* 370 A.2d 547 (N.J. Super. 1977) (contract to supply and install overhead doors; while the prefabricated disassembled doors were useless without a substantial amount of labor, the court noted that services always play an important role in the use of goods, but the predominant reason for the contract was procurement of overhead doors with the installation service incidental).

Cases finding primarily a sale of services and, therefore, no Article 2 coverage include

- *Higgins v. Lauritzen*, 530 N.W.2d 171 (Mich. Ct. App. 1995) (contract for drilling of well and installation of piping and water pump; plaintiff's affidavit stated the "primary purpose" of the agreement was for defendant "to provide the service of improving my property by drilling a well to provide water for domestic and farming purposes" and that he had sought out defendant to do the installation after two previous failed drilling attempts by others; complaint alleged improper installation of water pump and damage to health of his cattle from stray voltage);

- *Care Display, Inc. v. Didde-Glaser, Inc.*, 589 P.2d 599 (Kan. 1979) (contract for custom design and construction of themed booths for trade fair, where the overriding concern throughout the contract negotiations was development of an artistic or design concept with the actual construction of the booth incidental); and

- *Heuerman v. B&M Construction, Inc.*, 833 N.E.2d 382 (Ill. Ct. App. 2005) (contract with trucking company to supply and deliver gravel; contract specified type of vehicle to be used, that the loads were to be "dumped" at a particular site, and called the purchaser "Customer" rather than "Buyer"; itemized costs showed two-thirds was attributable to hauling and one-third to the cost of procuring rock from gravel companies).

 Reading the Code

Question 1. If a mixed transaction is considered to be within the scope of Article 2, what happens if no part of Article 2 addresses the issue at stake? Read 1-103(b) and Comment 2. What effect does 1-103(b) have on contracts that are solely sale-of-goods contracts (not mixed transactions)?

C. The Gravamen Test: Alternative or Aberration?

In one mixed transaction case that is sometimes mentioned by commentators and courts, a court applied an alternative to the predominant purpose test. The case involved a contract for the installation of a swimming pool. The court conceded that service would have predominated over goods if the court applied the predominant purpose test (which had been adopted in that jurisdiction), but noted that the "gravamen" of the complaint (a breach of warranty claim) was focused on the goods component, not the services component. The court concluded that public policy warranted allowing the consumer-plaintiffs' breach of warranty claim, despite the outcome of the predominant purpose test.[6] Commentators and courts sometimes suggest that this precedent offers an alternative to the predominant purpose test, in which the focus of the inquiry shifts from the purpose of the contract to the nature of the legal complaint (the so-called "gravamen test"). However, the authors of this casebook have been unable to identify a single other case in which this test was actually applied.[7]

APPLYING THE CODE

For each of the problems below, articulate the arguments for and against determining that the specified contract is within the scope of Article 2. What questions would you ask the parties in order to collect additional information relevant to that determination? If you were the judge, how would you decide the issue? If you were advising one of the parties and they wanted the transaction to be covered by Article 2, how would you structure the contract to reach that result?

Problem 3-1.

Emmanuel sells his dry-cleaning business to Sue, including his equipment, his customer list, the business name, and transfer of the remainder of the lease term for the retail shop. In Problem 2-6, we considered whether the transaction "involves" a sale of goods and concluded it does. Now consider whether the mixed transaction is within the scope of Article 2.

Problem 3-2.

PerfectFit Tailors agrees to make a custom-fitted suit for Yang. In Problem 2-7, we considered whether the transaction "involves" a sale of goods and concluded it does. Now consider whether the mixed transaction is within the scope of Article 2.

---

[6] Anthony Pools v. Sheehan, 455 A.2d 434 (Md. 1983).
[7] Anthony Pools cited Newmark v. Gimbel's Inc., 258 A.2d 697 (N.J. 1969) and Worrell v. Barnes, 484 P.2d 573 (Nev. 1971). *See also* cases cited in In re Trailer and Plumbing Supplies, 578 A.2d 343, 346 (N.H. 1990).

Problem 3-3.

Charles agrees to buy a van from a dealer that specializes in customizing new vehicles. The purchase agreement specifies that the dealer will present two to four designs from which Charles will choose. Dealer will acquire the new van, hand paint the exterior in accordance with the design, modify the interior as agreed, and install a specified upgraded CD/DVD system and a custom sunroof. The custom items add 25% to the base cost of the van. Is the contract within the scope of Article 2?

Problem 3-4.

Tony's Pools is a licensed contractor for building in-ground swimming pools and also has a retail store location displaying and selling pool equipment. Peter Shepherd visits the store to discuss having a pool built in his backyard. After viewing catalog pictures of various pool styles, the parties sign a two-page "Pool Purchase Agreement." On the first page, Tony's Pools "agrees to construct for and sell to" Shepherd, called "Buyer," the "swimming pool and related equipment described below to be installed" at Shepherd's home for a fixed cash price. The pool is made of prefabricated fiberglass sections and a vinyl liner, manufactured by Tony's and assembled and sealed together on site. The agreement includes specifications for excavation, installation of steel reinforcement ribs, finishing the pool interior with hand-troweled waterproof plaster, and supplying and installing a six-inch band of water-line tile. The cost of the pool as a whole is $7980. Attached to the "Pool Purchase Agreement" is a list of "Optional Equipment Supplied," including a detachable diving board, two removable pool ladders, and a skimmer (an aquatic robot that continuously vacuums the water surface for debris), with prices specified for each, for a total of $1200 added on to the $7980 pool cost. If a dispute develops over the contractor's performance, should the contract be considered to be within the provisions of Article 2? Does it matter if the claim is about a defect in one of the fiberglass sections, in the quality of the excavation work, or in the quality of the diving board?

Problem 3-5.

True North Companies and RR Industries enter an agreement for the purpose of co-developing and building composite railcars, using a patented technology licensed to True North and a plan created by a team of engineers drawn from both companies. Under the agreement, True North will produce carbodies (the boxlike structures on railcars); RR will manufacture steel under-carriages (with platforms and wheels) at a site adjacent to the True North facility, which True North will lease to RR. True North will mount its carbodies on the completed undercarriages and RR will then market and sell the composite railcars. Because the engineering plan for the composite cars was preliminary, the agreement called for later amendment to the specifications as might be necessary. The agreement calls for production of 2000 railcars; RR is to pay True North a specified price per carbody for the first 500, priced to compensate True North for "tooling, equipment, and learning curve" costs associated with creating the carbody design for the project. The price to be paid to True North for the remaining carbodies is True North's costs of manufacture plus 15%. If RR's sales figures for the composite railcars show a profit of more than 20% on the railcar sales, RR and True North will share evenly in the additional profits. The agreement is entitled "Carbodies Supply Agreement" and sets forth "the rights and obligations regarding the production and sale of carbodies." Among other provisions, it contains one that addresses the nature of "warranties" on the carbodies.

When disputes arise between the parties, True North sues, claiming damages, including various forms of economic loss from business disruption. RR claims that the contract is for the sale of goods (carbodies), while True North claims the contract is not within the scope of Article 2. The outcome is significant because $6.7 million of the damages claimed by True North are consequential damages, not available to sellers under Article 2. What arguments would you make on behalf of each party and, if you were the judge, how would you decide the issue?

Assignment 4
Definition of Merchant
§ 2-104

Although Article 2 governs transactions by both merchants and non-merchants, Article 2 also includes some provisions that impose special obligations on merchants who enter contracts for the sale of goods. This Assignment considers the Article 2 standard for determining whether a party is a merchant and why being a merchant may matter.

LEARNING OUTCOMES AND OBJECTIVES

At the completion of this Assignment, you should be able to

- determine whether it matters if a party is a merchant;
- apply the Article 2 definition of merchant to determine whether a particular contracting party will be considered a merchant;
- distinguish between "goods" and "practices" merchants; and
- predict the likely outcome in "easy" cases and make a reasonable argument about best outcome in "hard" cases.

Section 2-104 describes two different kinds of merchants (goods merchants and practices merchants) and the consequences under the Code vary according to whether a contracting party is one or the other kind of merchant (or both). Keep that distinction in mind as you work through the remainder of this Assignment.

Reading the Code: §§ 2-102 and 2-104

Re-read 2-102.

Question 1. Recall that 2-102 specifies which transactions are within the scope of Article 2. Under 2-102, does whether a transaction is covered by Article 2 depend on the nature of the parties who entered the transaction (e.g., whether the contracting parties are individuals, corporations, consumers, farmers, or merchants)? Are transactions by any, some, or all such parties covered by Article 2?

Read 2-104 Comment 1.

Question 2. Why does Article 2 contain a definition of "merchant"?

Read 2-104(1).

Question 3.

(a) May a corporation be a "person" for the purposes of 2-104(1)?

(b) Careful attention to the multiple paths through the merchant definition is critical to understanding it. List the ways in which a "person" may be shown to be a merchant. You should come up with at least 3 ways. For a hint about the multiple pathways, read the first paragraph of Comment 2 and recall the note above about the kinds of merchants included in the 2-104 definition.

Read 2-104 Comment 2.

In answering Questions 4, 5, and 6 and in subsequent examples and problems in this Assignment, you will see that applying the merchant definition requires reference to sections of Article 2 that you have not yet studied. In each instance, you do not have to understand the substance of the referenced provision, only how it intersects with 2-104.

Question 4. Make a jot list of the 4 special provisions as to merchants identified in the second paragraph of Comment 2. What kind of "knowledge or skill" (2-104(1)) is required to qualify as a merchant for these provisions?

Question 5. Make a jot list of the 3 special provisions as to merchants identified in the third paragraph of Comment 2. What kind of "knowledge or skill" is required to qualify as a merchant for these provisions?

Question 6. Make a jot list of the 6 provisions as to merchants identified in the fourth paragraph of Comment 2. What kind of "knowledge or skill" is required to qualify as a merchant for these provisions?

Question 7. In the first phrase of 2-104(1), what does it mean to "deal" in goods of the kind? What effect does the use of the words "otherwise by his occupation" have on your answer to that question? What effect do the Comments have on your understanding of "deals"?

Question 8. Are the following statements accurate paraphrases of 2-104?

    (a) "A seller or buyer is a merchant for the purposes of 2-104 if he or she has specialized knowledge about the goods being bought and sold."

    (b) "An occasional, one time seller, who is not engaged in the business of selling the goods in question, or holding himself out as a person who deals in such goods, is not a 'merchant.'"

Question 9. Does a professional musician become a merchant with respect to cars by persistently announcing that she is an expert on them? Does a computer programmer become a merchant with respect to cars by studying about automobiles and actually knowing more about them than the average professional auto mechanic?

EXAMPLES AND ANALYSIS

Example A: *McGregor v. Dimou*[1]

Dimou owns a body and fender shop. He purchased a 1973 Volvo from a salvage bureau, did substantial body repair work on the vehicle, and installed a rebuilt transmission. He drove the car for about a year and then placed a notice in the publication "Buy Lines" advertising sale of a 1973 Volvo "in very good condition." Dimou had previously bought two or three vehicles from the same salvage company, repaired them, and sold them through "Dimou Collision."

Donald McGregor, having recently relocated from New Zealand to the United States, responded to Dimou's notice. McGregor drove to Dimou's home and, after a short test drive, negotiated for and bought the vehicle. McGregor later discovered that the car would start only in reverse gear and, when he took the car to be inspected, was told that the car was seriously defective, hazardous, and not repairable. He sued Dimou, claiming that Dimou was a merchant of cars under 2-104 and had breached the implied warranty of merchantability (2-314).

Analysis: The court concluded that Dimou was not a merchant with respect to cars. What arguments would you make to support the court's conclusion? What arguments would you make to support a conclusion that he *is* a merchant with respect to cars? If you were the judge, how would you rule? Assuming the court is correct, would the outcome be different if the sale had been made at his body and fender shop rather than at Dimou's home? If the question were whether he was a merchant with respect to practices for purposes of applying the statute of frauds (2-201)?

Example B: *Smith v. General Mills, Inc.*[2]

Monica Smith and her husband operated their family farm for almost 40 years before her husband's death. For the next 10 years, Monica's sons, Jack and Frank, operated the farm as partners. Jack went on to other pursuits but, after Frank's death, Monica made Jack the personal representative of

---

[1]   422 N.Y.S.2d 806 (Civ. Ct. 1979).

[2]   968 P.2d 723 (Mont. 1998).

the estate to operate the farm and also act on her behalf in farm transactions. Jack entered a contract with a General Mills-owned grain elevator for sale of feed wheat from the farm. Jack subsequently entered a second contract with a different General Mills-owned grain elevator to sell the same wheat, but at a higher price. When General Mills withheld the difference in price, Monica sued. The court had to decide if Monica was a merchant under 2-104 for the purpose of application of the statute of frauds (2-201).

Analysis: The court noted that there is a split of authority on the issue of whether farmers are merchants under 2-104, with a majority of courts holding that a farmer may be included under the definition of merchant in some instances. Whether a particular farmer qualifies as a merchant cannot be determined through application of a per se rule, the court said; rather, courts must analyze the party's status on a case-by-case basis. The court reviewed the facts considered by the trial court: Jack "had an operative knowledge of the grain marketing system, including how the buying and selling worked, how competition moved the market, and what factors affected price. He was familiar with all facets of marketing the grain, including knowledge of the product, how to produce it, how to store it, where and how to sell it, and how to negotiate the best terms possible for its disposition. Jack's experience in marketing grain spanned a period of many years, and he had even been entrusted with the marketing of grain in a fiduciary capacity for his mother and his brother's estate. Furthermore, Jack acknowledged in writing as part of the [second] elevator contract that he was a merchant for purposes of marketing the grain he produced." The court concluded that Jack, and, therefore, Monica, was a merchant for the purposes of the statute of frauds (2-201).

After considering the court's analysis, do you think that it is more likely a farmer would be considered a merchant as to practices (for purposes of 2-201) or a merchant as to goods (for purposes of 2-314)?

Example C: *Fear Ranches, Inc. v. Berry*[3]

Fear Ranches, through its president, Kenneth Fear, sought to expand his breeding herds and he viewed and later bought cattle from the ranch of H.C. Berry for that purpose. Berry had previously entered a transaction to sell the same animals to Kelly Perschbacker, a cattle trader, but Perschbacker

---

[3]   470 F.2d 905 (10th Cir. 1972).

did not complete payment. Berry had previously only sold cattle to meat packers. Berry's planned sale to Perschbacker was the result of "financial difficulties."

Because Perschbacker had not completed payment and had not taken possession of the cattle at the time of the sale to Fear, they were still branded as Berry's cattle. Both Berry and Perschbacker signed as sellers of the cattle. Some time after the sale, it was discovered that the cattle had a contagious disease that made them unsuitable as breeders and led to the infection of other cattle owned by Fear. Fear sued both Berry and Perschbacker for breach of implied warranties under 2-314, so he was required to establish that they were merchants of the cattle.

Analysis: The court concluded that Berry was *not* a merchant under 2-104 and 2-314, but Perschbacker was. What arguments would you make to support the court's conclusions about each seller? If you were the judge, how would you rule?

Example D: *Sea Harvest, Inc. v. Rig & Crane Equipment Corp.*[4]

Rig & Crane Equipment Corp. is in the business of leasing and sometimes selling hydraulic cranes and similar equipment. For the past four years, 10% of the company's inventory in those years was for sales and 90% for rentals. For one of those years, a financial statement showed gross revenue of $1,300,000 for sales and $425,000 for rentals. The company's advertising material offered equipment for sale.

Rig & Crane financed its purchases of cranes through loans from Allis Chalmers Credit Corp. Allis Chalmers maintains a security interest in the cranes it finances (a right to reclaim the equipment if Rig & Crane defaults on the loan). In order to give Allis Chalmers priority as a creditor against others with interests in the same equipment, the security agreement must be formally "filed" so other potential creditors can check filed financing statements to determine whether security interests exist.

Sea Harvest, Inc. is in the fishing business. It buys equipment for use in its fishing operations, and sells equipment when it is no longer useful in the business. Sea Harvest leased a hydraulic crane from Rig & Crane. The lease included an option to buy that Sea Harvest exercised after 2 years renting the crane. Allis Chalmers Credit Corp. had financed Rig & Crane's purchase

---

[4]   436 A.2d 553 (N.J. Super. 1981).

of the crane leased to Sea Harvest, and, shortly after Sea Harvest exercised its option to buy, Allis Chalmers notified Sea Harvest that Rig & Crane had defaulted on its loan and Allis Chalmers intended to reclaim the crane under the security agreement. Sea Harvest defended by claiming it was "a buyer in the ordinary course of business" from Rig & Crane.

Although the issues for decision in the lawsuit arose under UCC Article 9, the court considered whether Sea Harvest was a merchant under 2-104 in order to determine if Sea Harvest should have operated under the then-higher merchant standard of good faith.[5] The court also considered whether Rig & Crane was in the business of selling cranes in order to determine if Sea Harvest had bought its crane "in the ordinary course of business," a critical issue under Article 9.

Analysis: The court concluded that Sea Harvest did not operate as a merchant in its crane purchase and that Rig & Crane was in the business of selling cranes. What arguments would you make to support the court's conclusion that Sea Harvest was not a merchant in the purchase transaction? What arguments would you make on behalf of Allis Chalmers to support a claim that Sea Harvest was a merchant? If you were the judge, how would you rule? Would your answer or arguments be different if the "merchant" issue came up with respect to applying the statute of frauds (2-201)?

If called upon to decide whether Rig & Crane was a merchant under 2-104 in the transaction with Sea Harvest, how would you rule? Why?

APPLYING THE CODE

As you have seen, a party may be a merchant with respect to goods or a merchant with respect to practices. Which kind of merchant status matters depends on the claims made in the case. In order to analyze the problems below, you will need to determine which kind of merchant status is at issue in order to apply the appropriate part of the merchant definition. While the problems refer to other Code provisions

---

[5]   At the time, good faith for non-merchants required "honesty in fact"; good faith for merchants required both honesty in fact and the observance of reasonable commercial standards of fair dealing in the trade. Subsequent amendments to Articles 1 and 2 created a uniform standard for good faith in 1-201(b)(20), but a significant number of jurisdictions maintain the bifurcated definitions of good faith. For further discussion, see Assignment 6.

(e.g., the statute of frauds, 2-201, and the implied warranty of merchantability, 2-314), you need not understand the operation of those additional provisions in order to answer the questions regarding merchant status. These scenarios, like those presented in the Examples and Analysis above, illustrate how merchant questions may arise in commercial disputes.

Problem 4-1.

Koursa is in the business of leasing printing equipment to third parties. Manroland, Inc. acts as the United States' sales representative for printing presses manufactured by Manroland AG, a German company. Koursa entered a contract with Manroland, Inc. to buy a printing press manufactured by Manroland AG; the press was to be delivered to Kappa Graphics, pursuant to a lease agreement between Koursa and Kappa. The Koursa-Manroland contract also provided that Manroland would provide 300 hours of training in the use of the equipment, warranty support for an additional year, and reduced pricing on any parts ordered for a 24-month period. Manroland AG declared bankruptcy before the printing press was delivered. Representatives of Koursa and Manroland engaged in an extensive correspondence about whether Manroland would be able to meet the specified delivery deadline under the contract. When litigation ensued, a critical question was whether the special standard in 2-609(2) applicable to contracts "between merchants" would be used to determine if Koursa had reasonable grounds for insecurity and whether Manroland gave adequate assurances of performance. Does that special standard apply?

Problem 4-2.

State University operates several agricultural research stations at which it grows crops for research purposes, and has done so for several decades. One of the pieces of equipment at each station is a grain dryer, used to remove moisture from the grain before storage. The University periodically purchased a grain dryer for each facility, ordering the equipment through its centralized purchasing department. Five years ago, when the grain dryer at the Southwest research station had to be replaced, the superintendent of the station consulted an agricultural engineering professor in University's Department of Agricultural Engineering to help identify the specifications needed for the new grain dryer. The engineer advised on the fan size, BTU requirements, and other features that should be included. The superintendent made the purchase based on the recommendations of the engineer.

A few years after the grain dryer was installed, it caught on fire, damaging both the grain dryer and the structure to which the dryer was attached. University determined that the fire was caused by the failure of a solenoid valve that stops the flow of fuel to the unit when the air in the dryer reaches a certain temperature. University sued the manufacturer of the valve and the seller of the grain dryer, claiming that the valve had failed, causing the dryer to overheat and start the fire. Under what is known as the "economic loss doctrine" (covered in more detail in Assignment 22), economic loss (like the damage to the facility surrounding the grain dryer) cannot be recovered from a seller if the buyer is a merchant with respect to goods of the kind. Can University recover from the defendants for its "economic loss"?

Problem 4-3.

US Industries, Inc. (USI) was in the business of manufacturing and selling irrigation pipe. At the request of the company, one of the USI employees successfully copied a competitor's molding machine used in manufacturing end-caps for use and sale with irrigation pipe, modifying the machine slightly to permit it to use USI's hydraulic system rather than electricity as a power source. Several years later, before ceasing to operate as a business, USI sold all its assets to Ulysses Irrigation Company, including the molding machine. When the molding machine caused injury to a Ulysses employee, that employee sought recovery from USI, claiming breach of an implied warranty under 2-314. USI denied liability, claiming it was not a merchant and therefore made no implied warranty. Is USI correct?

Problem 4-4.

Rush Johnson owns two farms in two Missouri counties. He owns a third farm in partnership with Andrew Baer, and Baer carries out the actual farming operations on both the partnership land and the two farms belonging solely to Johnson. For many years, Johnson has sold soybeans to various grain elevators. Last year, when Johnson was getting ready to sell his annual crop, he checked with a number of elevators to determine the market price of soybeans. He called the Missouri Farmers Association elevator in Salisbury and asked that he be notified when beans reached $4.00 a bushel. The secretary at the elevator called Johnson on January 2 and told him the beans were selling at $4.02 a bushel. Johnson orally agreed to sell his crop, which he estimated would be between 5000 and 6000 bushels. The secretary sent a letter confirming a contract for sale of 5000 bushels of soybeans, which letter Johnson discarded. Johnson delivered less than 5000 bushels. Johnson sued the elevator for failure to pay the agreed price for the bushels he did deliver; the elevator counter-sued, claiming Johnson did not deliver the promised amount.

(a) Under 2-201, if both the MFA elevator and Johnson are merchants, the written confirmation from the elevator will be sufficient to allow enforcement of the contract for the entire 5000 bushels. If they are not both merchants, the elevator can enforce the contract only up to the number of bushels actually delivered. (*See* 2-201(3)(c).) How should the court rule on the question whether Johnson is a merchant for the purposes of applying 2-201?

(b) Assume the soybean crop was diseased and the MFA elevator sued Johnson for breach of implied warranty under 2-314. To succeed, the plaintiff elevator must show that Johnson is a merchant for the purposes of applying 2-314. How should the court rule on the question of whether Johnson is a merchant for this purpose?

Problem 4-5.

Start Plastics, Inc. designs and manufactures fiberglass products, including brine tanks, truck caps, sun visors, motorcycle trailers, lawnmower parts, funeral vaults, and custom fiberglass applications. When Start manufactures brine tank systems, it typically supplies only the tanks, without any conveyors. To satisfy a new customer, Maggio Cheese Company, Start agreed to deliver a complete brine tank system for the buyer's use in processing cheese. To accomplish that, Start contacted Marchetta Elevator Company and arranged for Marchetta to design, manufacture, and install a conveyor system to attach to the brine tanks. Marcheta delivered and installed the conveyor at Start's facility, and Start then delivered to Maggio the complete package; Maggio had no direct dealing with Marchetta and understood that Start did not typically provide conveyors with its brine tanks. Start subsequently provided two more complete systems of brine tanks with conveyors. When an employee of Maggio was later injured by the conveyor belt as he was cleaning the equipment, he sued Start, claiming breach of implied warranty under 2-314 in conjunction with the sale of the brine tank system to his employer. Start denied liability, claiming it is not a merchant and, therefore, did not give a warranty under 2-314. Is Start correct?

Problem 4-6.

Valley Iron & Steel, Inc. manufactures cast iron products. Richard Thorin established a new retail store to sell equipment and supplies for tree-planting contracts and workers. Thorin met with the manager of Valley Iron & Steel to ask if Valley could manufacture castings of hoedad collars. A hoedad is a forestry tool used for planting seedling trees. The collar of a hoedad secures the metal blade to a wooden handle. Thorin showed the manager a sample casting made by another company and asked him to duplicate the casting. Thorin noted that the planting operation would likely encounter some rocky terrain so the hoedads should be made from durable material; the manager suggested iron. The parties agreed on a price, and Thorin obtained and delivered a pattern for the collar. Valley delivered the completed hoedads to Thorin. Problems immediately developed with the finished product; Thorin's customers complained that the castings were breaking too easily. Thorin contacted another foundry that used the pattern to make castings out of steel, which turned out to be more durable than the iron castings. In the suit by Thorin against Valley Iron & Steel, Thorin alleged breach of an implied warranty of merchantability under 2-314. Valley denied liability, claiming it is not a merchant and therefore did not give a warranty under 2-314. Is Valley correct?

Chapter 3

Contract Formation and
Content of the Contract

Key Concepts

- General contract formation under § 2-204
- Acceptance by promise or conduct (§ 2-206)
- Irrevocable firm offers (§ 2-205)
- Sources of contract terms: express, implied, and default
- UCC approach to the "battle of the forms" (§ 2-207)
  - When is a contract formed if an acceptance contains additional or different terms from the offer? (§§ 2-207(1) & 2-207(3), first sentence)
  - If a contract is formed under such circumstances, what are its terms? (§§ 2-207(2) & 2-207(3), second sentence)
- Parol evidence rule guidance on the relationship between the written agreement and unwritten contract terms (§ 2-202)

In this Chapter, you will learn the Article 2 rules that govern the formation of contracts (offer and acceptance) and how to determine what terms become parts of contracts. The Article 2 rules on contract formation appear in sections 2-204 through 2-207, but these rules do not cover every aspect of contract formation; much of sale-of-goods contract formation remains governed by the common law, as invited by § 1-103(b). Similarly, although some interpretative principles are established by Article 2, as explained in Assignment 1, much of sale-of-goods contract interpretation is governed by interpretative principles from the common law of contracts. As you have seen in Assignment 1, the terms of a contract may come from agreement of the parties, as well as from mandatory or default terms supplied by Article 2.

Assignment 5

Contract Formation by Offer and Acceptance or by Conduct

§§ 1-205, 2-204, 2-205, 2-206, 2-207(1), first sentence of 2-207(3)

The Article 2 rules on the formation of contracts reflect the UCC's general orientation toward respecting the freedom of contract of private parties, as expressed in § 1-302 (see Assignment 1). Article 2 relaxes many of the common law's more technical rules of offer and acceptance that sometimes pose barriers to finding that a contract has been formed. As you will see, under Article 2, it is easy to find that a contract for the sale of goods has been formed. The consequence of this flexible attitude toward contract formation is the need for a more robust set of rules and concepts giving content to the contracts so easily formed; that will be the topic of Assignments 6 and 7.

LEARNING OUTCOMES AND OBJECTIVES

At the completion of this Assignment, you should be able to

- identify the ways in which Article 2 rules for contract formation contribute to the generous approach to contract formation in the Code;

- apply two contract formation rules peculiar to Article 2, involving "offers for prompt or current shipment" of goods and "firm offers"; and

- apply the 2-207 rules for the formation of contracts through communications containing different terms (the "battle of the forms"); in Assignment 7, you will learn the 2-207 rules for determining the terms of such contracts.

A. Contract Formation under Article 2: General Rules

Reading the Code:
§ 2-204

Read 2-204 and its Comment.

Subsection (1) of 2-204 identifies circumstances that result in creation of a contract, and subsections (2) and (3) identify circumstances that will not prevent a finding that a contract was made. This section was written to make uniform the rules governing contract formation for sales of goods, even though the common law of some states was to the contrary of one or more of its subsections. Courts have applied subsection (3) by analogy to non-sale-of-goods circumstances.

Question 1. Under 2-204(1), what must be established to prove contract formation?

Question 2. Under 2-204(2) and (3), what circumstances are identified as not preventing contract formation?

Question 3. What test is to be applied to determine whether a contract fails for indefiniteness when one or more terms are left open?

EXAMPLES AND ANALYSIS

Example A: *Jannusch v. Naffziger*[1]

Gene and Martha Jannusch were in the business of operating a food truck at summer festivals. They started negotiating with the Naffzigers to sell their business for $150,000. The Naffzigers paid the Jannusches a $10,000 down-payment, but said they were not in a position to sign a contract until they received a bank loan and consulted an

---

[1]   883 N.E.2d 711 (Ill. App. Ct. 2008).

attorney. While the loan was being processed and the written contract drafted, the Naffzigers took possession of the physical assets of the business—a truck, trailer, refrigerators, freezers, roasters, chairs, tables, fountain service, signs, and lighting equipment. The Naffzigers sold food at six festivals and were disappointed with the income. They returned the equipment to the Jannusches, arguing that they had never entered into a contract for the purchase of the business.

Analysis: The court held that the parties had an enforceable contract, even though they never signed a formal agreement. What parts of 2-204 and what facts support the court's judgment? What arguments and what parts of 2-204 support the position of the Naffzigers that they had never entered into a contract? How would the Naffzigers support a claim that the stricter common law rules on contract formation should apply, rather than the more flexible rules of Article 2?

Example B: *Dell's Maraschino Cherries v. Shoreline*[2]

Dell's Maraschino Cherries Co. entered into a written contract with Shoreline Fruit Growers to purchase 100 truckloads of Michigan Brine Cherries at a price of 49 cents per pound, in shipments averaging 10 loads per month over the next year. The contract specified the weight of a truckload of cherries and the terms of delivery and payment. When the market price of cherries rose significantly after about half the truckloads had been delivered, Shoreline stopped delivering cherries to Dell's. Shoreline argued that they did not have a valid contract, since they had not agreed on some key terms in the contract, such as the meaning of "10 loads per month average."

Analysis: The court enforced the contract, finding that the signed contract manifested agreement on essential terms of "quantity, price, and time and manner of delivery." The court emphasized that "[t]he UCC's standard for contract formation is quite liberal and does not require every contractual term to be spelled out in detail, with precision, or even to be spelled out at all."

Another court described the orientation of Article 2 as follows: "Practical business people cannot be expected to govern their actions with reference to nice legal formalisms. Thus, when there is basic agreement, however manifested and whether or not the precise moment of agreement may be determined, failure to articulate

---

[2]   887 F. Supp. 2d 459 (E.D.N.Y. 2012).

that agreement in the precise language of a lawyer, with every difficulty and contingency considered and resolved, will not prevent formation of a contract."[3] Would the outcome in Dell's dispute with Michigan Brine have been different if, instead of "10 loads per month average", the alleged contract had said "up to 10 loads per month"?

B. Offer and Acceptance under Article 2: General Rules

The generous approach to contract formation in Article 2 is evident in its general rules for offer and acceptance, found in §§ 2-206(1)(a) and 2-206(2).

Reading the Code:
§ 2-206(1)(a)

Read 2-206(1)(a) and Comment 1.

2-206 Comment 1 makes clear that Article 2 liberalizes the traditional and more restrictive common law rules of acceptance of offers, rejecting the notion that the medium of acceptance has to match the medium of the offer and other "technical rules." At the same time, Article 2 preserves the common law rule that an offeror who chooses to limit the manner of acceptance can do so, as long as the offer is quite clear about the limitation ("unless otherwise unambiguously indicated").

EXAMPLES AND ANALYSIS

Example C: *Marrs v. Walters*[4]

The buyer of a truck signed a "Retail Buyer's Order" specifying that "this order shall not become binding until accepted by the dealer or his authorized

---

[3]   Kleinschmidt Div. of SCM Corp. v. Futuronics Corp, 363 N.E.2d 701, 702 (N.Y. 1977).

[4]   2014 WL 356568 (Ky. Ct. App. 2014).

representative." The buyer and the dealer negotiated a trade-in value for the buyer's old car, and the buyer left the old car with the dealer and took the new truck. The dealer never signed the Retail Buyer's Order.

Analysis: The court held that a contract had been formed under 2-206(1), on the terms set forth in the Retail Buyer's Order. What facts and what parts of 2-206 support the court's result?

APPLYING THE CODE

Problem 5-1.

In the scenarios described below, what facts and what parts of 2-206 support finding that the final telephone call is an effective acceptance of an offer? What facts and what parts of 2-206 support a contrary result? If you were the judge, how would you rule? How would you use the facts and outcome in Example C to support your result?

(a) Ngeri visits Omeed's car dealership to buy a new truck. Ngeri finds a model that she likes and negotiates an acceptable price from Omeed, but she wants a different color than the one available on the lot. Ngeri and Omeed fill out a purchase order form with the pertinent details, and Ngeri signs it. The form includes this language: "I (the buyer) understand that this becomes binding only when signed by a person authorized to accept on behalf of Omeed's Car Dealership." The following form language appears at the very bottom of the page: "ACCEPTED BY _____." Omeed does not sign the form and tells Ngeri that he'll try to locate a truck in the preferred color. Two days later, Omeed calls Ngeri and says, "I found the right color; I accept your order."

(b) Assadullah sells baking ingredients, such as flour, sugar, eggs, and yeast, whose prices fluctuate on a daily basis. Cynthia, a small bakery owner, routinely calls Assadullah in the morning to ask about the price of various ingredients she needs. If Cynthia likes the price, she e-mails Assadullah a purchase order, listing the ingredients being ordered, the quantity, the unit price, the total price, her shipping address, and six "Terms of Contract," including the following: "Order/

price confirmation w/ship date must be faxed/e-mailed immediately."
When Assadullah receives one of these e-mails, he calls Cynthia back,
saying "I accept your order."

* * *

The liberal standard for contract formation in Article 2 can mean a contract is
formed even when parties cannot identify the "moment of its making" (§ 2-204(3)).
Since, under the rule set out in § 2-206(1), an offeree can accept an offer "in any
manner . . . reasonable in the circumstances," the Article 2 offeror risks being bound
to contracts by actions of the offeree that might not be directly communicated to the
offeror. Section 2-206(2) provides some protection to the offeror against this risk.

Reading the Code:
§ 2-206(2)

Read the text of 2-206(2) and Comment 3.

Question 4. What is the meaning of the term "reasonable time," and how
does it impact the acceptance of an offer?

Question 5. There are very few reported cases in which parties argue that an
offer lapsed under 2-206(2) for failure to notify an offeror of an acceptance
made by beginning performance. Why do you think that is the case?

C. Offer and Acceptance under Article 2: Special Rules

The UCC sets forth two special rules for acceptance that apply to two specific
types of offers commonly used by merchants engaged in commercial practice—
offers for immediate shipment and offers that state that they will be kept open for
a specified period of time.

1. Offers for Prompt or Current Shipment

Buyers are frequently more interested in getting needed goods promptly than in waiting for completion of an orderly process of contract negotiation. Long before the enactment of the UCC, merchants had developed the practice of treating offers calling for prompt, immediate, or current shipment of goods as offers that could be accepted by actually shipping the goods. This practice has been codified in § 2-206(1)(b) of the UCC.

Reading the Code:
§ 2-206(1)(b)

Read the text of 2-206(1)(b) and Comments 2 and 4.

Question 6. What are the meanings of "seasonable" and "notify"?

Question 7. Select the statement that best describes the relationship between 2-206(1)(a) and (1)(b) (up to the comma):

(a) They cover the same factual circumstances.

(b) They cover entirely different factual circumstances.

(c) Their coverage overlaps partially but not completely.

(d) Subsection (a) is a subset of (b).

(e) Subsection (b) is a subset of (a).

Question 8. What must a seller do to prevent a non-conforming shipment from being an acceptance? Be specific about the actions to be taken.

Question 9. In the last clause of 2-206(1)(b) (after the comma), what does "such a shipment of nonconforming goods" constitute, if it is not an acceptance?

Question 10. If "such a shipment of nonconforming goods" is an acceptance, what else is it? (See Comment 4.)

EXAMPLES AND ANALYSIS

Example D: *Enpro Systems, Ltd. v. Namasco Corp.*[5]

On July 19, a manufacturer of pressure vessels placed an order with a steel plate supplier, with whom it had done business for 25 years, for a specific quantity of steel plates to be used in the construction of an oil refinery. On July 23, the supplier shipped the steel plate, before reviewing the terms of the purchase order.

Analysis: The court held that this shipment constituted acceptance of the offer under 2-206(1)(a), reasoning that the "purchase order confirmation and sales order form, which together identify quantities of steel plate of specified dimensions to be delivered . . . within days, evidence [supplier's] placement of an order for prompt shipment." Cases interpreting 2-206 tend to demonstrate a fairly generous application of this section in finding formation of contracts, typically as one of many possible reasons for concluding that the parties formed a contract. The focus of the courts is typically more on the fact of prompt shipment in response to an offer than on a careful analysis of any precise language in the offer. As one pre-UCC court explained of the pre-Code practices codified by 2-206, "[T]here is nothing mystic or ritualistic about the phrase 'prompt shipment.' It is used by practical men of affairs to indicate an immediate shipment." *Stallman v. Francis A. Cundill & Co.*, 288 F. 643 (S.D.N.Y. 1922).

2. Firm Offers

Under the common law, an offer may be withdrawn before acceptance unless consideration has been paid to keep it open, thereby creating an option contract. An offer may be made irrevocable under the common law in other situations described in the Restatement of Contracts (Second) §§ 45 and 87.

> **Restatement (Second) of Contracts §§ 45 & 87(2).**
>
> **§ 45** applies to offers for unilateral contracts; when an offeree begins performance, the offeror may not revoke the offer until the offeree has had a reasonable time to finish performing.
>
> **§ 87** provides for the creation of option contracts supported by reliance as well as by consideration.

---

[5]   382 F.Supp. 2d 874 (S.D. Tex. 2005). Note that this case was also discussed in Example A in Assignment 1.

Section 2-205 offers an additional means by which an offer may be made irrevocable, through what is referred to as a "firm offer."

Reading the Code:
§ 2-205

Read 2-205 and its Comments.

Question 11. What are the requirements under 2-205 for an offer to be irrevocable?

Question 12. For how long is such an offer irrevocable?

Question 13. If an offer otherwise meeting 2-205 is expressly stated as irrevocable for more than three months, is 2-205 inapplicable? If not, what is the result? Does your answer change if the offeree gave consideration to keep the offer open?

Question 14. What does the final "but" clause in 2-205 mean? Why is it needed?

Question 15. Which of the following phrases would satisfy the requirements to make a signed written offer from a merchant a "firm offer" under 2-205? If more than one might qualify, which is the best formulation?

(a) "This offer lapses after May 31."

(b) "This offer is irrevocable through May 31."

(c) "This offer is good until June 1."

APPLYING THE CODE

Problem 5-2.

Farmer Kasey is having lunch at the local diner owned by Alexa. After eating a particularly delicious serving of strawberry shortcake, he mentions to Alexa that he has a bumper crop of strawberries ready to harvest. He tells her, "If you order ten bushels from me before the end of the week, I will let you have them for a bargain price of $20 per bushel." Has Kasey made Alexa a "firm offer"?

D. Contract Formation in a "Battle of the Forms": § 2-207(1) & (3)

The general rules of contract formation discussed above demonstrate a generous attitude about the nature of the communications between parties that can lead to the formation of a contract. These general rules form the backdrop for considering one particularly troublesome (and increasingly common) scenario for contract formation: at some point during contract negotiations, one or both parties send the other a communication containing that party's proposal for the terms of the contract. The communications sent are frequently standard forms, such as purchase orders or acknowledgments and confirmations of orders, often generated automatically by companies buying or selling goods. At some point, the deal breaks down, and the parties (or their lawyers) have to determine whether the parties had a contract, and, if so, what its terms are. This scenario is often referred to as the "battle of the forms."

Section 2-207 contains the Article 2 rules for resolving the issues raised in these battles of the forms. The section deals with two distinct issues: (1) whether a contract is formed and (2) if so, what its terms are. Section 2-207(1) and the first sentence of § 2-207(3) deal with contract formation and will be covered in this Assignment. Section 2-207(2) and the remainder of § 2-207(3) provide rules for determining the terms of the contracts formed through the mechanisms of § 2-207; they will be covered in Assignment 7. Assignment 6 will cover the general rules in Article 2 for determining the terms of contracts.

1. The Scope of § 2-207(1)

Reading the Code:
§ 2-207(1)

Read 2-207(1) and Comment 1.

Question 16. What two different fact situations does 2-207(1) cover?

APPLYING THE CODE

Problem 5-3.

As you saw in Question 16, Comment 1 explains that 2-207 covers two different fact situations: (1) written confirmations of oral or informal agreements and (2) offers and acceptances. Identify which situation is described in each of the following scenarios.

Sam is the owner of an ice cream shop.

(a) At a trade show, he visits Sarah's booth and examines her display of freezers. Sam has been buying freezers from Sarah for over 15 years. Sarah shows him the latest model. Sam loves the new features and is satisfied with the price she quotes him. He tells her, "O.K., I'm in! You know where to send it. I'll write you the check as soon as it's installed." Two days later, Sam gets an e-mail from Sarah informing him that the freezer will be shipped out within 3 days.

(b) Sam sends an e-mail to Matthew's Dairy using Sam's standard purchase order form, requesting 500 gallons of cream, to be delivered the following Monday. Matthew's Dairy replies with an e-mailed acknowledgement of Sam's purchase order on its acknowledgement form, which includes the standard term, "Delivery due within 48 hours of sending of this acknowledgement form."

2. How § 2-207(1) Applies to Offers and Acceptances

Reading the Code:
§ 2-207(1)

Question 17. Creating an if/then paraphrase of a rule puts the rule in a format that identifies the elements that must be established to satisfy the rule (If . . .), what elements will prevent satisfaction (Unless . . .), what circumstances will not interfere with satisfying the rule (Regardless of . . .), and the legal consequences of satisfying the rule (Then . . .). Rewriting a rule in this fashion is a helpful way to break down a dense rule into its component parts to understand and apply it more effectively.

Ignoring for the moment the phrase "or a written confirmation which is sent within a reasonable time," reorder the clauses of 2-207(1) into if/then/regardless of/unless form.

IF _____ ,

THEN _____ ,

REGARDLESS OF _____ ,

UNLESS _____ .

Question 18. Recall that non-sale-of-goods contracts are governed by the mirror image rule, under which the acceptance must match the offer. Re-read 2-207 Comment 1 and read the first sentence of Comment 2.

   (a) Identify what part of the language of 2-207(1) displaces the common law mirror image rule.

   (b) Does this change from the common law rule likely increase or decrease the number of contracts formed?

   (c) How does this change fit with the general approach to contract formation displayed in 2-204?

EXAMPLES AND ANALYSIS

Example E: *Princess Cruises, Inc. v. General Electric Co.*[6]

Princess Cruises, Inc. (Princess) sought to schedule routine inspection services and repairs to its cruise ship SS Sky Princess to be performed by General Electric Company (GE), the original manufacturer of the ship's main turbines. In October, Princess issued to GE a Purchase Order for the repairs that included the proposed contract price, a brief description of the services to be performed, and Princess's standard terms and conditions, including a warranty of the work to be done. GE responded with a Final Price Quotation that contained its own standard terms and conditions, including strict limitations on damages and a disclaimer of any liability for consequential damages, lost profits, or lost revenue. Princess gave GE permission to proceed after receiving GE's Final Price Quotation. GE's repairs took more time than Princess expected, and Princess was forced to cancel cruises scheduled for both Christmas and Easter.

Princess paid GE the agreed-upon contract price for the repairs, then sued GE for breach of contract, claiming consequential damages and lost profits from the two cruises. The jury awarded Princess over $2.5 million in consequential damages, based on the District Court's instructions that understood the contract to be created under 2-207(1) by the exchange of documents, which (for reasons to be addressed in Assignment 7) meant the Princess warranty terms (rather than GE's disclaimer of warranties) were part of the final contract.

Analysis: The Court of Appeals overturned this verdict, limiting Princess' recovery to a refund of the cost of the repairs. The court held that Article 2 did not apply to the transaction,[7] so the common law's mirror image rule applied. Under 2-207(1), GE's Final Price quotation might have been an acceptance of Princess's Purchase Order, but under the mirror image rule, GE's Final Price Quotation was a rejection of it and a counteroffer. This counteroffer was accepted by the parties' subsequent behavior. Thus, the contract included GE's disclaimer of consequential damages. Why did Article 2 not apply to the transaction?

---

[6]   143 F.3d 828 (4th Cir. 1998), cert. denied, 525 U.S. 982 (1988).

[7]   Because admiralty law applied to the transaction, the first question was whether admiralty law should adopt Article 2 for all admiralty contracts or instead adopt it only when it would apply to a transaction under state law enactments of the UCC. The district court thought the former rule should apply. The court of appeals rejected that approach, interpreting admiralty law to be consistent with Article 2 as it is applied in the various states adopting it.

Although the *Princess Cruise* case provides a modern illustration of the potentially significant consequences of the application of the strict common law mirror-image rule, most jurisdictions have modified the rule's severity by, for example, interpreting an offeree's modestly varying term as having been implied in the original offer so that the response does mirror the offer, or allowing a contract to be formed if the offeree's varying terms are solely in offeror's favor, or viewing offeree's varying term as a mere suggestion. This loosening of the mirror image rule has moved the results in common law cases a bit closer to the UCC result in 2-207(1).

3. How § 2-207(1) Applies to Confirmations

Recall that § 2-207(1) applies not only to "definite and seasonable expressions of acceptance," but also to written confirmations.

Reading the Code:
§ 2-207(1)

Re-read 2-207(1) and Comment 1.

Focus on how the phrase "or a written confirmation which is sent within a reasonable time" fits into that sentence.

Comment 1 explains that a confirmation is a document sent "where an agreement has been reached either orally or by informal correspondence between the parties and is followed by one or both of the parties sending formal memoranda embodying the terms so far as agreed upon and adding terms not discussed." Note that a "confirmation" does not create a contract; the contract has already been formed "either orally or by informal correspondence." A "confirmation" merely confirms the existence and terms of a contract. Thus, § 2-207(1) creates a legal fiction with respect to a confirmation by saying that a confirmation "operates as an acceptance." It does this in order to apply § 2-207(2) to confirmations to determine whether the additional or different terms in the confirmation become part of the contract (which we will cover in Assignment 7).

4. Does § 2-207(1) Apply to Oral Acceptances?

Reading the Code:
§ 2-207(1)

Question 19. Subsection 2-207(1) specifically applies to "written" confirmations, but it does not limit its application to acceptances that are written. Which portions of 2-207 and its comments furnish arguments for or against applying 2-207(1) to oral acceptances? The answer to this question determines the scope of application of the rules in both 2-207(1) and (2).

5. Formation of Contracts under § 2-207(3)

Reading the Code:
§ 2-207(3), first sentence

Read the first sentence of 2-207(3) and Comment 7.

Question 20. Restate the first sentence of subsection 2-207(3) as an if/then paraphrase.

IF _____ ,

THEN _____ .

6. The Relationship of § 2-207(1) to § 2-207(3)

Can counsel choose freely between § 2-207(1) and § 2-207(3) as the source of authority for finding a contract exists? (As we will see in Assignment 7, the route to contract formation will determine which rules we follow to determine what the terms of that contract are.) The language of the two sections establishes that the two rules are mutually exclusive, and § 2-207(1) must be applied first. In a battle of the forms scenario, either the writings form a contract under the modified offer and acceptance analysis of § 2-207(1), or they do not. Only if the writings do not establish a contract under § 2-207(1) does § 2-207(3) apply. Look carefully again at the language of § 2-207(3): conduct can form a contract "although the writings of the parties do not otherwise (e.g., under the rules of § 2-207(1)) establish a contract."

E. Court Interpretations of Tricky Language in § 2-207(1)

The "battle of forms" under § 2-207 has been described as "a defiant, lurking demon patiently waiting to condemn its interpreters to the depths of despair."[8] Those are not just the sentiments of frustrated law students; courts across the country struggle with the complexities raised by the aggravating ambiguities of the section's language.

Two particular phrases of § 2-207(1) have been the subject of significant interpretation by the courts:

- "definite and seasonable expression of acceptance," and

- "expressly made conditional on assent to the additional or different terms."

We will examine the meaning of each of these phrases, and the role they play in the § 2-207 rules for contract formation.

1. What is a "Definite and Seasonable Expression of Acceptance," and Why Does It Matter?

a. Does the Response Demonstrate a "Definite and Seasonable Expression of Acceptance"?

The application of § 2-207(1) starts with determining whether a response to an offer constitutes "a definite and seasonable expression of acceptance." If a response is a definite and seasonable expression of acceptance, a contract is created. If there is no definite and seasonable expression of acceptance, there is no contract—yet. It is important to keep in mind that when parties argue about whether a communication is an acceptance, they are usually arguing not about whether a contract existed at all (especially where both parties have performed parts of the contract). They are instead arguing about which communication or conduct created

---

[8]   Reaction Molding Techs, Inc. v. Gen. Elec. Co., 585 F. Supp. 1097, 1104 (E.D. Pa. 1984), amended, 588 F. Supp. 1280 (E.D. Pa. 1984).

the contract and therefore, most important- ly, what terms are in the contract. The real legal battle in these situations is over the terms of the contract. We will address the weapons of that part of the battle of the forms in Assignments 6 and 7.

What satisfies the requirement that there be a "definite and seasonable expression of acceptance"? Comment 2 indicates that "a proposed deal which in commercial understanding has in fact been closed is recognized as a contract" even though the acceptance contains additional or different terms. According to one commentator:

> **Restatement (Second) of Contracts §§ 24 & 50(1).**
>
> **§ 24:** "An offer is the manifestation of willingness to enter into a bargain, so made as to justify another person in understanding that his assent to that bargain is invited and will conclude it."
>
> **§ 50(1):** "Acceptance of an offer is a manifestation of asset to the terms thereof made by the offeree in a manner invited or required by the offer."

> [T]he response of the offeree operates as an acceptance if a reasonable [person] in the position of the offeror would assume that an agreement had been made despite differences in the exchanged forms. In this connection, reasonable belief that the contract has been made must take into account the words that were used by the offeree, where they appeared in his form, whether they were printed, typed, or handwritten, along with the total commercial setting of the transaction, including course of dealing and usage of trade. In case of doubt, the court ought to decide in favor of the existence of a contract, because the chances are good that both parties intended to create one when they exchanged their forms, and moreover, the ambiguities of the offeree's purported acceptance ought to be resolved against him in close cases . . . .[9]

Determining whether a party's response to an offer constitutes a "definite and seasonable expression of acceptance" is the first (and sometimes the last) step in determining whether that response operates as the acceptance of the offer, creating a binding contract.

---

[9]   William D. Hawkland, Uniform Commercial Code Series § 2-207:2 (2001).

EXAMPLES AND ANALYSIS

Example F: *Standard Bent Glass Corp. v. Glassrobots Oy*[10]

Standard Bent Glass entered into negotiations with Glassrobots for the purchase of a glass fabricating system. During the course of their negotiations, in which the parties exchanged at least six documents with varying terms, the following occurred:

- After an earlier offer was rejected, Standard Bent sent an offer specifying quantity, price, payment terms, and warranties. The letter, dated February 1, ended by saying "Please sign this ORDER and fax to us if it is agreeable."

- Glassrobots did not return or refer to Standard Bent's letter. Instead, on February 2, it responded with its own cover letter, invoice, and standard form. The Glassrobots letter said, "Please read it through and let me know if there is anything you want to change. If not, I'll send you 2 originals, which will be signed."

- Later on February 2, Standard Bent faxed a return letter that "apparently accepted" Glassrobots' standard sales agreement, but requested five specific changes (using wire transfer instead of letter of credit, payment terms, late penalty for shipment delays, site visits, and technical specifications). The letter closed by saying, "Please call if the above is not agreeable."

- On February 4, Standard Bent wired a down payment to Glassrobots. One day later, Glassrobots sent Standard Bent a revised sales agreement that incorporated most, but not all, of Standard Bent's changes. The accompanying letter said: "Attached you'll find the revised sales agreement. . . . Please return one signed to us; the other one is for your files." One section of the sales agreement said the agreement "shall come into force when signed by both parties." Standard Bent never signed the revised sales agreement.

- Standard Bent sent one more document, a few days later, notifying Glassrobots of a change required in one of the technical specifications.

Glassrobots delivered and installed the glass fabricating system and Standard Bent paid the contract price. Defects appeared in the equipment but

---

[10]   333 F. 3d 440 (3d Cir. 2003).

the parties disagreed on the cause. In the ensuing litigation, the court had to decide whether there was a valid agreement between the parties and whether that agreement contained a binding arbitration clause that was referenced in Glassrobot's standard sales agreement.

Analysis: The court rejected Standard Bent Glass's argument that it had never agreed to a contract with Glassrobots. Standard Bent had pointed to the lack of a signed agreement and "the failure of the parties to achieve a meeting of the minds on all contract provisions," but the court noted that both parties had performed, which established that a contract existed, though not necessarily how it was created. In applying 2-207 to identify the terms of the contract, the court said that Standard Bent's February 2 return letter and February 4 wire transfer of funds "demonstrated its intent to perform under the essential terms of Glassrobots' standard sales agreement" and thus constituted "a definite and seasonable expression of acceptance" of Glassrobots' offer. The court also said that "Standard Bent Glass's conduct constituted a definite and seasonable expression of acceptance that evinced the formation of a contract rather than a counteroffer or rejection."

It is unclear from the two quoted statements whether the court found a writing that constituted "a definite and seasonable expression of acceptance" under 2-207(1) or "conduct by both parties which recognizes the existence of a contract" under 2-207(3). Which do you think is the correct application of 2-207? (Either way, a contract would be created, but whether the arbitration provision is part of the contract depends on which way the contract was formed, as you will see in Assignment 7.)

b. "Significant Divergence in Dickered Terms"

Many courts applying § 2-207(1) have interpreted "definite . . . expression of acceptance" as meaning that the document responding to the offer manifests acceptance and does not "diverge[] significantly as to a dickered term."[11] Considering whether there has been significant divergence in dickered terms is a useful way of determining whether an acceptance has occurred even if a jurisdiction has not expressly adopted that test.

---

[11]   U.S. Industries, Inc. v. Semco Manufacturing, Inc., 562 F.2d 1061, 1067 (8th Cir. 1977).

i. What is a "Dickered Term"?

A "dickered term" (or some use the phrase "dickered-for term") is a contract term that the parties have negotiated and agreed upon, or a term specified by a party in non-form language. One court explained, "The 'dickered terms' are those that are unique to each transaction such as price, quality, quantity, or delivery terms as compared to the 'usual unbargained terms on the reverse side [of a form] concerning remedies, arbitration, and the like.'"[12] There are many ways in which parties can indicate that particular terms are the subject of their "dickering." They could be specifically identified in a cover letter accompanying a draft or in the e-mail to which a draft is attached. If parties are exchanging standard forms, dickered terms might be considered to be what is added to the blank spaces in the form contracts. The fact that the party sending the document has to fill in the blank spaces, and the party receiving the document has its attention drawn to what has been put into the blanks, signals the 'dickering' over those terms. This can be contrasted with the form language on the back (or front) of those forms, containing what are often characterized as "standard terms and conditions." Although such terms are often of crucial significance, and are often the focus of subsequent litigation raising § 2-207 issues, they are not "dickered terms."

Examples of items commonly considered "dickered terms":

- Type of goods[13]

- Price and payment terms[14]

- Quantity of goods

- Delivery date[15]

ii. What is a "Significant Divergence" in a Dickered Term?

Determining whether a divergence is "significant" is a fact-specific determination, giving attorneys the chance to argue based on the particular context and industry practices.

---

[12] Matrix Intern. Textiles, Inc. v. Jolie Intimates Inc., 801 N.Y.S.2d 236 (Civ. Ct. 2005), quoting White & Summers, Uniform Commercial Code, § 1–3 [West Group 2000].)

[13] Id.

[14] General Electric Co. v. G. Siempelkamp GmbH & Co., 29 F.3d 1095, 1098 (6th Cir. 1994); LaForce, Inc. v. Pioneer General Contractors, Inc., 75 UCC Rep. Serv. 2d 624 (Mich. Ct. App. 2011).

[15] Alliance Wall Corp. v. Ampat Midwest Corp., 477 N.E.2d 1206 (Ohio Ct. App. 1984).

Examples of "significant divergences" in dickered terms:

- A divergence was found to be "significant" when an offer listed the price as $1.55 per ton and the responsive document listed the price as $1.85 per ton.[16] The court in that case also cited an example from White & Summers' UCC treatise finding significant divergence between an offer for 200,000 pounds of lard at 10¢ per pound and an acknowledgment at 15¢ per pound.

- A would-be acceptance was found to diverge significantly as to the dickered terms where the offer (a subcontractor's bid to a general contractor) gave an 8% payment discount if contractor paid in full within ten days of invoice, while the response gave an 8% discount but required contractor to pay only 90% of the cost of materials furnished within the preceding month, and allowed contractor to retain 10% of the price until completion of the project.[17]

APPLYING THE CODE

Problem 5-4.

Consider the following facts. Are any contracts created? If so, by which actions?

(a) After negotiations, Buyer orders 1,000 units of goods at $50 per unit in a purchase order that also contains a set of standard terms. Seller sends Buyer an acknowledgment promising to send 900 units, on a form that contains standard terms that differ from the Buyer's. After Buyer receives the acknowledgment but has done nothing else, Seller denies that a contract exists.

(b) After negotiations, Buyer orders 450 "red" seat cushions at $50 per unit in a purchase order that also contains a set of standard terms. Seller sends Buyer an acknowledgment promising to send 450 "scarlet" seat cushions on a form that contains standard terms that differ from the Buyer's. After Buyer receives the acknowledgment, Seller denies that a contract exists.

---

[16] Howard Construction Co. v. Jeff-Cole Quarries, Inc., 669 S.W.2d 221, 229 (Mo. Ct. App. 1983).

[17] Herm Hughes & Sons, Inc. v. Quintek, 834 P.2d 582, 585 (Utah Ct. App. 1992).

(c)   Buyer sends purchase order. Seller responds with a pre-printed "Order Verification" postcard that says, "Your order has been received and is being processed."

2. What is an Acceptance "Expressly Made Conditional on Assent to the Additional or Different Terms," and Why Does It Matter?

A "definite . . . expression of acceptance" does not operate to create a contract under § 2-207(1) if it is "expressly made conditional on assent to the additional or different terms." What language in an acceptance satisfies that rule?

a. Courts Agree That the Condition Must Be "Express"

The courts are unanimous that, to have an acceptance that is "expressly made conditional on assent to the additional or different terms" the condition must be express (not implied), using language such as "provided that," "subject to," "but only if," or other language that makes it clear that the would-be acceptance is effective only if the additional or different terms are included in the agreement. In this sense, § 2-207(1) is consistent with the policy and effect of § 2-206(1), which indicates that an offeror can specify how the offer is to be accepted but must do so unambiguously. Similarly, the offeree can specify whether the response is or is not intended to be an acceptance, but must do so expressly and unambiguously.

b. But Courts Disagree About What Makes an Acceptance "Expressly Conditional"

The courts take two different views of precisely what the acceptance has to be expressly conditional on. Must the acceptance be conditional on the offeree's proposed additional or different terms? Or must the acceptance be conditional on the offeror's assent to the offeree's additional or different terms? The following two cases illustrate the two approaches to this question.

Non-Uniformity Alert:
Construction Aggregates and *Dorton*

Construction Aggregates Corp. v. Hewitt-Robins, Inc.,

404 F.2d 505, 508 (7th Cir. 1968)

Construction Aggregates Corp. (Buyer) was hired to build dikes to be used in the process of extracting minerals from the Dead Sea. Buyer entered into negotiations with Hewitt-Robins, Inc. (Seller) to buy a conveyor system to move sand, gravel and rock to the construction site. Seller responded to Buyer's purchase order with a letter stating that their acceptance was "predicated on the following clarifications, additions or modifications to the order," including a substitute warranty clause. Buyer made no written objection to the terms in Seller's letter but requested only a change in the payment terms, which Seller granted. The court ruled that Seller's letter was a counter-offer, rather than an acceptance, because it was expressly conditional on the stated modifications.

Dorton v. Collins & Aikman Corp.,

453 F.2d 1161, 1168 (6th Cir. 1972)

Dorton (Buyer), a carpet retailer doing business as The Carpet Mart, purchased carpets from Collins and Aikman (Seller), a carpet manufacturer, in a series of over 55 transactions. The transactions were typically initiated by oral orders placed over the telephone or during visits by Seller's sales representatives. After each oral order, the current price and Buyer's credit status with Seller would be verified by Seller; if all was in order, Seller would send Buyer a printed acknowledgment form in one of two versions. One version of the form stated that "acceptance of your order is subject to all of the terms and conditions on the face and reverse side hereof, including the provisions for arbitration." The other version of the form stated that "your order is subject to" those same terms and conditions. The court held that neither version was "expressly made conditional on assent to the additional or different terms." The court held that a response to an offer is expressly conditional and therefore not an acceptance only if it "clearly reveals that the offeree is unwilling to proceed with the transaction unless he is assured of the offeror's assent to the additional or different terms therein." "Expressly" means "directly and distinctly stated or expressed rather than implied or left to inference." The court explained, "it is not enough that an acceptance is expressly conditional on additional or different terms; rather, an acceptance must be expressly conditional on the offeror's assent to those terms." This more stringent approach, requiring that the acceptance expressly demand affirmative approval of the additional or different terms, seems to be the majority approach.

Question 21. You have a retail sales client who wants to be sure her form sales agreement, not the buyer's, becomes the basis for any contract she enters. The first step in accomplishing that result, she thinks, is to make sure that no contract is formed when she sends her acknowledgment back to the buyer with her own sales agreement attached. What should she put in her cover letter (a) in a *Construction Aggregates* jurisdiction? (b) in a *Dorton* jurisdiction? How would you explain the difference to her?

Question 22. What happens if the buyer in Question 21 responds, "I agree"? What happens if the buyer does not respond but the seller delivers the goods and the buyer pays? What happens if the buyer responds with another form? Does it matter what language is in the other form? Does 2-207 govern the analysis in all three cases? If so, what section of 2-207 governs the analysis—2-207(1) or 2-207(3)?

EXAMPLES AND ANALYSIS

Examples of Language Courts Have Found to Satisfy the Stricter *Dorton* Standard for "Expressly Made Conditional":

- "Seller's acceptance of Buyer's order and shipments made pursuant thereto are subject to and expressly conditioned upon Buyer's acceptance of the terms and conditions herein. . . ."[18]

---

[18] Coastal & Native Plant Specialties, Inc., 139 F. Supp. 2d 1326, 1328 (N.D. Fla.2001).

- "Seller's acceptance of any offer by Purchaser to purchase the Products is expressly conditional upon the Purchaser's assent to all the terms and conditions herein, including any terms additional to or different from those contained in the offer to purchase."[19]

- "Where this agreement is found to be an acknowledgement, if such acknowledgement constitutes an acceptance of an offer such acceptance is expressly made conditional upon Buyer's assent solely to the terms of such acknowledgement, and acceptance of any part of Product(s) delivered by Company shall be deemed to constitute such assent by Buyer."[20]

- "[A]cceptance of [this] offer [is] subject to the express condition that the Seller assent that this Purchase Order constitutes the entire agreement between the Buyer and Seller with respect to the subject matter hereof and the subject matter of such offer."[21]

Examples of language courts have found did not satisfy the stricter *Dorton* standard for "expressly conditional":

- "Execution of this agreement constitutes an acceptance expressly limited to the terms herein and any additional or different terms suggested by Seller are hereby rejected unless expressly agreed to in writing by Buyer."[22]

- "The Buyer has 14 calendar days . . . to contest . . . any aspect of the invoice and the General Sales Conditions . . . relating to the Goods received from the Seller. The Buyer shall be deemed to have accepted the terms of any invoice (including the General Sales Conditions referred to therein) if the Seller fails to receive a notification from the Buyer within such time period.[23]

Analysis: What is the difference between the language found to have satisfied the stricter *Dorton* standard and the language that failed to satisfy that test? What words seem to make a difference in the outcome? Would you counsel clients to

---

[19] PCS Nitrogen Fertilizer, L.P. v. Christy Refractories, 225 F.3d 974, 976 (8th Cir. 2000).

[20] Belden Inc. v. Am. Elec. Components, Inc., 885 N.E.2d 751, 755 (Ind. Ct. App. 2008).

[21] White Consol. Indus., Inc. v. McGill Mfg. Co., 165 F.3d 1185, 1191 (8th Cir. 1999).

[22] Westinghouse Elec. Corp. v Nielsons, 647 F. Supp. 896, 898 (D. Colo. 1986).

[23] Option Wireless, Ltd. v. OpenPeak, Inc., 79 U.C.C. Rep. Serv. 2d 216 (S.D. Fla 2012).

include language that clearly satisfies the *Dorton* standard in all of their standard forms? What would be the advantages and the risks of doing so?

APPLYING THE CODE

Problem 5-5.

Consider the following facts. Does a contract exist? If so, created by which actions?

(a) Buyer sends purchase order. Seller responds with a pre-printed "Order Verification" that says, "We will ship your order in 4-6 business days. Please note that all sales are made subject to terms noted below." The Order Verification contains form language with several terms additional to and different from those contained on the original purchase order.

(b) Buyer sends purchase order. Seller responds with a "Purchase Acknowledgment" saying "We accept your order, but only if you agree to the terms in our standard contract, listed on the back of this confirmation." The pre-printed terms on the back of the Purchase Acknowledgment list several terms additional to and different from those contained on the original purchase order.

(c) Same facts as (b) above. There is no further communication between the parties. Seller later ships the ordered goods. Buyer receives and keeps the goods without objection.

F. Pulling It All Together

It can be tempting to jump immediately into § 2-207 battle gear whenever you sense the presence of more than one form document. However, it is important to consider all the possibilities for contract formation. The general Article 2 rules of contract formation should not be neglected, as illustrated in the following case. As you read *Mantaline Corp. v. PPG Industries*, consider the following questions:

(1) Why was Mantaline's price quotation not an offer? How would you amend the language in Mantaline's price quotation to change that conclusion? Why might Mantaline not want to make that change?

(2) Both the majority and the dissent agreed that the contract was formed by the parties' conduct, rather than by a formal verbal "acceptance" of the contract. Do they agree on what conduct constitutes the "acceptance"?

(3) What section of the UCC do the majority and dissent argue governs the formation of this contract?

(4) If Mantaline's price quotation had contained different language, and were found to constitute an offer, would PPG's purchase order have been an acceptance? If not, under these facts, could the court have found a valid contract?

MANTALINE CORP. V. PPG INDUSTRIES, INC.

2000 WL 799337 (6th Cir. 2000)
(Unpublished Opinion)

NELSON, CIRCUIT JUDGE

Case summary

This is an appeal from a summary judgment in a commercial law case that turns on the question whether a contract of sale contained an arbitration provision. Concluding that the question is governed by 2-207(3) of the Uniform Commercial Code, . . . the district court held that an arbitration clause set forth in the buyer's purchase order was not part of the contract. Upon *de novo* review, we conclude that UCC 2-207 is not controlling here and that under UCC 2-206 . . . the offer contained in the purchase order, with all of its terms, was accepted without qualification when the goods were delivered. Accordingly, and because we find no waiver of the right to arbitrate, we shall reverse the challenged judgment.

Facts and procedural history

PPG Industries . . . purchased gaskets from Mantaline . . . for use in installing windows at the Security Life building in Denver, Colorado. The gaskets allegedly leached sulphur, causing damage to the building. . . . PPG then commenced arbitration proceedings in Pittsburgh for resolution of its claims against Mantaline. Mantaline sought a declaratory judgment and injunction against this arbitration. . . . PPG then moved to dismiss Mantaline's action or stay the proceedings and compel arbitration. . . . Having determined that the contract between the parties did not contain the arbitration and indemnification provisions relied on by PPG, the district court ultimately ruled in favor of Mantaline on cross-motions for summary judgment. This appeal followed.

. . . .

Prior to purchasing the gaskets, PPG solicited price quotations from several companies, including Mantaline. Mantaline sent PPG a price quotation form in response to the solicitation. . . . Mantaline's standard price quotation form . . . contained a sentence reading as follows: "Any order placed in response to this quotation shall be deemed an express acceptance of each and every term and condition of sale contained herein and on the reverse side hereof." On the reverse side, the form said this:

> "This proposal is for immediate acceptance only and is subject to change at any time before orders are accepted by us. This proposal and our acceptance of your orders, signed by a representative of our Company, together with your order, constitutes the entire contract between us. Modifications, changes, additions, cancellations or suspensions will not be binding upon us unless accepted by a representative of our Company in writing upon terms which will indemnify us against all loss. The terms and conditions contained in this quotation shall prevail over any inconsistent terms contained in buyer's purchase order."

Following receipt of the quotation, PPG sent a purchase order to Mantaline. The purchase order contained the following declaration:

> "THIS PURCHASE ORDER IS EFFECTIVE AND EXPRESSLY CONDITIONAL ON SUPPLIER'S ASSENT TO ALL TERMS AND CONDITIONS IN THIS PURCHASE ORDER THAT ARE ADDITIONAL TO OR DIFFERENT FROM THOSE STATED IN SUPPLIER'S QUOTATION OR OTHER OFFERING DOCUMENTS. SUPPLIER'S ASSENT TO THIS PROVISION WILL BE MANIFESTED BY DELIVERY OF ANY PORTION OF THE GOODS DESIGNATED HEREIN."

The reverse side of the purchase order included provisions stating that the "[s]eller agrees to indemnify" PPG and agrees to binding arbitration for the resolution of any disputes "arising out of or relating to this Purchase Order, or breach thereof."

After receiving PPG's purchase order, and without objecting to any of the provisions contained therein, Mantaline shipped the gaskets.

Analysis and Discussion

The district court correctly determined that Mantaline's price quotation form did not constitute a "formal 'offer' under traditional contract analysis." "An 'offer,'" as the district court explained, "has been defined in Ohio case law as the 'manifestation of willingness to enter into a bargain, so made as to justify another person in understanding that his assent to that bargain is invited and will conclude it.'" . . . The Mantaline form specifically reserved to Mantaline final acceptance of any purchase order and conditioned the formation of any contract on the signature of a Mantaline representative accepting the purchase order.

Notwithstanding that PPG's purchase order, unlike Mantaline's price quotation form, did constitute an "offer" under traditional contract analysis, and notwithstanding that Mantaline shipped the gaskets without adding or disclaiming any contract terms once the purchase order had been received, the district court concluded that the arbitration and indemnification terms proposed by PPG were excluded from the contract under [2-207(3), which] reads as follows:

> "Conduct by both parties that recognizes the existence of a contract is sufficient to establish a contract for sale although the writings of the parties do not otherwise establish a contract. In such case, the terms of the particular contract consist of those terms on which the writings of the parties agree, together with any supplementary terms incorporated under any other provisions of [this Act]."

[2-207(3)] does not exist in isolation. . . . [W]e cannot ignore [2-206, which] provides in relevant part as follows:

> "Unless otherwise unambiguously indicated by the language or circumstances:

(1) an offer to make a contract shall be construed as inviting acceptance in any manner and by any medium reasonable in the circumstances;

(2) an order or other offer to buy goods for prompt or current shipment shall be construed as inviting acceptance either by a prompt promise to ship or by the prompt or current shipment of conforming or non-conforming goods. . . ."

Consistent with the express terms of PPG's purchase order, [2-206(2)] thus says that a purchase order shall be construed as inviting acceptance by the prompt shipment of conforming goods. An exception to this principle is recognized where the order itself or the circumstances "unambiguously" indicate otherwise, but we are not persuaded that the exception applies here. The language of the order certainly does not indicate that it should be construed as anything other than an offer inviting acceptance by the prompt shipment of conforming goods, and it does not seem to us that the provision on the reverse of Mantaline's earlier price quotation form—a provision which the district court assumed neither party had actually read—rises to the dignity of a "circumstance" that "unambiguously" negates [2-206(2)]. The price quotation form was simply an invitation to deal, after all, and not an offer capable of ripening into a contract upon acceptance by PPG. That being so, and Mantaline having shipped the goods–without any contemporaneous disclaimer–in response to PPG's purchase order, [2-206(2)] would seem to be directly applicable. If so, PPG's purchase order ripened into a contract when Mantaline accepted it by the prompt shipment of conforming goods.

[The Court then analyzes the District Court's application of 2-207(3) in deciding that the arbitration terms were excluded from the contract.] However, as we read it, subsection (3) is relevant only where subsection (1) applies–that is, where the "expression of acceptance . . . states terms additional or different from those offered. . . ." Subsection (1) has no application to the case now before us, because Mantaline gave no "expression of acceptance" stating terms different from those offered by PPG. [2-207], in our view, is thus inapplicable here. There were, to quote the caption of [2-207], no "[a]dditional terms in [the] acceptance or confirmation."

We are strengthened in this conclusion by *Litton Microwave Cooking Prods. v. Leviton Mfg. Co., Inc.,* 15 F.3d 790 (8th Cir.1994). In *Litton*, the Eighth Circuit held that [2-207] tells the courts how to resolve a "battle of the forms" only in a situation where a boilerplate offer is accepted by a form that contains additional or different terms: "For a 'battle of the forms' to arise and trigger the provisions of 2-207, there must be conflicting forms to begin with, each of which satisfies the common-law or statutory requirements for an offer. If the first form is not an offer, there can be no battle." *Id.* at 794 (emphasis supplied).

In the case now before us, as the district court correctly found, Mantaline's price quotation form did not satisfy the requirements for an offer. Thus, following *Litton*, there was no "battle" here that could trigger the provisions of section [2-207].

. . . .

In sum, the forward-looking language in Mantaline's invitation to deal (the price quotation form) fell by the wayside when the contract was formed. Because PPG's purchase order constituted the sole "offer," and Mantaline's shipment of conforming goods constituted an unqualified "acceptance" of the offer, the resulting contract included the terms of PPG's purchase order providing for indemnification and arbitration of disputes.

SILER, Circuit Judge, dissenting.

I would affirm the district court's decision. The district court correctly found that Mantaline's quotation form could not be construed as a formal offer under traditional contract analysis, because Mantaline's form reserved to it the final acceptance of any purchase order, and no contract could be formed unless one of Mantaline's representatives signed the order. As the court noted, under Ohio law, an offer must be the "manifestation of willingness to enter into a bargain, so made as to justify another person in understanding that his assent to that bargain is invited and will conclude it." . . .

The district court also correctly held that even if PPG's purchase order technically represented an "offer" to Mantaline, Mantaline did not accept PPG's offer on PPG's terms. I agree with the district court that [2-207(3)] governs . . . .

Here the actions of the parties, in shipping, receiving and paying for the gaskets, acknowledge the existence of the contract. The competing forms of the parties, on the other hand, indicate that the parties disagreed about mandatory arbitration and indemnification. Mandatory arbitration and indemnification thus were not terms of the contract.

[Citing a prior 6th Circuit opinion, Judge Siler argued that 2-207(3)] is to be broadly applied:

> The problem underlying any "battle of the forms" is that parties engaged in commerce have failed to incorporate into one formal, signed contract the explicit terms of their contractual relationship. Instead, each has been content to rely upon standard terms which each has included in its purchase orders or acknowledgements, terms which often conflict with those in the other parties' documents. . . . This case presents a situation typical in any battle of the forms: it is not that the parties' forms have said too little, but rather that they have said too much yet have expressly agreed upon too little.
>
> . . . .

Here, even if Mantaline accepted PPG's "offer" by shipping the gaskets, its price quotation form indicated in advance its objection to any inconsistent terms in PPG's purchase order. Nothing indicates that Mantaline intended to agree to mandatory arbitration and indemnification. Therefore, PPG did not acquire a contractual right to arbitration and indemnification.

APPLYING THE CODE

Problem 5-6.

Lisa was president of the local Gary Puckett fan club, which was hosting the national Gary Puckett fan club convention on September 1. For the welcome packets handed out to fans upon registration, Lisa ordered 5,000 copies of Puckett's "Greatest Hits" Compact Disc from CD Suppliers, at the $7.98 price listed on its website. Her purchase order consisted of a signed fax with the following language: "Please send me, at the address listed above, 5,000 copies of Gary Puckett's "Greatest Hits" CD, at a price of $7.98 per CD. Prompt shipment is required. Speed is of the essence, as these are needed for the Gary Puckett convention beginning next week." CD Suppliers was out of the "Greatest Hits" CD. Rather than disappoint 5,000 Gary Puckett fans, CD Suppliers immediately shipped Lisa 5,000 copies of Gary Puckett's "Golden Classics Edition" CD, at a price of $12.99 per C.D. What risks does CD Suppliers incur by this action, and what should it do to ameliorate these risks?

Problem 5-7.

Pam, a supply clerk at Universal Standard Technics (UST), ordered 5,000 memo pads from Dunder Mifflin (DM), a paper supply company. She used UST's standard purchase order form, filling in blanks for the name of the supplier, item ordered, the number of units ordered, the price, and the delivery date. She found the price in last year's DM catalogue. When DM received the purchase order, it automatically generated its standard acknowledgment form in response, and mailed it to UST. There were two differences in the two forms. One dealt with the time of delivery. UST's purchase order specified delivery by May 1; DM's acknowledgment specified delivery, "within five business days of the date of this order", which would be May 5. The second dealt with the place of delivery. UST's purchase order specified delivery to UST's headquarters in Minneapolis, Minnesota; DM's form specified delivery to UST's supply depot in St. Paul, Minneapolis. When DM's clerk, Dwight, started processing this order, he realized that the price for the memo pads had risen substantially in the last year. He sent a message to his boss, Michael, asking what he should do. Michael was on vacation and did not respond until he returned on May 10. DM never sent the memo pads. What, if any, breach of contract claims does UST have against DM?

Problem 5-8.

The Christmas Boutique (CB) ordered 500 glass Christmas tree ornaments from Ornaments, Inc. (OI). CB used its standard purchase order form, filling in the only blanks on the form—blanks for the name of the supplier, items ordered, the number and type of items ordered, the delivery terms, and the delivery date. The order was submitted by e-mail. OI responded almost immediately with an automatically generated standard order acknowledgment form in a reply e-mail. The two forms were exactly the same, except for the differences between the two excerpts from the forms set forth below. Neither party has yet taken any further actions with respect to this transaction. Has a contract been formed?

CB Purchase Order

- 500 glass Christmas tree ornaments, cushioned in bubble wrap

- All complaints about items purchased must be brought within 60 days of the date of purchase.

- This offer is expressly conditioned on acceptance of the terms of this purchase order.

OI Order Acknowledgment

- 500 glass Christmas tree ornaments, cushioned in environment-friendly straw

- All complaints about items purchased must be brought within 30 days of the date of purchase.

- Please note that all sales are expressly subject to the terms noted in this Acknowledgment.

Assignment 6

Determining the Content of Sales Contracts: Express and Implied Terms, Default Provisions

§§ 1-201(b)(3), (12), (20), (40), 1-303, 1-304, 2-305, 2-306, 2-307, 2-308, 2-309

In Assignment 5, you learned how contracts are created under Article 2 and saw that its flexible rules mean that contracts may be created even though the parties have omitted some terms (§ 2-204) or have exchanged documents that disagree on the terms included (§ 2-207). As a result, under Article 2, parties can easily find themselves bound to incomplete agreements. Recognizing this, the drafters of Article 2 developed tools to help determine the content of contracts. In this Assignment, you will learn about the Article 2 rules for filling gaps in contracts and about the meaning of the obligation to act in good faith. In Assignment 7, you will learn how § 2-207 determines the content of contracts formed in a battle of the forms containing different and additional terms.

LEARNING OUTCOMES AND OBJECTIVES

At the completion of this Assignment, you should be able to

- formulate arguments for the interpretation of Article 2 contracts when parties have not negotiated particular terms;

- distinguish among contract provisions arising from the express language of the contract, terms implied in fact, and provisions supplied by the default rules of Article 2 (implied in law);

- complete contracts left incomplete with respect to quantity or price, delivery terms, payment due dates, and timing of performance obligations; and

- articulate the meaning of the obligation of "good faith" under Article 2 in the many different contexts in which it is used.

Reading the Code:
Reviewing the Components
of a Contract

Review the equations you created to illustrate the meaning of "contract" and "agreement" in your response to Question 10 in Assignment 1. If you need to, review the UCC's definitions of all of the components of these equations.

Recall that 1-201(b)(12) establishes that the "contract" between two parties represents "the total legal obligation" between two parties under the UCC. That obligation includes, but is not limited to, the "agreement", which 1-201(b)(3) makes clear means the complete bargain in fact between the parties. The "agreement" is found in a combination of the express language (which need not always be in writing), from circumstances, and from the parties' dealings, arising as a course of performance, course of dealing, or usage of trade.

A. Express Language of the Contract

Reading the Code:
Reviewing Hierarchy of
Contract Terms

Review your responses to Questions 11 and 12 in Assignment 1, in which you articulated the hierarchy among sources of contract provisions.

Although it is clear that the express language of an agreement is only one source of contract obligations, it is a privileged source. Under 1-303(e), the express language occupies the highest rank and takes precedence over provisions that might otherwise arise from default rules (though the resulting terms may be waived or amended). Thus, the starting point for determining the content of the contract will always be the express language that supports a party's position, interpreted in accordance with the general rules of interpretation applied to common law contracts.

The next sections of this Assignment explore the interaction between such express language and implied (in fact and in law) provisions. Note that this is the starting point but not the ending point for determining the content of a contract. As already noted, inconsistent language included in a "battle of the forms" requires special treatment to determine which portion of that express language is considered part of the contract (Assignment 7). And under the parol evidence rule, the content of the written contract may take precedence over inconsistent express language appearing outside the written contract (Assignment 8). Ultimately you will need to apply all these rules when interpreting a contract, but considering express and implied terms is the first step.

B. Terms Implied-in-Fact

As you may recall from your Contracts class, sometimes terms that are not found in the express language of the contract are supplied by a court based on an analysis of what the parties most likely intended (or would have intended had they considered the matter), based on clues provided in the express language of the contract and the circumstances of the transaction. Such terms are often called "implied-in-fact" terms. Implied-in-fact terms are to be distinguished from the "implied-in-law" provisions that we will be discussing in the rest of this Assignment. "Implied-in-fact" terms are considered to be part of the express contract between the parties As one court explained,

> [t]erms are implied not because they are just or reasonable, but rather for the reason that the parties must have intended them and have only failed to express them . . . or because they are necessary to give business efficacy to the contract as written, or to give the contract the effect which the parties, as fair and reasonable men, presumably would have agreed on if, having in mind the possibility of the situation which has arisen, they contracted expressly in reference thereto.[1]

---

[1]   Barco Urban Renewal v. Housing Auth., 674 F.2d 1001 (3d Cir. 1982) (as cited in Calamari & Perillo on Contracts 141 (6th ed. 2009)).

The terms supplied by "course of performance," "course of dealing," and "trade usage," introduced in Assignment 1 are terms implied in fact. They are derived from the factual circumstances and context of the particular contract being interpreted. Section 1-201(b)(3) defines "agreement" as "the bargain of the parties in fact, as found in their language or inferred from other circumstances, including course of performance, course of dealing, or usage of trade." (If you need to refresh your memory of the meaning of these three concepts, review your responses to Questions 7 through 10 in Assignment 1 in which you detailed what must be established to show their existence.)

C. Provisions Implied in Law under Article 2

The total legal obligation of parties to a contract under Article 2 consists not only of the "agreement," but also of provisions that become part of the "contract" by operation of law. See § 1-201(b)(12). Those include both default provisions added by Article 2 to fill in "blanks" that the parties did not expressly negotiate and some general mandatory legal obligations, the most significant of which is the obligation of good faith.

1. Key Default Rules in Article 2

Article 2 provides busy merchants a robust set of default provisions that are automatically incorporated into contracts if the parties do not agree to any alternative.

APPLYING THE CODE

Problem 6-1.

(a) Review your responses to Question 6 in Assignment 1, where you created a "jot list" for a set of Article 2 default provisions. Supplement your "jot list" for the following Article 2 sections by specifying the default provision that will be added for the following:

· Quantity for an output or requirements contract [2-306(1)]

· Delivery in single or several lots [2-307]

· Payment due date [2-307]

· Place of delivery [2-308]

· Time for any action under a contract [2-309].

(b) What happens if the parties actually "fill in the blank" in their agreement by specifically agreeing, in writing, to a term other than the default provisions listed in (a)?

2. Open Price and Quantity Provisions

Although one might think that express agreement to the price and quantity of goods sold is essential, Article 2 permits parties to omit both of those terms sometimes, to specify them imprecisely, or leave them for later determination. Section 2-305 provides flexibility in specifying the price of goods. Section 2-306 provides flexibility in specifying quantity in output, requirements, and exclusive dealing contracts.

Reading the Code:
Open Price Terms
§ 2-305

Read 2-305.

Question 1. Subsection (1) says that a contract for sale may be formed "even though the price is not settled." Subsection (4) says that if the price "is not fixed or agreed, there is no contract." Explain how these subsections can be reconciled.

Question 2. Under what two sets of circumstances may one party to a contract set the sales price?

Question 3. Under what three sets of circumstances may a court choose a "reasonable price" to establish the price of goods in a sales contract?

Although courts can incorporate a default price ("a reasonable price at the time for delivery") in a contract if the parties intend to be bound without agreeing on a price, there is no parallel provision allowing for incorporation of a default quantity. There is simply no way for a court to determine a "reasonable quantity" of goods if the parties omit a quantity term. On the other hand, parties may specify a flexible range, for example, indicating a minimum, a maximum, or both a minimum and maximum quantity, leaving it (explicitly or implicitly) for the buyer or seller (or both together, by later agreement) to set a precise figure at the appropriate time. Similarly, the parties may decide to identify the quantity by relating it to the "output" of the seller (the quantity the seller produces or has available for distribution) or the "requirements" of the buyer (how much the buyer needs for its own operations). Section 2-306 governs such sales contracts.

Reading the Code:
Output and Requirements Contracts
§ 2-306(1)

Read 2-306(1) and Comments 1 through 4.

Question 4. What guidance do 2-306 and the Comments provide to help regulate the quantities that may be demanded by the buyer or tendered by the seller in an output or requirements contract?

Question 5. Is it possible that the quantity bought or sold in an output or requirements contract could be zero?

Reading the Code:
Exclusive Dealing Contracts
§ 2-306(2)

Read 2-306(2) and Comment 5.

Question 6. Section 2-306(2) governs an "exclusive dealing" contract between buyer and seller. How does this differ from an "output" or "requirements" contract?

Question 7. Section 2-306(1) introduces a standard of "good faith" in the quantity determinations. Does 2-306(2) use the same standard or a different one? If it is a different standard, why is it different, and how does it differ from "good faith"? Keep these questions in mind when considering the meaning of "good faith" in the following discussion.

3. Good Faith

As sections 2-305 and 2-306 illustrate, some default rules apply a "good faith" standard to the actions of the parties under a particular contract provision. Section 1-304 goes further, imposing an obligation of good faith on every contract in the UCC.

 Reading the Code:
§ 1-304

Read 1-304 and Comments 1 and 2.

Question 8. Does the obligation of good faith apply to contract negotiations?

Question 9. Comment 1 says that 1-304 "does not support an independent cause of action for failure to perform or enforce in good faith," and "does not create a separate duty of fairness and reasonableness which can be independently breached." How, then, would a party raise the obligation of good faith in a breach action?

While all contracts under Article 2 include an obligation to perform and enforce the contract in good faith, precisely what that obligation will entail depends on the particular obligations of that contract and an understanding of accepted and acceptable business practices.

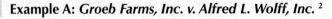

EXAMPLES AND ANALYSIS

Example A: *Groeb Farms, Inc. v. Alfred L. Wolff, Inc.* [2]

Groeb Farms, a company located in Michigan, entered into two contracts to purchase honey from an importer, Alfred L. Wolff, Inc. The first contract was for 2,045,890 pounds of honey originating from Korea. The second was for 4,466,074 pounds of honey originating from India. The first contract contained the following clause (with an almost identical clause in the second contract):

> In event of FDC/USDA rejection or non-shipment by original vendor of all or part of goods represented in this sale, Seller does not guarantee replacement. Due to unpredictability of USA/Import regulations and country of origin export regulations and remoteness of source, Seller does not guarantee total fulfilment of this order. Deliveries are guaranteed for price & quantity but precise weeks or months of delivery cannot be guaranteed. We intend to deliver according to the projected delivery periods indicated in this contract but we will extend delivery if circumstances beyond our control occur without liability on part of Alfred L. Wolff Inc. for any reasonable delays.

Wolff never delivered any honey to Groeb. Because there were no other sources of honey at comparable prices and quantities, Groeb sought specific performance of the contracts with Wolff. In its complaint, Groeb claimed breach of an obligation to deliver honey and breach of the duty of good faith when Wolff tried to deliver Chinese honey that was barred by the Department of Homeland Security because Chinese honey was subject to anti-dumping duties and tariffs. Wolff moved for summary judgment, claiming that the quoted contract clause meant it was excused from performing.

Analysis: The court denied Wolff's motion for summary judgment on the breach of contract claim, concluding that Groeb might be able to show that Wolff had violated the contract by trying to deliver honey from China when the contract required honey from Korea or India, or that Wolff had violated an obligation to deliver promised quantities at a later time after the rejection of the Chinese honey. However, the court dismissed Groeb's allegation that Wolff breached the

---

2   68 UCC Rep. Serv. 2d 539 (E.D. Mich. 2009).

duty of good faith, stating that 1-203 "does not serve to create an independent cause of action for failure to perform or enforce in good faith" but can only be enforced "as an element of [the party's] breach of contract claim."

How might Groeb's attorneys have characterized Wolff's alleged "bad faith" to avoid having the claim dismissed in summary judgment?

Under Article 2, good faith carries with it an obligation to perform each contractual duty in good faith. But what does it mean to perform those duties "in good faith"? The UCC defines "good faith," but this definition has not been adopted uniformly in all jurisdictions.[3]

Non-Uniformity Alert: Definitions of "Good Faith"

Prior to the 2001 revision of Article 1, Article 1 and Article 2 each had its own definition of "good faith." The 2001 revision proposed a new uniform good faith definition that would apply except in Article 5, and directed jurisdictions adopting the revised Article 1 to delete the nonconforming definition from Article 2. The effort to create a single definition of good faith failed, however. Although almost all states have now adopted the 2001 revision of Article 1, a substantial minority has chosen to retain the older Article 2 definition for transactions falling within that Article.

Consider the three definitions of "good faith" that you might find in the UCC adopted in different states (as well as reflected in newer and older case law):

> Revised Article 1 definition of good faith: "honesty in fact and the observance of reasonable commercial standards of fair dealing." 1-201(b)(20) (revised)

> Pre-revision Article 1 definition of good faith (retained by some jurisdictions when adopting revised Article 1): "honesty in fact in the conduct or transaction concerned." 1-201(19) (unrevised)

---

[3]   As of Jan. 1, 2016, 13 of 49 states that had adopted the 2001 revision did not adopt the new definition of good faith proposed in the revision. Note that Article 5 contains its own definition of good faith.

Pre-revision Article 2 definition of good faith (retained by some jurisdiction when adopting revised Article 1): "in the case of a merchant means honesty in fact and the observance of reasonable commercial standards of fair dealing in the trade." 2-103(1)(b)

Question 10. If a jurisdiction has retained the pre-revision Article 2 definition of good faith, what definition of good faith applies to (a) merchants and (b) consumers?

Question 11. If a jurisdiction has adopted the revised Article 1 definition of good faith and deleted the Article 2 definition, what definition of good faith applies to (a) merchants and (b) consumers?

Question 12. Which definition of good faith has been adopted in the jurisdiction in which you expect to practice law?

Reading the Code: § 1-201(b)(20)

Read the Comment associated with 1-201(b)(20).

Question 13. The comment suggests that the two different aspects of good faith ("honesty" and "commercial reasonableness") are distinguished by a significant difference in how they are to be assessed. What is that difference?

(a) Describe how you would prove that some act violated the good faith duty to be "honest." Who would you call as witnesses, and what would you want to get from their testimony?

(b) Describe how you would prove that some act violated the good faith duty to act with "commercial reasonableness." Who would you call as witnesses, and what would you want to get from their testimony?

Example B: *Mathis v. Exxon Corp.[4] and Casserlie v. Shell Oil Co.[5]*

The franchise contract between Exxon Corporation and its gas station franchisees contained an open price term, providing that Exxon would deliver gasoline to the stations at "EXXON's price in effect at the time of the loading of the delivery vehicle." In performing the contract, Exxon charged the franchisees the industry-standard "dealer tank wagon price." The franchisees contended, however, that Exxon charged them prices that were consistently higher than prices Exxon charged non-franchisees, a practice that the franchisees argued was intended to drive the franchisees out of business. The franchisees sued Exxon, claiming violation of the 2-305(2) obligation to fix prices under open price terms "in good faith."

Analysis: The jury in the case found Exxon had indeed intended to drive the franchisees out of business and thus had acted in bad faith, and the verdict was affirmed on appeal. In a very similar case against Shell Oil, however, (*Casserlie v. Shell Oil*) another court refused to inquire into the motive of the gasoline seller and found the use of the dealer tank wagon price sufficient to demonstrate good faith.

What actions by Exxon might be seen as violating the good faith requirements? Why were these actions in "bad faith"? How would you support the result in the case against Exxon? In the case against Shell? Would it matter what definition of "good faith" applied in the relevant jurisdiction? Both courts discussed Comment 3 to 2-305, especially the last sentence, but they came to opposite conclusions as to its meaning. Do you think that sentence supports the result in the case against Exxon or in the case against Shell?

---

[4]   302 F.2d 448 (5th Cir. 2002).
[5]   902 N.E.2d 1 (Ohio 2009).

APPLYING THE CODE

Problem 6-2.

The Latino/a Law Students Association (LLSA) started selling Chipotle burritos to members of the law school community every Friday, at a price of $7.00. People interested in buying a burrito were required to come to LLSA's office and sign their names on an order sheet by 5:00 p.m. on the preceding Thursday. The order sheet contained only a caption that said: "Order your burrito for this Friday for $7.00 by signing below and indicating what filling you want. Pay when you pick up your burrito, on Friday at noon." For the first four weeks, LLSA delivered the burritos to a table set up on the second floor of the law school building. Then, LLSA added a monthly plan. People interested in purchasing burritos every Friday for the month signed a separate order sheet in LLSA's office that contained only a caption that said: "Order burritos for the entire month by prepaying $25.00; sign below and indicate what filling you want." For the first three weeks of this new deal, LLSA members hand-delivered burritos to the offices of the faculty members who signed up for the monthly program. Assume that none of the order sheets or any of LLSA's advertisements about the burritos said anything about where the burritos were to be delivered. Assuming Article 2 of the U.C.C. applies to these sales, to which location is LLSA contractually obligated to deliver burritos to faculty members on the monthly plan next week—LLSA's office, the second floor station, or the faculty members' offices?

Problem 6-3.

Harrison signed an exclusive dealership agreement with Auto-Chlor Systems, Inc., for Harrison to sell Auto-Chlor's commercial dishwashing machines to restaurants and other customers. These machines used specially-developed chemical products to efficiently wash dishes in low temperature water. In their first agreement, signed in 1971, Auto-Chlor agreed to sell Harrison both the machines and all required machine parts, as well as the special chemical cleaning products, at the price "established from time to time by written notice from the company to the Dealer, taking into consideration geographic location and local conditions before establishing prices." In a later version of their agreement, signed in 1981, the only term governing price provided: "Auto-Chlor agrees to sell, and Dealer agrees to buy from Auto-Chlor, *virtually at cost,* all necessary and integral parts of apparatus, devices, and basic equipment, including dishwashing machines, as available, necessary to efficiently operate the Auto-Chlor System for washing and sanitizing eating utensils." In 1976, Auto-Chlor was purchased by a large corporate conglomerate. In order to generate more revenue, Auto-Chlor began charging independent dealers like Harrison significantly more than it charged company-owned retail outlets for both dishwashers and chemicals. Company-owned retail outlets were charged the total cost to Auto-Chlor, which included materials plus a flat labor charge. For independent dealers, the cost was calculated by doubling the labor rate, and multiplying the result by a factor anywhere from two to three times. When Harrison discovered this, he consulted you to ask whether he might be able to sue Auto-Chlor for violating 2-305(2), based on the price disparity he had uncovered. Might he have a valid claim under the 1971 version of the agreement? What about under the 1981 version of the agreement? Would your answer depend on whether Harrison is suing about the price disparities on the dishwashing machines or on the chemical products?

Problem 6-4.

Acme Automobile Corporation (Acme) entered into a contract with Best Ball Bearings (Best), pursuant to which Acme agreed to purchase all the ball bearings used at its Duluth assembly line from Best, for two years, at a fixed price of $.05 per ball bearing. For the first year after signing the contract, Acme ordered an average of 5,000 ball bearings a month from Best. At the beginning of the second year, however, Acme ordered only 300. In an e-mail accompanying that order, Acme explained, "Consumer demand for sustainable technology has required us to re-engineer many of our automobile models, resulting in a significantly lower demand for your ball bearings." The next few months' orders were similarly small. Best has heard rumors that Acme's President recently married the owner of Carter's Ball Bearings, a competitor in the manufacture of ball bearings. Describe Best's strongest arguments for breach of contract by Acme.

Problem 6-5.

Bario Todd is an artist whose medium is raku pottery. (Raku is a process that uses reduction rather than oxidation to produce iridescent and black finishes.) Todd is contemplating selling his bowls, vases, and plates at a local gallery, Exclusive Collections. Todd is excited about the opportunity to showcase his work in this venue. Todd thinks his items will sell at higher prices in the gallery than in his own shop or at art shows to which he usually travels, and that the higher prices at the gallery will also let him charge more elsewhere. The gallery has proposed a two-year arrangement under which Todd would furnish enough raku pieces so that the gallery could satisfy the demand from its customers. The gallery has suggested it might contemplate an exclusive distribution agreement, if demand is high enough to warrant that in the first year of the contract. Todd is anxious to get some sort of a deal with the gallery that will afford him exposure to their customers, but is concerned about whether he will be able to satisfy the gallery's expectations. Advise Todd as to the alternatives for contracts that afford some flexibility, yet offer him some control over production. What are the risks of the various alternatives? What sorts of protections might he want to include in his contract with the gallery?

Assignment 7

Determining the Content
When Offer and Acceptance Differ:
Battle of Forms

§ 2-207(2), (3)

Assignment 6 addressed the general rules in Article 2 for determining terms of contracts. You saw that the contract is created from the parties' express language, supplemented by commercial context (course of dealing, course of performance, and usage of trade) and default and mandatory provisions. As you also saw in Assignment 5, however, parties may create a contract even though the express language of the parties does not show agreement on the terms discussed. This Assignment returns to the issue (raised in Assignment 5) of determining the terms of a contract if a contract was formed under § 2-207(1) or § 2-207(3).

LEARNING OUTCOMES AND OBJECTIVES

At the completion of this Assignment, you should be able to

- apply the "knock out rule" to contracts formed by conduct under 2-207(3);

- articulate the interpretational issues raised by ambiguities in the language of 2-207 on which there is no clear consensus among the courts;

- identify the difference between "different" and "additional" terms in an acceptance; and

- apply the 2-207 rules for determining the terms of contracts formed under 2-207(1) by communications that contain terms different from or additional to the terms of the offer.

A. Terms in Contracts Created by Conduct under § 2-207(3)

As you saw in Assignment 5, when the communications of the parties disagree, if a contract is not created by the exchanged communications under § 2-207(1), a contract may still result under § 2-207(3) based on the conduct of the parties. Section 2-207(3) specifies how to determine the resulting contract's terms. The rule in § 2-207(3) is often referred to as the "knock-out rule." The following exercise should help you understand why.

Reading the Code:
§ 2-207(3)

Read 2-207(3) and Comment 7.

Question 1. The second sentence of 2-207(3) states a rule for determining contract terms. The first sentence (already covered in Assignment 4) tells you when that rule applies. Rewrite and paraphrase the subsection as an if/then statement:

IF these facts are established:

THEN this is the rule for determining the contract terms:

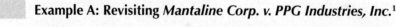

EXAMPLES AND ANALYSIS

Example A: Revisiting *Mantaline Corp. v. PPG Industries, Inc.*[1]

Both the dissenting opinion and the lower court opinion in the *Mantaline v. PPG* case included in Assignment 5 argued for the application of the rule of 2-207(3). If they had prevailed, 2-207(3)'s knock-out rule would have applied. Under that rule, since the arbitration provision was not a term on which both Mantaline's price quotation and PPG's purchase order agreed, it would not have become part of the contract.

---

[1]   225 F.3d 659 (6th Cir. 2000).

APPLYING THE CODE

Problem 7-1.

A purchasing clerk at Troy Industries, Inc. uses a standard company purchase order form to order business cards from Annie's Business Printing. On the back of that standard form is a clause stating, "Purchaser has 90 days after receipt of goods to return goods for defects." Annie's Business Printing responds with a "Purchase Acknowledgement" saying, "We accept your order, but only if you consent to the terms in our standard contract set forth on the back of this confirmation, by initialing this form and returning it to us." The preprinted terms on the back of the Purchase Acknowledgement include one that says, "Return of goods due to defects must be made within 30 days of receipt." Troy Industries receives the business cards and pays for them. How long does Troy Industries have to return the goods if it finds an error on the business cards?

B. Terms in Contracts Created by the Exchange of Forms under § 2-207(2)

1. Distinguishing between "Different" and "Additional" Terms

Reading the Code:
§ 2-207(1) & (2)

———————————

Read 207(1) and (2).

Question 2. 2-207(1) directs that under certain conditions, a response to an offer can operate as an acceptance even though the purported acceptance "states terms additional to or different from" those offered. What is the difference between "additional terms" and "different terms"? Does the text of 2-207(2) refer to additional terms, to different terms, or to both situations?

As you can see, § 2-207(2) is silent about "different" terms. Whether this silence was the consequence of careless drafting or an intentional omission is one of the many open questions under Article 2. Before looking at the different ways courts have addressed that issue, let us first consider the application of § 2-207(2) to the relatively straight-forward situation explicitly addressed: when a purported acceptance adds new terms to an offer.

2. The Application of § 2-207(2) when a Purported Acceptance Contains Additional Terms

Reading the Code:
§ 2-207(2)

Read 2-207(2).

Question 3.

(a) If the parties are not both merchants, what happens to additional terms in the acceptance? Under what circumstances will such terms become part of the contract?

(b) If the parties are both merchants, what happens to additional terms in the acceptance? Under what circumstances will such terms become part of the contract?

(c) Read the first sentence of 2-207 Comment 6. Why is this statement incorrect if read literally?

a. Examples of Language Invoking § 2-207(2)(a) and (c)

EXAMPLES AND ANALYSIS

Example B: *Tunis Manufacturing Corp. v. Mystic Mills, Inc.* [2]

A purchaser's written purchase orders contained a provision that said that "no change in orders can be effected except by a writing signed by" the

---

[2]   337 N.Y.S.2d 150 (App. Div. 1972).

purchaser. The seller shipped the requested goods, along with invoices containing an arbitration clause. The seller requested the purchaser to sign the invoices, but the purchaser refused. The court held that the purchase order expressly limited acceptance to the terms of the offer. Accordingly, under 2-207(2)(a), the arbitration clause did not become part of the agreement.

Example C: *Oskey Gasoline & Oil Co. v. OKC Refining, Inc.*[3]

In contrast to Example B, a purchaser's offer stated that the offeree "must acquiesce in writing to all the terms contained herein." The court noted that the offeror "did not use language that clearly indicated it was attempting to avail itself of 2-207(2)(a) and limiting any acceptance to the terms of the offer."

Analysis of Examples B and C: What is the significant difference between the language in Example B and the language in Example C? Can you draft a clause that would convince the court in Example C that 2-207(2)(a) should apply?

Example D: Notifications of Objection to Proposed Terms

2-207(2)(c) provides that a notification of objection to proposed terms may be made either before or after an acceptance with additional terms is received. As an example of an objection made *before* the acceptance, a court held that language in a seller's price quotation stating that "[n]o waiver, alteration, or modification of the provisions [of the quotation] shall be binding on [Seller] unless agreed to in writing", was sufficient "as the required notification of objection" under 2-207(2)(c) to a force majeure clause in the buyer's purchase order.[4] As long as they are specific and documentable, objections made *after* the acceptance can be informal oral objections.[5] Whether they are timely will depend on the specific facts of the case. An objection first lodged five months after performance under a contract was rejected as untimely.[6]

---

[3]   364 F. Supp. 1137 (D. Minn. 1973).

[4]   Power Engineering & Mfg., Ltd. v. Krug Int'l, 501 N.W.2d 490 (Iowa 1993).

[5]   Genecco Produce, Inc., v. Sol Group Marketing Co., 2006 WL 328385 (W.D.N.Y. 2006).

[6]   Oskey Gasoline & Oil Co. v. OKC Refining, Inc., 364 F. Supp. 1137 (D. Minn. 1973).

Analysis: How is 2-207(2)(c) different from 2-207(2)(a)? What is the difference between language that the court in Example B found satisfied 2-207(2)(a), and the language that the court in Example D found satisfied 2-207(2)(c)? How do these provisions relate to language that satisfies 2-207(1)'s standard for making an acceptance "conditional on assent to the additional or different terms"?

APPLYING THE CODE

Problem 7-2.

For the following two scenarios, determine (1) which subsection of 2-207 (if any) determines which terms are in the contract, and (2) whether the offeror's or offeree's terms control or what standard you would use to answer that question. Assume all parties are merchants.

(a) Offeror sends a purchase order saying, "This offer may be accepted only on the terms specified herein." Offeree responds with a document saying "Your order is accepted" but the document adds a new term on a minor subject not covered in the original purchase order. Would your answer be different if the purchase order instead said, "This offer expressly conditioned on your acceptance of these terms"?

(b) Offeror sends a purchase order with a set of standard terms and a cover letter specifying that seller must agree to all of buyer's terms. Offeree responds with a "Confirmation" containing standard terms (some of which differ from those in the offer) and specifying that "Acceptance is subject to agreement to all terms contained herein." There is no further written communication. Offeree ships the ordered goods within the time specified in the order. Offeror receives and keeps the goods.

b. What Constitutes a "Material Alteration" under § 2-207(2)(b)?

Under § 2-207(2)(b), additional terms proposed in an acceptance or confirmation will not become part of the contract if the new terms "materially alter" the contract.

Reading the Code:
§ 2-207(2), Comments 4 and 5

Read Comments 4 and 5 to 2-207.

Comments 4 and 5 provide lists of specific examples of terms that would or would not normally constitute a "material alteration." But they also suggest a more general standard for determining whether an additional term would "materially alter" the contract. Comment 4 describes material alterations as clauses that would "result in surprise or hardship if incorporated without express awareness by the other party." Comment 5 describes non-material alterations as clauses that "involve no element of unreasonable surprise."

Comment 4 gives the following examples of clauses that *would* normally materially alter a contract:

- Negating implied warranties that would normally attach to a sale;

- Demanding near perfect compliance with quantity terms where usage of trade allows greater leeway;

- Reserving to seller the power to cancel the entire contract if buyer doesn't pay a single invoice when due; and

- Requiring that complaints be made much sooner than usual or reasonable.

Comment 5 gives the following examples of clauses that *would not* typically materially alter a contract:

- Giving seller the same or a slightly greater exemption from performance than already granted by article 2 under circumstances of impracticability;

- Requiring that complaints be made within a time limit that is customary and reasonable;

- If the goods are being sold for immediate resale, providing for inspection by the ultimate purchaser;

- Providing credit terms or interest within the range of trade practice, and not interfering with credit bargained for; and

- Limiting remedies in a reasonable manner in accordance with the relevant Article 2 provisions.

Reading the Code:
§ 2-207(2), Comments 4 and 5

Question 4. From reviewing these examples and considering the general standard set forth in the Comments, what questions might you ask a client to help you determine whether an additional term would be considered a material or nonmaterial alteration?

The next two examples illustrate both how courts rely on the Comment 4 and 5 examples, and the case-by-case nature of the analysis of materiality. The court in the case described in Example F explains: "the test for whether an additional term would be a material alteration to the contract is 'whether the addition constitutes an unreasonable surprise to one of the bargaining parties.' . . . In determining whether an additional term constitutes an unreasonable surprise, courts may consider the course of conduct and prior dealings between the parties, as well as customary industry usage of the term. . . . The determination is made on a case-by-case basis."

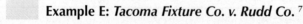

EXAMPLES AND ANALYSIS

Example E: *Tacoma Fixture Co. v. Rudd Co.* [7]

Tacoma Fixture Company regularly ordered paint and varnish products from Rudd Company, Inc., to use in manufacturing cabinets. For a number of years, Rudd responded to Tacoma's telephone or faxed orders with invoices containing additional terms that Tacoma never expressly accepted. When Tacoma began experiencing significant discoloration and cracking of the cabinets made with Rudd's product, it sued Rudd for breach of warranties.

[7] 174 P.3d 721 (Wash. Ct. App. 2008).

Rudd attempted to assert as a defense one of the additional terms on its invoice in which it disclaimed all warranties.

Analysis: Citing the official comments to 2-207, the court ruled that the warranty disclaimer did not become part of the contract under 2-207(2), because "a clause negating standard warranties, such as that for merchantability or fitness for a particular purpose, materially alters the contract."

Suppose Rudd could prove that it is an almost universal trade practice in the paint and varnish industry to disclaim all warranties. Would that make a difference in the analysis? Suppose Rudd's invoice contained not a complete waiver of all warranties, but rather stated, "claims for breach of warranty must be brought within two months of the application of the product." Could such a term become part of the contract under 2-207(2)?

Example F: *Jada Toys, Inc. v. Chicago Import, Inc.* [8]

Over the course of eight years, Chicago Import, Inc. purchased more than $4,000,000 worth of toy cars from Jada Toys, Inc. Hundreds of orders were initiated by Chicago Import, most often by telephone. Jada responded to each order with a written confirmation in the form of an invoice, followed by prompt shipment of the ordered goods. Each invoice contained the following provision on the front: "Delinquent accounts are subject to a service charge of 1½% per month. If it becomes necessary to file suit for the collection of any account, costs including reasonable attorneys' fees shall be paid by the buyer." The relationship soured when Chicago Import discovered that Jada was selling the toys to another distributor for lower prices. Jada sued Chicago Import for unpaid invoices, accrued interest for delinquencies in the unpaid invoices, and attorney's fees.

Analysis: In considering whether the additional terms regarding delinquency interest and attorney's fees became part of the contract under 2-207(2), the Court cited binding precedent in that jurisdiction holding that "between merchants, the party opposing the inclusion of additional terms has the burden of proving that one of the exceptions applies." Because Chicago Import had provided no evidence that either 2-207(2)(a) or (c) applied, the only question was whether the two terms materially altered the contract.

---

[8] 2009 WL 3055370 (N.D. Ill. 2009).

The interest charge for overdue invoices was held to be "a textbook example of a term that does not materially alter a contract," citing Comment 5. The court continued, "Chicago Import has provided no evidence that an interest charge on an overdue balance is uncommon in commercial transactions like the ones at issue here, or that the interest charge was outside the range of trade practice. Moreover, Chicago Import was familiar with Jada's forms, terms, and practices, including its asserted right to charge interest, because the parties had engaged in hundreds of transactions using the form with the interest charge provision on it."

Similarly, the attorney's fee provision was held not to materially alter the contract, based largely on their extensive past dealings. The court explained, "Jada and Chicago Import engaged in hundreds of transactions over the course of seven years, all of which involved written confirming invoices stating on the front that if it became necessary to file suit for the collection of any account, the buyer would be liable for Jada's reasonable attorneys' fees. Courts in Illinois and this circuit have found that additional terms posed no unreasonable surprise in situations where there had been far fewer prior dealings between the parties."

Suppose this were only the parties' third transaction together. How might that change the court's conclusion on either the interest charge or the attorney's fee provision? What if it were the third transaction, but the first one had been the subject of a lawsuit? Would it make a difference if the language of the attorney's fee provision required Jada to pay "costs including all attorney's fees"? Would it make a difference if the language about attorney's fees were on the back of the invoice or in a separate listing of "standard terms and conditions" referenced on the front of the invoice?

Example G: *Colorado-Arkansas-Texas Distrib., L.L.C. v. American Eagle Food Prods., Inc.*[9]

Colorado-Arkansas-Texas Distributing (CAT) ordered cashew nuts from American Eagle Food (AEF) for a number of years. During that time, the parties followed a practice common in the nut industry: CAT would make an oral order, and AEF would follow up by sending CAT a "Sales Order Form" containing the following language on the front of the form:

> This contract is entered into subject to the terms, conditions, and agreements printed on the back hereof.

---

[9]   525 F.Supp.2d 428 (S.D.N.Y. 2007).

Arbitration: Any controversy or claim arising out of this contract shall be settled in binding arbitration by the Association of Food Industries, Inc., of New York in accordance with its rules then obtaining.

Thank you for your business. If this confirmation is incorrect, please contact us immediately. If it is correct, sign and return one copy immediately.

CAT frequently (but not always) signed and returned the sales order forms, but for a number of years the parties performed whether or not CAT signed the form. At some point, CAT ceased to accept further nut deliveries from AEF. In August, AEF submitted a demand for arbitration before the Association of Food Industries. Arbitration was initially scheduled for the following January, but was rescheduled for March at the request of CAT's attorney. The day before the scheduled arbitration, CAT attempted, unsuccessfully, to enjoin the arbitration, claiming there were no agreements to arbitrate because CAT had not signed the sales order forms. After an arbitration award was entered for AEF, CAT sued to enjoin enforcement of the arbitration award.

Analysis: The court confirmed the arbitration award in favor of AEF. The court reasoned that the arbitration provision constituted an additional term in confirmation of an oral agreement. Both parties were merchants, and CAT did not claim to have ever objected to the inclusion of the arbitration provision. Whether the inclusion of an arbitration clause materially alters the oral agreement had to be determined on a case-by-case basis with "the burden of proving the materiality . . . on the party that opposes inclusion." That party "must establish that, under the circumstances, it cannot be presumed that a reasonable merchant would have consented to the additional term." In this case, CAT conceded that it was aware of the arbitration provision, and the court found that arbitration clauses were "common, if not customary, in the nut industry."

Suppose CAT had raised its objection to the arbitration proceeding in August, rather than March. Why might that have made a difference in the court's conclusion? Suppose the arbitration provision in AEF's Sales Order Form had been on the back of the form instead of on the front? Arbitration provisions are frequently challenged as material alterations, but as they become increasingly common in many industries, it becomes more difficult to argue that they constitute unreasonable surprises or hardship.

3. The Application of § 2-207(2) when a Purported Acceptance Contains Different Terms

Now that you understand the operation of § 2-207 with respect to *additional* terms, we must consider what effect the section has on *different* terms.

a. Distinguishing between "Different" and "Additional" Terms (Reprise)

Reading the Code:
§ 2-207(2) Applied to Different Terms

Re-read 2-207(1) and (2).

Question 5. In answering Question 2, you saw that 2-207(2) explicitly refers only to "additional" terms, not to "different" terms. Read Comment 3 to 2-207, the caption for 2-207, and 1-107. Based on these sources, what more can you say about how to treat different terms appearing in an acceptance?

b. The Three Different Approaches to Purported Acceptances with Different Terms

Your answer to Question 5 should convince you that § 2-207(2) fails to give clear guidance regarding how to treat different terms. One logical possibility might be to apply § 2-207(2) to different terms as well as to additional terms, even though the section does not explicitly say to do so. What would be the result of applying § 2-207(2)? Would the different terms always, never, or sometimes become part of the contract?

- Between non-merchants, § 2-207(2) would tell us that different terms are to be construed as "proposals for addition to the contract." They would not become part of the contract unless the other party accepts them. By definition, since they are different from the terms in the offer, they have not been accepted. Thus, the different terms would never become part of the contract.

- Between merchants, § 2-207(2)(b) would tell us that the different terms do not become part of the contract if they "materially alter" it or if "notification of objection to them has already been given . . . ." Anything that differed from what was proposed in the offer might be seen as a material alteration, because changing a term already expressly chosen by the other party might cause unreasonable surprise. However, the outcome might be different depending on the importance and consequences of the different terms. More generally, one might conclude that the different term would never become part of the contract because the offeror had provided notification of objection by inclusion of different terms in the offer.

Thus, for both merchants and non-merchants, it is possible to conclude that applying § 2-207(2) to different terms would mean that the different terms in the acceptance or confirmation would never become part of the contract (though exactly how § 2-207(2)(b) and (c) would apply to small differences in terms is not clear).

So applying § 2-207(2) does not provide clear directions regarding the handling of different terms. To complicate matters, further, applying § 2-207(2) to different terms is not the only option. Read the following case, which discusses three different approaches courts have taken to handling different terms. As you read *Daitom v. Pennwalt*, consider the following questions:

Focusing first on the theories of contract formation offered by the parties and courts in this case:

(1) How does the district court conclude the contract was formed in this case, and how does that conclusion support its determination that Pennwalt's 1-year statute of limitations applies to this contract?

(2) What two alternative theories of contract formation does Daitom assert in this case, and how does each support Daitom's argument that a 4-year statute of limitations applies to the contract?

(3) How does the court of appeals conclude the contract was formed in this case, and how does that affect the outcome with respect to the statute of limitations?

(4) What theory of contract formation does Judge Barrett adopt in his dissent? What is his disagreement with the majority opinion?

Focusing next on the alternative approaches to dealing with "different terms" under 2-207(2):

(5) Identify the three alternatives to handling different terms described by the court of appeals.

(6) How is each alternative supported by reference to the Code, Comments, and policy underlying the Code?

(7) Do you agree with the court's description of how 2-207(2) would work if applied to different terms?

(8) Which alternative does the court of appeals adopt, and why? What does the adoption of that alternative mean for Daitom's claim?

(9) If you were the judge, which alternative would you adopt, and why?

DAITOM, INC. V. PENNWALT CORP.

741 F.2d 1569 (10th Cir. 1984)

WILLIAM E. DOYLE, CIRCUIT JUDGE

I. STATEMENT OF THE CASE

This is an appeal from the grant of summary judgment against Daitom, Inc. (Daitom), the plaintiff below. The result was dismissal by the United States District Court for the District of Kansas of all three counts of Daitom's complaint.

Daitom had brought this diversity action in federal court on March 7, 1980 against Pennwalt Corporation and its Stokes Vacuum Equipment Division (Pennwalt). Counts I and II of Daitom's complaint alleged breach of various express and implied warranties [in connection with] certain rotary vacuum drying machines sold to and used commercially by Daitom in the production of a vitamin known properly as dextro calcium pantothenate and commonly as Vitamin B-5. [Count III alleged a claim based on negligent design and manufacture, which was dismissed under the Economic Loss Doctrine addressed in Assignment 22.]

Daitom is a Delaware chartered corporation having its principal place of business in Kansas. . . . Pennwalt is a Pennsylvania chartered corporation with its principal place of business in Pennsylvania.

Daitom requests a reversal of the district court's grant of summary judgment against Daitom on all counts of its complaint and seeks a remand for a trial on the merits.

We have concluded that there should be a reversal with respect to Counts I and II, together with a remand to the district court for a trial on the merits of those claims. . . .

II. FACTS

The essential facts so far as they pertain to the issues presented in this appeal are as follows.

. . . Daitom planned to construct and operate a manufacturing plant to commercially produce dextro calcium pantothenate. The design of the plant was undertaken and handled on behalf of Daitom by Kintech Services, Inc. (which company will be referred to as Kintech), an engineering design firm located in Cincinnati, Ohio. Kintech had the responsibility not only for designing the plant; it also was responsible for investigating various means of drying the product during the production process, and for negotiating the purchase of certain equipment to be used in the plant. Included in the equipment was automated drying equipment to be used in removing methanol and water from the processed vitamin as part of the purification process.

There were numerous tests made and conducted at Kintech's request by equipment manufacturers. Kintech formulated specifications for the automated drying equipment (Kintech Specification 342). On behalf of Daitom, Kintech invited various vendors to bid on the needed equipment.

Pennwalt, on September 7, 1976, submitted a proposal for the sale of two rotary vacuum dryers with dust filters and heating systems to dry dextro calcium pantothenate. The typewritten proposal specified the equipment to be sold, the f.o.b. price, and delivery and payment terms. A pre-printed conditions of sale form was also attached to the proposal and explicitly made an integral part of the proposal by the typewritten sheet.

Kintech recommended to Daitom that Pennwalt's proposal be accepted and on October 5, 1976, well within the thirty-day acceptance period specified in the proposal, Daitom issued a purchase order for the Pennwalt equipment. The purchase order consisted of a pre-printed form with the identification of the specific equipment and associated prices typewritten in the appropriate blank spaces on the front together with seventeen lengthy "boilerplate" or "standard" terms and conditions of sale on the back. In addition, on the front of the purchase order in the column marked for a description of the items purchased, Daitom typed the following:

> Rotary vacuum dryers in accordance with Kintech Services, Inc. specification 342 dated August 20, 1976, and in accordance with Stokes proposal dated September 7, 1976.

The two rotary vacuum dryers and the equipment that went along with them were manufactured by Pennwalt and delivered to Daitom's plant in early May 1977. For the reason that there had been no construction of Daitom's plant, the crated equipment was not immediately installed. Instead, it was stored outside in crates. On June 15, 1978, the dryers were finally installed and first operated by Daitom. Daitom notified Pennwalt of serious problems with the operation of the dryers on June 17, 1978.

Daitom's contention was that the dryers suffered from two severe defects: 1) they were delivered with misaligned agitator blades causing a scraping and damaging of the dryer interiors and an uneven distribution of the products being dried; and 2) they were undersized necessitating an overloading of the dryers and a "lumping up" of the product rendering it unsuitable for further use. Pennwalt's repair personnel visited the Daitom plant to investigate the alleged operating difficulties, but Daitom contends the dryers were not repaired and have never performed as required under the specifications and as represented by Pennwalt. This was the basis for the lawsuit.

. . . .

III. DISCUSSION

A. The Issues

It is to be noted that the district court granted summary judgment against Daitom on Counts I and II of the complaint, finding the breach of warranties claim barred by the one-year period of limitations which was set forth in Pennwalt's proposal. In ruling against Daitom the court followed a three step analysis. First, it concluded that pursuant to U.C.C. § 2-207(1), a written contract for the sale of the rotary dryers was formed by Pennwalt's September 7, 1976 proposal and Daitom's October 5, 1976 purchase order accepting that proposal. Second, the court found that the one year period of limitations specified in Pennwalt's proposal and shortening the typical four-year period of limitations available under the U.C.C. became part of the contract of sale and governed the claims for breach of warranties. Thus, the court accepted the proposal that was contained in the documents that had been submitted by the defendant-appellee. . . .

Daitom has challenged the district court's findings as to the terms which became a part of the contract. Daitom argues that its October 5, 1976 purchase order did not constitute an acceptance of Pennwalt's September 7, 1976 proposal. Instead, Daitom claims that its purchase order explicitly made acceptance conditional on Pennwalt's assent to the additional or different terms in the purchase order. As a consequence, Daitom argues, pursuant to U.C.C. § 2-207(1), the exchanged writings of the parties did not form a contract, because Pennwalt failed to assent to the additional or different terms in the purchase order. The most relevant additional or different terms Daitom alleges were in its purchase order were the terms reserving all warranties and remedies available in law, despite Pennwalt's limitation of warranties and remedies in its proposal. In a sense Pennwalt argues it enjoyed an exclusive right to set the conditions.

Daitom argues that on their face the writings failed to create a contract, and, instead, that a contract was to be formed by the conduct of both parties, pursuant to § 2-207(3), and the resulting contract consisted of the terms on which the writings agreed, together with "any supplementary terms incorporated under any other provision of [the UCC]." Therefore, Daitom concludes, the resulting contract governing the sale of the rotary dryers incorporated the U.C.C. provisions for express warranties (§ 2-313), implied warranties (§§ 2-314, 2-315), and a four year period of limitations.

As an alternative argument, Daitom contends that even if its October 5, 1976 purchase order did constitute an acceptance of Pennwalt's September 7, 1976 proposal and did form a contract, all conflicting terms between the two writings were "knocked out" and did not become part of the resulting contract, because of their being at odds one with the other. Therefore, Daitom concludes once again that the resulting contract consisted of only those terms in which the writings agreed and any supplementary or "gap-filler" terms incorporated under the provisions of the U.C.C.; specifically §§ 2-313, 2-314, 2-315, 2-725.

. . . .

After considering the record in the instant case, it is apparent that the substantive law was not correctly applied and that summary judgment against Daitom on Counts I and II was improper. The fundamental feature with respect to this is this court's determination of whether any terms in the parties' writings conflicted and, if so, which terms became part of the resultant contract.

B. The Applicable Law

The district court found the dispute between Daitom and Pennwalt involved a "transaction in goods," between persons who are "merchants" and, therefore, was governed by Article 2 of the U.C.C. U.C.C. §§ 2-102, 2-104. The district court also stated that the dispute is a classic example of the "battle of the forms."

As previously noted, there has been agreement that the law of Pennsylvania governs these claims for breach of warranty and Pennsylvania has adopted the provisions of the U.C.C. Section 2-207 of the U.C.C. was specifically drafted to deal with the battle of the forms and related problems. U.C.C. § 2-207, Comment 1.

Section 2-207 has been commented on in one case as a "murky bit of prose," and as "one of the most important, subtle, and difficult in the entire code, and well it may be said that the product as it finally reads is not altogether satisfactory." . . . The Pennsylvania Supreme Court has not addressed the issues presented by this case. In the absence, therefore, of an authoritative pronouncement from the state's highest court, our task is to regard ourselves as sitting in diversity and predicting how the state's highest court would rule. . . .

C. The Writings and the Contract

[The court concluded that Daitom's purchase order was an acceptance of Pennwalt's proposal, despite its inclusion of terms additional to and different from those in the offer. The court rejected Daitom's claim that certain provisions made the acceptance expressly conditional on assent to the additional or different terms, applying the standard articulated in *Dorton v. Collins & Aikman Corp.*, 453 F.2d 1161 (6th Cir. 1972).]

Having found an offer and an acceptance which was not made expressly conditional on assent to additional or different terms, we must now decide the effect of those additional or different terms on the resulting contract and what terms became part of it. The district court simply resolved this dispute by focusing solely on the period of limitations specified in Pennwalt's offer of September 7, 1976. Thus, the court held that while the offer explicitly specified a one-year period of limitations in accordance with § 2-725(1) allowing such a reduction, Daitom's acceptance of October 5, 1976 was silent as to the limitations period. Consequently, the court held that § 2-207(2) was inapplicable and the one-year limitations period controlled, effectively barring Daitom's action for breach of warranties.

While the district court's analysis undertook to resolve the issue without considering the question of the application of § 2-207(2) to additional or different terms, we cannot accept its approach or its conclusion. We are unable to ignore the plain implication of Daitom's reservation in its boilerplate warranties provision of all its rights and remedies available at law. Such an explicit reservation impliedly reserves the statutory period of limitations; without such a reservation, all other reservations of actions and remedies are without effect.

The statutory period of limitations under the U.C.C. is four years after the cause of action has accrued. U.C.C. § 2-725(1). Were we to determine that this four-year period became a part of the contract rather than the shorter one-year period, Daitom's actions on breach of warranties were timely brought and summary judgment against Daitom was error.

We realize that our conclusion requires an inference to be drawn from a construction of Daitom's terms; however, such an inference and construction are consistent with the judicial reluctance to grant summary judgment where there is some reasonable doubt over the existence of a genuine material fact. . . . When taking into account the circumstances surrounding the application of the one-year limitations period, we have little hesitation in adopting the U.C.C.'s four-year limitations reservation, the application of which permits a trial on the merits. Thus, this court must recognize that certain terms in Daitom's acceptance differed from terms in Pennwalt's offer and decide which become part of the contract. The district court certainly erred in refusing to recognize such a conflict. FN6

FN6. There is some indication in its memorandum and order that had the district court considered the effect of the conflicting terms, it would have applied § 2-207(2)(b) and concluded that the terms in Pennwalt's offer controlled because Daitom's conflicting terms would have materially altered the content. . . . Because we hold, *infra*, that conflicting terms should not be analyzed pursuant to § 2-207(2), this conclusion of the district court is also in error.

The difficulty in determining the effect of different terms in the acceptance is the imprecision of drafting evident in § 2-207. The language of the provision is silent on how different terms in the acceptance are to be treated once a contract is formed pursuant to § 2-207(1). That section provides that a contract may be formed by exchanged writings despite the existence of additional or different terms in the acceptance. Therefore, an offeree's response is treated as an acceptance while it may differ substantially from the offer. This section of the provision, then, reformed the mirror-image rule; that common law legal formality that prohibited the formation of a contract if the exchanged writings of offer and acceptance differed in any term.

Once a contract is recognized pursuant to § 2-207(1), 2-207(2) provides the standard for determining if the additional terms stated in the acceptance become a part of the contract. Between merchants, such additional terms become part of the resulting contract unless 1) the offer expressly limited acceptance to its terms, 2) the additional terms materially alter the contract obligations, or 3) the offeror gives notice of his or her objection to the additional terms within a reasonable time. Should any one of these three possibilities occur, the additional terms are treated merely as proposals for incorporation in the contract and absent assent by the offeror the terms of the offer control. In any event, the existence of the additional terms does not prevent a contract from being formed.

Section 2-207(2) is silent on the treatment of terms stated in the acceptance that are different, rather than merely additional, from those stated in the offer. It is unclear whether "different" terms in the acceptance are intended to be included under the aegis of "additional" terms in § 2-207(2) and, therefore, fail to become part of the agreement if they materially alter the contract. Comment 3 suggests just such an inclusion. FN7

FN7. Comment 3 states (emphasis added): Whether or not *additional or different* terms will become part of the agreement depends upon the provision of subsection (2). . . .

It must be remembered that even official comments to enacted statutory text do not have the force of law and are only guidance in the interpretation of that text. *In re Bristol Associates, Inc.*, 505 F.2d 1056 (3rd Cir.1974) (while the comments to the Pennsylvania U.C.C. are not binding, the Pennsylvania Supreme Court gives substantial weight to the comments as evidencing application of the Code).

However, Comment 6 suggests that different terms in exchanged writings must be assumed to constitute mutual objections by each party to the other's conflicting terms and result in a mutual "knockout" of both parties' conflicting terms; the missing terms to be supplied by the U.C.C.'s "gap-filler" provisions. FN8

FN8. Comment 6 states, in part:

> Where clauses on confirming forms sent by both parties conflict each party must be assumed to object to a clause of the other conflicting with one on the confirmation sent by himself . . . . The contract then consists of the terms expressly agreed to, terms on which the confirmations agree, and terms supplied by the Act, including subsection (2).

At least one commentator, in support of this view, has suggested that the drafting history of the provision indicates that the word "different" was intentionally deleted from the final draft of § 2-207(2) to preclude its treatment under that subsection. The plain language, comments, and drafting history of the provision, therefore, provide little helpful guidance in resolving the disagreement over the treatment of different terms pursuant to § 2-207.

Despite all this, the cases and commentators have suggested three possible approaches. The first of these is to treat "different" terms as included under the aegis of "additional" terms in § 2-207(2). Consequently, different terms in the acceptance would never become part of the contract, because, by definition, they would materially alter the contract (i.e, the offeror's terms). Several courts have adopted this approach. . . .

The second approach, which leads to the same result as the first, is that the offeror's terms control because the offeree's different terms merely fall out; § 2-207(2) cannot rescue the different terms since that subsection applies only to additional terms. Under this approach, Comment 6 (apparently supporting a mutual rather than a single term knockout) is not applicable because it refers only to conflicting terms in confirmation forms following oral agreement, not conflicting terms in the writings that form the agreement. This approach is supported by Professor Summers. J.J. White & R.S. Summers, Uniform Commercial Code, § 1-2, at 29 (2d ed. 1980).

The third, and preferable approach, which is commonly called the "knock-out" rule, is that the conflicting terms cancel one another. Under this view the offeree's form is treated only as an acceptance of the terms in the offeror's form which did not conflict. The ultimate contract, then, includes those non-conflicting terms and any other terms supplied by the U.C.C., including terms incorporated by course of performance (§ 2-208), course of dealing (§ 1-205), usage of trade (§ 1-205), and other "gap fillers" or "off-the-rack" terms (e.g., implied warranty of fitness for particular purpose, § 2-315). As stated previously, this approach finds some support in Comment 6. Professor White supports this approach as the most fair and consistent with the purposes of § 2-207. White & Summers, *supra*, at 29. Further, several courts have adopted or recognized the approach. . . .

We are of the opinion that this is the more reasonable approach, particularly when dealing with a case such as this where from the beginning the offeror's specified period of limitations would expire before the equipment was even installed. The approaches other than the "knock-out" approach would be inequitable and unjust because they invited the very kind of treatment which the defendant attempted to provide.

Thus, we are of the conclusion that if faced with this issue the Pennsylvania Supreme Court would adopt the "knock-out" rule and hold here that the conflicting terms in Pennwalt's offer and Daitom's acceptance regarding the period of limitations and applicable warranties cancel one another out. Consequently, the other provisions of the U.C.C. must be used to provide the missing terms.

This particular approach and result are supported persuasively by the underlying rationale and purpose behind the adoption of § 2-207. As stated previously, that provision was drafted to reform the infamous common law mirror-image rule and associated last-shot doctrine that enshrined the fortuitous positions of senders of forms and accorded undue advantages based on such fortuitous positions. . . . To refuse to adopt the "knock-out" rule and instead adopt one of the remaining two approaches would serve to re-enshrine the undue advantages derived solely from the fortuitous positions of when a party sent a form. . . . This is because either approach other than the knock-out rule for different terms results in the offeror and his or her terms always prevailing solely because he or she sent the first form. Professor Summers argues that this advantage is not wholly unearned, because the offeree has an opportunity to review the offer, identify the conflicting terms and make his or her acceptance conditional. But this joinder misses the fundamental purpose of the U.C.C. in general and § 2-207 in particular, which is to preserve a contract and fill in any gaps if the parties intended to make a contract and there is a reasonable basis for giving an appropriate remedy. U.C.C. §§ 2-204(3); § 2-207(1); § 2-207(3). Thus, this approach gives the offeree some protection. While it is laudable for business persons to read the fine print and boilerplate provisions in exchanged forms, there is nothing in § 2-207 mandating such careful consideration. The provision seems drafted with a recognition of the reality that merchants seldom review exchanged forms with the scrutiny of lawyers. The "knock-out" rule is therefore the best approach. Even if a term eliminated by operation of the "knock-out" rule is reintroduced by operation of the U.C.C.'s gap-filler provisions, such a result does not indicate a weakness of the approach. On the contrary, at least the reintroduced term has the merit of being a term that the U.C.C. draftpersons regarded as fair.

We now address the question of reverse and remand regarding Counts I and II. The result of this court's holding is that the district court erred in granting summary judgment against Daitom on Counts I and II of its complaint. Operation of the "knock-out" rule to conflicting terms results in the instant case in the conflicting terms in the offer and acceptance regarding the period of limitations and applicable warranties cancelling. In the absence of any evidence of course of performance, course of dealing, or usage of trade providing the missing terms, §§ 2-725(1), 2-313, 2-314, 2-315 may operate to supply a four-year period of limitations, an express warranty, an implied warranty of merchantability, and an implied warranty of fitness for a particular purpose, respectively. The ruling of the district court on Counts I and II does not invite this kind of a broad inquiry, and thus, we must recognize the superiority in terms of justice of the "knock-out" rule. Consequently, the ruling of the district court on Counts I and II must be reversed and the matter remanded for trial consistent with this court's ruling.

. . . .

BARRETT, Circuit Judge, dissenting:

I respectfully dissent. Insofar as the issue of contract formation is concerned in this case, we are confronted with a "battle of the forms" case involving the interpretation and application of U.C.C. § 2-207. I would affirm.

. . . .

The "knock-out" rule should not, in my view, be reached in this case. It can be applied only if, as Daitom argues and the majority agrees, the "conflicting terms" cancel each other out. The "knock-out" rule does have substantial support in the law, but I do not believe it is relevant in this case because the only conflicting terms relate to the scope of the warranty. In this case, it is not an important consideration because, pursuant to the express time limitations contained in Pennwalt's "offer," Daitom lost its right to assert any warranty claim. There was no term in Daitom's purchase order in conflict with the express one-year limitation within which to bring warranty actions. . . .

4. Putting it All Together: Surveying All the Possibilities with Additional and Different Terms in Acceptances

APPLYING THE CODE

Problem 7-3.

Consider the following chart, which displays four possibilities of agreement and disagreement between offer and acceptance as to a particular term. "Version A" represents one substantive choice of term, e.g., "1% monthly interest on unpaid balances." "Version B" represents a different substantive choice on the same subject matter, e.g., "No interest on unpaid balances." Fill in the final column, indicating which version of the term, if any, will be in the contract, or what rule will be used to select the term.

Term in the Offer	Term in the Acceptance	Term in the Contract
Version A	Version A	
Version A	(Silent)	
(Silent)	Version A	
Version A	Version B	

Reading the Code:
The Effect of § 2-207 on the Common Law "Last Shot" Rule

Consider your results in the chart above, as well as the rationale given by the majority opinion in *Daitom*.

Question 6. Under the common law, if an offer and acceptance did not match, the "acceptance" would be considered a counteroffer. If the parties nonetheless began performance, the counteroffer would often be considered the articulation of contract terms that had been accepted by performance of the other party, thereby giving preference to the "last form" exchanged between the parties. This was sometimes referred to as the "last shot" rule. Under similar circumstances, does 2-207 give a preference to the first form, the last form, or neither, in determining which terms are part of the contract?

C. Don't Forget Confirmations!

Up to this point, we have been considering how § 2-207 treats additional and different terms in an *acceptance*. But recall that in Assignment 5 we learned that § 2-207 also applies to confirmations of contracts. A typical scenario would involve two parties who enter into an oral contract, after which one or both sends the other a "confirmation" of their agreement. Under § 2-207, what happens if the confirmation contains terms in addition to, or conflicting with, the terms of the contract already formed? What if both parties send confirmations, and some terms in the two confirmations conflict with each other? The following exercises will help you understand the answers to those questions.

Reading the Code:
§ 2-207(2) Applied to Confirmations

Re-read 2-207(1), (2), and Comment 6 (except for the first sentence).

Question 7.

(a) Under 2-207(1) and (2), what happens to additional terms in a confirmation sent by one of the parties to the transaction?

(b) Recall the meaning of "confirmation" as used in 2-207(1). According to Comment 6, what happens if both parties send confirmations that contain additional terms that conflict with the terms on the other confirmation?

(c) What happens if one or both parties send a confirmation that contains terms that conflict with the agreement reached before the confirmation was sent?

APPLYING THE CODE

Problem 7-4.

Consider the following chart, which displays the range of scenarios that may occur regarding agreement, disagreement, and silence when one or both parties send confirmations after they agree to a contract. As in Problem 7-3, "Version A" represents a term on a particular subject matter (e.g., "Complaints as to delivered goods must be made within 60 days"), while "Version B" and "Version C" represent different terms on the same subject matter (e.g., "All complaints of defect to be made within 90 days" and "Seller must be notified of any defects within 120 days"). Fill in the final column, indicating what the term in the contract will be or what rule will be used to select the term.

Term agreed to before confirmation(s) sent	Term in confirmation from first party	Term in confirmation from second party	Term in final contract
(Silent)	Version A	(Silent)	
(Silent)	Version A	Version B	
Version A	(Silent)	(Silent)	
Version A	Version B	(Silent)	
Version A	Version B	Version B	
Version A	Version B	Version C	

Problem 7-5. Overview of 2-207.

Before proceeding to the review problems below, you should construct a flowchart or other rewrite of 2-207 based on the analysis reflected in your answers to Problems 7-1 to 7-4. This exercise will help you pull together your understanding of the parts of 2-207 and will serve as a foundation for applying the section. You may use the partially-completed flow-chart below as a starting point, but if you do, you should modify it to make it most understandable and useful to you.

Sample Flow-Chart for 2-207

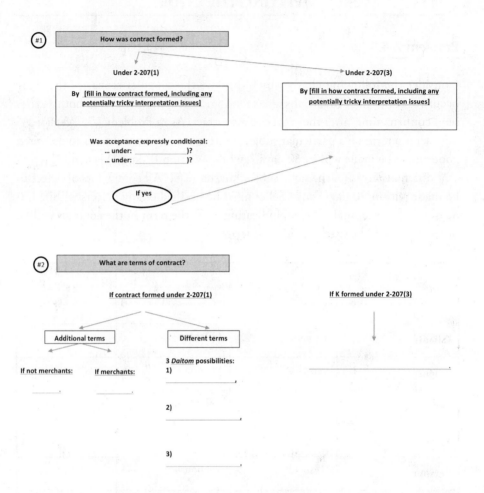

Problem 7-6.

Consider the following short scenarios, designed to ensure that you can navigate your way through the multiple paths in 2-207. For each one, identify (1) which subsection of 2-207 (if any) determines which terms are in the contract, and (2) whether the offeror's or offeree's terms control or what standard you would use to answer that question. Assume all parties are merchants. In answering these questions, you will find it helpful to consider first whether the contract is formed by offer and varying acceptance, by prior agreement followed by one or more confirmations, or by conduct.

(a) Offeror sends purchase order with no mention of a delivery date. Offeree responds with a preprinted "Order Verification" saying, "Your order is accepted. Shipment will be made in three business days."

(b) Same as (a), but the "Order Verification" also contains on the reverse side a pre-printed term specifying, "Goods sold without warranty."

(c) Offeror sends an offer to sell a specified quantity of goods to Buyer at a specified price. On the back is a pre-printed set of terms, including one that specifies, "Seller warrants against defects for six months" and another that provides for arbitration of disputes. Offeree responds with a "Purchase Order" repeating the quantity and price from Seller's form. On the reverse side is a pre-printed term specifying "One Year Warranty Against Defects." *So is the Wm. not a term either as offeree didn't accept it? K = silent?*

(d) Ritz Department Store sends a purchase order for perfume gift sets on Friday, December 3, specifying delivery of goods by December 14. Offeree responds on December 8 with a "Sales Verification" repeating the quantity and price from the purchase order and stating, "Shipment will arrive within ten business days."

(e) Buyer and Seller agree by phone on sale of goods to Buyer at a specified price. Buyer and Seller each send confirming documents repeating the agreed-upon terms on quantity and price. On the back of Buyer's form is a pre-printed provision specifying that Seller will pay any attorney fees that Buyer incurs if enforcement of the contract in court is necessary and identifying the law of Texas (where the Buyer is located) as the law to be applied to any such dispute. On the back of Seller's form is a preprinted provision specifying that the law of New York (where Seller is located) will apply to any dispute.

Problem 7-7.

Apple Aircraft Rentals ("Apple") sends the following communication to Primara Aircraft on June 1:

> We are ordering from you ten (10) Primara Cloudgrazer aircraft at the price stated in your price quotation, subject to our standard terms and conditions (attached).

The standard terms include this one:

> Vendor agrees to reimburse Apple for any amounts owed by Apple to third parties because of defects in vendor's product.

The next day, Primara sends the following response:

> We accept. Please note that the sale includes the terms contained on the back of this acceptance form.

The back of the form contains the following terms:

(i)   Any claims of defect in equipment must be submitted in writing within 60 days of detection;

(ii)   Primara will not pay any consequential damages to Buyer for any liability of Buyer to third parties arising from use of Primara's aircraft;

(iii)   Any dispute between us is to be governed by binding arbitration.

There is no further correspondence between the two companies relating to terms. Three weeks later Primara seeks to deliver the aircraft to Apple. Apple refuses to accept the planes, claiming there was no contract. Primara claims breach of contract and seeks to enforce the binding arbitration provision that it asserts is part of the contract.

(a)   Do these communications create a contract? If so, which of the terms specified by Apple or Primara are part of the contract, and why? In formulating your answer, consider the following information about arbitration procedure, drawn from an American Arbitration Association publication:

> · Under the standard AAA [American Arbitration Association] rules, the procedure is relatively simple: legal rules of evidence are not applicable; there is no motion practice or court conference; there is no requirement for transcripts of the proceedings or for written opinions of the arbitrators. Although there is no formal discovery process, the AAA's rules allow the arbitrator to require production of relevant documents, the deposition of factual witnesses, and an exchange of reports of expert witnesses.

· The arbitrator shall be the judge of the relevance, materiality, credibility and weight of the evidence offered, and conformity to legal rules of evidence shall not be necessary.

· The arbitrator may grant any remedy or relief that the arbitrator deems just and equitable and within the scope of the agreement of the parties.

· The parties may provide by agreement that the arbitrators give effect to substantive rules of law, but in the absence of such an agreement, the arbitrator is not bound to do so.

· Judicial review of arbitration awards is limited, and awards generally may not be challenged on the grounds that they do not follow substantive or procedural rules of law.

(b) Would your answer to (a) be different if the communications concerned a single Primara Cloudgrazer aircraft being purchased by a flying enthusiast for use in pleasure excursions?

(c) Would your answer to (a) be different if a previous dispute between Primara and Apple had been handled by arbitration?

(d) Would your answer to (a) be different if the order by Apple was the fifth such order from Primara and after each order Primara sent the same response, including the three terms on the back of the acceptance form?

INTEGRATING ASSIGNMENTS 5, 6, AND 7

Problem 7-8.

At this point in the course, you should review and try to synthesize the material in Assignments 5, 6, and 7. Review the *Mantaline* case from Assignment 5. What are *all* the ways that contracts can be formed under Article 2—both generally, and in battle of forms situations? What are *all* the ways provisions in addition to the express terms in a unified, single written contract can become part of a contract under Article 2—generally, and under the rules of 2-207? Supplement the flow chart you created in Problem 7-5 to include the materials covered in Assignments 5 and 6.

Problem 7-9.

On July 11, 2013, Great Lakes received a catalog for J&J Tomato Farms (J&J), which contained a list of the various types of tomatoes sold, prices, and delivery information. Great Lakes completed the order form provided with the catalog and ordered a shipment of 1,800 boxes of grape tomatoes from J&J, submitting the form through the J&J website. J&J shipped the grape tomatoes ordered by Great Lakes on July 13, 2013, to the railroad yard closest to Great Lakes. Great Lakes sent one of its drivers to pick up the shipment. The driver signed a bill of lading for the shipment prepared by J&J, dated July 13, 2013. The bill of lading listed the quantity (1,800 total boxes) of bulk grape tomatoes but did not include a price per unit, and indicated the total amount due was $0.00. J&J also sent Great Lakes an invoice by mail dated July 15, 2013, for $28,710.00, which Great Lakes alleges arrived a week later on July 22, 2013. By the time the invoice arrived, Great Lakes had already received the shipment and distributed the tomatoes to its customers. Both the bill of lading and invoice included the following language, which was not on the order form or in the catalog:

> Interest shall accrue at 1.5% per month (18% per annum) on all unpaid invoices. The buyer agrees to pay all costs of collection, including attorney fees.

Upon receipt of the invoice, Great Lakes did not contact J&J to object to the contractual terms. Both Great Lakes and J&J use attorney fees provisions in their standard invoices, and such provisions are commonplace in the produce industry. This transaction was the first and only transaction between the parties because Great Lakes was not pleased with the quality of the grape tomatoes, having received several complaints from its own customers.

After Great Lakes failed to pay the invoice and J&J's collection efforts proved unsuccessful, J&J filed litigation in November 2014 for breach of contract.

(a) Was a contract formed in this scenario, and if so, how?

(b) Does the contract require Great Lakes to pay attorney fees?

Assignment 8
Parol Evidence Rule
§ 2-202

Assignments 5, 6, and 7 showed how sale-of-goods contracts are created and how the content of the contract is built from the express language of the parties and implied-in-fact and implied-in-law provisions. In particular, you saw that the parties' express language takes precedence over other sources of contract provisions, unless superseded by mandatory provisions or later modifications. One more Article 2 rule must be explored to fully ascertain the contract terms that will govern performance, however. In certain circumstances, application of the parol evidence rule (§ 2-202) may bar consideration of aspects of the parties' alleged agreement-in-fact when the fact-finder determines what terms are in the contract. As a result, application of the parol evidence rule is required to see if there is a risk that parts of the alleged agreement will not be effective.

LEARNING OUTCOMES AND OBJECTIVES

At the conclusion of this Assignment, you should be able to

- articulate the purpose and policy of the Code's parol evidence rule;
- identify contract documents that are in the categories of writings protected by the parol evidence rule from modification by other evidence of agreement;
- identify which kinds of evidence are barred by the parol evidence rule and which kinds of evidence are not barred;
- articulate the arguments parties may use to support or oppose introduction of evidence based on the parol evidence rule; and
- predict the likely outcome of parol evidence disputes.

A. Why is it Called the Parol Evidence Rule?

When parties to a contract seek to prove the content of their contract, any evidence showing what they agreed is relevant. Examples of relevant evidence might include details of the negotiations leading up to the adoption of a written contract document; notes written on documents exchanged during the negotiation; conversations that might help to explain ambiguous words in the contract document; dictionary definitions of words used in the document; and discussions held after the signing of the contract document.

In order to be considered by the fact-finder, evidence that is relevant to prove the content of a contract must also satisfy—or not violate—the usual evidentiary standards on admissibility. For example, relevant evidence tending to show that the parties agreed to a particular term might be excludable as hearsay, and documents containing relevant evidence regarding contract terms might be excludable if not properly authenticated.

Section 2-202 establishes an additional set of rules forbidding the use of certain otherwise relevant and admissible evidence to prove contract terms, based on policy concerns relating to the importance of written contract documents. Although § 2-202 is not technically a rule of evidence, it operates like such a rule by forbidding the fact-finder from using certain evidence to determine the content of a contract.

That helps to explain why it is called the parol *evidence rule,* as it is in common law contract doctrine. But why *parol* evidence? "Parol" is usually understood to mean "oral" or "unwritten," and it is true that § 2-202 is often applied to oral conversations and agreements. But as you will see, the rule also applies to some written agreements, so the name of the rule is a bit misleading. The title of § 2-202 is more accurate: "Final Written Expression: Parol or Extrinsic Evidence." The section applies to parol (oral) evidence and other extrinsic (outside) evidence, that is, evidence from sources outside the final written expression. It is helpful to keep that longer title in mind as you work through this Assignment, though we will bow to common usage and will often refer to § 2-202 as "the parol evidence rule."

B. The Policy Underlying § 2-202

As indicated by the section title, § 2-202 addresses the handling of evidence that lies outside the "final written expression" of the parties. The rule in § 2-202 is based on the notion that if parties go through the trouble of negotiating the language of and signing a written contract to memorialize their agreement, the best evidence of what the parties intended is most likely the language of that written contract. Evidence based on things the parties might have said to one another, or written down on other pieces of paper during the negotiations leading up to the final written contract, are less reliable. The more explicitly the parties express their intent that the written contract be considered their final agreement, the more suspect other forms of evidence outside the written contract become.

To implement this objective, the parol evidence rule comes into play whenever (1) there is some writing that arguably expresses the parties' ultimate agreement (their "final written expression"); and (2) one party is attempting to introduce some evidence about what the parties agreed that comes from some other (parol or extrinsic) source. When there is no "final written expression" by the parties, or when a party seeks to introduce parol or extrinsic evidence for some purpose other than demonstrating the parties' agreement, the parol evidence rule has no effect, so the evidence is governed by all the usual rules of evidence and may well be admissible.

The parol evidence rule is concerned with (1) protecting written agreements that are the "final written expression" (2) from parol or extrinsic evidence (3) about agreements occurring outside the written document. Accordingly, analyzing whether the parol evidence rule bars admission of particular evidence is controlled by the answer to three questions, which you should keep in mind throughout this Assignment:

(1) **What kind of document(s) memorialize the contract?** Did the parties intend one document (or a particular collection of documents) to express their ultimate agreement? Did the parties intend that document to express all of their agreement, or just some of it?

(2) **What is the source of the evidence offered?** Was the evidence the party is trying to introduce generated during the negotiations leading up to that agreement, or from some other point in the transaction? Because the policy of the parol evidence rule is directed to protecting the final written expression from allegations of prior agreement that undermine its finality, the rule applies only to circumstances that precede the written memorialization of the agreement and to evidence of oral agreements made at the same time that the written agreement was signed.

(3) **For what purpose is the evidence offered?** Is the party attempting to prove agreement about a contract term (adding a term to those in the writing or contradicting something in the writing)? On the assumption that the written agreement is the best evidence of the parties' intent, attempts to prove terms outside the writing are problematic. If the party is trying to introduce the evidence for some other purpose (e.g., to resolve an ambiguity

in the written contract, or show that no contract or an avoidable contract exists), the assumption that the written agreement is the "best evidence" is not really relevant.

C. What Kind of Document Memorializes the Contract?

1. The Three Kinds of Writing Identified in § 2-202

As you will see as you read through the statutory language, section 2-202 privileges three identified types of writings: (1) *"confirmatory memoranda of the parties"* containing terms *"with respect to which [the memoranda] agree"*; (2) writings *"intended by the parties as the final expression of their agreement with respect to such terms as are included therein"*; and (3) writings *"intended also as a complete and exclusive statement of the terms of the agreement."* We will refer to these types of writings as (1) confirmations; (2) final expressions; and (3) complete and exclusive statements. The first two types of writings are given the same privilege vis-à-vis other forms of evidence under § 2-202; the last type of writing is given greater privilege. Before we dive into the intricacies of these privileges, make sure that you clearly understand the differences among the kinds of writings and can identify where each of these writings appears in the structure of § 2-202 by answering the next set of questions.

**Reading the Code:
Identifying the Three Types
of Writings in § 2-202**

Read 2-202 and Comment 1(a).

Mark where in 2-202 you find the italicized language quoted above, which identifies the three different types of writings addressed in the section.

Question 1. What is the difference in parties' intent between a "final expression of their agreement with respect to such terms as are included therein" and "a complete and exclusive statement of the terms of the agreement"? What questions would you ask your client to determine which the client intended the written agreement to be?

Question 2. Thinking about a single contract document signed by both parties to the contract:

(a) Could the document be both a final expression and a complete and exclusive statement?

(b) Could it be a final expression but not a complete and exclusive statement?

(c) Could it be a complete and exclusive statement but not a final expression?

(d) Could it be neither a "final expression" nor a "complete and exclusive statement"?

2. How Does a Court Decide What Kind of Document the "Contract" Is?

Section 2-202 does not explain how a court should decide whether a particular contract document is a final expression, a complete and exclusive statement, or neither. The language does indicate that the question is whether the parties intended the document to be a final expression as to the terms contained in it, or whether the writing was intended to also be a complete and exclusive statement. How would a court decide intent? As you would expect under general principles of contract interpretation, a court would start by looking at the document itself for clues and then consider the surrounding circumstances: Is the document called a "Contract" or a "Letter of Intent" or is it stamped "Draft"? Is it signed? Do its length and complexity suggest a completely negotiated transaction, or are there gaps? Did the parties use a template for the contract and fill in blanks or did they write the document from scratch? Is the industry practice to rely exclusively on a written contract or do parties regularly rely on promises made outside a document? Was legal counsel involved in the drafting? What did the parties say to each other about the contract document before and at the time it was signed?

As you may recall from your Contracts class, the presence of a clause specifically stating that the contract is intended to be a final or complete and exclusive statement of the terms (often called an "integration" or "merger" clause) can be powerful evidence of such intent. Examples of such clauses include the following:

- This agreement supersedes all prior agreements and representations, written or oral, concerning the subject matter herein.

- The parties agree that all past representations and agreements are merged into this writing.

- This agreement sets forth the entire understanding of the parties.

- There are no contract terms beyond the four corners of this document.

- This contract integrates all previous oral or written agreements, if any, between the parties, and constitutes the entire agreement between the parties.

However, there is a growing line of cases in which courts have concluded that a merger clause does not represent (or at least definitively represent) the intent of the parties in some situations. Factors a court might consider when interpreting a contract with a merger clause include the following:

- Did the parties talk about adding terms even as they signed the document with the merger clause in it?

- Was the merger clause boilerplate on a preprinted form?

- How sophisticated are the parties?

- What is the likelihood the parties knew of the existence and meaning of the merger clause?

- Are there elements of unconscionability or duress present?

Although all courts will consider the contract document itself in determining whether the document was final or complete and exclusive, courts are divided on whether evidence outside the four corners of the document should be considered for that purpose. Some courts conclude that, because the purpose of the parol evidence rule is to exclude from consideration evidence appearing outside the document, to look at any such evidence to decide whether the document is final or complete and exclusive would defeat the aim of the rule. Other courts conclude that all relevant evidence ought to be considered for the limited purpose of deciding whether the document was intended to be final or complete and exclusive. Some courts will look at all extrinsic evidence except the evidence about agreement to the term alleged to have been approved outside the writing, since that is the very evidence the parol evidence rule may exclude. It is certainly true that if the court first looks at the extrinsic evidence about agreement (e.g., considers testimony about promises allegedly made but not later incorporated into the writing) and is convinced that the parties reached an agreement about such terms, that will be persuasive evidence that the writing was not final or complete and exclusive.

D. Application of § 2-202 to the Three Kinds of Documents

In this section, you will learn how the rules in § 2-202 apply to each of the three kinds of contract documents identified in the previous section. Later in this Assignment, in Section G, Question 15 will ask you to record in a diagram the rules that you will discover as you work through the material below. You may find it helpful to refer to the diagram as you answer Questions 4 through 14 and perhaps even complete the diagram step-by-step, rather than waiting until you reach the diagram later in the Assignment.

1. Application to Final Expressions

If you have determined that the contract is, or arguably is, recorded in a "final expression," the next issue is what evidence § 2-202 bars from consideration.

**Reading the Code:
How § 2-202 Applies to
Final Expressions**

Read all of 2-202, including (a) and (b), but ignore for now
the last clause of (b) (starting with "unless the court finds . . . .").

Question 3. As you may have noticed, 2-202 is written as one very long sentence, with multiple clauses, passive voice, and confusing grammar. To figure out how to apply the section, you first have to break the sentence into component parts to make sense of it.

(a) What is the subject in the sentence? (Hint: there are actually two subjects, written as phrases connected by "or," and each subject-phrase starts with the first word in the section.)

    (b) What are the verb phrases associated with those two subject-phrases? (Hint: The verbs appear in both negative and positive form not long before sub-parts (a) and (b).)

Question 4. Once you have identified the two subject-phrases and the two verbs, you should be able to answer the next set of questions. Assume the parties have created a document that is indisputably a "final expression of their agreement with respect to such terms as are included therein."

    (a) What does 2-202 say about the use of evidence contradicting a term in the written document? Does the outcome depend on whether the promise was written or oral, or when it took place?

    (b) What does 2-202 say about the use of evidence that would add a term not mentioned in the document? Does the application of the rule depend on whether the statement was written or oral, or when it took place?

———————————

Read Comment 1(b) & (c) and 2; review 1-303 and its Comments.

Question 5. Assume, as in Question 4, that the parties have created a document that is a "final expression."

    (a) What does 2-202 say about the consideration of evidence of usage of trade, course of dealing, and course of performance?

    (b) If evidence of usage of trade, course of dealing, or course of performance is admitted under the parol evidence rule, what does 1-303 say about the effect of such evidence when considered with the words in the document?

    (c) In order to introduce usage of trade, course of dealing, or course of performance, does a party have to demonstrate that the contract is ambiguous on the relevant point?

Question 6. The text of 2-202 says that terms in a final expression may be "explained" or "supplemented" by the evidence described in 2-202(a) and 2-202(b). Which of the resulting combinations is not plausible?

    (a) Explaining terms by course of performance, course of dealing, or usage of trade

(b) Supplementing terms by course of performance, course of dealing, or usage of trade

(c) Explaining terms by evidence of consistent additional terms

(d) Supplementing terms by evidence of consistent additional terms

Question 7. If 2-202 does not say anything about how to handle particular kinds of evidence, is that evidence admissible?

EXAMPLES AND ANALYSIS

Example A. After several phone conversations to negotiate terms of a sale of goods, seller and buyer signed a four-page document titled "Purchase Agreement." The document contains price and quantity terms, a full description of the items being sold, and a statement that the goods are being sold with a six-month warranty against defects. Both parties read through the contract before each signed it. The document discusses the manner of delivery but does not include information on when the goods will be delivered. There is no merger clause in the document. When a dispute between the parties ends up in court, the buyer seeks to introduce evidence that the seller promised the goods would work satisfactorily for one year from the time of purchase and that the seller promised to deliver the goods within a week of the signing of the contract, so delivery after two months was a breach. The seller objects on the basis of the parol evidence rule.

Analysis: The document is likely to be considered final as to the terms contained in it because the parties negotiated terms before signing a reasonably lengthy sales contract that contains specific choices about price, quantity, warranty, and manner of delivery. It is possible but not likely the document would be considered complete and exclusive. Although the document leaves out a delivery date, the parties might have meant that to be filled in by 2-309 (within "a reasonable time"). On the other hand, most often you would expect the parties to name an expected delivery time, so its absence suggests the document is not complete. Assuming, then, that the document is final, the evidence about delivery time would be admitted under 2-202(b) as a consistent additional term. The evidence about a one year warranty would not be admitted because it is evidence of an alleged prior agreement that would contradict a term in the writing.

Example B. As detailed in Example A, the parties have negotiated and then signed the four-page Purchase Agreement that includes a six-month warranty against defects but does not mention anything about when the goods will be delivered. When the dispute ends up in court:

(a) The seller seeks to introduce evidence that there is an applicable usage of trade that buyers are charged a 1% fee each month the buyer does not pay the outstanding invoice. The buyer objects on the basis of the parol evidence rule.

(b) The buyer seeks to introduce evidence that there is an applicable usage of trade that sellers provide one-year warranties against major defects in the goods and that in a previous contract between the parties that also contained a six-month warranty provision, the seller had repaired goods that failed eight months after purchase, telling buyer that "we say six months to protect against small complaints after that time, but we are happy to respond if there is a major defect that appears after that." The seller objects on the basis of the parol evidence rule and argues in the alternative that the written six-month warranty in the Purchase Agreement prevails even if the buyer's evidence is admitted.

Analysis: As in Example A, the Purchase Agreement is likely a final agreement, not a complete and exclusive statement of the agreement of the parties. The evidence that the seller seeks to introduce (the 1% a month fee) is a usage of trade that would supplement the written agreement, so it would be admissible under 2-202(a). The evidence that the buyer seeks to introduce consists of a usage of trade and a course of dealing. The usage of trade (a one-year warranty for major defects) seems directly contrary to the six-month warranty in the writing, but it would still be admissible under 2-202. Section 2-202 bars evidence of prior agreements or contemporaneous oral agreements that contradict the writing, but a usage of trade is not a prior agreement. Nothing else in 2-202 bars admission of the evidence. Under 1-303, however, the written term in the document takes precedence over the contradictory usage of trade, so the buyer will not be able to show that the usage of trade was part of the contract. The buyer also seeks to introduce a course of dealing from a prior contract. Like the usage of trade, this evidence is also admissible under 2-202. Nothing in 2-202 bars its consideration. In addition, the buyer may claim that the course of dealing explains rather than contradicts the written term, as it shows what the parties meant by a six-month warranty. If understood that way, 2-202(a) says expressly that it is admissible and 1-303(e) says the course of dealing and the express written term should be construed as consistent with each other whenever reasonable, allowing buyer to argue that it has a greater-than-six-month warranty for major defects. Of course, the seller will argue that the course of dealing cannot reasonably be understood as consistent with the six-month warranty. Seller is likely to prevail, as "six months for minor defects but longer for major defects" seems to be inconsistent with an express six month warranty.

2. Application to Confirmatory Memoranda

Reading the Code: How § 2-202 Applies to Confirmatory Memoranda

Re-read 2-202, leaving out the words that refer to final expressions. What remains is the rule applying to confirmatory memoranda.

Question 8. Note that the treatment of confirmatory memoranda is the same as the treatment of final expressions. Why does it make sense that confirmations and final expressions are treated the same way under the parol evidence rule?

Question 9. 2-202 says terms with respect to which the confirmatory memoranda of the parties agree may not be contradicted by evidence of any "prior agreement." Does this rule bar use of evidence prior to the date of the first of the confirmatory memoranda, or prior to the date of the second confirmation? (Neither the Code nor the Comments answer this question expressly. You will have to reason out the better answer based on your understanding of 2-202 and the policies underlying it.)

3. Application of § 2-202 to Complete and Exclusive Statements

Reading the Code: How § 2-202 Applies to Complete and Exclusive Statements

Re-read 2-202, now including the final phrase in 2-202(b).

Question 10. Assume you have a contract document that is indisputably "a complete and exclusive statement of the terms of the agreement." Considering for the moment only the part of 2-202 up through the end of subsection (a), does 2-202 operate the same way or differently on that document than if it were only a "final expression"?

Question 11. Now look again at 2-202(b). What effect does 2-202(b) have with respect to final expressions? What effect does the "unless" clause have when 2-202 is applied to a complete and exclusive statement?

Question 12. Can "confirmatory memoranda of the parties" that have "terms with respect to which [the memoranda agree]" constitute a "complete and exclusive statement of the terms of the agreement"?

EXAMPLES AND ANALYSIS

Example C. As in Examples A and B, a buyer and seller negotiate terms of a sale of goods, and seller and buyer sign a four-page document titled "Purchase Agreement." In this instance, however, the document contains all the terms one would expect to have in a sales contract of this kind (except the time when delivery is expected), was reviewed by both the attorneys for each party as well as the parties themselves, and contains a merger clause that was separately initialed by the parties. When a dispute between the parties ends up in court, the buyer seeks to introduce evidence (1) that the seller promised the goods would work satisfactorily for one year from the time of purchase, (2) that the seller promised to deliver the goods within a week of the signing of the contract, (3) that there is a usage of trade that sellers provide one-year warranties against major defects, and (4) that there was a course of dealing as described in Example B. The seller seeks to introduce evidence that there is a usage of trade that buyers are charged a 1% fee for each month the buyer does not pay an outstanding invoice. Each party objects to the other's evidence based on the parol evidence rule.

Analysis: The Purchase Agreement is a complete and exclusive statement of the contract. Even though there arguably is a term missing (the delivery time), there is substantial evidence that the parties intended the document to be complete and exclusive. Both were represented by counsel, the document was thoroughly reviewed, all expected terms are included, and the parties gave specific assent to the merger clause. Course of dealing and usage of trade evidence is treated the same for a complete and exclusive statement as it is for a final agreement (admissible, but subject to the hierarchy of interpretation in 1-303) so the seller's usage-of-trade evidence and the buyer's items (3) and (4) are admissible, but the written agreement will prevail over anything contradictory in that evidence. The evidence of a contradictory oral agreement (buyer's item (1)) is not admissible, just as for a final agreement. Buyer's item (2), which would be admissible if the document was a final agreement, is not admissible in this Example, because 2-202(b) bars admission of evidence of consistent additional terms if the agreement is a complete and exclusive statement of the terms.

E. What is the Source of the Extrinsic Evidence?

Section 2-202 contains some clauses that expressly permit and some that expressly forbid use of particular kinds of evidence, as we have seen. We have also seen that, if a kind of evidence is *not* mentioned, its admissibility is controlled solely by the rules of evidence, unaffected by the parol evidence rule. As a result, § 2-202 does not forbid use of evidence if it comes from a source that is either expressly permitted or not mentioned at all in the statutory provision. The next question will help you recognize which sources of evidence § 2-202 does and does not address.

Reading the Code: § 2-202 and the Source of Extrinsic Evidence

Re-read 2-202 looking for references to the source of offered evidence.

Question 13. Which of the following sources of evidence are always admissible under the provisions of 2-202?

    (a) Oral statements made before the time of the contract document(s)

    (b) Written documents exchanged before the time of the contract document(s)

    (c) Oral statements made at the time the contract document was signed

    (d) Written document exchanged at the time the contract document was signed

    (e) Oral statements made after the contract document was signed

    (f) Written documents exchanged after the contract document was signed

    (g) Evidence of the existence of a course of dealing, course of performance, or usage of trade

F. For What Purpose is the Extrinsic Evidence Being Offered?

Just as section 2-202 expressly permits and forbids the use of particular *kinds* of evidence, it expressly permits and forbids the use of evidence only *for particular purposes*. If a party offers evidence for a purpose not mentioned in § 2-202, admissibility is again controlled solely by the rules of evidence, not by the parol evidence rule. Section 2-202 does not forbid use of a particular piece of evidence if it is offered for a purpose either expressly permitted or not mentioned at all in the statutory provision. What uses of evidence are and are not addressed in § 2-202? The next question will help you recognize which purposes § 2-202 does and does not address.

Reading the Code: § 2-202 and the Purpose of the Evidence

Re-read 2-202 looking for references to the purpose of offered evidence.

Question 14. For which of the following purposes is evidence always admissible under the provisions of 2-202?

   (a) To prove an additional term

   (b) To modify a term in the writing

   (c) To explain a term in the writing

   (d) To prove there was no offer and acceptance of the contract

   (e) To prove there was a mutual mistake

   (f) To prove there was a misrepresentation during contract negotiations

   (g) To prove there was a condition that did not occur, thus preventing contract obligations from taking effect as the parties had agreed

   (h) To prove there was a condition that did not occur, thus excusing contract performance as the parties had agreed

G. Diagramming § 2-202

To help you review and reinforce your understanding of the parol evidence rule, complete the following chart, documenting in a concise way the rules expressed in § 2-202. There are no "new" questions here. Every entry flows directly from the analysis already undertaken and can be answered as well by your skillful rereading of the Code language.

Question 15. Answer "yes" or "no" in the chart to this question: If the contract document is as described (top row), is the particular evidence specified (left column) admissible for the purpose indicated?

	Final Expression/ Exchanged Confirmations	Complete and Exclusive Statement	Neither Final nor Complete and Exclusive
Evidence is from prior agreement, contemporaneous oral agreement, offered to contradict			
Evidence is from prior agreement, contemporaneous oral agreement, offered to supplement with additional term			
Evidence is from usage of trade, course of dealing, course of performance offered to supplement or explain			
Evidence is from subsequent oral or written agreement			
Evidence is offered to explain a written term			
Evidence is offered to show fraudulent inducement, mistake, duress, absence of consideration, lack of assent, condition to contract formation			

[handwritten margin note: You said no to explaining terms by evidence of consistent additional terms?]

Your answers in the above chart should make clear that the only kind of evidence that § 2-202 *always* bars from consideration in cases involving confirmations, final expressions, and complete and exclusive statements is evidence that *contradicts* terms in the writing (or both writings, in the case of exchanged confirmations).

The parol evidence rule bars evidence offered to *supplement* the terms of a writing only when the writing at issue is a complete and exclusive statement.

A large part of the legal battle in any parol evidence case will center around the proper characterization of the written contract (top row), source of the evidence (first four rows), and purpose for which the evidence is offered (last two rows). You have already seen in Section C above the complexities that may surround arguments about the proper characterization of the written contract. Determining the source of the evidence or the purpose for which a party offers the evidence is typically more straightforward. But knowing which "box" you are in tells you only the rule to be applied. How the rule works in practice raises additional complications, addressed in the sections that follow.

H. Explaining/Supplementing/Contradicting the Terms

1. Does the Extrinsic Evidence "Explain," "Supplement," or "Contradict" the Writing?

Whether evidence is *offered* to explain or to supplement or to contradict terms in the writing will matter in determining whether § 2-202 permits or forbids use of the evidence. But it is the court or the jury that must determine whether the evidence can or should be understood as explaining, as supplementing, or as contradicting the writing. That determination is sometimes straightforward and sometimes more difficult, as the following examples illustrate.

EXAMPLES AND ANALYSIS

Example D: *Empire Gas Corp. v. UPG, Inc.*[1]

The contract as written stated that the price per gallon of propane to be purchased was "Seller's established price in effect at the time of delivery for the customer category of which Buyer is a member (which price may be revised from time to time during the period this Agreement is in full force and effect)." The buyer wanted to introduce evidence that the seller had promised a permanent two-cent-per-gallon discount beyond the "established

---

[1]   781 S.W.2d 148 (Mo. Ct. App. 1989).

price." The buyer claimed that the alleged discount was an additional term because the contract did not mention a discount from the established price.

Analysis: The court concluded that the buyer's alleged term contradicted the express contract term because the "customer category" mentioned in the clause referred to the seller's established practice of discounting between a half-cent and two cents a gallon for all customers, depending on the quantity of gas that was purchased in the relevant time period. Understood that way, the price clause in the contract indirectly stated that a particular discount would be given to the buyer based on quantity, which conflicted with a claim that a two-cent-a-gallon discount would be given no matter how much gas was purchased.

Example E. *Goaltex Corp. v. Association for the Blind and Visually Impaired*[2]

Association for the Blind and Visually Impaired (Goodwill Industries) issued a series of purchase orders to Goaltex to buy sneakers, specifying quantities and prices. Based on discussions predating the purchase orders, Goaltex claimed the existence of an agreement for Goodwill to buy all sneakers that Goaltex would order from the manufacturer on behalf of Goodwill while the contract was in effect, even if no purchase order had been issued. Goodwill asked to exclude evidence of the discussion on the basis of the parol evidence rule.

Analysis: The court ruled that the earlier discussions could not be considered. The earlier discussions were "parol or extrinsic evidence which contradict the Purchase Orders," there was "no assertion of some prior course of dealing or performance that might explain or supplement the clear terms of these Purchase Orders," and the alleged agreement to purchase all sneakers ordered from Goaltex's manufacturer "is not a 'consistent' additional term." Do you agree with the court's ruling? What arguments would you make to support use of the evidence Goaltex offered?

---

2   979 N.Y.S. 2d 481 (Sup. Ct. 2014).

Example F: Analyzing a Hypothetical Contract

Ben agrees to purchase Sasha's used car and the two of them sign a simple sales contract written by Sasha:

> Ben and Sasha agree to the sale of a 2005 Toyota RAV4, identification number 123456789, for $3000, as is, sale to include the spare tire, a set of extra snow tires, tire-changing tools in the trunk, and the GPS installed in the car.

Assume that the writing is a "final expression." When a dispute arises, Ben or Sasha want to testify that several more things were agreed or discussed before or during contract formation:

(a) The exchange of car for money would be made on September 12.

(b) The car would be washed and waxed before delivery.

(c) The sale includes the Minnesota Winter Safety Kit in the trunk (candles, matches, blanket, sand, shovel, chocolate bar, flashlight, and whistle).

(d) There are 2 extra snow tires.

(e) The tools in the trunk include road flares but no lug wrench.

(f) Ben would receive the portable Yakima equipment rack and luggage compartment Sasha used for long trips with the car.

(g) The price would be reduced by $200 if paid in cash.

(h) Ben would be excused from performing if he fails his upcoming driver's license examination.

(i) The car being sold was actually a 2006 Toyota Camry.

Analysis: For each of the terms, how would you argue that it (a) explains, (b) supplements, or (c) contradicts the written terms? Is the evidence likely to be admitted or not? On what basis?

Example G. *Nanakuli Paving & Rock Co. v. Shell Oil Co.*[3]

In considering *Nanakuli* in Assignment 1, you saw that evidence of commercial context may convince a fact-finder that even seemingly clear terms (sale at a "posted price") may be understood to mean something quite different (sale at a lower price based on understandings of price protection for transactions the buyer has already underway) when the fact-finder follows the instructions in 1-303 to construe express terms and any applicable course of performance, course of dealing, or usage of trade "whenever reasonable as consistent with each other." Once admitted, for any purpose, evidence about communications between the parties may have a powerful influence in the interpretation process. That is especially true with respect to evidence of commercial context.

While the meaning of the contract is governed by the hierarchies established in 1-303, whether the evidence of course of dealing, course of performance, and usage of trade is admissible requires consideration of the provisions of 2-202. The trial court in *Nanakuli* had ruled that some evidence of course of dealing was not admissible, relying on:

- Paragraph H, a boilerplate clause in Shell's printed-form contract in the "Remedies/Waivers" section that evidence of dealings or waivers was disallowed as affecting "Shell's right to require specific performance of buyer's obligations";

- Paragraph E, a "classic integration or merger clause"; and

- A belief that there was no ambiguity in the express price term of "posted price at time of delivery."

Analysis: The court of appeals expressed disapproval of the trial court's rulings on admission of evidence of course of dealing, indicating that all the offered evidence should have been considered by the fact-finder. What language in 2-202 and its Comments would you cite to support that result?

2. The Effect of Comment 3

We have seen that, if a contract document is a final expression of the parties' agreement, but not a complete and exclusive statement, the document may be supplemented "by evidence of consistent additional terms." If evidence is offered

---

[3]   664 F.2d 772 (9th Cir. 1981).

that contradicts an express term in the writing, the evidence will be excluded. Are there nonetheless some additional terms that do not contradict anything explicitly written into the contract, yet that are excluded as not consistent with the terms that are in the document?

 **Reading the Code:
§ 2-202 Comment 3**

Read 2-202 Comment 3.

Question 16.

(a) The first sentence of Comment 3 paraphrases the rule expressed in 2-202(b) ("[C]onsistent additional terms . . . may be proved unless the court finds that the writing was intended by both parties as a complete and exclusive statement of all the terms."). The second sentence says certain evidence "must be kept from the trier of fact." What evidence is barred in that sentence?

(b) How does the rule expressed in the second sentence of Comment 3 apply to final expressions? What evidence, if any, would be allowed according to the text of 2-202 but be excluded by the Comment?

(c) How does the rule expressed in the second sentence of Comment 3 apply to complete and exclusive statements? What evidence, if any, would be allowed according to the text of 2-202 but be excluded by the Comment?

Comment 3 seems to mean that even though the document is only a final expression, there are certain terms that are to be excluded because the court concludes the parties would not have left such a term out of the written contract if they had agreed to it. Such a term does not contradict an express term but it is, nonetheless, inconsistent with the agreement as written and so must be excluded.

EXAMPLES AND ANALYSIS

As described by one court, "'inconsistency' as used in 2-202(b) means the absence of reasonable harmony in terms of the language and respective obligations of the parties."[4] Based on that understanding, courts have invoked Comment 3 to exclude evidence that

- sale of 35,000 tons of scrap metal was conditional on the seller's ability to obtain the goods from its supplier;[5]

- sale and installation of carpet for 228 apartments could be unilaterally rescinded by either party;[6]

- the parties had agreed the buyer would forego cover damages (the difference between the price under the contract and the price of obtaining substitute goods) because that would "disrupt the delicate balance, the harmony, that the written contract establishes among the 'respective obligations' of the parties;"[7] and

- the parties had agreed the debtor would not have to pay back the full amount of a collateralized loan if he returned the purchased goods and they were sold for less than the remaining debt on the loan.[8]

Under the analysis used by these courts, the excluded terms contradict the usual understanding that a sale of goods does not depend on the seller's ability to acquire or produce the goods, does not allow termination at the will of one or both of the parties, and that performance is not dependent on other unstated conditions. In effect, when a court excludes evidence on the basis of Comment 3, it is concluding that the contract had an implied-in-fact term—an unstated but understood assumption of the parties—contradicted by the proposed parol evidence. Under this line of analysis, a final expression, while not complete and exclusive as to all terms in the contract, is complete and exclusive as to some particular terms. As expressed by White and Summers in their handbook on the UCC, the question is not the completeness of the document as to the entire agreement, but the completeness of the agreement with respect to the specific matter in question.[9]

---

4 Snyder v. Herbert Greenbaum & Assoc., Inc., 380 A.2d 618 (Md. Ct. Spec. App. 1977).

5 Luria Bros. & Co., Inc. v. Pielet Bros. Scrap Iron & Metal, Inc., 600 F.2d 103 (7th Cir. 1979).

6 Snyder v. Herbert Greenbaum & Assoc., Inc., 380 A.2d 618 (Md. Ct. Spec. App. 1977).

7 ARB (American Research Bureau), Inc. v. E-Systems, Inc., 663 F.2d 189 (D.C. Cir. 1980).

8 Norwest Bank Billings v. Murnion, 684 P.2d 1067 (Mont. 1984).

9 J. White & R. Summers, Handbook of the Law under the Uniform Commercial Code, § 2-10 (2d ed., 1980).

However, a narrower understanding of this kind of inconsistency under Comment 3 has been articulated and applied by some courts. One court described an alleged term as being consistent unless it could be "precluded as a matter of law or as factually impossible." Based on that understanding, courts have permitted evidence that

- the parties agreed that an option to purchase stock stated in unconditional form was to be exercised by the potential buyer only if the seller of the stock solicited a bid from a third party during the pendency of negotiations;[10]

- the parties orally agreed that the seller would supply as much stainless steel solids as he could up to 500 tons, despite the existence of an express contract term that the seller would supply "500 gross ton;"[11] and

- the parties agreed that jewelry purchased "on approval" would have to be returned by the Monday evening following the purchase in order to receive the stated credit, so a "seasonable" return (see 2-327) the next Wednesday did not comply with the requirement.[12]

Example H: *Nanakuli Paving & Rock Co. v. Shell Oil Co.*[13]

When the trial court in *Nanakuli* ruled course-of-dealing evidence regarding price protection inadmissible (see Example G), the court also appeared to rely on 2-202 Comment 3, saying "[I]f that point [price protection] is so important, at the time the contract was entered into, why wasn't it stated in the contract?"

Analysis: The court of appeals rejected the trial court approach, noting that "price protection might well not be written into a contract between parties with a long and close relationship. Certainly Shell would not be likely to put its agreement never to charge more than Chevron charged H.B. into writing." Do you agree with the trial court or the appellate court with respect to the application of Comment 3?

---

[10] Hunt Foods & Industries, Inc. v. Doliner, 270 N.Y.S.2d 937 (App. Div. 1966).

[11] Michael Schiavone & Sons, Inc. v. Securalloy Co., Inc., 312 F. Supp. 801 (D. Conn. 1970).

[12] George v. Davoli, 397 N.Y.S.2d 895 (City Ct. 1997).

[13] Nanakuli Paving & Rock Co. v. Shell Oil Co., 664 F.2d 772 (9th Cir. 1981).

Example I. Revisiting Ben and Sasha

Analysis: Look back at the contract terms at issue in Example F. What additional arguments might be made for exclusion of the alleged terms based on 2-202 Comment 3?

3. Is Ambiguity Required before Admitting Evidence to Explain a Term?

As we have already seen, contract terms that appear clear on their face may come to seem less clear when considered in context. That is true with respect to evidence of commercial context (recall *Nanakuli*), but it is equally true with respect to other kinds of parol evidence. If parol evidence is always admissible to explain, and explanatory evidence can support a reading of a contract term quite different than written, what remains of the policy that written terms should be privileged over terms agreed to before the writing is signed?

It is that concern that leads some courts to require a finding that a term is ambiguous before allowing introduction of any parol evidence purportedly to explain the term, and to base the determination of ambiguity solely on the four corners of the document. A similar concern—and a view that language can be understood with clarity simply by reading it in the contract—leads some courts to hesitate before finding ambiguity (in effect looking for "clear ambiguity," as oxymoronic as that phrase may seem).

Other courts take the view that language must always be understood in context, and that anything relevant to the contract phrase should be admissible to try to explain the term, even if the new evidence raises a sense of ambiguity where none existed before. Such courts rely on the fact-finder not to be swayed unduly by the parol evidence; the evidence may be admissible to try to explain the term, but sensible juries and judges will not change their understanding of the written words without good reason.

The fact that courts disagree about whether ambiguity, and how much ambiguity, is required before parol evidence is considered to explain the contract adds another level of complexity to arguments about what evidence may and may not be received in court. Especially because you may not know to which court or judge your dispute will be brought or the attitudes of the judge to whom the case is assigned, it is always advisable to lay a foundation for entering parol evidence by trying to establish ambiguity on the face of the contract document based on plausible understandings of the deal as expressed in the document. Of course, the best plan is to have the meaning of the contract appear in the express terms, without the need to introduce parol evidence at all—but the many parol evidence and interpretation disputes in court demonstrate the difficulty of doing that in every instance.

APPLYING THE CODE

In the following problems, if the analysis depends on a determination for which you do not have sufficient information (e.g., whether the contract document is a final expression), you should argue all relevant and plausible branches (e.g., what happens if it is a final expression, what happens if it is not), identify the facts that lead to one or the other branch, and think about what questions you might ask your client to settle the uncertainty.

Problem 8-1.

JNK Machine Corp., a wholesale truck equipment and parts dealer, entered into a written agreement to sell to TBW, Ltd. for $650,000 "the entire inventories" of two stores owned by JNK. JNK sued to collect the price of the goods when TBW did not pay. In defense and counterclaim, TBW offered testimony about an oral agreement regarding the quantity and price of goods to be sold and about JNK's breach of an oral agreement permitting TBW to use the computer inventory program owned by JNK for as long as was needed. JNK objected on the basis of the parol evidence rule.

Problem 8-2.

After stopping at the display booth of MarineMax at a boat show and then visiting the company's showroom, Michael Stock purchased a yacht from MarineMax LLC for $1,925,000, naming it The Naughty Monkey in honor of Curious George, the main character in a series of popular children's books.[14] As the court noted, "unlike the Man in the Yellow Hat, Michael Stock quickly lost patience with his Naughty Monkey" and tried to return the boat to MarineMax under the following provision in the written purchase agreement:

---

[14]   Curious George is a mischievous money named George, brought from his home in Africa by "The Man with the Yellow Hat" to live with him in a big city. *See* H.A. Rey and Margret Rey, Curious George (1973).

TRADE VALUE GUARANTEED TO 15% LOSS WITHIN 18 MONTHS (PER ANDREW SCHNEIDER) SUBJ. TO MARINE SURVEY AND FINANCING.

Stock believed the clause entitled him to a partial cash refund if he returned the boat within eighteen months of its purchase; he sought to buy a used boat for $2,900 plus a cash refund of $1,633,350. MarineMax refused, saying that the clause allowed Stock only to trade the boat for credit toward the purchase of a larger boat made by the same manufacturer.

To prove the meaning of the clause, the parties offered to introduce the following evidence:

- Dictionary definitions of the word "trade";

- Testimony from Stock that the parties had discussed his concern about getting cash back from a trade and that the parties understood the trade value clause would provide that option;

- Testimony from Stock that he thinks the word "guaranteed" in the clause would have no meaning unless he could trade the boat for cash;

- Testimony from the owner of MarineMax that he understood the clause merely established a guaranteed minimum or floor value in the event Stock sought to trade the boat back;

- Language in an earlier version of the agreement between the parties, superseded by the final purchase agreement, which referred to Stock's "refundable" deposit on the boat, to show that the final boat payment was not "refundable" as Stock alleged; and

- Testimony from Stock that he had been told between July 7 (the date of the first agreement) and July 31 (the date of the superseding agreement) that the purpose of the trade clause was to allow him to exit the Naughty Monkey transaction and trade it for anything that MarineMax had regardless of size.

Which of these pieces of evidence should the court permit under 2-202?

Problem 8-3.

Clean Burn Fuels, LLC entered a written contract for purchase of corn from Perdue BioEnergy LLC, the corn to be delivered at the buyer's plant for use in the production of ethanol. Two years later, Clean Burn Fuels closed its plant and entered bankruptcy. At that time, there were 600,000 bushels of corn in the bins at the plant, delivered by Perdue but not yet processed. In bankruptcy court, the trustee, protecting the assets of the debtor, claimed that the corn was owned by Clean Burn Fuels. Perdue claims it retained ownership of the corn.

Section 7 of the Feedstock Supply Agreement between Clean Burn Fuels and Perdue specifies that delivery of the corn is "complete once Perdue delivers the corn to the Clean Burn Fuels site."

Section 11(h) of the Master Agreement, incorporated by reference in the Feedstock Supply Agreement, provides that "[n]o course of prior dealings between the Parties, and no usage of trade, except where expressly incorporated by reference, shall be relevant or admissible to supplement, explain, or vary any of the terms of this Master Agreement, the Goods and Services Agreements or the Confidentiality Agreement even though the accepting and acquiescing Party has knowledge of the nature of the performance and an opportunity to object."

Perdue offers to introduce evidence from a deposition that the parties did not intend delivery to occur until the corn crossed the weighbelt to enter the ethanol production cycle. Should the court permit introduction of that evidence? Why or why not?

Problem 8-4.

Nancy Gilmore is the owner of Gilmore Farms, which breeds Beefmaster Cattle. Kerry Haliburton, interested in expanding from showing horses to showing cattle, entered a contract with Gilmore with respect to three head of cattle (Clara's Jade, Hope's Cracker Jack, and Clara Belle). Haliburton claims that the cattle were sold to him and that he later sent the animals to Gilmore for breeding purposes after the cattle exceeded the age at which they could be shown, on the understanding they would eventually be returned to Haliburton. When Gilmore refused to return the cattle, Haliburton sued Gilmore. Gilmore claims that the arrangement was for Gilmore to retain majority ownership in the cattle, for Haliburton to show the cattle and then return them to Gilmore, and that Haliburton would have a percentage interest in any offspring of the three after breeding but Gilmore would own and still owns the cattle.

At trial, Haliburton introduced Certificates of Breeding for the cattle that showed him as the owner. As explained by the court:

Beefmaster cattle are registered with the Beefmaster Breeders United (BBU) organization. Registration and ownership of a cow is reflected by a Certificate of Breeding. Kerry explained that registration with the BBU is like the registration of a car. When a registered Beefmaster cow is sold, ownership of the cow is assigned to the new owner and reflected by completing the transfer form on the back of the Certificate of Breeding. The transfer form provides, "When the ownership of the animal named on this Certificate changes, the Seller must immediately complete the transfer and return the Certificate to Beefmaster Breeders United." The form then states, "I/We hereby authorize the transfer of this Certificate of Breeding on the records of Beefmaster Breeders United to the buyer indicated below," under which the "Seller," who must be the current registered owner, identifies himself or herself, the "Buyer," and the "Date of Sale" and then signs the form. Once the transfer form has been completed, the Certificate is then submitted to the BBU, after which the BBU issues a new Certificate of Breeding listing the "Buyer" on the previous Certificate's transfer form as the new "Current Owner."

For each of the cattle in question, Haliburton introduced an original Certificate of Breeding showing Gilmore as the original owner with a completed transfer form on the back showing transfer to Haliburton and a new Certificate of Breeding from BBU showing him as the "Current Owner." For one of the transactions, Haliburton also introduced a completed BBU "Bill of Sale" that indicated the cow was being sold by Gilmore to Haliburton. Neither the Bill of Sale nor any of the Certificates of Breeding indicated a price for the transaction, but Haliburton testified that the price for each sale was $5000.

At trial, Gilmore testified that the transaction was not a sale, that the transfer of the Certificate of Breeding was completed so Haliburton could show the cattle at cattle shows, that the cattle were expected to be returned to Gilmore once their showing careers were over, and that Haliburton was to have a 25% ownership in both the three named animals and in any resulting calves. Gilmore also testified that Kerry Haliburton—who was a lawyer as well as a horseman—was supposed to draft a contract memorializing the agreements about ownership but never did. Gilmore introduced one email from Haliburton's wife saying "Kerry has been out of town all week but will get to the contract as soon as possible." Gilmore said that she was told several more times that Haliburton was going to get her a contract, but it never happened. The cattle were returned to Gilmore Farms after they were shown; according to Gilmore, Haliburton asked that they remain registered in his name so that they could show any future calves in a "bred and owned show," and Gilmore agreed.

The trial court found in favor of Gilmore, concluding that she owned the cattle. On appeal, Haliburton argues that Gilmore's testimony was parol evidence that should not have been admitted or considered. Without that evidence, he argues, the contract unambiguously shows a sale of the cattle and that he is thus entitled to return of the animals. How would you rule and why?

Chapter 4

Contract Enforceability
(Statute of Frauds)

Key Concepts

- Scope of the Article 2 statute of frauds writing requirement (§ 2-201(1))
- Explicit exceptions to the requirement of a writing (§ 2-201(3))
- Requirements for satisfying the writing requirement and the special rule for merchants (§ 2-201(2))
- Use of promissory estoppel to overcome statute of frauds defenses

Section 2-201 establishes that a writing is required in order to enforce certain contracts within the scope of Article 2 and identifies the kind of writing required. Even though a contract might satisfy all the Article 2 provisions governing contract formation, a party may nonetheless be prevented from enforcing that contract if it does not satisfy the requirements of § 2-201. If § 2-201 renders the contract unenforceable, the court will not consider the merits of the contract claim. The statute of frauds thereby permits a party to end a breach of contract action early in litigation, based on the determination that a writing is required by § 2-201 and a sufficient writing does not exist.

Although we are addressing these issues as arising after formation of an otherwise valid agreement, parties entering contracts should more properly consider these questions before, at the time of, or shortly after contract formation so the proper steps can be taken at that time to ensure enforceability. From the perspective of a transactional lawyer, the issue is how to document an obligation so that it is enforceable. From the perspective of a litigator, the issue is whether a statute of frauds defense is available. If so, a party must raise the failure to satisfy the statute as an affirmative defense in the earliest stages of the lawsuit. Such failure may result in dismissal of the suit before the court considers on other grounds whether a contract existed.

Assignment 9:
Statute of Frauds

§ 2-201

As you will recall from your Contracts class, the general term "statute of frauds" is used to refer to all the various laws preventing enforcement of certain types of contracts if they are not memorialized in some sort of written memorandum, or subject to some exception to the requirement of a writing. These laws are descendants of the English Act for Prevention of Frauds and Perjuries of 1677; they were initially enacted to address concerns about fraudulent efforts to enforce putative oral contracts. England repealed most of its statute of frauds in 1954, based on a consensus that it was "a product of conditions which have long passed away," that it is "out of accord with the way in which business is normally done," and that it "promotes more frauds than it prevents."[1] As discussed in Assignment 27, the Convention on the International Sale of Goods dispenses with any writing requirement. Nevertheless, many statutes of frauds survive in the American legal system, including the one in Article 2. As you learn more about the scope and requirements of § 2-201, consider both the historical purposes of statutes of frauds and the modern skepticism about the continued validity of such requirements. This context should help you make sense of both the requirements and the exceptions to these requirements.

LEARNING OUTCOMES AND OBJECTIVES

At the completion of this Assignment, you should be able to

- identify what kinds of contracts require some form of writing in order to be enforceable;
- identify what kinds of contracts fall within the three statutory exceptions to the writing requirement;
- draft a writing that satisfies the requirements of § 2-201;
- identify the kind of writing that satisfies the writing requirement imposed on merchants; and

---

[1] John E. Murray, Jr., Murray on Contracts § 69, at 335 (5th ed. 2011) (citing Report of the English Law Revision Committee on the Statute of Frauds and the Doctrine of Consideration (Sixth Interim Report, Cmd. 5449, 1937), reprinted in 15 Can. B. Rev. 585, 589 (1937).

> • identify how to employ the statute of frauds strategically in litigation, either to avoid or to enforce a contractual obligation.

A. Structuring the Statute of Frauds Inquiry

Section 2-201 begins by establishing a broad category of contracts that require a writing in order for the contract to be enforceable. The statute then explicitly carves out three specific circumstances that will remove the requirement of a writing, even though the contract otherwise fits within that broad category. Finally, the statute specifies what kind of writing is required, both for contracts between merchants and for other contracts. Based on that sequence, in analyzing whether § 2-201 requires a particular contract to be in writing, you should structure your inquiry using the following three questions, each addressed in a separate section below:

(1) Is the contract in the category of agreements for which § 2-201 requires a writing?

(2) Does one of the exceptions in § 2-201 apply to eliminate the requirement of a writing?

(3) If a writing is required, is there a writing that satisfies § 2-201, taking into account whether both parties are merchants?

B. Is the Contract within the Class of Contracts for which § 2-201 Requires a Writing?

Reading the Code:
§ 2-201(1)

Read the first sentence of 2-201(1).

Question 1. "Except as otherwise provided" elsewhere in the section, for what kinds of contracts does 2-201(1) require "some writing"?

C. What Are the Three Exceptions to the Writing Requirement in § 2-201?

Reading the Code:
§ 2-201(3)

Read 2-201(3) and Comments 2 and 7.

Question 2. For each part of 2-201(3), what would a party have to prove in order to establish that the contract at issue can be enforced without the existence of "some writing," even though 2-201(1) would otherwise require one? Be specific in identifying the facts the party would have to establish.

Question 3. For each part of 2-201(3), is all or only part of the unwritten contract enforceable?

EXAMPLES AND ANALYSIS

Example A: *The Barrington Group, Ltd. v. Classic Cruise Holdings*[2]

For some period of time, Regent, a luxury cruise line, purchased from Barrington a variety of items marked with the Regent logo, to sell or give as gifts to its passengers. When Regent attempted to cancel outstanding shipments, Barrington sued for breach of contract. Regent raised the statute of frauds as a defense to the claim. Barrington moved for summary judgment, claiming the goods were specially manufactured, so no writing was required.

Analysis: The court denied the motion, explaining:

In determining whether or not the goods are specially manufactured, the crucial inquiry is whether the manufacturer could sell the goods in

---

2   2010 WL 184307 (N.D. Tex. 2010).

the ordinary course of his business to someone other than the original buyer." The focus of the exception is on the goods themselves. "If with slight alterations the goods could be so sold, then they are not specially manufactured; if, however, essential changes are necessary to render the goods marketable by the seller to others, then the exception does apply."

Barrington contends that the products at issue were specially manufactured to bear Regents marks or logo. In opposition, Regent points to evidence that with minor alterations, those marks or logos could be removed or covered up, making it possible to resell the goods. This fact dispute is material, rendering summary judgment inappropriate. . . . Further, Barrington has not submitted conclusive evidence that, at the time of Regent's attempted cancellation, it had made "either a substantial beginning of their manufacture or commitments for their procurement."

Which party is invoking 2-201, and which party is invoking an exception under 2-201(3)? Which exception is being invoked? For what strategic purpose is each party invoking 2-201: *defensively* (that is, to get out of a contractual obligation), or *offensively* (that is, to hold the other party to a contractual obligation)? Which party is trying to get summary judgment based on the statute of frauds? Given their strategic goals, who "won"? Do you agree with the court's reasoning? Should a seller be obliged to change the specialty goods into non-specialty goods? Is this a proper consideration for purposes of the statute of frauds if the goods were specialized at the time of the breach?

Example B: *Associated Home & RV Sales, Inc. v. R-Vision, Inc.* [3]

Darrell Higgins was the Regional Sales Manager for R-Vision, a manufacturer of recreational vehicles (RV's). At a trade show, Higgins entered into discussions with an RV dealer, Associated Home, about possibly having Associated replace R-Vision's current dealer in Albuquerque, Rocky Mountain. Higgins notified Rocky Mountain that R-Vision was considering replacing it as dealer. Associated Home sent R-Vision an application to become a dealer, as well as an order for four RV units. In the course of their discussions about the order for the four RV units, Higgins had a telephone conversation about the models ordered. Higgins wanted Associated Home to order four of a

---

[3]   62 UCC Rep. Serv. 2d 180 (D.N.M. 2006).

specific model of RVs, but Associated Home preferred to try to sell two different models first, promising to order more if the first ones sold well. In the course of that conversation, Higgins said to Associated Home: "Fine. That's good enough, we'll do it that way."

In the meantime, Rocky Mountain objected to being terminated as R-Vision's dealer and ordered additional RVs from R-Vision. Then, Higgins was laid off by R-Vision. Associated Home never received any RVs from R-Vision and sued R-Vision for breach of contract. The court dismissed the suit on summary judgment for lack of a written contract. One of Associated Home's arguments was that Higgins's statement ("Fine. That's good enough. We'll do it that way"), to which he testified in his sworn deposition, was an admission in court of the contract.

Analysis: The court rejected this argument, because:

> [E]ach time Higgins declared that R-Vision had made a contract with Associated Home, one of the . . . requirements was missing. When Higgins initially told Associated Home that the order forms were sufficient . . . he was not making those statements in court. When Higgins testified to the same effect in his deposition, he was no longer R-Vision's agent, because he had been laid off. . . . To allow Higgins, who is no longer R-Vision's agent, to bind R-Vision to the alleged oral contract would undermine the purpose of the agent admission exception, which is that a party cannot shield himself behind the Statute of Frauds while admitting that a contract exists.

Which party is invoking 2-201, and which party is invoking an exception under 2-201(3)? Which exception is being invoked? For what strategic purpose is each party invoking 2-201: *defensively* (that is, to get out of a contractual obligation), or *offensively* (that is, to hold the other party to a contractual obligation? Do you agree with the court's reasoning? Why is it not sufficient that Higgins was an agent at the time the oral agreement was made? Is this fair to Associated Home?

Example C: *Feldt v. Kan-Du Construction Corp.*[4]

A buyer ordered a modular home, paying the full purchase price. The builder installing the home negligently damaged the home and eventually

---

[4] 2013 WL 27733 (D. Kan. 2013).

abandoned the installation. The buyer incurred more than $40,000 in costs to complete the home, and expert testimony established that repairing the damages caused by the builder would cost $130,000 more. The buyer sued the seller for breach of contract, and the seller moved for summary judgment, based on the statute of frauds.

Analysis: The court denied summary judgment to the seller under 2-201(3), finding that the goods had been received and paid for. Which party is invoking 2-201, and which party is invoking an exception under 2-201(3)? Which exception is being invoked? For what strategic purpose is each party invoking 2-201: *defensively* (that is, to get out of a contractual obligation), or *offensively* (that is, to hold the other party to a contraction obligation)? Do you agree with the court's reasoning?

APPLYING THE CODE

Problem 9-1.

Matthew was the owner of a tea store called Your Tea Emporium (YTE). YTE's specialty was creating personalized blends of tea for its customers called "Your Unique Blend." These blends were created based on an extensive customer survey and interview to determine the customer's health condition, diet, exercise patterns, stress level, and taste preferences. Caitlin filled out a survey and engaged in a lengthy interview. Matthew offered Caitlin a special bulk deal on her personalized blend—a full year's worth of tea for a discounted price of $600. To take advantage of this offer, though, she would have to make a down-payment of half that amount in advance, in order for YTE to begin assembling her personalized blend. Caitlin paid the $300 in cash. A few days later, Caitlin called Matthew to tell him that she had changed her mind about the purchase. Matthew protested, saying, "We've already blended your tea!" Caitlin responded, "Too bad for you. You've got nothing in writing, so go ahead and sue me!" In an ensuing lawsuit, if Caitlin files a motion to dismiss for failure to satisfy 2-201, how might Matthew use the exceptions in 2-201(3) to defend? Would he be successful?

D. What Kind of a Writing is Required by § 2-201?

1. What Counts as a Writing?

Like the common law, the UCC has a generous attitude toward what qualifies as a "writing," defining it to include "printing, typewriting, or any other intentional reduction to tangible form." § 1-201(b)(43). As many of the following cases illustrate, courts routinely find that exchanges of e-mails and other documents can be used to satisfy the writing requirement, as long as the other requirements of § 2-201 are met.[5]

2. Using Multiple Writings

As you probably remember from your Contracts class, the writing requirement of most statutes of frauds can be satisfied by piecing together multiple signed writings or even a signed writing that refers to or is attached to or enclosed with unsigned writings. Many jurisdictions also go a step further, piecing together any writings that show sufficient connection to the same transaction. In applying § 2-201(1), the same dynamic applies.

EXAMPLES AND ANALYSIS

Example D: *Ellig v. Molina*[6]

On a world cruise, Mr. and Mrs. Ellig met Molina, a jeweler. They became close personal friends, travelling together frequently over the years. As Mrs. Ellig's 65th birthday approached, Molina suggested that Mr. Ellig buy her a large diamond ring. Mr. Ellig was fiscally conservative, investing primarily in municipal bonds. He told Molina that he would consider purchasing a ring that large only if it were an investment as well as a gift. Molina said that diamonds were safe investments, and told Mr. Ellig that, if he bought the ring and they were unhappy with it for any reason at all, Molina would buy it back within a year for the full purchase price plus a guaranteed 10%. Mr. Ellig and Molina had a number of conversations about the ring; in

---

[5] As we will discuss in greater detail in Assignment 14, statutes outside of the UCC addressing electronic commerce offer courts more direct authority for this point, but decisions reaching the conclusion that e-mails qualify as "intentional reductions to tangible form" predate the enactment of these statutes.

[6] 996 F. Supp.2d 236 (S.D.N.Y. 2014).

each conversation, the terms of this guarantee were mentioned, but they were not put in writing. When the conversations about the ring began, Mr. Ellig was considering a gift in the range of a few hundred thousand dollars. In the end, he bought a ring for over $700,000, in reliance on the specific and repeated representations of Molina regarding the buy-back promise. He paid for the ring in two separate wire transfer payments and received invoices for each payment.

From the first time Mrs. Ellig saw the diamond, she expressed some concerns about its blue florescence. Although Molina repeatedly assured her that this added to its value, her continued concern caused her to obtain some third-party valuations, which were all much lower than the purchase price. Ten months after the purchase, the Elligs decided to return the ring. Molina sent them a letter containing the following:

> When we discussed the risk of you purchasing the diamond, I made several statements to both of you.
>
> 1. If you decide that you do not want the diamond a year from now, I would get your money back and a 10% return on your money. I understand that is your understanding that I committed to buy the stone and you are correct. The only gray area is that for me to do so I have to sell the stone. (I am prepared to provide you with a financial note that guarantees the funds and a return.) . . .

The "gray area" referred to in the letter is Molina's claim that returning the purchase price plus 10% was contingent on finding another buyer for the ring at that amount.

Molina claimed that their oral contract was not enforceable because there was no writing that satisfied 2-201.

Analysis: The court rejected Molina's defense based on the statute of frauds, holding that Molina's letter, together with the invoices and written records of the wire transfer, were sufficient to confirm the contract between the parties. The one essential term not mentioned in that letter—the purchase price—was evidenced in the invoices and the wire transfers. Why would the Elligs want to include as the "writing" satisfying the statute of frauds a piece of paper that contains the qualification to the buy-back guarantee that they are arguing is not part of their contract? Would the court's conclusion have been different if the parties were disputing the purchase price for the diamond, as well as the terms of the buy-back guarantee?

3. What Constitutes a "Sufficient" Writing?

Keeping in mind that the "writing" satisfying the Article 2 statute of frauds need not be one single piece of paper (or even a piece of paper at all), let us examine more closely the § 2-201 requirements for a writing.

Reading the Code:
§ 2-201(1)

Read all of 2-201(1), as well as Comments 1, 5, and 6. Be sure to look at relevant definitions referenced in the UCC and Comments.

The following questions focus on the three basic requirements for a writing as they are articulated in 2-201. You should answer each question based on a careful reading of the text of the UCC and Comments, before looking at the illustrations of each point that follow.

Question 4. What are the three items that must be included in a writing for it to be "sufficient" under 2-201(1) and Comment 1?

Question 5. What forms of signature are identified in 2-201(1) and related sections as being sufficient to consider a writing "signed" for the purposes of 2-201? Which party must sign?

Question 6. What is the one term that must be included in the writing?

Question 7. Is it possible to satisfy the statute of frauds if the writing no longer exists—for example, if it was discarded or burned in a house fire?

a. "Sufficient to indicate that a contract for sale has been made between the parties"

The writing or set of writings offered by a party in satisfaction of § 2-201 must "indicate that a contract for the sale has been made between the parties." Comment 1 indicates that the writing may be satisfactory though it includes significantly less than the entire contract: "The required writing need not contain all the material terms of the contract and such material terms as are stated need not be precisely stated. All that is required is that the writing afford a basis for believing that the offered oral evidence rests on a real transaction." However, the writing does have to give evidence that the parties actually entered into a contract. In this respect, Article 2 demands more of the writing than may be required under the common law. As formulated in § 131(b) of the Restatement (Second) of Contracts, the writing must be "sufficient to indicate that a contract with respect thereto has been made between the parties *or offered by the signer to the other party.*" Under Article 2, the writing has to offer evidence that a contract was formed rather than merely offered.

One court explains:

> [T]he spirit of the comments seems to be that "sufficient to indicate" is roughly equivalent to "more probably than not." . . . In other words, if it is more probable than not that the writing evidences a deal between the parties, then the writing should be found sufficient.

> Most courts have required that the writing indicate the consummation of a contract, not mere negotiations. Thus, a writing which contained language indicating a tentative agreement has been found insufficient to indicate that a contract for sale had been made. ([E.g.,] check inscribed with 'tentative deposit on tentative purchase' held insufficient because it indicated no final commitment had been made). Writings which do not contain words indicating that a binding or completed transaction has occurred have been found insufficient. ([E.g.,] mere purchase orders which did not refer to previous agreement [have been] held insufficient.) Some courts have required that the writings completely acknowledge the evidence of an agreement. Even those courts giving a liberal interpretation to the requirement that the writing evidence an agreement have insisted that the terms of the writing at least must allow for the inference that an agreement had been reached between the parties. ([E.g.,] the words "confirmation of purchase" allow for inferences that writing confirmed some agreement previously made by the parties; . . . the terms of the purchase order were so specifically and clearly geared to the desires of the party to be charged that the purchase order reflected a completed contract.)[7]

---

[7]   Howard Construction Co. v. Jeff-Cole Quarries, 669 S.W.2d 221, 227 (Mo. Ct. App. 1983) (citations omitted).

EXAMPLES AND ANALYSIS

Example E: *Maghsoudi Enterprises, Inc. v. Tufenkian Import/Export Ventures, Inc.* [8]

Tufenkian, an importer of fine carpets, entered into discussions with a carpet dealer, Gallerie One. Under the terms of an alleged oral contract between these two parties, Gallerie One was to purchase $75,000 worth of carpet samples to show potential customers; in exchange, Tufenkian would fill all orders for any of their carpets Gallerie One might sell. Gallerie One paid for the samples and enjoyed sixteen months of profitable sales of Tufenkian carpets. Then, Tufenkian opened its own showroom close to Gallerie One's shop and informed Gallerie One that it would no longer be filling orders for Gallerie One's customers. Gallerie One brought suit for breach of contract. The only writings offered as evidence of the contract were the letter from Tufenkian indicating that it was terminating its business relationship with Gallerie One and the response from Gallerie One indicating that it was returning all its consigned merchandise and the samples. (Both of these writings are reprinted below.) Neither party raised the statute of frauds as an issue, but the court considered the issue on its own.

Analysis: The court granted summary judgment to Tufenkian based on the statute of frauds, noting that "Neither letter . . . indicates the existence of a contract between the parties, nor indicates its terms." Who is asserting the statute of frauds, and for what purpose? What aspect of the writing or writings arguably shows a contract of sale was made between the parties? Do you agree with the court's ruling? What advice would you give to contracting parties or their lawyers to avoid the outcome here? Why do you think the parties did not have a sufficient writing?

---

[8] 2008 WL 4449881 (N.D. Ill. 2008).

TUFENKIAN

ARTISAN CARPETS

March 12, 2007

Mr. Marc Maghsoudi
Gallerie One
222 Merchandise Mart Plaza, Suite 600
Chicago, IL 60654

Dear Mr. Maghsoudi;

I am writing to advise you that Tufenkian Carpets has made a unilateral decision to terminate the relationship with your Company.

Please advise us of any projects your sales personnel have been developing. The projects should be registered and the list sent to me by March 31st. The rugs must be ordered by April 30, 2007. Effective immediately, all orders will be purchased on a cash before delivery basis. However, nothing will be shipped until all consignment rugs have been returned to Tufenkian. As of April 1, 2007 Tufenkian Carpets will supply only custom or back-ordered rugs that have been paid in full.

Sales Support will issue return authorizations for any rugs consigned to you. These need to be returned within 30 days in order for you not to be invoiced.

Sales Support will also issue a return authorization for any promotional materials you may have. You will have 30 days to return these items as well. Credit will be issued once the items have been inspected and found to be in a re-sellable condition.

We appreciate your past business and wish you the best in your future endeavors.

Regards,

Harry Fry
Vice President, Sales & Marketing

Gallerie One

Distinctive Rugs

12/5/07

Eric Jacobson,

Gallerie One has decided to return all the consignment merchandise as well as $27,500 worth of Tufenkian invoiced and paid for samples against our open invoices.

You may have your representative pick this merchandise up next week December 10th through the 14th with paperwork indicating the proper credits to our account the same day prior to the merchandise removal from the showroom. I ask that you call to set up a time for this prior to your representative's arrival.

It is still unclear to me how the advertising credit has been applied and how it affects the open invoices. Of the $5950.00 advertising cost for 2007, how much of this has been credited to our open invoices. I would like a detailed explanation of this.

Marc Maghsoudi

Example F: *Howard Construction Co. v. Jeff-Cole Quarries*[9]

Howard Construction (Howard) entered into negotiations to purchase rock from Jeff-Cole Quarries (Jeff-Cole) for use in constructing a highway. In a meeting, they discussed the purchase of both "base rock" and a number of different types of asphaltic rock. The final contract signed by both parties referenced only the base rock. Howard sued Jeff-Cole for breaching an alleged oral contract with respect to the asphaltic rock. To satisfy the statute of frauds, Howard offered a typewritten "Proposal" created and signed by Jeff-Cole, listing prices for both kinds of rock, and containing hand-written notes amending these prices (Exhibit 1 below). Howard testified that these notes evidenced the oral agreement reached by the parties at their meeting and argued that they satisfied the statute of frauds. Among the other documents generated by the parties was a purchase order signed by Howard that mentioned only the base rock (Exhibit 2 below). The trial court dismissed the case on summary judgment based on the statute of frauds; the ruling was appealed.

Analysis: The appellate court affirmed the lower court's dismissal of the case. The court held that "no words on the writing allow for the inference that any agreement was reached between the parties. . . . At best, they evidence negotiations for the sale of asphaltic rock and a separate and completed contract for the sale of base rock." The court gave some suggestions for when a writing might evidence a contract for sale: "The words 'as per our agreement,' 'in confirmation of,' or 'sold to buyer,' would indicate that the parties had reached an agreement. Even the terms of the writing itself might be so specific and favorable to the party against whom the writing is offered that the court at least could draw the inference that an agreement had been reached."

Who is asserting the statute of frauds, and for what purpose? What aspect of the writing or writings arguably shows a contract of sale was made between the parties? Do you agree with the court's ruling? What advice would you give to contracting parties or their lawyers to avoid the outcome here? Why do you think the parties did not have a sufficient writing?

---

[9]   669 S.W.2d 221 (Mo. Ct. App. 1983).

EXHIBIT 1

JEFF-COLE QUARRIES, INC.
GENERAL CONTRACTORS
HIGHWAY 54 SOUTH
JEFFERSON CITY, MISSOURI 65101

NOVEMBER 21, 1972

P R O P O S A L

RE: MISSOURI STATE HIGHWAY
PROJ. DP-F-54-3(37)
ROUTE 54, COLE COUNTY

ITEM NO.	DESCRIPTION	QUANTITY	UNIT	UNIT PRICE	TOTAL AMOUNT
301-20.00	MINERAL AGGR. BITUM. BASE	85,795.0	TONS	1.55 1.65	1.70
304-01.02	TYPE 1 AGGR. FOR BASE	99,600.0	TONS	1.55	
310-50.02	GRAVEL (A) OR STONE (B)	3,908.0	TONS	1.84 1.85	2.43
390-90.00	TEMPORARY SURFACING	150.0	TONS	1.46 1.85	
403-70.00	1" MIN'L AGGR. TYPE "B" ASPH.	13,996.0	TONS	2.45	2.65
403-80.00	½" MIN'L AGGR. TYPE "C" ASPH.	13,117.0	TONS	2.45	2.65

TOTAL FOR PROJECT...............

WE HAVE THREE (3) SITES AVAILABLE ON THE PROJECT. SITE A IS BETWEEN STA. 763+00 AND STA. 775+00, APPROX. 500 FT. OFF RT. 54. SITE B IS BETWEEN STA. 815+00 AND STA. 830+00, APPROX. 2000 FT. OFF RT. 54. SITE C IS BETWEEN STA. 940+00 AND STA. 970+00, APPROX. 500 FT. OFF RT. 54.

WE PREFER SITE____, HOWEVER, IT WILL BE OUR OPTION TO SELECT THE SITE AFTER FINAL DETERMINATION OF THE ROCK QUALITY IS MADE. AN ASPHALT PLANT SITE WILL BE AVAILABLE AT ALL 3 LOCATIONS.

THE PRICE FOR TYPE 1 AGGR. FOR BASE ABOVE INCLUDES PUGGING. IF YOU PREFER TO USE HIGHWAY DEPARTMENT BATCH WEIGHTS IN LIEU OF OUR SCALE WEIGHTS ON THE MINERAL AGGR. BITUMINOUS BASE AND AGGR. FOR TYPES "B" & "C" ASPHALT MIX, ADD THE FOLLOWING:

MINERAL AGGR. BITUM. BASE   10%
MINERAL AGGR. TYPE "B"   15
MINERAL AGGR. TYPE "C"   1.70

RESPECTFULLY SUBMITTED,

HARRY H. ADRIAN, PRESIDENT
JEFF-COLE QUARRIES, INC.

EXHIBIT 2

PURCHASE ORDER   Nọ   322

Howard Construction Company
& AFFILIATED COMPANIES
1504 North Osage — Sedalia, Missouri

SOLD TO: Jeff Cole Quarries
Highway 54 South
Jefferson City, Missouri

PROJECT: DP-F-54-3(37)
Route 54
Cole, County

PLEASE INVOICE HOWARD CONSTRUCTION COMPANY.
☐ BRIDGE
☒ CONSTRUCTION COMPANY.
☐ QUARRIES

Job #91

PRICES AS PER QUOTATION DATED: 1/2/73

QUANTITY	ITEM	UNIT PRICE	TOTAL PRICE
99,600 Tons	Type 1 Aggregate for Base (Pugged)	1.55	154,380.00
3,908 Tons	Crushed Stone (B)	1.80	7,034.40
150 Tons	Temporary Surfacing	1.80	270.00
85,795 Tons	Mineral Aggregate (Bit. Base)	1.70	145,851.50
33,000 Tons	Crushed Rock for Type B & C Asphalt	2.65	87,450.00

Rock for Mineral Aggregate (Bit. Base) and Type B & C Asphalt will be batch weights from job mix approved by the M.S.H.D.

Net 15 Days   TOTAL

ALL MATERIAL TO MEET THE MINIMUM REQUIREMENTS OF THE SPECIFICATIONS FOR THE PROJECT SHOWN ABOVE.

Jake Moore
General Supt.

ACCEPTED BY:
Title:

b. "Signed by the party against whom enforcement is sought"

To satisfy § 2-201, a memorandum must be "signed" and the signature must be that of the "party against whom enforcement" of the contract is sought.

In response to Question 5, you will have seen that the UCC understanding of "signature" is expansive, including "any symbol executed or adopted with present intention to adopt or accept a writing." § 1-201(b)(37). The signature requirement of § 2-201 is commonly held to be satisfied by the sender's name on an e-mail. As one court explained: "Neither the common law nor the UCC requires a *handwritten* signature . . . , even though such a signature is better evidence of identity than a typed one. It is not customary, though it is possible, to include an electronic copy of a handwritten signature in an e-mail, and therefore its absence does not create a suspicion of forgery or other fraud—and anyway an electronic copy of a signature could *be* a forgery."[10]

The Comments to § 1-201 and § 2-201 confirm both the generous understanding of the sort of symbol that might constitute a "signature" (e.g., initials, thumbprint, letterhead) and the importance of the requirement that this symbol must have been intentionally executed or adopted by the necessary party with "the present intention to adopt or accept the writing." The following examples illustrate the application of these concepts.

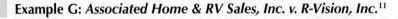

EXAMPLES AND ANALYSIS

Example G: *Associated Home & RV Sales, Inc. v. R-Vision, Inc.*[11]

Recall from Example B that, based on the lack of a written contract, the court dismissed on summary judgment the breach of contract suit brought by the RV dealer Associated Home against the RV manufacturer R-Vision. Associated Home had also argued that the order forms it submitted to R-Vision for four RVs satisfied the statute of fraud writing requirement. The only signatures on those forms were those of agents for Associated

---

[10]   Cloud Corp. v. Hasbro, Inc., 314 F.3d 289, 295 (7th Cir. 2002). As we will discuss in greater detail in Assignment 14, statutes addressing electronic commerce give courts even more direct authority for this point. This case discussed the validity of this analysis prior to the effective date of these statutes.

[11]   62 UCC Rep. Serv. 2d 180 (D.N.M. 2006).

Home, but the order forms were pre-printed forms supplied by R-Vision, containing R-Vision's logos.

Analysis: The court rejected Associated Home's argument that these logos satisfied the signature requirement, explaining:

> While the Official Comment . . . recognizes that non-traditional forms of identification, including initials, thumbprints, billheads, and letterheads, may satisfy the Statute of Frauds, the proper inquiry is whether R-Vision executed or adopted the symbol with present intention to authenticate the writing. Associated Home points to no evidence that establishes that R-Vision intended to use its logos as an authentication of a contract between the parties; that the logos were printed on the order forms before Associated Home received them . . . suggests, if anything, that R-Vision did not use the logos as a stamp of approval on a subsequent contract between it and Associated Home.

The court suggests that a logo on an order form *might* satisfy the signature requirement, if it were "adopted with the present intention to authenticate the writing." How might a party in Associated Home's position argue that the other party did use a logo on an order form with such an intent?

Example H: *East Lynn Fertilizers, Inc. v. CHS, Inc.*[12]

In July, East Lynn Fertilizers entered into an oral agreement with CHS to buy 360 tons of anhydrous ammonia, to be delivered the following April. The terms of the agreement were confirmed in an e-mail from East Lynn, as well as in a written contract that CHS sent to East Lynn. East Lynn signed the contract and returned it to CHS with a 10% down payment. CHS never signed the contract; according to its normal practices, it simply filed the contract. The following November, the price of ammonia had dropped significantly. After an unsuccessful attempt to renegotiate the price, East Lynn informed CHS that there was no binding contract, since CHS had never signed it. East Lynn sued CHS to get back its deposit, and CHS counter-sued for breach of contract. East Lynn moved for summary judgment based on the absence of a signature by CHS.

---

[12] 2010 WL 5070752 (C.D. Ill. 2010).

Analysis: The court rejected East Lynn's motion for summary judgment because "[CHS's] signature is not required to enforce the contract against [East Lynn] because [CHS] is not the party to be charged." Why is CHS not "the party to be charged"? How do you know which party is the party to be charged and therefore has to have signed the writing?

c. Quantity Term

As you have already seen, "[t]he required writing need not contain all the material terms of the contract and such material terms as are stated need not be precisely stated." And from Assignment 6 you also know that many omitted terms can be added using the gap-fillers in Part 3 of Article 2. But there is no gap-filler for a quantity term; there is no way to fill in a "reasonable amount" if the parties have not specified a quantity. As you saw in Question 6, though § 2-201 itself says only that "the contract is not enforceable . . . beyond the quantity of goods shown in such writing," Comment 1 makes clear that "[t]he only term which must appear is the quantity term" though it need not be accurately stated. Parties may specify the quantity less specifically, however. Requirements contracts ("all the buyer will need"), output contracts ("all the seller can supply"), and exclusive dealing contracts are permitted ways of specifying a quantity.

EXAMPLES AND ANALYSIS

Example I: *United Galvanizing, Inc. v. Imperial Zinc Corp.*[13]

A buyer and seller of zinc had a lunch meeting during which they discussed the buyer's need for an additional supplier of zinc. Afterwards, the buyer sent an e-mail to the seller that said:

> Good afternoon. Could you please ship United a load of the zinc metal we discussed at lunch the other day. I would like to give a load a try? Please advise earliest delivery date.

---

[13] 73 UCC Rep. Serv. 2d 448 (S.D. Tex. 2011).

The seller responded with an email saying "I will call am tomorrow and get a ship date for you. Thank you for the business." The seller later sent an order confirmation for 45,000 pounds of "remelt zinc."

The buyer later sued the seller, claiming an enforceable contract and breach of an obligation to supply a particular quality of zinc. The court considered whether there was an enforceable contract with a quantity term specified.

Analysis: The court held that the reference to "a load" satisfied the quantity requirement of 2-201. Do you agree with the court's conclusion? Do you think the case would come out the same way if the order confirmation had not been sent? If the responsive email had not been sent?

APPLYING THE CODE

Problem 9-2.

Seller sends buyer a document on its letterhead saying, "Thank you for your recent purchase order for 500 widgets at $5 each." Would this communication satisfy the requirements of 2-201(1) in an enforcement action by the seller? By the buyer?

Problem 9-3.

Buyer sends seller a document on its letterhead saying, "Confirmation of agreement for our purchase from you at $30 per bushel of all the apples produced in the next harvest from your Fairfax orchard." The named orchard annually produces 5000 to 6000 bushels of apples. Would the buyer's document satisfy the requirements of 2-201(1) in an enforcement action by the seller? By the buyer?

4. The Merchant Confirmation Exception of § 2-201(2)

Section 2-201(2) establishes an alternative set of requirements for a "sufficient" writing if the contract is between merchants.

Reading the Code:
§ 2-201(2)

Read 2-201(2) and Comment 3.

Question 8. What would a party have to prove in order to establish that the contract at issue can be enforced under the provisions of 2-201(2)? Be specific in identifying the facts required.

Question 9. What does "sufficient against the sender" mean in 2-201(2)?

Question 10. Why might this rule be dubbed the "merchants-must-read-their-mail" exception to the requirements of 2-201(1)?

Your careful reading of § 2-201(2) and your responses to the questions above should reveal that this exception modifies the requirements of § 2-201(1) in some respects, allowing some contracts between merchants that do not have the correct party's signature to satisfy the statue of frauds. However, the other requirements of § 2-201(1) must be met, as indicated by the requirement that the writing must be "sufficient against the sender."

The case that follows illustrates the application of the "merchants" rule in § 2-201 and how that rule intersects with the remaining requirements of § 2-201(1). In reading *Brooks Peanut Co v. Great Southern Peanut*, consider the following questions:

(1)   What is the purpose of § 2-201(2), as explained by the court in its footnote 2?

(2)   Is it the buyer or the seller that raises the statute of frauds as a defense?

(3)   What writing does the other party offer as satisfying the statute of frauds? Would that writing satisfy the requirements of § 2-201(1)? If not, why not?

(4)   Using the text of § 2-201(2) and the list you created in answering Question 8 above, identify how the writing satisfies the requirements of § 2-201(2).

(5)   Remember that, even if a party establishes that there was a writing that satisfies § 2-201(1) or § 2-201(2), that party must also prove that the parties in fact agreed to the contract and establish the terms that the party claims were breached. What defenses to the contract's existence are raised by Great Southern Peanut? Which of those defenses, if any, were resolved by the court of appeals? Which of those defenses, if any, remain for the trial court to consider after the remand?

Brooks Peanut Co. v. Great Southern Peanut, LLC

746 S.E.2d 272 (Ga. Ct. App. 2013)

Ellington, Presiding Judge.

Brooks Peanut Company, Inc. ("Brooks Peanut") appeals from an order of the Superior Court of Lee County granting summary judgment to Great Southern Peanut Company, LLC ("GSP") on Brooks Peanut's claims for breach of contract, promissory estoppel, negligent misrepresentation, fraud, and attorney fees arising out of a commodities transaction. The superior court found that GSP's alleged promise to sell peanuts to Brooks Peanut was unenforceable under the Statute of Frauds, OCGA § 11-2-201. . . . For the following reasons, we reverse the court's grant of summary judgment to GSP.

Brooks Peanut contends that it produced evidence showing that a writing sufficient to satisfy the Statute of Frauds exists; therefore the trial court erred in concluding that GSP's Statute of Frauds defense bars Brooks Peanut's claims as a matter of law. We agree.

. . . .

Brooks Peanut is a peanut shelling company operating in Samson, Alabama. GSP is a competing peanut sheller located in Lee County, Georgia. Because there is no established peanut commodities market, peanut shellers and other businesses handling peanut products often use brokers to buy and sell peanuts. Typically, the broker's fee is paid by the seller. The commodities transaction at issue in this case was brokered by Mazur & Hockman, Inc. ("M & H"). Brooks Peanut and GSP have both used M & H, as well as other brokers, to buy and sell peanut products on their behalf.

In mid-September 2010, Barrett Brooks, president of Brooks Peanut, called Richard Barnhill and Jay Strother, peanut brokers with M & H, and asked them to find peanuts for his company to buy and to have delivered to his shelling facility. Brooks requested that Brooks Peanut not be identified as the buyer when M & H contacted potential sellers. According to Brooks and Strother, that is not an unusual practice. M & H solicited offers from several peanut shellers, including GSP, and conveyed them to Brooks. After reviewing the offers, on September 20, Brooks asked Strother to communicate a counteroffer to GSP's manager, Doug Wingate. Specifically, the counteroffer was an offer to buy 3,168,000 pounds of 2010 crop medium runner shelled peanuts for $.4675 per pound, to be delivered monthly throughout 2011.

According to Strother, Wingate accepted the counteroffer that same day, September 20. After Wingate accepted these terms, Strother revealed that Brooks Peanut was the buyer. According to Strother, Wingate "sighed" upon learning that a competitor was involved in the transaction; however, he did not reject the deal. Wingate testified that, although he initially accepted the deal, he declined to consummate it when he learned that Brooks Peanut was the buyer.

On the same day, M & H prepared and then faxed to GSP and Brooks Peanut a written confirmation of the sale of peanuts. The confirmation stated: "We confirm a Sale and Purchase Transaction as described below[.]" The confirmation was printed on M & H letterhead and listed the names and addresses of the seller and the buyer, as well as terms covering price, quantity, quality, crop year, delivery schedule, and payment method. Spaces for the seller's contract number and the buyer's purchase order number were left blank. The confirmation stated that "[t]his confirmation is subject to the following condition[ ]: Seller's contract and Buyer's purchase order to follow[.]" . . .

The confirmation was signed by M & H's Strother. GSP and Brooks Peanut each received the faxed confirmation from M & H. It is undisputed that GSP did not issue a contract and that Brooks Peanut did not issue a purchase order. After Strother sent the confirmation to GSP and Brooks Peanut, he continued communicating with the parties to finalize the logistics of the deliveries. For example, on September 21, he told Brooks that GSP had offered to haul the peanut loads. They also discussed increasing the monthly shipments, but Wingate stated that he wanted "to stay at 6 loads a month on the [B]rooks [Peanut] contract for right now[.]"

GSP did not raise any objection to the fax confirmation until late January 2011, almost four months after M & H sent it. Wingate testified that he "did not see the need" to object to the confirmation. Beginning in January 2011, GSP took the position that, despite the confirmation, GSP and Brooks Peanut had not entered into that particular transaction because Wingate had rejected the sale when he learned that it involved his company's competitor, that M & H was not authorized to confirm the sale or to send the confirmation, and that a condition precedent had not occurred because GSP had not issued a written contract.

The evidence adduced shows that M & H had routinely brokered thousands of peanut sales between other peanut companies, shellers, and manufacturers using the same form of trade confirmation at issue here. Further, it is undisputed that GSP agreed to sell peanuts to Brooks Peanut in June 2009 and April 2010 and that such agreements were memorialized solely by M & H sending the parties confirmations that were substantially similar to the one at issue in this case.

. . . .

Section 2-201(1) is the UCC's general Statute of Frauds provision. Section 2- 201(2), sometimes referred to as the "merchant confirmation rule," "the reply doctrine," or the "merchant's exception," has somewhat modified requirements concerning oral agreements between merchants, primarily dispensing with the necessity of the confirmation recipient's signature. [FN2]

FN2. . . . UCC § 2-201(2) was drafted to correct an unfair condition which developed under other statutes of frauds when one contracting party sent a letter to the other contracting party to confirm an oral contract made by them. The party sending the confirmatory letter often could not invoke the statute of frauds as a defense because he had signed a writing which satisfied the statute. The party receiving the confirmatory writing had not signed the confirmatory writing. If the contract proved to be advantageous for the receiving party, he was able to enforce it against the sending merchant. But if the contract was not to the receiving party's advantage, he could refuse to perform, assert the statute of frauds as a defense and prevent the sending party from enforcing the oral contract. UCC § 2-201(2) attempts to remove this inequity and thereby encourage the sending of writings to confirm oral contracts.

As one treatise explains,

While § 2-201(2) stands as an exception to the UCC's general statute of frauds, § 2-201(1), it is not entirely separate from that provision. The courts have generally held that the language in § 2-201(1) to the effect that a writing relied upon to satisfy the statute of frauds must be "sufficient to indicate" a contract is equally applicable to § 2-201(2), although there is authority to the contrary. Similarly, the condition stated in § 2-201(1) to the effect that a contract is not enforceable under the code beyond the quantity stated in the writing used to overcome the statute of frauds has been expressly held applicable to § 2-201(2), as well as by implication. [82 A.L.R.4th 709 § 2[a].]]

The record demonstrates that Brooks Peanut and GSP are merchants within the meaning of the UCC and that the transaction at issue is one "between merchants." Thus, we resolve this claim of error with reference to both subsections (1) and (2) of OCGA § 11-2-201.

The confirmation in this case indicates that the parties entered into a transaction for the sale of a specific quantity of goods for a price exceeding $500 . . . . The confirmation at issue also puts the recipient on notice that it confirms a prior oral agreement concerning the sale of goods sufficient to trigger a response by the recipient and, thus, is sufficient under OCGA § 11-2-201(2).

GSP argues, however, that the confirmation is insufficient to show that the parties had reached a final agreement because it contains a condition that was not fulfilled, that is, that a seller's contract was "to follow."

A formal, written agreement may be a condition precedent to the formation of a binding contract, when the parties so intend. When the parties intend to memorialize with a formal document an agreement that they have already reached, on the other hand, the execution of the document is not an act necessary to the creation of an enforceable contract. In this case, there is no evidence that the parties intended the execution of the seller's contract to be a condition precedent, especially since the parties had previously consummated deals using broker confirmations only.

The record also contains evidence showing the applicability of OCGA § 11-2-201(2) in that GSP received the written confirmation within a reasonable time, given that the record shows that it was sent by fax and received on the same day that the oral agreement was allegedly reached. Further, GSP had reason to know of the confirmation's contents, given that Wingate had been a party to the negotiations. And it is undisputed that GSP failed to object to the confirmation in writing within [10] days.

. . . .

[T]he record [also] contains evidence from which the factfinder could infer that the writing was signed by both parties to the transaction through their agent and that the confirmation was signed by the sender's agent such that it was sufficient against the sender. Consequently, GSP is not entitled to summary judgment based upon its Statute of Frauds defense, and the trial court's order must be reversed.

APPLYING THE CODE

Problem 9-4.

In a telephone conversation on December 4, Interstate Chemical Corporation (ICC) agreed to purchase one barge (containing 420,000 gallons, or 10 mb[14]) of methanol from Mitsubishi International Corporation (MIC) at a price of $2.55 per gallon. Later the same day, ICC sent MIC an e-mail staying: "We would like to purchase your methanol barge. Please give me a call." MIC responded with an email that said: "We confirm 10 mb @ $2.55/gal loading Dec 20 or later." MIC also sent ICC a contract and asked ICC to sign it and send it back; ICC never signed or returned it. On December 18, ICC informed MIC that it was having trouble getting Coast Guard approval for receipt of the barge at the intended destination and attempted to cancel the delivery. MIC eventually sold the barge to another buyer at a price of $2.05 per gallon and sued ICC for breach of contract. What arguments does MIC have that either of the two writings described satisfy the statute of frauds?

---

[14] An "mb" is an abbreviation used in Canada and the United States to refer to 1000 barrels of oil; each barrel contains 42 gallons.

E. Promissory Estoppel and the Statute of Frauds.

As you will likely recall from your Contracts course, promissory estoppel is a common law doctrine that permits parties to enforce agreements that otherwise would be unenforceable because of the absence of consideration or some other requirement for establishing the existence of a contract. Is it appropriate to use promissory estoppel to permit enforcement of an alleged contract that would otherwise be unenforceable under § 2-201 because it is not in writing? On the one hand, promissory estoppel is designed to make a promise binding even though it is missing one of the requirements for enforcing it, as long as the elements of a promissory estoppel are established, so it seems suited to doing just that if the requirement of a writing is not satisfied. On the other hand, permitting enforcement of an oral promise on this basis would allow parties to circumvent a statutory writing requirement, sometimes facilitating a fraud, and would encourage parties to rely on oral promises rather than put their agreements in writing.

> **Restatement (Second) of Contracts § 90(1):**
>
> A promise which the promisor should reasonably expect to induce action or forbearance on the part of the promisee or a third person and which does induce such action or forbearance is binding if injustice can be avoided only by the enforcement of the promise. The remedy granted for breach may be limited as justice requires.

Most courts have permitted parties to invoke promissory estoppel when the oral promise was about the writing requirement itself, e.g., when a party promised to put the agreement in writing and then did not, or when a party promised not to rely on the statute of frauds and then later raised that defense. In those limited situations, applying promissory estoppel might be said to prevent a party from using the statute of frauds as an affirmative instrument of fraud.

But when faced with the broader question whether promissory estoppel should be available for enforcement of simple oral contracts that would otherwise be unenforceable under § 2-201, the courts have reached conflicting conclusions. Before looking at how the courts have handled the issue, we start with an important first question: what arguments for and against the use of promissory estoppel can be derived from closely reading the relevant statutory text and Comments?

Reading the Code:
Promissory Estoppel and the
Statute of Frauds

**Read 1-103 and Comment 1, and review all of 2-201,
paying particular attention to the opening clause.**

Question 11. Section 2-201 says that the writing requirements specified in the section apply "unless otherwise provided in this section." In light of 1-103 and Comment 2 and 2-201 and its Comments, how would you argue that the opening phrase permits only those exceptions explicitly included in 2-201(2) and (3)?

Question 12. How would you argue that the opening phrase does not restrict exceptions only to those explicitly included in 2-201(2) and (3) but instead allows use of common law exceptions like promissory estoppel?

Question 13. If you were a judge facing a promissory estoppel claim for enforcing a contract within the scope of Article 2, which of these two meanings would you attribute to the opening phrase of 2-201? Why?

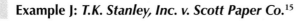

EXAMPLES AND ANALYSIS

Example J: *T.K. Stanley, Inc. v. Scott Paper Co.*[15]

Scott Paper Company and T.K. Stanley both operated hardwood sawmills. Stanley alleged that Scott had entered into an oral agreement to sell Stanley the timber rights to a particular tract of land. This oral agreement induced Stanley to buy that land from the third-party owner; however, Scott never conveyed the timber rights to Stanley, and in fact logged the land itself. The court granted summary judgment to Scott based on the lack of a written contract, rejecting Stanley's attempt to assert promissory

---

[15] 793 F. Supp. 707 (S.D. Miss. 1992).

estoppel. The court distinguished between Mississippi law that permitted the assertion of promissory estoppel in cases involving general statutes of frauds, and Mississippi law that prohibited the assertion of promissory estoppel in cases involving 2-201. The court cited cases holding that the clear language of the UCC, "which provides that the writing requirement controls 'except as otherwise provided in this section' . . . thus [leads to the conclusion] that the legislature had provided the only exceptions in sections 2-201(2) and (3). . . . [E]stoppel is not a supplementary exception to the UCC statute of frauds. . . ."

Example K: *Atlantic Paper Box Co. v. Whitman's Chocolates*[16]

Atlantic Paper Box Co. made specialty candy boxes, "primarily heart-shaped boxes used for Valentine's Day candy." Approximately 40% of its business consisted of producing candy boxes for Whitman's Chocolates. Industry practice in this business is to place orders for Valentine's Day candy boxes 15 months before the candy is to be sold. In October 1992, Atlantic started discussions with Whitman's concerning the 1994 Valentine's Day boxes. Atlantic alleged that Whitman assured Atlantic that it would place orders with Atlantic in February 1993. Atlantic also alleged that Whitman's did place telephonic orders in February totaling over $1,000,000 worth of boxes. At the time of these negotiations, Atlantic was aware that Whitman's was for sale. Atlantic expressed concern about whether Russell Stover was a potential buyer, because Russell Stover produced its own candy boxes, and would thus not need Atlantic's boxes if it purchased Whitman's. Whitman's assured Atlantic that Russell Stover was not a potential buyer. In fact, Russell Stover did acquire Whitman's and terminated all business with Atlantic.

Atlantic sued Whitman's, seeking damages under both breach of contract and promissory estoppel theories. Whitman's argued that the statute of frauds bars claims for promissory estoppel in the absence of proving either a writing satisfying 2-201(1) or some exception to the writing requirement. While the court agreed that, "[o]n its face, defendant's argument that the Pennsylvania UCC bars a claim for promissory estoppel appears correct," it went on to permit the promissory estoppel claim on the theory that Whitman's telephone orders, which were confirmed by subsequent purchase orders, together with the industry practice of placing orders 15 months in

---

[16] 844 F. Supp. 1038 (E.D. Pa 1994).

advance of the sale date, arguably constituted a waiver of the statute of frauds defense. These allegations provided a sufficient basis for denying Whitman's motion to dismiss the promissory estoppel claims.

Analysis of Examples J and K: Both courts rely on state court holdings that 2-201 bars the use of promissory estoppel in the absence of a writing satisfying the Code provisions. Why did the court in Example K nonetheless allow the promissory estoppel claim to go forward even without a writing sufficient under 2-201? If the state courts in each case instead thought that 2-201 was not a bar to applying promissory estoppel, would you apply promissory estoppel in the circumstances of Example J? Example K? Why or why not?

Example L: *Hitzke v. Easterday*[17]

Easterday operates a horse stable primarily engaged in boarding and breeding horses. She occasionally gets involved in the sale of horses. Hitzke learned that Easterday was trying to sell a show pony owned by Kasten. Kasten had bought the pony on the condition that, when he no longer wanted it, Easterday would buy it back for its purchase price ($25,000). Kasten no longer wanted the pony, so Easterday was trying to find another buyer for it. During the negotiations between Hitzke and Easterday, Hitzke expressed some concerns about the pony's condition and the price. According to the trial court's finding of facts:

> [H]e didn't want to lose the investment. He was concerned about that. And that he wanted this, as he described it, an exit strategy. The horse still needed a vet check according to him, that his wife thought it was too expensive. And so he was getting some cold feet on the transaction. And this is what he said Ms. Easterday said: If this horse does not work out, I would give you a guaranteed buy back of the horse.

> Based upon that he felt that if it didn't work out, he could sell it back. Got that from [Easterday], and then talked to his wife, and they agreed that they would proceed with the sale. He would not have done that purchase without the assurance.

Hitzke eventually agreed to buy the pony from Kasten for $25,000, conditioned on Easterday's "guaranteed buy back" for the same price. There was

---

17   2005 WL 1459699 (Wis. Ct. App. 2005).

no writing memorializing that agreement. When Hitzke tried to exercise the guaranteed buy back, Easterday refused to buy it back herself; instead, she found another buyer who purchased it for $21,800. Hitzke sued Easterday for the balance of the buy back guarantee. Easterday argued that their oral contract was unenforceable under the statute of frauds.

Analysis: The trial court found for Hitzke. It rejected Easterman's statute of frauds argument for two reasons, both of which were rejected by the appeals court. First, the trial court ruled that 2-201 did not apply because the parties were not merchants. Second, the trial court reasoned that, even if 2-201 applied, the transaction fell within the exception in 2-201(3) for goods for which payment has been made and accepted. The appeals court rejected this argument because, "while it is true that money changed hands, both when Hitzke bought and sold the pony, payment was not made by Hitzke to Easterday nor was payment made by Easterday to Hitzke." Although the appeals court rejected the trial court's reasoning, it also found for Hitzke, based on promissory estoppel, even though Hitzke had not pled promissory estoppel. The appeals court pointed to the portion of the trial court's factual findings cited above, and ruled that "the relevant facts supporting the doctrine were found by the trial court." Further, the court cited precedent in the jurisdiction for the proposition that "[t]he Statute of Frauds is not applicable in an action involving promissory estoppel."

Why is the trial court's first reason for declining to apply the statute of frauds clearly wrong? Do you agree with the trial court or the appeals court with respect to the second reason for declining to apply the statute of frauds? Was the appeals court correct to raise the promissory estoppel argument even though Hitzke had not done so? Do these facts present a strong case for applying promissory estoppel to overcome a statute of frauds argument?

APPLYING THE CODE

Some tips on solving statute of frauds problems:

- To demonstrate that a writing is not required for enforcement, you must show either that the contract is not one for which 2-201(1) requires a writing or that it fits any one of the exceptions in 2-201(3).

- To demonstrate that a writing is required, you should show that a writing is required by 2-201(1) and that none of the exceptions in 2-201(3) applies or is satisfied.

- If a writing is required, the writing will be sufficient if it satisfies the requirements of 2-201(1) or 2-201(2). If it is arguable that a writing is required, you should determine whether a writing exists that satisfies that requirement.

Problem 9-5.

Winona, an art gallery owner with a large personal art collection, visits Artexpo Chicago, an annual juried expo that brings art galleries and collectors together with both established and emerging artists. She is particularly attracted to the work of a young sculptor, Thomas Wright, who specializes in marble renderings of wildlife. Since none are quite what she's looking for, Thomas agrees to create one to order for her, for a price of $10,000. (Each set of facts below is independent of the others.)

(a) Winona is buying the sculpture for personal use, to display in her home. She gives Thomas $1,000 toward the purchase price, paying by personal check without other notation on it. Thomas cashes the check and begins work on the sculpture, cutting a block of marble of the type and in the size appropriate for Winona's special order. A week later, Winona calls Thomas to cancel the order. Thomas seeks to enforce the contract in court. Winona raises 2-201 as a defense and seeks dismissal of the lawsuit. Will Winona be successful? Why or why not?

(b) Winona is buying the sculpture for personal use, to display in her home. She gives Thomas her business card and writes her home address and phone number and the word "sculpture" on the back. Thomas gives Winona a receipt marked "Special order sculpture $10,000, estimated delivery date: 6 weeks." The receipt has "Tom's Sculptures" stamped at the top. At the end of the day, Winona decides she was too hasty in ordering the sculpture and calls Thomas to cancel the order. She leaves a message on his voicemail, which he receives when he returns to his workshop at the end of the Art Expo. Thomas seeks to enforce the contract in court. Winona raises 2-201 as a defense and seeks dismissal of the lawsuit. Will Winona be successful? Why or why not?

(c)   Winona agrees to buy the sculpture to resell it in her own gallery. Thomas gives Winona his business card and marks on the back "Agreement for special order sculpture, $1,000, delivery on 10/15." Five days later, Winona calls Thomas to tell him she is no longer interested in purchasing the sculpture. Thomas seeks to enforce the contract in court. Winona raises 2-201 as a defense and seeks dismissal of the lawsuit. Will Winona be successful? Why or why not?

(d)   Winona agrees to buy the sculpture to resell it in her own gallery. Thomas realizes the price he quoted to Winona is too low. Since she made no payment and he gave her no receipt, Thomas decides to cancel the contract. He writes Winona a letter in which he says "I am not able to supply the sculpture you ordered at the price quoted so will have to cancel our arrangement. If you would pay $2000 more than the agreed price, I would reinstate the order." Winona seeks enforcement of the contract, and Thomas raises 2-201 as a defense. Will Thomas be successful? Why or why not?

(e)   Thomas files a complaint, seeking to enforce his agreement with Winona. Her answer says: "The parties' contract for sale of the sculpture is not enforceable because there is no writing to satisfy the statute of frauds." Will Winona be successful when she seeks dismissal on the basis of 2-201? Why or why not?

(f)   If Thomas seeks to enforce his agreement with Winona and is successful in meeting the requirements of 2-201, is he then entitled to summary judgment on his breach of contract claim?

Problem 9-6.

Pullman (a merchant) started negotiating to buy sugar from Labudde (also a merchant). Labudde sent the following e-mail to Pullman:

Pullman,

Here's what we need to proceed:

(1)   a firm offer in writing saying that you will pay $.17/lb "as is," FOB Baltimore, MD and will ship everything over the next 30 days.

(2)   a written guarantee that you will remove the sugar from the packaging and that packaging will be destroyed

(3)   payment terms such as wire transfer each day to cover the product that will pick up or a lump sum wire up front to cover X amount of shipments, etc.

Also, a reminder that there is still a chance that half of this 5.4 million pounds will have to go to another customer.

Thanks,

Labudde

Pullman promptly responded with the following e-mail: "Here is your offer. Please email me back the signed confirmation or fax it back to me."

Attached to the e-mail was a document signed by Pullman, stating the following:

This offer lies between Pullman Sugar of 700 E. 107th Street, Chicago, IL 60628 and Labudde Group of 1239 12th Ave, Grafton, WI 53024.

· Pullman Sugar offers to pay Labudde Group $.17/lb FOB for all 5,419,916 lbs of sugar located in Baltimore, MD.

· Pullman Sugar guarantees that all of the product coming from Baltimore, MD will be taken out of its original packaging and the packaging will be destroyed.

· Payment terms—Pullman Sugar will wire transfer the money to Labudde Group in increments as the product is picked up from the warehouse.

· Acceptance of this offer is needed by today, February 15, 2008.

The Offer also included a blank signature line below Pullman's signature. Labudde did not sign or return this document. Labudde then sold the sugar to another party. Pullman alleges that the parties had a contract for the sugar and that Labudde breached that contract. Labudde moves to dismiss the lawsuit on summary judgment, relying on the statute of frauds. Will Labudde be successful? Why or why not?

Chapter 5

Warranties

Key Concepts

- Nature of warranties that may be made by a seller of goods:
    - Implied warranty of title and against infringement (§ 2-312)
- Implied warranty of merchantability by merchant sellers (§ 2-314)
- Implied warranty of fitness for the buyer's particular purpose (§ 2-315)
- Express warranties arising from seller's words and conduct (§ 2-313)
- Seller's disclaimer of warranties (§ 2-316)
- Rights of third parties to warranty protections made by sellers to buyers (§ 2-318)

As you saw in Chapter 2 (Assignments 1 and 6), Article 2 includes a number of gap-filling default provisions that become part of a contract if the parties do not agree otherwise As you also saw, some implied-in-law provisions are mandatory and cannot be abrogated by the parties' agreement. This Chapter continues the exploration of contract terms, focusing on warranties (express and implied) that become part of the contract. We begin by looking at the nature of warranties and the ability of the parties to vary the default warranty provisions of Article 2.

We often think of a warranty as the piece of paper that comes inside a box when we purchase goods, but warranty protections go much beyond what may be written there. Warranties include all contractual guarantees about the quality of the goods that the buyer is to receive, forming the basis for the buyer's enforcement of its expectations about the goods it is purchasing. If the buyer believes the goods have failed to live up to those guarantees, the buyer will attempt to claim breach of warranty. The buyer must establish the existence and content of the warranty provisions, express and implied, and address any claims by the seller that it effectively limited or disclaimed warranties on the goods.

Because the quality of the goods sold is at the core of the buyer's expectations in a sale-of-goods contract, much Article 2 litigation involves disputes over the existence and breach of warranties. Article 2 provides for creation of both implied-in-law and express warranties. Implied warranties, covered in Assignment 10, are warranties furnished by Article 2 as default terms and include (i) the implied warranty of title and against infringement (§ 2-312); (ii) the implied warranty of merchantability (§ 2-314); and (iii) the implied warranty of fitness for a particular purpose (§ 2-315). Express warranties, covered in Assignment 11, are the explicit and implied-in-fact promises about the goods that arise from the seller's words and conduct in the contract formation stage (§ 2-313). Article 2 also provides rules about how to read all those warranties together (§ 2-317) and if, and how, a seller may exclude or modify either implied or express warranties (§ 2-316), covered in Assignment 12. Assignment 12 also explores a related but independent source of warranty protection, the Magnuson-Moss Warranty Act. Finally, Article 2 provides guidance as to when third parties may claim protection of warranties made by the seller to the buyer (§ 2-318), covered in Assignment 13.

Assignment 10
Creation of Implied Warranties
§§ 2-312, 2-314, 2-315

Implied warranties are not the result of an express agreement by the parties, but rather reflect assumptions about the warranties that typically accompany (or, in the eyes of the UCC drafters, should accompany) the sale of goods, in some or all contexts. Depending on the facts of the sale, under Article 2 a buyer might receive any or all of the following implied warranties: title, non-infringement, merchantability, and fitness for a particular purpose. All of these warranties are "implied" in the sense described—they become part of the contract based on the circumstances of the sale without express agreement of the parties—but Article 2 chooses to call only the warranties of merchantability and fitness for a particular purpose "implied warranties" to differentiate them from the warranties of title and non-infringement with respect to certain consequences. We will call all of those warranties "implied warranties" to mark the distinction from express warranties, but we will alert you to the consequences of the different Article 2 nomenclature.

> ### Implied-in-Fact Terms
>
> Recall from Assignment 6 that terms that are not found in the express language of the contract may nonetheless be understood to be included in the agreed terms based on the circumstances of the transaction. Such implied-in-fact terms are considered to be part of the bargain between the parties (their "agreement").

Because all of the implied warranties are based on assumptions about the usual or generally expected warranties that accompany sales of goods, the parties may "agree otherwise," meaning that sellers may disclaim or modify the otherwise expected implied warranties. Assignment 12 explores how sellers can disclaim or modify the implied warranties of merchantability and fitness for a particular purpose (the ones called "implied warranties" in Article 2). The modification or disclaimer of the warranties of title and against infringement are discussed in this Assignment.

At the completion of this Assignment, you should be able to

- identify the circumstances when implied warranties (as differentiated from express warranties) are included in a sales contract;
- determine when the implied warranties of title and non-infringement attach and what they protect;
- distinguish between the implied warranty of merchantability and the implied warranty of fitness for a particular purpose; and
- apply the relevant portions of Article 2 to determine whether a given set of facts provides the basis for the inclusion of any implied warranties so as to bind the seller in the event of its breach.

A. Warranties of Title and against Infringement under § 2-312

Ordinarily, a buyer expects to acquire good title to purchased goods and does not expect to be subjected to a lawsuit to protect title. Similarly, a buyer typically expects to be free of claims that its use of the purchased goods infringes on intellectual property rights created by patents, copyrights and trademarks. Such a claim might occur, for instance, if a seller of goods does not have a license for the intellectual property that is part of the goods that are sold. Section 2-312 extends to the buyer protection consistent with those normal expectations of the buyer to be able to use the goods without exposure to a lawsuit.

As noted above, the warranties of title and against infringement are "implied" warranties because, unless disclaimed, they are provided by operation of the Code, but they are not formally defined as "implied warranties" under the Code. Therefore, they are not subject to the general provisions on disclaimers in § 2-316 that we will take up in Assignment 12. Section 2-312 offers a more specific provision for disclaiming these warranties.

Reading the Code:
§ 2-312

Read 2-312(1) and (3).

Question 1. Reword 2-312(1) and (3) in one or more if/then paraphrases, using the form indicated below:

    (a) 2-312(1): If ____, then there is a warranty that ____ and _____

    (b) 2-312(3): If____, then there is a warranty that ____except that___

Question 2. What does "security interest" mean in 2-312(1)? See 1-201(b)(35).

Question 3. Recall the hierarchy of contractual provisions discussed in Assignment 1. The implied warranties in 2-312 are (choose one):

    Mandatory provisions

    Express terms

    Implied-in-fact terms

    Default provisions

Question 4. If a course of performance, course of dealing, or usage of trade runs contrary to one of the implied warranties above, which will prevail?

1. Warranty of Title

Section 2-312(1) specifies two expectations concerning the title to goods sold: (1) that the title is good and the transfer rightful; and (2) that the goods are delivered free of any security interest, lien, or encumbrance of which the buyer has no knowledge. There is no requirement that the seller have knowledge or notice of the title defect and there is no requirement that the seller be a merchant. (Compare to the warranty against infringement in § 2-312(3), discussed in section 3 below.)

The language of this section contains a number of qualifications to the protections afforded the buyer. As indicated explicitly in § 2-312(1), a buyer who at the time of contracting has knowledge of a security interest, lien, or encumbrance on the goods cannot claim violation of the warranty of title. And as noted in Comment 2, as with any breach, a buyer must provide a seller with notice within a "reasonable time" of a breach of the warranty of title in order to be able to make a claim.

EXAMPLES AND ANALYSIS

Example A: *Saber v. Dan Angelone Chevrolet, Inc.*[1]

Dan Angelone Chevrolet sold a used 1985 red Chevrolet Corvette equipped with an automatic transmission to George Saber for $14,900. After Saber experienced problems with the Corvette on a number of occasions, he researched the car's history. His research revealed discrepancies with the title application for the Corvette, which described the car as black with a manual transmission. Believing the car might be stolen, Saber contacted the state police.

The state police performed a visual inspection and discovered discrepancies, including ones with respect to the vehicle identification number (VIN) and major components of the Corvette. The plate that contained the VIN was blistered and painted over and the identification numbers on the car's frame, engine and transmission did not correspond to the VIN on the window. The VIN normally located on the door of the car was missing. The state police impounded the car and told Saber he could not have it back. Further investigation revealed that the Corvette was not stolen, but rather had been destroyed in a fire and subsequently rebuilt using parts from other cars. Dan Angelone Chevrolet did not reveal any of these facts to Saber; it was unclear whether the seller, who took the car as a trade-in, was aware of the problems.

Although the state police returned the car to Saber, he brought an action against the seller for breach of contract, including a claim for breach of warranty of title. The seller moved for summary judgment on the warranty-of-title claim because the car was not stolen and Saber had valid legal title to the car.

Analysis: The court denied summary judgment to the seller and ultimately held in favor of Saber, finding a "substantial shadow" on Saber's title. Which part(s)

---

[1]   811 A.2d 644 (R.I. 2002).

of 2-312 support that result? If representing Saber, what questions would you ask your client to elicit facts that might support his claim? If representing Dan Angelone Chevrolet, what questions would you ask your client to help counter the claim? In its opinion, the court, relying on Comment 1 to 2-312, determined that a buyer could establish a breach of warranty of title by showing disturbance of quiet possession. Do you agree? Is it appropriate to read the provision as requiring more than a simple legally valid title? Is that reading necessary to support the outcome here?

Do you agree with the outcome in this case? Why or why not? What part of 2-312 and its Comments support your position?

2. Disclaiming the Warranty of Title

Section 2-312(2) explains how parties may disclaim (exclude) or modify the implied warranty of title.

Reading the Code:
§ 2-312(2)

Read 2-312(2) and Comment 5.

Question 5. Write a statement that you would include in a sales agreement to exclude or modify the warranty of title as specified in 2-312(2). What characteristics make the statement effective as an exclusion or modification?

Question 6. What "circumstances" would communicate exclusion or modification of the warranty of title under 2-312(2)? For ideas, look at Comment 5.

3. Warranty against Infringement

As you have seen, § 2-312(3) imposes a requirement only on merchants regularly dealing in goods of the kind that the goods be free of rightful claims of infringement. Thus, this provision would not apply to occasional sellers or sales made by consumers. As noted in Comment 3, "[w]hen the goods are part of the seller's normal stock and are sold in his normal course of business, it is his duty to see that [there is] no claim of infringement." Notice that there is no requirement that the infringement actually prevents the buyer from using the goods. See § 2-312, Comment 4. Protection from a notice of infringement may be important in a commercial environment that values intellectual property rights and in which those rights are defended vigorously.

A buyer who has provided its own specifications for the goods, though, will not be able to claim protection of the provision respecting infringement if the infringement arose "out of compliance with the specifications." As noted in Comment 3, the buyer rather than the seller is responsible "when the buyer orders goods to be assembled, prepared or manufactured on his own specifications," whether the claim is against the buyer or the seller.

Subsection (3) begins with qualifying words ("unless otherwise agreed") that expressly permit the parties to negotiate their own provisions excluding or modifying the implied warranty against infringement.

EXAMPLES AND ANALYSIS

Example B: *Big Lots Stores, Inc. v. Luv N' Care*[2]

Luv N' Care is in the business of manufacturing and selling infant care products, such as crib mobiles, photo albums, books and towel sets. As part of its business, Luv N' Care obtains licenses to various trademarks and copyrighted images that it prints on its products. Luv N' Care obtained a license from Frederick Warne & Co. (Warne) for the use on its products of the Peter Rabbit images created by Beatrix Potter. The license was to last for a two-year period with all rights and title to the product reverting back to Warne after the license expiration. After the license expiration, Luv N' Care could not lawfully sell the Beatrice Potter products anywhere, except for a one-year sell-off period to reduce remaining inventory. The license also contained a restriction whereby Luv N' Care was permitted to sell Beatrix Potter products only to Walmart, Target and Toys "R" Us stores within the United States.

---

[2]   62 UCC Rep. Serv. 2d 522 (S.D. Ohio 2007).

During the license period, Luv N' Care made several sales of Beatrix Potter products to Big Lots Stores. Luv N' Care also made sales to Big Lots after the expiration of its license from Warne. Luv N' Care never discussed the expiration of the license with Big Lots or inform them of the restriction on sales in the United States.

Big Lots resold the Beatrix Potter products purchased from Luv N' Care throughout North America and Latin America, and some products even arrived in England. Warne discovered the sales outside the license territory and outside of the license period and ordered the sellers to cease the sales. Big Lots demanded that Luv N' Care accept return of the Beatrix Potter products, reimburse it for costs and expenses, and indemnify it for any future infringement action brought by Warne.

When the parties failed to agree on how to resolve outstanding invoices and liability, Big Lots brought suit for breach of warranty. Luv N' Care denied liability and counterclaimed, seeking payment on the unpaid invoices.

Analysis: The court ultimately held in favor of Big Lots based on 2-312. Which part of 2-312 could support that outcome? If representing Big Lots, what questions would you ask your client to elicit facts that might support his claim? If representing Luv N' Care, what questions would you ask your client to help counter the claim? In its opinion, the court determined that Luv N' Care was a merchant for purposes of 2-312. Do you agree? Can you explain why merchant status would matter? Do you agree with the outcome in this case? Why or why not? What part of the Code supports your position? Read Comment 3. Could this affect the outcome in the case brought against Luv N' Care?

B. Implied Warranties of Quality

Article 2 provides two implied warranties that relate to the quality of goods: the warranty of merchantability and the warranty of fitness for a particular purpose. Like the warranties of title and against infringement discussed above, these warranties attach automatically without any specific actions of the parties if the circumstances described in the statutory provisions are met. The warranty of merchantability satisfies buyers' typical expectation that purchased goods will be of generally acceptable commercial quality (to be "merchantable"). We will explore the meaning of "merchantability" as defined in § 2-314. The warranty of fitness satisfies buyers' expectations that, if they communicate special needs to a seller, the goods will satisfy those needs. We will explore the particular circumstances specified in § 2-315 to establish that coverage.

1. Implied Warranty of Merchantability under § 2-314

 Reading the Code:
§ 2-314(1), (2)

Read 2-314(1).

Question 7. Assuming a contract for the sale of goods exists and there is no exclusion or modification under 2-316, what is the single other requirement to establish that an implied warranty of merchantability exists?

Question 8. Read Comment 3. What does the Comment add to your understanding of the meaning of the merchantability warranty? To your understanding of the sellers who are understood to provide a merchantability warranty? Does the warranty of merchantability attach in the sale of used as well as new goods?

Question 9. Read Comment 4. Under what circumstances would 2-314 provide protection to a buyer even if the seller is not a merchant with respect to goods of the kind?

Read 2-314(2).

Subsections (a) through (f) contain a list of promises that are part of the implied warranty of merchantability, likely drawn from "the steadily developing case law on the subject" (see Purposes of Changes in the Official Comment).

Question 10. Read Comment 6. Does the list in (a) through (f) completely define the meaning of merchantability?

Question 11. Read Comment 8, which indicates that 2-314(c) contains the promise that is "fundamental" to the section. Does the promise that the goods are "fit for the ordinary purpose for which such goods are used" protect buyers who purchase the goods for resale rather than use?

Question 12. What is the difference between 2-314(2)(e) and (f)? See Comment 10.

Question 13. Read Comment 13. Who has the burden of demonstrating that the goods were not merchantable when sold? What evidence does the Comment say will help the buyer establish its claim? What evidence does the Comment say will help the seller defend against the claim?

EXAMPLES AND ANALYSIS

Example C: *Tamayo v. CGS Tyres US, Inc.*[3]

CGS Tyres manufactures and sells tires, including a tractor tire marketed under the name Continental. CGS Tyres sold tires to Hi-Line, who in turn sold and installed them for customers. Miguel Tamayo, an experienced tire technician at Hi-Line, had installed the Continental tires many times without problems or incidents. Lynn Frederick, a farmer, called Tamayo for new tractor tires and requested installation of the Continental tires. Tamayo obtained the tires and traveled to Frederick's farm for installation, but when he released the jack during the installation, the tire exploded, injuring Tamayo. Upon inspection of the tire, Tamayo concluded that the wire bead in the tire broke and failed to hold the tire together on the rim of the tractor. When Tamayo installed a replacement Continental tire on the tractor, it did not explode and the farmer was able to use the tractor without incident.

Tamayo gave CGS Tyres notice of the explosion and later brought suit for claims that included a breach of the implied warranty of merchantability. CGS Tyres moved for summary judgment, asserting that Tamayo had failed to prove that the tire was not merchantable.

---

[3]   2012 WL 2129353 (D. Neb. 2012).

Analysis: Denying the motion, the court held that Tamayo had presented evidence that the tire was not merchantable. The purpose of the Continental tire is to function as a tractor tire. The tire exploded even when installed by an experienced technician. Which parts of section 2-314(2) provide the basis for Tamayo's argument that the tire was not merchantable? If representing Tamayo, what questions would you ask your client to elicit facts that might support his claim? If representing CGS Tyres, what questions would you ask your client to help counter the claim?

Example D: *In re Sigg Switzerland (USA), Inc. Aluminum Bottles Marketing & Sales Practices Litigation*[4]

Sigg manufactures and sells water bottles advertised by Sigg to be "BPA-free." After discovering that the bottles did have BPA, plaintiffs, who purchased the bottles, filed a class action that included a claim for breach of the warranty of merchantability.

Sigg moved for dismissal, asserting that the bottles were merchantable because the water bottles were for drinking liquids and because the bottles held liquids, they did not breach the warranty.

Analysis: Agreeing with Sigg, the court held that a seller's express statement about goods does not define the "ordinary purpose" of the goods for purposes of the warranty of merchantability. Thus, whether goods conform to the "ordinary purpose" is determined in broad terms, rather than by the seller's statements. Do you agree with the court's reasoning? Would 2-314(2)(f) provide any recourse for the buyer?

Applying the reasoning of the case, would a washing machine that stopped washing mid-cycle and required a restart be merchantable because it washed clothes?[5] What about a car that did not have a license plate holder as required by state law?[6] The court noted that the plaintiff had become aware of the "potential harm" associated with BPA. Might the outcome have been different if there was definitive proof as to the adverse health effects of BPA?

---

4   2011 WL 159940 (W.D. Ky. 2011).

5   *See* Tietsworth v. Sears Roebuck & Co., 2009 WL 3320486 (N.D. Cal. 2009).

6   *See* Strauss v. Ford Motor Co., 439 F. Supp. 2d 680, 685 (N.D. Tex. 2006).

Reading the Code:
§ 2-314(3)

Read 2-314(3) and Comment 12.

Question 14. Recall that warranties that arise from a usage of trade or course of dealing are part of the "agreement" of the parties (the "bargain in fact"). *See* 1-201(b)(3) and the discussion of these terms in Assignment 1. Why are they considered "implied warranties" in Article 2?

2. Implied Warranty of Fitness for Particular Purpose under § 2-315

Unlike the implied warranty of merchantability, which (unless disclaimed or modified) attaches to all sales by merchants with respect to goods of the kind, the implied warranty of fitness for particular purpose attaches to only some sales transactions and there is no requirement that the seller be a merchant at all. The implied warranty of fitness is, as suggested by its title, a warranty that the goods are fit for the particular special purpose for which the buyer intends to use the goods, rather than for the general ordinary purpose of such goods, as with the implied warranty of merchantability. Not surprisingly, the warranty of fitness attaches only if the special purpose is made known to the seller, as you will see reflected in the particular requirements of § 2-315.

Reading the Code:
§ 2-315

Read 2-315.

Question 15. What are the elements that 2-315 requires the buyer to prove in order to establish its right to a warranty of fitness?

Question 16. Does the warranty of fitness have to be in writing?

Question 17. May the seller exclude or modify the warranty of fitness?

Question 18. Read Comment 1. What kind of evidence may establish that the seller "has reason to know" the particular purpose and the buyer's reliance even though the buyer does not "bring home to the seller actual knowledge"?

Question 19. Read Comment 2. How does "particular purpose" under 2-315 differ from "ordinary purpose" under 2-314(2)(c)? Consider something you recently bought and identify

(a) what the ordinary purpose of the item would be; and

(b) a particular purpose for which someone might purchase the item.

EXAMPLES AND ANALYSIS

Example E: *Keahole Fish LLC v. Skretting Canada Inc.* [7]

Keahole Point Fish, the operator of a fish farm, contacted Skretting Canada, a seller of fish feed, and requested that Skretting prepare a custom diet for its fish. Skretting provided four options for feed, including one that would substantially reduce the cost of the food by substituting poultry

---

[7] 971 F. Supp. 2d 1017 (D. Haw. 2013).

meat for some fishmeal. Keahole purchased the poultry meal feed and initially experienced good fish survival. After a number of months, however, Keahole reported poor eating and slowed growth, as well as increased mortality of the fish. In response to Keahole's inquiry, Skretting denied that it had changed the feed's nutritional components. Keahole switched to a high fishmeal feed from a competitor of Skretting, and the fish improved quickly and dramatically.

Keahole brought a number of claims against Skretting, including breach of the implied warranty of merchantability and the implied warranty of fitness for particular purpose. Skretting counterclaimed for unpaid invoices. Skretting moved for summary judgment against both warranty claims.

Skretting argued that no warranty of merchantability attached to the custom-designed fishmeal because there could not be an "ordinary purpose" for custom-made goods since there is no way to determine standards for ordinary performance. Keahole argued that a warranty of merchantability attaches to all products irrespective of any customization.

Skretting also claimed that the warranty of fitness for a particular purpose did not attach because it did not make feed recommendations to Keahole. Keahole's president said that he "relied on Skretting's global expertise and skill in formulating fish feed in deciding to continue to purchase the Kona Pacific feed from Skretting." He further explained that he was aware of Skretting's expertise through websites, advertisements, and the product sheet.

Analysis: The *Keahole* court denied Skretting's motion for summary judgment. The court concluded that there was a genuine issue of material fact whether Keahole could establish the elements of an implied warranty of fitness. The court agreed with Keahole that there could be both a warranty of merchantability and a warranty of fitness, declining to follow other cases that have found a "custom product exception" to the warranty of merchantability. While the court thought the custom product exception could apply to new products, the fishmeal at issue had been sold by Skretting for a number of years before the problems arose, so a standard for merchantability was ascertainable. Do you agree with the court's judgment on these points? What support can you offer from 2-314, 2-315, and their Comments?

What is the "ordinary purpose" for which the feed in *Keahole* would be used? What is the "particular purpose" claimed by Keahole? Are they the same or different? Even for standard products (not custom made), courts disagree about whether a particular use of goods can be both an "ordinary purpose" under 2-314 and a "particular purpose" under 2-315. In *Keahole*, the court allowed the buyer's case on both the implied warranties to proceed. Other courts might have determined that if goods are bought for a particular purpose, the warranty of merchantability cannot be claimed with respect to that purpose. Which do you think is the proper result? Note that, even if both claims are allowed, a buyer claiming breach of both warranties ultimately can prevail and get relief only on one theory.

Sometimes, a buyer claims a breach of the fitness warranty in addition to, and separate from, a claim for a breach of the warranty of merchantability. The case of *Gared Holdings v. Best Bolt Products* that follows presents an opportunity to see how one court looked at the combination of these two implied warranties. As you read the case, consider these questions:

(1) What facts support Gared's claim of a breach of merchantability?

    (a) What part of § 2-314 does Gared rely on for its breach claim?

    (b) On what basis did the court find Best Bolt to be a merchant with respect to goods of the kind? Do you think the court reached the correct result?

    (c) What are the elements of a merchantability cause of action? Read § 2-314, Comment 13.

(2) What facts support Gared's claim of breach of the warranty of fitness? Which language from § 2-315 proves troublesome for Gared's claim? See Comment 1.

(3) Which facts persuaded Judge Robb that the majority was not correct as to the warranty of fitness? Do you agree with the majority or the minority opinion?

GARED HOLDINGS, LLC v. BEST BOLT PRODUCTS, INC.

991 N.E.2d 1005 (Ind. Ct. App. 2013)

CRONE, Judge.

Case Summary

Gared Holdings, LLC ("Gared"), approached Best Bolt Products, Inc. ("Best Bolt"), to see whether Best Bolt could supply pulleys for use in basketball goal systems that Gared manufactures. Gared provided Best Bolt with samples of the pulleys that it had been using, but also indicated that there were problems with those pulleys. Gared did not provide detailed specifications to Best Bolt and did not specifically request a lubricated bushing, a cylindrical part that fits between the wheel and axle to reduce friction. Best Bolt produced some samples, and Gared had some testing performed on the pulleys, but did not discover that the pulleys lacked a lubricated bushing. The lack of lubrication caused the pulleys to seize up soon after the basketball goals were sold.

. . . .

Facts and Procedural History

. . . .

At issue in this case are two orders that Gared placed for pulleys. Gared uses pulleys in the basketball goal systems that it manufactures. The basketball goals are designed to hang from the ceiling and can be raised and lowered. The facts favorable to the judgment reflect that, during one of Sparks's regular sales calls in 2006, Turner asked him if Best Bolt could supply pulleys. Turner indicated that their current supplier, Inventory Sales, was going to raise the price, and she was hoping to find a less expensive pulley. Turner also indicated that there was a problem with cables slipping off the wheel and becoming lodged between the wheel and the side plate. Turner provided samples pulleys in two sizes, #3 and #5. Sparks told Turner, "I'll see what I can do." Sparks did not tell Turner that neither he personally nor Best Bolt generally had ever sold pulleys before.

. . . .

Best Bolt decided to source the pulleys through Dakota Engineering, which would manufacture the pulleys in China. The sample pulleys from

Gared were sent to Dakota's engineer in China, who sent back a sample. Joe Connerly, the engineering manager for Gared, examined the samples, measured the diameter, and looked for a proper gap between the wheel and side plate. He did not take the samples apart because they "appeared to be correct." Although he could not tell for sure without taking the pulley apart, he believed that the pulley contained a lubricated bushing because there was a small gap on each side of the wheel between the wheel and the side plate. However, the sample pulleys did not actually have a bushing.

Gared then sent the samples to St. Louis Labs, which performed the standard pull and side pull tests . . . .

On June 27, 2007, after receiving the test results, Turner placed an order with Best Bolt for 4995 #5 pulleys. On April 14, 2008, Turner placed an order for 2000 #3 pulleys and an additional 5000 #5 pulleys.

. . . .

In the fall of 2008, one of Gared's customers reported that a basketball goal had fallen part way to the floor. Connerly examined the goal system and determined that the pulley had stopped turning. . . . Connerly took the pulley apart and realized for the first time that the pulley did not have a bushing and was not lubricated in any way. Without any lubrication, the wheel and axle had become "frozen" together. Connerly conducted a cycling test on two Best Bolt pulleys, which involves repeatedly lifting and lowering a load. The pulleys each seized up after twenty-one cycles.

. . . .

A bench trial was held on June 5 through 7, 2012. It was undisputed that Gared did not specifically request that the pulley have a lubricated bushing. However, Gared attempted to show that a lubricated bushing was a standard or essential component of a pulley, and therefore a buyer would not typically need to make a specific request for a lubricated bushing. Connerly testified that he considered pulleys to be an "off-the-shelf" item that could be purchased from a catalog without needing to provide a drawing. He testified that a buyer would not have to specify that it have a lubricated bushing or bearing because "[t]hat's standard in the industry." Connerly stated that the pulleys that Gared has purchased from suppliers other than Best Bolt have all had lubricated bushings and did not have problems with seizing up. Connerly testified that a pulley without a lubricated bushing could work only "[f]or a short period of time," but not for the "expected life of the . . . pulley." He stated that the Best Bolt pulleys started failing less than a year after the basketball goal systems were sold, and he would expect a pulley to last more than a year. Connerly testified that he had not opted to perform a cycle test on the pulleys before approving them for purchase because "the pulleys that . . . are normally manufactured . . . it's a requirement of that pulley to be able to rotate. So when you purchase a pulley you expect it to be able to rotate and it was really no reason to do a cycle test at that point in time." After the problem arose with the Best Bolt pulleys, Connerly made a detailed drawing of a pulley "so that if we chose to go to . . . another supplier who was not a normal manufacturer of pulley[s] they would understand the requirements of manufacturing a pulley." However, when Gared started purchasing pulleys from Block, it did not provide the drawing to Block because Block had its own drawing.

[The trial court ruled against Gared on both warranty of merchantability and warranty for fitness for a particular purpose.]

As to Gared's claim for breach of the warranty of merchantability, the court's order states: "The evidence demonstrated that this was the first and last sale of pulleys by Best Bolt. In fact Best Bolt was merely the distributor and Gared was aware that Best Bolt was trying to find a company to manufacture the pulleys at a price acceptable to Gared."

As to Gared's claim for breach of the warranty of fitness for a particular purpose, the court's order noted that Gared was required to prove three things: (1) that Best Bolt had reason to know of Gared's particular purpose; (2) that Best Bolt had reason to believe that Gared was relying on Best Bolt's skill and judgment; and (3) that Gared in fact had relied on Best Bolt's skill and judgment. The court found that Best Bolt knew that the pulleys would be used in basketball goal systems. However, the court found that the evidence was unclear as to the second element and that Gared had not established the third element. . . .

Discussion and Decision

. . . .

II. Implied Warranty of Fitness for a Particular Purpose

. . . .

In an action for breach of the warranty of fitness for a particular purpose, the buyer must show: "(1) that seller must have had reason to know buyer's particular purpose, (2) that seller must have had reason to believe buyer was relying on seller's skill and judgment, and (3) that buyer in fact had relied on seller's skill and judgment." *Paper Mfrs. Co. v. Rescuers, Inc.,* 60 F. Supp. 2d 869, 881 (N.D. Ind. 1999). The trial court found that Gared proved the first element, that the evidence was unclear as to the second element, and that Gared had not proven the third element by a preponderance of the evidence.

On cross-examination, Connerly was questioned about whether Gared relied on Best Bolt's judgment:

Q. Knowing that your standard operating procedure was to check specifications and[/]or a drawing and[/]or a narrative and based upon your testimony that you did that in this case and that you tested . . . The pulleys the way you wanted and that you inspected them the way that you wanted to, isn't it a fact that you were not relying on Best Bolt's judgment as to what Gared needed for this Number Five (#5) pulley?

A. That would be correct.

. . . .

Q. Would you agree that Best Bolt never advised Gared that the Best Bolt pulley would do whatever it was that Gared required?

A. Not to my knowledge.

Q. In fact Gared made its own independent analysis that the pulleys would meet its requirements, isn't that right?

A. That's correct.

On redirect, Connerly testified as follows:

Q. [D]id you ever have any expectation that the Best Bolt pulleys would not have a lubricated bearing?

A. No.

Q. Or a bushing?

A. No.

Q. [D]id you rely on them to provide that?

A. Yes.

Connerly initially testified that Gared did not rely on Best Bolt's judgment, and while he later stated that he relied on Best Bolt to provide a lubricated bushing, it is clear from his testimony as a whole that he knew that the pulley needed to have a lubricated bushing and assumed that Best Bolt would know that, too. Gared again notes that the testing that was performed on the pulleys was not designed to show whether the pulley was properly lubricated. However, the evidence reflects that Gared determined what testing would be performed and did not rely on Best Bolt to perform any testing. The drawing that Connerly later produced demonstrates that Gared knew what it needed in a pulley and was capable of specifying its needs; Gared simply failed to do so. *See Adsit Co. v. Gustin*, 874 N.E.2d 1018, 1024-25 (Ind. Ct. App. 2007) (seller of vehicle seat covers did not breach warranty of merchantability by supplying seat covers that did not match interior of vehicle where buyer did not provide vehicle's VIN number or other information that would enable seller to determine the exact color needed). The evidence favorable to the judgment supports the trial court's conclusion that Gared failed to establish that it relied on Best Bolt's judgment to select a suitable pulley.

III. Implied Warranty of Merchantability

The trial court ruled that the implied warranty of merchantability did not apply because Best Bolt is not a merchant as that term is defined by Indiana's version of the Uniform Commercial Code. . . . The comments to [2-314] state, "A person making an isolated sale of goods is not a 'merchant' within the meaning of the full scope of this section and, thus, no warranty of merchantability would apply." Ind. Code § 26-1-2-314, cmt. 3. . . . The comments to [2-104] state that, in the context of the implied warranty of merchantability, the term "merchant" is restricted "to a much smaller group than everyone who is engaged in business and requires a professional status as to particular kinds of goods." Ind. Code § 26-1-2-104, cmt. 2. At the same time, our cases hold that the implied warranty of merchantability "is imposed by operation of law for the protection of the buyer and must be liberally construed in favor of the buyer." *Frantz v. Cantrell*, 711 N.E.2d 856, 859 (Ind. Ct. App. 1999).

Regarding Gared's claim for breach of the warranty of merchantability, the court's order states: "The evidence demonstrated that this was the first and last sale of pulleys by Best Bolt. In fact Best Bolt was merely the distributor and Gared was aware that Best Bolt was trying to find a company to manufacture the pulleys at a price acceptable to Gared." Appellant's App. at 20. The term "merchant" is not limited to manufacturers, and Best Bolt does not cite any authority that supports the proposition that a distributor cannot be a merchant.

Furthermore, the court's order is incorrect insofar as it states that Best Bolt made only one sale of pulleys. Best Bolt made two sales to Gared, and we also note that Best Bolt's vice president testified that Best Bolt would be willing to continue selling pulleys if it had a buyer.

. . . .

We conclude that the trial court erred by focusing on the fact that Best Bolt was a distributor rather than a manufacturer because that fact is not relevant to the analysis. We also conclude that the trial court erred by characterizing Best Bolt's experience with pulleys as a single sale where the undisputed evidence reflects that Best Bolt made two sales and was willing to continue selling pulleys if it had a buyer. *See McHugh v. Carlton*, 369 F. Supp. 1271, 1277 (D.S.C. 1974) (service station that would procure and sell recapped tires upon request of customer was a merchant of recapped tires even though service station did not regularly stock and sell recapped tires). Based on the authorities that we have examined, we conclude that Best Bolt is a merchant with respect to pulleys.

We turn then to whether Best Bolt breached the implied warranty of merchantability. . . .

The undisputed evidence establishes that the ordinary purpose of a pulley is to bear a dynamic load. Several of Gared's witnesses testified that a lubricated bushing was an essential part of a pulley, that lubricated bushings were standard in the industry, that it was unreasonable to make pulleys without lubricated bushings, and that a pulley without a lubricated bushing would inevitably have a short useful life. On the other hand, Hylton testified that he was aware of pulleys made without lubricated bushings and opined that "under certain load—static load or . . . very low dynamic loads a non[-]bushed pulley could work just as well as a bushed pulley." Because the evidence is in conflict and the trial court did not reach the issue, we remand for the trial court to determine whether Best Bolt breached the warranty of merchantability. Depending on the trial court's resolution of this issue, it may also be necessary to reconsider the portion of Best Bolt's counterclaim dealing with #5 pulleys.

Conclusion

We conclude that the trial court's judgment on Gared's claims of breach of contract and breach of the implied warranty of fitness for a particular purpose is supported by the evidence, and we affirm as to those issues. However, we conclude that the trial court erred in ruling that Best Bolt was not a merchant. We therefore remand for the trial court to determine whether Best Bolt breached the implied warranty of merchantability, and if so, whether that alters the result of Best Bolt's counterclaim.

Affirmed in part and remanded.

ROBB, CHIEF JUDGE, concurring with separate opinion

I concur in the majority's result with respect to Gared's breach of contract and implied warranty of merchantability claims. I respectfully dissent, however, from the resolution of the implied warranty of fitness for a particular purpose claim.

The implied warranty of fitness for a particular purpose occurs where the seller has reason at the time of contracting to know of any particular purpose for which the goods are being purchased and the buyer is relying on the seller's skill or judgment in choosing suitable goods for that purpose. See *Irmscher Suppliers, Inc. v. Schuler*, 909 N.E.2d 1040, 1048 n.4 (Ind. Ct. App. 2009). The trial court found that Gared had proved Best Bolt knew of the particular purpose for which the goods would be used—to raise and lower basketball backboards. I believe when Gared asked Best Bolt to procure pulleys and Best Bolt agreed to do so, Gared was relying on Best Bolt to offer a pulley that would suit this purpose and further, that Gared demonstrated that reliance when it did not test the pulleys for lubrication because, as the majority notes in the discussion of the implied warranty of merchantability, there was testimony indicating a lubricated bushing is an essential part of a pulley and is standard in the industry. Non-lubricated bushings could bear a static load or low dynamic load, but not the load Best Bolt knew these pulleys would be bearing. Gared gave Best Bolt a sample pulley, and although Gared did not want an exact replica of that pulley because they were having quality issues with the cable separating and jamming between parts of the pulley, there were no quality issues with the lubricated bushing and Best Bolt, offering to procure a suitable replacement, held itself out to have the ability to judge what would be suitable.

I would reverse the trial court's judgment in favor of Best Bolt on the implied warranty of fitness for a particular purpose claim.

APPLYING THE CODE

Problem 10-1.

After Irving purchased a used Audi car from Frankfurt Motors, he tried to register the car. The Department of Motor Vehicles informed Irving that he could not register the car because it was stolen. Did Frankfurt Motors breach its contract with Irving? What if, instead, after Irving received the car, Jane brought an action to recover it from Irving and asserted that she, rather than Irving, was the owner? Assume Irving successfully defended the action brought by Jane, but had to rent a car while his Audi was impounded by the authorities and had to pay legal fees that were not recoverable from Jane. Would Irving have any redress against Frankfurt Motors?

Problem 10-2.

Pure Country Weavers (Pure Country) is engaged in the manufacture and sale of textile art. Bristar imports and sells products. Paradise Shops is engaged in the retail business of gifts and specialty stores. Pure Country owns the copyright for a design called "In the Wild," which includes an African safari motif with animal skin patterns and animal depictions. Bristar sold bags and luggage to retailers including Paradise Shops that included the In the Wild design. Does Pure Country have any claim against Bristar or Paradise Shops? *See* 2-312 Comment 3.

Problem 10-3.

Assume that a warranty under 2-314 has been created. Determine which particular parts of 2-314(2) have been breached in each set of facts. If more than one subsection may apply, determine which breach will be easier to establish.

(a) A restaurant patron orders a glass of wine and is cut by a glass chip on the rim of the glass. (Assume the warranty is given by the restaurant, not the restaurant's supplier.)

(b) The manager of a delicatessen orders four gallon-size bottles of colossal-size olives (this is a size specified in a federal regulation), containing 90 olives apiece. The label on each bottle says that a bottle contains "90 colossal-size olives." The four bottles delivered to the deli are gallon size and contain colossal olives only, but the bottles contain 110, 85, 90, and 80 olives, respectively.

(c) A buyer purchases from Boat and Motor Mart an Osprey 30 sport-fishing boat, which occasionally leaks. During routine maintenance and repainting of the hull, the repair facility informs the buyer that the hull of the boat and is flawed because of a number of poorly designed patches, where Osprey had converted the hull from an inboard to an outboard engine. An expert concludes that the patches will entirely fail at some point during the boat's useful life.

(d) The seller represented to the buyer of a trailer that the trailer was a year 2000 model when in fact it was a 1999 model.

Problem 10-4.

These fact situations explore issues surrounding the meaning of the warranty in 2-314(2)(c). For each scenario, consider whether the goods "are fit for the ordinary purpose for which such goods are used." What are the best arguments for and against that conclusion? Assume the goods are bought from a merchant who deals in goods of this kind. Are there additional facts you would want to know?

(a) A couple purchased new windows when remodeling their home, which was built in 1800. Some of the windows were equipped with screens that the owners could pull down to prevent the entry of insects while the windows were open to obtain fresh air. The screens did not function properly, and many insects entered the home when the owners opened the windows.

(b) A restaurant patron chips a tooth on a chicken bone in what the menu says is "homemade chicken salad." Would your analysis be affected if the restaurant is run by a sole proprietor who makes everything from fresh ingredients? If the chicken salad is very chunky? Finely ground up? Not billed as "homemade"?

(c)   A buyer of a new motor home develops asthma and can no longer use the vehicle because of formaldehyde fumes from the plywood paneling. Assume that the buyer can prove that this level of formaldehyde fumes is harmful to 8% of the population.

(d)   A cigarette lighter is taken out of a purse by the purchaser's child, who starts a serious fire while playing with the lighter. You represent the purchaser seeking recovery for injury from the manufacturer of the lighter. You discover that each year, fires started under similar circumstances cause an average of 120 deaths, 750 personal injuries, and $300 million in property damage.

Problem 10-5.

Consider 2-315 Comment 2 when analyzing the following facts, which are designed to expand your understanding of the difference between fitness for an ordinary purpose (2-314(2)(c)) and fitness for a particular purpose (2-315).

(a)   Golden wanted new dental veneers that were "super white." After seeing an advertisement from Den-Mat Corp., Golden contacted the company and received a brochure, and Den-Mat referred Golden to Dr. Gill, a nearby dentist, who was authorized to apply its veneers. After Dr. Gill applied the veneers, they faded, developing a gray cast within the first fifteen months. Was a warranty of merchantability (fitness for the ordinary purpose) created and, if so, was it breached? Might there be a 2-314(3) warranty here based upon industry standards for veneers? Was a warranty of fitness for a particular purpose created and, if so, was it breached?

(b)   The Chases purchased a four-wheel all-terrain vehicle (ATV) for their children, ages 14 and 12 from Honda of Columbus. The manufacturer designed the ATV for drivers age 16 and older, but the salesman indicated the ATV was suitable for the Chase children. A month after the purchase, when the children drove the ATV and tried to apply the brakes to avoid a pothole and stop the ATV, it did not stop and the children were injured. Investigation reveals that the ATV's brakes were out of adjustment. The ATV owner's manual included a section related to maintenance and adjustment of the ATV's brakes. Was a warranty of merchantability (fitness for the ordinary purpose) created and, if so, was it breached? Was a warranty of fitness for a particular purpose created and, if so, was it breached?

(c)   These scenarios involve sales of house paint. Assume the paint was bought from a paint store. Also assume that most house paint is sold with a label that says it should be used when the temperature will remain above 40° F for six hours. For each set of facts below, was a warranty of merchantability (fitness for the ordinary purpose) created and, if so, was it breached? Was a warranty of fitness for a particular purpose created and, if so, was it breached?

1.   Label on exterior house paint says to paint only when temperature remains above 40° F for six hours. Buyer tells salesperson she wants to paint at 35-40° F. Salesperson points to a specific paint and responds, "You can use this paint all the way down to 30° F." Buyer paints when it is 35-40° F, but the paint crystallizes and flakes off because the salesperson is wrong.

2.   Label on exterior low-temperature paint says to apply paint only between 35° and 45° F. Buyer applies it at 50° F, and it dries almost immediately with streaks and brush marks.

(d)   Buyer manufactures liquid wheatgrass, which it sells in a bottle. Buyer contracted with seller for bottle caps, providing seller the specifications of its bottles. Unfortunately, seller's bottlecaps did not provide the appropriate seal on the bottles, allowing air to penetrate and spoil the wheatgrass and causing some of the bottles to leak. Was a warranty of merchantability, fitness, or both created and breached here by the seller?

Problem 10-6.

Dr. Muther informed Griffin that his medical partnership needed a spinal scanner that would produce acceptable scans for neurological and psychiatric purposes. Griffin assured Dr. Muther that the Pfizer CT Scanner would produce acceptable scans. With this understanding, Dr. Muther purchased the Pfizer CT Scanner. Upon installation, though, the scanner did not perform acceptable scans for diagnosis, and Dr. Muther was unable to use the scanner for routine spinal purposes. What implied warranties, if any, were created? Were any such warranties breached? Assume that the seller's agents after installation told Dr. Muther that the scanner would produce the spinal scans and that any problems with the scanner could be resolved. Would the parol evidence rule bar the introduction of such statements?

Problem 10-7.

Lisa visited Pete's Exercise Boutique, an exercise equipment shop that advertises widely as "The Place to Go for Personalized Exercise Equipment." She consulted personally with the owner, Pete, explaining that she had just had a baby, and was looking for exercise equipment to help her get back into her pre-baby physical condition in three months, when she was due to resume her job as a fitness instructor. In the store, she asked Pete what equipment he'd recommend to target the muscles in her stomach and waist. He showed her a display labeled "Trimming the Stomach and Waist," and said, "Anything in this section should do the trick. However, if you really want to attack that area, I'd recommend that you try something else." He took her to a display labeled "Trimming the Thighs," and said, "If you take this Thighslimmer 2000X, and bend it around like this, and use it to do stomach crunches instead of thigh presses for at least 10 minutes every day, I guarantee you'll lose at least three inches off your waist in three months. Many people have started using this on their stomachs this way, and they're reporting good results." Lisa responded, "Humphhh. I don't believe that for a second. But, I did read a good review of this in the latest issue of Consumer Reports, and I do need to work on the thighs, too, so I might as well buy it." Lisa bought the Thighslimmer, which did not come with any sort of packaging or labeling. She used it faithfully every day for 10 minutes of stomach crunches in the way Pete had demonstrated, as well as for 10 minutes of thigh exercises. After three months, Lisa had lost 2 inches off her waist and 2 inches off her thighs. Does Lisa have a claim for breach of a warranty of merchantability? Does Lisa have a claim for breach of a warranty of fitness for a particular purpose?

Assignment 11
Creation of Express Warranties
§ 2-313

This Assignment continues to explore the first step in analyzing warranties, identified at the beginning of the Chapter: determining what warranties are included in a contract. Assignment 10 focused on implied warranties. We now turn our attention to express warranties. An express warranty is a warranty made affirmatively by words or actions of the seller promising something about the goods. All contracts for sale of goods contain at least the express warranty that the goods are what is named in the contract (e.g., a car, a cow, a bushel of wheat). As we will see, contracts for sale may contain a host of other express warranties as well. Although contracts for sale may also include other kinds of promises, the promises about the goods—the warranties—are among the most important promises and often form the basis of complaints about problems that arise in contract performance.

Determining the nature of express warranties given by the seller involves several related inquiries: What words or actions sufficiently indicate that a promise has been made about the goods, and when do the promises amount to mere "puffing" that don't really promise anything? At what point in the contract-for-sale transaction does the promise have to be made to constitute a warranty? Can a remote seller (e.g., one who sells the goods to a third party, who then sells them to the buyer) be found to have made a warranty promise to the buyer? This Assignment will help you answer these questions.

LEARNING OUTCOMES AND OBJECTIVES

At the completion of this Assignment, you should be able to

- differentiate express warranties made by a seller from implied warranties made by a seller;
- explain how express warranties are created, as well as when a seller's words and conduct do not result in the creation of a warranty; and
- determine whether particular circumstances result in creation of an express warranty that binds the seller in the event of its breach.

A. Creating an Express Warranty

Express warranties are, as the name suggests, warranties that are expressly made by the seller, not implied by law from the circumstance. Although "express" connotes affirmative "expression" (i.e, from words used to communicate), express warranties may also arise from conduct. Section 2-313 governs express warranties from the seller to the *immediate* buyer. In Assignment 13, we will consider how these warranties might be extended to parties other than the immediate buyer.

Express warranties are particularly important to buyers, as they represent a buyer's opportunity to recover when goods do not perform as promised. While express warranties may be formal promises about the goods made to a buyer as part of a warranty document or booklet, express warranties may also arise from less formal representations made by the seller to the buyer outside the confines of what the seller calls a "warranty." For example, advertising and oral statements made by a salesperson may create express warranties. Because of the broad range of words and conduct that may create an express warranty, it is sometimes difficult to determine if an express warranty was made and, if so, the nature of the warranty.

Generally, an express warranty may be created by three types of representations by sellers, none of which depend upon the use of words like "warranty" or "guarantee" and none of which need to be in writing. First, "affirmations of fact or promises" made by the seller to the buyer that relate to the goods (such as oral statements by a seller) can be express warranties. Second, "descriptions of the goods" (such as product labels) can be express warranties. Finally, any "sample or model" provided by the seller can create an express warranty. Of course, the more formal the communication from the seller to the buyer is, the more likely the representations will form the basis for an express warranty (such as a contract proposal, package insert, or photograph). Due to the expansive recognition of express warranties, a seller may not even realize a communication constitutes an express warranty.

Each of the three ways to create an express warranty arises from a particular way in which a seller communicates with a buyer regarding the goods and must relate in a specific way to the goods sold. Express warranties are "agreed upon" by the parties, so they are more difficult to later disclaim by agreement (as we will see in Assignment 12).

As you will see in the examples below, buyers sometimes make claims against the immediate seller (the person from whom the buyer bought the goods) and sometimes make claims against remote sellers (those who sold the goods up the distribution chain). At the end of this Assignment and in Assignment 13 we will consider under what circumstances a remote seller will be found to have made express warranties or otherwise be held liable to a remote buyer. For now, as you read through the examples in this Assignment, concentrate only on whether an express warranty is created by the representations made and assume that both direct and remote sellers in the examples may be found to have created express warranties.

Reading the Code: § 2-313(1)

Read 2-313(1).

Question 1.

List (separately) the elements the buyer would have to establish to prove the existence of a warranty under subsection (a), under subsection (b), and under subsection (c). What is the content of the warranty created in each instance? What does the word "express" mean in this context? See Comment 1.

EXAMPLES AND ANALYSIS

Example A: *Stanley v. Central Garden & Pet Corp.*[1]

Stanley purchased a "Nylabone" Double Action Chew toy for her French bulldog, which became ill after chewing off and swallowing a piece of the toy. Stanley claimed that the seller breached an express warranty through its general marketing program and other assertions, through statements found in Nylabone literature that "Nylabone manufactures dog chews, bones, treats and toys designed to meet the chewing need of any dog—no matter the breed, size, or chew strength." Moreover, guidelines for the chew toys are provided on the back of the packaging, under a tab that advises buyers to "review guidelines for more products and tips." The guidelines stated:

---

[1]   891 F. Supp. 2d 757 (D. Md. 2012).

NON-EDIBLE CHEW PRODUCTS (Plastic, Rubber, Nylon), although non-toxic, are NOT intended for consumption. During normal chewing, tiny bristle-like projections are raised, which help clean teeth. If they are ingested, they should pass through. A dog should not be able to break off large pieces of any Nylabone Non-Edible Chew. If you think your dog swallowed a large piece of a Non-Edible Chew, take the chew away and contact your veterinarian for advice.

No dog chew toy is totally indestructible. Frequently inspect any chew before giving it to your dog to make sure it's whole and intact, with no missing pieces. Replace a Non-Edible Chew when knuckle ends are worn down, or if it becomes too small to chew safely.

Analysis: The court granted the seller's motion to dismiss the express warranty claim, finding that the statement did not create an express warranty that the product was safe for her particular dog. The court observed that the advertising statement indicated that Nylabone manufactures a wide variety of products. What arguments support Stanley's claim under the text of 2-313? What arguments support the court's finding that the advertising statement did not create an express warranty under the text of 2-313? Do you agree with the court's reading of the Code? What does the outcome in *Stanley* tell you about the generality or specificity of the promise required to create a warranty under 2-313?

1. "Part of the Basis of the Bargain" and its Relationship to Reliance

Note that, while the types of representations made by sellers listed in §§ 2-313(1) (a), (b), and (c) are different, all of the parts of subsection (1) require a buyer to prove the communication is "part of the basis of the bargain." Accordingly, this is a key Code requirement for creation of express warranties. Under the Uniform Sales Act, the predecessor statute to Article 2, a promise or an affirmation of fact created an express warranty "if the natural tendency of such affirmation or promise is to induce the buyer to purchase the goods, and if the buyer purchases them relying thereon." In effect, the older rule required that the buyer have reasonably relied on the affirmation of promise. Under Article 2, the requirement that the representation be "part of the basis of the bargain" is undefined, and courts have come to varying conclusions about the meaning of the phrase, disagreeing about whether reliance by the buyer is necessary for the creation of a warranty, as it was under the Uniform Sales Act.

Even though "basis of the bargain" is part of the requirements of § 2-313, courts do not always explain the reasoning behind their conclusions that a buyer has or has not proven the element. Courts that have discussed the issue expressly tend to follow one of three different approaches regarding how and when a representation becomes part of the basis of the bargain. These approaches are summarized below with a short-hand name for each for ease of reference. All turn on how the court views whether and how reliance is required to establish "basis of the bargain."

- *Reliance approach:* This approach is similar to the pre-UCC requirement of reliance. A seller's representation about the goods becomes part of the basis of the bargain and therefore becomes an express warranty if the buyer can prove, by a preponderance of the evidence, that it decided to buy the goods based, at least in part, on the seller's representation. Of course, the seller can prevent the buyer from sustaining its burden of proof by challenging the buyer's factual showing or by directly establishing the buyer's non-reliance on the representation, perhaps showing that the buyer knew nothing of the representation at the time of contract formation, or that the representation was a draft term that the parties did not agree on, or that the buyer had reason to doubt the truth of the representation and therefore did not rely on it.

- *Comment 3 approach*: Based on § 2-313 Comment 3 (and to a lesser extent, on Comment 8), some courts have concluded that the buyer need only show that the seller made a representation about the goods during the bargain preceding the formation of the parties' contract, but need not show reliance. This interpretation focuses the inquiry on the seller's conduct in making a representation, not on the buyer's awareness of or reaction to that conduct. The buyer's showing creates a rebuttable presumption that the seller's representation was part of the basis of the bargain. The seller can rebut that presumption by clear affirmative proof that the buyer did not rely at all on the seller's representation in deciding to buy the goods.

- *Non-reliance:* This approach is also based on part of Comment 3. Under this approach, the mere fact that the seller made a statement in the process of marketing the goods is sufficient to make it part of the basis of the bargain in a subsequent sale transaction, regardless of buyer's non-reliance or even lack of knowledge of the representation. In the cases adopting this approach, the representations were made directly to the buyer, accompanied the goods in the packaging, or were part of a catalog or other public advertising issued prior to the contract being formed between buyer and seller.

Reading the Code:
§ 2-313

Read 2-313 Comments 3 and 8.

Question 2. Using the text of 2-313 and the language of Comments 3 and 8, how would you support adopting (a) the reliance approach, (b) the Comment 3 approach, and (c) the non-reliance approach?

EXAMPLES AND ANALYSIS

Example B: *Goldemberg v. Johnson & Johnson Consumer Companies, Inc.*[2]

Goldemberg brought a breach of warranty action against Johnson & Johnson, claiming the Aveeno personal care products the buyer purchased were not made from natural ingredients as marketed. The seller moved to dismiss the claim.

Analysis: Denying the motion as to the express warranty, the court held that under New York law, a buyer must plead: (i) a material statement amounting to a warranty; (ii) reliance on the warranty; (iii) breach of the warranty; and (iv) injury caused by the breach. The buyer satisfied the pleading requirements by alleging reliance on the labelling and advertising containing the "Active Naturals" statements concerning the Aveeno products. Which of the three approaches to "basis of the bargain" described above did this court take?

---

[2]   8 F. Supp. 3d 457 (S.D.N.Y. 2014).

Example C: *In re Hydroxycut Marketing & Sales Practices Litigation*[3]

The buyers of weight loss products brought a nationwide class action against the retailers for claims, including breach of express warranty. The retailer moved to dismiss the warranty claims.

Analysis: The court, granting the motion, held that in California "[a]lthough reliance may not need to be proven to establish the formation of an express warranty, at minimum, the buyer must have heard, seen, or received the representations in order for them to form the basis of the bargain." Which of the three approaches to "basis of the bargain" described above did this court take?

In making out its case for the existence of an express warranty, the buyer might introduce facts to establish one or more of the following:

- That the seller made a particular representation before the contract was entered.

- That the buyer knew of the representation before entering into the contract.

- That the buyer relied on the seller's representation in entering the contract.

In rebutting the buyer's case, the seller might be able to introduce facts to establish one or more of the following:

- That the seller did not make a particular representation before the contract was entered.

- That the buyer did not know of the representation before entering into the contract.

- That the buyer did not rely on the seller's representation in entering the contract.

Question 3.

(a) In a reliance jurisdiction, which of the facts above must a buyer prove by a preponderance of the evidence to establish that the

---

[3]   299 F.R.D. 648 (S.D. Cal. 2014).

representation was "part of the basis of the bargain"? Which of the facts above should a seller seek to establish in rebuttal?

(b) In a Comment 3 jurisdiction, which of the facts above must a buyer prove by a preponderance of the evidence to establish that the representation was "part of the basis of the bargain"? Which of the facts above should a seller seek to establish in rebuttal?

(c) In a non-reliance jurisdiction, which of the facts above must a buyer prove by a preponderance of the evidence to establish that the representation was "part of the basis of the bargain"? Which of the facts above should a seller seek to establish in rebuttal?

(d) Look back at your list of elements of an express warranty in Question 1. How would you modify that list in view of your understanding of "part of the basis of the bargain?

Question 4. Which statement is true in both a Comment 3 jurisdiction and a reliance jurisdiction? Why are the others not true?

(a) Buyer establishes a warranty merely by proving that it was aware of the seller's representation.

(b) A representation cannot be part of the basis of the bargain if seller proves buyer's non-reliance.

(c) A buyer will always be able to prove basis of the bargain by producing the packaging with which the goods were sold.

(d) The seller's representation must be the sole reason motivating buyer to buy the goods.

2. Representations in Advertising

Because so many claims about products occur in sales literature and advertisements, whether such promotional materials become part of the basis of the bargain is a point of contention in many suits brought by disgruntled buyers. In *Cipollone v. Liggett Group, Inc.*, 893 F.2d 541 (3d Cir. 1990), a consumer injured by years of smoking cigarettes sued the sellers, including a claim for breach of express warranties in its advertisements (claims that the cigarettes were "mild," and that the brand cigarettes the plaintiff smoked were "better and safer for you" or had filters that made them cleaner and safer). The sellers sought to introduce evidence that the plaintiff knew about health consequences of smoking and so could not have relied on the statements in the advertisements. The court applied § 2-313 and formulated the following approach for assertions made in advertisements:

- To gain a presumption that the buyer relied on the representations in an advertisement and that they are therefore part of the basis of the bargain, the buyer must show that, at the time of purchase, the buyer had read, heard, or seen the advertisement containing the representations. This is similar to the requirement in Comment 3 jurisdictions that the buyer show the seller made the representations during the bargaining process.

- The seller may rebut that presumption with proof that the buyer did not believe the advertisement, which would create a rebuttable presumption of non-reliance.

- The buyer may counter the seller's proof of non-belief (and its presumption of non-reliance) with proof that the buyer nonetheless relied on the seller's representations, even without believing them. In effect, *Cipollone* allows a buyer to rely not on the truth of the assertion, but on the seller's apparent willingness to stand behind the assertions made in the advertisement. The court noted that "[i]t is possible to disbelieve, but still rely on the existence of a warranty. In this sense, the buyer can 'buy' a lawsuit." (But, the court also noted, such a buyer could receive only economic damages, not consequential damages, which could have been avoided or mitigated.)

Cippollone has been adopted by a minority of jurisdictions and has so far been applied only to advertising claims (though none of the jurisdictions has defined "advertisement"). In theory, the conclusion—that a buyer may rely on claims it does not believe—could be applied in reliance and Comment 3 jurisdictions as well, though no court has done so. Similarly, the *Cippolone* "reliance despite unbelief" could also be applied by analogy more broadly to other representations made by sellers.

Reading the Code

Question 5. Return to the list preceding Question 3 of facts that buyer or seller might be able to prove related to a warranty claim. In a *Cipollone* jurisdiction, assuming that the representation was in an advertisement, which of the facts listed must a buyer prove by a preponderance of the evidence to establish the advertisement was "part of the basis of the bargain?" If the buyer gains a presumption by showing those facts, what is the nature of the presumption? Which of the facts listed in Question 3 should the seller seek to establish in rebuttal? What additional facts not listed might the buyer or seller introduce to establish that the advertisement was, or was not, part of the basis of the bargain?

B. The Defense of "Puffing"

As you probably understand from seeing and hearing the wide range of advertisements and sales claims made in the marketplace, some statements made by sellers about goods are not the kind that buyers do or ought to rely upon in making purchases because they are too general or vague or promotional. These statements might be thought of as "just sales talk." Statements of that kind are known as "puffing" or "puffery" and do not create express warranties under § 2-313. But just what statements fit into that category?

Reading the Code:
§ 2-313(2)

Read 2-313(2) and Comments 4 and 8.

Question 6. From 2-313(2) and the Comments, make a list of what additional factors matter in determining whether a statement creates an express warranty.

Section 2-313(2) may be seen as furnishing an additional element to 2-313: a statement of value or seller's opinion or commendation of the goods does not constitute an express warranty. Alternatively, the provisions on puffing may be seen not as adding an element, but as clarifying when a representation is not "part of the basis of the bargain" or identifying when no promise or affirmation of fact has been made, thus amplifying the elements established by 2-313(1)(a).

Courts have held that a seller's statement is puffing if a reasonable person would not take the representation seriously. Seller's statements of opinion or commendation of the goods also are puffing because opinions are not measurable or objective and because their meaning varies from person to person. Seller's commendations often exaggerate the degree of quality of the product, and such exaggerations are reasonably to be expected of a seller. Cases frequently use the following test for differentiating between warranty and opinion: "whether the seller asserts a fact of which the buyer is ignorant or merely states an opinion or judgment on a matter of which the seller has no special knowledge and on which the buyer may be expected also to have an opinion and to exercise his judgment." *See, e.g., Royal Bus. Mach., Inc. v. Lorraine Corp.*, 633 F.2d 34, 41 (7th Cir. 1980); *Artistic Carton Co. v. Thelamco, Inc.*, 70 UCC Rep. Serv. 2d 621 (N.D. Ind. 2009); *Vladmir Ltd. v. Pac. Parts Supply Co., Inc.*, 2009 WL 3719566 (W.D. Tex. 2009), *on reconsideration in part*, 75 Fed. R. Serv. 3d 80 (W.D. Tex. 2009); *Tribe v. Peterson*, 964 P.2d 1238 (Wyo. 1998); *Garriffa v. Taylor*, 675 P.2d 1284 (Wyo. 1984); *Helm v. Kingston*, 2011 WL 6746064 (Tex. Ct. App. 2011); *Carpenter v. Alberto Culver Co.*, 184 N.W.2d 547 (Mich. Ct. App. 1970).

UCC case law on what is and is not puffing is fairly consistent at either end of the spectrum, but very inconsistent in the middle. According to leading commentators, "[A]nyone who says he can consistently tell a 'puff' from a warranty is a fool or a liar. . . ." White et. al., *Uniform Commercial Code*, § 9.4 (6th ed. 2009). For instance, in sales of used goods between two consumers, the following statements have been held to be puffing and therefore not express warranties: that the car was "in good shape," was "in excellent condition," and that an outboard motor was in "perfect running condition" (in conjunction with a description of damage to the motor). In other sales of used goods between consumers, the following statements were held to be express warranties and not puffing: that the car was in "good mechanical shape or condition," was "a good reliable car," was in "A-1 shape" and "mechanically perfect," had "no problems," was "road ready" (after buyer said it wanted a car without mechanical problems).

The puffing defense arose in the mid-1800s when caveat emptor ("buyer beware") ruled the marketplace. There often was just a single buyer and seller, and the buyer often had the opportunity and ability to inspect the goods before the contract was entered into. Accordingly, some courts have allowed the defense primarily when the buyer is capable of checking the veracity of the seller's statement because, in such circumstances, the buyer's loss is caused by the buyer's failure to check rather than by the seller's faulty statement. However, other courts have refused to impose on the buyer a duty to check the veracity of the seller's statements and have not allowed the puffing defense on that basis.

The defense of puffing is not limited to claims of breach of warranty; it also is a defense to misrepresentation and false advertising, so applications of the definition in cases litigating those claims are relevant to defining puffing for the purposes of Article 2. The following factors often influence courts toward determining that a seller's statement is puffing and may be used as a starting place for argument:

- General rather than specific statement

- Hedged rather than unqualified statement

- Phrased as opinion rather than fact

- Medium of communication (oral rather than written, or in informal statement rather than in formal written contract)

- Experimental rather than standard goods

- Statement refers to a consequence of buying the goods rather than to an aspect of the goods

- Defect is not a hidden or unexpected nonconformity

- Claim is not capable of objective measurement or being adjudged true or false

- Unreasonableness of buyer's reliance on the statement

- Seller not significantly more sophisticated or knowledgeable than buyer

- Bargain price rather than premium price for the goods

- Usage of trade suggests buyer should not rely on statement

EXAMPLES AND ANALYSIS

Example D: *In re Scotts EZ Seed Litigation*[4]

The seller and manufacturer sold Scotts Turf Builder EZ Seed (EZ Seed), a combination mulch-grass product. The EZ Seed was labeled with certain qualities, in particular:

- Is "WaterSmart"

- "Grows Anywhere! Guaranteed"

- "Makes the Most Of Every Drop"

- "Grows in Tough Conditions! Guaranteed!"

- Is "Drought tolerant"

- Is "[t]he revolutionary seeding mix that takes care of the seed for you, so you can grow thick, beautiful grass ANYWHERE," including "Dry, sunny areas," "Dense shade," and "Even grows on pavement!"

- Is a "premium quality" product that "is developed to thrive in virtually every condition—harsh sun, dense shade, and even spreads to repair wear and tear. The result—thicker, beautiful, long lasting grass!"

The EZ Seed package promised superior performance and even included a picture depicting a patch of grass grown using EZ Seed and one of a patch of grass grown using ordinary seed. Next to the pictures the label described the potential growth further: "50% THICKER WITH HALF THE WATER††" and "††Results 32 days after planting; each watered at half the recommended rate for ordinary seed. Results may vary. (Subject to proper care.")" Home Depot and Lowe's in-store advertising displays contained these same statements, but the sellers were not involved with the manufacture of the EZ Seed.

The buyers brought suit on claims that included breach of express warranty, alleging that the EZ Seed did not grow grass when used as directed by the manufacturer.

Analysis: The court found that many of the labeled statements concerning the seed were only opinions, and therefore puffing, and did not create express

[4] 2013 WL 2303727 (S.D.N.Y. 2013).

warranties, including the statements "WaterSmart," "Drought tolerant," "Grows Anywhere! Guaranteed," "Makes the Most of Every Drop," and "Grows in Tough Conditions! Guaranteed!" The court found that other statements, though, were not puffing and could create express warranties, including the statements that the seed grows grass "50% thicker with half the water" compared to "ordinary seed" and that the seed was "developed to thrive in virtually every condition—harsh sun, dense shade, and even spreads to repair wear and tear," because these statements promised that the seed would perform in specific and measurable ways.

In addition, the court held that the buyers could state a breach of implied warranty of merchantability claim against the sellers because grass seed that does not grow any grass is not fit for its ordinary purpose.

What arguments would you make to support a judgment on the merits in favor of the buyers based on the text of 2-313 and the Comments? What arguments would you make in favor of the seller on the merits? Review Comment 8. Do you agree with the outcome in this case? Why or why not?

C. Representations Made after Contract Formation

The descriptions of the three approaches to determining whether a warranty is "part of basis of the bargain" indicated that a representation must be made before the contract is formed between seller and buyer in order to create an express warranty. Most representations that become warranties are, indeed, made during the formation process, but there is some flexibility in this requirement. Comment 7 to § 2-313 states:

> The precise time when words of description or affirmation are made or samples are shown is not material. The sole question is whether the language or samples or models are fairly to be regarded as part of the contract. If language is used after the closing of the deal (as when the buyer when taking delivery asks and receives an additional assurance), the warranty becomes a modification, and need not be supported by consideration if it is otherwise reasonable and in order (§ 2-209).

Not all statements made after the sale become part of the contract. The Supreme Court of New Mexico ruled in *Salazar v. D.WB.H., Inc.*, 192 P.3d 1205 (N.M. 2008) that a comment by an employee of an automobile repair shop to a customer picking up her repaired car indicating she should return the car if she had any problems with the used engine the shop had installed did not constitute an express warranty. The court noted that an express warranty can be made after a contract is formed, but must still be part of the basis of the bargain. This statement, the court concluded, was merely a part of "good customer service," as the employee stated, not part of the basis of the bargain. *Id. See also* Comment 7.

EXAMPLES AND ANALYSIS

Example E: *Kraft v. Staten Island Boat Sales, Inc.* [5]

Kraft purchased from Staten Island Boat Sales, Inc. (Staten Island) a power boat that had been manufactured by Silverton Marine Corporation (Silverton). Upon delivery of the boat, a Staten Island representative and Kraft discovered leaking between the hull and the deck. Even after repairs, the boat continued to leak. Eventually, black mold developed in the hull of the boat. Kraft brought claims, including breach of express warranty, against both Staten Island and Silverton. Kraft's documents in support of the express warranty claim against Staten Island included the seller's pre-delivery service record (PDSR). The PDSR was a 53-point checklist completed by the retailer upon sale of a boat covering categories such as "pre-launch" through "final check." Several of the boxes noted "no leaks." The PDSR, which was completed eight months after Kraft entered into the contract to buy the boat, was part of the process required by the manufacturer to trigger its warranty obligations.

Staten Island moved for judgment on the pleadings, and Silverton moved for summary judgment on the buyer's warranty claims.

Analysis: Which part(s) of 2-313 might be at issue here? How should the court rule on the seller's motion for summary judgment? Was the PDSR "part of the basis of the bargain"? Which of the facts, if true, would support an argument in favor of Kraft? Why might the much-later-delivered PDSR not be considered part of Kraft's bargain? Did Kraft rely on the PDSR? In the actual case, the court held that the PDSR did not by itself create an express warranty. Instead, it was part of the manufacturer's warranty provided to the buyer.

---

[5] 715 F. Supp. 2d 464 (S.D.N.Y. 2010).

D. Representations by Remote Sellers

As noted earlier in this Assignment, statements about purchased goods may be made not only by the immediate seller, but also (or instead) by a manufacturer, distributor, or other remote seller. Figure 1 below gives an overview of how a sale of goods might be traced through multiple parties.

Figure 1.

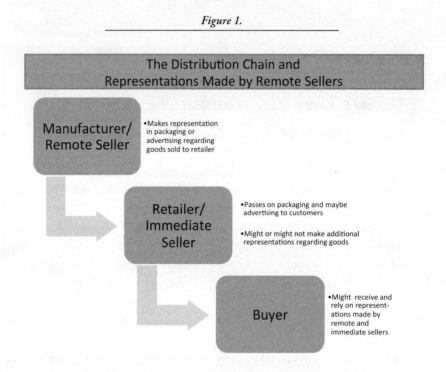

Figure 1 illustrates a simple sale of goods from manufacturer to retailer to buyer, but the chain of distribution may be longer. For example, a manufacturer may market goods to a wholesale regional distributor, which sells the goods to a local warehouse/distributors, which sells the goods to retailers, which sells to end users. Sometimes only the manufacturer and the retailer make representations about the goods, but in theory, each party in the chain can add its own representations that accompany the goods.

Section 2-313 suggests that warranties for a buyer can be created only by the immediate seller, not by a seller further up the distribution chain. This is implicit in the requirement that the representation be made "by the seller to the buyer" and particularly that it be "made part of the basis of the bargain" between the seller and the buyer. Comment 2 to § 2-313 makes this point explicit by noting that "this section is limited in its scope and direct purpose to warranties made by the seller to the buyer as part of a contract for sale."

However, Comment 2 continues: "[W]arranties need not be confined either to sales contracts or to the direct parties to such a contract. . . . [T]he matter is left to the case law with the intention that the policies of this Act may offer useful guidance in dealing with further cases as they arise." In response, courts often have expanded warranty coverage beyond the direct seller-buyer relationship, especially when the remote seller has made representations knowing they would be passed on to later purchasers. Remote sellers thus may have obligations to remote buyers that are virtually identical with § 2-313 warranties, though based on a court-created extension of § 2-313 rather than through direct application of § 2-313. The representation must still satisfy the other aspects of § 2-313 (be an affirmation of fact, promise, description, or sample or model, not be puffing, and be part of the basis of the bargain in the immediate sales transaction).

> **Third Party Beneficiaries**
>
> In this Assignment, you learn about warranties made to the buyer by remote sellers, imposed by courts as an extension of § 2-313 based on packaging and advertising aimed at consumers. But sellers up the distribution chain may also make representations to their own direct buyers (e.g., manufacturer to distributor) that do not reach the buyer. In Assignment 13, you will learn that such warranties may also sometimes protect a buyer later in the distribution chain, through application of § 2-318.

EXAMPLES AND ANALYSIS

Example F: *Westport Marina, Inc. v. Boulay*[6]

Clean Seas Company (Clean Seas) designed an enzymatic boat coating intended to inhibit marine growth on the bottom of boats. The coating's label provided: "Keeps hull exceptionally clean from marine growth! Increase speed, Reduce drag, Maximize efficiency!" Several wholesale distributors purchased the coating from an intermediary for resale to retailers, who resold the coating to customers. Moreover, the intermediary marketed and advertised the coating at trade shows and other situations. After the distributors received complaints about the coating the distributors suffered losses

---

[6]   783 F. Supp. 344 (E.D.N.Y. 2010).

on sales to end users. Because the distributors' immediate seller was out of business, the distributors sued Clean Seas, the company that designed and patented the Product, claiming breach of express and implied warranties.

Clean Seas moved for summary judgment, arguing that even though it was the manufacturer, it did not make any statement regarding performance of the coating to the buyers. It argued that the intermediary, rather than Clean Seas, had applied the labels and made the marketing statements to the purchasers. Further, Clean Seas argued that, even if it was responsible for the representations made in the labeling, the distributors could not prevail in an action for breach of express warranty because they did not rely on the representations in making purchases of the coating (reliance being required in New York). None of the distributors had read or seen the coating's label or marketing literature prior to making their purchases.

Analysis: Which part(s) of 2-313 might be at issue here? Which of the described facts, if true, would support an argument in favor of the plaintiffs? In the actual case, the United States District Court for the Eastern District of New York granted summary judgment in favor of the defendant manufacturer. Why might the court have granted the motion to dismiss the express warranty claims? Should the manufacturer be bound by oral representations made by intermediaries? The court held that the intermediary was not an agent of Clean Seas. Why does this matter? Should a purchaser of a failed product be required to show reliance on advertising literature in all cases? If a product has a general reputation in the marketplace, can that satisfy a reliance requirement, where applicable?

E. Pulling it All Together

The following opinion in *Avola v. Louisiana-Pacific Corp.* presents a typical illustration of how the interwoven concepts of reliance, basis of the bargain, puffing, and liability of remote sellers arise in a claim of express warranty in a single case. As you read the case, consider these questions:

(1) What are the elements of an express warranty cause of action according to the *Avola* court?

(2) What approach did the court use to evaluate whether any statements became part of the basis of the bargain under 2-313? Is the statement that "LP SmartSide products work and cut just like traditional wood, taking nails and screws with ease" puffing? Why or why not?

(3) Did the communication by the Home Depot employee induce Avola to purchase the siding? What about the advertisement of Louisiana-Pacific? Why or why not?

(4) Does a seller like Home Depot, that recites the manufacturer's statements, describes the manufacturer's warranty, or provides a manufacturer's warranty to a buyer, make a warranty of its own? Why or why not?

(5) The court held that even if the statements were made, there was no reliance by Avola. Does his status and training as an employee help or hurt his claim here?

(6) How does Avola make his claim that the siding "caused" his injury? How might a buyer go about proving causation?

Avola v. Louisiana-Pacific Corp.

81 UCC Rep. Serv. 2d 509 (E.D.N.Y. 2013)

PAMELA K. CHEN, District Judge.

This action is about an advertisement that reads: "LP SmartSide products work and cut just like traditional wood, taking nails and screws with ease." Defendants Louisiana-Pacific Corporation ("Louisiana-Pacific") and Home Depot U.S.A., Inc. ("Home Depot") seek summary judgment, dismissing Plaintiffs' breach of express warranty and false advertising claims based on this advertisement ("Motion"). The Motion is GRANTED in part and DENIED in part, for the reasons set forth below.

I. Background

A. Avola's Carpentry Experience

Plaintiff Anthony Avola ("Avola"), a carpenter's son and self-described "master carpenter," has had over three decades of experience in the carpentry industry. Avola was also a member of the local carpenters' union for more than two decades.

. . . .

B. Avola's Employment at Home Depot

In early-to-mid 2000, around the age of 70, Avola took a part-time job as a sales associate at the Home Depot store in Commack, New York (the "Home Depot Store" or the "Store"). In spite of his extensive experience in carpentry, Avola was assigned to work in the Store's plumbing department. Avola admitted that he only "knew enough about plumbing to tell [the customers] what they needed," from having observed the plumbers at one of his prior jobs.

Like Avola, other employees of the Store were also assigned to work in departments for which they had little-to-no prior experience . . . . [as] the Store expected its employees to "work every department," regardless of the department to which they were assigned.

In terms of the information that the Store's employees were required to possess regarding the products sold, Pretty [, another employee,] stated that Home Depot offered different department-specific classes, such as a "very basic class on all the materials in the department" and classes "sponsored by a vendor." Specifically, having worked for three years in the lumber department, Pretty also stated that "I'm sure at one point in a class [LP SmartSide] was gone over," though she denied ever having read materials regarding, or practiced using, this product. Pretty stated that, as such, the employees could only "answer with a basic knowledge of the products" in their departments.

C. Avola's Purchase of LP SmartSide

Home Depot sells siding products to cover the outside of buildings and other structures. Among these products is LP SmartSide, a type of "composite wood" siding product created by combining wood byproducts and chemicals. On its website, Louisiana-Pacific advertises LP SmartSide, touting, in relevant part, that "LP SmartSide products work and cut just like traditional wood, taking nails and screws with ease" (the "Advertisement").

According to Pretty, Home Depot also sells other types of siding products, such as "vinyl" and actual "wood." Information from Home Depot's website, which Plaintiffs introduce into evidence, indicates that the actual "wood" siding products include mostly products made from white cedar and T1-11 Siding, a product made from longleaf pine. The product page for T1-11 Siding specifically describes this product as plywood with a "traditional wood siding *look.*" Plywood is created by layering thin strips of actual wood.

On the afternoon of October 1, 2009, Avola went to the Home Depot Store, where he was still employed, to buy a siding product for the extension to the shed in his backyard. According to Avola, he had previously used T1-11 Siding for the shed. This time, Avola had also purchased T1-11 Siding, and was about to leave the Store when an unnamed, Home Depot sales associate in the lumber department approached him. The sales associate suggested that Avola try LP SmartSide, as an alternative, stating that it "nails just like wood," "works as easy as traditional wood siding," and can be installed the same way as T1-11 Siding (the "Related Statements"). According to Avola, this was the first time that he had heard about LP SmartSide.[FN6] Avola subsequently purchased LP SmartSide.

FN6. Avola did not visit Louisiana-Pacific's website, nor view the actual Advertisement for LP SmartSide, until after the accident, when he was researching this product.

D. Avola's Accident

On the morning of November 3, 2009, Avola started installing LP SmartSide on the extension to the shed. For nailing into this "composite wood" siding product, Avola adhered to the same procedures that he had previously followed for "wood" siding products. . . . .

Avola began nailing in the panels of LP SmartSide from the back to the front of the shed. According to Avola, even in the beginning, the nails refused to stay in place after he hammered them once; he had to hammer each nail two or three times for it to hold, before letting go with his left hand and fully hammering in the rest of the nail. Avola also stated that, in some places, the nails "fell to the floor," and elsewhere "it was hard to nail, so I would skip the area and go to a different area to nail." . . .

By mid-afternoon, Avola had hammered about 100 nails into seven panels of LP SmartSide. Shortly thereafter, as he was nailing in the eighth and last panel, Avola stooped down slightly, tapped one of the nails into place, let go of it, and hammered it again once or twice, at which point it ricocheted into his left eye . . . .

Avola stated that, six months after the accident, upon his recovery, he finished nailing in the eighth panel of LP SmartSide using the same type of nails, except that this time he *predrilled* the nails into the panel.

. . . .

II. Discussion

. . . .

C. Surviving Claims: Breach of Express Warranty and False Advertising

This Court turns to Plaintiffs' surviving claims under New York law: breach of express warranty and false advertising.

New York breach of express warranty claims require (i) a material statement amounting to a warranty; (ii) the buyer's reliance on this warranty as a basis for the contract with his immediate seller; (iii) the breach of this warranty; and (iv) injury to the buyer caused by the breach. . . . .

In spite of the fact that the buyer might not have contracted with the manufacturer, the buyer may still bring a claim against the manufacturer based on the manufacturer's advertisements, upon which the buyer relied when contracting with his immediate seller. 28 N.Y. Prac., Contract Law § 19:4; *see Randy Knitwear, Inc. v. Am. Cyanamid Co.*, 11 N.Y.2d 5, 12, 226 N.Y.S.2d 363, 181 N.E.2d 399 (1962) (rejecting "manufacturer's denial of liability [for breach of ex-press warranty] on the sole ground of the absence of technical privity," in light of the fact that "the significant warranty, the one which effectively induces the purchase, is frequently that given by the manufacturer through mass advertising . . . to consumers with whom he has no direct contractual relationship").

. . . .

1. Materiality Element

Judge Learned Hand once wrote about commercial puffery being a non-actionable "basis of an action for deceit":

There are some kinds of talk which no sensible man takes seriously, and if he does he suffers from his credulity. If we were all scrupulously honest, it would not be so; but, as it is, neither party usually believes what the seller says about his own opinions, and each knows it.

Vulcan Metals Co. v. Simmons Mfg. Co., 248 F. 853, 856 (2d Cir. 1918). Defendants argue that Louisiana-Pacific's Advertisement and the Home Depot sales associate's Related Statements were mere puffery, which no "reasonable jury" could find were "material" for purposes of Plaintiffs' claims against them. This Court disagrees.

. . . The patchwork of district court decisions in such cases discuss, but do not create, a workable test for puffery. This Court, however, discerns several factors on which these decisions rely: (i) vagueness; (ii) subjectivity; and (iii) inability to influence the buyers' expectations.

. . . .

Here, however, the Advertisement and Related Statements can reasonably influence the buyers and shape their expectations. By representing that LP SmartSide acts like "traditional wood" siding products, these statements are not so overblown that they imply more than the buyers ought to anticipate from a siding product. Nor should the buyers expect to hear these statements from the manufacturers of other siding products that do not act like "traditional wood" siding products but have other distinguishing characteristics.

Defendants have failed to demonstrate that the Advertisement and Related Statements constitute puffery as a matter of law. Accordingly, the materiality element for Plaintiffs' claims still presents factual issues for trial.

2. Reliance Element

i. Claims Against Louisiana-Pacific

Defendants argue that, as Avola did not see the Advertisement before buying LP SmartSide, no "reasonable jury" could find reliance for Plaintiffs' claims against Louisiana-Pacific. This Court disagrees: the jury could find that Avola relied on the Advertisement, as recited by the Home Depot sales associate in his Related Statements at the time of Avola's purchase.

The threshold issue is whether to consider Avola's testimony from his affidavit and deposition, as evidence that the Home Depot sales associate actually made the Related Statements upon which Avola allegedly relied. . . .

Avola's testimony must sufficiently show that the Related Statements recited Louisiana-Pacific's Advertisement, such that Avola relied on the Advertisement for the claims against Louisiana-Pacific. In *In re Scotts*, the district court held that the statements on the grass seed manufacturer's labeling, as well as in-store advertising displays by Home Depot and Lowe's parroting these statements, supported the reliance element for the breach of express warranty claim against the manufacturer. This Court finds that this holding applies with equal force to the situation where, as here, the sellers orally repeated the manufacturer's statements, as opposed to repeating these statements on their in-store advertising displays. . . . .

Here, Plaintiffs have put forth enough evidence, in the form of Avola's testimony, to suggest that the Home Depot sales associate recited, and thereby induced, Avola's reliance on the Advertisement. Plaintiffs' claims against Louisiana-Pacific should therefore survive summary judgment. A "reasonable jury" might find that at least two of the Related Statements—that LP SmartSide "nails just like wood" and "works as easy as traditional wood siding"—parroted the Advertisement stating that "LP SmartSide products work and cut just like traditional wood, taking nails and screws with ease." The fact that the jury might also make the opposite finding merely indicates that the reliance element raises triable issues that this Court should not resolve on summary judgment.

ii. Claims Against Home Depot

. . . .

The evidence presents two possible theories for finding such reliance. The first theory. . . [A]ssum[es] the Home Depot sales associate "passively" recited Louisiana-Pacific's Advertisement in his Related Statements to Avola, without separately promising more, the sole "basis of [Avola's] bargain" would be the Advertisement. Plaintiffs would have the right to sue Louisiana-Pacific, but not Home Depot . . . .

The second theory depends on the finding that the Home Depot sales associate not only recited the Advertisement, but separately represented that LP SmartSide can be installed the same way as T1-11 Siding, a siding product with which Avola was familiar. Even assuming that Avola relied on the sales associate's independent representation regarding T1-11 Siding, as Defendants point out, Plaintiffs cannot show that Avola was acting as Home Depot's agent for this purpose. . . .

Regardless of whether the jury finds that the Home Depot sales associate recited the Advertisement in his Related Statements, it cannot ultimately find that Avola relied on these statements for the breach of express warranty and false advertising claims against Home Depot. Thus, there are no triable issues with respect to the reliance element for either claim.

3. Breach/Falsity and Causation Elements

Relying on the "characteristics" of LP SmartSide and Avola's "description of how the accident happened," as well as certain other evidence, a jury may reasonably conclude, without the aid of experts, that the Advertisement and Related Statements, by virtue of their breach or falsity, were the cause of Avola's accident. *Voss,* 59 N.Y.2d at 111, 463 N.Y.S.2d 398, 450 N.E.2d 204. The Advertisement and Related Statements represented that LP SmartSide had the same working quality and ability to take nails as "traditional wood" siding products. The evidence suggests that LP SmartSide might not have performed accordingly: arguably, it did not work and take nails like any wood used in construction, much less "traditional wood" siding products, and, uncharacteristic of wood used in construction, a nail ricocheted into Avola's eye.

. . . .

Knowledgeable about different types of wood, after working in the carpentry industry for over three decades, Avola attested that only "soft woods" are used in construction. This type of wood is easy to nail into: one can hammer the nail once to get it to hold, before hammering in the rest of it; and drilling is never necessary. For the shed, Avola had previously used without incident T1-11 Siding, a product belonging to the same category of actual "wood" siding products as "traditional wood" siding products. By contrast, for the extension on the shed, Avola used LP SmartSide, for which he had to hammer not once, but two or three times to get the nails to hold. After the accident, Avola was only able to finish nailing in the panels of LP SmartSide with a drill. This evidence, even without expert testimony, establishes enough issues as to the breach/falsity element for Plaintiffs' claims to survive summary judgment.

Avola also attested that, at most, the nail falls but never flies out of the "soft woods" used in construction. From the beginning, however, Avola was finding that, in certain spots, the nails either fell off or would not go into the panels of LP SmartSide. When the accident finally occurred, the nail flew into Avola's eye with force that felt to him like a bullet. The fact that Avola had hammered about 100 nails into seven panels up to this point tends to rebut the possibility that the accident resulted from issues in his technique, such as hammering at the wrong angle, or the size of the nail that he used. As such, absent expert testimony, there still remain factual issues for trial regarding the causation element for Plaintiffs' claims.

. . . .

For all of the above reasons, the Motion is GRANTED as to Plaintiffs' breach of express warranty and false advertising claims against Home Depot, given the absence of any issues regarding the reliance element for these claims. The Motion, however, is DENIED as to the same claims against Louisiana-Pacific.

. . . .

APPLYING THE CODE

Problem 11-1.

The following fact situations are drawn from real cases. Which of the factors listed in Section B of this Assignment weigh in favor of the statements being puffing, and which ones weigh against? Do enough of the factors tilt in one direction to allow you to determine that the statement is puffing or not? Does the nature of the defects influence your determination as to whether or not the statements are puffing? Should it?

> (a) In 2006, a seller from Nevada advertised a used 1995 Mercedes Benz automobile on eBay as "gorgeous" and with just minor blemishes "to the best of my knowledge," including a missing master key, CD cartridge and spare tire. The buyer did not inquire about the vehicle or its history or hire mechanics to inspect the car before purchase. Upon arrival of the car to the buyer in New York, the buyer discovered the car had been damaged in an accident and had been painted, the upholstery was stained, the undercoating was worn out and parts

were rusted, body work would cost $1,741.66, and electrical and other repairs exceeded $10,000.

(b) Ford sells an E350 van, described as a "15-passenger" van that is "America's Most Trustworthy" and a "very safe vehicle." A buyer of the van finds that it cannot safely carry 15 passengers due to a high center of gravity that leads to a high rollover rate and an increased risk of death or injury.

(c) Hewlett-Packard (HP) made available to the public a technical specification document and maintenance and service brochures regarding its Pavilion computer. The HP statements indicated that the computer was compatible with certain graphics cards allowing users to attain the "most cinematic graphics and special effects." The buyers found that the graphics cards were incompatible with their computers, rendering the cards inoperable.

(d) An experienced dealer in racehorses tells a buyer (who owns and races standard-bred horses as an avocation) that the horse can "leave like a deer, take a forward position, and if you brush him from the head of the stretch home, he would just jog home in preferred company every week." In fact, the horse is later found to suffer from temporary tendinitis and thrombosis. At trial, the seller testifies that, among horse traders, it is "not a common thing" to guarantee a horse and that he has never guaranteed a horse unless he had an "understanding" that an ignorant buyer was relying totally on a knowledgeable seller not "to make a mean deal." The buyer does not contradict this testimony.

(e) In a non-reliance jurisdiction, seller shows buyer a diamond bracelet and says that the bracelet is worth a lot more than $15,000, but the shop needs to "move the bracelet," so the sale price is $15,000. Buyer later phones seller to say he wants to buy the bracelet and will stop by the next day to complete the purchase. Seller fills out and signs a form with the following language: "This is our estimate, for insurance purposes only, of the present retail replacement cost of identical items, and not necessarily the amounts that might be obtained if the articles were offered for sale. Estimated value: $25,000.00." When Buyer comes the next day, Seller shows Buyer the estimate form and then puts it in the box. Buyer pays Seller and leaves with the bracelet. The bracelet is later found to be worth $13,000.

(f) Buyer tells the salesperson at a used-car business that she needs a reliable car to drive 700 miles and back home again, with her 7-month-old daughter, to visit her husband at the army base at which he is serving. She wants to spend less than $1000. The salesperson points to a car on the lot and says that it is in "good condition," that he has driven the car and can recommend it, and that the car is in "A-1 shape." Buyer purchases the car, which breaks down after seventy-five miles and leaves the buyer and her daughter stranded in a very small town for two days while the repairs are being made.

Problem 11-2.

Among your own purchases of "goods," locate packaging or enclosed written material that contains an affirmation of fact, a promise, a description, and puffing.

(a) Bring the packaging or enclosed written material to class and be prepared to identify which language fits into each category and to defend your conclusions.

(b) If you did not buy the goods directly from the manufacturer (or other person who packaged the goods), did the seller from whom you bought make any warranties (express or implied) to you based on the packaging? (Assume that you are in a non-reliance jurisdiction.) Does it matter whether the manufacturer or the immediate seller made the warranty?

Problem 11-3.

In (a) through (c) below, do the immediate seller's representations become part of the basis of the bargain under any of the approaches to "part of the basis of the bargain"? Consider them in the order of most to least favorable to the buyer: non-reliance, Comment 3, *Cipollone* (if applicable), reliance.

(a) Buyer shows that she told the sales agent she wanted a van that has anti-lock brakes and that the agent told her the van she was looking at has such brakes. The owner's manual, which was delivered in the glove box of the van a week later, says that the van has an "anti-skid feature that's particularly well suited to front-wheel drive vans," but that the van does not have anti-lock brakes.

(b)   Buyer, a hospital, shows that its purchasing agent received a brochure listing the characteristics of an MRI machine before she ordered the machine for the hospital. Unfortunately, she left her job and moved away soon after, so neither party can depose her about whether she actually read or relied on the brochure in making the purchase.

(c)   Buyer shows that she saw Seller's TV infomercial that showed its paint remover could strip four layers of paint off a radiator overnight. Buyer admitted on cross-examination that she did not believe the infomercial's demonstration, but bought the paint remover anyway because she figured that Seller would stand behind its word.

Problem 11-4.

Beverly is a purchasing manager for a company that runs a catalog business for consumer garden tools and projects. Devon, a vendor's representative for a garden tool company, visits Beverly's company and shows Beverly a new line of specialty hardened steel tools. Devon takes Beverly to a remote section of the parking lot and says, "Watch what these tools can do," as he uses the hoe and the shovel to pry and break up the edge of the asphalt pavement. He makes no oral or written representations as to the tools' strength. Beverly is very impressed and orders 200 of each for the next season. Unfortunately, the tools break easily when they are used to pry stones out of the ground (a frequent task in some gardens). The customers who bought the tools from Beverly's company return the broken tools in droves, and her company cheerfully refunds the price, to keep goodwill. She is then astonished when the vendor refuses to reimburse her company for those returned tools. The vendor says that the tools were not covered by an express warranty, and even if they were, that warranty was not breached. See 2-313 Comment 6.

(a)   Has Devon's company made any express warranties to Beverly's company? If so, what are they, and have they been breached? (Assume that the jurisdiction's case law is confused as to whether this is a reliance, comment 3, or non-reliance jurisdiction, so your answer needs to consider all three possibilities.)

(b)   Would your answer to (a) be any different if Devon tells Beverly that the hoe and shovel he is demonstrating are prototypes of the products that will be available next month, but that the factory has not yet geared up to make those particular hoes and shovels?

Problem 11-5.

Buyer visits a local grocery store where he sees seller's product labeled "100% Pure Olive Oil," which he purchases. Buyer, who is health conscious, would not have purchased the product if not 100% pure olive oil. Later, buyer discovers that the product is not pure olive oil, but a secondary product referred to as "pomace." Whereas olive oil is made from olives that are harvested and quickly processed with no heat or chemicals, pomace is made from the residue material left after the olive oil is extracted from the olives and is superheated, bleached, deodorized and treated with solvents. Has the seller made either express or implied warranties here? Could the seller defend any claim by arguing that the label was not a warranty, but rather a product description without any assurance of product performance levels?

Problem 11-6.

The parol evidence rule (Assignment 8) can directly impact whether a buyer can prove a seller made warranties and whether a claim is within any warranty so made. For this problem, draw upon your knowledge from Assignment 8 and Assignment 11.

A commercial buyer solicited bids for a new boiler. The seller responded with its quote for a 600 BHP (brake horsepower) boiler with a burner fueled by "No. 2 oil" and "natural gas," specifying the capacity, design and operating pressures, steam quality, and motor power of the boiler. The buyer says he told the seller by telephone that, to meet state requirements, the boiler had to be "Lo-NOx." (Lo-NOx means there are lower emissions of nitrogen (NOx), which has a role in the production of smog and acid rain as well as indoor air pollution.) The seller's quote did not indicate any Lo-NOx emissions specifications. The buyer ordered the specified boiler model and all the boiler's specifications were clearly delineated on the purchase order and confirmatory memorandum. There was no Lo-NOx specification in the purchase documents. The seller did include a warranty for repair or replacement for specified failures, good for five years from the date of shipment. The terms and conditions specifically included the following integration clause:

> No representations or guarantees other than those contained herein shall be binding upon the seller unless in writing and signed by an official of the seller.

Which of the following warranty claims (if any) might be successfully asserted by the buyer? What effect (if any) might the parol evidence rule have on these claims?

(a) Failure of a heating coil within the first year of the boiler's installation, whether or not seller knew of the problems.

(b) Failure of all heating coils more than five years after delivery, but within five years after the seller made repairs to the boiler.

(c) Failure of the boiler to have Lo-NOx emissions.

Problem 11-7.

Recall Problem 10-7 concerning Lisa, Pete's Exercise Boutique and the Thighslimmer 2000X. Does Lisa have a claim for breach of an express warranty?

Assignment 12
Warranty Disclaimers and Conflicts
§§ 2-312, 2-316, 2-317

This Assignment continues to explore the first question raised at the beginning of the Chapter—determining what warranties are included in a contract. Assignments 10 and 11 examined how implied and express warranties are created. This Assignment shows how to resolve conflicts among warranties and how those warranties may be disclaimed by seller's language or action.

LEARNING OUTCOMES AND OBJECTIVES

At the completion of this Assignment, you should be able to

- identify the ways in which different types of warranties are disclaimed;

- evaluate when a seller's attempt to disclaim may be ineffective, often because it does not comply with statutory requirements such as conspicuousness;

- compare the mandates of the Magnuson-Moss Warranty Act and its restrictions on a seller's ability to disclaim implied warranties, facilitating consumer suits against sellers on warranties; and

- apply the relevant portions of Article 2 to evaluate a seller's claim that it disclaimed warranties so as to bar a buyer's claims regarding the quality of the goods sold.

A. Disclaiming Express Warranties

We saw in Assignment 11 that sellers create express warranties through representations, whether through affirmations of fact or promises, descriptions, or samples or models that become part of the basis of the bargain. Because manufacturer sellers and immediate sellers may make representations not only in the formal contract itself but also in advertisements and other descriptions of the goods, one of the tasks for a seller's attorney is to review not only the formal terms and conditions in the sales contract, but also marketing and advertising materials used by the seller to ensure that the seller is aware of warranties it may be making and that it limits warranties if it desires to do so. Moreover, because disclaiming express warranties is difficult, as we shall see, it is often better to focus on avoiding the creation of a warranty in the first place, rather than attempting to avoid liability through disclaimer. The safest strategy to reduce a seller's exposure for warranty is to be careful about the promises made concerning the product in the first place.

Two Notes on Terminology

Exclusions and Modifications: Although 2-316 is titled "Exclusion or Modification of Warranties," a common synonym is "disclaimer of warranties." This Chapter uses "disclaimer" to describe either an exclusion or a modification of a warranty.

Remedy Limitations and Warranty Disclaimers: A warranty disclaimer is designed to limit the seller's liability by restricting the scope of seller's representations about the nature of the goods being sold. Sellers can also (or alternatively) limit their liability by limiting the remedies available to buyers once a breach of warranty is established. Assignment 24 takes up this latter issue.

EXAMPLES AND ANALYSIS

Example A: *Kraft v. Leonard's Healthcare Corp.*[1]

Kraft purchased a "no-slip ice carpet" advertised in a mail order catalogue with the following clause:

Get a grip and prevent falls for good!

NO-SLIP ICE CARPET

Just place over ice or snow—and away you go! Get out of the house without shoveling, salting or scraping! Rugged coil fibers grip to ice, snow and your shoes! Just place on walkway or stairs for improved traction even in the worst conditions. Flexible in sub-freezing temperatures. Use it every winter.

The Krafts ordered the ice blanket through a mail order catalog, which came with the following instructions:

---

[1]   646 F. Supp. 2d 882 (E.D. Mich. 2009).

Ice Carpet with Built-in-traction

The Ice Carpet prevents slips, skids and tumbles on your entrance walk and sidewalk. Even on thick accumulations of ice and snow, just lay down the ice carpet for improved traction. With proper care it can be used year after year. Helps provide surefootedness, no matter what the weather. No installation is necessary. Stays where you place it. For a longer or wider walk, two or more can be placed together. When walking on ice, it is a good idea to observe your next step and caution should be taken. Brush any accumulation off the ice carpet with a broom. Store in a dry place.

Kraft slipped and fell the first time he used the carpet, fracturing his wrist and injuring his hand. He brought suit claiming breach of express warranty. Both the buyer and the seller moved for summary judgment on the express warranty claim.

Analysis: The court granted summary judgment to the buyer and denied summary judgment to the seller. Which statements would the court likely have found created an express warranty under 2-313 that was possibly breached by the buyer's fall? Assuming a warranty would be created by that language, do you think the seller should be permitted to disclaim such a warranty after making the statements? Why or why not? Use your common sense, since we haven't read the Code provisions yet, but be as specific as possible. How might you revise the sales literature to avoid creating the express warranty in the first place? Would you advise the seller to make those changes? Why or why not?

Reading the Code:
§ 2-316(1)

Read 2-316(1).

Question 1. Section 2-316(1) contains two rules of law dealing with disclaimer of express warranties. Rewrite those rules in if/then paraphrases. How do those two rules relate to each other?

2-316(1): If _____, then _____.

2-316(1): If _____, then _____.

Question 2. Does section 2-316(1) prevent a seller from disclaiming warranties made during the sales process?

Question 3. Consider again *Kraft v. Leonard's Healthcare Corp.* from Example A above. Would the outcome of the case change if, before completing the sale, the seller provided a statement to the buyer that the seller "disclaims all express warranties?" What language from 2-316(1) supports your position?

Question 4. A prospective seller and buyer negotiate over purchase of an item, and during the course of the negotiations the seller makes oral or written representations about the goods. The parties then sign a written contract that contains a clause disclaiming all express warranties not appearing on the face of the contract. The contract also contains a merger clause. Would the disclaimer be effective under 2-316(1)? Be sure to consider the effect of "the provisions of this Article on parol or extrinsic evidence," as referenced in 2-316(1). Would your answer change if there were no merger clause?

How do you reconcile the seemingly conflicting language of 2-316(1) and 2-202?

The underlying policy of 2-316 is to "protect the buyer from unexpected and unbargained language of disclaimer by denying effect to such language when inconsistent with language of express warranty . . . ." Comment 1. Attempts to deny or modify the existence of a clearly stated warranty promise will fail because they are inconsistent with "words or conduct relevant to the creation of an express warranty" (2-316(1)). For instance, in *Kraft v. Leonard's Healthcare Corp.* in Example A above, where the seller made specific and repeated affirmations regarding the goods, the seller could not disclaim those warranties by including a statement that the goods were being sold "as is" or that all express warranties were disclaimed. As we will see, the federal Magnuson-Moss Warranty Act also provides buyers some protection from warranty disclaimers.

While the Code protects buyers by making disclaimer of express warranties difficult, there are two limitations to that protection. First, the rule in § 2-316 is "subject to the parol evidence rule." A disclaimer that is inconsistent with an express warranty will not be effective, but if evidence of the express warranty cannot be introduced because of the parol evidence rule, there is no such inconsistency and the disclaimer will prevail. If a contract appears to have language of express warranty and a disclaimer of that warranty, you must always consider first if the parol evidence rule bars evidence of the warranty before considering whether the two are inconsistent.

Second, § 2-316 says a warranty and a disclaimer may be read together if they are not inconsistent with each other. This rule may apply if there are two sellers in a transaction and one seller gives an express warranty while the other seller disclaims warranties. In such a case, the warranty and disclaimer are not inconsistent with each other because they are given by different parties. The rule may also apply if a warranty promise is ambiguous or may be read as being either broad or narrow; the existence of a disclaimer may support adopting the narrower interpretation that allows the disclaimer to be effective.

The following examples should help you see when warranties and disclaimers will be considered consistent or inconsistent.

EXAMPLES AND ANALYSIS

Example B: *Brothers v. Hewlett-Packard Co.*[2]

Michael Brothers and others purchased computers with video graphics cards from Hewlett–Packard (HP). In technical specifications, maintenance and service guides, and other materials provided on or with plaintiffs' computers, HP stated that the computers at issue "contain and are compatible with the 'NVIDIA GeForce FX Go5700 with 64-MB video memory' and with the 'NVIDIA GeForce FX Go5700 with 128-MB video memory.'" In its product specifications made available on the internet and at retailers, HP stated that the computers the plaintiffs bought have "NVIDIA GeForce GPU with 8X AGP for the most cinematic graphics and special effects." The plaintiffs claimed that the graphics cards proved to be incompatible with their computers, rendering them completely inoperable, and that HP breached an express warranty through its product specifications. HP claimed that the statements in its materials were "puffery" and that, even if an express warranty was created, HP properly disclaimed the

---

[2]   62 U.C.C. Rep. Serv. 2d 76 (N.D. Cal. 2007).

warranty through its written "Limited Warranty" that expressly disclaimed warranties not contained in that document.

Analysis: The court concluded that HP had created express warranties with its specific statements about both the compatibility of the computers and graphics cards and its statements about "the most cinematic graphics and special effects." The court further concluded that HP did not effectively disclaim those express warranties, "reasoning that allowing the disclaimers to exclude a manufacturer's express representation of product specifications would be unfair." Do you agree with the court's reading of the Code? Using 2-313 and 2-316, how would you support the court's judgments that a warranty was created and not effectively disclaimed? What arguments might you make for HP?

Example C: *Avram v. Samsung Electronics America*[3]

Avram and others purchased Samsung refrigerators bearing the Department of Energy (DOE) Energy Star label indicating they met specified standards of energy efficiency. Such appliances cost more to purchase but lead to savings for users through the energy efficiency. Some time after purchase, the DOE found the appliances did not meet the Energy Star criteria. The buyers brought suit for breach of express warranty against Samsung (the manufacturer) and Lowe's (the retail seller). The manufacturer and the retail seller moved for dismissal, pointing to the Limited Warranty, which said it "covers manufacturing defects in materials and workmanship encountered in normal, noncommercial use of the product." The Limited Warranty also provided "THERE ARE NO EXPRESS WARRANTIES OTHER THAN THOSE LISTED AND DESCRIBED ABOVE. . . . SAMSUNG SHALL NOT BE LIABLE FOR . . . FAILURE TO REALIZE SAVINGS OR OTHER BENEFITS. . . ."

Analysis: Denying the motion to dismiss the express warranty claims, the court concluded that the attempt to disclaim the energy benefits was "ineffective" in the face of the express warranty created with the Energy Star logo. The court noted "the potential for unfairness if an express warranty is displayed to the purchaser when he parts with his money at the store, but the disclaimer appears at page 42 of a manual sealed inside the product's packaging."

---

[3]   81 U.C.C. Rep. Serv. 2d 48 (D. N.J. 2013).

Using 2-313 and 2-316, how would you support the court's judgments that a warranty was created and not effectively disclaimed? What arguments might you make for Samsung and Lowe's? Do you agree with the court's reading of the Code?

B. Disclaiming Implied Warranties

We saw in Assignment 10 that there are several types of implied warranties that become part of the seller's obligation regarding the goods—implied warranties of title and against infringement, of merchantability, and of fitness for a particular purpose. As implied warranties, they are imposed without being agreed to by the sellers, and sellers may accordingly wish to limit or eliminate these warranties.

One might start by asking whether such disclaimers should be allowed at all. After all, implied warranties are included in a contract because the drafters of the Code considered them to be the standard protections reasonably to be expected by buyers under the circumstances of the sale. Perhaps, like express warranties, once they attach under the relevant Code provisions, they should be difficult if not impossible to disclaim. On the other hand, the Code seeks to enforce the bargain actually made by the parties, and by definition implied warranties are not part of that bargain. Returning to a distinction discussed in Assignment 1, the implied warranties are considered default terms, not mandatory terms. Sellers are permitted to disclaim them, but must do so in the manner prescribed. As we have already seen, the policy of § 2-316 is to protect buyers from "unexpected and unbargained language of disclaimer." The focus is to ensure that disclaimers are done in a manner that effectively confirms that the parties understood that the transaction did not include the implied warranties.

EXAMPLES AND ANALYSIS

Example D: *Wilke v. Woodhouse Ford, Inc.* [4]

Elizabeth and Mark Wilke purchased a used Ford cargo van from Woodhouse Ford (Woodhouse). Woodhouse sold the van "as is" and disclaimed

---

[4]   774 N.W.2d 370 (Neb. 2009).

all implied warranties. The same day as the purchase, Elizabeth was injured when her 3-year-old daughter was able to pull the gearshift out of park when the key was not in the ignition and without depressing the brake pedal, causing the van to roll. According to Federal Motor Vehicle Safety Standards, vehicles with an automatic transmission must prevent removal of the key unless the shift is locked in park to reduce rollaway occurrences. The Wilkes brought suit for negligence and breach of implied warranty of merchantability. The trial court granted summary judgment to Woodhouse, and the Wilkes appealed.

The Wilkes claimed that because of concerns for public safety, it was against public policy for a used car dealer to disclaim the warranty of merchantability.

Analysis: The Nebraska Supreme Court disagreed. It ruled that the legislature had established public policy in 2-316, which allows such a disclaimer so long as the seller complies with its provisions. The court reversed the summary judgment entered below on the buyer's negligence claim, however. The court ruled that used car dealers, even those who disclaim all warranties, have a duty to conduct a reasonable inspection of vehicles prior to sale to determine if there are any patent defects that would make the vehicles unsafe.

Which part of 2-316 supports Woodhouse? Which supports the Wilkes? Do you agree with the court's reasoning relative to allowing disclaimers where public safety is implicated? Why or why not? Notice that the court allowed summary judgment on the contract claims, but not the tort claims. Should warranty law play a role in these situations? Which party was in the best position to avoid this accident? Was the disclaimer here bargained for?

As we turn to further consideration of the formalities that are required by § 2-316, recall the terminology associated with the warranties of title and against infringement in § 2-312: even though they are in effect implied warranties (that is, they are imposed based on the circumstances of the sale, not because the parties included them in their agreement), they are not called "implied warranties" by the Code. As noted in Assignment 10, the result of that semantic choice is that the 2-316 provisions on disclaiming "implied warranties" do not apply to disclaiming the warranties in § 2-312. We will return later in this Assignment to consider how § 2-312 warranties are disclaimed.

Reading the Code:
§ 2-316(2) and (3)

Read 2-316(2) and (3) and all the Comments.

Question 5. Subsection (2) of 2-316 contains three rules of law pertaining to disclaimer of implied warranties. Subsection (3) contains three additional means of implied warranty disclaimer. Some of the rules apply to the implied warranty of merchantability. Some apply to the implied warranty of fitness. And some apply to both. In the chart below, set forth for each of those implied warranties the multiple ways a seller may disclaim that warranty. Jot down the subsection number and letter of the part of 2-316 or the paragraph number of the Comment that provides the rule you are relying on. As you make the list, consider the relationship between subsections (2) and (3), as indicated by the statements that subsection (2) is "subject to subsection (3)" and subsection (3) applies "[n]otwithstanding subsection (2)."

How to disclaim an implied warranty of merchantability	How to disclaim an implied warranty of fitness for a particular purpose

Question 6. Subsection (3) includes two "safe harbor" provisions that tell sellers a particular set of words that will be counted as disclaiming some or all implied warranties. What are those words and what do they disclaim? Are there any other requirements on seller to ensure that those words have the desired effect?

Question 7. Read 2-316 Comment 8 again. What does Comment 8 add to your understanding of 2-316(3)(b)? Under 2-316(3)(b), if seller demands and buyer examines or refuses to examine the goods, what warranties are disclaimed?

As you have seen in responding to the questions above, § 2-316 does not bar disclaimer of the implied warranties of merchantability and fitness but instead prescribes particular formalities for making effective disclaimers of those warranties. The message in the Code is that buyers can be sufficiently protected by such formalities, and that sellers can rely on those formalities to protect themselves from unwanted liability. Of course, applying those rules is not always easy or straightforward, as you will see in the examples below.

1. Is the Disclaimer Conspicuous under § 2-316(2)?

Remember that in order to satisfy the formalities of § 2-316(2), the language must be "conspicuous." Whether particular language meets the conspicuousness requirements of § 2-316(2) depends on the individual circumstances, because "conspicuous" is defined in § 1-201(b)(10) to refer to "a term [that is] so written, displayed, or presented that a *reasonable person* against which it is to operate ought to have noticed it."

**Reading the Code:
"Conspicuous"**

Read 1-201(b)(10) and Comment 10.

Question 8. If you were the deciding judge, would you think that boxed, large font, or colored text was conspicuous? What about the first or last clause in a three-page agreement? What about a disclaimer in all capital letters, when the rest of the agreement was also in all capital letters? What about a disclaimer in the middle of a long clause labeled with the heading "Warranty"? As a contracting party, what would make a clause conspicuous for you? As a contract drafter, what would you do to make a clause conspicuous?

With the limited guidance offered by § 1-201(b)(10), courts have different opinions on what it means to make a disclaimer conspicuous.

EXAMPLES AND ANALYSIS

Example E: *Salazar v. D.W.B.H., Inc.*[5]

D.W.B.H (d/b/a Santa Fe Mitsubishi) sold Sandra Salazar a used engine for her car and installed it. When Salazar picked up the car, the documents included an "Exclusion of Warranties." The provision stated "that dealer makes no warranties of any kind, express or implied, and disclaims all warranties including warranties of merchantability or fitness for a particular purpose . . . ." After installation of the used engine, the car smoked, lost oil rapidly, and eventually stopped working. When Salazar returned the car to Santa Fe Mitsubishi, it advised her she needed another new engine. Unbeknownst to Salazar, Santa Fe Mitsubishi had given a 90-day warranty on the labor but not on the used engine itself. By the time Salazar returned the car, the warranty had expired. Santa Fe Mitsubishi informed Salazar that labor had been covered under the 90-day warranty, but not the engine itself. As a result, Salazar would have to buy another replacement engine. Salazar brought suit against Santa Fe Mitsubishi for breach of express and implied warranty and other claims.

Analysis: The trial court found that a statement made by an employee that she could return the car if she had any problems qualified as an express warranty. The New Mexico Supreme Court disagreed, finding the employee's statement was not part of the basis of the bargain. This statement, the court concluded, was merely a part of "good customer service," as the employee stated.

---

5   192 P.3d 1205 (N.M. 2008).

As to implied warranties, the trial court found that Santa Fe Mitsubishi breached the implied warranty of fitness. The court of appeals disagreed, finding that the Exclusion of Warranties provision satisfied 1-201(b)(10) and was conspicuous as a matter of law because Santa Fe Mitsubishi set the provision off to one side of the page with a heading in a capital letters. The supreme court did not decide the issue of conspicuousness, but cast doubt on the conclusion that the Exclusion was conspicuous, finding the provision had extremely small lettering that was smaller than other print on the page. Key to the court's conclusion was the fact that Salazar did not separately sign the Exclusion of Warranties provision, even though the provision called for a customer signature and even though Salazar had signed another portion of the document to authorize repairs. The lack of signature indicated that Salazar did not agree to the exclusion of warranties. The court noted that "when reviewing exclusion provisions, we must look both to the provision's form and its language. In this case, we cannot ignore the specific language in the provision that requires a buyer's agreement in order to exclude warranties." Without an effective exclusion, Santa Fe Mitsubishi did not disclaim the implied warranties and thus had warranted the engine as merchantable.

Which part of 2-316 supports Salazar? Santa Fe Mitsubishi? Do you agree with the reasoning of the trial court, the court of appeals, or the supreme court? Why? Do you agree with the outcome here? Why or why not?

Example F: *US Airways, Inc. v. Elliott Equipment Co.* [6]

The City of Philadelphia, through a contract with Global Ground Support, LLC, purchased boom assemblies and de-icing equipment from Elliott Equipment Company, Inc. for operation by US Airways, Inc. While US Airways was using the de-icing equipment, one of the assemblies sustained a structural failure and collapsed, injuring an employee and damaging an Airbus 330 airplane. U.S. Airways brought suit against Elliott for breach of express and implied warranties and other claims. Elliott's twelve-month warranty included the following language:

> 7.1. [Elliott] warrants that each Item, parts thereof, spare parts and repaired or replacement parts manufactured or modified to [Elliott's] detailed design and specifications, be free from defects in material, workmanship, process of manufacture and design and be suitable for

---

6   2008 WL 4461847 (E.D. Pa. 2008).

the intended purpose. [Elliott] shall not be liable for defects or failure caused by [Global's] misuse, negligence or failure resulting from noncompliance with [Elliott's] operating, maintenance and overhaul manuals. [Elliott] does not warrant any components, which have been specified or supplied by [Global].

7.2. [Elliott] agrees that its warranty, with respect to defects in material, workmanship, process of manufacture and design shall extend as outlined and will be warranted for a period of no less than twelve months.

Elliott claimed this language operated as a limitation on implied warranties as to the equipment.

Analysis: The court disagreed, finding the language did not meet the requirements of conspicuousness and did not use the required language of disclaimer. Specifically, the court noted, "[T]he language of the alleged disclaimer was not conspicuous, as these provisions are in the same size print as the remainder of the document and in regular type in the middle of a long agreement." The court found that "it would be difficult to conclude that Elliott intended these sections to serve as a disclaimer of implied warranties." The court held that a reasonable person would not have noticed these provisions.

What did Elliott do wrong here if it truly intended to make a disclaimer of implied warranties? Could you fix the language to accomplish a disclaimer? Should courts have a uniform understanding of conspicuousness?[7]

2. Disclaiming the Warranties of Title and against Infringement

Recall that under § 2-312, the warranties of title and against infringement protect the buyer's typical interest in receiving good, clear title to the purchased goods and in not being exposed to lawsuits in order to protect against title, liens, or intellectual property claims. The Code also recognizes that a transaction may involve transfer of less than good title and less protection against infringement claims, so

---

[7]   *See* Warren W. Fane, Inc. v. Tri-State Diesel, Inc., 2014 WL 1806773, 83 UCC Rep. Serv. 2d 574 (N.D.N.Y. 2014) (upholding disclaimer that a reasonable person would have noticed as it "sets out clearly, in capital letters and [was] set apart in a section entitled "warranty disclaimer and limitations of liability," that [seller] offers no warranty of merchantability or fitness for a particular purpose"); Alongi v. Bombardier Rec. Prods., 2013 WL 718755 (E.D. Mich. 2013) (finding disclaimer of implied warranties conspicuous when "written in all capital letters within the body of the warranty such that a reasonable person ought to have noticed it").

the Code provides for disclaimer of those warranties. As noted earlier, however, those disclaimers are not covered by § 2-316 but instead appear in § 2-312.

Reading the Code:
§ 2-312 (2), (3)

Read 2-312(2) and (3)

Question 9. How is the warranty of title disclaimed under 2-312(2)? Does the inclusion of "circumstances" in addition to contractual "language" as a means of disclaimer undermine the usefulness of this warranty? How is the warranty of non-infringement disclaimed under (3)? What did the drafters mean when they used the language "unless otherwise agreed"?

EXAMPLES AND ANALYSIS

Example G: *Rochester Equipment & Maintenance v. Roxbury Mountain Service, Inc.*[8]

Rochester Equipment & Maintenance purchased a used construction vehicle from Roxbury Mountain Service, Inc. After the buyer refurbished the vehicle, the Department of Motor Vehicles seized the vehicle as stolen property. The buyer brought an action against the seller for breach of the warranty of title. The seller defended the action by pointing to the "as is" clause in the purchase.

Analysis: Ruling in favor of the buyer, the court held that the buyer had no reason to know that the seller did not have title to the vehicle and the "as is" clause related to the operability of the vehicle, not to title. Which part of 2-312 supports the buyer? Could the seller rely on its 2-316 disclaimer here? Why or why not? *See* Example H below.[9]

---

[8]   891 N.Y.S.2d 781 (App. Div. 2009).
[9]   *See also* Moore v. Pro Team Corvette Sales, Inc., 786 N.E.2d 903 (Ohio Ct. App. 2002) (language in sales

C. Cumulation and Conflict of Warranties

What happens when the parties' various writings and oral assurances regarding the goods contain conflicting warranties, even after any disclaimers are applied? When faced with potentially conflicting contract terms, the Code prefers a construction toward harmonization whenever "reasonable." *See* § 1-303. This is consistent with the value the Code places on the context of the transaction in deciding the totality of the parties' agreement, as we saw in Assignment 6.

Reading the Code:
§ 2-317

Read 2-317 and the Comments.

Question 10. Does 2-317 limit the ability of a seller to disclaim warranties?

Question 11. How might a court heed the instruction to construe apparently conflicting warranties as consistent? Recall in Example A the seller expressly advertised a "no-slip" ice carpet. How would 2-317 apply if the seller included a disclaimer in the box with the carpet that provided, "Seller disclaims all express and implied warranties?"

Question 12. Why are samples given more weight than contract descriptions? Why are technical specifications given an even higher weight under 2-317(a)?

Question 13. Why is the implied warranty of fitness given a higher status than other implied warranties under 2-317(c)?

Section 2-317 provides for harmonization among the various express and implied warranties made by a seller, ensuring that they are interpreted "cumulatively," and therefore in favor of the buyer, unless such construction is "impossible or unreasonable." *See* § 2-317 Comment 1. Like other contractual provisions, the

---

contract stating "[a]ll warranties pursuant to O.R.C. 1302.25 (U.C.C. 2–312) (warranty of title and against infringement) are hereby excluded from this transaction" found to express a limit on the seller's liability only and was not sufficiently clear to disclaim the warranty of title as it did not convey a limit on what title the seller purported to transfer).

warranties given by the seller (express and implied) are interpreted to give effect to all contractual promises where possible.

EXAMPLES AND ANALYSIS

Example H: *N.J. Transit Corp. v. Harsco Corp.*[10]

Harsco Corp. sold the N.J. Transit Corp. (Transit) a new track geometry inspection vehicle (TGIV). As required in the bidding documents, Harsco provided a one-year express warranty on "the car and all equipment and components installed on it." After the one year period, the TGIV caught fire during normal operations and was a total loss. Transit brought suit for, among other claims, breach of implied warranties of merchantability and fitness for a particular purpose. The trial court granted summary judgment to Harsco, finding there were no warranties after expiration of the one-year limited warranty. Transit appealed.

Transit argued that it was given both a one-year express limited warranty and the implied warranties of merchantability and fitness, because the express warranty did not mention merchantability or fitness and so did not satisfy 2-316. Harsco argued that the one-year limitation in the express warranty drafted by and required by Transit applied to all warranties.

Analysis: The Third Circuit Court of Appeals upheld the summary judgment for Harsco. With respect to the implied warranty of fitness, it ruled that there was no warranty because Transit did not rely on the skill of the seller, because Transit specified what it required in its bidding request. Applying 2-317, the court also ruled that it was reasonable to construe the express warranty and the warranty of merchantability together as both having a duration of one year. To construe the implied warranty of merchantability to have a longer duration than the express warranty would make it inconsistent with the express warranty. The court based its reasoning on the extremely broad warranty that was drafted by the buyer in the transaction. The court emphasized that sellers reviewing Transit's bidding materials would have read the required warranty carefully and priced their TGIV accordingly with the one-year warranty period in mind.

---

[10]   497 F.3d 323 (3d Cir. N.J. 2007).

Which part of 2-317 supports Transit? Harsco? Do you agree with the court's reasoning and result? Why or why not? Would your opinion differ if Harsco had drafted the limited warranty? Should it? In this case, the court found no implied warranty of fitness. If the warranty of fitness had attached, same result?

APPLYING THE CODE

Problem 12-1.

Jerry Johnson, owner of Jerry's Jalopies, a used car dealer, has come to you for legal advice. In each of the sales entered by his company, Jerry's Jalopies includes in the written sales agreement a minimal express warranty in compliance with state statutes regulating used car sales. He does not wish to make any additional express or any implied warranties. He knows, however, that no matter what he tells his sales force, some of the sales representatives will make assorted promises and representations about the cars when they talk with prospective customers. Jerry wants to be sure that when the customer signs the sales agreement, the only warranties will be the ones mandated by the state law, as already included in the written sales agreement. What alternatives will you suggest to him, taking into account 2-313, 2-314, 2-315, 2-316, 2-317, and 2-202? For each alternative you suggest, how could a customer ensure that an oral promise made during the negotiations nonetheless becomes part of the contract?

D. Magnuson-Moss Warranty Act

1. Background

Article 2 is supplemented by a federal statute called the Magnuson-Moss Warranty Act, 15 U.S.C. § 2301 et seq. (Magnuson-Moss or the Act), which was enacted in 1975 to supplement the warranty protection offered by the UCC; the accompanying regulations appear in 16 C.F.R. Parts 700-703. As you have seen, Article 2 provides for several default warranties but no mandatory warranties, and it permits disclaimer of most or all of the default warranties. Magnuson-Moss adds additional protections for consumers, and it can be an especially important tool for litigators because it permits access to federal court for controversies over $50,000 or class actions with more than 100 plaintiffs. It makes breach of a state law warranty a violation of the Act and provides consumer protection in cases that might not otherwise be brought due to the smaller value of the goods involved.

Although the statute and its regulations may appear in your statutory supplement, the statutory language is difficult to follow, even by an experienced UCC reader, so the most salient provisions connected with Article 2 are summarized here to help prepare you for reading and using the statute. In general, Magnuson-Moss

(1) Mandates clearer labeling of warranties, to provide guidance to consumer buyers;

(2) Restricts the extent to which Article 2 implied warranties may be disclaimed and how such disclaimers are to be accomplished;

(3) Restricts remedy limitations (covered in Assignment 24); and

(4) Facilitates consumer lawsuits against warrantors by making the breach of warranty also a violation of federal law and allowing the recovery of costs and attorneys' fees.

2. Definitions and Scope

Several key definitions are useful to understanding the reach of Magnuson-Moss:

(1) A "**consumer product**" is goods normally used for personal, family, or household purposes, such as an automobile or a typewriter, whether or not, in the particular contract at issue, the goods were bought for such a use. The Act protects anyone, including a business, buying a consumer product. *See* 16 C.F.R. § 700.1(a).

(2) A "**written warranty**" is (1) a written affirmation of fact or promise by a supplier of goods (direct or indirect) that affirms or promises that the material or workmanship of the goods is defect-free or will meet a specified level of performance over a specified period of time, or (2) a supplier's written undertaking to refund, repair, replace, or take other remedial action as to the goods upon the failure of the goods to meet contract specifications, so long as (1) or (2) is contained in a writing that becomes part of the basis of the bargain between the supplier and the buyer.

(3)   A "**service contract**" is a written contract to perform maintenance or repair services over a fixed period of time.

The Act does not require any seller to give a warranty. However, when a "warrantor" (a seller, manufacturer, or supplier) offers a "written warranty" on a "consumer product," the Act requires that the warranty satisfy specified disclosure requirements and minimum federal standards, outlined below. The same requirements apply when a warrantor enters into a "service contract" as to a consumer product, either at time of sale or within ninety days after the sale. An express warranty created orally or by conduct (based on a sample or model) is not covered by Magnuson-Moss. On the other hand, Magnuson-Moss covers some "service contracts," which often are outside the scope of UCC Article 2 unless they are within a contract that has sale of goods as its predominant purpose.

EXAMPLES AND ANALYSIS

Example I: S*keen v. BMW of North Am., LLC*[11]

Buyers of MINI Coopers brought a class action in federal court against the manufacturer claiming the vehicles contained a latent defect in a part of the engine known as the "timing chain tensioner" that caused the part to fail prematurely. The vehicles came with an express warranty of 48 months or 50,000 miles, whichever came first. For each of the buyers, the alleged defect manifested after the term of the warranty expired. The buyers alleged that, though the alleged defects manifested after the warranties expired, the manufacturer knew of the problem and manipulated the warranty to avoid the cost. Their claims included breach of express warranty, breach of implied warranties, and violation of Magnuson-Moss. The manufacturer moved to dismiss the action.

Analysis: The court allowed the buyers to proceed with their implied warranty of merchantability claim and their claim that the express warranty was unconscionable. Because the buyers adequately pled a breach of the state law warranties, the court allowed them to proceed also with a Magnuson-Moss claim. What was the "consumer product" here? Did the seller provide a "written warranty"?

---

[11]   2014 WL 283628 (D.N.J. 2014).

Why could the buyers bring the case in federal court under Magnuson-Moss? How would you articulate the express warranty and implied warranty of merchantability claims?

Example J: *In re Frito-Lay North America, Inc. All Natural Litigation*[12]

Buyers of Tostitos, Sun Chips and Fritos Bean Dip products labeled "All Natural" brought a class action against the manufacturer, claiming the products contained genetically modified organisms. The defendant moved to dismiss the Magnuson-Moss claim.

Analysis: The court granted the defendant's motion. The court held that the "All Natural" label was not a "written warranty" for purposes of the Act. Therefore, there was no Magnuson-Moss claim. What was the "consumer product" here? Why could the buyers not bring the case in federal court under Magnuson-Moss? If there was not a "written warranty" in this case, what was the nature of the buyer's warranty claim?

Figure 1
"Express Warranty" and "Written Warranty"

Unique to Article 2 "express warranty":

definition in 2-313

promise or affirmation of fact relating to something other than material or workman-ship being defect-free or meeting a specified level of performance over specified period of time, or relating to a non-consumer-product; description; sample; model; promise or affirmation of fact not in writing

Overlap between Article 2 "express warranty" and MMWA "written warranty":

written promise or affirmation of fact relating to material or workmanship being defect-free or meeting a specified level of performance over specified period of time, if basis of bargain

Unique to MMWA "Written Warranty":

written promise to take remedial action, made with respect to consumer product (contract for sale of goods may also have such remedial promises, but nothing in Article 2 relates directly to such promises)

---

[12]   2013 WL 4647512 (E.D.N.Y. 2013).

3. Full and Conspicuous Disclosure of Warranty Terms

Magnuson-Moss requires that any written warranty given to the buyer "fully and conspicuously" disclose all the "terms and conditions of such warranty." If the goods cost more than $15,[13] certain specified terms (*see* 16 C.F.R. § 701.3) must be clearly and conspicuously displayed in a single document in simple and readily understood language, including, for example, the following statement which will look familiar if you have ever read through written warranties accompanying products you have purchased:

> Some states do not allow the exclusion or limitation of incidental or consequential damages, so the above limitation or exclusion may not apply to you. This warranty gives you specific legal rights, and you may also have other rights which may vary from state to state.

4. Mandatory Two-Tier System of Warranty Labeling

The Act sets up a choice between two labels or titles to be attached to "written warranties": "Full [duration] Warranty" or "Limited Warranty." If a "written warranty" is not so labeled, a small line of cases has held that it becomes a Limited Warranty by default.

If the warranty is labeled a "Full [duration] Warranty," the warrantor cannot exclude or modify any UCC implied warranty, including limiting its duration. That is much more restrictive than Article 2, of course, which permits full disclaimer of implied warranties. The regulations also forbid the warrantor from requiring the buyer of a consumer product to return a warranty registration card as a condition precedent to warranty coverage and performance, unless the warrantor can prove that the duty is a reasonable one. *See* 16 C.F.R. § 700.7. In addition, the Act restricts a warrantor's ability to limit remedies and provides some additional remedy provisions. Those aspects of the Act will be covered in Assignment 24 on remedy limitations.

If the warranty is labeled a "Limited Warranty" or becomes one by default, the warrantor cannot exclude any UCC implied warranty and cannot limit its duration to a period shorter than the supplier's written warranty of reasonable duration. Again, that is more restrictive than Article 2. Moreover, any limitation of implied

---

[13] While the statutory provisions contain $5 and $10 thresholds, the applicable regulations cover goods more than $15.

warranty duration must be conscionable, must be in clear and unmistakable language, and must appear prominently on the face of the written warranty.

Reading the Code:
Magnuson-Moss §§ 102-104

Read 101(1), 101(6), 102-104, and 108.

Question 16. Does a supplier have to make a written warranty? If a supplier gives no written warranty, do the provisions governing Full and Limited Warranties apply to the transaction? Recall Examples I and J earlier in this Assignment.

Question 17. Of the provisions in 102-104 and 108, which ones supplement the Article 2 rules? Which ones change Article 2 rules?

Question 18. Magnuson-Moss restricts a seller's ability to limit "the duration" of an implied warranty. Article 2 does not seem to contemplate a time-length for the implied warranties of merchantability or fitness. What might Magnuson-Moss mean when it says an implied warranty may sometimes be limited in duration? Can that be reconciled with the absence of a time limit in Article 2?

Question 19. Does Magnuson-Moss have any effect on the warranties created under 2-312?

You have seen how a seller creates both express and implied warranties, how a seller may attempt to limit those warranties, and the additional requirements and restrictions imposed by the Magnuson-Moss Act. The following case will illustrate how warranty creation, disclaimers, and the Magnuson-Moss Act work together. As you read *Fleisher v. Fiber Composites, LLC,* consider the following questions:

(1) What are the elements of an express warranty cause of action according to the *Fleisher* court?

(2)   Why did the court reject the seller's argument that it had disclaimed the express warranties?

(3)   What approach did the court use to evaluate whether any statements became part of the basis of the bargain under 2-313? Was this the end of the plaintiff's express warranty claim? Why or why not?

(4)   Did the seller disclaim the implied warranty of merchantability? Why did the court allow the implied warranty of merchantability claim to proceed?

(5)   What was the relationship between the buyers' state law warranty claims and the federal Magnuson-Moss claim? Did the court allow the plaintiffs' Magnuson-Moss claim to proceed? Why or why not? What was the advantage to the buyers to also have the Magnuson-Moss claim?

FLEISHER v. FIBER COMPOSITES, LLC

79 U.C.C. Rep. Serv. 2d 20 (E.D. Pa. 2012)

PADOVA, J.

Plaintiffs bring this putative class action for breach of warranty and other claims arising out of Defendant Fiber Composites, LLC's ("Fiber") sale of defective deck materials to named Plaintiffs in Pennsylvania, New Jersey, New York, and Massachusetts. Presently before the Court is Fiber's Motion to Dismiss. For the reasons that follow, we grant the Motion in part and deny it in part.

I. BACKGROUND

A. Introduction

The First Amended Complaint ("FAC") alleges the following facts. Defendant Fiber manufactured, advertised, and sold Portico™ Series Decking products, including Portico™ Advantage and Eclipse composite decking (collectively "Portico") to consumers throughout the United States. Unlike natural wood decking products, Portico is made up of a composite material comprised of equal parts of wood fiber and polyethylene, a thermoplastic material. Portico is manufactured by direct extrusion, a process by which

304 • Learning Sales Law •

polyethylene and wood fibers are mixed together and melted in an extruder, then forced through a die to form a finished structural part. This process is designed to completely encapsulate the wood fibers in the polyethylene, rendering them virtually moisture proof. (*Id.*) Portico products were sold at nearly double the price of natural wood products.

Fiber expressly warranted Portico for a twenty-year period, guaranteeing that "the Decking & Railing will not check, splinter, peel, rot, or suffer structural damage from fungal decay." This warranty was limited by the following disclaimer:

> THE FOREGOING WARRANTY IS EXCLUSIVE AND IN LIEU OF ANY AND ALL OTHER WARRANTIES WITH RESPECT TO PORTICO™ FIBER COMPOSITE MATERIAL. WARRANTOR DISCLAIMS ANY AND ALL OTHER WARRANTIES, INCLUDING WITHOUT LIMITATION ANY IMPLIED WARRANTY OF MERCHANTABILITY OR FITNESS FOR A PARTICULAR PURPOSE.

> Purchaser's sole remedy for any claim whatsoever arising out of the purchase, use, storage, or possession of Portico™ Fiber Composite Material (whether such claim arises in contract, warranty, tort, strict liability or otherwise) including without limitation any claim that Portico™ Fiber Composite Material failed to perform as warranted above, shall be replaced with new Portico™ Fiber Composite Material in an amount equal to the volume of defective material as scheduled on the prorated warranty schedule.

Fiber made the following representations regarding Portico that appeared on its website and on contractors' websites: Portico is unlike "[t]raditional wood decking [that] fades, molds, cracks, splinters, and needs to be treated and sealed regularly for the deck to maintain its original look and feel"; "Portico Eclipse is slip resistant, has a quality surface finish that reduces dirt and mold buildup and will not check, split, or warp"; Portico has "just about eliminated the problems associated with typical wood decking"; Portico is "able to resist moisture penetration and degradation from fungal rot as the plastic encapsulates and binds the wood together"; "[l]ong after installation, [Portico] . . . will stay beautiful and provide you with years of outdoor enjoyment"; and Portico has "consistent color throughout the board."

The named Plaintiffs are consumers from Pennsylvania, New Jersey, New York, and Massachusetts, who purchased Portico decking materials. Soon after installation, Plaintiffs noticed dark spotting on the surface of their decks, which has been determined to be extensive mold, mildew, and/or fungal growth ("fungal growth") resulting in discoloration of the deck surface. The fungal growth is due to a uniform latent defect in Portico that occurs regardless of proper installation, maintenance, and cleaning, and cannot be prevented or remediated. The Portico manufacturing process causes this latent defect because it does not result in complete encapsulation of the wood fibers, making Portico susceptible to moisture and microbe penetration to the internal wood fibers. This moisture and microbe penetration is the foundation for the fungal growth that caused the dark spotting on Plaintiffs' decks. In addition, Portico was manufactured with Micro-DOME technology, which creates an embossed surface on the boards which collects standing water and promotes fungal growth. Fiber failed to inform customers that moisture would immediately invade Portico and the decking surface would be enveloped with irremediable dark spotting caused by fungal growth.

After discovering the fungal growth on their decks, four of the five named Plaintiffs complained to Fiber. Fiber refused to refund the named Plaintiffs for the costs of cleaning their decks or to replace their Portico under the Limited Warranty, but merely advised Plaintiffs to chemically clean their decks. Plaintiffs cleaned their decks as directed, but the chemical products only worked briefly, or failed to work altogether, resulting in recurrence of the fungal growth. To this day, Fiber has not provided any further relief.

. . . .

III. DISCUSSION

A. Breach of Express Warranty[FN1]

Fiber argues that Plaintiffs' breach of express warranty claim should be dismissed because: (1) the FAC does not allege a breach of a term in the Limited Warranty; (2) no other express warranties were created in Fiber's promotional materials; (3) if other express warranties were created, Fiber properly disclaimed them in its Limited Warranty; and (4) if any express warranties were created, they did not become part of the basis of the bargain in Plaintiffs' purchase of Portico.

Plaintiffs contend that the FAC contains allegations of fact that support a claim for breach of Fiber's Limited Warranty as well as breach of express warranties created by Fiber's representations in promotional materials describing Portico's quality and characteristics. An express warranty is "a promise . . . that a good will conform to a specific description." *Knipe v. SmithKline Beecham*, 583 F. Supp. 2d 602, 625 (E.D. Pa. 2008) (citation omitted). . . .

In order to survive a motion to dismiss, a complaint asserting a claim for breach of an express warranty must "provide more than 'bald assertions,' and identify specific affirmations by Defendant that could be found to constitute an express warranty." *Snyder v. Farnam Cos., Inc.*, 792 F. Supp. 2d 712, 722 (D.N.J. 2011).

FN1 Plaintiffs' claim for violation of the Magnuson-Moss Consumer Products Warranty Act (the "Magnuson-Moss Act"), their first claim for relief, depends upon the existence of either an express or implied warranty. Consequently, we address Plaintiffs' arguments with respect to Plaintiffs' breach of express warranty (Second Claim for Relief) and breach of implied warranty (Third Claim for Relief) first.

1. The Limited Warranty

The Limited Warranty guarantees that Portico products "will not check, splinter, peel, rot, or suffer structural damage from fungal decay." Fiber argues that the FAC does not allege that any terms of the Limited Warranty were breached by Portico's latent defect that caused fungal growth, as the FAC does not allege that Plaintiffs' decks suffer "rot" or "structural damage from fungal decay." The FAC alleges that Plaintiffs suffered damage to their decks in the form of, inter alia, "incurable dark spotting" "unsightly and extensive discoloration"; "extensive discoloration in the form of unsightly black and gray spots"; and "irremediable staining from fungal growth." The FAC does not allege, and Plaintiffs do not argue, that these damages constitute "rot" or "structural damage from fungal decay" as stated in the Limited Warranty. Accordingly, we conclude that the FAC does not state a claim upon which relief may be granted based on a breach of the terms of the Limited Warranty.

2. Promotional Materials

Plaintiffs maintain that the FAC alleges that Fiber made representations in promotional materials that also constitute express warranties. Specifically, the FAC alleges that Fiber expressly warranted the following:

"Your choice of decking design and material will influence the overall appearance of your home and ultimately, its resale value. At some point, homeowners will sell their homes and the homebuyer does not want to be faced with a series of expensive home improvements."

"Long after installation, Portico's composite decking material will stay beautiful and provide you with years of outdoor enjoyment."

Portico products have "consistent color throughout the board" and "have the look of a hardwood floor."

Portico "has a quality surface finish that reduces dirt and mold buildup."

Portico is "able to resist moisture penetration and degradation from fungal rot as the plastic encapsulates and binds the wood together."

Fiber argues that the FAC does not assert a plausible claim for breach of warranty based on these statements because the FAC does not allege the existence of any statement made by Fiber "inside or outside the express warranty . . . that constitutes an affirmation of fact or promise that . . . Portico products would not stain as a result of fungal growth on the decks." Whether these representations constitute express warranties depends upon whether they constitute an "affirmation of fact or promise . . . which relates to the goods." 13 Pa. Cons. Stat. § 2313(a). Of the five alleged representations, all of which concern the quality and characteristics of Portico to resist fungal growth, we find that two constitute express warranties:[FN3] (1) that Portico products have "a quality surface finish that reduces dirt and mold buildup;" and (2) that Portico products are "able to resist moisture penetration and degradation from fungal rot." These representations are not exaggerations or overstatements "expressed in broad, vague, and commendatory language," *Castrol Inc. v. Pennzoil Co.*, 987 F.2d 939, 945 (3d Cir. 1993), but rather specifically describe Portico's ability to resist moisture and fungal growth. Accordingly, we conclude that the FAC alleges two representations that constitute express warranties made by Fiber as to the quality and characteristics of Portico products, and we limit further discussion of this issue to these two representations.

[FN3] The FAC also alleges that Portico samples were available at retail stores and that those samples constitute express warranties as to Portico's quality. However, the FAC fails to plead sufficient facts to support this claim because it does not describe the qualities or characteristics of the samples with respect to their ability to resist fungal growth.

3. The Limited Warranty's Disclaimer

Fiber argues that the disclaimer in the Limited Warranty precludes liability for breach of warranty in this case. As we discussed earlier, the Limited Warranty contains a disclaimer of "any and all other warranties." (Limited Warranty.) "[C]ontractual provisions limiting warranties, establishing repair or replacement as the exclusive remedy for breach of warranty and excluding liability for special, indirect and consequential damages in a commercial setting are generally valid and enforceable" under Pennsylvania law. *New York State Elec. & Gas Corp. v. Westinghouse Elec. Corp.*, 387 Pa. Super. 537, 564 A.2d 919, 924 (Pa. Super. Ct. 1989) (citations omitted). Fiber maintains that the Limited Warranty contains the sole terms of its warranty, and that the disclaimer in the Limited Warranty is enforceable and effectively limits warranty terms to those set out in the Limited Warranty.

However, the Uniform Commercial Code provides that "[w]ords or conduct relevant to the creation of an express warranty and words or conduct tending to negate or limit warranty shall be construed wherever reasonable as consistent with each other." 13 Pa. Cons. Stat. § 2316(a). "This section 'seeks to protect a buyer from unexpected and unbargained language of disclaimer by denying effect of such language when inconsistent with language of express warranty.'" *Morningstar v. Hallett*, 2004 PA Super 337, 858 A.2d 125, 131 (Pa. Super. Ct. 2004) (quoting 13 Pa. Cons. Stat. § 2316(a) cmt. 1). In other words, "[a] provision that there are no express warranties will be ignored when clearly inconsistent with statements that were made and that, by themselves, would constitute express warranties." Larry Lawrence, *Anderson on the Uniform Commercial Code* § 2-316:101 (3d ed. 2009).

Consequently, when otherwise valid disclaimers conflict with existing express warranties, the disclaimers are deemed inoperative. *See Pocono Artesian Waters Co. v. Leffler Sys.*, Civ. A. No. 90-1928, 2012 U.S. Dist. LEXIS 157343, 1991 WL 22075, at *3 (E.D. Pa. Feb. 19, 1991) (refusing to enforce a disclaimer of express warranties that was inconsistent with express warranty made by defendant); *Effanzee Assocs. v. Thermo Electron Corp.*, Civ. A. No. 92-6583, 1994 U.S. Dist. LEXIS 773, 1994 WL 6885, at *5 (E.D. Pa. Jan. 6, 1994) (enforcing a disclaimer that was "not inconsistent with any express warranty which may have been created by [the defendant's] promotional material"); *see also Viking Yacht Co. v. Composites One LLC*, 496 F. Supp. 2d 462, 470 (D.N.J. 2007) (recognizing that an otherwise enforceable disclaimer may be inoperable if unreasonably inconsistent with an express warranty).

The Limited Warranty contains specific guarantees that Portico "will not check, splinter, peel, rot, or suffer structural damage from fungal decay," and includes a clear disclaimer of all other express warranties. (Limited Warranty.) At the same time, the FAC alleges the existence of two express warranties regarding the ability of Portico to resist fungal growth. These express warranties guarantee that Portico has "a quality surface finish that reduces dirt and mold buildup," and is "able to resist moisture penetration and degradation from fungal rot." Fiber's attempt to disclaim other express warranties is thus unenforceable because it is inconsistent with the language of its express warranties. Therefore, we conclude that the FAC alleges the existence of express warranties regarding Portico's resistance to fungal growth that are not limited by the disclaimer contained in the Limited Warranty.

4. Basis of the Bargain

Fiber also argues that Plaintiffs' claims for breach of those two express warranties must be dismissed because the FAC does not allege that these warranties formed part of the basis of Plaintiffs' bargain in their purchase of Portico. . . .

Nonetheless, a warranty does not become part of the basis of the bargain unless plaintiffs show that they "read, heard, saw or knew of the advertisement containing the affirmation of fact or promise." *Cipollone v. Liggett Grp., Inc.*, 893 F.2d 541, 567 (3d Cir. 1990) (interpreting New Jersey law), *rev'd on other grounds* 505 U.S. 504, 112 S. Ct. 2608, 120 L. Ed. 2d 407 (1994). Where alleged express warranties appear on a defendant's website, the plaintiffs must prove that they "read, heard, saw or knew of the statements made on defendants' website prior to the purchase of [the product] or that they were induced to buy [the product] based on these statements." *Parkinson v. Guidant Corp.*, 315 F. Supp. 2d 741, 752 (W.D. Pa. 2004) (applying Pennsylvania law); *see also Yurcic v. Purdue Pharma, L.P.*, 343 F. Supp. 2d 386, 395 (M.D. Pa. 2004) (applying Pennsylvania law and rejecting plaintiff's argument that his awareness of the warranties could be inferred from allegations that the warranties were made publically where the complaint did not also allege that he was aware of the statements).

The FAC alleges that Fiber "advertised its Portico products directly to consumers, including by way of advertisements and its Internet web site." The FAC does not, however, allege that Plaintiffs read, heard, saw, or knew of the express warranties alleged in paragraphs 49 and 46 of the FAC regarding Portico's resistance to fungal growth prior to purchasing Portico. We therefore conclude that the facts alleged in the FAC do not support a reasonable inference that the express warranties alleged in paragraphs 49 and 46 of the FAC became part of the basis of Plaintiffs' bargain. Fiber's Motion to Dismiss is, accordingly, granted as to Plaintiffs' breach of express warranty claim.[FN4]

[FN4] At the same time, however, we grant Plaintiffs' request for leave to amend the FAC to allege facts showing that Fiber's express warranties became part of the basis of the bargain for Plaintiffs' express warranty claims. . . .

B. Breach of the Implied Warranty of Merchantability

Fiber argues that Plaintiffs' breach of implied warranty claim should be dismissed because the FAC fails to allege that Portico decking materials are not fit for their ordinary purpose. [FN5]

[FN5] We note that Fiber has not argued that Portico's implied warranties, if any, were disclaimed by the Limited Warranty.

. . . .

In arguing that the FAC does not allege that Plaintiffs' decks are unfit for ordinary use, Fiber asserts that the ordinary purpose of a deck is structural in that it provides an outdoor recreational space. Fiber argues that the spotting alleged in the FAC is not alleged to have made the decks unusable, as the FAC does not allege that Plaintiffs cannot sit, walk, or entertain on their Portico decks. Fiber further notes that the FAC does not assert that the alleged fungal growth and spotting caused the boards to rot or caused their decks to fail.

Plaintiffs urge us to reject Fiber's essential proposition that decking material is merely purchased and used for its structural, rather than its aesthetic, characteristics and contend that the "ordinary purpose" of decking materials is to "look beautiful and [] enhance the appearance of their homes." Plaintiffs maintain that Portico's latent defect caused fungal growth and ugly spotting that rendered it unfit for ordinary use as decking material. *See Isip v.*

Mercedes-Benz USA, LLC, 155 Cal. App. 4th 19, 65 Cal. Rptr. 3d 695, 700 (Cal. Ct. App. 2007) (rejecting the notion that a car is fit for its ordinary purpose merely because it can provide transportation and explaining that "[a] vehicle that smells, lurches, clanks, and emits smoke over an extended period of time is not fit for its intended purpose"); *Stearns v. Select Comfort Retail Corp.*, Civ. A. No. 08-2746, 2009 U.S. Dist. LEXIS 48367, 2009 WL 1635931, at *8 (N.D. Cal. June 5, 2009) (allowing a claim for breach of the implied warranty of merchantability to proceed because "the fact that a person still may sleep on a moldy bed does not bar as a matter of law a claim for breach of the implied warranty of merchantability").

The FAC alleges that Fiber "marketed, promoted and sold Portico products to increase the aesthetic appeal, as well as to enhance the outdoor enjoyment, of a consumer's properties." We agree with Plaintiffs that, based on these allegations in the FAC, it is reasonable to infer that the ordinary use of outdoor decking material, and the use for which Fiber intended Portico, is in part to "increase the aesthetic appeal" and "enhance the outdoor enjoyment" of Plaintiffs' residential properties. (*Id.*) Thus, the FAC adequately alleges that under the warranty of merchantability, the minimum quality required of Portico is one which the consumer expects to satisfy a certain aesthetic expectation. . . [FN6] The FAC alleges that Fiber breached this warranty by selling a defective product that develops ugly and irremediable dark spotting.

[FN6] Fiber relies on *Carey v. Chaparral Boats, Inc.*, 514 F. Supp. 2d 1152, 1155-56 (D. Minn. 2007), for the proposition that defects in a product's cosmetic appearance do not violate the implied warranty of merchantability. In *Carey*, the district court concluded, on a summary judgment motion, that "overwhelming evidence demonstrates that cracks in the boat's finish are a cosmetic problem and in no way impact the boat's ordinary use." *Carey*, 514 F. Supp. 2d at 1156. In contrast, here the FAC alleges that Plaintiffs spent considerable money to "increase the aesthetic appeal" of their homes by installing Portico decks, and thus the latent defect in Portico's design and manufacture impaired the decks' ordinary use as aesthetic goods.

Therefore, we conclude that the FAC has adequately pled a claim for breach of the implied warranty of merchantability, and accordingly, we deny Fiber's Motion to Dismiss as to Plaintiffs' claim for breach of the implied warranty of merchantability.

C. Magnuson-Moss Consumer Products Warranty Act

Fiber argues that Plaintiffs' Magnuson-Moss Act claim should be dismissed because Fiber did not breach its express warranties and implied warranty of merchantability as required to state a claim under the Magnuson-Moss Act. The Magnuson-Moss Act, 15 U.S.C. § 2301 et seq., provides a private right of action in federal court for consumers who are "damaged by the failure of a supplier, warrantor, or service contractor to comply with any obligation . . . under a written warranty, [or] implied warranty." 15 U.S.C. § 2310(d)(1). "A claim under the [Magnuson-Moss Act] relies on the underlying state law claim."

. . . .

Fiber argues that Plaintiffs' Magnuson-Moss Act claim should be dismissed because the FAC fails to plead a state law claim for breach of express warranty or breach of the implied warranty of merchantability upon which relief may be granted. As we have concluded that the FAC adequately pleads a claim for breach of the implied warranty of merchantability, it follows that Plaintiffs' claim under the Magnuson-Moss Act for breach of the implied warranty of merchantability is also adequately pled and should not be dismissed. See 15 U.S.C. § 2301(7) (defining "implied warranty" under the Magnuson-Moss Act as "an implied warranty arising under State law"). Therefore, we conclude that the FAC adequately pleads a claim for breach of the Magnuson-Moss Act, and we deny Fiber's Motion to Dismiss as to Plaintiffs' Magnuson-Moss Act claim.

. . . .

IV. CONCLUSION

For the foregoing reasons, Fiber's Motion to Dismiss is denied in part and granted in part. . . .

APPLYING THE CODE

Problem 12-2.

Richard La Trace has come to you with a problem regarding some lamps he bought at a B&B Antiques auction recently. B&B Antiques sent Richard a brochure for an upcoming auction. Intrigued, Richard attended the auction and spent $56,200 on lamps described in the brochure as "Tiffany" brand lamps. B&B Auction personnel reassured La Trace after the auction that the lamps were made by Tiffany. When Richard tried to resell the lamps, Dean Lowry, an expert in Tiffany products, told him they were only reproductions and not authentic Tiffany lamps.

The B&B Antiques brochure contained the following statement under the heading "Conditions of Sale":

> 1. All property is sold AS IS WHERE IS, and we make NO guarantees, warranties or representations, expressed or implied, with respect to the property or the correctness of the catalog or other description of authenticity of authorship, physical condition, size, quality, rarity, importance, provenance, exhibitions, literature or historical relevance of the property or otherwise. No statement anywhere, whether oral or written, shall be deemed such a guarantee, warranty or representation. Prospective bidders should inspect the property before bidding to determine the condition, size and whether or not it has been repaired or restored and no refunds or credits shall be issued.

Richard signed a similar statement as part of the "Conditions of Auction," and the sales slips stated the merchandise was sold "as is." Does Richard have a claim against B&B for breach of express warranty that the lamps were "Tiffany"? To what extent can a seller provide a disclaimer upfront (and regularly thereafter), yet still have responsibility for express statements made about the goods? Does it matter whether Richard has attended other B&B Antiques auctions? Would the outcome be different if in the brochure the auction company had included a statement that any descriptions of the items being sold were to be used "only as a guide," and the auctioneer did not make any statements about Tiffany at the auction itself?

Problem 12-3.

Recall Problems 10-7 and 11-7 concerning Lisa, Pete's Exercise Boutique, and the Thighslimmer 2000X. Suppose Lisa and Pete both signed a contract for the

Thighslimmer, which set forth the price, the conditions for repair and return, and the following language in bold print, surrounded by a border and shaded:

LIMITED WARRANTY

This product is warranted against defects for 1 year from date of purchase. Within this period, Pete's Exercise Boutique will repair it without charge for parts and labor. Simply bring your sales slip as proof of purchase date to Pete's Exercise Boutique. Warranty does not cover transportation costs. Nor does it cover a product subjected to misuse or accidental damage. EXCEPT AS PROVIDED HEREIN, PETE'S EXERCISE BOUTIQUE MAKES NO WARRANTIES, EXPRESS OR IMPLIED, INCLUDING WARRANTIES OF MERCHANTABILITY AND FITNESS FOR A PARTICULAR PURPOSE. PETE'S EXERCISE BOUTIQUE HAS NO LIABILITY FOR ANY INCIDENTAL OR CON-SEQUENTIAL DAMAGES.

How would this affect Lisa's ability to bring any of the warranty claims discussed in your responses to Problems 10-7 and 11-7?

Problem 12-4.

Your client, Materials, Inc., sells wood veneers that buyers use to make furniture products. Materials is concerned that it might have warranty exposure on the wood veneers after the buyer fabricates it into furniture. Materials uses the following language in its Purchase Order:

> All products distributed by Materials Inc. (MI) are manufactured to meet the standard industry specifications of our suppliers. Since MI has no control over end products fabricated with the materials sold, no warranty is expressed or implied. All products must be inspected upon purchase. MI makes every effort to check and match product specifications, colors, species, dimensions, etc. of the merchandise ordered. However we cannot guarantee an accurate match. Please check merchandise before installation. MI's responsibility shall be limited to the replacement of the materials proven to be defective in material and/or workmanship, or incorrectly shipped, if claimed within 10 days of delivery. MI makes no warranty based on any usage of trade or

fitness for any particular use. Buyer assumes all risks resulting from the use with other substances or in any process.

Has Materials effectively disclaimed all warranties? If not, how would you recommend changing the language to accomplish the disclaimer?

Problem 12-5.

Your client, Cullen, was injured after she fell while filling her new walk-in tub with water and became wedged in the front of the tub. Cullen was stuck in water in the tub for thirty hours, because the tub failed to drain when the chain attached to the stopper broke. Cullen wants to make a claim against the company and has provided you the sales agreement. The one-page sales agreement was signed by Cullen at the bottom of the page and in the middle of the page. In the middle of the page, in large, bold, capital letters, the agreement says, "I have read, understood and agree with the conditions overleaf before having signed this agreement." In the two-page "conditions overleaf," the only paragraph in all capital letters says, "The express warranties, if any, contained herein are in lieu of all other warranties, either expressed or implied, including without limitation any implied warranty of merchantability or fitness for a particular purpose, and of any other obligation on the part of the manufacturer." Cullen has told you she never read the conditions overleaf. Is she bound by it? Does it preclude her claim? Do we know if the seller has complied with Magnuson-Moss?

Problem 12-6.

In each of the fact situations below, what express and implied warranties have been created? Which, if any, have been effectively disclaimed? Breached?

(a) Sarah is shopping for a camp stove from a store that sells outdoor recreational equipment. She is concerned about her friends' stories about camp-stoves flaring up with large flames while being lit. She tells the store employee that she wants a stove that lights without producing large flames. The employee helps her to select a model with a butane tank, which avoids the flare-up problem of stoves with white gas. The particular stove that Sarah later buys is on display, out of its package, and assembled. The salesperson suggests that Sarah carefully look over the stove because it is a floor sample and to see if it has all the features Sarah wants. Sarah glances at the stove to make sure it is the model recommended to her, then takes it to the register and pays for it.

(b)   Sarah is shopping for a sleeping bag from a store that sells outdoor recreational equipment. The label sewn onto the bottom of one of the sleeping bags says that the bag is "machine washable in warm water with a mild soap and an extra rinse cycle." Sarah reads the label, then asks a salesperson whether the bag is really machine washable. The salesperson says that machine washing shortens the life of the bag by weakening stitching and decreasing the insulating quality so he would recommend dry cleaning. Sarah buys the sleeping bag. When Sarah washes the bag according to the label instructions, the insulation bunches up into lumps that cannot be completely separated.

(c)   Sarah is shopping for a new washing machine. She finds a top-loading Kenmore Elite brand machine at Sears labeled and advertised as a "High Efficiency" machine featuring "extra high" spin speeds of 1050–1100 RPM, along with a system that prevents or minimizes vibrations, for smooth, quiet operation during use, so laundry dries faster than washing machines that do not have high efficiency capabilities. Sears sold the machine with a limited warranty that covered defects in materials and workmanship for one year from the date of purchase with an exclusive remedy of repair or replacement. From the very beginning, Sarah experienced unbalanced loads that caused the machine to shake violently, make banging noises, and rock from side to side. The "violent movement" of her machine was so severe that the machine would shift or "walk itself" away from the wall on which it was positioned. In order to keep the machine from damaging the dryer positioned next to it, Sarah used a plastic trash can as a "buffer" to help absorb the "shock of the shaking machine" and "attempt to keep it in place." Sarah did not complain to Sears about the alleged defects until more than a year had passed after her purchase of the machine. After the United States Consumer Products Safety Commission recalled the washing machine due to risk of personal injury and property damage, Sears repaired Sarah's machine by lowering the spin speed so that it did not operate at the advertised "extra high" spin speeds.

Problem 12-7.

Katie has bought a powerful new gas stove for her kitchen. She is having problems getting the stovetop burners to simmer liquids at a low enough temperature to prepare particularly delicate sauces like Hollandaise, even though the burners are adjusted correctly. Assume that the following occurred before the contract was entered:

- The seller's salesperson simmered a small pan of Hollandaise sauce on the same model stove at the store.

- The seller's salesperson said that the 15,000 BTU burners "have the power to stir fry and sear meat at very high temperatures, but also to simmer delicate sauces at very low temperatures."

- The seller's brochure about the stove, given to Katie by the seller, says that the lowest burner setting heats at 180°F. (The stove meets these latter specs, but to properly prepare some sauces requires the burners to heat at 150° F.)

- Assume that the contract also contains an implied warranty of merchantability but not a warranty of fitness for a particular purpose.

Which express warranties have been created? Which of these warranties cannot reasonably be construed consistently with each other? How does 2-317 resolve the conflict(s)?

Assignment 13
Extending Warranties to
Third-Party Beneficiaries
§ 2-318

In Assignments 10 and 11, we explored express and implied warranties made by a seller to the immediate buyer in sales transactions. We also saw that warranty liability may be created for a remote seller (often a manufacturer or wholesaler) by written warranty language packaged with the goods and passed on to a remote buyer, and by the remote seller's advertisements seen by a remote buyer. But what about other third persons not a party to a sales transaction? For example, when a seller creates a warranty with respect to goods, is the buyer's spouse or other family member protected by that warranty if the goods fail to conform while the goods are in their hands? What about the buyer's friend? Or a bystander? If warranties are made by a manufacturer to a wholesaler, is the retailer who buys from the wholesaler covered by the original warranty? What about the retailer's customer? Are any of these "third parties" (those not part of the original contract) beneficiaries of the warranty provisions made in the sale by the original warrantor?

LEARNING OUTCOMES AND OBJECTIVES

At the completion of this Assignment, you should be able to

- evaluate when third parties (someone other than the immediate buyer) who use, buy, or are exposed to goods may be protected by UCC warranties made to the immediate buyer;

- identify when lack of privity of contract will bar an action for breach of warranty and when it will not; and

- evaluate when a warranty made by a seller may be disclaimed as to third parties.

A. The Historical Requirement of Privity

We started this Assignment with a set of questions about whether a variety of third parties—non-parties to the sales transaction—would be protected by warranties given by the seller to the buyer. Under older common law rules, the answer to all these questions was "no." Only persons in "privity of contract"—the direct parties to the sale—were permitted to sue for relief under a contract, which meant that only the immediate buyer in a sales transaction was protected by a seller's warranty. This direct relationship is sometimes referred to as being "in privity." *See* Figure 1 below. As explained in Assignment 11, some courts have concluded that sellers are liable to remote buyers for written representations passed through to those buyers and made part of the basis of the bargain, e.g., warranty booklets in new cars, or warranty provisions appearing on the outside of packaged goods. Liability for such "pass-through warranties" is not based on being in privity, but is supported by Comment 2 to § 2-313. These indirect relationships are sometimes referred to as "horizontal privity" or "vertical privity" because they operate to connect individuals up and down a distribution chain. Horizontal privity refers to the non-privity relationship of someone who used or consumed the goods but was not a buyer. Vertical privity refers to the non-privity relationship of the buyer and those, such as manufacturers, with whom the buyer does not have a direct relationship. But the rules regarding vertical privity protect only buyers, not others who may be injured by a breach of warranty, so protection for those in horizontal privity is sometimes afforded under the Code. Moreover, a remote buyer is protected by this extension of § 2-313 only if the written warranty was part of the basis of the bargain in the sale, under the standard applicable in the jurisdiction.

The common law has offered one other way for an injured person to circumvent the privity obstacle to liability: a seller/warrantor might be held "indirectly" liable to customers or others not in privity under a combination of tort and contract principles. For example, if a car dealer provides a warranty against defects to a car buyer, and a third party is injured in an accident when the steering mechanism fails while the buyer is driving, the third party would not be in privity with the seller and therefore could not collect directly from the seller for breach of warranty. However, the third party might sue the driver (buyer) for tortious injury and the buyer might then seek recovery from the car dealer (seller) for any tort damages the buyer owed to the third party as a result of the dealer's warranty breach.

Similarly, imagine that AC/DC, Inc. manufactures and sells batteries to Ford, warranting their quality. Ford installs those batteries in some of its cars, which it then sells to dealers with an implied warranty of merchantability. A dealer subsequently sells the cars to consumers with an implied warranty of merchantability. If one of the batteries causes an engine fire, the consumer could seek relief from the car dealer for breach of the dealer's warranty; the dealer could seek reimbursement by claiming against Ford for breach of Ford's warranty to the dealer; and Ford could seek relief against AC/DC under AC/DC's warranty made to Ford. Liability of AC/DC or Ford for injury to ultimate purchasers would thus depend upon a series of contractual warranty provisions (AC/DC to Ford; Ford to the dealer; and dealer to the consumer). The procedural obstacles are evident, and liabilities up the "warranty chain" depend on the nature of the warranty given (or disclaimed or excluded) in each contract.

Figure 1.

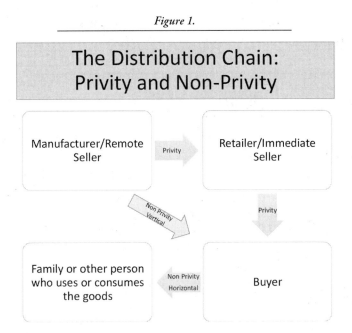

B. The Modern Relaxation of Privity

To respond to problems created by such privity rules, courts during the twenti-eth century gradually relaxed the rules requiring privity of contract, and Article 2 followed that trend. Moreover, because states have had differing attitudes about how much to relax the requirement of privity, Article 2 offers three alter-native versions of third-party warranty liability within § 2-318, and some states have created their own versions. By a recent count, twenty-nine jurisdictions have enacted Alternative A,[1] nine use Alternative B,[2] and six have adopted

---

[1] Alaska, Arizona, Arkansas, Connecticut, District of Columbia, Florida, Georgia, Idaho, Illinois, Indiana, Ken-tucky, Maryland, Michigan, Mississippi, Missouri, Montana, Nebraska, Nevada, New Jersey, New Mexico, North Carolina, Ohio, Oklahoma, Oregon, Pennsylvania, Tennessee, Washington, West Virginia, and Wisconsin have adopted Alternative A.

[2] Alabama (applying some modifications); Colorado (excluding the word "natural"); Delaware, Kansas, and (excluding the word "natural"); New York, South Carolina, and South Dakota (combining B & C); and Vermont and Wyoming (excluding the word "natural") have adopted Alternative B.

Alternative C.[3] A number of states adopting each alternative have modified the § 2-318 text to suit local preferences, however, so one cannot rely on those numbers to determine which is the majority or plurality rule.[4]

Each of the three alternatives provides some coverage for third party beneficiaries, but in different ways. Accordingly, the ability of third parties to bring claims against the sellers, distributors, and manufacturers of goods depends on the alternative chosen by the state.

Reading the Code:
§ 2-318

Read 2-318 and its Comments.
Also find and read your own state's version of that section.

Question 1. Reading 2-318, you will see that 2-318 Alternative A does not mandate warranty coverage for affected individuals unless they are in the family or household of the buyer or are a guest in the buyer's home. Similarly, section 2-318 Alternatives A and B do not mandate warranty coverage for individuals who suffer property damage rather than personal injury.

Question 2. Note that each version of 2-318 indicates: (i) *the category of persons* to whom the seller's warranty extends (beyond the immediate buyer); and (ii) *the nature of the injury or injuries* included in the extension of warranty protection. In the final sentence of each version, the section *restricts the ability of sellers to modify the effect of the section.* Fill in the following chart and note the differences among the versions:

---

3   Hawaii, Iowa, Minnesota, North Dakota, Utah, and the U.S. Virgin Islands (with some variation) have adopted Alternative C.

4   Gary L. Monserud, Blending the Law of Sales with the Common Law of Third Party Beneficiaries, 39 Duq. L. Rev. 110, 129-34 (2000). Although the majority of jurisdictions have adopted Alternative A, in many of those states, the courts have adopted common law liability rules approximating the broader coverage in Alternatives B and C.

	Who else is protected by seller's warranty besides the immediate buyer?	For what kind of injury?	Limits on seller's power to restrict 2-318 protection
Alternative A (See note below)			
Alternative B			
Alternative C			
Your state's version			

Note: In construing Alternative A, consider whether the "his" in "his buyer" and the "his" in "in his home" refer to the same party to the transaction.

Read 2-318 Comment 3 and 2-313 Comment 2.

May a court extend warranty coverage to include individuals or injuries not granted warranty protection by the state legislature through its adoption of Alternative A or B? In view of the text of the Comments, is there a reason to treat differently (a) extending coverage for personal injury to an otherwise excluded individual, and (b) extending coverage for property damage to someone already protected against personal injury?

APPLYING THE CODE

Problem 13-1.

Revco launches a new perfume, "Gracie," which it sells to a retailer, Pharmco, where Harriet purchases a bottle.

  (a) What type of privity does Revco have with Pharmco? With Harriet? See Figure 1 above.

  (b) If Revco does not disclaim the implied warranty of merchantability and, further, makes an express warranty that the perfume is defect-free, what warranties will Harriet have under each of the 2-318 alternatives? How would your answer change if Revco disclaimed just the implied warranty of merchantability here?

  (c) If Revco disclaims all express and implied warranties properly under Article 2 in its contract with Pharmco, what warranties, if any, will Harriet have for the perfume under each of the 2-318 alternatives?

  (d) If Harriet's teenage daughter, Sandy, uses the perfume and develops hives, would Sandy have the benefit of those warranties in Alternative A, B, and C states?

EXAMPLES AND ANALYSIS

Example A: *Jensen v. Bayer AG*[5]

Jensen, a resident of Illinois, purchased Baycol, prescribed by his doctor for cholesterol, which he purchased at a pharmacy. Later, the manufacturer, Bayer, discontinued the drug due to adverse health effects that could be fatal. Jensen brought suit against the manufacturer for—among other claims—breach of the implied warranty of merchantability.

Analysis: The court ruled that the buyer, who took a prescription cholesterol drug that was later removed from the market, could not assert an action against the manufacturer based on the implied warranty of merchantability because

[5]   62 N.E.2d 1091 (Ill. App. Ct. 2007).

he bought the drug from the pharmacy and, therefore, lacked privity with the manufacturer.

Which part of 2-318 supports Bayer? Might it matter for Jensen's case that the case was decided under Illinois law, which is an Alternative A state? Would the answer be different in a state that adopted Alternative B? Alternative C?

A number of states have adopted their own versions of § 2-318 that vary, dramatically or slightly, from the alternatives in the UCC. Consider the following non-uniform versions.

Reading the Code:
§ 2-318 Variations

Read the Texas and Virginia versions of 2-318, reprinted below.

Texas § 2-318

This Chapter does not provide whether anyone other than a buyer may take advantage of an express or implied warranty of quality made to the buyer or whether the buyer or anyone entitled to take advantage of a warranty made to the buyer may sue a third party other than the immediate seller for deficiencies in the quality of the goods. These matters are left to the courts for their determination.

Virginia § 2-318

Lack of privity between plaintiff and defendant shall be no defense in any action brought against the manufacturer or seller of goods to recover damages for breach of warranty, express or implied, or for negligence, although the plaintiff did not purchase the goods from the defendant, if the plaintiff was a person whom the manufacturer or seller might reasonably have expected to use, consume, or be affected by the goods; however, this section shall not be construed to affect any litigation pending on June 29, 1962.

Question 3.

   (a) How does the Texas statute compare to Alternatives A, B, and C?

   (b) Who decides in Texas whether a third party, such as Sandy in Problem 13-1(d), has the benefit of any warranties made by the manufacturer/remote seller or retailer?

   (c) Can a warrantor exclude or limit the operation of the Texas statute?

Question 4.

   (a) How does the Virginia statute compare to Alternatives A, B, and C?

   (b) Would Sandy from Problem 13-1(d) have the benefit of warranties made by Revco if the claim arises in Virginia? For what kind of injuries might Sandy be protected in Virginia?

   (c) Can a warrantor exclude or limit the operation of the Virginia statute?

EXAMPLES AND ANALYSIS

Example B: *American Aerial Services, Inc. v. Terex USA, LLC*[6]

American Aerial Services, Inc. (American) supplies cranes and labor in the construction industry in Maine. In need of a new crane, American purchased a Terex Model T-780 truck crane manufactured by Terex USA, LLC (Terex) from a Terex distributor, Empire Crane Company (Empire). The crane turned out not to be just off the assembly line, but one that had been in an open air lot in Iowa for several months. Shortly after delivery by Empire, a technician discovered the crane's engine was low on coolant and had likely been driven from Iowa to Maine in that condition. American sent Empire a notice of revocation of acceptance, but retained the crane, as Empire and Terex attempted numerous repairs over many months. Unable to resolve the issues, American brought suit for breach of contract and

---

[6] 39 F. Supp. 3d 95 (D. Me. 2014).

warranty, among other claims. The seller and distributor filed a motion for summary judgment.

Analysis: The court granted summary judgment on the contract claim, finding the crane was new, as it had not been previously sold or put to use. The court denied the motion with respect to the warranty of merchantability, however. The court explained that Maine has a non-uniform version of 2-318 which provides:

> Lack of privity between plaintiff and defendant shall be no defense in any action brought against the manufacturer, seller or supplier of goods for breach of warranty, express or implied, although the plaintiff did not purchase the goods from the defendant, if the plaintiff was a person whom the manufacturer, seller or supplier might reasonably have expected to use, consume or be affected by the goods.

Based on Maine's version of 2-318, American could bring suit for breach of the implied warranties. Moreover, under Maine law, Terex's attempted warranty disclaimer and limited product warranty did not bind American because Terex did not deliver the disclaimers to American. Finally, the only exclusions delivered to American on a data sheet concerning the crane were not conspicuous or clear as to exclusion, so they did not satisfy the requirements of a disclaimer under 2-316. The court found that the implied warranty of fitness did not apply.

How did the non-uniform rule in Maine affect the outcome in this case? Compare the result in *American Aerial Services* with *MAN Engines & Components, Inc. v. Shows*, 434 S.W.3d 132 (Tex. 2014), in which the court applied Texas law to find that a subsequent buyer could sue the manufacturer for breach of the implied warranty of merchantability, but that a manufacturer's valid disclaimer would be binding on the later buyer, and *Gunn v. Hytrol Conveyor Co., Inc.*, 80 UCC Rep. Serv. 2d 948 (E.D.N.Y. 2013), holding that while privity rules are relaxed in New York law, the employee of a conveyor belt company who was injured and brought suit against the manufacturer was bound by the warranty disclaimer of the manufacturer. Which of the court's judgments do you support? Why?

What would the result in *American Aerial Services* have been under Alternatives A, B, and C?

At times, a state's approach to relaxation of privity has gone even further:

Example C: *Anunciacao v. Caterpillar Inc.*[7]

Caterpillar Inc. (Caterpillar) licensed its trademark to a Japanese company that manufactured a Caterpillar excavator. The plaintiff was run over by the excavator and sustained serious injuries. Caterpillar did not manufacture or sell the specific excavator, but the machine bore the Caterpillar name, address, and trademark pursuant to the licensing agreement. Moreover, Caterpillar had assisted the licensor with the design and development of the excavator. Caterpillar moved for summary judgment, arguing that trademark licensors, in this situation, should not be liable for breach of the implied warranty of merchantability.

Analysis: The court disagreed with Caterpillar, holding that under Massachusetts law a non-seller trademark licensor can be liable for breach of the implied warranty of merchantability under the "apparent manufacturer" doctrine. The court noted that 2-318, as adopted in Massachusetts, imposes liability on manufacturers and suppliers, as well as sellers, irrespective of privity, which could include entities that participated substantially in the "design, manufacture, or distribution" of the goods.

Should privity be a bar in cases like this where the company did not actually manufacture or sell the goods? Do you agree or disagree with the court's reasoning here regarding the "apparent manufacturer" doctrine? Did the non-uniform provision make a difference here? *But see First Choice Armor & Equip., Inc. v. Toyobo Am., Inc.*, 839 F. Supp. 2d 407 (D. Mass. 2012) (stipulating that the relaxation of privity did not extend under Massachusetts law to a remote commercial retailer bringing contract-based claims).

While the cases surely indicate a tendency toward relaxation of privity, that relaxation is not without limitations, as can be seen in the next Example.

---

[7]   2011 WL 4899969 (D. Mass. 2011).

Example D: *Mosley v. Wyeth, Inc.*[8]

The buyer of the drug Reglan brought a breach of warranty claim against the manufacturers of the brand-name drug. The manufacturers moved to dismiss on the grounds that the buyer had used a generic form of the drug, not one purchased from the manufacturer, directly or indirectly. The buyer of the drug argued that the manufacturers disseminated inaccurate information about the drug knowing that others would rely so they should be liable.

Analysis: The court agreed with the manufacturers, recognizing that 2-318 allows for actions by those who lack privity, but does not permit an action by someone who was not a consumer of the manufacturer's product. That is, there is no action against a "brand name" manufacturer by someone who used a generic product.

Which part of 2-318 supports the manufacturers? Should privity be a bar in cases like this where the manufacturer gets the approval from the Federal Drug Administration and knows that others will make and distribute generic drugs based on its information? Perhaps the cause of action is simply not in warranty? *See Wyeth, Inc. v. Weeks*, No. 1101397, 2014 WL 4055813 (Ala. Aug. 15, 2014) (allowing a claim for fraud to proceed against the manufacturers in this case).

The following case, *Babb v. Regal Marine Industries, Inc.,* illustrates the effect of privity on a remote buyer's claim against a manufacturer. As you read the case, consider these questions:

(1)   Why didn't Babb bring a claim against the seller of the boat?

(2)   Washington is an Alternative A state. Why didn't 2-318 help Babb? Would 2-318 have helped Babb if Washington were an Alternative B or Alternative C state?

(3)   Did the sales invoice establish privity with the manufacturer for Babb? Why or why not?

---

[8]   719 F. Supp. 2d 1340 (S.D. Ala. 2010).

(4) Why did Babb raise a claim that he was a third-party beneficiary? How does such a claim differ from a claim under Article 2?

(5) Did the court find that Babb was an intended third–party beneficiary? Why or why not? Under what circumstances will a buyer be able to claim protection as a third-party beneficiary?

(6) Why might courts be more likely to relax privity standards for express warranties than for implied warranties?

BABB V. REGAL MARINE INDUSTRIES, INC.

186 Wash. App. 1003 (2015)

JOHANSSON, J.

. . . .

FACTS

In 2007, Babb shopped for a new boat, researching the boat market and reading product reviews which, according to Babb, rated Regal positively. Babb visited a local boat dealership, PBNW, where he purchased a Regal. By the terms of a contract between PBNW and Regal, PBNW was an authorized Regal dealer.

Regal provides a limited warranty for its boats. The warranty specifies that the dealer will repair or replace any defective parts for one year from delivery. But the warranty lists exceptions not covered: engines, aftermarket accessories, gelcoat surfaces, damage caused by user negligence, accident, or misuse, among others. The boat's Volvo engine had its own warranty.

. . . .

Over the 2007 to 2008 winter, Babb stored his boat, and in spring 2008, his son-in-law, Shane Hagen, used it. Hagen reported that the boat "repeatedly stalled and had to be towed back into shore." Babb phoned [a representative of Regal] named Rainey . . . in July 2008, and Rainey told Babb to take the boat to CSR Marine, a repair shop, and to tell them that Rainey "ok'ed it." Rainey also sent Babb a new wake board tower for his boat when Babb reported that the existing tower had broken welds.

CSR Marine inspected Babb's boat and informed Babb that the boat's engine had a small engine head crack caused by freeze damage. Babb phoned Regal again in December 2008, indicating that he needed to repair his boat and that his dealer, PBNW, had gone bankrupt. He spoke with Regal Manager of Customer Service, Mark Skrzypek, and explained the cracked engine head. Skrzypek informed Babb that he believed that the cracked engine was caused by improper winterization not a manufacturing defect. Skrzypek convinced CSR to reduce the storage fees it had charged Babb, but told Babb that Regal's warranty did not cover the Volvo engine.

Dissatisfied when Skrzypek advised him that Regal would not cover the engine repairs, Babb sued Regal on numerous grounds, including . . . breach of express and implied warranties, among others. . . .

The trial court granted summary judgment in favor of Regal on each of Babb's claims. Babb appealed, and we affirmed the summary dismissal of his claims for . . . breach of express warranties. . . . But we reversed the trial court's order dismissing Babb's claim that Regal breached implied warranties because there was no evidence in the record to demonstrate that Babb had negotiated a waiver of those claims.

. . . .

On remand from our Supreme Court, we are asked to determine whether Babb's claim that Regal breached its implied warranty of merchantability is precluded by the lack of contractual privity between Babb and Regal.

ANALYSIS

Babb does not dispute that contractual privity is required to maintain a claim for breach of an implied warranty of merchantability. Rather, Babb argues that (1) he has satisfied the privity requirement by virtue of the sales invoice that identifies Regal as a party to the agreement, or (2) because he is an independent third party beneficiary of the contract between Regal and PBNW, an exception to the privity requirement applies. We hold that Babb's claim for breach of implied warranty of merchantability is precluded by his lack of contractual privity with Regal.

Article 2 of the UCC, as adopted in Washington, governs warranties arising from the sale of goods. RCW 62A.2-313, 2-318. Unless excluded or modified, a warranty that goods are merchantable "is implied in a contract for their sale" so long as the seller is a "merchant with respect to goods of that kind." RCW 62A.2–314(1). This implied warranty of merchantability assures that the goods "are fit for the ordinary purposes for which such goods are used." RCW 62A.2–314(2)(c); *Tex Enters., Inc. v. Brockway Standard, Inc.*, 149 Wn.2d 204, 208, 66 P.3d 625 (2003).

Lack of contractual privity has historically been a defense to claims of breach of warranty. The "vertical" nonprivity plaintiff is a buyer who is in the distributive chain, but who did not buy the product directly from the defendant. Our Supreme Court has upheld dismissals of remote purchasers' claims for breach of implied warranties of merchantability where privity between purchaser and manufacturer was absent.

Here, Babb contracted to purchase his boat from PBNW, not from Regal directly. Accordingly, Babb is a vertical nonprivity plaintiff because he is a buyer in the distributive chain but who did not buy the product directly from the defendant.

A. DIRECT PRIVITY

Nonetheless, Babb argues that privity between he and Regal exists because (1) the sales invoice issued by PBNW identifies Regal as a party to the agreement, and (2) neither PBNW, Babb, nor Regal signed the invoice's waiver of implied warranties. Babb contends that had he signed that waiver, Regal would have argued that Babb made a conscious waiver of the implied warranties, and in doing so, Regal would implicitly recognize the existence of privity between the two parties.

First, Babb does not cite to the record to substantiate his claim that the sales invoice issued by PBNW identifies Regal as a party to the agreement. Instead the record shows that the invoice simply names Regal as the maker of the boat. Nothing in these documents establishes that Regal was party to the contract between Babb and PBNW.

Second, Babb's argument about the waiver of the implied warranties rests on speculative assertions regarding a hypothetical scenario. We do not address hypothetical questions. Instead, we conclude that Babb had no contractual relationship with Regal and, therefore, no privity with Regal. To allow implied warranties to arise without reliance on an underlying contract is inconsistent with our court's prior approach to implied warranties. This is evident because "the plain language of both RCW 62A.2-314 and -315 requires that implied warranties only arise out of contractual relationships." *Tex Enters.*, 149 Wn.2d at 211. We reject Babb's attempt to establish direct privity for the forgoing reasons.

B. THIRD PARTY BENEFICIARY

Babb next argues that Regal is responsible for breach of its implied warranty of merchantability because Regal was obligated to process warranty claims brought by the dealership's customers. In Babb's view, this fact entitles him to recovery as an intended third-party beneficiary of the contract between Regal and PBNW. We disagree. Babb is not an intended third-party beneficiary under the "sum of the interaction" test for purposes of his claim for breach of the implied warranty of merchantability.

Although lack of contractual privity is ordinarily a defense to a claim for breach of implied warranty of merchantability, our Supreme Court has created an exception to the requirement. Specifically, our courts have allowed a remote purchaser to pursue claims for breach of implied warranties of merchantability notwithstanding lack of vertical privity when the remote purchaser can show that it was an intended third-party beneficiary of a contract involving the manufacturer. Our courts apply the "sum of the interaction" test essentially to determine whether the manufacturer was sufficiently involved in the transaction (including post-sale) with the remote purchaser to warrant enforcement of an implied warranty.

In support of his position that he was an intended third-party beneficiary of the contract between Regal and PBNW, Babb relies on *Lidstrand v. Silvercrest Industries*, 28 Wn.App. 359, 365, 623 P .2d 710 (1981), where Division One of this court held that warranties made by a mobile home manufacturer extended to subsequent purchasers of the home as intended third party beneficiaries notwithstanding a lack of contractual privity between the parties. Importantly, however, *Lidstrand* involved express warranties. 28 Wn. App at 363. And our courts have long recognized that the privity requirement is relaxed when the claims involve a manufacturer's express representations rather than those implied warranties that arise automatically by operation of a sale. Babb has cited no authority to support his claim against Regal for breach of implied warranty.

Babb does not argue that he is an intended third-party beneficiary under the "sum of the interaction" between the parties, but even when we apply the test, Babb's claim fails nonetheless.

Our Supreme Court first applied the test to a claim for a breach of an implied warranty of merchantability in *Touchet Valley*. . . .

. . . [T]he *Touchet Valley* court concluded that the owner of a collapsed grain-storage facility could maintain an implied warranty action against a subcontractor with whom there was no privity because the owner was the intended third-party beneficiary of the contract between the general contractor and the subcontractor. In so holding, the *Touchet Valley* court determined that the subcontractor knew Touchet Valley's identity, its purpose, and its requirements for the storage building. 119 Wn.2d at 346. The subcontractor had also designed the building to the purchaser's specifications and delivered components to the construction site. And when the building first began to collapse, the subcontractor helped to attempt repairs.

. . . .

Here, Regal did not know Babb's identity or his purpose nor did it build the boat specifically with his requirements in mind. Rather, Regal merely built a version of one of its ostensibly ordinary models at its headquarters in Florida, and then sold and shipped that boat to one of its dealers in Arizona. Ultimately, PBNW arranged delivery to its location, where Babb made his purchase.

After he began to experience trouble with his boat, and once he determined that PBNW had gone bankrupt, Babb had a series of contacts with Regal. According to Babb, Regal representatives assured him that they would take care of his problems. Regal then sent Babb a new wake board tower and instructed Babb to take his boat to a marine repair shop presumably to conduct repairs with Regal's permission. But the record does not establish that the repair shop ever did any work on Babb's boat with or without Regal's approval. Instead, when the result of the repair shop's investigation revealed a broken engine, it appears from the record that although Regal offered to assist in obtaining parts at wholesale cost, it otherwise refused to cover any repair costs because the engine had a separate warranty through its own manufacturer.

Accordingly, aside from the replacement of his wake board tower, the extent of the interaction between Regal and Babb was a series of post-sale phone calls related to the repair of a boat that Regal did not build specifically for Babb. The facts here are distinguishable from those in . . . *Touchet Valley*. Consequently, we hold that Babb's claim for breach of implied warranty of merchantability fails as a matter of law because there is no privity between Babb and Regal and because Babb was not an intended third-party beneficiary of the contract between Regal and PBNW.

Affirmed.

APPLYING THE CODE

Problem 13-2.

This problem asks you to consider a sale of goods that begins with a manufacturer, proceeds through multiple sales, and ends with the product in the hands of a third party. The product fails, injuring both the third party and others, and you are asked to determine what warranties are available to the injured parties from each seller in the distribution chain. To help you answer that question, as you read the facts you should make a note of each sale in the chain and the warranties made and disclaimed by each seller to its immediate buyer. That list will help you determine which of those warranties extend beyond the immediate buyer.

- Elektron, Inc. sells 10,000 tablet devices (with earbugs) and 500 mini-tablets to Tabmart Products, Inc., a regional wholesale distributor of Elektron products. Elektron expressly warrants to Tabmart Products that the goods have no defects in materials or workmanship. Because Elektron is a merchant with respect to goods of the kind, the goods are also covered by an implied warranty of merchantability.

- Tabmart Products sells 1000 Elektron tablets and 100 mini-tablets to Better Buy Discounts, making no express warranties,[9] and disclaiming all implied warranties.

- Better Buy sells one tablet and one mini-tablet to Vicki Quesada and provides a one-year warranty against defects, but disclaims the implied warranty of merchantability.

---

[9] Of course, even if Tabmart Products tries to avoid making any express warranties, it will almost certainly have at least made a warranty of description (e.g., that the item sold is an Elektron tablet). Such warranties are not relevant for this problem so, for the sake of simplicity, we will assume no express warranty was made.

- The day after her purchase, Quesada gives the tablet to her friend, Hawo Abukar, as a birthday present.

- For the purposes of this question, assume Elektron made *no* warranty directly to Quesada in any package inserts, brochures, or manuals, or on the package.

The following occurs within a month of Quesada's purchase:

- The electrical connections in Quesada's mini-tablet short out, resulting in a house fire that causes considerable damage.

- The tablet given to Abukar has a feature that is supposed to prevent the unit from playing too loudly but the feature fails suddenly and the resulting extremely loud blast of music damages Abukar's ears permanently.

- When the defect in Quesada's mini-tablet is publicized, neither Tabmart Products nor Better Buy is able to sell any more Elektron mini-tablets from their inventory.

  (a) Complete the chart on the following pages, indicating for each of the three sellers in the distribution chain (Elektron, Tabmart Products, Better Buy), which of the injured parties (Tabmart Products, Better Buy, Quesada, Abukar) would be covered by that seller's warranty (and for which injury) under the three 2-318 Alternatives. Note whether the warranty coverage is direct (under 2-313 or 2-314) or indirect (through the operation of 2-318). (You will probably find it easier to fill in the chart one row at a time.)

	Elektron	Tabmart Products	Better Buy
Alternative A	Tabmart _____ _____ _____ Better Buy _____ _____ Quesada _____ _____ _____ Abukar _____ _____ _____ _____	Better Buy _____ _____ _____ _____ Quesada _____ _____ _____ Abukar _____ _____ _____ _____	Quesada _____ _____ _____ _____ _____ Abukar _____ _____ _____ _____ _____
Alternative B	Tabmart _____ _____ _____ Better Buy _____ _____ Quesada _____ _____ _____ Abukar _____ _____ _____ _____	Better Buy _____ _____ _____ _____ Quesada _____ _____ Abukar _____ _____ _____ _____	Quesada _____ _____ _____ _____ _____ Abukar _____ _____ _____ _____ _____

	Elektron	Tabmart Products	Better Buy
Alternative C	Tabmart _____ _____ _____	Better Buy _____ _____ _____	Quesada _____ _____ _____
	Better Buy _____ _____	Quesada _____ _____	Abukar _____ _____
	Quesada _____ _____ _____	_____ _____ _____	_____ _____ _____
	Abukar _____ _____ _____ _____	Abukar _____ _____ _____ _____	_____ _____ _____ _____

(b) Would the result under any of the 2-318 alternatives change if Quesada gave Abukar her present at a birthday party Quesada held in her home? Read Comment 3 to 2-318.

(c) Does the Magnuson-Moss Warranty Act operate to change any of the warranties in operation in this scenario?

Problem 13-3.

As we have seen in Assignment 12, a seller may disclaim or limit warranties given to an immediate buyer as long as the seller does so in accordance with the provisions of 2-316 and within the limits of the Magnuson-Moss Warranty Act. We know as well that, under the first sentence of each version of 2-318, whatever warranties are given to the immediate buyer—whether full or more limited—will extend to some additional persons. Thus, if the seller includes in its initial sale an effective warranty disclaimer, that disclaimer will be effective as well against any person who makes a claim pursuant to 2-318.

But can the seller distinguish between the immediate buyer and others in the "distributive chain" by contracting for a greater degree of warranty protection for the immediate buyer than for others? That is, can the seller specify that its warranty protections extend *only* to the immediate buyer, thereby altering the extension of warranty protection granted by 2-318? Parts (a), (b), and (c) below will help you answer that question.

    (a)   Read the last sentence of 2-318 Alternative B and all of 2-318 Comment 1. What effect, if any, would the last sentence of Alternative B have on the following clauses, if included in a sales contract? (Assume the sale does not involve consumer products, so no issues are raised under the Magnuson-Moss Warranty Act.)

        1. Seller expressly disclaims the implied warranty of merchantability.

        2. Seller and Buyer expressly agree that in the event of a breach of warranty, Buyer's sole remedy shall be to return the item to Seller for repair or replacement, and in no event shall Seller be liable for any consequential damages.

        3. The muffler you are buying for your car is guaranteed for as long as you own your car.

    (b)   The last sentence of Alternative C differs from the last sentences of Alternatives A and B. Write a clause for a seller that makes use of the additional power that sellers are given in Alternative C to restrict warranty coverage.

    (c)   How does your own state's version of 2-318 compare to Alternatives A, B, and C with respect to the limit on the seller's power to disclaim?

Problem 13-4.

Suzanne is the proud owner of an amazing 7.35-carat pear-shaped diamond given to her by her mother. Her mother purchased the diamond from a jeweler, Stanley & Sons (S&S), several years ago. Suzanne took the diamond to another jeweler for insurance purposes, which recommended she obtain an appraisal and certification from the Gemological Institute of America, Inc. (GIA). The GIA will not return the diamond to Suzanne, as it is in possession of a theft report involving a diamond with the same characteristics. Suzanne has asked you if she has a claim for breach of the warranty of title by S&S if she is unable to get back the diamond. Does it matter which 2-318 alternative has been adopted in the state where Suzanne lives?

Problem 13-5.

Steven lives in a state that uses Alternative A to 2-318. Steven was out hunting deer when he fell from his deer stand and suffered injuries to his hip and elbow. Steven used a safety strap with a separate buckle made by National Molding, but it broke when he fell to the ground after falling asleep. Steven did not purchase the buckle from National Molding, but rather from a third party. National Molding has notified distributors as follows:

> WARNING: THIS PRODUCT IS NOT FOR USE IN ANY PRODUCT INTENDED TO PROVIDE SAFETY OR PROTECTION TO ANY PERSON.
>
> You must independently evaluate the suitability of, and test each product for their use in your application. National Molding Corporation disclaims any liability resulting from its use. National Molding Corporation's only obligations are those in our Standard Terms and Conditions of Sale and in no case will National Molding be liable for an incidental, indirect, or consequential damage arising from the sale, resale, use or misuse of its products.

Does Steven have a claim for breach of express or implied warranty against National Molding?

Problem 13-6.

Delgado, who lives in New Jersey, purchased a boat manufactured by Carver Boat Corporation (Carver) from Staten Island Boat Sales (SIBS), an independent boat dealer in New York, for $994,500. Carver gave Delgado an express limited warranty, which provides for repair or replacement for the duration of the one year warranty. The boat needed repairs and was out of the water for eighty days following the purchase. Delgado has complained about vibration, electrical, and construction problems with the boat. Carver has offered to repair under the limited warranty, but Delgado has not allowed further repairs. Delgado is unhappy with the boat and wants to bring an action for breach of contract and express and implied warranties.

(a) Recall that New York has adopted Alternative B and New Jersey has adopted Alternative A. What effect on the buyer's claim would the court's choice of New York or New Jersey law have?

(b) Can Delgado make a claim for breach of contract against Carver?

(c)   Can Delgado make a claim for breach of express warranty against Carver?

(d)   Can Delgado make a claim for breach of the warranty of merchantability against Carver?

(e)   Can Delgado make a claim for breach of the implied warranty of fitness against Carver?

(f)   What would Delgado need to prove in order to have a claim against Carver under the Magnuson-Moss Warranty Act?

Problem 13-7.

Cayemberg's Office Products (COP) is a family-owned manufacturer of office supplies located in Salt Lake City, Utah (an Alternative C state). It sells fifty industrial strength, high-powered, battery-operated staplers to Deckert's Office Supplies (DOS), a family-owned local office supply store. These staplers are for business use only; they have no possible use for personal, family, or household purposes. COP's contract with DOS includes this language:

> Seller expressly warrants to Buyer that the products sold have no defects in materials or workmanship and meet all applicable safety standards. This warranty does not extend to any third parties. **EXCEPT AS PROVIDED HEREIN, SELLER MAKES NO WARRANTIES, EXPRESS OR IMPLIED, INCLUDING WARRANTIES OF MERCHANTABILITY AND FITNESS FOR A PARTICULAR PURPOSE.**

DOS sells one of these staplers to Utah-based Foschi Real Estate Company (FRE). There is no written contract between FRE and DOS, and they had no conversations about the sale. It turns out that some staplers were defective, exploding during use. The explosion started a fire that caused significant property damage to FRE's offices and seriously burned Goff, the real estate agent using the stapler at the time of the explosion. What causes of action do FRE and Goff have for breach of warranty, and against whom?

Chapter 6

Sales Contracts in
the 21st Century

Key Concepts

- Scope of the Uniform Electronic Transactions Act (UETA) and Electronic Signatures in Global and National Commerce Act (E-SIGN)

- Impact of electronic contracting statutes UETA and E-SIGN on the Article 2 rules of contract formation

- Including "terms in the box" with shipment of purchased goods

- Effect of "terms in the box" on contract formation and modification under Article 2

- Effect of "terms in the box" on warranties and warranty disclaimers

The rise of electronic commerce has introduced new methods of contract formation that do not always fit comfortably within the old-fashioned paradigm of contract formation upon which the basic offer and acceptance rules of Article 2 rest. The rules addressed in Assignments 5 and 7 originated in the days when a contract was typically formed by the issuance of some communication that could be identified as an "offer," followed by a responsive communication or an act that could be identified as an "acceptance." In the new world of electronic contracting, offers and responses to such offers are often generated by computer programs that may be programmed to act automatically upon receipt of certain communications from other computers. Such programs may also enter an electronic battle of the forms, with communications sent back and forth that are not read by the other party to the transaction. The use of electronic contracting on one or both sides of a transaction posed challenges for application of the offer and acceptance rules in Article 2. Similarly, the use of electronic communications raised questions about the application of the Article 2 statute of frauds, which focused on the existence of "a writing." Finally, the expansion of electronic commerce has highlighted a long-standing question about contract formation in the sale of goods: what is the effect on contract formation and on contract terms when the seller provides goods accompanied by packaging that purports to add terms that were not discussed in previous communications between the parties (referred to as "terms in the box")?

After an unsuccessful attempt to amend Article 2 to address at least some aspects of electronic contracting, which failed along with the other changes proposed in 2003 (see Chapter 1), separate statutory and common law developments occurred that have helped answer some, though not all, the questions about how the contract formation rules of Article 2 will operate in the context of electronic commerce. Federal law (the Electronic Signatures in Global and National Commerce Act, or E-SIGN) and a uniform state law (the Uniform Electronic Transactions Act, or UETA) were adopted to address some of the basic formation and statute of frauds issues raised by electronic contracting. Assignment 14 covers the provisions of UETA and E-SIGN and how they interact with Article 2. The questions raised by "terms in the box," especially in the electronic contracting arena, have proved more intractable. Courts have attempted to address the issues by applying the existing offer and acceptance rules. Unfortunately for students of Article 2 (and perhaps for merchants and consumers who might be better-served by certainty about the rules of contract formation), the courts have not reached uniform conclusions, leaving us with a patchwork of possible approaches to questions raised by scenarios involving terms in the box. Assignment 15 considers these developments.

Assignment 14
Electronic Contracting
§§ 2-204, 2-206, 2-207, 2-209

> **LEARNING OUTCOMES AND OBJECTIVES**
>
> At the completion of this Assignment, you should be able to
>
> - identify when and how UETA and E-SIGN apply to a contract for sale of goods; and
>
> - apply the Article 2 rules on contract formation and the statute of frauds to contracts negotiated and formed using modern electronic communications such as e-mails and texts.

A. "Business as Usual"? UETA and E-SIGN's Legal Infrastructure for Electronic Commerce

The meteoric rise of electronic commerce in the 1990s triggered debates about whether e-commerce was "business as usual" that could be governed by existing rules of law, or whether it was a "brave new world"[1] of commerce that needed new rules for contracting. Meanwhile, the courts began to confront issues such as whether the writing requirement of the statute of frauds could be satisfied with an electronic memo, and whether requirement of a written notice could be satisfied with an electronic communication. Because "writing" was defined as an "intentional reduction to tangible form," the courts reached inconsistent conclusions on these issues. Similar issues began to crop up about how an electronic communication is "signed" by means of a "symbol" that is "executed or adopted with present intention to adopt or accept a writing," § 1-201(b)(37)). Again, the courts' rulings were inconsistent.

---

[1]   *Cf.* Aldous Huxley, Brave New World (1931). Huxley's novel famously imagines a dystopia raising concerns about the changes wrought by the technological and social developments of the early 20th Century.

This inconsistency in judicial outcomes led the National Conference of Commissioners on Uniform State Law (NCCUSL)[2] to add new terms and definitions to the UCC, allowing writing requirements to be satisfied by either paper or electronic means.[3] These changes found their way into revised Articles 5 and 8, into the Article 2 amendments that ultimately failed,[4] and eventually into revised Articles 1, 7, and 9. Key to the success of the UCC changes was the addition of the new term "record," defined as including both written and electronic information.[5]

Meanwhile, NCCUSL drafted and promulgated the Uniform Electronic Transactions Act (UETA) in 1999. As of December 2015, it has been enacted in 47 states, the District of Columbia and the Virgin Islands.[6] Like the UCC revisions and amendments, this uniform state law expands paper-based rules to cover electronic transactions, and it uses the term "record" to encompass information in both written and electronic media. UETA applies to "electronic records and electronic signatures relating to a transaction,"[7] as long as both parties to a transaction have "agreed" to conduct the transaction by electronic means.[8] "Agreed" is defined consistently with the UCC's broad definition of "agreement,"[9] so that "[w]hether the parties agree to conduct a transaction by electronic means is determined from the context and surrounding circumstances, including the parties' conduct." This construction ensures that UETA has broad applicability. The Comments to UETA note, for example, that a person can agree to conduct transactions electronically by presenting a business card with an e-mail address or by ordering books from an on-line vendor.[10]

---

2   NCCUSL is now known as the Uniform Law Commission (ULC). See http://www.uniformlawcommission.com/.

3   Patricia Brumfield Fry, X Marks the Spot: New Technologies Compel New Concepts for Commercial Law, 26 Loy. L.A. L. Rev. 607 (1993), available at http://digitalcommons.lmu.edu/llr/vol26/iss3/7; Christina L. Kunz, The Definitional Hub of e-Commerce: "Record", 45 Idaho L. Rev. 399 (2009), available at http://open.mitchellhamline.edu/facsch/176/.

4   See Chapter 1.

5   See Christina L. Kunz, The Definitional Hub of e-Commerce: "Record", 45 Idaho L. Rev. 399 (2009), available at http://open.mitchellhamline.edu/facsch/176/.

6   The three states that have not adopted UETA (Illinois, New York, and Washington) have enacted non-uniform laws addressing electronic commerce in ways similar to UETA. http://electronicsignature.com/ueta-uniform-electronic-transactions-act/. Puerto Rico has enacted an Electronic Transaction Act modelled after UETA, with some variations. P.R. Laws Ann. Tit 10, §§ 4081–4096 (2015).

7   UETA § 3(a).

8   UETA § 5(b). See also § 3 (exclusions from scope).

9   UETA § 2(1).

10   UETA § 5 cmt. 4.

Figure 1

Only in UETA:

Admissibility of evidence, whether paper or electronic

When/where record is "sent", "received"

Presentation of record

Attribution & effect of record

Effect of change or error

Provisons in both UETA & E-SIGN:

Definitions of record, e-record, e-signature, e-agent

Enforceability of record, signature, contract--whether paper or electronic

Automated transactions with e-agent(s)

Record retention

Notarization, acknowledgement

Transferable records

Only in E-SIGN:

§ 101(c) consumer protection (see next ¶ in text below)

Applicability to federal & state governments

International e-commerce principles

A year later, in 2000, Congress enacted a similar federal statute, Electronic Signatures in Global and National Commerce Act (E-SIGN),[11] to apply to "any transaction in or affecting interstate or foreign commerce."[12] Accordingly, E-SIGN's definitions and rules are the law in every jurisdiction with regard to transactions touching on interstate or foreign commerce. E-SIGN copied many UETA provisions and added a few additional rules to cover national concerns.

Consumer advocates succeeded in convincing Congress to add the following consumer protection provision in E-SIGN § 101(c):

- If any law requires that information relating to an interstate commerce transaction be furnished to a consumer in writing, an electronic record can instead be used if

  - the consumer receives a clear and conspicuous statement of the following:

    · that the consumer is not required to consent, that any consent is revocable, and that consent covers the specified transactions;

    · how to revoke consent, and how to get a paper copy; and

    · the system's hardware and software requirements; and

---

[11]   Public Law 106-229 (codified at 15 U.S.C. §§ 7001-7031) (June 30, 2000).

[12]   E-SIGN § 101(a). See also § 103 (exclusions from scope).

- the consumer then consents (or confirms assent) electronically using his or her own computer, to assure his or her ability to access the system.

Although the Supremacy Clause of the United States Constitution would allow E-SIGN to pre-empt UETA, E-SIGN explicitly allows states to enact laws that modify, limit or supersede much of E-SIGN if the state law either (1) is an enactment of UETA; or (2) has alternative procedures or requirements for use or acceptance of electronic records and signatures, so long as they are consistent with E-SIGN and do not favor one technology over another (and if enacted after E-SIGN, they specifically refer to E-SIGN). This unusual provision allows a state statute to take precedence over E-SIGN, to the extent the two statutes are inconsistent.[13] If a state enacts a non-uniform version of UETA, it might still be treated as an "enactment of UETA" if the variations are minor. But a non-uniform version of UETA with less-than-minor variations would probably need to meet the requirement of the "alternative procedures or requirements" in order not to be pre-empted by E-SIGN.

Both acts adopt the principle of "media neutrality," saying that a signature, contract, or other record may not be denied legal effect, validity, or enforceability solely because it is in electronic form.[14] Rules of law that are "media-neutral" can govern an entire transaction regardless of the parties' chosen media for communication and information storage. This approach allows parties to vary their communications among paper and electronic media without raising issues about which rules of law apply. For instance, a party may initiate a transaction with an inquiry on a website, the other party may mail a packet of paper information, the recipient may phone back an offer, and the other party may accept by email. The same rules of law apply to the entire transaction without regard to the medium of communication.

Thus, the enactment of UETA and E-SIGN reflect the view that electronic commerce is "business as usual," rather than a "brave new world," because these acts allow the existing rules of law to apply to all transactions, rather than making new rules for electronic transactions. At both the state and federal level, the two acts allow the legislatures to effectively extend hundreds of thousands of statutes and regulations to apply to electronic commerce without having to amend those statutes and regulations.

---

[13]   E-SIGN § 102(a).
[14]   E-SIGN § 101(a)(1); UETA § 7(b)-(d).

B. Applying UETA and E-SIGN to Contract Formation

Reading and Applying
UETA and E-SIGN

Following is a set of questions based on a common scenario in electronic commerce. Each question asks you to consider specific pertinent sections of these two statutes (some of which have been paraphrased for ease of understanding), illustrating the commonalities and differences between them. The exercise will introduce you to the terminology used in the statutes and how the statutes interact with the Article 2 formation rules.

Scenario: A bookseller sets up a web site on which customers can order used books. The web site terms of use say that all orders are "subject to availability," a statement that appears at the top of the ordering screen. Each customer can fill an electronic "shopping cart" with items from an electronic catalog, and then must furnish a credit card number and agree to pay the listed price by clicking a clearly labeled "I Agree" button. The web site software then checks the bookseller's automated inventory report to make sure that the ordered books are in stock and issues an automated e-mail to the customer stating when the ordered items will be shipped. The buyer receives the e-mail. The bookseller ships the ordered books to the customer, who receives them and finds them to be acceptable.

Question 1. Identify the "electronic records" used between the parties. Use the definitions below.

Definition	Authority
"Record" means information that is inscribed on a tangible medium or that is stored in an electronic or other medium and is retrievable in perceivable form.	**E-SIGN § 106(9)** **UETA § 2(13)**
"Electronic record" means a record created, generated, sent, communicated, received, or stored by electronic means.	**E-SIGN § 106(4)** **UETA § 2(7)**
"Electronic" means relating to technology having electrical, digital, magnetic, wireless, optical, electromagnetic, or similar capabilities.	**E-SIGN § 106(2)** **UETA § 2(5)**

Question 2. Have any of the electronic records you identified in Question 1 been "sent" or "received", using the UETA rules below? If so, identify when. Note any additional facts you need to know. (E-SIGN has no pertinent rules.)

Definition	Authority
(a) unless otherwise agreed, an electronic record is sent when it (1) is addressed properly or otherwise directed properly to an information processing system that the recipient has designated or uses for the purpose of receiving electronic records and from which the recipient is able to retrieve the electronic record, (2) is in a form capable of being processed by that system, and (3) enters an information processing system outside the control of the sender.	**UETA § 15(a)**
(b) Unless otherwise agreed between a sender and the recipient, an electronic record is received when it (1) enters an information processing system that the recipient has designated or uses for the purpose of receiving electronic records and from which the recipient is able to retrieve the electronic record and (2) is in a form capable of being processed by that system.	**UETA § 15(b)**
(e) An electronic record is received under subsection (b) even if no individual is aware of its receipt.	**UETA § 15(e)**

Question 3. Did the electronic records you found in Question 1 contain any "electronic signatures"? If so, identify them. Use the definition below.

Definition	Authority
"Electronic signature" means an electronic sound, symbol, or process attached to or logically associated with a record and executed or adopted by the person with the intent to sign the record.	**E-SIGN § 106(5)** **UETA § 2(8)**

Question 4. Are any "electronic agents" involved in the contract formation process? If so, identify them. Use the definition below.

Definition	Authority
"Electronic agent" means a computer program or an electronic or other automated means used independently to initiate an action or respond to electronic records or performances in whole or in part, without review or action by an individual.[1]	E-SIGN § 106(3) UETA § 2(6)

Question 5. Which actions, if any, form a contract between the bookseller and the customer? Use the rules below, as well as common law rules.

Definition	Authority
Record, signature, or contract cannot be denied legal effect or enforceability solely because it is in electronic form.	E-SIGN § 101(a) UETA § 7(a), (b)
A contract may be formed between an electronic agent and an individual or between two electronic agents.[2]	E-SIGN § 101(h) UETA § 14(1)
A contract may be formed by the interaction of an electronic agent and an individual, acting on the individual's behalf or for another person, including by an interaction in which the individual performs actions that the individual is free to refuse to perform and which the individual knows or has reason to know will cause the actions electronic agent to complete the transaction or performance.	UETA § 14(2)
The terms of the contract are determined by the substantive law applicable to it.	UETA § 14(3)

Question 6. Would your answers to Question 5 be different in a jurisdiction not enacting UETA, if you used just UCC Article 2 and common law?

---

[1] Note that an "electronic agent" is not really an "agent," because agency law requires an agent to be a person. Computer software running on a computer is a machine programmed by a person and set in motion by a person, but it is not an agent.

[2] Such as when software programmed as a shopping "bot" buys from an automated web site.

C. Applying UETA and E-SIGN to the Statute of Frauds

EXAMPLES AND ANALYSIS

Example A: *International Casings Group, Inc. v. Premium Standard Farms, Inc.*[15]

For more than six years, a pork producer sold hog casings to a company that described itself as "a global leader in the natural sausage casings industry,"[16] under long-term output contracts. The parties terminated the long-term contracts and began renegotiating their relationship. Through a series of e-mail exchanges over a period of approximately five months, the parties negotiated the details of their future relationship, while continuing to perform under the terms of their prior contracts. The e-mails were short messages between two agents of the seller and buyer, neither of whom used automatic signature blocks on their e-mails, although the agent for the seller did occasionally end his messages with "Thanks, Kent." When the seller informed the buyer of its intent to terminate their business relationship and begin selling its casings to a third party, the buyer sought a preliminary injunction against the seller, arguing that the seller was already contractually obligated to the buyer.

Analysis: The court granted the buyer's injunction, applying general common law to reach the conclusion that the e-mail exchange evidenced a "meeting of the minds" sufficient to find a contract. The court rejected the seller's argument that any contract formed would not satisfy the Article 2 requirement of a "writing" with a "signature" under the statute of frauds provisions in 2-201. The court concluded that UETA would apply because "a fact finder will probably infer from the objective evidence that the parties agreed to negotiate and eventually reach the terms of an agreement via electronic mail based on their ongoing e-mail negotiations."

The court rejected the seller's argument that UETA did not apply to this transaction. What argument might the Seller have made, and why would the court have rejected it? How was the "signature" requirement satisfied in this scenario? What would the result in this case have been if UETA did not apply?

---

[15]   358 F. Supp. 2d 863 (W.D. Mo. 2005).
[16]   See http://casings.com/our-company/.

APPLYING THE CODE

Problem 14-1.

Review Problem 5-2 and your response.

(a) Would your answer change if Farmer Kasey's offer was not oral, but rather in the form of a text to Alexa's phone number?

(b) Would it make a difference if Farmer Kasey (1) found Alexa's phone number for the text by looking up her website after eating at the restaurant, or (2) had her phone number because Farmer Kasey had been using it to make informal arrangements to supply her diner with seasonal fruits for the past three years?

Problem 14-2.

Tuvia met with Gerrard to discuss the possible purchase of 1,600,000 pairs of jeans stored in Gerrard's warehouse. They agreed that Tuvia would buy the entire inventory at a price between $3.00 and $3.50 per item, subject to Tuvia's visual inspection of the items. When Tuvia visited the warehouse on September 29, he learned that approximately 700,000 pairs of jeans had been sold to a third party. Tuvia spent the entire day spot-checking the remaining merchandise to determine whether an agreement could still be reached. Although the remaining jeans differed from the description given by Gerrard in their initial conversation, Tuvia was still willing to buy the bulk of the remaining inventory of jeans, at $2.50 per item. Gerrard allegedly accepted the offer orally that day. Gerrard subsequently sold its inventory to another buyer at a higher price.

Tuvia brought suit for breach of contract by Gerrard. Tuvia produced a copy of a letter, addressed to Gerrard and sent by e-mail on September 30 from Tuvia's assistant, on behalf of Tuvia. The e-mail's subject line read: "Total Inventory Purchased," and the electronically-attached letter, on Tuvia Inc. letterhead, stated:

> As per our agreement with Gerrard, we would like to inform you that Tuvia Inc. has bought the 747,096 of the jeans inspected at your warehouse yesterday. The purchased jeans consist of all of the inventory listed on your Sep. 29 Inventory, less the following: Kohls men 8,000 pcs; Structure men 22,000 pcs; Express junior 10,000 pcs, Express missy 19,200 pcs. Please

send us a proforma invoice in order for us to proceed in preparing our Letter
of Credit for payment. Please ship all samples per our conversation to Tuvia
Inc. at the address listed above.

The letter closed with Tuvia's typed signature. Tuvia said that he did not receive
a reply to his e-mail.

Gerrard claimed to recall neither seeing the e-mail message nor opening its
attachment.

Gerrard moved for summary judgment, based on failure to satisfy the statute of
frauds. Should Gerrard win?

Problem 14-3.

Harrison and Hart met at a home furnishing trade show. Harrison manufactured
all-natural floor mats and rugs made out of bamboo. Hart owned a large home
furnishing store. After looking at Harrison's brochures and hearing his pitch about
the beauty and durability of his products, Hart told him she might want to buy a
large quantity (500) to sell in her store. Hart asked whether Harrison could provide
volume discount, and he pointed her to the page in the brochure with pricing that
included volume discounts. Hart told Harrison that she thought the price seemed
fair, and asked if he had enough in stock to send her 500 by July 15 (2 weeks from
then). Harrison said that he did. Hart replied, "Well, I think we have a deal, if I
can just see one of them to make sure they live up to your hype." Harrison agreed
to send her some samples the next week, and they exchanged business cards with
the relevant contact information. When Hart got the samples, she sent Harrison
an e-mail with the caption "Bamboo Mat Order." The e-mail read:

> The mats are great! This will confirm our contract for 500 mats to be deliv-
> ered to my store by July 15, at the price listed in your brochure. I'll pay you
> by wire transfer upon receipt of the mats.
>
> Yours truly,
>
> L. Hart
>
> President, Hart's Home Furnishings

The mats were not delivered on July 15. When Hart called to ask why, Harrison replied, "Gee, when I didn't hear back from you, I sold my entire supply to
another buyer, who was so anxious to buy that he offered to pay more than the
list price. Sorry!"

When Hart sued him for breach of contract, Harrison claimed that Hart's e-mail was caught up on Harrison's spam filter, and he never saw it. Harrison moves for summary judgment, based on the statute of frauds. Will he win?

Assignment 15
Terms in the Box
§§ 2-204, 2-206, 2-207, 2-209

The rise in the volume of electronic commerce has highlighted a long-standing question about contract formation: when and how do contract terms contained in the packaging of purchased goods become part of the contract for the purchase of those goods? When you buy a boxed item in a store, it is likely that, when you take it out of the box, you will find a pamphlet in the packaging. You may (or may not) consult the pamphlet for set-up or operating instructions. You may (or may not) toss the pamphlet into a file or drawer where you collect such pamphlets "just in case." Being a law student who has taken a Contracts course and is now taking a Sales course, you may read (or think about whether you should read) the pamphlet more carefully. If you undertake this task, you will see that the pamphlet contains significant terms that the seller expects to be part of your sales contract (and some of which you may favor as well): terms governing warranties and remedies, limiting warranties or remedies, or mandating arbitration of disputes. Are those terms part of the sales contract, even if you did not see them before or when you purchased the goods?

Consider the increasingly typical scenario in which a buyer orders goods "electronically" (either by phone or, more commonly now, through a website) and receives the goods in a shipping box along with documents that purport to contain terms of the contract. Are the documents in the box to be considered acceptances or confirmations so that the effect of their contents is governed by § 2-207(2)? Does § 2-206(1) furnish any guidance about which terms become part of a contract formed by shipment of the goods? Does it matter if the seller's documents say the goods should be returned if the additional terms are not satisfactory? If the parties agreed to price, quantity, and other particulars before shipment, is the contract already formed, so that the documents are an offer to modify the contract under § 2-209? If the terms in the box include representations that might constitute express warranties under § 2-313, are they "part of the basis of the bargain"? Should "warranty disclaimers in the box" be effective to disclaim implied or express warranties?

This Assignment will explore how the Article 2 rules for contract formation and modification apply in situations in which significant contract terms are delivered inside the packaging of goods, typically not seen by the purchaser before the goods are acquired.

LEARNING OUTCOMES AND OBJECTIVES

At the completion of this Assignment, you should be able to

- recognize the different lines of reasoning that have been developed by courts in a series of cases dealing with significant terms placed in the packaging of goods ordered by telephone and over the internet;
- identify the different conclusions about the process of contract formation that underlie these different lines of reasoning; and
- apply these lines of reasoning to questions about contract formation and about the creation and disclaimer of warranties.

A. "Terms-in-the Box" Contracting: Conflict in the Courts

Article 2 originated in a time when a contract was typically formed by the issuance of some communication that could be identified as an "offer," followed by a responsive communication or an act that could be identified as an "acceptance." The battle-of-forms provisions in § 2-207 address the situation arising when a buyer and a seller exchange an offer and an acceptance and proceed with their transaction without expectation (or practice) that the other party actually reads or responds to the forms issued. With the growing use of electronic contracting, offers or responses to such offers are often generated by computer software, programmed to act automatically upon receipt of certain communications from other computers. These same automatic programs can interact with automated inventory systems and warehouses to generate shipments of goods. Such shipments may include documents purporting to be offers or acceptances and may contain significant contract terms that the seller intends to be part of the contract for sale (the "terms in a box"). Because the offer and acceptance rules of Article 2 do not directly address some of the issues raised by these scenarios, the courts faced with such questions have had to use what they can from Article 2 and then return to common law principles of contracts.

A number of early cases involving purchases of computer hardware and software generated two lines of reasoning about whether such "terms in the box" become part of the contract. These two lines differ fundamentally in their understanding of when and how the contract was formed. Because many sellers and buyers are affected by these kinds of "terms in a box," you should be familiar with the competing cases and rationales and should be able to determine whether a particular jurisdiction has controlling authority on this point. This remains a highly contested issue related to sales of goods.

1. Cases Holding "Terms in the Box" are Part of the Contract

In this line of cases, the courts concluded that the contract was formed only after the buyer received all of the "terms in the box" from the seller; the buyer accepted the contract (and the terms in the box) by some act designated by the seller as acceptance.

EXAMPLES AND ANALYSIS

Example A: *ProCD, Inc. v. Zeidenberg*[1]

Zeidenberg bought from a retail store a CD-ROM compiled by ProCD, containing data from over 3,000 telephone directories. The box in which the CD-ROM was packaged contained a notice that the enclosed software was restricted according to the terms of an enclosed license; the license was printed in the manual enclosed in the box, encoded in the CD, and appeared on a user's screen whenever the software ran. (Licenses delivered in this manner are often called "shrink-wrap licenses", referring to the fact they often contain language purporting to make them effective when the "shrinkwrap" plastic or cellophane covering the CD is torn open.) The license restricted use of this data to noncommercial purposes. When Zeidenberg used the data for a commercial venture, ProCD sought an injunction based on the terms of the license.

Analysis: The court of appeals granted the injunction, concluding that the contract was formed under 2-204 in the following manner: "A vendor, as master of the offer, may invite acceptance by conduct, and may propose limitation on the kind of conduct that constitutes acceptance. And that is what happened. ProCD proposed a contract that a buyer would accept by *using* the software after

---

[1] 86 F.3d 1447 (7th Cir. 1996).

having an opportunity to read the license at leisure. This is what Zeidenburg did." Section 2-207 was held to be irrelevant because there was only one form.

The court of appeals reversed the lower court's holding that "placing the package of software on the shelf is an 'offer,' which the customer 'accepts' by paying the asking price and leaving the store with the goods." (Under that understanding of contract formation, the lower court had concluded that Zeidenberg was not bound by terms that were "hidden" inside the box at the time of acceptance.) The court of appeals acknowledged that contracts *can*, indeed, be formed in the manner described by the lower court, but that "the vendor, as master of the offer" chose a different mechanism for contract formation. (As we will see shortly, subsequent courts have been critical of the *ProCD* court's rationale for its conclusion about contract formation.) Which account of the moment and manner of acceptance makes the most sense to you? Can you think of any other possibilities?

Is the court correct that 2-207 does not apply if there is only one form? As we will see shortly, many courts disagree with this conclusion.

Example B: *Hill v. Gateway 2000, Inc.*[2]

The buyer ordered a computer by telephone from the manufacturer, who shipped the computer in a box containing additional terms, including an arbitration clause and a statement that those terms became part of the contract unless the buyer returned the computer within thirty days. Buyer did not return the computer, and the manufacturer sought to enforce the arbitration clause.

Analysis: The court held that the terms (including the contested arbitration clause) were an offer from the manufacturer, which the buyer accepted by not returning the computer.

Both the *ProCD* and the *Hill* decisions were written by the same judge (Seventh Circuit Judge Frank Easterbrook), and both relied on the Supreme Court decision of *Carnival Cruise Lines, Inc. v. Shute.*[3] The *Hill* case was the first one to squarely address the "terms in the box" situation. The contract at issue in *Carnival* was for the purchase of passage on a cruise ship (thus a service, not a good) bought

---

[2]   105 F.3d 1147 (7th Cir. 1997).
[3]   499 U.S. 585 (1991).

through a travel agent; the disputed forum selection clause was included in the ticket later sent by the cruise line. The Supreme Court upheld the unnegotiated clause in the form contract because the buyers received notice of the forum clause before the cruise and because the clause was enforceable under previous precedents on enforceable forum-selection clauses. The contract at issue in *ProCD* involved primarily the purchase of software (thus arguably not a good), and the manual in the box containing the license limitation was only one of a number of possible ways in which the license limitation arguably became part of the contract; the license limitation was also encoded in the software and appeared every time the program was used. In contrast, in *Hill*, there is no question that the contract involved a sale of goods governed by Article 2, and there was no possible source for the disputed term other than a "term in a box." Do these distinctions in the facts of these three cases raise any questions about the validity of *Hill*'s analysis of the contract formation issues?

2. Cases Holding "Terms in the Box" are Not Part of the Contract

In another line of cases, courts held either that the contracts were created *before* the additional terms in the box were received by the buyer, or that the additional terms were included in the seller's acceptance. The courts then used § 2-207 or § 2-209 to determine whether those additional terms became part of the contract.

EXAMPLES AND ANALYSIS

Example C: *Step-Saver Data Systems, Inc. v. Wyse Technology*[4]

Buyer, a value-added retailer, ordered multiple copies of software by phone, and seller, the software manufacturer, promised to ship. Buyer then sent a purchase order detailing the terms, and seller responded with shipment and an invoice with nearly identical terms (price, quantity, shipping, payment). On each software package was printed a "box-top license," which specified that buyer had a non-transferable license, disclaimed all warranties except a single express warranty, limited buyer's remedies to return and replacement,

---

[4]   939 F.2d 91 (3d Cir. 1991).

excluded all damages, provided that the box-top license was the final and complete agreement of the parties, specified that buyer's opening of the box was acceptance of the box-top terms, and instructed buyer to return the box unopened within fifteen days for a refund if buyer did not accept the terms. The parties repeated this sequence over perhaps six to eight shipments for a total of 142 software copies.

Analysis: The court concluded that the box-top terms were *not* part of the final contract. The court's analysis has been criticized because it includes a number of errors. Despite (and perhaps because of) these errors, it is an interesting case, illustrating both the myriad possible avenues for finding contract formation in this context, and some of the troubles courts have had in applying Article 2 to the terms-in-the-box situation. The court held:

(1) The parties' performance (seller's shipment and buyer's acceptance of the goods and payment) had formed a contract.

(2) The contract was sufficiently definite under 2-204(3) without the box-top term.

(3) Buyer never agreed to the box-top license as a final expression or modification of the parties' agreement so the integration clause was not binding.

(4) The box-top license was similar to a written confirmation under 2-207(1) rather than a conditional acceptance.

(5) The warranty disclaimer and the remedy limitation in the box-top agreement would materially alter the parties' agreement under 2-207(2) and so did not become part of the agreement.

Can you identify the errors in this analysis? Compare steps (1) and (4) above. The fundamental error is that the court began with the conclusion that the contract was formed by the behavior of the parties through the shipment of goods and payment, presumably under 2-207(3). Thus, under 2-207(3), the knock-out rule should have dictated that the box-top terms were not included. The court did not satisfactorily explain why it needed to analyze the issue of conditional acceptance under 2-207(1) (Step 4) when the parties had already formed a contract by that point. (A subsequent decision, the *Arizona Retail Systems* case discussed next, noted that the *Step-Saver* court's approach was erroneous in this respect and refused to follow that part of the *Step-Saver* reasoning.) The *Step-Saver* court seemed to use 2-207(3) for its analysis of the parties' contract formation by performance, then shifted to 2-207(1) to analyze seller's conditional acceptance arguments, and finally used 2-207(2)(b) to determine whether the disclaimer and remedy limitation were added to the agreement (Step 5). The final two steps were erroneous.

Example D: *Arizona Retail Systems, Inc. v. Software Link, Inc.*[5]

Buyer ordered some software from the manufacturer (who was also one of the defendants in *Step-Saver*). The manufacturer sent both an evaluative copy and a live copy of the software, which were wrapped together in shrink-wrap plastic with an attached license agreement that claimed to be triggered upon buyer opening the plastic; accompanying materials stated that buyer could return the materials if not satisfied. The additional terms in the license agreement included a disclaimer of virtually all warranties and significant limitations on remedies. Buyer tested the evaluation disk, read the license agreement, and decided to keep the software.

Subsequently, buyer made numerous purchases of the same software by phone with manufacturer, who promised to ship it promptly and did not mention the license agreement. Manufacturer then shipped the software with a shrinkwrap license agreement attached to the packaging.

Analysis: The court held that buyer accepted the license terms with respect to the first shipment of the evaluative and live copy of the software either by not returning the software or by tearing open the shrinkwrap plastic. With respect to these subsequent purchases, the court adopted *Step-Saver's* conclusion that the contract was formed by the prompt shipment of the goods. The license agreement sent with the shipment was either

(1) an additional set of terms in a confirmation that were material alterations under 2-207(2)(b) and therefore were not part of the contract, or

5   831 F. Supp. 759 (D. Ariz. 1993).

> (2) a proposal to modify under 2-209 to which buyer did not expressly consent.

Can you see how the court's conclusion that the contract was formed before the goods were received affects the characterization of the terms in the box? Which of the court's two different possible characterizations of the additional terms do you find most plausible? Does it matter which characterization the court adopts?

Example E. *Klocek v. Gateway, Inc.*[6]

In this case, the record was "woefully unclear" as to how and where a contract was formed so the court considered multiple contract formation scenarios. The buyer purchased a computer and scanner from the manufacturer, who shipped the goods or gave the goods to the buyer in person, with its "Standard Terms and Conditions" enclosed in the box. The terms included an arbitration clause and also stated that buyer would be deemed to have accepted those terms by not returning the goods within five days.

Analysis: The court rejected two of the conclusions in *ProCD* and *Hill*: (1) that 2-207 does not apply in cases involving only one form; and (2) that the vendor is necessarily the "master of the offer." On the latter point, the court noted that, in fact, "[i]n typical consumer transactions, the purchaser is the offeror, and the vendor is the offeree." Thus, for purposes of ruling on a motion to dismiss, the court assumed that the buyer made an offer in person or by catalog order, which offer the seller accepted either (1) by completing the sales transaction in person or (2) by agreeing to ship the catalog order or shipping the computer to buyer, per 2-206.

The court then reasoned that the terms enclosed with the shipment were not conditional and so not a counteroffer, but instead were either an expression of acceptance or a written confirmation under 2-207(1). Because buyer was not a merchant, those enclosed terms did not become additional terms to the contract under 2-207(2) unless buyer agreed to them. Buyer's lack of assent caused the same result under 2-209. Buyer never assented to the five-day return term and so could not be said to have assented to the enclosed terms by keeping the goods

---

[6] 104 F. Supp. 2d 1332 (D. Kan. 2000).

for more than five days, nor did buyer assent to the enclosed terms in any other way. "Express assent cannot be presumed by silence or mere failure to object." The court denied the manufacturer's motion to dismiss.

Where did the court find the offer and the acceptance in this transaction? How does this differ from the analysis in Examples C and D? How did this court nonetheless come to the same ultimate conclusion (that the terms in the box are not part of the contract) as the courts in Examples C and D?

APPLYING THE CODE

Problem 15-1.

The *ProCD/Hill* and *Step-Saver* lines of cases reached different outcomes because they reached different conclusions regarding when and how the sales contracts were formed. To help clarify those analyses, consider the following chart. Column 1 describes the moment of contract formation, according to the courts in these cases.

- For each moment of formation identified in column 1, what section of Article 2 would you point to as establishing or governing that contract formation? Place your answers in column 2.

- For each theory of contract formation identified in column 1, do the seller's terms in the box become part of the contract? What statutory provisions support your result? Place your answers in column 3.

- Which of these lines of reasoning makes the most sense to you? Why?

(1) Moment of contract formation	(2) UCC section governing contract formation	(3) Do terms in the box become part of the contract? If so, under what UCC section?
Pro-CD; Hill v. Gateway: When buyer received goods and did not return them		

(1) Moment of contract formation	(2) UCC section governing contract formation	(3) Do terms in the box become part of the contract? If so, under what UCC section?
AZ Retail: When seller ships goods: · buyer's order = offer · shipment = acceptance by act		
Klocek v. Gateway: When seller sends "confirmation of order" (with the goods): · buyer's order = offer · seller's confirmation = acceptance with additional/ different terms		
Possible variation on Klocek's version of offer & acceptance: By action of parties recognizing contract: · buyer's order = offer · seller's confirmation = acceptance "made expressly conditional on buyer's agreement to additional terms" · buyer never expressly agreed · so the writings did NOT form contract		

Problem 15-2.

Consider the following transaction: A consumer buyer places an order for goods on the seller's web site, providing a credit card for payment. Consumer receives an automatic e-mail "confirming" the purchase. Seller ships the goods and includes in the shipment a "Confirmation of Order" that contains additional terms and instructs the buyer to return the goods if the terms are not acceptable.

(a) In the chart below, apply the reasoning of the courts identified in column 1 to identify the moment of contract formation in this scenario. Place your answers in column (1).

(1) Moment of contract formation	(2) UCC section governing contract formation	(3) Do terms in the box become part of the contract? If so, under what UCC section?
Under *Hill v. Gateway* line of reasoning:		
Under *Klocek v. Gateway* line of reasoning:		

(b) For each moment you identified in column 1, what section of Article 2 would you point to as establishing or governing that contract formation? Place your answers in column 2.

(c) For each theory of contract formation you noted in columns 1 and 2, do the seller's terms in the box become part of the contract? What statutory provisions support your result? Place your answers in column 3.

Problem 15-3.

Given the variations reflected above, as the lawyer for a manufacturer who sells products directly to buyers, both merchants and non-merchants, through catalog and web purchases as well as in its own retail locations, what advice would you give to help your client maximize the chances that its terms will be binding on buyers?

Problem 15-4.

Peter ordered a diamond engagement ring from Gateway Jewelers' web site for his fiancée, Anna. Nothing on the web site mentioned arbitration. When Gateway received Peter's electronic order, it sent Peter an automatic e-mail acknowledging the order, packed the ring in a box, and shipped it to Peter. In the box with the ring was a document setting forth Standard Terms and Conditions, including a mandatory arbitration clause. The document stated that the buyer would be deemed to have accepted the enclosed Standard Terms and Conditions unless the ring was returned within 10 days. A month later, when Peter presented the ring to Anna, she immediately spotted a flaw. She does not want to return the ring, because she is sentimental about keeping the ring he put on her finger when she accepted his proposal. Peter, though, wants to sue Gateway for breach of its express warranty that the diamond was flawless, hoping to get a refund of part of the purchase price. Compare how a court following the rationale in *Hill v. Gateway* would find that a contract was formed with how a court following the rationale in *Klocek v. Gateway* would find that a contract was formed in this transaction. Explain how both courts would decide the issue of whether Peter would have to arbitrate this dispute rather than sue Gateway in court.

B. Express Warranties and Warranty Disclaimers "In the Box"

1. Express Warranties "In the Box"

As discussed in Assignment 11, whether any representation becomes "part of the basis of the bargain" depends on when the representation was made, when the contract was formed, and whether the applicable jurisdiction has adopted the reliance, Comment 3, or non-reliance test. The same is true for a "representation in the box." Recall from Assignment 11 that Comment 7 to § 2-313 says that a representation may become part of the basis of a bargain even if the contract was formed before the representation was made. An affirmation of fact, promise, or description that comes "in the box" after a contract was formed thus can arguably be part of the basis of the bargain.

To complicate matters, even un-assented-to terms, including "terms in the box," may sometimes be binding, by way of an equitable doctrine like promissory estoppel or equitable estoppel. A buyer may have a promissory estoppel claim because of justifiable and foreseeable detrimental reliance on seller's "promises in the box." Or a seller may be equitably estopped from objecting to "terms in the box" becoming part of the contract, because the seller placed the terms into the box and intended the buyer to receive them after the contract was formed, so the seller should be estopped from raising defenses like the buyer not having assented to the terms or the representation not being "part of the basis of the bargain."

Therefore, determining whether "terms in a box" can be the basis of an express warranty claim requires a highly fact-dependent inquiry about when the contract was formed and whether the term became part of the basis of the bargain, as well as whether an equitable doctrine applies.

APPLYING THE CODE

Problem 15-5.

Charles visits Cooks-Are-Us, a local restaurant and kitchen supply store, to look at food processors. He asks the salesperson to show him which models are good at both slicing vegetables and grinding meat. The salesperson shows Charles several models and recommends one, manufactured by KitchenArt, as providing the best value for the money. Charles takes a box containing that food processor to the counter to purchase it. He signs the credit card receipt and takes the food processor home. The outside of the box (which Charles does not read until he gets the box home) says, "Slices, Dices, AND Grinds Meat!" Inside the box is a pamphlet that Charles saves but does not read. The pamphlet contains the following text:

Limited Six-Month Warranty

KitchenArt warrants this product against all defects in material and workmanship for a period of six months from purchase. Normal wear and tear is excluded.

Is there an express warranty between Charles and Cooks-Are-Us based on the pamphlet? What about between Charles and KitchenArt? In your answer, consider whether and when a contract was formed and whether the representation was part of the basis of the bargain. If you think that the likely answer to either issue is no, determine whether other arguments from the discussion above favor the enforcement of the representation, even if no contract is formed or even if the representation is not part of the basis of the bargain.

2. Warranty Disclaimers "In the Box"

In contrast to "representations in the box," whether "warranty disclaimers in the box" become part of the contract depends only on whether the buyer assented to the terms. Because disclaimers are not covered by § 2-313, a disclaimer does not have to be "part of the basis of the bargain." The equitable doctrines of promissory estoppel and equitable estoppel apply only to prevent a party (here, the seller) from withdrawing a promised benefit (e.g., the express warranty) to someone else, so they are irrelevant to whether seller gets the benefit of a disclaimer term. The chart below shows the difference between the questions raised when considering whether express warranties and warranty disclaimers "in the box become part of a contract."

	Express warranties "in the box"	Warranty disclaimers "in the box"
Did buyer assent to the term?	✓	✓
Was the express warranty "part of the basis of the bargain"?	✓	
Promissory estoppel based on seller's promise	✓	
Equitable estoppel against seller	✓	

Note that a buyer who wants the court to uphold an express warranty in the box must prove both assent and basis-of-the-bargain or, alternatively, promissory estoppel or equitable estoppel. However, a seller who wants to defeat an express warranty in the box must prevail against all three alternatives. On the other hand, a seller who wants the court to uphold a warranty disclaimer in the box must prove the buyer's assent, and the buyer must counter the proof on that issue.

The buyer's assent could be understood differently when the question is whether the buyer assented to a largely favorable warranty term than when the issue is the buyer's assent to a generally unfavorable disclaimer term (and differently again if the disclaimer is packaged with a favorable warranty). For example, a buyer may argue that evidence sufficient to show that the buyer agreed to a favorable term (that is, the inaction of not sending back delivered goods) may not be sufficient to show that the buyer agreed to an unfavorable term. On the other hand, a seller may argue that fairness dictates that all "terms in the box" be treated the same, no matter who benefits from the term, and that the seller's warranty and disclaimer terms are a package to which the buyer assents (or does not assent) as a whole.

APPLYING THE CODE

Problem 15-6.

Assume that the Limited Six-Month Warranty in Problem 15-5 also contains the following language in bold type:

> **The seller undertakes no responsibility for the quality of the goods except as provided in this contract. The seller assumes no responsibility that the goods will be fit for any particular purpose for which you may be buying these goods, except as otherwise provided in the contract. These goods are not covered by warranties of merchantability or fitness.**

Does the quoted language above disclaim any implied warranties and express warranties between Charles and Cooks-Are-Us? What about between Charles and KitchenArt?

Chapter 7

Performance Issues: Living in the Contract and Escaping from the Contract

Key Concepts

- Identification of goods (§ 2-501)
- Tender of delivery (§ 2-503), receipt of goods (§ 2-103(1)(c)), and passing of title (§ 2-401)
- Shipment contracts vs. destination contracts (§§ 2-503, 2-504 and Incoterms)
- Risk of loss to the goods (§§ 2-509, 2-510)
- Buyer's right to reject the goods: the "perfect tender rule" (§ 2-601)
- Process and timing of rejection of the goods (§§ 2-602, 2-605)
- Reasonable opportunity to inspect the goods (§ 2-513)
- Buyer's duties with respect to handling rejected goods (§§ 2-602, 2-603, 2-604, 2-711)
- Seller's right to cure (§ 2-508)
- Process and consequences of acceptance of the goods (§§ 2-606, 2-607)
- Revocation of acceptance of the goods (§ 2-608)
- Reasonable grounds for insecurity and adequate assurances of performance (§ 2-609)
- Repudiation (§ 2-610)
- Excuse (§§ 2-613 to 2-616)

The preceding Chapters have covered how to create enforceable contracts for the sale of goods, how to determine what terms are included, and how to understand the promises that were made about the quality and performance of the goods. This Chapter addresses the next phase in the life of a contract—what happens in the "performance" stage. As stated in § 1-301, the obligation of the seller is to "transfer and deliver" as required by the contract and the obligation of the buyer is to "accept and pay in accordance with the contract." The first step in understanding those aspects of the parties' performance duties is to explore the nature of the delivery and payment responsibilities, some of which are covered by terms in the agreement and some of which are supplied by the provisions of Article 2. That is the subject of Assignments 16, 17, and 18, which address what we call "living in the contract." Sometimes, however, events that occur after the contract is created may allow the parties to be excused from performance, which we call "escaping from the contract," covered in Assignment 19.

A brief overview of the questions that arise with respect to delivery and payment will establish a context to help you learn the complex web of interconnected sections that govern contract performance and the parties' rights and remedies that flow from the provisions. Consider, for example, a farmer who in May enters into a contract to sell a thousand bushels of wheat to a flour mill to be delivered the following September. The sections of Article 2 covered in this Chapter address many of the complications that can arise in the months between May and September. Among the issues addressed:

- How is delivery from seller to buyer to be accomplished under the contract? If the wheat is to be transported, who is responsible to make arrangements for the transportation, who pays for it, and who bears the risk if the grain is lost or damaged while in transit? Assignment 16 introduces a set of Article 2 shipping terms, as well as the Incoterms® from the International Chamber of Commerce, any of which may be used by the parties to specify these aspects of the contract terms. Assignment 18 will cover additional aspects of risk of loss.

- When does the buyer gain ownership of (title to) the grain, and why might that matter? (Assignment 16)

- Does the buyer have a right to inspect the goods before paying? (Assignment 17)

- What does the Code say the buyer may or should do if the goods (the wheat) is not as promised? Under what circumstances may the buyer reject the wheat, and when is the buyer required instead to accept it and seek damages? How do the Code's answers to those questions compare to the common law "substantial performance" rule? (Assignments 17 and 18)

- If the goods are rejected, what should the buyer do with the rejected goods? And does the seller have the right to attempt again to perform (to "cure")? (Assignments 17 and 18)

- What happens if, in mid-summer, either buyer or seller (the flour mill or the farmer) learn facts that suggest the other party may not perform (e.g., the harvest is predicted to be unusually bad or the flour mill has reduced demand from its customers)? What if one party explicitly tells the other party it will not perform? What recourse does the other party have? (Assignment 19)

- Finally, if circumstances make it difficult or impossible for either party to perform, when might that party be excused from performing? (Assignment 19)

Assignment 16

Identification, Tender of Delivery, Risk of Loss, and Passage of Title

§§ 2-319, 2-320, 2-401, 2-501, 2-503, 2-504, 2-509

A. Unbundling the Passage of Ownership

In real property law, title is a "bundle of sticks," each stick representing a different aspect of property ownership. Unless the buyer and seller agree otherwise, the entire bundle of sticks usually is passed at one instant from seller to buyer. As a result, the moment of title passage for real property has enormous significance for a wide range of legal sub-issues, like risk of loss to the transferred property, responsibility for real estate taxes, right to exclude trespassers, right to convey security interests attached to the real estate, and so on. Predictably, because so much of realty law depends on title, the cases deciding when title to land passes have sometimes been inconsistent, varying in result by which underlying ownership right was at issue. (For instance, risk-of-loss cases might determine that title passes at different times than do cases on real estate taxes.)

Article 2 diverges from this "unitary title" concept often applied to real property. Karl Llewellyn, the reporter for the Article 2 drafting committee in the 1940s and 1950s, persuaded the committee to abandon the unitary-title convention and instead "unbundle" the sticks, so that each right or obligation of ownership is transferred at the most sensible time, but not necessarily the same time that other rights and obligations are transferred. As the Comment to § 2-101 states, "the purpose is [1] to avoid making practical issues between practical [people] turn upon the location of an intangible something, the passing of which no [one] can prove by evidence and [2] to substitute for such abstractions proof of words and actions of a tangible character." This change was a radical innovation that has worked quite well, freeing Article 2 from the inconsistent case law results that have occurred in real property cases determining the moment of title passage. As a result, it has meant that § 2-401 on title passage has a very small role in determining the parties' rights and obligations under Article 2. That is, the default provisions in the Code allocate most rights and obligations to the buyer or the seller according to a common sense determination of who should have the particular right or bear the particular burden, regardless of who has title to the goods at that time. Thus, the actual passage of title becomes just one possible time for buyer and seller to acquire some of the unbundled sticks. In reality, the other moments in time are more important.

This Assignment covers the following aspects of ownership and events related to ownership: identification of goods, tender of delivery, risk of loss, receipt of goods, responsibility to pay for transportation or freight, and passing of title. The order of the discussion roughly follows the order in which these events might occur in a typical transaction for the sale of goods, though that order might be affected by the terms of the contract, as you will see.

LEARNING OUTCOMES AND OBJECTIVES

At the completion of this Assignment, you should be able to

- identify the legally significant stages in the delivery of goods from a seller to a buyer, from the initial identification of goods to a particular contract to the passage of title to the goods to the buyer;
- distinguish among and apply the default shipment terms provided by Article 2 and the International Chamber of Commerce to specify the various possible arrangements between sellers and buyers concerning responsibilities for

  · delivering the goods,

  · making arrangements for shipment,

  · paying for freight and insurance, and

  · the risk of loss upon destruction of or damage to the goods, absent fault of either party.

B. Identification of Goods

1. Requirements for Identification

After contract formation, identification is often the next (or concurrent) event that affects rights and duties between the parties. As you saw in Assignment 2, identification is the process of designating which particular items are the goods that buyer will receive. For purposes of our discussion of the scope of Article 2 in Assignment 2, this general understanding of the concept of identification sufficed. Now, however, we need to delve into the details of the technical requirements of identification in § 2-501.

> **Make the Connection to Assignment 2**
>
> You learned about "identification" in Assignment 2 in connection with discussion of the scope of Article 2. Article 2 applies to contracts for sale of goods; 2-105(1) defines goods generally as "all things . . . which are movable *at the time of identification to the contract for sale*." 2-105(1)

Reading the Code: § 2-501

Read the first sentence of 2-501(1).

Question 1. Do goods have to exist to be identified?

Question 2. Do goods have to conform to the contract requirements in order to be identified?

Read the second sentence of 2-501(1).

Question 3. How and when does identification occur under this provision?

Read the third sentence of 2-501(1), which contains subparts 2-501(1)(a), (b), and (c), and read the Comments to 2-501.

Question 4. When do none of these subsections apply?

Question 5. Under what circumstances does 2-501(1)(a) apply? If it does apply, when are the goods identified? (Note: there is an unfortunate circularity in the language of 2-501(1)(a), which can be confusing in determining the answer to this question. How might you rewrite this section to avoid that circularity? Hint: look at the language in 2-501(1)(b).)

Question 6. Under what circumstances does 2-501(1)(c) apply? If it does apply, when are the goods identified?

Question 7. Does 2-501(1)(c) specify the time of identification of the goods in a contract for sale of crops if the crops are already growing at the time the contract is entered into?

Question 8. Under what circumstances does 2-501(1)(b) apply? To answer, you must read 2-105(2), which contains an important definition. If 2-501(1)(b) does apply, when and how are the goods identified?

A careful reading of § 2-501 reveals that determining when goods are "identified" in the technical sense of that section requires answering two questions:

(1)   When was the contract formed?

(2)   When were the particular goods at issue designated to that particular contract?

EXAMPLES AND ANALYSIS

Example A: *In re Carman*[1]

Bonner signed a contract with Carman Boats for Carman to build a 46-foot motorboat. The contract listed boat specifications and provided for progress payments, but did not address delivery. For the next three years, the boat was under construction, and some progress payments were made. At one point, Carman prepared and filed paperwork with the Coast Guard to register the boat in Bonner's name, but the paperwork was

---

[1]   399 B.R. 158 (Bankr. D. Md. 1991).

rejected because it lacked Carman's signature. Bonner became impatient with the slow construction and told Carman he was going to have another company finish the boat. Before Bonner could make arrangements with another company, Carman filed for bankruptcy. When the bankruptcy trustee proposed to sell the boat at auction, Bonner objected, claiming that ownership to the boat had passed to him at the time that the contract was entered into, under 2-401(3)(b) (addressed in greater detail in Section H of this Assignment), which provides that, if delivery is to be made without moving the goods, title passes at the time and place of contracting "if the goods are at the time of contracting already identified and no documents of title are to be delivered."

Example B: *Jones v. One Fifty Foot Gulfstar Motor Sailing Yacht*[2]

Jones entered into negotiations to purchase a 50-foot Gulfstar sailing yacht from Underwood Marine. After taking an inspection sail on a prototype, she entered into a contract to purchase a yacht at a base price of $59,000, as soon as a hull became available to Underwood Marine. At that time, she provided a $1,000 down payment. A month later, she was informed that Hull No. 01 had become available. After an inspection and trial sail, she agreed to purchase the yacht, selecting numerous options for the interior. Over the next month, Underwood installed fabric, carpet, and other gear. Jones initiated procedures for registering the yacht under Florida's boat registration laws under the name "Cast Off," and Underwood sent her a revised sales agreement. She signed the agreement and wired the remainder of the purchase price to Underwood. A month later, when Jones was to take delivery, she was instead informed that Underwood was closed for business, and General Electric Credit Corporation, which had financed the construction of the hull for Underwood, had taken possession of the yacht based on its security interest. Jones argued that title to the yacht had passed to her, giving her interest in the boat ahead of G.E., under 2-401(3)(b), which (as we saw in Example A), provides that, if delivery is to be made without moving the goods, title passes at the time and place of contracting "if the goods are at the time of contracting already identified and no documents of title are to be delivered."

---

[2]   625 F.2d 44 (5th Cir. 1992).

Analysis of Examples A and B: The bankruptcy court rejected Bonner's argument, holding that the boat was not in existence at the time the contract was signed. Therefore, there could be no identification under either 2-501(1)(a) or 2-501(1)(b), and title could not have passed to Bonner under 2-401(3)(b). In contrast, in Example B, the Fifth Circuit held that Jones did have title to the Gulfstar yacht under 2-401(3)(b).

What is the difference in the two cases? In Example A, did the bankruptcy court hold that the boat was not identified to the contract at all, or was the crucial distinction one of timing?

APPLYING THE CODE

Problem 16-1.

When does identification occur in each of the following scenarios? Consider both of the questions posed before the Examples and Analysis: when was the contract formed, and when were the goods designated to the contract? Identify the part of 2-501 that provides the answer in each scenario.

(a) Customer takes an apple from the produce section of a grocery store, brings it to the cash register, and pays for it.

(b) Customer at SportsPlace selects a canoe from those on the display floor. She takes the product designation slip for that model of canoe to the cash register and pays for the canoe. After Customer drives around to Customer Pick-up, a warehouse worker takes a canoe of the correct model from storage, carries it to the loading dock, and lashes it to the top of the Customer's car.

(c) Buyer, an appliance manufacturer, orders 300 electrical motors of a certain model from Seller. When the order arrives electronically at Seller's warehouse, the Seller's employee promptly locates the motors in the warehouse, wraps 300 of them in plastic on several pallets, labels them with Buyer's address and account information, and uses a fork lift to move the pallets to the loading dock of the warehouse. Seller's truck driver picks up the pallets at the loading dock and delivers them to Buyer's factory as directed by Buyer.

(d)   Lois visits a restaurant at which she orders lobster and then, at the invitation of the waiter, she goes to the restaurant's tank to select a live lobster. The kitchen prepares it for her dinner. (Recall the second sentence of 2-314, if you are wondering about the scope issue.)

(e)   In February, a farmer contracts to sell the wheat crop that he will harvest the upcoming September. Planting will be in May. Will your answer differ if he enters into the contract in June, after the crop is planted?

2. Consequences of Identification

Examples A and B illustrate one of the potentially significant consequences of identification—its effect on some title determinations. Once identification occurs, the following additional consequences (among others) follow:

- The buyer obtains an insurable interest in the goods (§ 2-501).

- The buyer acquires the right to inspect the goods at any reasonable place and time and in any reasonable manner, except in a few situations (§ 2-513(1)).

- The buyer obtains a "special property" in the goods (§ 2-501), which allows the buyer to recover the goods from an insolvent seller under certain limited circumstances (§ 2-502).

- If the goods are identified when the contract is made and those identified goods are necessary for performance of the contract, under certain circumstances the damage or loss of those goods will excuse the seller from performance rather than causing a breach (§ 2-613).

- If the seller fails or refuses to deliver the goods and buyer is unable to locate a reasonable substitute for those goods, buyer can replevy the goods (§ 2-716(3)).

- If the buyer refuses to take goods that have been identified to the contract, the seller will still be able to recover the purchase price of those goods if the seller is unable to resell them (§ 2-709(1)(b), (2)).

- If the buyer repudiates or otherwise breaches while the risk of loss to the goods otherwise remains on the seller, the risk of loss nonetheless may be considered to be on the buyer to the extent that seller has under-insured the conforming goods (§ 2-510(3)).

You do not need to memorize this list of consequences, but you need to be alert to references to identification to the contract when applying these sections of the Code.

C. Tender of Delivery

Once the goods have been identified, the next event often is the seller's tender of delivery. Goods can be "delivered" in a variety of ways:

- The buyer can take possession of the goods at the time of sale.

- The seller's truck can deliver the goods to the buyer.

- The seller can enter into a contract with a third party (a "carrier") to deliver the goods to the buyer.

- The seller can enter into a contract with a third party who owns a warehouse to hold the goods at the warehouse for the buyer to pick them up.

Which delivery method is used will depend upon the terms of the agreement and the provisions of Article 2.

The buyer and seller are acutely interested in determining when the seller has completed its delivery obligations, because that determination is relevant: (i) for allocating responsibility for accidental loss to the goods (e.g., from fire or theft) and (ii) for determining whether seller or buyer is responsible for pursuing remedies for problems caused by the carrier or the warehouse (e.g., delivery to the wrong location, late delivery, damage to goods, or refusal to hand the goods over to the buyer). In the absence of credit terms, seller's delivery usually also triggers buyer's obligation to pay. *See* § 2-301.

It is tempting to imagine that seller's completion of delivery triggers shifting risk of loss from seller to buyer and also causes title to pass. Sometimes that is true, and sometimes it is not. You have to "unbundle" these items from each other and consider them as separate legal concepts.

1. Basic Requirements for Tender of Delivery

Section 2-503 is the umbrella section dealing with "tender of delivery."

Reading the Code:
§ 2-503

**Read 2-503(1)–(3) and Comments 1 to 4,
and skim 2-503(4) and (5).**

Question 9. Subsection (1) sets out the basic rules governing tender of delivery, which apply regardless whether the goods are to be shipped, delivered at a warehouse, or handed over directly from seller to buyer. What must a seller do to comply with the basic requirements for tender of delivery in 2-503(1)?

EXAMPLES AND ANALYSIS

Example C: *Hansen-Mueller Co. v. Gau*[3]

In August 2010, Gau, a farmer, entered into a contract to sell 7500 bushels of yellow corn to Hansen-Mueller, a company that operated a grain elevator in Council Bluffs, Iowa. The corn was to be shipped between June 1 and June 30, 2011. During the month of June, Gau called Hansen-Mueller repeatedly, requesting to deliver the corn. Hansen-Mueller refused to accept the delivery, claiming that storage at this particular grain elevator was impractical due to the threat of impending flooding in the area. (However, Hansen-Mueller did accept other deliveries of grain at that elevator for purposes of creating a blend of grain that could be removed from the elevator.) Gau offered to deliver the corn to a different Hansen-Mueller grain elevator, but Hansen-Mueller refused. In July, Gau cancelled the contract, claiming that it was void because Hansen-Mueller

---

3   838 N.W.2d 138 (Iowa Ct. App. 2013).

refused to take delivery. Both parties sued each other for breach of contract. Hansen-Mueller argued that Gau never tendered the corn for delivery, because tender required Gau to physically bring the corn to the elevator or extend a written offer of performance.

Analysis: The court granted Gau summary judgment against Hansen-Mueller. The court emphasized that, under 2-503(1), tender is not the same as delivery. Although mere inquiry would not meet the requirements of tender, Gau did more than inquire about delivery. His repeated phone calls to Hansen-Mueller asking to deliver the corn, as well as his offer to bring the corn to another facility, clearly established that Gau was prepared to deliver the 7500 bushels of corn during the time frame required by the contract. Gau placed the grain at Hansen-Mueller's disposition and provided the notification reasonably necessary to enable it to take delivery, thereby satisfying the requirements of 2-503(1) for tender.

The contract specified delivery to the Council Bluffs elevator. Does this constitute determination of the "time, manner and place for tender" by agreement under 2-503(1)? Why should Gau's offer to deliver to another elevator be relevant to whether Gau tendered in accordance with the terms of the agreement?

Example D: *TVI, Inc. v. Infosoft Technologies*[4]

TVI operated a national chain of thrift stores. For a number of years, it leased computer software and purchased various kinds of computer hardware, including cash registers and printers, from Infosoft. In December 2005, TVI entered into a contract with Infosoft to purchase 99 cash registers, paying for them in full. The contract did not specify any terms regarding the timing or method of delivery of the cash registers. By April 2006, Infosoft had delivered only 32 cash registers to TVI. Around that time, Infosoft informed TVI that it was terminating their business relationship because TVI had started purchasing equipment from another company. According to deposition testimony, during their negotiations to resolve their outstanding agreements and accounts, Infosoft told TVI, both verbally and by e-mail, that if Infosoft did not receive payment of all outstanding invoices on other contracts by April 15, it would send the cash registers back to the manufacturer. TVI disputed the amount outstanding on the invoices, and

---

[4]   2007 WL 2710950 (E.D. Mo. 2007).

demanded that Infosoft deliver the remaining cash registers to their trucking company immediately and make arrangements for the delivery of other equipment. Both parties sued each other for breach of contract. Infosoft responded to TVI's summary judgment motion by alleging that there was a genuine issue of material fact about whether it had, in fact, tendered the cash registers to TVI. This argument was supported by an affidavit from Infosoft's President that Infosoft had made the cash registers available to TVI for pick-up, but that TVI had not picked them up.

Analysis: The court granted TVI's summary judgment motion against Infosoft, concluding that Infosoft had not tendered delivery. The conclusory assertions in the President's affidavit contradicted the sworn statements made in the deposition and thus could not be used to establish an issue of fact. According to the deposition statement and the e-mail, Infosoft had told TVI that it would return the cash registers to the manufacturer unless outstanding invoices were paid. This undermined Infosoft's argument that it had tendered delivery under 2-503(1).

Since the contract did not specify any of the delivery terms, what was the time and place for tender in this contract? Which requirement of 2-503(1) did TVI not meet?

2. Tender of Delivery via Carrier or Warehouse

The remaining subsections of 2-503 deal with particular types of tender of delivery—by carrier, by warehouse, and with delivery documents. A "warehouse" is a person engaged in the business of storing goods for hire. See § 7-102(a)(13). A "carrier" is a person engaged in the business of transporting or forwarding goods for others who enters into a contract with a buyer or seller to transport the goods.[5] Note that a seller cannot be its own third-party bailee and hence cannot be a "carrier." If a seller is using its own vehicle to the goods, the goods are not being tendered by carrier.

---

[5]   This definition is derived from amended § 7-102(a)(2), which defines "carrier" as "a person that issues a bill of lading." Under § 1-201(6) (§ 1-201(b)(6) in revised Article 1), a bill of lading is "a document evidencing the receipt of goods for shipment issued by a person engaged in the business of transporting or forwarding goods."

Deliveries by carrier or warehouse may be accomplished using documents of title (often called simply "documents"). Assignments 20 and 21 cover the meaning and use of documents of title. For the purpose of this Assignment, think of these documents as simply receipts that may be presented to claim the goods from the carrier or warehouse.

If the seller is tendering the goods to the buyer by way of a carrier, tender of delivery may occur by what the trade calls a "shipment contract" or by what the trade calls a "destination contract." Subsection (2) of § 2-503 refers to § 2-504, which establishes the requirements for "shipment contracts." Subsection (3) of § 2-503 establishes the requirements for "destination contracts." Subsection (4) sets forth the requirements for tender of delivery if the seller is storing the goods in or delivering the goods to a third-party warehouse, where the buyer is to retrieve them. The next Problem explores differences among these types of tender of delivery.

APPLYING THE CODE

Problem 16-2.

Fill in the third column in the chart below, indicating what the seller has to do to satisfy its tender obligations for each type of delivery.

Section or subsection	Delivery type	Seller's obligations
2-503(1)	Buyer picks up goods at seller's business	
2-503(2), which refers to 2-504	Shipment contract, by carrier	
2-503(3)	Destination contract, by carrier or seller's vehicle	
2-503(4)	Warehouse	(Do not fill in this square; these tender obligations will be treated in Assignment 20.)

In this Assignment, "tender" means tender of delivery of conforming goods, as detailed in Question 1 and Problems 16-1 and 16-2. However, Article 2 occasionally uses "tender" to mean a tender of nonconforming goods or a tender of documents. Consider the context in order to determine which meaning governs. See § 2-503 Comment 1.

D. Risk of Loss in Absence of Breach[6]

Now that we have examined identification and tender of delivery, we need to explore the links between those two events and risk of loss. The shifting of risk of loss has important consequences:

If the seller still has the risk of loss when the goods are lost, damaged, or delayed (whether the seller still has the goods or they are already in the possession of a carrier or warehouse), the seller usually is still contractually obligated to deliver conforming goods to the buyer in a timely manner or pay the buyer damages for the loss, damage, or delay. In an appropriate case, seller may be able to recover some of its losses by pursuing remedies against a carrier or warehouse or under its own insurance coverage.

On the other hand, if the buyer has the risk of loss when the goods are lost, damaged, or destroyed, the buyer is still contractually obligated to pay the seller for the goods. In an appropriate case, buyer may be able to recover some of its losses by pursuing remedies against a carrier or warehouse or under its own insurance coverage.

In other words, the parties' contractual obligations are not modified by damage to or loss of the goods. A buyer must still pay at the contract rate even though the goods were damaged or destroyed, if the buyer had the risk of loss. A seller must still deliver conforming goods—or pay damages for not doing so—even though the goods were damaged or destroyed, if the seller had the risk of loss. There are a few exceptions to this rule, however, including common law excuse doctrines (e.g., impossibility) and provisions appearing in § 2-613 (casualty to identified goods), § 2-614 (substituted performance), and § 2-615 (excuse by failure of presupposed conditions). We will cover these sections in Assignment 19.

---

[6] Assignment 18 covers risk of loss when buyer or seller has breached.

Reading the Code:
§ 2-509

Read 2-509(1) and Comments 1 and 2.

This section establishes the risk of loss when the goods are to be transported by a carrier. Note that it contains similar phrases to those you already read in 2-504 on shipment contracts and in 2-503(3) on destination contracts. In particular, subsection (1)(a) of 2-509 establishes the risk of loss for deliveries that do "not require [seller] to deliver [the goods] at a particular destination"—a Code phrase that refers to shipment contracts. Subsection (1)(b) establishes the risk of loss for deliveries that do "require [seller] to deliver [the goods] at a particular destination"—a Code phrase that refers to destination contracts. Remember that a seller cannot be its own third-party bailee and hence cannot be a "carrier," so delivery in seller's vehicle is not within the scope of 2-509(1)(a).

Read 2-509(2) and Comment 4.

This section covers contracts "where the goods are held by a bailee to be delivered without being moved"—a Code phrase that refers to seller's delivery by way of a third-party warehouse. This same phrase appears in 2-503(4) on tender in warehouse deliveries.

Read 2-509(3) and Comment 3.

This section is a catch-all provision that covers all other types of deliveries, including when the buyer picks up the goods from the seller's business or residence or the seller delivers the goods in its own vehicle.

Read 2-509(4) and Comment 5.

This section emphasizes that the parties' agreement can displace these default provisions on risk of loss.

APPLYING THE CODE

Problem 16-3.

Fill in the third column in the chart below, when 2-509 says that the risk of loss shifts for each type of delivery. In the bottom row, consider whether it makes any difference whether seller is a merchant as to goods or as to practices.

Subsection	Delivery type	When risk of loss passes
2-509(1)(a)	Shipment contract, by carrier	
2-509(1)(b)	Destination contract, by carrier[1]	
2-509(2)	Warehouse	(Do not fill in this square; risk of loss for warehouse contracts will be treated in Assignment 20)
2-509(3)	Buyer picks up goods from seller, or seller's vehicle delivers goods	

[1] Note that 2-509(1)(b) applies only when a carrier is used for delivery. The tender requirements of 2-503(3) do not mandate use of a carrier for a destination contract.

Reading the Code:
§ 2-509

Read Comment 1 to 2-503.

The questions below ask about the meaning of four important 2-509 phrases that describe the actions that a seller must take to pass the risk of loss in particular kinds of deliveries. What portions of 2-503, 2-504, and the definitions in Articles 1 and 2 assist you in discerning the meaning of those phrases?

Read 2-509(1)(a) and Comment 2.

Question 10. What does it mean to "duly deliver" the goods to the carrier, in 2-509(1)(a)? Must the seller satisfy all or only some of the requirements of 2-504 in order to "duly deliver"?

Read 2-509(1)(b).

Question 11. What does it mean to "duly tender" the goods at a particular destination?

Read 2-509(3).

Question 12. What does "receipt" mean?

Question 13. What does "tender of delivery" mean?

APPLYING THE CODE

Problem 16-4. Implications of Risk of Loss.

Based on your understanding of risk of loss so far:

(a)   Would a seller prefer a shipment contract or a destination contract?

(b)   Would a buyer prefer a shipment contract or a destination contract?

(c)   Which party (buyer or seller) should carry insurance on the goods during a shipment contract?

(d)   Which party (buyer or seller) should carry insurance on the goods during a destination contract?

(e)   If the agreement calls for a shipment contract, may seller use its own vehicle?

(f)   If the agreement calls for a destination contract, may seller use its own vehicle? If seller does, are there any risk-of-loss consequences for that choice?

(g) If the parties agree that the goods be sent by carrier, but they fail to agree on whether it is a shipment or destination contract, what is the default provision? See 2-503 Comment 5. What does that default provision mean in terms of when tender occurs and who has the risk of loss while the carrier has the goods?

E. Delivery Terms under the UCC

Carrier contracts are referred to in acronyms that create a daunting alphabet soup, but the UCC fortunately deals with a limited set of carrier contracts. We will consider only four types of UCC carrier contracts:

- F.O.B.[7] place of shipment

- F.O.B. place of destination

- C.I.F.

- C. & F. or C.F.

Reading the Code:
§§ 2-319 & 2-320

Read the sections listed below,
pertaining to the identified type of carrier contract:

F.O.B. place of shipment: 2-319(1)(a)

F.O.B. place of destination: 2-319(1)(b)

C.I.F.: 2-320 and Comments 1 and 2

C. & F. or C.F.: 2-320(1) & (3)

Question 14. Do the seller's obligations under each of these four types of carrier contracts end upon delivery to a carrier ("shipment contract") or, instead, upon delivery at the destination ("destination contract")? Place

---

7   F.O.B. originally meant "free on board," but you should ignore that meaning and instead focus on the use of the word in Article 2.

each kind of carrier contract in the proper column below, creating a handy reference chart.

Shipment contracts	Destination contracts

EXAMPLES AND ANALYSIS

Example E: *Windows, Inc. v. Jordan Panel Systems Corp.*[8]

Jordan, a construction company installing window wall panels at an air cargo facility at John F. Kennedy Airport in New York City, ordered custom-made windows from Windows, a South Dakota window manufacturer. The contract specified: "All windows to be shipped properly crated/packaged/boxed suitable for cross country motor freight transit and delivered to New York City." The windows were constructed according to Jordan's specifications, and delivered intact and properly packaged to a common carrier. During the course of the shipment, however, the goods were significantly damaged. Due to "load shift," approximately two-thirds of the shipment had broken glass and gouged and twisted window frames. In an attempt to stay on its contractor's schedule, Jordan salvaged as much of the shipment as it could and ordered a new shipment from Windows, which was delivered with no problem. Jordan sued Windows for incidental and consequential damages resulting from the damage.

---

[8]   177 F.3d 114 (2nd Cir. 1999).

Analysis: Jordan's claim against Windows was dismissed on summary judgment, because the risk of loss had shifted to Jordan when Windows put the goods, properly packaged, into the possession of the carrier for shipment. The court interpreted the delivery language as creating a shipment contract, rather than a destination contract, under 2-503. The court cited commentary and a case to support the idea that there is a "strong presumption" favoring shipment contracts; Comment 5 states the same presumption. That strong presumption can be overcome only by explicit language imposing on the seller the obligation to deliver to a particular destination, the court noted, and the language of this contract did not do so.

Does Jordan have any recourse for the damage to the windows? The opinion notes in a footnote that one of the judges suggested that the contract was not a destination contract under 2-503(3) because it used the phrase "delivered to New York City" rather than "delivered at New York City." Do you think this is a valid distinction?

Example F: *Stampede Presentation Products, Inc. v. Productive Transportation, Inc.*[9]

Stampede, a distributor of presentation equipment, entered into a contract with 1SaleADay, an Internet discount retailer, to buy 960 flat-screen TVs. This contract was evidenced by a Purchase Invoice, which identified 1Sale-ADay as the "vendor" and directed the items to be shipped to Stampede's resale customer in Napierville, Illinois. Stampede then hired Productive Transportation to handle the shipping, pursuant to a Uniform Straight Bill of Lading designating Productive as the "delivering carrier" and indicating that the TVs were to be shipped "FOB Origin" by the "Shipper" (identified as Stampede) from a warehouse in California to Stampede's customer in Illinois. Productive subcontracted with another carrier to pick up the goods. This trucker picked up the TVs at the warehouse and then stole or lost them. Stampede sued both Productive and 1SaleADay. 1SaleADay moved to dismiss, arguing that the contract was clearly a shipment contract, pursuant to which the risk of loss passed to Stampede upon delivery of the goods to the carrier at the California warehouse. Stampede countered that 1SaleADay's reliance on 2-509 was a "pure red herring,"

---

[9]   80 UCC Rep. Serv. 2d 927 (W.D.N.Y. 2013).

since the facts in the complaint set forth a plausible claim that 1SaleADay breached the contract by delivering the TVs to someone other than the carrier authorized by Stampede.

Analysis: The court dismissed Stampede's breach of contract claim against 1SaleADay, finding that their contract was a shipment contract under 2-504, and that the risk of loss passed to Stampede when the goods were delivered to the carrier under 2-509(1)(a). The terms of the purchase agreement clearly expressed the parties' understanding that Stampede would be designating a carrier to make the shipment to the customer. There is no express language anywhere giving 1SaleADay any obligation to deliver the TVs to a particular destination. This conclusion was strengthened by the use of the term "FOB Origin" on the Bill of Lading and the "strong presumption" favoring shipment contracts, noted in Example E.

Does Stampede have any recourse for the loss of the TVs? What was Stampede trying to say by characterizing 1SaleADay's reliance on 2-509 as a "pure red herring"? The court responded to this argument by writing: "To the contrary, since the parties are merchants as that term is defined in [2-104(1)], and the transaction at issue is for the sale of goods as defined in [2-105(1)], it cannot be disputed that the allocation of the risk of loss to the goods during the transaction is covered by UCC Article 2." Do the risk of loss provisions of 2-509 apply only to merchants?

Example G: *Ron Mead T.V. & Appliance v. Legendary Homes, Inc.*[10]

Mead, a merchant selling household appliances, sold a set of appliances to a builder, Legendary Homes, for installation in a home that was under construction. When the Mead delivery truck arrived at the construction site, the builders were gone and the home was closed. The garage was unlocked, so the deliveryman put the appliances in the garage and locked the door behind him. During the night, the appliances were stolen. Mead sued Legendary Homes for the price of the appliances.

---

[10]   746 P.2d 116 (Okla. Civ. App. 1987).

Analysis: The court held for Legendary Homes, reasoning that the risk of loss had not passed from Mead at the time of the theft under 2-509(3), because Legendary Homes had not "received" the goods. "Receipt" is defined in 2-103 as taking physical possession of the goods, and leaving them in the garage did not give Mead the opportunity to take physical possession.

Do you agree with this ruling? Would the result have been different if Mead were a homeowner who sold the appliances to Legendary Homes at a garage sale? Would the result have been different if the contract called for delivery of the goods to Legendary Homes by a third-party delivery service?

F. Paying for the Freight

Yet to be discussed is the separate question of who is responsible for paying the cost of transporting the goods from the seller to the buyer. This cost of transport is known as "freight." The contract price does not always include freight; in fact, the norm is that it usually does not. Nor is it reliable to assume that the party who has the risk of loss during transport is the party paying the freight. Nor does the distinction between shipment and destination contracts always dictate who pays the freight. Instead, one must know which particular shipping term is involved. To figure out who pays the freight, we need to read the shipping provisions and associated Code definitions with particular care.

Note that, when this textbook asks who pays the freight, it is asking who has the ultimate legal responsibility to pay the freight. With respect to the actual mechanics of payment, many possible arrangements abound. Either party may choose a carrier with whom it has a regular account or has negotiated a flat fee for local deliveries; in that case, that party may both make the initial payment and take on the ultimate responsibility for the cost of the freight. Or the seller may pay the freight to the carrier, and then bill the buyer for it. Or the buyer may pay the carrier at the end of the trip, and then offset that cost against the cost of the goods when buyer pays the seller. Such arrangements may be reflected in the contract terms or in the commercial context (e.g., course of dealing, course of performance, or usage of trade). While you should be alert for such specifications, the starting point must be determining who ultimately bears responsibility for paying.

Reading the Code:
§§ 2-319 & 2-320

Re-read the subsections pertaining to the four types of
carrier contracts identified in Question 14:

F.O.B. place of shipment: 2-319(1)(a)

F.O.B. place of destination: 2-319(1)(b)

C.I.F.: 2-320 and Comments 1 and 2

C. & F. or C.F.: 2-320(1) & (3)

Question 15. For each of the four types of carrier contracts, what part of
the transportation must the seller ultimately furnish or pay for, and what
part of the transportation must the buyer ultimately pay for? Note that these
sections say what the seller must pay for; by implication, the rest of the cost
of delivery is the buyer's cost.

G. Domestic Shipping Terms from Sources other than the UCC

The shipping terms in Article 2 are not the only options for parties shipping
goods.[11] In contracts for shipping goods internationally, parties often choose to
use the shipping terms known as "Incoterms®" (short for "International Commercial Terms"), published by the International Chamber of Commerce.[12] Incoterms
consist of a set of eleven shipping terms that specify in great detail the same basic
issues addressed by the UCC's shipment terms: passage of risk of loss, which parties
have responsibility for delivery to what particular place, and which parties have
responsibility for what shipping costs. The Incoterms also address who has the
responsibility for customs declarations.

---

[11] For a discussion of additional sources of alternative shipping terms in international trade, see Alain Frecon,
Practical Considerations in Drafting F.O.B. Terms in International Sales, 3 Berkeley J. Int'l L. 346 (1986).

[12] International Chamber of Commerce Incoterms 2010 (I.C.C. Publ. No. 715E, 2010 Edition).

The ICC zealously guards the copyright to its expensive materials, even for educational purposes, so the complete Incoterms 2010 are not listed here. However, if you have access to a law library or employer that has purchased any Incoterm books or posters, take the opportunity to look at the color diagrams of the shipping process with their easy-to-understand graphics.

Various commercial websites have fashioned their own useful graphics that summarize Incoterms 2010. You can locate them easily by doing a Google images search for "Incoterms 2010." Make sure that the graphic pertains to Incoterms 2010 with 11 terms, not the earlier version with 13 terms.

Compare the following descriptions of the meanings of select Incoterms, provided on the website of the International Chamber of Commerce,[13] and compare their meaning to the meanings of the Article 2 shipping terms discussed above.

Reading the Code: Comparing Incoterms and Article 2 Shipping Terms

Incoterms FOB and CIF

Incoterms FOB and CIF (note that the Incoterms versions have no periods between the letters as the Article versions do) are used only for transportation by sea or inland waterway. They do not apply to land-based transport, like trucks and railroads. Read the following definitions of these Incoterms:

- **FOB:** "'Free On Board' means that the seller delivers the goods on board the vessel nominated by the buyer at the named port of shipment or procures the goods already so delivered. The risk of loss of or damage to the goods passes when the goods are on board the vessel, and the buyer bears all costs from that moment onwards."

- **CIF:** "'Cost, Insurance and Freight' means that the seller delivers the goods on board the vessel or procures the goods already so delivered.

---

13   See iccwbo.org. Reproduced with the permission of the ICC Business Bookstore, which sells the complete version at iccbooks.com.

The risk of loss of or damage to the goods passes when the goods are on board the vessel. The seller must contract for and pay the costs and freight necessary to bring the goods to the named port of destination."

Question 16. Besides the limitation of these definitions to transport by ship, how (if at all) do these definitions differ from Article 2's definitions of these shipping terms?

_____

Incoterms FCA, CPT, and DAP

Other Incoterms apply to any mode of transport. Read the following definitions of these Incoterms:

- **FCA:** "'Free Carrier' means that the seller delivers the goods to the carrier or another person nominated by the buyer at the seller's premises or another named place. The parties are well advised to specify as clearly as possible the point within the named place of delivery, as the risk passes to the buyer at that point."

- **CPT:** "'Carriage Paid To' means that the seller delivers the goods to the carrier or another person nominated by the seller at an agreed place (if any such place is agreed between parties) and that the seller must contract for and pay the costs of carriage necessary to bring the goods to the named place of destination."

- **DAP:** "'Delivered at Place' means that the seller delivers when the goods are placed at the disposal of the buyer on the arriving means of transport ready for unloading at the named place of destination. The seller bears all risks involved in bringing the goods to the named place."

Question 17. What are the closest analogues to these three shipping terms under Article 2? How (if at all) do these definitions differ from those Article 2 analogues?

If the parties agree upon a particular Incoterm, the contract should specify not only the three-letter term, but also the fact that it is from Incoterms 2010, not a previous version and not some other set of shipping terms. So, for instance, a contract might specify "FCA (Incoterms 2010)."

Although Incoterms have been developed for international trade, parties to purely domestic contracts sometimes choose to use Incoterms. And, of course, both the Article 2 definitions and the Incoterms are merely default terms. Parties to any contract can specify either type of shipping term and can even alter any part of a definition for purposes of their own contract. Parties can also draft shipping clauses from scratch, or choose not to address shipping terms at all, relying instead on course of performance, course of dealing, and usage of trade.

APPLYING THE CODE

Problem 16-5.

Read the following contract clause used in an actual contract between two merchants in a long-term relationship involving multiple deliveries of goods in response to purchase orders submitted by the buyer from time to time. (The "Vendor" is the seller; "TSC" is the buyer.) Which parts of this contract clause incorporate Article 2's definitions of F.O.B. shipment or destination, Incoterms' definitions of FCA or CPT or DAP, or some variation of these terms?

> **Title and Risk of Loss:** The Vendor is responsible, at its cost, for insuring the goods to the FOB point for full replacement value, including freight, and the Vendor shall file all claims for loss or damage. All uncollectible portions of concealed damage claims shall be charged back to the Vendor. All transportation costs or expenses incurred by TSC because of the Vendor's failure to comply with the terms of this Vendor Agreement and any additional or excess transportation charges due to split shipments, errors in classification of merchandise, or any other compliance error shall be charged to the Vendor.
>
> For prepaid FOB Destination Purchase Orders, no liability shall be incurred by TSC, and the risk of loss shall not pass to TSC until the legal title passes upon delivery of the goods to TSC's final destination in the condition required by this Vendor Agreement and the goods are accepted by TSC.
>
> For FOB Origin Purchase Orders, liability and legal title passes to TSC or its carrier at the time the goods are picked up and loaded at Vendor's dock by a TSC specified carrier.

H. Passage of Title

As you can see from the preceding sections on identification, tender of delivery, risk of loss, and freight, many of the traditional indicia and consequences of holding title are handled separately from title in Article 2. Title is still important for some purposes, but most of them are outside of the UCC (for example, the timing of a "sale" for purposes of sales tax liability, whether the buyer or the seller can enforce tort liability for damage to or interference with the goods, whether certain actions interfering with the goods amount to criminal theft or other crimes, and insurance coverage of "owner's goods"). You may wish to review Examples A and B, which illustrate some situations in which the timing of passage of title is significant under the UCC, as well as the importance of the concept of "identification" to passage of title under § 2-401(3).

Reading the Code: § 2-401

Read 2-401(2) and (3).

The parties may pass title at any time agreed upon, subject to the limitations in 1-102(3). The default rule is that title passes when the seller completes its performance with regard to physical delivery of the goods. Subsections (2) and (3) elaborate on this rule in particular delivery settings, using some phrases that parallel those used in 2-503 and 2-509.

Question 18. Fill in the chart below.

Delivery Type	Applicable portion of 2-401	When and where title passes
Shipment Contract		
Destination Contract		
Buyer picks up goods at seller's location		

APPLYING THE CODE

Problem 16-6. Tying It All Together.

Using your answers from many of the previous problems, fill in the following charts by recording the pertinent section number and the answer it gives to the question in the top row for the type of delivery in the left column. If more than one provision is needed to fully answer the question, jot down each provision in order of analysis.

(a) Tender of delivery and payment of freight

Delivery Type	How does seller complete "tender of delivery"?	Who pays freight?
Buyer picks up goods at seller's location		no freight paid
Shipment contract, by carrier		
Destination contract, by carrier or seller's truck		

Delivery Type	How does seller complete "tender of delivery"?	Who pays freight?
Warehouse (fill in only # of section or subsection)		no freight paid

(b)   Passage of risk of loss and title

Delivery Type	When does risk of loss pass to buyer (if no breach)?	When does title pass to buyer?
Buyer picks up goods at seller's location	If seller is merchant: If seller is not merchant:	If goods identified at time of contracting: If not:
Shipment contract, by carrier		
Destination contract, by carrier or seller's truck	If carrier: If no carrier:	
Warehouse (fill in only # of section or subsection)		

Problem 16-7.

Tina is remodeling the kitchen in her home. She visits a stone supply company to select the granite for her countertop from among 33 representative slabs of different granites. Each type of granite is displayed vertically with only the top one of several similar slabs visible. She signs an agreement to purchase the granite, to have it cut to fit her kitchen, and to have it installed. The cost of cutting and installation is $585, while the retail cost of the granite is $1900. The agreement reserves to the stone supply company the right to select the particular granite slabs to be used from among the slabs of the same type of granite. Tina makes a down payment of $1500 and arranges dates for measuring and for installation.

A company employee comes to Tina's house and measures the kitchen precisely. He selects two slabs for Tina's kitchen and places her name on masking tape on the back of each slab. He cuts, polishes, and "edges" the granite to fit the measurements. Two employees come to Tina's house and install the granite. Tina pays the remaining amount due. When are the goods identified to the contract? Consider 2-501 and Comments 1, 2, and 4, as well as 2-704, which allows the seller to take certain actions after buyer breaches by refusing to take the goods.

Problem 16-8.

Seller proposes to sell specified goods for "$500, F.O.B. seller's loading dock, ship to buyer's plant."

   (a)   Buyer instead seeks "F.O.B. buyer's plant." Will the buyer's proposal cause the seller to want a change in the price?

   (b)   Buyer instead seeks "F.O.B. buyer's plant, buyer to pay freight." Will the buyer's proposal cause the seller to want a change in the price?

Problem 16-9.

Agreement between fish merchant in Duluth and a seafood restaurant in New Orleans calling for the sale of "500 lbs. No. 1 Quality Walleye, F.O.B. Duluth, ship to port of New Orleans. Payment due five days after goods arrive in New Orleans." The goods are shipped via a refrigerated container and loaded on a boat that travels the Mississippi River. Seller gets a bill of lading and forwards it to buyer. During shipment, the container malfunctions, and the fish spoil.

(a)   Who has the risk of loss for the spoilage of the fish, and why?

(b)   Will your answer in (a) change if the agreement instead specifies "C.I.F. New Orleans"?

Problem 16-10.

Bianca orders $180 worth of clothes for her children on a web site run by Terra Children, Inc., a company with high quality clothing and particularly good prices. The web site says in its posted terms and conditions that purchased clothes will be sent by United Parcel Service (U.P.S.) within fourteen days. Terra Children gives the clothes to U.P.S. for shipment and sends Bianca a postcard saying that her clothes have been shipped and providing the U.P.S. tracking number. No additional documents are necessary for Bianca to obtain delivery. Thirty days after her order, Bianca contacts Terra Children to say that the clothes have not yet arrived. Terra Children says that U.P.S. picked up the clothes three days after her order. (Assume, for purposes of this problem, that U.P.S. is within the meaning of "carrier" in the UCC. Also assume that Bianca's credit card payment may be rightfully suspended only for defective goods or missing goods that are the seller's responsibility.)

(a)   Bianca asks Terra Children to track the order for her with U.P.S., but Terra Children refuses, saying that Bianca bears the responsibility of tracking things down with (or making a claim against) U.P.S. once Terra Children gives Bianca the U.P.S. tracking number. Is Terra Children correct?

(b)   Terra Children also tells Bianca that she still must pay Terra Children for the clothing (so she cannot rightfully suspend payment on her credit card). Is Terra Children correct?

(c)   If Bianca's homeowner's insurance policy covers the loss of goods that she "owns," regardless of where they are, will her policy cover the loss of this clothing if she never receives it?

Assignment 17
Buyer's Rights and Duties after Tender, Part I: Rejection and Cure

§§ 2-508, 2-601, 2-602, 2-603, 2-604, 2-605, 2-612

This Assignment picks up where Assignment 16 left off—at the seller's tender and delivery of goods pursuant to the contract. At that point in the transaction, the buyer can judge whether the goods, the means and timing of delivery, and the documents conform to the contract (§ 2-106(2)). The buyer can then decide whether to "accept" the goods (§ 2-606) or to "reject" them (§ 2-602), and whether to seek damages for any nonconformity. Even if the buyer accepts the goods, under certain circumstances the buyer may be allowed to "revoke acceptance" of the goods (§ 2-608). If the buyer rejects or revokes acceptance of the goods, the seller may have a right to "cure" any nonconformity (§ 2-508).

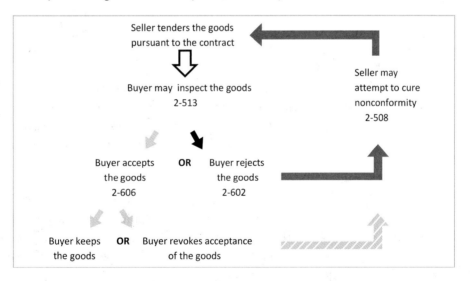

In this Assignment, we will address inspection, buyer's rejection, and seller's cure (following the grey arrows in the flowchart above). Assignment 18 will complete the picture by addressing buyer's acceptance and revocation of acceptance (following the blue arrows in the flowchart above). Buyer's remedies for breach and their interrelationship with any payments that the buyer has made will be treated in Assignment 20.

A. Rejection of Goods by Buyer

Some of the Code sections that govern rejection, considered below, also refer to revocation of acceptance. For now, consider only the language dealing with rejection. We will return to these sections in Assignment 18 and consider their application to revocation of acceptance.

As you consider the Code sections related to a buyer's rejection of goods, it is important to distinguish between the buyer's right to reject and the process the buyer must use to reject properly. Article 2 uses the terms effective rejection and ineffective rejection based on whether the buyer took the required steps to reject. An effective rejection may be rightful or wrongful depending on whether the buyer is permitted to reject the goods. We will consider first the question of when a rejection is rightful: Under what circumstances does a buyer have the right to reject, and what special rules apply for a buyer rejecting only a portion of the goods or rejecting goods that are the subject of an installment contract? Then we will consider the question of when a rejection is effective: How does a buyer effectively communicate a rejection of the goods?

1. When is a Rejection Rightful?

a. The Perfect Tender Rule

In most circumstances, Article 2 gives the buyer the right to reject goods for any deficiency in either the goods themselves or in any aspect of the contractual obligation with respect to the delivery of goods. This generous standard for rejection is colloquially known as the "perfect tender rule." The "perfect tender rule" is a significant deviation from the common law of contracts, which typically gives a party the right to reject the other party's performance only if the breach is a "material breach." Non-material breaches are typically deemed to constitute "substantial performance." Under the common law, a party faced with a non-material breach (having received substantial performance) has the right to damages caused by the breach, but may not "reject" the nonconforming performance, either by suspending its performance or cancelling the contract. Under the perfect tender rule of Article 2, in contrast, even the most trivial defects in performance under the contract may justify rejection of the goods (though, as we will see, that is only the beginning, not the end, of the story about the rights and remedies of the parties with respect to nonconforming goods).

> **Restatement (Second) of Contracts §§ 241 and 242**
>
> These provisions list factors to consider when determining if a breach is "material," justifying the suspension of performance by the non-breaching party, and when a material breach becomes "total," discharging all the remaining duties of the non-breaching party.

Reading the Code: § 2-601

Read 2-601.

Question 1. Does the standard for rejection found in 2-601 literally mean that the goods must be perfect?

Read 2-601, 2-504 (final paragraph), and 1-304.

Question 2. Under what circumstances can a buyer rightfully reject goods?

EXAMPLES AND ANALYSIS

Example A: *Jauregui v. Bobb's Piano*[1]

Jauregui entered into a contract to buy a new piano from Bobb's Piano. The piano that was delivered was damaged and was not new.

Analysis: The trial court denied any recovery by the plaintiff, finding that, "even in its defective condition, the piano was worth as much or more than plaintiff actually paid." On appeal, this ruling was reversed. Citing 2-601, the appeals court explained: "[T]he purchaser of non-conforming goods like the offending piano retains the option to claim either the difference in value or, as the plaintiff clearly did in this case, in effect, to cancel the deal and get his money back. . . . This principle is based on the common sense idea that the purchaser is entitled to receive what he wanted to buy and pay for and that the seller is not free to supply any non-conforming item she wishes just so long as the deviant goods are worth just as much." Which court (trial or appeals) applied the common law rule of "substantial performance," and which court applied the Article 2 perfect tender rule?

Example B: *Alaska Pacific Trading Co. v. Eagon Forest Products, Inc.*[2]

In April, Alaska Pacific Trading Co. (ALPAC) agreed to sell 15,000 cubic meters of logs to Eagon Forest Products. The logs were to be shipped from Argentina to Korea between the end of July and the end of August. Over the next few months, the market for logs began to soften, with the price falling rapidly. Representatives of ALPAC and Eagon engaged in a series of meetings and letters, with ALPAC seeking assurance that Eagon would

---

[1]   922 So. 2d 303 (Fla. Dist. Ct. App. 2006).

[2]   933 P.2d 417 (Wash. Ct. App. 1997).

purchase the logs, and Eagon seeking reductions in the price and volume of logs. While these negotiations continued, ALPAC cancelled the ship it had reserved for the logs. By August 31, the logs had not been loaded or shipped, though the parties continued to negotiate. Eventually, ALPAC sued Eagon for breach of contract, and Eagon responded with a motion for summary judgment, arguing that ALPAC had breached by failing to deliver the logs by the end of August. ALPAC argued that it did not breach the contract by failing to deliver the logs by that date, because time of delivery was not a material term of the contract.

Analysis: The court sided with Eagon. It reasoned that, because the contract was for a sale of goods and thus covered by Article 2, the perfect tender rule replaced the common law doctrine of material breach. Under the perfect tender rule, since the contract specified a date for shipment, and the logs were not shipped by that date, Eagon was released from its duty to accept the goods.

What might a seller in ALPAC's position do to avoid this result, during the time period in which it is attempting to salvage a contract that appears to be headed for breach? How might the concept of "good faith" help a seller in ALPAC's position? Suppose ALPAC had not cancelled the ship it had reserved for the logs, but instead had loaded the logs onto the ship and sent them on their way, but held off notifying Eagon that it had done so while it continued the negotiations. Would that have made any difference in the result in this case? Hint: would it make a difference if this were a shipment contract or a destination contract?

Example C: *Patitucci v. Consumers Warehouse*[3]

Patitucci ordered kitchen cabinets from Consumers Warehouse. The "Sales Order" generated by Consumers Warehouse after Patitucci submitted his order read:

> MATERIAL: CHERRY...
>
> END CONSTRUCT: ENGINEERED WOOD...
>
> YOUR CABINETRY IS CONSTRUCTED USING MANY PIECES OF SOLID WOOD AND WOOD VENEERS. GRAINING DIFFERENCES AS WELL AS NORMAL COLOR CHANGE CAN BE EXPECTED.

---

3   851 N.Y.S. 2d 72 (App. Term 2007).

When the cabinets were delivered, Patitucci rejected them. He was displeased that the sides and backs of the cabinets were made of pressed wood, rather than solid wood.

Analysis: The court concluded that the contract did not specifically call for solid wood, but rather clearly stated that the cabinets were of "engineered wood." Thus, the cabinets conformed to the contract, and Patitucci did not have grounds to reject them. Do you agree with the court's ruling?

b. Rejection of Portions of Goods: The Concept of "Commercial Units"

Reading the Code: § 2-601

Read 2-601 Comment 1 and 2-105(6).

Question 3. What factors should be considered to decide if a buyer is justified in rejecting only some of the goods?

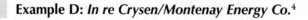

EXAMPLES AND ANALYSIS

Example D: *In re Crysen/Montenay Energy Co.*[4]

Crysen and Con Edison entered into an agreement whereby Crysen agreed to sell Con Edison approximately 4.4 million barrels of oil, with delivery to occur in installments over the next year. The agreement required any oil delivered to meet a minimum temperature of 135° F. When the first shipment of oil was delivered, however, it was found to have an average temperature of 114.3° F. Con Edison permitted Crysen to start discharging

---

[4]   23 UCC Rep. Serv. 2d 748 (S.D.N.Y. 1993).

the oil from the cargo ship into Con Edison's shore tanks, but the lower temperature increased the viscosity of the oil, significantly slowing the delivery rate. After 31½ hours of discharging the oil, Con Edison halted the delivery. Con Edison paid for the oil that was delivered (99,716.02 barrels), but rejected the rest. Because oil prices had dropped since the contract was entered into, Crysen had to sell the undelivered oil to another buyer at a loss. Crysen sued Con Edison, arguing, among other things, that the commercial unit applicable to this agreement was the entire cargo load on that ship, and thus Con Edison had no right to reject only the undelivered barrels of oil.

Analysis: The court rejected Crysen's argument, holding that the applicable commercial unit was the barrel, and that Con Edison rightfully rejected the undelivered barrels. The court relied on the language of the contract, which expressly designated barrels as the unit for price and quantity purposes, and on the fact that, on several occasions in the past, "less than an entire cargo load had been delivered by Crysen and accepted by Con Edison, with the balance sent elsewhere. In those instances, the shipment prices were determined at a per barrel rate."

Using the terms introduced in Assignment 1, what would you call the practice described in the second rationale given by the court? Of what relevance here is the fact that Crysen had to sell the undelivered barrels at a loss? Consider the language of 2-105(6), as well as Comment 1 to 2-601.

Example E: *A.W. Fabrizio & Son, Inc. v. Fort Lauderdale Produce, Inc.*[5]

Fabrizio & Son ordered from Fort Lauderdale Produce a mixed truckload of fresh lettuce, consisting of 10 packages of boston lettuce, 10 packages of escarole, 40 packages of endive, and 80 packages of romaine. When the truck arrived, Fabrizio accepted part of the truckload, and attempted to reject 140 packages of lettuce. The rejected lettuce was sold to another buyer, at a substantially lower price.

---

[5]   28 UCC Rep.Serv. 680 (U.S.D.A. 1980).

Analysis: The U.S. Department of Agriculture found that the entire truckload was one "commercial unit," for the following reasons:

> First, as far as the perishable agricultural commodities industry is concerned, a truckload of mixed produce, rather than each individual lot contained in such truckload, is generally viewed as "a single whole for purposes of sale," due to the excessive burden which the opposite view would place on the seller. This stems from the fact that when a truckload composed of perishable agricultural commodities is rejected by the buyer, the seller is essentially at the buyer's mercy if such seller is located a great distance from the buyer's place of business with a corresponding lack of control over the produce. Under these circumstances, if the buyer does not promptly resell such produce on the seller's behalf, the produce will soon be worthless due to its perishable nature. If the buyer's right of rejection extended to the individual perishable agricultural commodities contained in a mixed truckload, thus treating them as separate commercial units, the seller's burden would be much greater. Second, when a particular perishable agricultural commodity from a mixed truckload is rejected, its value becomes "materially impaired," as there usually is little market for such a small amount of produce.

Using the terms introduced in Assignment 1, what would you call the practice described in the Department of Agriculture's first argument? Of what relevance here is the fact that Fort Lauderdale Produce had to sell the rejected packages of lettuce at a loss? How is this scenario different from the one in Example D?

c. Rejection in Installment Contracts

**Reading the Code:
§ 2-612**

Read 2-612(1) and Comments 1 through 3.

Question 4. Under what circumstances does 2-612 rather than 2-601 govern acceptance and rejection of a shipment?

Read 2-612(2) and (3) and Comments 4 through 6.

Question 5. What standards govern the buyer's rejection of goods under 2-612? What rationale is suggested for the difference between 2-612 and 2-601?

EXAMPLES AND ANALYSIS

Example F: *Holiday Mfg. Co. v. B.A.S.F. Systems, Inc.*[6]

B.A.S.F. entered into an installment contract to purchase six million plastic cassette tapes from Holiday Manufacturing Co., to be manufactured according to specifications provided by B.A.S.F. Over the course of the next year, Holiday made numerous deliveries of tapes to B.A.S.F., many of which were rejected and returned for various defects, such as sinking in of the cassette cases, cracks, discrepancies in size, and incorrect spacing of guideholes. As these defects were identified, B.A.S.F. worked with Holiday to correct the defects. At no time did B.A.S.F. express concerns about the fact that the deliveries were behind schedule from the start. After a year, however, B.A.S.F. notified Holiday that it was cancelling the entire contract due to "continuous quality problems and delivery delays." Holiday sued B.A.S.F. for wrongful cancellation of the contract.

Analysis: The court agreed with Holiday, reasoning that B.A.S.F. had not established that the nonconformities substantially impaired the value of the whole contract for B.A.S.F. With respect to the delivery delays, the court concluded that B.A.S.F. considered this project "a potentially very profitable business venture and that the delays which occurred in development of this relatively new product by a manufacturer unfamiliar with cassette production were liberally tolerated by B.A.S.F." With respect to the quality problems, the court found that, despite the undisputed defects, on balance they did not substantially impair the value of the whole contract for B.A.S.F. because (1) B.A.S.F. did not evidence any protest or serious displeasure over delays in fixing defects, (2) most of the defects were

---

[6] 380 F. Supp 1096 (D. Neb. 1974).

fixed, and (3) B.A.S.F. continued to place orders for more tapes, indicating that "B.A.S.F. had confidence that Holiday could produce acceptable tapes."

Was Holiday making an argument under 2-612(2) or 2-612(3)? Given your answer to this question, what was the significance for the court of the fact that Holiday was able to cure most of the defects in performance?

Example G: *ebm-papst Inc. v. AEIOMed, Inc.*[7]

AEIOMed makes continuous positive airway pressure ("CPAP") machines used to treat sleep apnea. AEIOMed entered into a multi-year installment contract with ebm-papst, which manufactures a component in CPAP machines knowns as "blowers." The first installments of blowers were delivered, accepted, and built into CPAP machines. Those machines, however, began to fail, due to defective blowers. The field return rate on CPAP machines built with ebm-papst blowers was 1.48%. After in-house testing revealed that the failures were due to problems with the blowers, AEIOMed stopped paying for blowers and refused further deliveries. Then ebm-papst sued AEIOMed for breach of contract.

Analysis: The court denied ebm-papst's motion for summary judgement, holding that a genuine issue of fact existed as to whether the value of the contract was "substantially impaired" by the defective blowers. In support of its motion, ebm-papst argued that the blower defects did not substantially impair the contract, since only 1.48% of the blowers were defective. AEIOMed countered with evidence that (1) the total cost to AIEOMed in dealing with the returned CPAP devices was significant; (2) the blower failures had led the FDA to require AEIOMed not to sell CPAP machines made with ebm-papst blowers, and (3) 1.48% is an unacceptable failure rate in the medical device industry.

If you were a member of the jury hearing this case, how would you hold, based on the summary of the evidence given above? Why?

---

[7] 2010 WL 4720848 (D. Minn. 2010).

2. When Is a Rejection Effective?

a. The Process of Rejection

Now that you understand when a buyer has the right to reject, let us turn to the process a buyer must follow to effectively reject under Article 2. The sections that govern the "how" of rejection, which we explore below (§§ 2-602, 2-603, and 2-604), say that they apply only to "rightful" rejection (see all three titles and § 2-602 Comment 3), but courts consistently use the sections to establish whether rejection effectively occurred whether the rejection is rightful or not.

Reading the Code: § 2-602

Read 2-602(1) and Comment 1.

Question 6. What must the buyer do to effectively reject goods?

Question 7. Why is it not an effective rejection if a buyer says to the seller, "I'm not satisfied with the goods you sent, they don't work"?

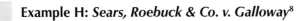

EXAMPLES AND ANALYSIS

Example H: *Sears, Roebuck & Co. v. Galloway*[8]

Galloway purchased a boiler from Sears in January 1986 for $5,400. After Sears installed the boiler, Galloway complained that it was not functioning properly. Sears serviced the boiler and found nothing wrong. In response to Galloway's continued complaints, Sears offered to reduce the sales price by $1,000, or to remove the boiler and credit Galloway's account. Galloway refused these offers and continued to use the boiler, although she had paid only $162 of the purchase price. In July 1989, Sears sued Galloway, asking

---

[8] 600 N.Y.S. 2d 773 (App. Div. 1993).

for either payment due of the balance of the purchase price or return of the boiler.

Analysis: The court did not accept Galloway's argument that she had rejected the boiler, holding that "mere complaint about the goods does not constitute a clear and unequivocal act of rejection," and "the undisputed evidence of defendant's continued retention and use of the boiler for a substantial period of time, covering several heating seasons, despite plaintiff's offers to remove the boiler and credit her account, constitutes an acceptance."

Example I: *Ferraro v. Perry's Brick Co.*[9]

Ferraro purchased a $12,000 door from Perry's Brick Co. on the belief that he was purchasing a solid oak door. In fact, the door was a veneer oak door, consisting of a laminated wood core covered with a veneer of solid oak. Ferraro learned that the door was not solid oak when the worker hired to install the door could not insert the expensive decorative lock Ferraro had purchased for the door, because only a solid oak door could support this particular lock. Ferraro complained to Perry's about the door, asking it to take the door back because it was a veneer oak door rather than a solid oak door. Perry's would not take the door back, but rather worked with Ferraro and the manufacturer over the course of the next few months to fix various other problems with the door: it was too short for the frame, bowed, and contained gaps between the panels through which both air and water leaked. Ferraro sued Perry's, seeking return of the purchase price.

Analysis: Although the court concluded that Perry's had violated an express warranty that the door was solid oak, it did not accept Ferraro's argument that he had rejected the door. The court explained:

Although Ferraro timely notified Perry's Brick that the door was defective and was not of solid wood, he never effectively rejected the door. His mere complaints that he never bargained for a veneer door does not constitute a rejection. His testimony was equivocal as to whether he ever told Perry he did not want the door. Furthermore, he was more focused on having the . . . employees fix the various alleged defects in the door, such as the

---

[9] 2011 WL 182088 (NY Civ. Ct. 2011).

lock and spaces between the frame and door, than he was in returning the door due to its being veneer. Given the primary emphasis plaintiff placed upon the door not being made of solid wood, it begs all reason for him to have requested that Perry's repair the various defects in the door, since the composition of the door was unalterable and non repairable.

Contrasting Examples H and I: In these two examples, how significant was the seller's response to the buyer's complaint about the goods? How significant was the buyer's retention of the goods? What did each buyer communicate about the goods to the seller? What should each buyer have said or done to clearly communicate rejection? Does the court's holding that the buyer in each case had not rejected the goods mean the buyer is without any remedy for the seller's breach?

Reading the Code: § 2-605

Read 2-605 and Comments 1 to 3.

Question 8. Under what circumstances must a buyer communicate to a seller the particular defects leading to rejection? What are the consequences of failing to convey such information?

b. Time for Rejection and the Reasonable Opportunity to Inspect

Under § 2-602, to be effective, a rejection must occur "within a reasonable time after . . . delivery or tender." What constitutes a "reasonable time" depends on the "nature, purpose and circumstances" of the act of rejection (*see generally* § 1-205). Comment 1 to § 2-602 adds that "reasonable time" must be understood in connection with Article 2 provisions giving buyer the right to inspect the goods (*see* § 2-513). Consequently, the buyer must be given a reasonable opportunity to inspect and discover defects, but the rejection must occur quickly enough to protect the seller's interests as well. In Assignment 18, we will take an even closer look at

§ 2-513 and what constitutes "a reasonable opportunity to inspect"and therefore a reasonable time for rejection, as we explore the consequences of failing to reject before a reasonable opportunity to inspect has passed. For now, it is enough to know that case law has suggested that the following factors are relevant to determining whether the rejecting buyer has acted within a reasonable time:

- Whether delay will result in deterioration of the goods;

- Whether delay will impair seller's ability to cure;

- The ease or difficulty of communicating notice of rejection;

- Whether the value of the goods threatens to decline, so that delay would further injure the seller; and

- Whether the contract specifies a reasonable time for rejection.

EXAMPLES AND ANALYSIS

Example J: *Oda Nursery, Inc. v. Garcia Tree & Lawn, Inc.*[10]

Garcia Tree & Lawn ordered 985 spreading juniper plants from Oda Nursery for a beautification project for the City of Albuquerque. When the plants arrived in Albuquerque in March, they were inspected by one of Garcia's employees, who claims that she called Oda at that time and complained that the plants did not look "up to snuff." Oda denied such a phone call. For the four months following delivery, the plants remained in their 5-gallon shipping containers. They were watered and fertilized, but not planted until July and August. By October, some of them had begun-to die. Eventually, about 700 of the trees were removed and found to be root-bound. In December, Oda filed suit for payment; Garcia's response, asserting that the trees were root-bound was, according to Oda, the first notice it had received regarding any defects in the plants.

Analysis: The court noted, "Of course, Garcia must be allowed a certain amount of time within which to inspect the plants." However, the court found that Garcia's phone call after delivery did not constitute a rejection, because it did not specify the particular defect in a way that would have permitted cure. The court

---

[10] 708 P.2d 1039 (N.M. 1985).

also rejected Garcia's argument that its response to the lawsuit constituted a rejection, holding that "[n]otice of a root-bound condition in growing plants eleven months after delivery is not seasonable notice."

The court found that Garcia's response was not an effective rejection because it happened after a "reasonable time for inspection" passed. Which of the factors identified in the text preceding this Example are relevant to the court's holding here? The phone call would have been timely, but it fails two other requirements for an effective rejection that we have already covered. Can you identify them?

c. Handling Goods after Rightful Rejection

Reading the Code:
§§ 2-602, 2-603, 2-604, 2-711

**Read 2-602(2) and Comment 2, 2-604
and its Comment, and 2-711(3) and Comment 2.**

Note that a "security interest," referred to in 2-711(3), is an interest in goods or other collateral granted to a person who makes a loan or otherwise extends credit to a person with an interest (ownership or less) in the goods. That security interest allows the creditor (now the secured party) to seize the collateral under certain circumstances and resell it to satisfy the debt. Security interests are governed largely by UCC Article 9.

Question 9. What must a buyer do with rejected goods in buyer's possession?

Question 10. What may a buyer do with them, and under what circumstances?

Read 2-603(1) and Comments 1 and 2.

Question 11. What additional responsibilities does a merchant buyer have with respect to rejected goods, and under what circumstances?

Example K: *Ford v. Starr Fireworks, Inc.*[11]

In spring, Starr Fireworks sold a shipment of fireworks to Ford. Some of the fireworks delivered to Ford's warehouse were unsalable because of water damage and packaging problems. Ford called Starr to report the problems and asked Starr to replace them. Starr refused to do so unless Ford either returned the fireworks or paid for them. Starr twice sent employees to Ford's warehouse to pick them up. On the first trip, on July 2, Ford refused to return any fireworks. On the second trip, on August 3, Ford returned a small portion of the fireworks. Ford sent some of the fireworks to his various retail outlets, where some were sold to consumers. Ford alleges that he returned the remaining fireworks to Starr's Denver office on August 13. A Starr sales representative told Ford to deliver them to a responsible person, but Ford testified that no one was in the offices, so he left them outside the office door. Starr never received those fireworks. Starr sued Ford for the price of the fireworks not returned, and Ford countersued for expenses incurred in returning fireworks to Starr, lost profits, and damage to reputation.

Analysis: The court held that Ford's failure to make the rejected goods available to Starr's employees for at least two months after providing notice of rejection was unreasonable, particularly in an industry with "seasonal sale peaks." Furthermore, the court concluded that "leaving the fireworks unattended on a busy street is unreasonable" and that "Ford failed to follow reasonable instructions in returning the fireworks." Did Ford have a duty to return the fireworks to Starr? What aspects of Ford's behavior, if any, violated 2-602(2)(a)? 2-602(2)(b)? 2-603(1)?

Example L: *Design Plus Store Fixtures, Inc. v. Citro Corp.*[12]

Design Plus entered into a contract with Citro to manufacture display tables that Design was to assemble and deliver to its customer, Springmaid. The tables were delivered late, with substantial defects making them impossible to assemble. Design notified Citro of the defects promptly and refused to pay for the tables. Citro made no offer to cure and gave no instructions as to the disposal or return of the tables. In order to meet its deadline on the contract with Springmaid, Citro redrilled holes in the delivered tables and sent them to Springmaid, with the understanding

---

[11] 874 P. 2d 230 (Wyo. 1994).
[12] 508 S.E.2d 825 (N.C. Ct. App. 1988).

that they would ultimately be replaced with conforming tables. After Springmaid was finished using the tables, Design gave them away to a charity. Design sued Citro for expenses incurred, and Citro countersued for breach of contract.

Analysis: The court determined that Citro had not accepted the tables by redrilling the holes and sending them to Springmaid. The court reasoned that a buyer like Citro, who has given reasonable notification of rejection of nonconforming goods but receives no instructions from the seller with respect to disposition of the goods, is not limited to the three specific options listed in 2-604 (storing, selling, or reshipping). Repairing the tables in order to allow Springmaid to use them when needed was a reasonable step taken in good faith toward realization on or preservation of the goods, and thus did not constitute acceptance of the tables. However, the court held that giving the tables away without notifying or obtaining the consent of Citro was "an unreasonable act, inconsistent with ownership, where the tables had some salvageable value," and thus constituted acceptance by Design Plus.

The court relied heavily on the Comment to 2-604 in its analysis. What parts of the Comment support the court's holding? Why is 2-604 entitled and characterized in the Comment as a "salvage" section?

B. Cure of Nonconformity by Seller

As noted above, the buyer's right to reject is expansive under the Code (the "perfect tender rule"), broader than the injured party's rights under the common law (which uses a "substantial performance" rule). The buyer's right to reject is tempered, however, by the seller's right under certain circumstances to cure the defect in performance that led to the buyer's rejection.

1. Seller's Right to Cure

Reading the Code:
§ 2-508

Read 2-508(1) and Comment 1.

Question 12. Under what circumstances is a seller permitted to cure a nonconformity in tender or goods under this subsection? What must the seller do to cure?

Read 2-508(2) and Comments 2 and 3.

Question 13. How does a seller's right to cure under (2) differ from a seller's right to cure under (1)? What must the seller do to cure under (2)?

Question 14. Is a seller required to cure a nonconforming delivery? Should a seller cure a nonconforming delivery?

2. Expanding the Definition of Cure

You have seen above how § 2-508 defines when the seller has a right to cure and generally how a cure is effectuated. The case below expands upon the meaning of cure and how it works in particular circumstances. As you read *Wilson v. Scampoli,* consider these questions:

(1)   What does this case add to your understanding about how a seller may effectuate a cure?

(2)   What does this case illustrate about the consequences if the buyer refuses to allow the seller to cure after rejection?

(3)   Was the seller in this case exercising its right to cure under 2-508(1) or 2-508(2)? When was performance due under the contract?

WILSON V. SCAMPOLI

228 A.2d 848 (D.C. Ct. App. 1967)

MYERS, ASSOCIATE JUDGE.

This is an appeal from an order of the trial court granting rescission of a sales contract for a color television set and directing the return of the purchase price plus interest and costs.

Appellee purchased the set in question on November 4, 1965, paying the total purchase price in cash. The transaction was evidenced by a sales ticket showing the price paid and guaranteeing ninety days' free service and replacement of any defective tube and parts for a period of one year. Two days after purchase the set was delivered and uncrated, the antennae adjusted and the set plugged into an electrical outlet to "cook out." When the set was turned on however, it did not function properly, the picture having a reddish tinge. Appellant's delivery man advised the buyer's daughter, Mrs. Kolley, that it was not his duty to tune in or adjust the color but that a service representative would shortly call at her house for that purpose. After the departure of the delivery men, Mrs. Kolley unplugged the set and did not use it.

On November 8, 1965, a service representative arrived, and after spending an hour in an effort to eliminate the red cast from the picture advised Mrs. Kolley that he would have to remove the chassis from the cabinet and take it to the shop as he could not determine the cause of the difficulty from his examination at the house. He also made a written memorandum of his service call, noting that the television "Needs Shop Work (Red Screen)." Mrs. Kolley refused to allow the chassis to be removed, asserting she did not want a "repaired" set but another "brand new" set. Later she demanded the return of the purchase price, although retaining the set. Appellant refused to refund the purchase price, but renewed his offer to adjust, repair, or, if the set could not be made to function properly, to replace it. Ultimately, appellee instituted this suit against appellant seeking a refund of the purchase price. After a trial, the court ruled that "under the facts and circumstances the complaint is justified. [The court ordered the set returned to the defendant and the purchase price returned to the plaintiff.]

Appellant does not contest the jurisdiction of the trial court to order rescission in a proper case, but contends the trial judge erred in holding that rescission here was appropriate. He argues that he was always willing to comply with the terms of the sale either by correcting the malfunction by minor repairs or, in the event the set could not be made thereby properly operative, by replacement; that as he was denied the opportunity to try to correct the difficulty, he did not breach the contract of sale or any warranty thereunder, expressed or implied.

. . . .

A retail dealer would certainly expect and have reasonable grounds to believe that merchandise like color television sets, new and delivered as crated at the factory, would be acceptable as delivered and that, if defective in some way, he would have the right to substitute a conforming tender. The question then resolves itself to whether the dealer may conform his tender by adjustment or minor repair or whether he must conform by substituting brand new merchandise. The problem seems to be one of first impression in other jurisdictions adopting the Uniform Commercial Code as well as in the District of Columbia.

Although the Official Code Comments do not reach this precise issue, there are cases and comments under other provisions of the Code which indicate that under certain circumstances repairs and adjustments are contemplated as remedies under implied warranties. In *L & L Sales Co. v. Little Brown Jug, Inc.*, 12 Pa. Dist. & Co. R. 2d 469 (Phila. County Ct.1957), where the language of a disclaimer was found insufficient to defeat warranties under §§ 2-314 and 2-315, the court noted that the buyer had notified the seller of defects in the merchandise, and as the seller was unable to remedy them and later refused to accept return of the articles, it was held to be a breach of warranty. In *Hall v. Everett Motors, Inc.*, 340 Mass. 430, 165 N.E.2d 107 (1960), decided shortly before the effective date of the Code in Massachusetts, the court reluctantly found that a disclaimer of warranties was sufficient to insulate the seller. Several references were made in the ruling to the seller's unsuccessful attempts at repairs, the court indicating the result would have been different under the Code.

While these cases provide no mandate to require the buyer to accept patchwork goods or substantially repaired articles in lieu of flawless merchandise, they do indicate that minor repairs or reasonable adjustments are frequently the means by which an imperfect tender may be cured. In discussing the analogous question of defective title, it has been stated that:

The seller, then, should be able to cure [the defect] under subsection 2-508(2) in those cases in which he can do so without subjecting the buyer to any great inconvenience, risk or loss. Hawkland, *Curing an Improper Tender of Title to Chattels: Past, Present and Commercial Code*, 46 Minn. L. Rev. 697, 724 (1962). *See also* Willier & Hart, *Forms and Procedures under the UCC* 24.07(4); D.C. Code § 28:2-608(1)(a) (Supp. V 1966).

Removal of a television chassis for a short period of time in order to determine the cause of color malfunction and ascertain the extent of adjustment or correction needed to effect full operational efficiency presents no great inconvenience to the buyer. In the instant case, appellant's expert witness testified that this was not infrequently necessary with new televisions. Should the set be defective in workmanship or parts, the loss would be upon the manufacturer who warranted it free from mechanical defect. Here the adamant refusal of Mrs. Kolley, acting on behalf of appellee, to allow inspection essential to the determination of the cause of the excessive red tinge to the picture defeated any effort by the seller to provide timely repair or even replacement of the set if the difficulty could not be corrected. The cause of the defect might have been minor and easily adjusted or it may have been substantial and required replacement by another new set—but the seller was never given an adequate opportunity to make a determination.

We do not hold that appellant has no liability to appellee, but as he was denied access and a reasonable opportunity to repair, appellee has not shown a breach of warranty entitling him either to a brand new set or to rescission. We therefore reverse the judgment of the trial court granting rescission and directing the return of the purchase price of the set.

Reversed.

3. Cure after Performance is Due

As you have seen in the case above, under § 2-508(2), a seller may cure even if the time for performance has expired if the seller "had reasonable grounds to believe [that the nonconforming tender] would be acceptable." The following case (and another look at *Wilson*) explores what "reasonable grounds" for such a belief might be. As you read *Bartus v. Riccardi*, consider these questions:

(1)   Did the seller in *Bartus* know of the nonconformity at the time of tender? What about the seller in *Wilson*? How do your answers to these questions affect each court's analysis of what constitutes "reasonable grounds to believer [the tender] would be acceptable"?

(2)   If the seller in *Bartus* had offered the buyer a discount on the hearing aid at the time it was first delivered, would the buyer still have been able to reject the hearing aid? Would the seller still have had a right to cure?

(3)   If, after the buyer in *Bartus* rejected the hearing aid, the seller offered buyer a price discount on the rejected goods, would that constitute an attempt to cure? If not, what is it?

BARTUS V. RICCARDI

284 N.Y.S.2d 222 (City Ct. 1967)

HAROLD H. HYMES, JUDGE.

The plaintiff is a franchised representative of Acousticon, a manufacturer of hearing aids. On January 15, 1966, the defendant signed a contract to purchase a Model A-660 Acousticon hearing aid from the plaintiff. The defendant specified Model A-660 because he had been tested at a hearing aid clinic and had been informed that the best hearing aid for his condition was this Acousticon model. An ear mold was fitted to the defendant and the plaintiff ordered Model A-660 from Acousticon.

On February 2, 1966, in response to a call from the plaintiff the defendant went to the plaintiff's office for his hearing aid. At that time he was informed that Model A-660 had been modified and improved, and that it was now called Model A-665. This newer model had been delivered by Acousticon for the defendant's use. The defendant denies that he understood this was a different model number. The hearing aid was fitted to the defendant. The defendant complained about the noise, but was assured by the plaintiff that he would get used to it.

The defendant tried out the new hearing aid for the next few days for a total use of 15 hours. He went back to the hearing clinic, where he was informed that the hearing aid was not the model that he had been advised to buy. On February 8, 1966, he returned to the plaintiff's office complaining that the hearing aid gave him a headache, and that it was not the model he had ordered. He returned the hearing aid to the plaintiff, for which he received a receipt. At that time the plaintiff offered to get Model A-660 for the defendant. The defendant neither consented to nor refused the offer. No mention was made by either party about canceling the contract, and the receipt given by the plaintiff contained no notation or indication that the plaintiff considered the contract canceled or rescinded.

The plaintiff immediately informed Acousticon of the defendant's complaint. By letter dated February 14, 1966, Acousticon writing directly to the defendant, informed him that Model A-665 was an improved version of model A-660, and that they would either replace the model that had been delivered to him or would obtain Model A-660 for him. He was asked to advise the plaintiff immediately of his decision so that they could effect a prompt exchange. After receiving this letter the defendant decided that he did not want any hearing aid from the plaintiff, and he refused to accept the tender of a replacement, whether it be Model A-665 or A-660.

The plaintiff is suing for the balance due on the contract. Although he had made a down payment of $80.00, the defendant made no claim for repayment of his down payment until the case was ready to go to trial. The plaintiff objected to the counterclaim as being untimely. There is nothing in the pleadings to show that such a claim had been previously made by the defendant and, therefore, the court will not consider any counterclaim in this matter.

The question before the court is whether or not the plaintiff, having delivered a model which admittedly is not in exact conformity with the contract, can nevertheless recover in view of his subsequent tender of the model that did meet the terms of the contract.

The defendant contends that since there was an improper delivery of goods, the buyer has the right to reject the same under §§ 2-601 and 2-602(2)(c) of the Uniform Commercial Code. He further contends that even if the defendant had accepted delivery he may, under § 2-608(1)(b) of the U.C.C., revoke his acceptance of the goods because "his acceptance was reasonably induced . . . by the seller's assurances." He also relies on § 2-711, claiming that he may recover not only the down payment but also consequential damages.

The defendant, however, has neglected to take into account Section 2-508 of the Uniform Commercial Code which has added a new dimension to the concept of strict performance. This section permits a seller to cure a non-conforming delivery under certain circumstances. Subparagraph (1) of this section enacts into statutory law what had been New York case law. This permits a seller to cure a non-conforming delivery before the expiration of the contract time by notifying the buyer of his intention to so cure and by making a delivery within the contract period. This has long been the accepted rule in New York. (*Lowinson v. Newman*, 201 App. Div. 266, 194 N.Y.S. 253; *Portfolio v. Rubin*, 196 App. Div. 316, 187 N.Y.S. 302).

However, the U.C.C. in sub-paragraph (2) of Section 2-508 goes further and extends beyond the contract time the right of the seller to cure a defective performance. Under this provision, even where the contract period has expired and the buyer has rejected a non-conforming tender or has revoked an acceptance, the seller may "substitute a conforming tender" if he had "reasonable grounds to believe" that the nonconforming tender would be accepted, and "if he seasonably notifies the buyer" of his intention "to substitute a conforming tender." (51 NY Jur. Sales, p. 41).

This in effect extends the contract period beyond the date set forth in the contract itself unless the buyer requires strict performance by including such a clause in the contract.

"The section (2-508(2) U.C.C.) rejects the time-honored and perhaps time-worn notion that the proper way to assure effective results in commercial transactions is to require strict performance. Under the Code a buyer who insists upon such strict performance must rely on a special term in his agreement or the fact that the seller knows as a commercial matter that strict performance is required." (48 Cornell Law Quarterly 13; 29 Albany Law Review 260).

This section seeks to avoid injustice to the seller by reason of a surprise rejection by the buyer. (Official Comment, McKinney's Cons. Laws of N.Y., Book 62½, Uniform Commercial Code, Section 2-508).

An additional burden, therefore, is placed upon the buyer by this section. "As a result a buyer may learn that even though he rejected or revoked his acceptance within the terms of Sections 2-601 and 2-711, he still may have to allow the seller additional time to meet the terms of the contract by substituting delivery of conforming goods." (Bender's U.C.C. Service—Sales and Bulk Transfers—Vol. 3, Section 14-02(1)(a)(ii)).

Has the plaintiff in this case complied with the conditions of Section 2-508?

The model delivered to the defendant was a newer and improved version of the model than was actually ordered. Of course, the defendant is entitled to receive the model that he ordered even though it may be an older type. But under the circumstances the plaintiff had reasonable grounds to believe that the newer model would be accepted by the defendant.

The plaintiff acted within a reasonable time to notify the defendant of his tender of a conforming model. (Section 1-204 U.C.C.). The defendant had not purchased another hearing aid elsewhere. His position had not been altered by reason of the original non-conforming tender.

The plaintiff made a proper subsequent conforming tender pursuant to Section 2-508(2) of the Uniform Commercial Code.

Judgment is granted to plaintiff.

APPLYING THE CODE

Problem 17-1.

In early October, Maloney ordered 500 pumpkins from Marrinan's Pumpkin Farm in Duluth, Minnesota, planning on selling them at his roadside stand in New Orleans during the two weeks before Halloween (October 31). Their contract said, "500 pumpkins, C.I.F. Port of New Orleans, delivered to Maloney's Roadside Pumpkin Stand, New Orleans. Delivery guaranteed in New Orleans no later than October 17. Down payment of $200 due at time of order; balance of $300 due 30 days after delivery." On October 10, Marrinan loaded the 500 pumpkins on a ship to New Orleans, and e-mailed Maloney to tell him that the goods had been shipped and that he had received Maloney's down payment. Due to an early ice storm on October 13 that delayed traffic on the Mississippi, the pumpkins did not arrive in New Orleans until October 27. Maloney was following the weather news, and realized there would be a risk that the pumpkins would not arrive on time. He immediately set about ordering pumpkins from other suppliers to meet the pre-Halloween demand. When Marrinan's shipment of pumpkins arrived at his stand, Maloney called Marrinan and said they were too late, and that he would have to have someone come pick them up. Marrinan responded, "Maloney, could you please try to sell them for me? You're the first customer I've ever sent anything to in New Orleans; I don't know anyone else down there. I don't even know how long it's going to take me to find someone to pick them up, and those pumpkins are going to start rotting really soon, if you just leave them out in the hot Louisiana sun much longer!" What should Maloney do?

Problem 17-2.

Brady's Books is planning a reading and book signing event with an author and orders 100 copies of the author's most recent novel to be delivered "at least two days before author's visit scheduled for April 25." The books arrive on April 23, but all copies have been badly damaged by water during transit. Assuming the seller had the risk of loss during transit and buyer rejects the books, does seller have a right to cure? If so, when must seller effect the cure?

Problem 17-3.

Charles buys a new car, which he picks up from the dealer on April 1, the promised delivery date. The next day, Charles discovers the spare tire compartment in the trunk is empty and the car has a CD player rather than the double USB ports that he had ordered. He calls the dealer, describes the problem, and says he does not want to keep the car. The dealer asks Charles to bring the car back, but Charles refuses, telling the dealer the car will be parked in front of his home and can be picked up at any time. Did Charles rightfully and effectively reject? Does seller have a right to cure? Should Charles have brought the car back to the dealer?

Problem 17-4.

Nancy purchases a new car. Three days later, the car stalls, and when she starts it again, it makes loud clanging noises. The dealer inspects the car, reports that the engine blew out, and says it will put in a new engine and return the car to her. Can Nancy successfully demand that the dealer give her either a new car or her money back?

Problem 17-5.

(a)   On March 1, Buyer, a liquor store, enters a contract with Seller, a wine importer and distributor, for purchase of 50 cases of wine (10 cases each of 5 varieties, 24 bottles to each case), F.O.B. Buyer's store, delivery on April 1. When the wine is delivered, six of the cases have one or two broken bottles in them. Buyer receives the goods on Friday, March 30 and phones the seller to reject the whole shipment on Monday, April 2. Did Buyer rightfully & effectively reject? If Buyer did so, would Seller have a right to cure? If so, when must Seller effect the cure?

(b)   Same as (a), but Buyer rejects the six cases with broken bottles and accepts the rest. Did Buyer rightfully reject? Could Buyer reject the nine broken bottles and accept the rest?

Assignment 18

Buyer's Rights and Duties after Tender, Part II: Acceptance and Revocation of Acceptance of Goods, Inspection, Risk of Loss in Presence of Breach

§§ 2-508, 2-513, 2-601, 2-602, 2-603, 2-604, 2-605, 2-612

Recall the flowchart used in Assignment 17 to outline a buyer's handling of the goods after the seller's tender and delivery:

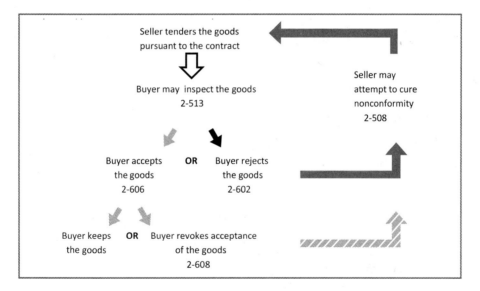

This Assignment will address acceptance and revocation of acceptance (following the blue arrows in the flowchart) and also return to the topic of risk of loss, exploring what happens when buyer or seller breaches.

LEARNING OUTCOMES AND OBJECTIVES

At the completion of this Assignment, you should be able to

- identify when a buyer has accepted goods and what legal consequences flow from acceptance;
- apply the factors that are used to determine whether the buyer had a reasonable opportunity to inspect the delivered goods, and recognize how this determination affects the analysis of whether a buyer has accepted goods;
- identify the circumstances under which a buyer has a right to revoke an acceptance; and
- recognize when and how a breach of a contract by either the seller or the buyer can affect the risk of loss rules that you learned in Assignment 16.

A. Acceptance of Goods

1. Three Means of Acceptance

**Reading the Code:
§§ 2-513, 2-606**

Read 2-513(1) and 2-606.

Question 1. Fill in the following blanks, based on 2-606(1)(a), (b), and (c):

To prove that the buyer accepted goods, the seller would have to prove that:

(a) the buyer _____

and then the buyer _____

OR

(b) the buyer _____

         as long as the buyer _____

OR

(c) the buyer _____

As your answers to Question 1 reveal, Article 2 provides three distinct ways for a buyer to "accept" goods: (1) communicating her acceptance to the seller (after a reasonable opportunity to inspect); (2) failing to effectively reject the goods (after a reasonable opportunity to inspect); and (3) acting in a way inconsistent with the seller's ownership of the goods. You have already been introduced to certain elements of each of these methods of acceptance in our discussion of rejection in Assignment 17. Both of the first two methods of acceptance depend on the passage of a "reasonable opportunity to inspect." In Assignment 17, you saw that a "reasonable time" for a rejection also depends on the buyer having had a reasonable opportunity to inspect. The third method of acceptance, acting in a way inconsistent with the seller's ownership, was relevant to our consideration in Assignment 17 of what a buyer can do with rejected goods still in her possession. As we consider these concepts again in connection with acceptance, be aware of the differences in the contexts in which these ideas arise in Article 2.

2. Communicating Acceptance to Seller

Communication of acceptance to the seller can be done through buyer's actions as well as the use of specific words. However, buyer's communication operates as an acceptance only if it takes place after a reasonable opportunity to inspect has passed.

EXAMPLES AND ANALYSIS

Example A: *Plateq Corp. of North Haven v. Machlett Laboratories, Inc.*[1]

Machlett Laboratories ordered from Plateq Corporation two lead-covered steel tanks, to be constructed according to specifications supplied

---

[1] 456 A.2d 786 (Conn. 1983).

by Machlett. The tanks were designed for the special purpose of testing x-ray tubes and were subject to federal standards for being radiation-proof. Since neither party had any prior experience with such tanks, they agreed that the tanks would be tested for radiation leaks after their delivery to and installation at Machlett's premises, and that Plateq would pay to correct any deficiencies discovered after installation. The goods were to be delivered "F.O.B. Origin." Plateq had trouble meeting both the contract specifications and the contract deadlines, which Machlett noted during during various inspections over the course of the construction period. At the final inspection, Machlett's engineer noted some remaining deficiencies, which Plateq promised to remedy by the next day so that the goods would then be ready for delivery. The engineer "gave no indication to the plaintiff that this arrangement was in any way unsatisfactory to the defendant. Not only did [he] communicate general acquiescence in the plaintiff's proposed tender but he specifically led the plaintiff to believe that the defendant's truck would pick up the tanks and the stands within a day or two." Instead of sending its truck, Machlett sent a telegram that said:

> This order is hereby terminated for your breach, in that you have continuously failed to perform according to your commitment in spite of additional time given you to cure your delinquency. We will hold you liable for all damages incurred by Machlett including excess cost of reprocurement.

Plateq sued Machlett to recover the purchase price of the goods.

Analysis: The court found that Machlett had accepted the tanks before it sent the telegram by "signifying" to Plateq its willingness to "take" the tanks despite possible remaining minor defects. It also held that the telegram did not constitute a rightful or a valid rejection. Based on the court's holding, how must it have understood the parties' agreement for testing of the tanks after delivery and installation at Machlett's premises? Why was the telegram neither a rightful nor a valid rejection? (You may want to review 2-602, 2-605, and 2-508.)

3. Revisiting "Reasonable Opportunity to Inspect" in the Context of Acceptance

Recall from Assignment 17 (Example J) that rejection must occur within a reasonable time after delivery or tender, and a "reasonable time" must include a reasonable opportunity for the buyer to inspect. A buyer's acceptance of the goods often also depends on the passage of a reasonable opportunity to inspect. Just what constitutes a reasonable opportunity to inspect is a question of fact highly dependent upon the circumstances of each case. In deciding whether the buyer has had a reasonable opportunity to inspect, courts consider factors such as the following:

- The contract terms (e.g., does the agreement indicate who will inspect or by when inspection is expected to occur?);

- Trade usages (e.g., is it the usual practice for wholesalers to inspect only when a resale contract is created?);

- The way the parties treated previous deliveries under this or other contracts;

- The circumstances of delivery (e.g., were the goods delivered to a remote location?);

- The availability of inspection facilities;

- The nature of the goods (e.g., are the goods likely to change condition rapidly and so should be inspected quickly? Are the goods complex, requiring more time and effort to inspect adequately? How long will it take to see if the product will perform as promised?);

- The nature of the defect (e.g., are the goods likely to have hidden defects? Can the particular defect at issue be found only after putting the goods to use? Should the alleged defects have been detectable quickly?);

- The nature of the buyer (e.g., is the buyer an expert who can detect defects more easily than the seller?); and

- Whether the seller promised and/or attempted to make repairs to defective goods, which will extend the inspection period.

A reasonable time to inspect must generally allow the buyer an opportunity to examine the product sufficiently to check for defects or put the product to its intended use or to test the product to verify its capability to perform as intended, depending on the nature of the goods. The reasonable opportunity to inspect may last as little as a day or as long as a year, depending upon the particular circumstances.

EXAMPLES AND ANALYSIS

Examples B and C: In one case, the court found rejection of an auctioned racehorse within 24 hours was untimely. Because such goods can change condition rapidly, inspection for detectable and easily caused problems (in this instance, a fractured bone in the horse's foreleg) must be conducted immediately after the sale.[2] In another case, the purchased horse was rejected because it was a gelding, not a colt, and rejection the day after delivery was considered to be timely.[3]

Example D: The court found no acceptance even though the buyer's representative inspected the purchased scrap plastic before shipment, because the particular defects could not be detected by a visual or manual inspection and the contract provided for inspection upon arrival of the goods.[4]

Example E: The court found that a reasonable opportunity to inspect had not passed even though the buyer had possession of the purchased flight simulator for 6 weeks. The agreement contemplated that testing would occur on buyer's property after delivery and that acceptance would occur only when the testing was completed and FAA certification received.[5]

Example F: The court found acceptance of the purchased airplane occurred before the buyer took possession of the aircraft because the buyer had inspected the plane visually twice and had sent the plane to a third party for inspection as provided in the purchase agreement.[6]

Example G: The court found the buyer's inspection of frozen pork bellies two months after purchase was timely because trade usage contemplated inspection of warehoused goods only when the buyer was ready to deliver the goods under a resale contract.[7]

---

[2]   Miron v. Yonkers Raceway, Inc., 400 F.2d 112 (2d Cir. 1968).

[3]   Brodsky v. Nerud, 414 N.Y.S.2d 38 (App. Div. 1979).

[4]   Askco Engineering Corp. v. Mobil Chemical Corp., 535 S.W.2d 893 (Tex. Civ. App. 1976).

[5]   United Air Lines, Inc. v. Conductron Corp., 387 N.E.2d 1272 (Ill. App. Ct. 1979).

[6]   Hidden Brook Air, Inc. v. Thabet Aviation, 241 F. Supp. 2d 246 (S.D.N.Y. 2002).

[7]   GNP Commodities, Inc. v. Walsh Heffernan Co., 420 N.E.2d 659 (Ill. App. Ct. 1981).

Example H: The Court found that rejection of carpet after nine months was timely because seller knew the buyer could not install the carpet until a construction strike ended and industry practice was to inspect only when the purchaser was ready to use the carpet.[8]

Example I: A "spin around the block" before purchase was not a reasonable opportunity to inspect a car.[9]

Example J: Thirty days was a reasonable time to inspect a boat to determine if it had a quiet, smooth, and dry ride, especially because the buyer had the opportunity to use the boat only on weekends.[10]

Analysis of Examples B–J: The reasonable opportunity to inspect always involves factual questions and balancing the kinds of factors listed above. Whenever you must determine whether acceptance has occurred (as in Problem 18-1, below), consider whether a reasonable opportunity to inspect has passed—and be creative in identifying arguments to extend or narrow the period of time allowed.

APPLYING THE CODE

Problem 18-1.

Each scenario below may or may not result in an acceptance under 2-606. For each scenario, make the best arguments for finding that acceptance has occurred, and the best arguments for finding that acceptance has not occurred. If you think one argument should clearly win, indicate the likely outcome. Be sure to note which subsection of 2-606(1) you rely on in each of your arguments.

(a) Buyer of a new car arrives at the showroom to pick up the vehicle. She signs all the final paperwork and pays for the car. The car is brought from the service bay to the front of the parking lot, the sales agent hands her the keys, and she drives the vehicle two miles to her

---

8 La Villa Fair v. Lewis Carpet Mills, Inc., 548 P.2d 825 (Kan. 1976).
9 Zabriskie Chevrolet, Inc. v. Smith, 240 A.2d 195 (N.J. Sup. Ct. 1968).
10 Don's Marine, Inc. v. Haldeman, 557 S.W.2d 826 (Tex. Civ. App. 1977).

home. Did acceptance occur when she signed the paperwork? When she received the keys? By the time she arrived home with the car?

(b)   Same as (a), but one week after Buyer drives the vehicle home, the salesperson calls the Buyer to "see how you like the new car." Buyer says, "It's great. Just what I wanted." Has Buyer now accepted the car? Would your answer be affected if Buyer tried to return the car one week later because the car began to vibrate severely at speeds above 60 miles per hour when she first took the car out on the highway?

(c)   Buyer purchases a sweater at a retail store. He puts it in his closet for 3 weeks before noticing a hole in the back of the collar. Is it too late for him to reject the sweater? Would your answer be affected by the existence of a store policy allowing returns with a receipt within 30 days?

(d)   A grocery store receives a shipment of apples it bought from an orchard. The next day, the buyer rejects 20% of the apples because of bruises to the fruit. The remainder of the shipment is set out on the grocery shelves. Has the grocery store accepted the apples not rejected?

(e)   Buyer of a piece of farm equipment notifies Seller upon delivery that the equipment is defective. Seller assures Buyer the problems can be corrected with minor repairs and adjustments. For six months, Buyer continues to use the equipment while Seller attempts unsuccessfully to fix the machinery. At the end of six months, Buyer notifies Seller it wants to return the equipment. Has Buyer already accepted the equipment?

(f)   Buyer is a wholesale distributor of electronic goods. Seller is the manufacturer of electronic fitness trackers that consumers wear on their wrists. Seller delivers 1000 trackers to Buyer, who immediately resells 100 of them to a retail store, still in unopened boxes. The retail store resells the trackers to its customers (still in unopened boxes), and only then discovers (because of customer complaints) that the trackers are accompanied by instruction manuals written only in Korean. It reports this problem to the distributor. Has the Buyer (the wholesale distributor) accepted the 100 trackers sold to the retail store? The 900 trackers remaining in its inventory?

4. Revisiting "Acts Inconsistent with Seller's Ownership" in the Context of Acceptance

Example L in Assignment 17 introduced you to the concept of "acts inconsistent with the seller's ownership of the goods," exploring the sometimes tricky boundary between what a buyer can do with rejected goods in the absence of a seller's instructions, and when a buyer's actions cross into acts inconsistent with the seller's ownership. We will explore that boundary more closely now.

**Reading the Code:
§§ 2-602, 2-606**

Read 2-606 Comment 4 (1st paragraph).

Question 2. What does it mean to say an action is "inconsistent with seller's ownership"? What kinds of action by the buyer with respect to the goods might fit that description?

Read 2-602(2)(a).

Question 3. When is an act inconsistent with seller's ownership wrongful as against the seller? What are the consequences if it is wrongful?

Review 2-603, 2-604, and 2-513.

Question 4. What actions by the buyer with respect to the goods will not constitute an acceptance under 2-606(1)(c)?

Review 2-711(3).

Question 5. Buyer takes delivery of defective goods. After notifying seller that the goods are rejected, Buyer resells them to recoup the prepaid contract price. Has Buyer accepted the resold goods?

EXAMPLES AND ANALYSIS

Example K: *Cartamundi USA, Inc. v. Bunky's Enterprises, Inc.*[11]

Bunky's, a publisher of collectible card games, created a game known as "Terminator 2—Judgment Day." It contracted with Cartamundi to print the cards for the game. According to their agreement, Cartamundi was to assemble packs consisting of common cards, "rare cards," and "ultra rare" cards. The cards were to be packaged in packs of five cards each. The packs would be assembled into display boxes (known as "POPs") consisting of 30 packs. Each POP was to contain two packs with a rare card and one pack with an ultra rare card. Bunky's paid the required 50% downpayment, and Cartamundi started production. The first few cases of cards were shipped to Bunky's owner, Gress, at a games convention. Gress opened up a number of packs to create a card catalogue to start advertising the game, but found that he could not create a full set of cards from the opened packs, and thought that the ratio of rare and ultra rare cards per POP was off. Gress gave away a couple of the packs to potential customers at the convention. Gress refused to pay for the balance of the cards, and Cartamundi retained the remaining cards in its warehouse. Cartamundi sued Bunky's for failure to pay the rest of the contract price.

Analysis: The court found for Cartamundi, holding that Bunky's had accepted the goods. If Bunky's meant to reject the cards, would it have had any obligation to return them to Cartamundi? Would it have made a difference to the outcome if Gress had not given any packs of cards to any customers, but had only opened them to catalogue them?

Example L: *Jorgensen v. Pressnall*[12]

Gordon and Kathryn Jorgensen bought a mobile home from Pressnall, giving up their old mobile home as down payment. Shortly after moving in, they discovered water and air leaks, gaps in the construction, and defective doors, cabinets, vents and walls. After numerous unsuccessful attempts to repair these defects, the Jorgensens sued Pressnall, rescinded their contract, tendered back the mobile home, and demanded return of

---

[11]   2012 WL 3933056 (Conn. Super. Ct. 2012).

[12]   545 P.2d 1382 (Or. 1976).

their down payment. They continued to live in the mobile home until three weeks before the trial.

Analysis: The court rejected Pressnall's argument that the Jorgensens' continued use of the goods was an act inconsistent with the seller's ownership, and thus an acceptance. The court found that "[c]ontinued occupancy was the most feasible method of protecting the mobile home from water damage. The alternative was to find covered storage which would have been expensive. Defendant suffered no loss as a result of plaintiffs' occupancy since the trial court awarded an offset to defendant for the rental value of the mobile home during plaintiffs' occupancy." While voluntary use of purchased goods frequently results in a finding that the buyer accepted them, courts have displayed some leniency when buyers of mobile homes continue to live in them as they continue to complain to the seller about serious defects. Such buyers often do not have the resources to abandon the mobile home and live elsewhere if the seller refuses to acknowledge the buyer's rejection of the goods. As in *Jorgensen*, courts faced with such circumstances may find rejection occurred but reduce the buyer's recovery by the value they received from living in the home.

The Jorgensens continued to live in their mobile home during the early course of the litigation on the advice of their attorney. Suppose their attorney had advised them to move out and store the mobile home. Would they have been able to recover the expense of storage from Pressnall? Recall our discussion of a buyer's responsibility for rejected goods in Assignment 17.

Example M: *Bowen v. Young*[13]

Young bought a new mobile home from Bowen. When it was delivered and hooked up to utilities, Young discovered many defects, including the fact that the heating system was electric rather than gas, and that it was equipped with a 3-ton air conditioning unit rather than the 3½-ton unit he had ordered. He made numerous complaints to Bowen to remedy the defects, to no avail. He finally wired the seller cancelling the order. Bowen would not return his deposit. Since Young was currently paying rent for another living space, storage fees for his furniture, and the cost of rental space for the mobile homes, he decided to move into the mobile home to

---

[13]   507 S.W.2d 600 (Tex. Civ. App. 1974).

minimize expenses. He lived in the mobile home for a year, during which time he converted the heating system from electric to gas.

Analysis: The court found that Young's actions constituted "a course of conduct clearly inconsistent with seller's continued ownership of the mobile home," and that he had thus accepted the home. As noted in Example L, courts show some leniency to mobile home buyers who continue to live in defective homes while seeking to rescind the sale, but the outcome may depend on the nature of the defects, the circumstances of the buyer, the firmness of the buyer's efforts to rescind, and the court's view of the legal standard to be applied in determining rejection.

Do you agree with the court's judgment in Example L? In Example M? What might justify the different outcomes?

5. Consequences of Acceptance

Reading the Code:
§§ 2-607 & 2-717

Read 2-607(1) to (4) and the associated Comments.

Question 6. May a buyer reject goods after accepting them?

Question 7. Does a seller have a right to cure after the buyer has accepted defective goods? Should a seller offer to cure?

Question 8. Who (buyer or seller) has the burden of establishing whether or not the goods were defective under each of the circumstances given below?

_____ A buyer rejects goods and then files suit, seeking damages.

_____ A buyer rejects goods and the seller files suit, claiming breach by the buyer.

_____ A buyer accepts goods and then files suit, seeking damages.

_____ A buyer accepts goods and refuses to pay full price, saying the goods were defective, and the seller than files suit, claiming breach by the buyer.

Read 2-717.

Question 9. Does 2-607(1) mean a buyer must pay full price for any accepted goods despite the existence of defects in the goods?

B. Notifying Seller of Breach

It is important to remember that acceptance of goods does not deprive a buyer of remedies for breach of contract; those remedies will be covered in Assignment 22. In order to preserve those remedies, however, a buyer who becomes aware of a defect in accepted goods is subject to certain notification requirements. In order to permit sellers to correct deficiencies, mitigate damages, prepare for litigation, and negotiate regarding defects in the goods or tender, buyers are required by § 2-607(3) to convey information to sellers about the defects.

 Reading the Code:
§ 2-607(3)

Read 2-607(3) and Comments 4 and 5.

Question 10. What information must a buyer convey to the seller after discovery of a defect in accepted goods?

Question 11. Is notice required only from the immediate buyer to the immediate seller?

Question 12. When must 2-607(3) notice be given?

Question 13. What happens if the buyer does not give the required notice?

It is noteworthy that, to further the purposes of the § 2-607 notice requirement, some courts have interpreted § 2-607(3) as requiring the buyer to give more detailed information to sellers than seems compelled by the language of the section and its comments. The consequences of failing to give adequate notice are sufficiently severe that buyers are well advised to include more rather than less information when notifying sellers of deficiencies.

Some courts have ruled that a buyer fulfills its duty to notify remote sellers that an injury has occurred by notifying the immediate seller who, it is assumed, will pass the information up the distribution chain. Caution nonetheless suggests that a buyer notify all those against whom the buyer may seek liability.

C. Revocation of Acceptance of the Goods

Once a buyer has accepted goods (whether by communicating acceptance or failing to reject within a reasonable time), the buyer may keep the goods or, in limited circumstances, the buyer may revoke acceptance. As with rejection, the Code provides standards for determining (1) whether a revocation of acceptance is justified or unjustified and (2) whether the revocation is effective or ineffective.

1. Under What Circumstances May a Buyer Revoke an Acceptance, and How?

Reading the Code:
§ 2-608

Read 2-608(1)(a) and Comment 2.

Question 14. Under 2-608(1)(a), what facts must a buyer prove to justify revoking acceptance of goods?

Read 2-608(1)(b) and Comment 3.

Question 15. Under 2-608(1)(b), what facts must a buyer prove to justify revoking acceptance of goods?

Read 2-608(2) and Comments 4, 5, and 6.

Question 16. What must a buyer do to effectively revoke acceptance?

Question 17. If a buyer effectively revokes acceptance, what are the buyer's responsibilities and options with respect to the goods?

Question 18. As your answers to the above questions should make clear, it is more difficult for a buyer to establish justification for revoking acceptance (§ 2-608) than for rejecting goods (§ 2-601). What might explain this difference in standards?

EXAMPLES AND ANALYSIS

Example N: *Trisler v. Carter*[14]

Carter bought a chest of drawers from Trisler, an antiques dealer. When he brought it home and cleaned it, he found nails protruding from the back of the chest. Trisler told him that he could return it for a store credit, but when he returned it, he found nothing in the store that he wanted. Carter sued Trisler, demanding a refund of the purchase price.

Analysis: The court found that Carter had no grounds for revoking his acceptance. Carter did not accept the chest on the assumption the non-conformity would be cured (2-608(1)(a)). The fact that he discovered the defect upon opening the drawers to clean the chest demonstrated that it was not difficult to discover the nonconformity, and there is no suggestion that Trisler prevented Carter from inspecting it fully before the purchase (2-608(1)(b)). Does the court's ruling mean that Carter has no remedy against Trisler? What was the acceptance in this case? Does Carter have an argument that he never accepted the chest in the first place?

---

[14]   996 N.E.2d 354 (Ind. Ct. App. 2013).

Example O: *Viking Packaging Technologies, Inc. v. Vassallo Foods, Inc.*[15]

Vassallo Foods, a noodle maker, ordered from Viking an automatic pasta bagging system. The system that Vassallo Foods ordered consisted of a bagger, a scale, a tin-tie applicator for sealing the bags of pasta, and a conveyer belt. The total purchase price was $178,074, with the tin-tie applicator priced at $47,173. When Vassallo Foods' representatives inspected the machine prior to shipping, the tin-ties did not regularly close up. Viking assured Vassallo Foods that the issue had been resolved, and Vassallo Foods approved the shipment. The system was installed on June 17. Over the next month, Viking made various adjustments to the system to correct problems with the scale and bagger, but the problem with the tin-ties persisted. On July 10, Viking informed Vassallo Foods that the tin-tie applicator could not be made to work with their product. Viking made no further attempts to fix the tin-tie applicator, and Vassallo Foods did not request any further efforts. On December 4, Vassallo Foods sent Viking an e-mail asking for a refund of the price paid for the tin-tie applicator. Viking responded with a lawsuit for the outstanding amount due on the system, totaling $34,110.22.

Analysis: The court rejected Vassallo Foods' arguments that its December 4 e-mail constituted an effective revocation of its acceptance, which had been made on the assumption that Viking was continuing to work on fixing the tin-tie applicator. The court held that Viking had known, or should have known, since July 10 that the tin-tie applicator would not work, and therefore the attempted revocation was ineffective.

Does the court's ruling mean that Vassallo Foods has no remedy against Viking? What was the acceptance in this case? Does Vassallo Foods have an argument that it never accepted the system in the first place? How might the concept of a "commercial unit" be relevant to your response?

Example P: *Nassar v. Wiz Leasing, Inc.*[16]

Steve and Karen Nassar told Frank, a used car salesman, that they were looking for a safe used car for Karen to use for driving with their children.

---

[15]   804 N.W.2d 507 (Wis. Ct. App. 2011).
[16]   2014 WL 7662478 (Conn. Sup. Ct. 2014).

Frank recommended a particular Mistubishi Diamante, assuring them that it was in good working order and telling them that it was the car he would purchase for his family. In fact, the car had not undergone a full safety check at Frank's dealership. The Nassars took it for a short test drive, gave the dealer a down-payment, and signed a purchase order acknowledging that the vehicle was being sold "AS IS" and that seller disclaimed all warranties. The Nassars returned to pick up the car a few days later. On their way home, Steve noticed that one of the fog lights on the Diamante was not working. Minutes later, the check engine light came on, and Karen pulled off the road. Karen returned the car to the dealership for servicing. A few weeks later, the check engine light came on again, and the Nassars returned to the dealer again. A few weeks after that, the check engine light came on, and various other mechanical problems became evident: problems starting the car, problems with the directional signals, and bucking and stalling. Seventy-three days after purchasing the car, the Nassars decided the car was unsafe and brought it back to the dealership to return it. Frank told them that they could not return it and that if they left it, he would consider it abandoned and leave it on the street. Steve removed the plates and registration from the car and left. The following week, Frank sent Steve a letter telling him the dealership was charging him an indoor storage fee of $40 per day until the Nassars removed the abandoned vehicle. The car was subsequently substantially damaged as a result of flooding from Hurricane Sandy. The Nassars sued the dealership.

Analysis: The court accepted the Nassars' argument that they had rightfully and effectively revoked their acceptance of the car under 2-608(1)(b). Do you agree with the court's ruling? Does the fact that the Nassars never conducted an independent inspection of the vehicle by an outside mechanic make a difference to your assessment of this case? Of what significance is the fact that the car was sold "AS IS"? How would you distinguish this case from the cases described in Examples N and O?

2. Cure after Revocation

Because § 2-508 refers only to a seller's right to cure after a buyer rejects goods, a majority of courts that have considered the issue have concluded that a seller has no right to cure after a buyer justifiably revokes acceptance.[17] Why might the drafters of the UCC have decided not to give the seller a right to cure after revocation of acceptance?

A minority of jurisdictions do permit cure after revocation.[18] These courts rely on the language in § 2-608(3) providing a purchaser revoking his acceptance "has the same rights and duties with regard to the goods involved as if he had rejected them," and apply § 2-508 by analogy to help determine when cure is appropriate and how long the seller has to effectuate a cure.

APPLYING THE CODE

Problem 18-2.

If a buyer seeks to return goods to the seller, the buyer often will argue in the alternative, claiming that it has rightfully and effectively rejected the goods before acceptance but also that, if acceptance already occurred, it has justifiably and effectively revoked acceptance. Full analysis of a problem therefore often requires consideration of both rejection and revocation of acceptance as possibilities and, as with the consideration of whether acceptance has occurred, the arguments and conclusions may be highly dependent on the factual circumstances. For each of the following scenarios, make the best arguments for finding that the buyer has rejected or in the alternative has revoked acceptance of the goods. What arguments would you expect from the seller in response? Can you predict a likely outcome?

    (a)   Buyer of a copy machine has problems with paper jamming and misfeeds that begin two weeks after the copier is delivered. Seller assures Buyer the problem will "solve itself" within a few days or seller will perform any necessary repairs. After two months, Seller's repairs have been unsuccessful, and the copier still jams. Buyer notifies Seller it wants a replacement copier.

    (b)   Same as (a), but in the two months Buyer has the copier, one of Buyer's employees spills a can of soda pop on the copier, causing a short circuit and sticking keys.

[17] See, e.g., Lile v. Kiesel, 871 N.E.2d 995 (Ind. Ct. App. 2007); Bowen v. Foust, 925 S.W.2d 211 (Mo. Ct. App. 1996); U.S. Roofing, Inc. v. Credit Alliance Corp., 279 Cal. Rptr. 533 (Cal. Ct. App. 1991).
[18] See, e.g., David Tunick, Inc. v. Kornfeld, 813 F. Supp. 988 (S.D.N.Y. 1993); Tucker v. Aqua Yacht Harbor Corp., 749 F. Supp. 142 (N.D. Miss. 1990); Conte v. Dwan Lincoln-Mercury Inc., 374 A.2d 144 (Conn. 1976).

(c)   Charles purchases a new car. One year later, Charles takes his car for servicing, and the mechanic notices rust developing on the underside. Charles discovers that the rustproofing and polymer coating listed on the invoice were not applied to the car. Charles tells the dealer he does not want to keep the car.

(d)   Buyer of a mobile home tells the salesperson that he needs a three-bedroom home that will fit on an existing foundation that is 70 feet long. The salesperson shows him several models, and he picks one costing $52,000. Several months later, the mobile home drifts off its foundation. Buyer discovers that the home is actually only 67 feet in length. Buyer writes to Seller indicating he wants Seller to take back the trailer home.

(e)   Same as (d), but Seller denies liability and refuses Buyer's demand that Seller take back the trailer and return the purchase price. Buyer continues to live in the trailer home and two months later sues Seller for breach.

* * *

The following case illustrates a seller's arguments that the buyer had accepted under all three of the modes of acceptance set out in § 2-606, and reaffirms the perfect tender rule in rejection, contrasting this rule with the standard for revocation. As you read *Yates v. Clifford Motors, Inc.*, consider these questions:

(1)   Why did the court assert that it is "ludicrous" to argue that Yates accepted under § 2-606(1)(a)?

(2)   Why did the court analyze arguments under § 2-606(1)(b) and § 2-606(1)(c) together? Are they, in fact, two different tests?

(3)   How did Yates notify Clifford of his rejection? What does the answer to this question tell you about what the court must have considered a "reasonable opportunity to inspect" in this case?

(4)   Why did the court reject Clifford's argument that Yates acted "inconsistent[ly] with Clifford's ownership" by keeping the truck for about six months and putting 9,000 miles on it? How is § 2-711 relevant to Yates' actions with respect to the truck, and how does it potentially function to limit Yates' recovery?

(5)   Even though the court did not specifically refer to the "perfect tender rule," it is relevant to this decision. How?

YATES V. CLIFFORD MOTORS, INC.

423 A.2d 1262 (Pa. Super. Ct. 1980)

PRICE, JUDGE:

STATEMENT OF THE CASE

The instant appeal is from the order and judgment in the court of common pleas awarding appellee, Walter Yates, $2,780.12 . . . in his suit against appellant, Clifford Motors, Incorporated, for damages resulting from rescission of a contract for the purchase of a Dodge pick-up truck. For the reasons that follow, we affirm the trial court's verdict as to the liability of appellant but reverse and remand on the issue of damages. . . .

FACTS

On January 13, 1977, appellee Yates test drove a Dodge club-cab pick-up truck and entered into a discussion with one Joe Farino, appellant's salesman, regarding the possible purchase of said vehicle. During the test drive, Yates detected a vibration in the front end of the truck and brought it to Farino's attention. Farino suggested that the problem possibly was caused by the icy road conditions and that if it was mechanically induced it could be alleviated by a minor adjustment. Following the test drive, Farino and Yates discussed the purchase price, the "extras" to be included within said price and the gas mileage which Yates could expect the truck to get. Yates ultimately agreed to purchase the truck for $2,000 plus the trade-in value of his 1976 Dodge Aspen.

On January 14, 1977, appellee returned to Clifford Motors to examine the truck with a friend. On this occasion, Yates detected a defect in the driver's side door which prevented the door from closing completely. Farino assured Yates that the door would be repaired and that there would be no other difficulties since the vehicle was new and under warranty. The truck thus remained with appellant. Yates returned, either on Monday, January 16 or Tuesday, January 17, 1977, to take delivery of the truck. When the truck was brought from the service area, however, it was apparent that the defective door had not been repaired. In addition, appellee observed scrapes and gouges in the finish on the passenger side door and rear quarter panel. Yates was again assured that the defects would be rectified but since the shop was closed for the day, Yates was instructed to take delivery of the truck, to schedule an appointment to have the truck repaired at a later date, and to make a list of any other defects which became apparent during the interim.

Appellee's subsequent use of the truck revealed numerous problems. Even unloaded, the truck would not travel a hill unless it was first driven several miles to warm the engine. Rather than the fifteen to seventeen miles per gallon of gasoline Yates was told to expect, the truck obtained only about five miles to the gallon. Although the vehicle was to have been equipped with Goodyear tires, tinted glass on all windows and a factory radio, as delivered, the tires were manufactured by General, only the windshield was tinted, and the radio installed by the dealer failed to fit properly in the dashboard. Besides these shortcomings, the heater failed to generate heat and thus had to be replaced. On at least four occasions, the truck was returned to appellant's repair shop to have the problems corrected. Although repair work was performed, the defect which prevented the door from being completely closed, the front end noise and vibration complained of during the initial test drive, and the marred finish on the door and quarter panel were never corrected.

Thereafter, appellee attempted unsuccessfully to contact appellant's owner on numerous occasions concerning the difficulties he was experiencing. Approximately one week before his first monthly payment was due, Yates contacted the Jermyn Bank, which bank financed appellee's purchase of the truck. Yates explained the difficulties with the truck as well as his inability to contact appellant's owner and informed the bank that he would make no payments on the truck until the appropriate repairs were made. The person to whom Yates spoke reportedly informed him that the bank would contact appellant and attempt to resolve the difficulties. Yates thus continued in his refusal to make payments and, although the Jermyn Bank apparently failed to fashion a solution, Yates received neither notification of the bank's failure nor a statement that his account was past due.

Nearly four months after Yates took delivery of the truck and some three months following his communication with the Jermyn Bank, the matter remained unresolved. On or about May 5, 1977, therefore, appellee filed a complaint in assumpsit against appellant, Clifford Motors. Two months later, during the first week in July, appellant repossessed the truck based upon appellee's failure to make the required payments. . . .

DISPOSITION AT TRIAL

On February 6, 1979, following a non-jury trial, a verdict was rendered in appellee Yates' favor and against Clifford Motors. The trial court reasoned, pursuant to section 2-606 of the Pennsylvania [U.C.C.], that Yates never accepted the contract for purchase of the truck or, alternatively, even accepting, arguendo, that Yates had accepted the truck, he would nonetheless have been entitled to revoke his acceptance pursuant to U.C.C. section 2-608. Consequently, the court concluded that Yates was "entitled to recover the value of the vehicle he traded in on the truck together with any cash outlay." Appellant, Clifford Motors, thereafter filed this appeal.

ANALYSIS

Appellant argues that appellee accepted the truck since he failed to seasonably notify Clifford Motors of his intent to reject as required by U.C.C. section 2-602. Further, appellant contends that the facts adduced at trial belie any assertion that appellee's acceptance was revoked pursuant to U.C.C. section 2-608. . . .

DID YATES ACCEPT UNDER 2-606(1)(a)?

We now address appellant's first contention that appellee Yates accepted the vehicle pursuant to U.C.C. section 2-606. That section posits a three-pronged test for determining whether a buyer has accepted a particular item of goods. First, acceptance occurs after the buyer has had a reasonable opportunity to inspect the goods and has advised the seller either that the goods are conforming or that he will take or retain the goods despite an existing nonconformity. Second, a buyer will be deemed to have accepted the goods if, after a reasonable opportunity to inspect, he fails to effectively reject. Last, a buyer who acts in a manner inconsistent with the seller's ownership rights may likewise be charged with acceptance of the goods in question. See U.C.C. § 2-606(1)(a)-(c). In view of the facts adduced at trial, it would be untenable to maintain that appellee accepted the truck based on the first prong of the test contained in U.C.C. section 2-606.[FN5]

FN5. Commencing with appellee's road test of the truck and ending with his ultimatum to the Jermyn Bank, appellee made it unequivocally clear that the truck was nonconforming. In addition to his testimony to that effect at trial, the truck's nonconformity is circumstantially confirmed by the fact that appellee scheduled and kept numerous appointments to have the truck repaired at appellant's expense. The record itself reveals that, absent assurances by appellant's sales personnel that the nonconforming vehicle would be repaired, appellee would never have taken delivery of the truck in the first instance. . . . It is ludicrous to argue, therefore, either that appellant was advised by Yates that the truck was acceptable or that he would accept it in spite of the numerous uncorrected defects.

DID YATES ACCEPT UNDER 2-606(1)(b) or (c)?

Accordingly, our analysis must focus on the latter two prongs of the Code's test to determine whether appellee properly and timely rejected and whether his conduct with respect to the truck was consistent both with his rejection and with appellant's ownership of the truck.[FN6]

[FN6]. U.C.C. section 2-602(2)(a) states that "after rejection any exercise of ownership by the buyer with respect to any commercial unit is wrongful as against the seller." Section 2-606(1)(c) provides that a buyer may be deemed to have accepted an item of goods if he "does any act inconsistent with the seller's ownership." Official comment no. 4 to section 2-606 states that: "Under paragraph (c) (of 2-606), any action taken by the buyer which is inconsistent with his claim that he has rejected the goods, constitutes an acceptance." Despite the fact that section 2-606 explains what constitutes acceptance, a claim of rejection is thus a condition precedent to analysis under the "inconsistent conduct" provisions of both sections. Accordingly, we make no attempt to treat the sections individually in our discussion of this issue.

Appellant argues that appellee failed to effectively reject the truck because: (1) the rejection, if any, occurred after an unreasonable passage of time; (2) appellee did not notify Clifford Motors that he was rejecting; (3) there was no offer to return the truck or tender of the same to Clifford Motors; (4) appellee's operation of the truck for some six months and 9,000 miles is inconsistent with a theory of rejection; and (5) the defects complained of were too insubstantial to justify rejection. We disagree.

"Rejection of goods must be within a reasonable time after their delivery or tender." U.C.C. § 2-602(1). What is a reasonable time, however, is generally deemed a question of fact to be resolved by the factfinder. . . . Instantly, the trial was before a judge without a jury and, accordingly, our scope of review is limited to a determination whether the court's finding that appellee rejected within a reasonable time is supported by competent evidence. . . . Section 1-204 of the U.C.C. provides that "a reasonable time for taking any action depends upon the nature, purposes and circumstances of such action." . . .

Instantly, appellee detected problems with the truck during his test drive and communicated to appellant his expectation that they would be alleviated. As each additional problem surfaced, appellee was assured that it would be remedied. Appellee continually returned the truck to Clifford Motors so that appropriate repairs could be made. While there was some evidence that appellee was advised that the defective doors could not or would not be repaired, there is no evidence to justify a conclusion that he was similarly advised regarding the marred finish, the abnormally low gas mileage, the vibrating front end, or the lack of engine power sufficient to enable the truck to negotiate a hill.

Thus, based upon appellee's testimony at trial, the court reasonably could have concluded that, from January 1977 until on or about May 5, 1977, the date on which appellee's complaint was filed, Yates was awaiting the repairs which had been promised by appellant's salesman at the time he first took delivery. On cross-examination, for example, counsel for Clifford Motors asked Yates the following question: "If the vehicle was not going to be repossessed, if they hadn't come to get it (in July of 1977), what was your intention to do with the vehicle?" . . . Appellee responded thus:

> They were supposed to be taking care of the vehicle. That is what I was waiting on. The bank said that he would take care of it. I was waiting for the owner of [Clifford] Motors or somebody to fix the vehicle the way it should be. That's why I kept the vehicle.

It is the function of the factfinder to pass upon the credibility of witnesses and to weigh the evidence. . . . Thus, it is of no moment that we might have been impelled to reach a contrary conclusion had we been confronted with this issue in the first instance. It is sufficient for us to note at this juncture that, if believed, the above evidence amply supports the conclusion that it was not unreasonable for appellee to wait some four to five months prior to rejecting the truck.

Appellant also contends that appellee's rejection was ineffective since he failed to give notice of such rejection to appellant. We disagree. Rejection "is ineffective unless the buyer seasonably notifies the seller." U.C.C. § 2-602(1). A party gives notice "to another by taking such steps as may be reasonably required to inform the other in ordinary course." U.C.C. § 1-201(26). "A person has 'notice' of a fact when . . . from all the facts and circumstances known to him at the time in question he has reason to know that it exists." U.C.C. § 1-201(25). Instantly, appellee made appellant aware of every defect of which he complained.[7]

FN7. In this regard, we note the underlying policy of U.C.C. section 2-605 . . . [The court cites Comments 1 and 2], then continues: The facts in the instant case belie any assertion that appellant was prevented from effecting a "cure" by lack of notice. Appellant had at least a five month period during which to cure the defects prior to the date on which appellee's complaint was filed.

In addition, he made no payments on the purchase of the truck and advised the Jermyn Bank that none would be forthcoming unless the problems were corrected. Ultimately, appellee filed a complaint in assumpsit requesting damages or, alternatively, the return of the Dodge Aspen which he had used as a trade-in, in return for which, appellee desired to return the defective truck. Since the U.C.C. is to "be liberally construed and applied," U.C.C. § 1-102(1), and given the circumstances of this case, we conclude that the complaint filed on May 5, 1977 was adequate notice that the truck was then being rejected.

Appellant further insists that appellee failed to effectively reject because he made no offer to return the truck to Clifford Motors. This contention is not only factually incorrect . . . but also legally erroneous. U.C.C. section 2-602(2)(b) requires only that a buyer hold the goods with reasonable care to permit the seller to remove them. This section imposes no obligation to formally return the goods to the seller. . . . Instantly, appellee testified that the truck was parked in his front yard during the months of April and May of 1977. The truck was in that same location when it was repossessed in July, 1977, and since there was no allegation that appellee in any way sought to prevent appellant from regaining possession of the truck, we can only conclude that appellee complied with the mandate of section 2-602.

Appellant also asserts that appellee's conduct with respect to the truck was inconsistent with his rejection of the same since he retained possession of the truck for approximately six months and allegedly travelled some 9,000 miles. We disagree. We have already concluded that notice of appellee's rejection was effectively communicated on or about May 5, 1977, the date on which appellee filed his complaint. Section 2-602(2)(a) and 2-606(1)(c) refer only to inconsistent acts occurring after a claimed rejection. Thus, only appellee's use of the truck from May 5, 1977 until the first week of July, 1977, the approximate time of repossession, is pertinent to our determination whether he acted in a manner consistent with his rejection of the truck.FN12

FN12. Even had we not reached this conclusion, we have already noted that the trial court could reasonably have concluded that appellee's use of the truck prior to May of 1977 was reasonable and thus not inconsistent with appellant's rights since appellee was operating on a rational assumption based upon the assurance of appellant's salesman that the truck would be repaired.

While indicating a pattern of frequent use prior to May 5, 1977, the evidence adduced at trial established that the truck was used only sparingly following that date and only for such essential purposes as trips to the grocery store. . . . Having exchanged his automobile for value toward the purchase price of the truck appellee had no other means of transportation. We do not believe that it would serve the ends of justice to penalize a consumer who exercises his right to reject by prohibiting that consumer from even the slightest use of the goods involved until the conclusion of litigation. This is particularly true where, as here, the "goods" in question, motor vehicles, have become such an essential means of transportation for even disadvantaged members of our society because of the mobility mandated by modern living conditions. Moreover, under U.C.C. section 2-711, a buyer who has rightfully rejected has a security interest in the goods in his possession to the extent of any payments made. Such a buyer may retain the goods and even sell them to recover the value of his security interest. Instantly, although appellee made none of his required monthly payments, he nonetheless retained a security interest for approximately $2,700, the value of the automobile that he traded in on the truck. To this extent, appellee's use of the truck subsequent to the filing of his complaint and prior to appellant's repossession must be deemed reasonable and not inconsistent with his rejection of the truck. However, the trial court failed to consider by what amount, if any, appellee's use exceeded his security interest in the truck. The court simply awarded appellee the entire value of the trade-in together with interest without adjusting that value in relation to the reasonable use. Accordingly, we find it necessary to remand to enable the trial court to adjust its verdict accordingly.

ARGUMENTS RELATED TO REVOCATION

Appellant's final point in support of his position that appellee failed to effectively reject is that the defects complained of were too insubstantial to warrant rejection. . . . This argument is patently untenable in light of the evidence adduced at trial. Of greater significance, however, is appellant's attempt to commingle the requirements of revocation of acceptance pursuant to U.C.C. 2-608 and the requisites of rejection under 2-602. Whereas revocation of acceptance is justified only where the value of the tendered goods is "substantially impaired" as to the buyer, see U.C.C. section 2-608(1), no such requirement obtains for rejection under U.C.C. section 2-602.... Thus, even assuming, arguendo, the validity of appellant's contention regarding the extent of defects in the truck, it would have no effect on our disposition of this case.

Appellant's second principal contention is that appellee failed to revoke his acceptance. Instantly, the trial court concluded only that appellee "would have been entitled to revoke his acceptance." ... The court did not determine that appellee in fact revoked his acceptance pursuant to U.C.C. section 2-608. We need not resolve this issue, however, because we have concluded that appellee never accepted the truck. *See* U.C.C. section 2-606.

Therefore, we affirm the trial court's verdict as to the liability of appellant. We reverse and remand, however, on the issues of damages, limiting the remand to the sole determination whether or not appellee's use of the vehicle exceeded his security interest therein.

D. Varying Rules of Acceptance, Rejection, and Revocation by Agreement

Recall that under § 1-102(3), the effect of most provisions of the Code may be varied by agreement. The provisions on acceptance, rejection, and revocation are not exceptions to this general rule. Parties may, for example, agree that the buyer will have no right to inspect before acceptance occurs, leaving the buyer with only alternative remedies to rejection. *See* § 2-513(1). As you answer the questions below, consider both the possibility of variation by agreement and the nature of the usual opportunity to inspect before acceptance.

Reading the Code: §§ 2-513 & 2-606

Read 2-513(3)(a) and 2-606 Comment 3.

Question 19. Buyer orders a watch C.O.D. Does acceptance occur when the package arrives, and buyer signs for delivery of the package and pays the contract price?

Question 20. Buyer of a new car arrives at the showroom to pick up the vehicle. She signs all the final paperwork, including a document entitled "Acknowledgment of Acceptance of Vehicle." She pays for the car, is given the keys, and drives the car off the lot. Does acceptance occur when the buyer signs the "Acknowledgment of Acceptance?"

E. Effect of Breach on Risk of Loss

In Assignment 16, we explored who has the risk of loss in the absence of breach by either party, as governed by § 2-509. Section 2-510 covers risk of loss in the presence of certain breaches by a buyer or a seller.

1. Effect of Seller's Breach on Risk of Loss

Reading the Code: § 2-510

Read 2-510(1) and Comments 1 and 2.

Question 21. What does a buyer have to prove in order to establish that the risk of loss did not shift to the buyer when the goods were delivered?

Question 22. If the buyer rightfully rejects goods and the seller sends replacement goods that conform to the contract, who has the risk of loss with respect to the original shipment of goods? With respect to the replacement goods?

Read 2-510(2).

Question 23. If a seller delivers seriously nonconforming goods but the buyer nevertheless accepts the goods, who then has the risk of loss? Does the risk of loss shift back to the seller if the buyer has a right to revoke acceptance? If the buyer justifiably revokes acceptance?

EXAMPLES AND ANALYSIS

Example Q: *Lykins Oil Co. v. Fekkos*[19]

One Saturday, Fekkos bought a tractor from Lykins Oil Co., paying by check. It was delivered to his house that afternoon. The next day, when Fekkos used it for the first time, he discovered that it had a dead battery, that it overheated while pulling either a mower or tiller, and that it was missing safety shields and a water pump. Monday morning, Fekkos stopped payment on the check and contacted Lykins with his complaint. Fekkos claims that Lykins told him it would pick the tractor up from his house the next day; Lykins claims it promised to pick up the tractor within the next few days. Fekkos' driveway was broken up because of a renovation, and his garage was inaccessible. Because the tractor would have to be jump-started due to the dead battery, Fekkos parked the tractor with the tiller attached in his front yard, at the end of the lawn as near as possible to the front door without driving it over his landscaping. The tractor was not picked up the next day. On the following day, at 6:00 a.m., Fekkos discovered that the tractor had been stolen, although the tiller had been unhitched.

Analysis: The court held that the risk of loss for the stolen tractor remained with Lykins, based on the defects in the tractor. The court found that Fekkos had

---

[19]   507 N.E.2d 795 (Ohio Ct. C.P. 1986).

acted reasonably in parking the tractor where he had, given the inaccessibility of his garage, and that Lykins knew where the tractor was parked and did not object. Based on the description of the case offered above, did Lykins retain the risk of loss under 2-510(1) or 2-510(2)? What would you have to know to answer this question?

Example R: *Eagle Jets, LLC v. Atlanta Jet, Inc.*[20]

Eagle Jets entered into a contract with Atlanta Jet to purchase a helicopter then located in Santa Cruz, Bolivia. The purchase agreement provided that, "title to the Aircraft . . . and risk to the Aircraft shall pass to Purchaser when the purchase price is paid in full to Seller." During the pre-purchase inspection of the helicopter in Bolivia, a number of defects were discovered. One was remedied on site in Bolivia, and the parties agreed to defer remedy of another until after the helicopter was delivered to Eagle Jets in Ft. Lauderdale, Florida. The parties executed an "Addendum" to the agreement entitled "Acceptance," noting the results of the inspection and the manner in which they would be resolved. Eagle Jets paid the purchase price by wire transfer. The helicopter crashed during its flight from Bolivia to Florida. Eagle Jets argued that, although 2-509(4) provides that parties may by contract vary the Article 2 default rules for risk of loss, 2-509 was subject to 2-510. Under 2-510(1), Eagle Jets argued, as a result of the unremedied defect in the helicopter, Atlanta Jet had not tendered a helicopter in conformance with the contract, and thus the risk of loss remained with Atlanta Jet.

Analysis: The court held that the risk of loss had passed to Eagle Jets before the crash, noting that 2-510 places the risk of loss on the seller only "until cure or acceptance." Eagle Jets had clearly accepted the goods with knowledge of the nonconformities while the helicopter was still in Bolivia. The court also upheld the jury's finding that 2-510 did not even apply, because Atlanta Jet had not breached the contract. How would Atlanta Jet have made this argument to the jury?

---

[20] 740 S.E.2d 439 (Ga. Ct. App. 2013).

2. Effect of Buyer's Breach on Risk of Loss

Reading the Code:
§ 2-510

Read 2-510(3), and review 2-509.

Question 24. If a buyer repudiates a contract while the seller is still completing manufacture of the goods, who has the risk of loss?

Question 25. The parties enter into an F.O.B. destination contract, and Seller delivers conforming goods to the carrier without obtaining insurance for the shipment. Buyer repudiates while the goods are in transit. The goods are damaged while in the hands of the carrier. Who has the risk of loss?

EXAMPLES AND ANALYSIS

Example S: *Shilling v. Campbell*[21]

George Shilling entered into a contract with Campbell Grain and Seed Co., to sell the company his crop of soybeans. The soybeans had been harvested and were being stored in bins on Shilling's land. The soybeans were to be picked up by Campbell when it had enough room in its elevator to store them. The cursory written confirmation of the transaction stated that delivery would be in "April," "f.o.b. bin on farm." At the end of April, Campbell contacted Shilling about picking up the beans. It had rained the night before, and Shilling told Campbell that he might get stuck if he tried to get the beans. Over the next few days, the rain continued. The parties discussed the possibility of flooding a number of times, but Campbell did not pick the beans up before the rising flood waters reached the bins and inundated the beans. This caused the beans to swell to such an extent that they were completely destroyed, and the bins were extensively damaged. Shilling sued Campbell for the purchase price of the beans.

---

[21] 186 N.E.2d 782 (Ill. App. Ct. 1962).

Analysis: The court determined that Campbell had breached the contract due to its failure to pick up the beans in April, and that the risk of loss therefore fell on Campbell. This case was decided before the adoption of the UCC in Illinois, under law that was largely consistent with the current Article 2 rule. Under the current 2-510(3), would Shilling be able to get his full purchase price from Campbell? What more would you need to know?

APPLYING THE CODE

Problem 18-3.

Bentley, a professional violinist, saw a notice indicating that Slavik was selling a rare Auguste Sebastien Philippe Bernardel violin made in 1835, with an appraised value ranging from $15,000 to $20,000. On Jan. 28, 1984, Bentley went to Slavik's home to inspect the violin. Slavik showed Bentley a certificate and appraisal indicating that it was an authentic Bernardel violin. Bentley played the violin for at least two hours and agreed to purchase it for $17,500. Bentley gave Slavik a $15,000 down payment, agreed to pay the balance of $2,500 by the middle of February, and took the violin home with her. She sent the second payment to Slavik on February 13, accompanied by a letter that said, "This violin is a Bernardel masterpiece! I am more than satisfied with its quality and sound; it has, in fact, exceeded my expectations." From the date of purchase until the end of 1985, Bentley played the violin for an average of eight hours a day. In November of 1984, the top of the violin was removed, a procedure considered "major surgery" in the bowed-stringed-instrument community. The repair was poorly done, leaving the violin with adhesive residue visible on its exterior. The violin also acquired cracks near the fingerboard and under the chin rest. The neck of the violin was broken in transit and reattached.

In April of 1985, a friend of Bentley's who curated a musical instrument museum examined the violin and offered the informal opinion that it could not possibly be a genuine Bernardel. Bentley demanded that Slavik return the purchase price and offered to return the violin, but Slavik refused to do so. For the rest of that year, she continued to play the violin, while attempting to get an expert appraisal. Eventually, two experts offered opinions that the violin was not a genuine Bernardel, and that it was probably worth between $700 and $2000 at the time that Slavik purchased it. What arguments might Bentley raise in court to get her purchase price back?

Problem 18-4.

Consider this agreement between a fish merchant in Duluth and a seafood restaurant in New Orleans calling for the sale of "500 lbs. No. 1 Quality Walleye F.O.B. Duluth, ship to port of New Orleans." The goods are shipped via a refrigerated container and loaded on a boat that travels the Mississippi River. Seller obtains and forwards to the buyer the needed documents. During shipment, the container malfunctions, and the fish spoil. After inspecting the spoiled fish, the buyer's agent claims that 20% of the fish were too small for "No. 1 Quality" in the first place.

(a) If the buyer's agent is right about the size of the fish, who has the risk of loss for the spoilage of the fish, and why?

(b) If the buyer's agent is wrong, who has the risk of loss for the spoilage of the fish, and why?

(c) If the contract had been F.O.B. New Orleans, who would have had the risk of loss for the spoilage of the fish? Would it have mattered if the fish had not been "No. 1 Quality"?

Problem 18-5.

Return to the facts in Problem 16-10. Assume now that Terra Children does not send a postcard to Bianca informing her the goods were shipped. The goods never arrived and Bianca seeks a replacement shipment or a refund from Terra Children. Is she entitled to receive such relief?

Problem 18-6.

Blissenbach ordered a new washing machine and dryer from Boyle's Appliance Mart and agreed to pay Boyle's to deliver and install the machines. The washing machine and dryer arrived at Blissenbach's home late in the afternoon. The children's nanny let the deliverymen into the house, and they completed the installation. When Blissenbach got home from work that evening, he saw that Boyle's had delivered and installed almond-colored machines instead of the white ones he had ordered. He made a mental note to call Boyle's in the morning to get the machines replaced, but Blissenbach was in the middle of a trial and forgot to do so. One week after delivery, a tornado ripped through his neighborhood, flooding his basement and destroying both machines. Assuming the sales contract says nothing about the risk of loss, who bears the risk of loss of the machines?

Assignment 19

Repudiation and Adequate Assurance of Performance; Excuse from Performance

§§ 2-609, 2-610, 2-611, 2-612, 2-613, 2-614, 2-615, 2-616

In Assignments 16, 17, and 18, you learned how to determine the delivery and payment responsibilities of buyers and sellers with respect to the goods being bought and sold. This Assignment steps back from that perspective and considers problems that may develop with respect to performance of the contract as a whole. These are of three types:

- Circumstances that lead one party to doubt the other party's ability to perform as promised (insecurity about future performance and a corresponding demand for adequate assurances);

- Statements or actions by one party that appear to indicate an intention not to perform future responsibilities under the contract (repudiation); and

- Circumstances that make performance much more difficult or even impossible and that might lead a court to allow rescission of the remaining parts of the contract (excuse).

Although we will treat these three concepts in separate sections below, the issues are interlocking. For example, statements that are not sufficient to constitute repudiation may nonetheless create insecurity about future performance, allowing the other party to demand assurances of performance. Circumstances that are not sufficient to excuse performance may nonetheless create insecurity about future performance, allowing the other party to demand assurances.

Note, too, that the provisions studied here also relate to upcoming assignments on breach and remedies. Missteps by one party in handling the performance issues raised in this Assignment (e.g., making an unjustified demand for adequate assurance or claiming excuse when none exists) may constitute a breach of the contract that triggers the other party's enforcement rights.

At the completion of this Assignment, you should be able to

- identify when a party has the right to demand adequate assurance of performance and how to make an effective demand;
- determine if a party has issued an anticipatory repudiation and identify appropriate action in response; and
- identify the elements necessary to establish an excuse for failure of performance and how to make effective arguments that excuse is, or is not, warranted.

A. Reasonable Insecurity about Future Performance

When circumstances lead one party to doubt whether the other party is still willing and able to perform, but no breach has as yet occurred, the concerned party is placed in an uncomfortable position. If she awaits performance that is never forthcoming, she may not be able to protect adequately against the consequences of the breach. If, instead, she ceases her own performance or repudiates to avoid further injury, she is likely to be the one who first breaches the contract and will then be liable for damages to the other. What the concerned party most wants is either to be reassured that the other party will indeed perform or to press the other party to repudiate so that she can consider the contract at an end and mitigate the damages that otherwise will accumulate.

As you may remember from your Contracts course, traditional common law offered insecure parties little or no recourse under such circumstances, so some parties took care of such concerns by writing contract clauses that allowed one or both parties to take protective steps if insecurity arose. Courts enforced such clauses if they appeared expressly in a contract. Over time, even without an express contract term, courts sometimes found a right to adequate assurance based on an implied contract term, at least in circumstances that the court believed justified an assumption that the parties would have intended such protection to be part of the arrangements. The drafters of Article 2 formalized the right to adequate assurance for all contracts for sale of goods. Comment 1 to § 2-609 articulates the rationale for including that right:

The section rests on the recognition of the fact that the essential purpose of a contract between commercial men [sic] is actual performance and they do not bargain merely for a promise, or for a promise plus the right to win a lawsuit and that a continuing sense of reliance and security that the promised performance will be forthcoming when due, is an important feature of the bargain. If either the willingness or the ability of a party to perform declines materially between the time of contracting and the time for performance, the other party is threatened with the loss of a substantial part of what he has bargained for.

We turn now to the particular provision adopted to address a party's insecurity about future performance.

Reading the Code: § 2-609

Read 2-609 and its Comments.

Question 1. May the parties provide in their contract that one or both parties have no right to demand adequate assurance of performance as described in 2-609?

Question 2. What do the Comments tell you about what constitutes "reasonable grounds for insecurity"?

Question 3. If a party has reasonable grounds for insecurity, what actions may that party take?

Question 4. What do the Comments tell you about what constitutes "adequate assurance of due performance"?

Question 5. If adequate assurance of due performance is forthcoming, what should the party who demanded assurance do?

Question 6. If adequate assurance of due performance is not forthcoming, what may or should the party who demanded assurance do?

As you will have realized in answering the set of questions above, the application of § 2-609 is heavily fact-dependent and requires reference to and an understanding of the commercial realities of operating in the context of uncertainty. The following examples should help you see the facts and arguments that will be taken into account and considered persuasive in disputes over the meaning of § 2-609.

EXAMPLES AND ANALYSIS

Example A: *Starchem Laboratories, LLC v. Kabco Pharmaceutical, Inc*[1]

Kabco Pharmaceuticals entered into a contract to manufacture 17,000 bottles of nutritional supplements for Starchem Laboratories. The raw materials and bottles for the manufacturing process would be supplied to Kabco by third-party vendors. The contract was memorialized in part in a June 4 purchase order that provided for payment 30 days after delivery of the supplements.

As of August 28, Starchem owed Kabco $3,192.60 on a previous purchase order and owed $27,880 to Futurebiotics, a sister company of Kabco, for past orders totaling $47,940. On August 28, Kabco sent a letter to Starchem that contained the following:

> The payment term set by Kabco for Starchem is net 30 days, while your credit limit is $25,000. This order far exceeds your credit limit.

> Your payment history for the previous orders was also not satisfactory as they were delayed. We have also been informed that Starchem has failed to live up to its payment obligations by not paying our sister Company (Futurebiotics) in spite of several written and verbal promises made to several Managers of Futurebiotics . . . .

> In view of the above, please be informed that your orders will be processed as soon as we receive a payment (bank certified check) for $165,120 towards [the June 4 purchase order]. The balance amount of $25,000 will be net 30 as per our agreed payment terms. We also would like you to pay the outstanding balance due to Futurebiotics.

---

[1] 2014 WL 1492118 (N.Y. Sup. Ct. 2014).

After receiving no reply from Starchem, Kabco emailed Starchem on September 4 and 5 saying it would begin manufacturing on September 8 if Starchem agreed to the $25,000 credit limit. Starchem responded by asking for credit in the amount of $60,000 to $90,000. Kabco emailed Starchem again, mentioning the unpaid Futurebiotics bill and asking for confirmation that someone from Starchem would be present on the following Monday to sample the first output of the manufacturing process. Starchem did not respond, but filed suit against Kabco for breach of contract when Kabco did not begin manufacturing the nutritional supplements. Kabco moved for summary judgment dismissing the complaint and for judgment in its favor on counterclaims for the outstanding invoices, claiming it had reasonable grounds for insecurity under 2-609 and had not received adequate assurances.

Analysis: The court noted that "[w]hether a seller has reasonable grounds for insecurity depends on various factors, including the buyer's exact words or actions, the course of dealing or performance between the parties, and the nature of the sales contract and the industry. Reasonable grounds for insecurity can arise from the sole fact that the buyer has fallen behind in his account with the seller, even when the items involved have to do with separate and legally distinct contracts, because it impairs the seller's expectation of due performance." The court ruled in favor of Kabco.

What facts support the court's conclusion that (1) Kabco had reasonable grounds for insecurity, (2) Kabco appropriately demanded adequate assurances, and (3) Starchem repudiated the contract?

Example B: *Rensselaer Polytechnic Institute v. Varian, Inc.*[2]

Rensselaer Polytechnic Institute (RPI) agreed to purchase a nuclear magnetic resonance (NMR) system and VectorShield from Varian for $2,250,000. The system was to be the centerpiece of a new biotech building at RPI. While awaiting performance, RPI became concerned about two aspects of Varian's performance. First, it viewed a similar shield at McGill University and saw that it was less striking in appearance than the one on the manufacturer's website. Second, RPI viewed website specifications indicating

---
[2]   66 U.C.C. Rep. Serv. 2d 152 (N.D.N.Y. 2008).

that the shield needed 22 feet of space when only 21 feet were allotted to the machine in the new building. RPI sought assurances from Varian that the system would fit.

A Varian representative examined the allotted space and provided a scale drawing showing that the system would fit in its anticipated placement. He also raised the possibility of having Varian deliver an actively shielded magnet for the system, which would have removed the need for including the VectorShield altogether, allowing the machine to fit more comfortably in the space.

After further communications indicating differences of opinion within RPI about whether the system would fit into the building, RPI wrote to Varian requesting that Varian stop production and, several months later, RPI cancelled the contract, requesting return of the $900,000 already paid. Varian returned $533,000, retaining $367,000 as damages caused by RPI's cancellation. RPI sued for the return of the remainder of the price paid, arguing it rightfully rescinded the contract because of the incorrect appearance of the unit and because it had reason to believe the system would not fit properly in the biotech building. Both parties moved for summary judgment.

Analysis: With respect to the appearance of the unit, the court determined that, *if* RPI had reasonable grounds for insecurity, its proper action would have been to ask for adequate assurances under section 2-609, but RPI never did so. With respect to the size of the unit, the court determined that RPI had asked for assurances and had received adequate assurances, so the size concern could not serve as a basis for RPI to withhold performance. Accordingly, the court held that RPI had wrongfully cancelled its order for the system, thereby breaching the contract.

Did RPI have reasonable grounds for insecurity with respect to the appearance of the unit (an issue not directly addressed by the court)? What should RPI have done to ask for adequate assurance of performance? What response from Varian would have been sufficient? With respect to the issue of size, do you agree with the court's judgment? If RPI remained unconvinced that Varian would perform, what should RPI have done?

Example C: *Partex Apparel International LTDA S.A. de C.V. v. GFSI, Inc.*[3]

Partex Apparel International, a company located in El Salvador with an office in Florida, and GFSI, Inc., a designer, manufacturer, and marketer of sportswear, had a long-standing relationship for Partex to manufacture sports apparel and deliver it to GFSI for marketing and distribution. In 2010, GFSI placed orders for $1,094,655.75 worth of clothing, which Partex manufactured and shipped. Partex issued invoices to GFSI for the apparel. GFSI thereafter learned that Partex had ceased manufacturing operations. GFSI also received demands from two other entities (Banco Centrroamerico Integracion Economica and Sartee) to pay the invoiced amount directly to them based on money they alleged they were owed by Partex. GFSI asked Partex in writing for "adequate assurances" as to which party should receive payment on the invoices. Partex did not respond to the demand so GFSI continued to withhold payment. Partex filed suit, claiming breach of contract.

Analysis: The court granted Partex's motion for summary judgment as to GFSI's breach of contract, rejecting GFSI's claim that it could suspend performance under 2-609.

What facts support the court's conclusion that GFSI failed to satisfy 2-609? Which part or parts of 2-609 were not satisfied? Was GFSI entitled to demand adequate assurance of performance? Did it do so appropriately?

APPLYING THE CODE

Problem 19-1.

Remuda Jet is a company formed by a group of pilot-investors to purchase six Mustang jets from Cessna. Remuda and Cessna signed a purchase agreement in January 2008 for delivery in late 2010 or early 2011 for a purchase price of $2,995,000 for each plane, with a $175,000 deposit at the time the contract was

---

[3]   2012 WL 1059854 (D. Kan. 2012).

entered and additional deposits due eighteen months and nine months before the anticipated delivery of each jet.

In April 2009, the pilot-investors were informed by another pilot that a Mustang had experienced frozen flight controls, that Cessna had been unable to fix the problem, and that the owner of the jet had ultimately returned it to Cessna. The problem was the subject of five Service Difficulty Reports (SDRs) published in a Federal Aviation Administration database. Two of the pilots (Greenspun and Wihl) reviewed the SDRs and made their own inquiries with other pilots and jet owners but found no other reported problems involving Mustangs. Greenspun raised the frozen flight control problem with Cessna and orally requested more information. A local Cessna sales representative and a regional sales manager informed Greenspun that only one Mustang had experienced the problem and that Cessna was working to identify the cause and engineer a solution.

Before the second deposit ($100,000 for each plane) was due, Greenspun wrote to Cessna and explained that Remuda Jet would withhold further payments until Cessna "has, to our satisfaction, solved the frozen flight control problems reported in the five SDRs. Given the unprecedented nature of a modern jet at 33,000 feet being uncontrollable, we want to make sure that this problem is fully understood before we go forward. A second issue of concern is the impact that these incidents will have on our ability to attract customers. Even if the flight control problem were to be solved eventually, customers may shy away from an aircraft perceived to be unsafe. We would like to know what Cessna is doing to reassure passengers that the Mustang is safe."

Greenspun identified twelve categories of information he "need[ed] to evaluate the situation," including requesting "any information that Cessna has obtained about other problems with the Mustang that could affect the safety of flight." In closing, he asked Cessna to "stop any work that you might be doing on the six airplanes" ordered, explaining that he would consider canceling the orders if "Cessna's response to this request for information does not satisfy Remuda Jet's experts." Remuda Jet made no further payments on the planes and subsequently sued Cessna for breach of contract; Cessna counterclaimed, claiming breach by Remuda.

Cessna has moved for summary judgment on Remuda Jet's breach of contract action, noting that it was Remuda Jet, not Cessna, that ceased performance. In response, Remuda Jet relies on 2-609, claiming that Cessna repudiated the contract by failing to provide adequate assurances regarding aspects of the planes' safety about which Remuda Jet was reasonably insecure.

Based on the information you have, what arguments would you make on behalf of Remuda Jet to support the assertion that Cessna repudiated by failing to provide adequate assurances? What arguments would you make on behalf of Cessna in response? How should the judge rule on the summary judgment motion? If the issue of repudiation under 2-609 proceeds to trial, what questions would you ask one or both parties (or others), as attorney for Remuda Jet? As attorney for Cessna?

B. Anticipatory Repudiation

Anticipatory repudiation refers to statements or actions by one party that indicate in advance that future performance will not be forthcoming—that the party is repudiating the contract. You know from the previous section that repudiation can occur if a party fails to provide adequate assurances upon justifiable demand by the other party. But repudiation may also occur directly, as established in § 2-610.

Reading the Code: § 2-610

Read 2-610 and its Comments.

Question 7. What do the Comments tell you about what words or actions will result in a conclusion that a party has repudiated the contract?

Question 8. 2-610 lists several actions a party may take after repudiation by the other party. Are those actions justified after all repudiations, or are there are some restrictions on when the non-repudiating party may act?

Question 9. What is the relationship among the options for action described in 2-610(a), (b), and (c)? Must the aggrieved party choose only one action to take? If not, what combinations of actions are authorized or contemplated? Is the initial choice made by the aggrieved party final?

Example D: *Al-Misehal Commercial Group, Ltd. v. Armored Group, LLC.*[4]

Al-Misehal Commercial Group, Ltd. (Al-Misehal), a Saudi Arabian company, ordered seven custom Ford Excursion sport utility vehicles from The Armored Group, LLC (TAG,) to be delivered on September 6, 2006. Al-Misehal requested TAG to armor three of the vehicles with remotely operated weapons and four with "BombJammers" to defend against improvised explosive devices. On April 10, 2006, TAG contracted with Homeland Security Strategies, Inc. (HSS) for the "BombJammers." Questions arose concerning HSS's ability to perform, so on May 13, 2006, TAG requested assurances from HSS. After TAG did not receive any assurances from HSS, Al-Misehal expressed concern about HSS's performance in an email to TAG. TAG and Al-Misehal discussed the possibility of using substitute jammers; at one point in the correspondence, Al-Misehal seemed to approve the substitution, but later said it was not willing to accept substitutes and indicated it was convinced HSS would not perform. As late as June 10, 2006, TAG assured Al-Misehal that it still believed HSS would perform on time. On June 29, 2006, Al-Misehal cancelled the contract with TAG, saying that HSS's failure to perform meant that TAG could not meet the September 6 delivery date. Al-Misehal sued TAG for breach of contract and moved for summary judgment alleging that TAG had repudiated the contract under 2-609 and 2-610.

Analysis: The court denied summary judgment, concluding that Al-Misehal had not sufficiently demonstrated an "overt communication of intention or an action which renders performance impossible or demonstrates a clear determination not to continue with performance." When the fact-finder considers at trial whether TAG repudiated the contract, what arguments would you expect each side to make? If you were the judge, how would you rule with respect to repudiation under 2-609? Under 2-610?

---

[4] 2011 WL 4543924 (D. Ariz. 2011).

Example E: *Doral Steel, Inc. v. Gray Metal Prods., Inc.*[5]

On July 1, 2008, Gray Metal Products (GMP) submitted to Doral Steel, Inc. a purchase order for hot dip galvanized steel of various widths and gauges. The purchase order called for 875 metric tons of steel to be delivered at the "end of July 2008" for a total purchase price of $1.24 million. On July 29, 2008, Richard Gray (Purchasing Manager for Gray Metal Products) sent an email to John Spoerl (Sales Rep for Doral) asking Doral to "move a couple hundred tons of steel to another customer," presumably because it was not needed. Spoerl refused to reduce the tons from GMP's order, but did agree to "work a little longer on the time frame and spread [the shipments] out in August." Starting in August 2008, GMP issued a number of partial releases on the purchase order authorizing Doral to ship some of the steel. GMP accepted and paid for all shipments of this released steel.

On August 8, 2008, Gray sent another email to Spoerl stating "you are going to need to work with us on this, or we will be forced to cancel some of the tonnage." During this time, the price of steel was declining dramatically. One month later, GMP placed an order for steel with a different vendor, which order was substantially the same as GMP's previous order from Doral. On September 26, 2008, Doral shipped to another customer coils of steel originally designated for GMP.

On September 30, 2008, Gray sent another email to Spoerl stating that GMP "will not be able to take any more of this material unless the pricing is adjusted drastically." Spoerl replied that Doral might be able to adjust the pricing if GMP were willing to take more tons than specified in the purchase order. However, the parties never reached an agreement to modify the price or quantity.

Gray sent another email to Spoerl on October 22, 2008:

> John, after reviewing the new proposal from you and looking at what we have in inventory along with the price of steel in the low .50 a pound range we can not bring in anymore material from Doral. I am sorry but this is the position we have to take to protect our companies. If the pricing was closer to current market conditions we would be able to probably do something but with the current drop we are being forced to adjust our pricing in several markets.

---

[5] 672 F. Supp. 2d 798 (N.D. Ohio 2009).

GMP did not issue any more releases and refused to accept any more steel after October 2008. There was no further contact between Doral and GMP until early February 2009, when Mike Crooks (Vice President of Doral) called Gray, who confirmed he would not take any more steel. On February 17, Doral's legal counsel sent GMP a letter demanding reasonable assurance that GMP would accept and pay for the remaining steel under the purchase order. GMP did not respond to the letter, and Doral filed a suit on April 1 claiming breach of contract.

Analysis: The court concluded that GMP repudiated the contract under 2-610 either at the end of October or by mid-November 2008. Why did the court choose those dates and not earlier or later? Would it have been possible for the court to conclude that GMP repudiated under 2-609?

C. Retraction of Repudiation

By definition, a repudiation occurs before performance is due and therefore before a breach has occurred. The repudiating party therefore may have an opportunity to retract the repudiation and restore the expectation that it will perform.

**Reading the Code:
§ 2-611**

Read 2-611 and its Comments.

Question 10. When is retraction no longer an option for the repudiating party?

Question 11. How does the repudiating party make an effective retraction?

Question 12. What are the consequences that flow from a retraction? What happens to performance responsibilities? Who is responsible for the costs or damages caused by any performance delays arising from the repudiation?

D. Excuse from Performance

Parties enter into contracts in order to plan future activity, knowing that their contractual obligations will remain the same even if (or especially if) circumstances change after the contract is formed. The market price of goods may rise, but the seller will still be committed to providing the goods at the contract price, protecting the buyer's expectations. The buyer's need or desire for the goods may change, but the buyer will still be committed to paying for the goods ordered, thus protecting the seller's expectations.

Because it is understood that contracts hedge against the risk of change, the early common law concluded that contractual duties were almost entirely absolute and not excusable merely because of unanticipated circumstances. But sometimes circumstances change drastically or in unexpected ways, so the common law and later the UCC developed a somewhat more flexible view of when inability or failure to perform might be excused rather than considered a breach of contract. Sections 2-613 to 2-616 establish the rules for excuse in Article 2, supplementing (but not entirely replacing) the common law doctrines of impossibility and frustration of purpose. As you will see, §§ 2-613 and 2-614 create limited exceptions to the absolute obligation to perform if the goods are damaged or destroyed or if the methods expected to be used for delivery or payment are not available. Section 2-615 creates a broader exception in circumstances of "commercial impracticability," but as you will see, that broad exception is only rarely invoked successfully to excuse performance, reflecting the underlying assumptions about the continuity of contractual obligation in the face of changing commercial realities.

1. Casualty to Identified Goods

Reading the Code:
§ 2-613

Read 2-613 and its Comments.

Question 13. Which party or parties may be excused under the provisions of 2-613?

Question 14. Ignoring for now the reference to a "no arrival, no sale" term, what are the four facts that must be established for the protected party to claim excuse under 2-613?

Question 15. When does 2-613(a) apply, and what are the consequences if it does? When does 2-613(b) apply, and what are the consequences if it does? What is the meaning of the final clause ("but without further right against the seller")?

Question 16. If the seller's negligence causes the damage to or destruction of the goods, may the seller invoke the protections in 2-613? What happens if the buyer's negligence causes the damage?

Question 17. For the purposes of applying 2-613, does it matter if the goods were already damaged when the contract was made (common law "mistake" doctrine) or instead were damaged after that time (common law "impossibility" doctrine)?

Question 18. What is a "no arrival, no sale" clause, and how does 2-613 apply if the contract contains one?

Question 19. May the parties agree that excuse under 2-613 will not be available to one or both parties?

EXAMPLES AND ANALYSIS

Example F: *Lane-Lott v. White*[6]

Harold and Anne White brokered a deal between Laura Lane-Lott and Gerald Gambrel for Lane-Lott to trade her quarter-horse mare, Ima Slow Lopin Dream, for Gambrel's mare, Kcees Time to Skeik, which was at the time being boarded at the Whites' farm for breeding. Lane-Lott testified that she accepted the swap offer because she was familiar with Kcees' bloodline, which in her estimation made the horse valuable. At the time of the swap, the horse delivered to Lane-Lott was pregnant. After the swap

---
6   126 So. 3d 1016 (Miss. Ct. App. 2013).

and after the mare gave birth, Lane-Lott attempted to register the foal with the American Quarter Horse Association. DNA testing revealed that the mare Lane-Lott had received was not Kcees, but a different horse, Miss Savannah. The parties later determined that Gambrel had mistakenly picked up Miss Savannah when that horse and Kcees were both being boarded at the Whites' farm earlier in the year; when the mare was returned to the Whites for breeding, both Gambrel and the Whites continued to believe the horse was Kcees. The Whites compensated the owners of Miss Savannah for what they mistakenly thought was the loss of their horse. The second horse (thought by all at the time to be Miss Savannah, but in fact Kcees) was never found. According to the court, "[w]hile it is unclear whether Kcees had gone to that great pasture in the sky or was just in another earthly pasture at the time of the agreement, what is clear is that both parties were laboring under the misconception that the mare that had been impregnated was Kcees."

Lane-Lott sued Gambrel and the Whites for breach of contract and fraud. The defendants moved to dismiss the breach claim, relying on 2-613.

Analysis: The court avoided the contract under 2-613, noting that the principle underlying the common law mistake doctrine "carries over" into Article 2 through 2-613. How would you expect the court to explain the result, citing to the particular facts and statutory language to support the outcome? What argument might you make on behalf of Lane-Lott that the requirements of 2-613 were not met?

2. Substituted Performance for Delivery or Payment

As indicated by its title, § 2-614 is about substituted performance rather than about excusing performance. It mandates that, under certain specified circumstances, the available substitute performance must be tendered by the performing party and must be accepted by the other party.

Reading the Code: § 2-614

Read 2-614 and its Comments.

Question 20. Rewrite 2-614(1) as an "If . . . Then . . ." statement to clarify the elements required to establish the obligation to tender and accept substitute performance. To which phrase or phrases does "but a commercially reasonable substitute is available" apply?

Question 21. 2-614(2) applies "[i]f the agreed means or manner of payment fails because of domestic or foreign governmental regulation." What are the consequences of such an event if the goods have not yet been delivered? What are the consequences if the goods have already been delivered?

EXAMPLES AND ANALYSIS

Example G: *Hansen-Mueller Co. v. Gau* [7]

Farmer Scott Gau agreed to sell to Hansen-Mueller, a grain elevator company, 7500 bushels of yellow corn at a price of $4.35 per bushel, to be shipped between June 1 and June 30, 2011, to the company's grain elevator in Council Bluffs, Iowa. Because of the threat of impending flooding in and around the area of the grain elevator in the spring and summer of 2011, Hansen-Mueller refused to accept the corn delivery from Gau, claiming storage at the facility had become impractical. Hansen-Mueller accepted other deliveries at Council Bluffs to blend with the supply on hand so the company could remove the grain. Gau offered to deliver the corn to another Hansen-Mueller elevator but the company refused. On July 18, Gau cancelled the contract because of Hansen-Mueller's failure to take delivery. Gau stored the corn until he sold it in October 2011 for $6.10 per bushel. Hansen-Mueller filed suit to recover $22,425, the difference between the

---

[7]   838 N.W.2d 138 (Iowa Ct. App. 2013). Note that this case was also discussed in Assignment 16.

parties' contract price and the market price on the date.g.u repudiated the contract. Hansen-Mueller claimed that it had not breached the contract when it refused delivery because delivery had become impracticable, so Gau did not have the right to cancel the contract for failure of performance. Gau counterclaimed for damages for costs of storage and transport of the corn. The trial court granted Gau's motion for summary judgment and dismissed Hansen-Mueller's claim, finding that Gau was justified in canceling the contract. Hansen-Mueller appealed.

Analysis: The court of appeals rejected Hansen-Mueller's claim of excuse, affirmed the grant of summary judgment for Gau, and remanded for consideration of Gau's counterclaim. Under 2-614, "a commercially reasonable substitute" for delivery to Council Bluffs was available, Gau tendered that substitute performance, and Hansen-Mueller was required to accept it. Section 2-614 rather than 2-615 was applicable because the impossibility of performance arose "in connection with an incidental matter" (place of delivery) rather than going "to the very heart of the agreement" (as in the case of total destruction of the source of supply).

Example H: *Macromex SRL v. Globex International, Inc.*[8]

Macromex, a Romanian company, agreed to buy from Globex International, an American company, 112 containers of chicken parts to be delivered in Romania by May 29, 2006. By June 2, 2006, Globex had shipped only 50 containers. On June 7, the Romanian Government declared, without notice, that no chicken could be imported into Romania unless it was certified by June 7. Globex was able to certify and deliver 20 more containers of chickens, but could not ship the remaining 42 containers to Romania. Macromex proposed that Globex ship to a port in Georgia, a nearby country. Another of Macromex's American suppliers had agreed to such a change in another contract, but Globex refused and resold the 42 containers of chickens at the now-higher market price. Macromex brought arbitration proceedings against Globex to recover the $608,323 excess Globex received in the resale. The contract was governed by the Convention on the International Sale of Goods, but the arbitrator relied on UCC 2-614 to clarify the CISG provisions and award relief to Macromex. Macromex petitioned the U.S. District Court for confirmation of the award; Globex petitioned to vacate

---

[8]   65 U.C.C. Rep. Serv. 2d 1033 (S.D.N.Y. 2008).

the award, claiming the arbitrator's application of 2-614 was "manifest disregard of the law."

Analysis: The court upheld the award, confirming that 2-614 was appropriately applied. How would you expect the court to support that result?

3. Excuse by Failure of Presupposed Conditions

Reading the Code:
§§ 2-615 and 2-616

Read 2-615 and Comment 1 and 2-616.

Question 22. According to 2-615, what is required to prevent "delay in delivery or non-delivery in whole or part by a seller" from being a breach of contract?

The wording of the excuse standard in § 2-615(a) is a bit convoluted, but in essence the provision excuses delay or non-delivery if the promised performance has become "impracticable" for one of two reasons:

(1) as a result of the parties' good faith compliance with a governmental regulation or order, or

(2) because the parties made a "basic assumption" about the context for contract performance that turned out to wrong. (Section 2-615(a) says the basic assumption was about "the non-occurrence" of a "contingency" that ended up occurring. Comment 1 talks about the occurrence of "unforeseen . . . circumstances" that were "not within the contemplation of the parties at the time of contracting.")

The seller must comply with § 2-615(b) and (c) by treating all buyers fairly if there is a delay or reduction rather than a total inability to deliver and by notifying the buyer seasonably about the delay or non-delivery. Under § 2-616, after such notification, the buyer has the option of taking the partial delivery "in substitution" or of terminating the contract and discharging the seller from responsibility for unexecuted portions of the contract. The buyer's silence will be understood as choosing the latter option.

You should already see that defining "impracticable" and "basic assumption" is crucial for applying § 2-615. Although the Comments will be somewhat helpful in that endeavor, the courts have provided most of the context for understanding the meaning of the section.

Reading the Code: § 2-615

Read Comments 1 through 11 of 2-615.

As you read each Comment, make a bullet list of each point that may help you further understand and then apply 2-615. Be sure you can answer the following questions:

Question 23. May the parties agree that excuse under 2-615 will not be available to the seller?

Question 24. Is it possible that a seller may be partially rather than fully excused from liability for delayed delivery or non-delivery?

Question 25. If the unexpected circumstances involve destruction of goods, does 2-615 apply?

Question 26. Will a seller be excused from performing if the cost of the seller's raw materials doubles?

EXAMPLES AND ANALYSIS

As noted above, 2-615 can only be understood in the context of court decisions delineating what kinds of events are "unforeseen" and "not in the contemplation of the parties" and what challenges to performance are considered to make the performance "impracticable." The following Examples should provide some guidance although, as one commentator has suggested, you may not find complete clarity or consistency.[9] The commercial impracticability issue is often raised in circumstances that also raise questions about good faith adjustments, demands for adequate assurances, and possible repudiation. As you will see, the courts rarely find contracting parties excused from performance based on supervening circumstances.

Example I: *BRC Rubber & Plastics, Inc. v. Continental Carbon Co.*[10]

Continental Carbon Co. (Continental) manufactures furnace-grade carbon black, a raw material filler used in tires and other rubber and plastic products. BRC Rubber & Plastics, Inc. (BRC) was a longtime customer of Continental, purchasing three grades of carbon black for incorporation into numerous rubber products it supplies to its customers. The parties entered a five-year supply agreement in 2010 that obligated Continental to supply and BRC to purchase all BRC's requirements of three grades of carbon black for the five-year term of the contract. The contract projected that BRC would purchase approximately 1.8 million pounds annually. It set a firm price schedule for amounts between 1.5 and 2.1 million pounds, but also specified a graduated price rebate for amounts above 2.1 or 2.2 million pounds and a graduated price penalty for amounts below 1.5 or 1.4 million pounds.

With the rebounding of both the automotive industry and the overall economy, BRC's requirements for carbon black increased, as did the demand for carbon black from other customers of Continental. Despite the high demand, Continental was operating at a loss and sought a two-cent-a-pound

---

9   "Despite the hope that section 2-615 and [Restatement 2d of Contracts] section 261 would lead to wide acceptance of commercial impracticability both under Article 2 and the common law, courts continue to rarely excuse a party under the doctrine of commercial impracticability. Even more rare, are judicial decisions discussing commercial impracticability in any meaningful way. The few cases that do discuss it developed muddled and inconsistent rules, leading to an unpredictable and confusing doctrine that fails to serve its intended purpose." Jennifer Camero, Mission Impracticable: The Impossibility of Commercial Impracticability, 13 U.N.H. Law Rev. 1, 6 (2015) (footnotes omitted).

10   949 F. Supp. 2d 862 (N.D. Ind. 2013).

increase in base price. All of Continental's customers except BRC agreed to the increase; BRC refused.

When Continental could not keep up with the demand for carbon black, it began allocating its available supply among its customers. When Continental failed to confirm some orders from BRC, BRC asked for adequate assurances of performance. Subsequently, there were conflicting messages from Continental employees, some indicating Continental would ship under the original contract, some indicating shipments would be withheld unless BRC agreed to the price increase. After Continental failed to fill some of BRC's orders, BRC terminated the agreement, filed suit, and moved for summary judgment. Continental defended by claiming that BRC ordered amounts of carbon black in bad faith and beyond what was contemplated by the requirements contract and that Continental's failure to deliver should be excused because of commercial impracticability based on increased demand for carbon black and the fact that one of the two carbon black reactors Continental used to produce the product was down for maintenance for several weeks.

Analysis: The court granted BRC's motion for summary judgment. With respect to Continental's claim that BRC had increased its ordering in bad faith, the court noted that, to be considered in good faith, "the buyer must be motivated by considerations 'independent of the terms of the contract or any other aspect of [the buyer's] relationship with [the seller].'" The court found that BRC ordered amounts to protect against fluctuations in the automotive market and to have adequate supplies on hand. It found "no evidence upon which a reasonable factfinder could find, or even infer, that BRC's purchasing methods changed in any way due to a shift in the carbon black market."

With respect to Continental's claim that BRC ordered amounts disproportionate to stated estimates (see 2-306), the court found the amounts within the contemplated range in the contract, especially since the contract expressly provided for purchase of larger amounts by specifying a price break above the top of the stated range.

The court found that Continental had repudiated the contract by failing to provide adequate assurances of performance after demand by BRC and by claiming, incorrectly, that it was not required to satisfy BRC's requirements, but only to send 1.8 million pounds per year. While a party may temporarily err in its interpretation of a contract without being found to have repudiated, Continental's continued refusal to send more carbon black constituted repudiation.

Finally, with respect to Continental's reliance on 2-615, the court concluded that no reasonable factfinder could excuse Continental's breach. Routine annual maintenance was not unanticipated and therefore could not constitute commercial impracticability as a matter of law. Further, the record contained "a plethora of evidence that Continental did not allocate among its customers in a fair and reasonable manner," but instead did so to maximize its profits. Continental refused to ship to BRC because BRC refused Continental's request for a price increase, and explicitly failed to ship to fourteen customers, including BRC, due to a negative gross profit on those contracts. In addition, during the alleged shortage period, several of Continental's customers received significantly more carbon black than was designated for them in Continental's Annual Operating Plan, and Continental supplied other customers in a month when it told BRC that it had no product "available at the moment."

BRC Rubber & Plastics demonstrates that, although determinations with respect to commercial impracticability (and repudiation) are often within the judgment of the factfinder, decisions as to both issues may be made as a matter of law where the evidence is especially strong or weak.

Example J: *Rochester Gas & Electric Corp. v. Delta Star, Inc.*[11]

On June 15, 2005, Delta Star agreed to sell to Rochester Gas & Electric Corp. (RG&E) eight electrical transformers for a total price of $5,586,664. On December 21, 2005, Delta Star wrote to RG&E asking for a price increase based on high demand (and consequently much higher prices) for core steel needed in constructing the transformers, as well as a need to modify some designs to accommodate substitute grades of core steel. RG&E refused the price increase, but agreed to discuss modification to the delivery dates and grades of steel to be used, as well as to loan Delta Star some funds to help it deal with the price increases. RG&E requested adequate assurances of performance but, in the words of RG&E, "instead received a diatribe 'venting' in attempt to intimidate and coerce [RG&E] to give in to Delta Star's demands." RG&E said it viewed Delta Star's

---

[11]   68 U.C.C Rep. Serv. 2d 130 (W.D.N.Y. 2009).

actions as a repudiation and terminated the agreement. RG&E sued for breach of contract. Delta Star raised the affirmative defense of commercial impracticability, and RG&E moved to strike the defense as insufficient.

Analysis: The court granted RG&E's application to strike the defense, ruling that the increase in price cannot excuse performance "unless the rise in cost is due to some unforeseen contingency which alters the essential nature of the performance" (Comment 4). Delta Star's allegation that government-run companies in China were buying up supplies of steel and causing a substantial shortage in this country was also not sufficient; "governmental interference cannot excuse unless it truly 'supervenes' in such a manner as to be beyond the seller's assumption of risk" (Comment 10). Applying a statement of the Second Circuit, the court noted that "[t]he mere fact that this undertaking may have become burdensome, as a result of subsequent, perhaps unanticipated, developments, does not operate to relieve [Delta Star] of [its] obligation."

Do you think it mattered that RG&E offered to discuss modifications to the transformer design using different grades of steel? Do you think the outcome would be different if no such substitutions would be possible?

Example K: *Mid-Am Building Supply, Inc. v. Schmidt Builders Supply, Inc.*[12]

Mid-Am Building Supply agreed to sell building supplies to Schmidt Builders Supply on credit. Kaw Valley Bank was a secured lender to Schmidt. Some time after Mid-Am delivered goods to Schmidt, Schmidt's business faced financial difficulties, resulting in a settlement agreement that terminated Schmidt's business operations and required Schmidt to surrender all of its assets to the bank. When Mid-Am sued Schmidt for breach of contract for failure to pay invoices in the amount of $455,739.49, Schmidt defended by claiming commercial impracticability under 2-615 because it could no longer make payments to Mid-Am. Mid-Am moved for summary judgment on its claim.

---

[12]   2013 WL 1308980 (D. Kan. 2013).

Analysis: The court granted summary judgment to Mid-Am. In rejecting the excuse of commercial impracticability, the court noted the following:

- Schmidt did not show that it was legally obligated to enter into the contract with the bank that terminated its business operations, so it did not demonstrate payment to Mid-Am was not possible.

- Schmidt failed to show that the non-occurrence of the contingency (the bank's closure of its business) was a basic assumption on which the contract was made, noting that the continued existence of certain market conditions or financial conditions of the parties is ordinarily not a basic assumption of contracting parties.

- Schmidt failed to establish that the closure of its business was unforeseeable and not an assumed risk. "When the contingency in question is sufficiently foreshadowed at the time of contracting, the contingency may be considered among the business risks that are regarded as part of the negotiated terms of the contract, either consciously or as a matter of reasonable, commercial interpretation from the circumstances." Similarly, if the promisor has no power to prevent the contingency but has superior knowledge of the possibility that it might happen, the promisor may be assumed to have taken the risk. Schmidt had been in the business of supplying construction materials from 1946 to 2011, and therefore would have superior knowledge about market conditions, its own financial situation, its debts to the bank and other creditors, and the possibility that financial difficulty would lead to business closure. Thus the possibility that Schmidt's business would close due to financial inability to make payments was "likely foreseeable" to Schmidt.

The court also rejected the common law defense of frustration of purpose because that defense, like commercial impracticability under 2-615, requires that the supervening events be unforeseeable.

As noted, the court based its determination partly on its conclusion that the changed circumstances were not "unforeseeable." The suggestion that an event must be "unforeseeable" is made in many cases, though neither 2-615 nor its Comments use that term. What is the difference between proving the event is "unforeseeable" and proving it was "unforeseen" (Comment 4) or that its non-occurrence was a "basic assumption on which the contract was made" (2-615(a))? Which formulation makes it more likely that an excuse may be found?

APPLYING THE CODE

For each of the problems below, determine which excuse provision(s) might apply and whether each of the required elements of that provision or provisions is likely satisfied for the seller or buyer claiming excuse. If you need more information to determine if an excuse provision applies or would be satisfied, identify the information you would seek and how the additional information would affect the application of the provision.

Problem 19-2.

Buyer and Seller enter a contract for sale of grain, to be shipped via railroad on April 28 for arrival on May 1. On April 27, Seller is notified of a shortage of rail cars for transport. Seller notifies Buyer that the grain will be shipped instead by truck and will arrive on May 3.

Problem 19-3.

Buyer, a retail jewelry store, and Seller, a manufacturer of watches, enter a contract for sale of two dozen watches, F.O.B. Buyer's store. The shipment of watches is damaged in transit when the truck carrying them is involved in an accident caused by the driver of another vehicle. Seller fails to deliver any watches to Buyer.

Problem 19-4.

Lunches To Go, Inc. (LTG) enters a contract to furnish milk to a school district for the entire school year at a designated price. LTG plans to purchase the milk wholesale on the market and package it in half-pint containers for delivery. Halfway through the school year, the market price of milk increases 50% due to unusually severe crop failures, which causes a large increase in the price of feed for dairy cows. LTG declines to deliver milk for the remainder of the year.

Problem 19-5.

In April, ALPAC Trading Company agreed to sell to Eagon Forest Products 15,000 cubic meters of logs at a designated price, to be shipped from Argentina to Korea between the end of July and the end of August. The contract was arranged by Setsuo Kimura, ALPAC's president, and C.K. Ahn, an Eagon vice president. In the months following the agreement, the market for logs began to soften (the price dropped), and ALPAC became concerned that Eagon would try to cancel the contract. In fact, Eagon internally expressed concern about the drop in timber prices; Eagon's vice president Ahn sent several memoranda to the home office noting that the corporation might not wish to go through with the deal given the drop in timber prices, but saying that acceptance of the logs was "inevitable" under the contract.

On August 23, Eagon received the following faxed letter from ALPAC:

> I understand, and recognize your troubles to sell, and concerns about the Korean market at this time. Therefore, as a seller, I (ALPAC) will offer you to reduce volume and price . . .

> We have approx. 21,000 cubic meters of logs around port of Campana, Argentina, now. Therefore, I hope you can find times to check logs with me toward end of August to early Sept.

> Please let me know by return fax when is the best time to go over there.

Eagon did not respond to the fax. In a business meeting soon afterward, ALPAC president Kimura asked Eagon's vice-president Ahn whether he intended to accept the logs. Ahn admitted that he was having trouble getting approval from the home office and noted that Eagon would be losing money if it accepted delivery of the logs. On August 30, Ahn sent a letter to the home office stating he would attempt to avoid acceptance of the logs, but that it would be difficult and suggesting that they hold ALPAC responsible for shipment delay.

ALPAC canceled the vessel that it had reserved for shipping the logs because it believed that Eagon was canceling the contract. The logs were not loaded or shipped by August 31, but Ahn and Kimura continued to discuss the contract into September. On September 7, Ahn told Kimura that he would continue to try to convince headquarters to accept the delivery and indicated that he did not want Kimura to sell the logs to another buyer. The same day, Ahn sent a letter to Eagon's home office indicating that "the situation of our supplier is extremely grave" and that Eagon should consider accepting the shipment in September.

On September 27, ALPAC sent a letter to Eagon saying that Eagon had breached the contract by failing to confirm it would take delivery of the logs; Eagon replied that ALPAC, not Eagon, had breached, by failing to ship the logs. ALPAC sued, claiming breach by Eagon. Eagon moved for summary judgment, arguing that ALPAC breached by failing to deliver the logs. ALPAC defended by claiming Eagon failed to provide adequate assurances of performance or had affirmatively repudiated the contract.

Assume that the UCC would apply to the contract between ALPAC and Eagon.

(a) Evaluate ALPAC's claim that Eagon had breached the contract, either by failing to provide assurances of adequate performance or by affirmatively repudiating.

(b) If you were representing ALPAC, what actions would you have taken in July after concerns were raised about whether Eagon would accept delivery of the logs to best protect your client's interests?

(c) Assume Eagon told ALPAC in August that it would not take delivery of the logs because the market in Korea had "bottomed out" so that the logs were worth only 10% of the contract price. Would Eagon have a viable excuse under 2-615 for not accepting delivery?

(d) Assume governmental environmental restrictions were placed on logging and exporting from Argentina in June, decreasing the supply of logs, doubling the production cost to ALPAC and increasing the market price for the logs by 60%. Would ALPAC have a viable excuse under 2-615 for failing to ship the logs to Eagon?

4. Force Majeure Clauses

Sections 2-613, 2-614, and 2-615 specify default presumptions about the power of buyers and sellers to claim excuse when circumstances change after the contract is entered. The parties may agree to modification of those default presumptions, typically in a "force majeure" clause.

A "force majeure" clause may be drafted to serve one or more of the following functions:

- Specifying and clarifying aspects of the excuse doctrine (e.g., articulating circumstances that the parties assume will continue and why that continuation is a basic assumption on which the contract is made; specifying which risks are allocated to which party; defining how much difficulty in performance is necessary to create impracticability);

- Adding events that can serve as excuses (for instance, strikes, economic downturns, technology failures, etc.); or

- "Contracting out" of the default rules on excuse.

In drafting and reviewing force majeure clauses, the parties should consider not only events that will impede seller's performance (e.g., labor actions, severe weather, transportation interruption, acts of war), but also those that might cause extraordinary difficulty for the buyer (changes in marketability for resale, changes that will impact buyer's need for the goods) as well as how to allocate the burdens that might arise from excuse.

APPLYING THE CODE

Problem 19-6.

The purchasing agent for your corporate client is negotiating a purchase agreement for electronic parts that your client needs in its manufacturing operation. Seller has proposed its standard clause for force majeure:

> The vendor is excused from breach in the event of war, nuclear holocaust, embargo of essential parts, strike, earthquake, fire, flood, and other sources of substantial delay or destruction beyond vendor's control.

The purchasing agent is seeking advice about whether to accept this clause or bargain for another alternative.

(a) How does this clause interact with the excuse rules in the UCC? Does it pre-empt, duplicate, or supplement?

(b) Which particular exemptions are inadvisable for practical, factual, or strategic reasons?

(c) What aspects of the clause could be drafted with greater clarity? Write better language.

(d) Would the force majeure clause above protect the buyer or seller in the circumstances presented in Problems 19-2 to 19-5? If not, what language might protect the party who otherwise would seek excuse? Would you advise your client to press for inclusion of such language in the contract?

Chapter 8

Engaging with Third Parties in Complex Sales Transactions

Key Concepts

- The function of documents of title and drafts in documentary transactions
- The difference between "negotiable" and "non-negotiable" documents of title and drafts
- The application of Article 2 rules for tender, risk of loss, buyer's obligation to pay, and buyer's right to inspect in documentary transactions
- The derivative title rule
- Voidable and void title
- Good faith purchasers for value
- Buyers in the ordinary course of business

Chapter 7 examined the complex practices and rules through which Article 2 regulates the rights and duties of buyers and sellers in the performance stage, when seller tenders and transfers title to the goods and buyer tenders payment. This Chapter explores two related issues: how title to the goods may be transferred and what happens if there is a defect in the title to the goods being sold.

Assignment 20 introduces you to the rules for documentary transactions. Documentary transactions are contracts for the sale of goods in which the parties choose to tender rights to the goods and rights to payment by using "documents of title" and "drafts," specialized documents defined in UCC Articles 3 and 7 and referenced in Article 2, instead of tendering the goods and payment directly. You will see how Article 2 accommodates the use of such documents and the variations that result in the general rules for tender, risk of loss, a buyer's obligation to pay, and a buyer's right to inspect.

Assignment 21 addresses issues that arise when a buyer resells goods bought from another but had defective title to the goods arising from her own purchase transaction. What are the rights of buyers further down the chain who may know nothing about the blemish on the title to the goods? These complex questions are addressed in § 2-403, the focus of Assignment 21.

Assignment 20

Shipping and Paying Using Documents of Title and Drafts

§§ 2-310, 2-503, 2-504, 2-505, 2-512, 2-513

LEARNING OUTCOMES AND OBJECTIVES

At the completion of this Assignment, you should be able to

- identify and define the kinds of documents that are part of a documentary transaction in a sale of goods;

- identify when article 2 permits or requires parties to use documents of title and drafts;

- identify how the buyer and seller perform their tender obligations in a documentary transaction; and

- determine if and when a buyer has the right to inspect the goods when documents of title are used.

As specified in § 2-301, "the obligation of the seller is to transfer and deliver and that of the buyer is to accept and pay in accordance with the contract." The transfer of goods and payment between the parties is straight-forward if the buyer and seller are in close proximity to one another. As explored in Chapter 7, the seller tenders the goods by delivering them to the buyer or making them available for pickup; title passes to the goods when they are physically delivered to the buyer; the buyer inspects the goods and then pays the seller, using cash, check, or electronic payment. If the seller is concerned about the seller's ability or willingness to pay, it may require advance payment in part or full. With no middleman involved, the seller has control over the goods until delivery and the buyer can see the goods before making payment.

However, many contracts involve buyers and sellers located at a distance from each other, with the parties using third party carriers to transport the goods. Under these circumstances, the transfer of goods and money presents additional challenges.

The seller may wish to retain control over the goods in the hands of the carrier until assured of payment by the buyer and be able to redirect the goods elsewhere if the buyer repudiates while the goods are in transit. Or the seller may wish to transfer its right to collect from the buyer to a third party. The seller may even sometimes ship goods to a distant location while still negotiating with prospective buyers in that market. And buyers in such transactions may want to be assured of delivery before turning funds over to the seller.

A mechanism developed to assist buyers and sellers in transferring goods and payment in the flexible manner desired is a "documentary transaction." Documents (which may be in paper or electronic format) are created that represent the right to take possession of the goods and the right to receive payment of allocated funds, and those documents can be placed into the hands of particular persons (individuals or commercial entities) to effectuate the "delivery" of goods and money by passing the paper (or its electronic equivalent) from hand to hand. Transfer of documents is easier, quicker, and more flexible than transfer of the underlying property (especially the underlying goods), so the delivery of goods and payment can be effectively manipulated while also protecting the interests of buyers and sellers separated by distance.

The two kinds of documents typically used in a sale-of-goods transaction are documents of title (representing the right to the goods) and drafts (representing the right to payment). Those two kinds of documents are governed by provisions in UCC Article 7 (Documents of Title) and Article 3 (Negotiable Instruments). In this Assignment, we will introduce important concepts from those two Articles of the Code, but the primary focus will be on the Article 2 provisions that specify whether parties are permitted or required by the contract to set up a documentary transaction and how the use of documents impacts tender and other Article 2 rules.

As already indicated, documentary transactions may be effectuated using actual pieces of paper (documents of title and drafts), but modern transactions increasingly involve documentary transactions represented electronically. For ease of reference, we will usually refer to "documents" and the transfer of "paper" representing goods and money, but you should understand throughout that all the documents may be electronic as well as tangible.[1]

---

[1]   UETA and E-SIGN (covered in Assignment 14) do not apply to documents of title or drafts (*see* 15 U.S.C. § 7003(a)(3); UETA § 3(b)(2)), but the sections of the UCC governing those types of documents offer their own accommodations to electronic commerce. Detailed discussion of those accommodations is beyond the scope of this book, but may be covered in a course on Payments Systems or Negotiable Instruments.

A. Documents of Title

A "document of title" is a "record" (a tangible or electronic representation of information) that identifies particular goods and gives the person possessing the document the right to "receive, control, hold, and dispose of *the record and the goods the record covers*" (§§ 1-201(b)(16), (31)) (emphasis supplied). A document of title is issued by a third party who takes possession of the goods—typically a warehouse or a carrier of goods, called a "bailee")—and given to the seller when the seller delivers the goods to be held or shipped. A document of title may be a bill of lading ("lading" means loading a vessel with cargo), a warehouse receipt, a dock warrant or receipt, a transport document, or an order for delivery of goods (all listed in § 1-201(b)(16)). In each case, it represents a receipt from the storage company or carrier acknowledging that the particular goods were received from the seller (the "consignor") and, if the goods will be transported, identifying where and to whom the goods will be sent (the "consignee"). An example of a simple document of title—in this instance, a bill of lading—is on the next page.

Because a document of title gives the holder the right to "receive . . . and dispose of the goods" it covers, the seller who receives the document of title from the bailee has the power to control whether and when the bailee will deliver the goods to the buyer. Even once the goods arrive at the shipping destination, the buyer will not have the right to receive the goods until the seller allows that to happen, and the seller can, if it chooses, wait to take that action until the buyer has paid or committed to paying.

In order to explain how that transfer happens, and the implications for both seller and buyer, we need to introduce you to another concept: negotiability.

1. Negotiable v. Non-Negotiable Documents of Title

Documents of title come in two varieties: "negotiable" and "non-negotiable." The difference between them is how the documents are transferred from person to person (e.g., seller to buyer or seller to bank to buyer) and whether the person who wants to get the goods from the bailee (e.g., the buyer) must have the custody and control of the document of title in order to do so.

If a bill of lading or warehouse receipt is *negotiable*, the holder of the document *must* deliver it to the carrier or warehouse in order to retrieve the goods held by the bailee, and the bailee may not deliver the goods to anyone but the holder of the document. As a result, once the buyer receives a negotiable document of title

Bill of Lading

ORIGINAL—NOT NEGOTIABLE

RECEIVED, subject to the classifications and tariffs in effect on the date of the issue of this Bill of Lading

DATE: [*date shipment is given to carrier*]
FROM: [*name of seller*]
ADDRESS: [*seller's address*]

the property described below, in apparent good order, except as noted

CONSIGNED TO: [*name of buyer*]
ADDRESS: [*address of buyer*]
DELIVERING CARRIER: [*name of carrier*]

❑ **Remit C.O.D.** [Shaded entries just below to be completed if delivery made C.O.D.]

    TO: [*name of seller*]
    ADDRESS: [*seller's address*]
    C.O.D. AMOUNT $ [*amount buyer owes*]

Number of Packages	Kind of Package, Description of Articles, Special Marks, and Exceptions	Weight	Rate	Charges

Note–Where the rate is dependent on value, shippers are required to state specifically in writing the agreed or declared value of the property.

The agreed or declared value of the property is hereby specifically stated by the shipper to be not exceeding $_____ per [unit, e.g., barrel, crate, kilogram].

SHIPPER   **CARRIER**

  [*name of seller*]   [*name of carrier*]

Per   [*signature of seller*]   Per   [*signature of carrier*] from the seller, the buyer can be certain that no one else has the power to retrieve the goods, and that the seller no longer has the ability to retain or reroute them. Similarly, if a bank or other financial institution holds in its possession a negotiable document of title for goods that serve as collateral for a loan, the bank can be sure that the borrower cannot transfer the collateralized goods without the bank's knowledge. In essence, the negotiable document of title serves as a substitute for the goods in financing and sales transactions and offers a high degree of certainty that the goods will remain available only to the person in possession of the document.

A *non-negotiable* document of title gives the person named in it the right to take possession of the goods or redirect their delivery, but the document itself need not (although it may) be delivered to the carrier or warehouse in order to do so. The non-negotiable document of title thus offers more flexibility than does a negotiable document of title in transferring the goods in commerce because there is no need to deliver the document itself in order to transfer ownership rights in the goods. For example, the person named in the document of title may simply instruct the bailee in writing to deliver the goods to another person. Parties to a sales transaction may prefer using non-negotiable documents because the parties could be hampered if delivery of the goods cannot occur until the document itself is delivered. What is lost by using non-negotiable documents of title, however, is certainty, especially for the buyer. Having possession of a non-negotiable bill of lading or warehouse receipt offers no guarantee to the buyer or bank that the seller has not resold the goods and ordered delivery to someone else, though that uncertainty may or may not be a significant concern.

Whether a document of title is negotiable or non-negotiable depends on how the instructions for delivery are given. Under § 7-104, use of particular words is required to create a negotiable document of title; the document must say the goods are to be delivered "To Bearer" or "To the Order of" a named person. No other form of words is sufficient (so "Deliver goods to ABC Corporation" makes the document of title non-negotiable), and the "magic words" may not be qualified (so "Deliver to bearer on receipt of proper instructions from Seller" makes the document of title non-negotiable). The appropriate instructions must be visible on the document itself so that buyers, sellers, financers, and bailees will know their rights and responsibilities under the document. There is also a practice of printing negotiable bills of lading on yellow paper while non-negotiable or "straight" bills of lading are printed on white paper, creating another marker of negotiability.

Article 7 also establishes a set of procedures for "duly" negotiating a negotiable document of title. If those procedures are followed, the person receiving the goods takes them free of certain defenses that might otherwise be available, offering additional protections to the buyer.

2. Using a Document of Title

Now that you understand how a negotiable or non-negotiable document of title works, you can understand what happens once the seller receives the document of title from the bailee (e.g., the warehouse or carrier). The seller may give complete delivery instructions and authority to the warehouse or carrier immediately upon giving the goods to the bailee, or the seller instead may obtain a document of title and have the warehouse or carrier store or transport the goods and await further instructions for delivery. If payment from the buyer is due before or upon delivery of the goods, the seller can refuse to deliver to the buyer a negotiable document of title or refrain from ordering delivery to the buyer under a non-negotiable document of title until the buyer has paid. For the buyer, delivery to her of the bill of lading at the time of payment offers some assurance (more in the case of a negotiable bill of lading) that the goods are available to her upon demand.

B. Negotiable Instruments (Drafts)

As noted earlier, a documentary transaction may involve not only use of a document of title representing the right to receive the goods but also use of a document (a draft) representing the right to receive the money owed by the buyer. Just as a document of title may be used by the holder of the document to direct and redirect delivery of the goods, a draft may be used by the holder of the draft to direct and redirect disposition of the buyer's payment. Because the draft may be written to be payable either immediately or at a date in the future, the holder of the draft may exercise the power over payment even before the payment is due. For example, if the purchase price is due only after delivery of the goods but the seller has an immediate need for cash to finance the sales transaction, the seller may transfer to a bank the right to collect the purchase price when the price becomes due, in exchange for the bank's immediate payment to seller of a smaller sum.

Just as there is a particular form for a document of title, which may be negotiable or non-negotiable, there is a particular form for creating a draft, which may be negotiable or non-negotiable. An example of a draft that might be part of a sale-of-goods transaction is on the next page.

```
┌─────────────────────────────────────────────────────────────────┐
│                                                                   │
│  To: [Seller] _____    Date: [date draft is signed] ___ │
│                                                                   │
│  On:  sight _____                                     │
│       ["sight" or specified date]                                 │
│                                                                   │
│  PAY to the order of   [name of seller] _____ │
│                                                                   │
│  the sum of  [contract price] _____  dollars.    │
│                                                                   │
│                            Signed: [signature of seller] _____  │
│                                                                   │
└─────────────────────────────────────────────────────────────────┘
```

The seller (as the person entitled under the contract to receive payment from the buyer) signs the draft, filling in the amount of money owed by the buyer pursuant to the contract terms and specifying that the draft be paid either "on sight" (immediately on presentation) or on a specified date, depending on the agreed payment arrangements under the contract. Because the buyer owes the seller the purchase price under the terms of the sales contract, the seller can order that the money owed be paid to the person holding the draft, and the buyer should be willing to pay that money at the specified time, assuming that the seller has by then fulfilled its contract obligations, probably by delivering to the buyer either the goods or the bill of lading representing the buyer's right to collect the goods. (We will return below to considering just when the buyer must pay; for now, concentrate on the way a draft works.)

Note the similarity between a draft and a check. A check, in fact, *is* a draft, but a special kind: one that is drawn on a bank. When you write a check, you are telling your bank—which owes you money, because you deposited funds with the bank or the bank agreed to make a loan to you—to pay the money it owes you to the named person (the phone company, or a magazine publisher, or a restaurant, etc.). Similarly, when the seller writes a draft, it is telling the buyer to pay the purchase price—which the buyer owes to the seller under the contract—to the bearer or a person named in the draft.

Just as is true with documents of title, drafts are negotiable or non-negotiable. To be negotiable (§ 3-104), a draft must be

- an unconditional order to pay a fixed amount of money, with no limitation or instruction by the person ordering payment (the seller) other than a small set of explicitly permitted ones;

- payable "To Bearer" or "To order" of a named person (the "magic words"); and

- payable on demand or at a definite stated time.

C. Using Both Documents of Title and Drafts

Using *both* a document of title *and* a draft, the seller can provide for transfer of the goods to the buyer and of the money to the seller, her bank, or her agent simply by moving paper (or electronic documents) through what are called "customary banking channels." Statutes and regulations outside Article 2 facilitate this set of transactions by creating obligations for both the bailee and the banks to handle the documents of title and the drafts in the manner that seller and buyer expect. The bank and the bailee would be liable to seller or buyer for failing to fulfill these duties, so both contracting parties can reliably assume that the transaction will proceed as planned.

The diagram on the next two pages illustrates the steps for conducting a sale of goods using documents of title and drafts. As you follow each step in the diagram, you will see the following sequence:

(1) The parties enter a contract for the sale of goods.

(2) The seller delivers the goods to a carrier. The carrier issues a bill of lading to the seller.

(3) The seller delivers to its local bank the bill of lading endorsed to the buyer and a draft ordering the buyer to pay the price, with instructions to send the documents to a bank local to the buyer, to present the draft for payment, and to deliver the bill of lading to the buyer when payment is made.

(4) The seller's local bank sends the documents to a bank near the buyer, using customary banking channels. Meanwhile, the goods are in transit.

(5) The bank local to the buyer presents the draft to the buyer, who pays (perhaps after inspecting the goods, if they have already arrived locally, though still in the hands of the carrier). When payment is made, the bank delivers the bill of lading to the buyer, giving the buyer the right to retrieve the goods.

(6)   The buyer presents the bill of lading to the carrier, which delivers the goods to the buyer. Meanwhile, the bank local to the buyer sends the payment through banking channels to the seller's local bank and to the seller.

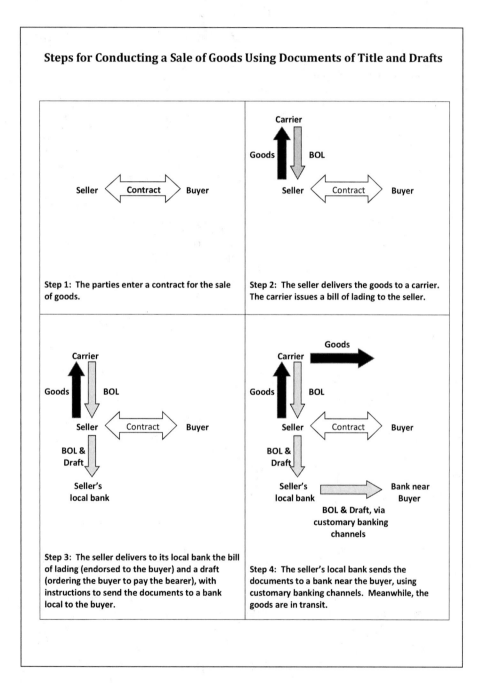

Steps for Conducting a Sale of Goods Using Documents of Title and Drafts

Step 1: The parties enter a contract for the sale of goods.

Step 2: The seller delivers the goods to a carrier. The carrier issues a bill of lading to the seller.

Step 3: The seller delivers to its local bank the bill of lading (endorsed to the buyer) and a draft (ordering the buyer to pay the bearer), with instructions to send the documents to a bank local to the buyer.

Step 4: The seller's local bank sends the documents to a bank near the buyer, using customary banking channels. Meanwhile, the goods are in transit.

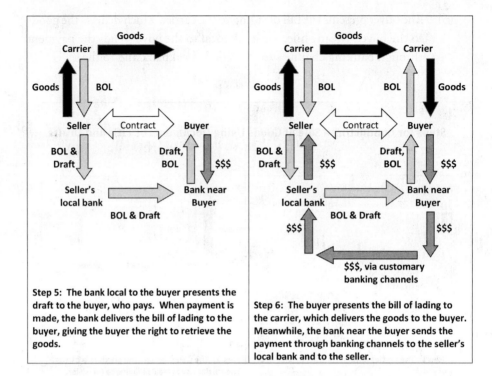

Step 5: The bank local to the buyer presents the draft to the buyer, who pays. When payment is made, the bank delivers the bill of lading to the buyer, giving the buyer the right to retrieve the goods.

Step 6: The buyer presents the bill of lading to the carrier, which delivers the goods to the buyer. Meanwhile, the bank near the buyer sends the payment through banking channels to the seller's local bank and to the seller.

D. Article 2 and Documents of Title

Now that you have a sense of how documentary transactions work and why contracting parties might want to use them, we turn attention to the Article 2 provisions that govern both how parties specify whether a documentary transaction will or may be used and the effect that use of documents of title and drafts have on the performance responsibilities of buyer and seller. We will address three different issues with respect to documentary transactions:

- Whether the contract permits or requires the seller to use documents of title, and what kind;

- The seller's responsibilities for tender of delivery if documents of title are used; and

- The effect of the use of documents of title on the buyer's right to inspect the goods and the timing of the buyer's responsibility to pay.

Although the Code provisions often combine these issues, we will address them separately in order to help sort through this complicated portion of Article 2.

1. Determining Whether Documents of Title May or Must Be Used

As is true with respect to most contract terms, whether documents of title may be used is controlled by the language of the contract and the default provisions of Article 2. First, the contract may contain explicit language saying documents of title may or must be used, or specifying exactly what kind of documents of title are permitted or mandated (e.g., "delivery by bill of lading," "negotiable bill of lading required"). As with other aspects of the contract, course of performance, course of dealing, or usage of trade may likewise mandate or permit use of documents of title.

Alternatively, parties may specify a documentary transaction by using standard terms that are defined in Article 2, and in certain circumstances, Article 2 provides a default choice regarding the use of documents of title.

Reading the Code: Documentary Transactions in §§ 2-310, 2-320, 2-503, 2-505

Read 2-310(b) up to the first comma, then read 2-505.

Question 1. What does it mean to say the seller is "authorized to send the goods"? If the seller is authorized to send the goods, may or must the seller use a document of title? What kind of document of title?

Read 2-320(2)(a) and (e) and 2-320(3).

Question 2. If a contract contains the term "C.I.F. [destination]" or "C. & F. [destination]," may or must the seller use a document of title? What kind of document of title?

Read 2-503(4).

Question 3. If a contract specifies that the goods are to be held by a bailee and delivered to the buyer without being moved, may or must the seller use a document of title? What kind of document of title?

---

2. Seller's Delivery Responsibilities Using Documents of Title

As explored in Assignment 16, the scope of a seller's tender responsibilities depends upon the contract's terms with respect to delivery. Now that you understand the nature of documentary transactions, we can revisit the provisions on tender and consider what they say about tender when documents of title are used.

Reading the Code:
Tender Using Documents of Title
under §§ 2-230, 2-503, 2-504

Question 4. As you may recall, 2-503 specifies the manner of seller's tender under a destination contract or a contract for delivery without shipment; 2-504 specifies the manner of seller's tender under a shipment contract; and 2-320 defines seller's responsibilities under a C.I.F. or C. & F. delivery term. The chart below identifies the subsections of those provisions that refer to tender using documents of title. For each, read that subsection, and list in the chart what the section says seller's tender responsibilities are when using documents of title.

Delivery term	Article 2 subsection	Seller's tender responsibilities with respect to documents of title
C.I.F., C. & F.	2-320(2)(e)	
Warehouse pickup	2-503(4)(a) and (b)	

Delivery term	Article 2 subsection	Seller's tender responsibilities with respect to documents of title
Shipment contract	2-504(b)	
Destination contract	2-503(3), Comment 2, ¶3	
Documents of title required	2-503(5), Comment 7, ¶1	

3. Risk of Loss and Documents of Title

Assignment 16 covered the risk of loss, the allocation of which to buyer and seller depends on the contact's terms with respect to delivery. Now that you understand more about the nature of documentary transactions, we can revisit the provisions on risk of loss and consider what they say about the allocation of risk when parties use documents of title.

**Reading the Code:
Risk of Loss under § 2-509
Using Documents of Title**

Read 2-509, with documents of title in mind.

Question 5. When does risk of loss pass if the seller ships the goods under a bill of lading (*see* 2-509(1))? In answering this question, recall from preparing the answer to Question 4 that "duly deliver" may require the seller to obtain a document of title and deliver it to the buyer.

Question 6. When does risk of loss pass if the goods are in a warehouse and delivered by document of title without being moved (2-509(2))?

4. Buyer's Obligation to Pay When Documents of Title Are Used

Previous sections of this Assignment have explored what the seller is allowed and required to do with respect to documents of title in order to fulfill delivery obligations. As might be expected, if the seller uses documents of title, the buyer must be given whatever documents are required for the buyer to get delivery of the goods from the carrier or warehouse that has possession of the goods. But when those documents are presented to the buyer, must the buyer immediately tender payment? Or can the buyer wait to pay until the buyer gets the goods themselves? The parties to the contract may specify explicitly when payment is required (e.g., "Payment by sight draft against bill of lading"), but what happens in the absence of such express terms?

Reading the Code: Buyer's Payment Obligation under §§ 2-310 and 2-320

Read 2-310(a), Comment 1 to 2-310, and 2-103(1)(c).

Question 7. Unless otherwise agreed and with no documents of title used, when is payment due from the buyer? What is the difference between receipt and delivery of the goods? Why is payment not due upon delivery?

Question 8. Buyer's payment obligations when documents of title are used appear in 2-320 for C.I.F. and C. & F. terms and in 2-310 for other circumstances. The chart below identifies the particular subsections that define when buyer must pay under various delivery circumstances. For each, read that subsection, and list in the chart what that section says about when the buyer must pay.

Delivery term	Article 2 subsection	When and where is payment due?
C.I.F. & C. & F.	2-320(4) & Comment 1	
Goods authorized to be shipped; seller chooses to ship under reservation	2-310(b) & Comment 2	
Parties agree goods will be shipped and delivery will be made with documents of title	2-310(c)[2]	
Parties agree goods will be held at warehouse and delivery will be made by using documents of title	2-310(c)	

5. Buyer's Right to Inspect the Goods

As you saw in Assignment 16, § 2-513(1) specifies that "unless otherwise agreed and subject to subsection (3), where goods are tendered or delivered or identified to the contract for sale, the buyer has a right before payment . . . to inspect them at any reasonable place and time and in any reasonable manner." Inspection before payment is thus the default—unless the parties otherwise agree or § 2-513(3) says otherwise. Subsection (3) governs certain kinds of delivery using documents of title.

---

[2]   Section 2-310(c) applies if delivery is "authorized and made by way of documents of title otherwise than by subsection (b)." Section 2-310(b) permits a seller who is simply authorized to ship the goods to choose to use documents of title, to ship under reservation. Delivery by way of documents of title is "otherwise" authorized if there is an agreement (through language, usage of trade, course of performance, and course of dealing) that documents may be used in delivering the goods.

Reading the Code:
Buyer's Right to Inspect When
Documents of Title are Used

Question 9. The buyer's right to inspect the goods when documents of title are used appears in 2-320 for C.I.F. and C. & F. terms and in 2-513 and 2-310 for other circumstances. The chart below identifies the particular subsections that define buyer's rights to inspect the goods before payment. For each, read that subsection and list in the chart what that subsection says about whether the buyer may inspect before paying. Be sure you can identify the statutory language that provides the answer.

Delivery term	Article 2 subsection	Does buyer have right to inspect before payment?
C.O.D. (Cash On Delivery)	2-513(3)(a)	
C.I.F. & C. & F.	2-320(4) & Comment 1, 2-513(3)(b)	
Goods authorized to be shipped; seller chooses to ship under reservation	2-310(b) & Comments 2 and 3	

Delivery term	Article 2 subsection	Does buyer have right to inspect before payment?
Parties agree goods will be shipped and delivery will be made with documents of title	2-310(c), 2-513(3)(b)	
Same, but contract says "hold documents until arrival of goods"	2-513 Comment 5	
Parties agree goods will be held at warehouse and delivery will be made by using documents of title	2-513(3)(b) & Comment 5 ¶ 3, 2-310(c)	(Hint: Consider (1) when the goods are available for inspection if held in a warehouse and (2) when payment is due if documents of title are used but the goods will *not* be shipped.)

Question 10. Read 2-512(1)(a) and Comments 1 through 3 and 2-513 Comment 1. If the buyer is required to pay before inspection, may the buyer refuse to pay because the goods are defective? If so, under what circumstances?

APPLYING THE CODE

The problems below ask you to determine whether the buyer has breached by demanding delivery or inspection of the goods before paying. To answer that question, you will need to determine what the seller's contract obligations are with respect to tendering goods *and* documents, to determine when and where the buyer is required to make payment upon the seller's proper tender, and to determine whether the buyer has a right to demand inspection before paying.

Problem 20-1.

Agreement between High Seas, a fish merchant in Boston, and Sea Coast, a restaurant in Minneapolis, calling for the sale of "300 lobsters, each 1 to 2 pounds, ship to Sea Coast Restaurant, lobsters to be alive at delivery." (Each problem below is independent of the others unless otherwise noted.)

(a) High Seas ships the lobsters, obtaining a bill of lading "to order of High Seas." When the lobsters arrive at the carrier's facility in Minneapolis, Sea Coast inspects the lobsters and finds them conforming. The agent for High Seas in Minneapolis demands payment before indorsing and releasing the bill of lading. Sea Coast refuses, claiming that payment is due only upon delivery of the lobsters to the restaurant, which the carrier refuses to do without an indorsed bill of lading. Has Sea Coast breached by refusing to pay until the lobsters are delivered?

(b) High Seas ships the lobsters, obtaining a bill of lading "to order of High Seas." While the lobsters are en route, the agent for High Seas in Minneapolis presents the sight draft to Sea Coast and demands payment, promising an indorsed bill of lading in return. Sea Coast refuses, claiming the right to inspect the lobsters upon delivery to make sure they are still alive. Has Sea Coast breached by refusing to pay?

(c) Same as (b), but agreement says "Delivery: C.I.F. Minneapolis." When Sea Coast demands inspection before paying against the sight draft, has Sea Coast breached?

Problem 20-2.

Agreement on October 1 between Commodities Corp. and Cereals Deluxe for sale of $50,000 worth of grain owned by Commodities Corp. and stored in a grain warehouse owned by Great Silos, Inc. Nothing is said in the agreement about the use of documents of title. (Each problem below is independent of the other.)

(a) On October 2, Commodities Corp. sends to Great Silos a letter authorizing delivery of the grain to Cereals Deluxe on November 1. When is Cereals Deluxe obligated to pay for the grain?

(b) On September 15, when the grain was delivered to Great Silos, Commodities Corp. obtained a negotiable warehouse receipt. On October 2, Cereals Deluxe seeks to inspect the grain stored at Great Silos, but the warehouse refuses to allow the inspection. On October 3, Commodities Corp. presents the warehouse receipt and sight draft to Cereals Deluxe and demands payment in exchange for the indorsed warehouse receipt. Does Cereals Deluxe have to pay upon this demand?

Assignment 21
Power to Transfer Title
§ 2-403

A sale of goods involves the passing of title of goods from seller to buyer, and we have seen that § 2-401 governs when title passes in a sales transaction. But what happens if the transaction purports to pass title to the buyer, but the seller does not have good title to the goods at the time of the sale? Although you might expect that the seller can pass on at most the title it holds, there are several circumstances under which the buyer can acquire good title even though the seller did not own the goods.

LEARNING OUTCOMES AND OBJECTIVES

At the conclusion of this Assignment, you should be able to identify and articulate the circumstances when the buyer takes less or more of a property interest in the goods than the seller had. In particular, you should be able to

- explain and apply the derivative title rule;
- explain the difference between void and voidable title and identify when a buyer will receive one or the other;
- explain and apply the rule that permits a good faith purchaser for value to receive good title even if the seller had only voidable title; and
- explain and apply the rule that permits a buyer in the ordinary course of business to receive good title from a merchant who was entrusted with the goods.

Section 2-403 specifies both the general rule (the buyer takes the same interest in the goods the seller had) and the exceptions that permit the buyer to take more (or less) of an interest in the goods. Because so much is packed into § 2-403, we will walk through the section sentence by sentence to help you understand the provision and how it works, as well as to consider why the Code treats title as it does in this section.

Note that the title problems dealt with in § 2-403 typically arise when the goods pass through not just a single transaction (e.g., seller to buyer) but through a series of transactions (e.g., seller to buyer 1, who resells to buyer 2; or owner to lessee, who unlawfully sells to buyer). You might diagram the relationships this way, with two transactions involved:

Transaction 1:   **Transaction 2:**

A to B   B to C

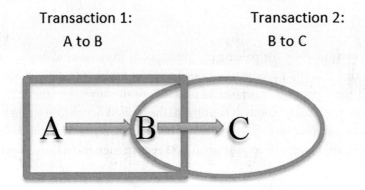

At times in the text below we will simply refer to a seller and buyer, but at other times we will refer to "transaction 1" and "transaction 2" to make clear which part of the series of transactions is being discussed. As you will see in the Examples, the chain of transactions can be longer, involving goods passing from hand to hand multiple times, but the principles remain the same in such circumstances.

A. The Derivative Title Rule

Reading the Code:
§ 2-403(1)

Read the first sentence of 2-403(1), the first two sentences of Comment 1, and the second paragraph of Comment 1.

Question 1. "Derivative" means "something that is based on another source." Focusing only on the part of the sentence before the word "except," why would the rule expressed there be called the "derivative title" rule?

Question 2. Now looking at the second part of the sentence, starting with the word "except," how might a buyer receive less than the title that the seller held?

Question 3. Notice that 2-403(1) refers not to a "buyer," "seller," and "sale" of goods but to a "purchaser," "transferor," and "transfer" of goods. Recall from Assignment 2 that Article 2 applies to "transactions" in goods (2-102), but that the scope of Article 2 is usually narrowed to transactions involving contracts for the sale of goods. The language used in 2-403(1) tells you that this is one part of Article 2 that applies beyond that context. "Transfer" and "transferor" are not defined in Articles 1 or 2, but "purchaser" is. How is a "purchaser" different from a "buyer"?

B. Transferring Better Title to the Buyer

Section 2-403 identifies two circumstances when a transferor (usually a seller) can pass good title to a purchaser (usually a buyer) even though the transferor did not have good title. The circumstances involve (1) "good faith purchase for value" from someone holding "voidable title" and (2) sale of goods to a "buyer in the ordinary course of business" by a merchant "entrusted" with the goods. In the sections below, we will see how § 2-403 states those exceptions and how they are understood and applied.

1. "Good Faith Purchaser for Value"

**Reading the Code:
§ 2-403(1)**

Read the second sentence of 2-403(1).

Question 4. The sentence refers to a person having "voidable title." We will explore below the meaning of voidable title. For now, it is enough to recognize that voidable title is less than "good title." Under what factual circumstances does 2-403(1) say a person having only voidable title has the ability to transfer good title to another? What other Code sections are applicable to fully identify those factual circumstances? (Think about definitions.)

Question 5. Does a person with voidable title always pass good title to the buyer in the transaction? In answering, recall your answer to Question 2 above.

2. Voidable Title

A person with "voidable title" has the power to pass good title, but the Code does not define "voidable title," so courts applying § 2-403(1) draw upon the common law of the relevant jurisdiction to define it. Typically, the common law says that a transferee receives voidable title if the transferor intended to and did transfer good title at the time of a transaction, but subsequent events or subsequently discovered facts entitle the transferor to rescind the transaction and regain title. Notice that the transaction is voidable (able to be voided), not void; the transferor still must perform the action of rescinding the transaction in order to regain title. If he or she does not, the right to rescind the transaction is eventually waived and lost.

EXAMPLES AND ANALYSIS

Example A: *Sherwood v. Walker*[1] *revisited*

One example of a defect that results in voidable title is mutual or unilateral mistake. Consider that famous cow case from first-year Contracts class, Sherwood v. Walker. Sherwood (a cattle breeder) arranged to sell the cow, Rose of Aberlone, to Walker (a banker), setting the price at $80 because both seller and buyer thought her to be sterile. After they entered into the contract, but before Rose was delivered to the buyer, Sherwood discovered that Rose was pregnant and therefore was worth between $750 and $1000, so he refused to deliver her. Because the cow had not yet been delivered, the banker-buyer asked the court to order the breeder-seller to deliver the cow. The court refused, ruling that the contract was voidable because of mutual mistake. No title issues were raised because the cow was never delivered.

If, instead, Sherwood had delivered the cow and then discovered she was not sterile, Sherwood might have (successfully) sued Walker to return the

---

[1]   33 N.W. 919 (Mich. 1887).

cow to him. Before that court judgment, Walker would have had "voidable title" to Rose: his title was good unless and until Sherwood was able to avoid the contract based on mistake. So what would happen if Walker sold Rose to a third party for $85 before he found out she was pregnant? Would the outcome be different if Walker learned she was pregnant and, fearing Sherwood would ask for the cow back, hurriedly sold Rose to a farmer for $200?

Analysis: As "a person with voidable title" based on his purchase of Rose, Walker "has power to transfer a good title to a good faith purchaser for value" under 2-403(1). If he sold Rose for $85 to a third party, not yet knowing she was not sterile, it would appear that the third party was a "good faith purchaser for value," so the third party would get good title. If Sherwood had sued Walker before that sale, he could have gotten the cow back on the basis of mistake. But if he sued the third party after the second sale, he could not get the cow back because Walker would have passed good title to the cow to the third party.

On the other hand, if Walker knew about the mistake he and Sherwood had made and quickly sold the cow for $200, it is possible a fact-finder could conclude that the third party was not a good faith purchaser (though he would have been a purchaser for value). The odd price of the cow—much more than her value if sterile but much less than her value if fertile—might suggest that the third party knew or should have known there was something unusual about the sale, so he might not have acted with "honesty in fact" and with "observance of reasonable commercial standards of fair dealing."

As illustrated in Example A, mistake in the original sale ("transaction 1" in the diagram in the introduction) provides voidable title to the buyer, who can then pass good title on to someone else. The third sentence of § 2-403 provides a list of other "transaction 1" circumstances that can result in a person having voidable title (subparts (a) through (d)). These are not the only circumstances that can lead to voidable title, but they describe circumstances common enough (and perhaps troublesome enough under pre-Code law) to include expressly.

Section 2-403(1)(a) through (d) describes four circumstances that may occur in "transaction 1" (party A transferring goods to party B) that do not prevent transfer of good title in "transaction 2" (party B transferring goods to party C).

Match each of the four scenarios below with the appropriate subpart of 2-403(1).

Example B: *U.S. v. Wyoming National Bank of Casper*[2]

On November 24, Riverton Auction and Livestock Co. sold cattle to Packers. Packers took immediate possession of the cattle, and they became part of its inventory. In payment for the cattle, Packers gave Riverton two checks totaling $10,155.38. Bank refused to pay one check because of insufficient funds and the other because of an insufficient indorsement. On December 6, an audit disclosed that Packers was in default under its loan and security agreement with Bank. On the next day Packers turned all of its assets over to Bank. Riverton has never been paid for the cattle and seeks return of the cattle or payment for the cattle from Bank.

Example C: *Charles Evans BMW, Inc. v. Williams*[3]

Williams agreed to sell his car to Hodge. Hodge provided a cashier's check, and Williams signed the certificate of title to allow transfer to Hodge. The next day, Hodge offered to sell the car to Car Dealer at a reasonable price, representing to Car Dealer that he was Williams and providing to Car Dealer the title signed by Williams. Car Dealer paid Hodge by check made out to Williams; Hodge cashed that check at a bank by representing himself again as Williams. Hodge's cashier's check was a forgery, so Williams sought return of the car, which Hodge had resold to Car Dealer.

Example D: *Jernigan v. Ham*[4]

Jernigan offered his 1954 Ford Jubilee tractor for sale in the front yard of his home. In December 1982, he was contacted by an individual named

---

2   505 F.2d 1064 (10th Cir. 1974).
3   395 S.E.2d 650 (Ga. Ct. App. 1990).
4   691 S.W.2d 553 (Tenn. Ct. App. 1984).

John Rickman, who expressed an interest in purchasing the tractor. Rickman inspected the tractor and offered to purchase the tractor and grader blade for $2,250.00. When Rickman returned and loaded the tractor and grader blade onto his trailer, he gave Jernigan a check. Jernigan stated that he did not want a check, but, rather, that he required cash. They agreed, however, that since the tractor was already loaded, Rickman could take it and return with the cash the next day at which time Jernigan would give him a bill of sale.

On the following day, Rickman took the tractor and blade to Memphis Ford Tractor, Inc., in Tennessee, and sold the equipment there to William Ham for $1,500.00. When Ham bought the tractor and blade from Rickman, he did not ask for a bill of sale. Ham testified that it is not customary to demand a bill of sale because "it's very doubtful that people could go back and dig up a bill of sale that they've had for years and years." Rickman told Ham that the tractor had been used at a deer camp. Ham testified that although the tractor was clean, most sellers clean their equipment before bringing it to sell. Ham also noticed that Rickman's truck had Arkansas license plates, but Ham stated that he often bought tractors from individuals from Arkansas and Mississippi. Ham had no prior or subsequent dealings with Rickman.

When Rickman failed to appear with cash to pay for the tractor, Jernigan began to search for Rickman and the tractor. He located the tractor on the lot of the Memphis Ford Tractor, Inc. The next day, Jernigan contacted Ham about the tractor and demanded possession, but Ham refused to return the tractor. Rickman never paid the check to Jernigan, and he was subsequently convicted of larceny by trick and passing bad checks.

Example E: *Iola State Bank v. Bolan*[5]

Biggs operated a feed and grain elevator, purchasing grain from farmers and selling grain to large grain dealers. He conducted his banking business with Iola State Bank, including the receipt of loans to finance his operations. Biggs bought grain from several farmers, issuing checks to the farmers dated between August 17 and December 2. At the time the checks were issued, there were sufficient funds in Biggs's accounts to pay for the grain.

---

[5]   679 P.2d 720 (Kan. 1984).

While reviewing its accounts in July, the Bank determined that Biggs had been unable to pay principal or interest on his loan balance, and, after giving Biggs 90 days to find other financing, the Bank refused further extensions on Biggs's payments. When the farmers began bringing Biggs's checks to the Bank starting December 7, the Bank refused to pay them.

The Bank sued Biggs to obtain payment of balances unpaid from his accounts; the farmers intervened, claiming ownership of the grain because Biggs's payment checks were not honored. In determining whether the Bank (through its security interest in the grain) and subsequent purchasers of the grain obtained good title to the grain from Biggs as compared to the farmers, the court noted the following: "Prior to the adoption of the Uniform Commercial Code, cash sales were governed by the 'cash sale doctrine.' A cash buyer did not receive title to the goods purchased until the seller was paid in full. A cash buyer who had not paid the seller in full could not pass title to a bona fide purchaser. A cash seller who was not fully paid for the goods retained title and could reclaim the goods from the purchaser. The cash sale doctrine restricted the free flow of goods in commerce. The cash sale doctrine was abolished by the adoption of [the state's version of the UCC]."

3. Void Title

Formal title can be passed in only two ways: (1) by the title-holder's voluntary and intentional transfer of title to a "purchaser" (remember the broad definition of that word) or (2) by some process of law that transfers title (e.g., a foreclosure). As we saw in the previous section, if person B tricks person A into selling a car by misinforming person A about person B's solvency, person B receives voidable title. If the transfer was voluntarily and intentionally made, the purchaser temporarily gets title, but because the transfer was made as the result of deceit, the transferor can rescind the transaction and regain title.

In contrast, if—prior to any sale—person B takes the car for a test drive and never returns it, person B has stolen person A's car. There was no voluntary and intentional transfer of title. Person B has "void title," which more accurately is no title at all. Person A retains title. Instead of title, person B has a right of possession that is superior to the rights of anyone else except person A. When goods are stolen, they do not become fair game for everyone else to steal from the thief. The thief can recover them from any subsequent thief (if he or she has the moxie!). But if the original owner can find the goods, the original owner can recover them from the thief or from anyone else, no matter how far down the chain of title they have passed.

EXAMPLES AND ANALYSIS

Example F: *Lieber v. Mohawk Arms, Inc.*[6]

In 1945, Philip Lieber, then in the United States Army, was among the first soldiers to occupy Munich, Germany. He and some companions entered Adolph Hitler's apartment and removed various items of Hitler's personal belongings. Lieber brought his share home to Louisiana. It included Hitler's uniform jacket and cap, and some of his decorations and personal jewelry. Lieber's possession of these articles was publicly known. Louisiana newspapers published stories and pictures about his collection, and he was the subject of a feature story in the Louisiana State University Alumni News in October 1945. In 1968 the collection was stolen by Lieber's chauffeur, who sold it to a New York dealer in historical Americana. The dealer sold it to Mohawk Arms, which purchased in good faith. Through collectors' circles, Lieber was able to discover the whereabouts of his stolen property, made a demand for its return that was refused, and commenced an action seeking the return. Mohawk Arms moved for summary judgment on the ground that Lieber "never obtained good and legal title to this collection" and that "the collection properly belongs to the occupational military authority and/or the Bavarian Government," not to Lieber.

Analysis: Because Lieber received void title (that is, no title at all) when he took the items, no one else in the chain (chauffeur, dealer, or Mohawk Arms) could receive good title from their transactions. It does not matter that the purchase by Mohawk Arms (and perhaps by the dealer) was made in good faith. Even though he had no title, Lieber had a right superior to any of the others, so he was entitled to return of the goods to him. Note that (1) if Lieber had had good title of the items, the chauffeur would have received void title when he stole them, resulting in the same outcome; and (2) if the collection did belong to the military authority or the Bavarian government (or anyone else), they could recover the items from Lieber (though none had tried to do so in the almost 25 years in which Lieber had publicly possessed them).

Mohawk Arms, at least, was blameless in the transaction, and the dealer too may have had no reason to suspect a problem with title when it bought the items. Still,

---

[6]   314 N.Y.S.2d 510 (Sup. Ct. 1970).

Lieber successfully reclaimed the goods from Mohawk Arms. What recourse might Mohawk or the dealer have to recover for their losses?

4. Buyer in the Ordinary Course of Business

The second exception to the derivative-title rule concerns the "buyer in the ordinary course of business" from a "merchant who deals in goods of that kind" to whom someone else has "entrusted" the goods.

Reading the Code: § 2-403(2) and (3)

Read 2-403(2) and (3).

Question 6. Rewrite 2-403(2) by creating a list of bullet points that specify what a buyer must establish in order to retain ownership of goods received from "a merchant who deals in goods of that kind." Be sure to include elements that must be established based on the definition of "entrusting" in 2-403(3) and "buyer in ordinary course of business" from 1-201(b)(9).

Question 7. What do the two "regardless of" clauses in 2-403(3) add to the list you created in response to Question 6? Describe a set of circumstances that would lead a buyer to invoke the "regardless of" clauses in proving her claim to the goods.

Question 8. Refer again to the diagram in the introduction showing "transaction 1" and "transaction 2." If party C could qualify both as a good-faith-purchaser under 2-403(1) and as a buyer-in-the-ordinary-course under 2-403(2), which subsection would likely produce the better outcome for party C?

Example G: *Two Typical Entrustments*

John takes his great-grandmother's ring to Wanda's Watch Repair and Jewelry Emporium to have the ring cleaned and re-sized so that he can give it to his fiancée for their engagement. The Emporium both repairs and sells jewelry, and its sales include both new items and previously owned items received from individuals and estate sales. After the work on John's ring is done, an employee mistakenly places the ring on a shelf containing used items for sale. Linda buys the ring, unaware that it is someone else's. John finds out that Linda bought the ring and sues her for return of the family heirloom.

Painter loans a painting to Dealer for the purpose of displaying it as part of an art show but makes clear the piece is not to be sold. Some but not all of the pieces in the show are for sale. Dealer is in the business of selling artwork as well as arranging for shows and loans of artwork to museums. Without authorization, Dealer sells the painting to Collector, intentionally misrepresenting it as available for purchase. Collector buys the painting without knowing it was not supposed to be for sale. Painter sues Collector for return of the artwork.

Analysis: Both Linda and Collector received good title to the purchased items so neither John nor Painter can recover their goods. Both owners "entrusted" their goods to the merchant (they delivered them voluntarily); Emporium and Dealer are each a "merchant who deals in goods of that kind," and both Linda and Collector bought the items, in good faith, "in the ordinary course from a person . . . in the business of selling goods of that kind" and "without knowledge that the sale violates the rights of another person." It does not matter that John and Painter understood that the items were to be returned to them or even that they each had an express agreement with the merchant that the items were not for sale ("regardless of any condition expressed between the parties to the delivery"). The result is the same whether the merchant mistakenly sold the item, as Emporium did, or intentionally resold it without authority, as Dealer did ("regardless of whether . . . the possessor's disposition of the goods [was] such as to be larcenous under the criminal law"). Note that, although neither John nor Painter can recover their goods from the purchasers, they will likely have recourse against the seller for breach of contract or conversion.

As you can see here and in the additional examples below, the "buyer in the ordinary course" rule can have harsh results for the person who delivered goods to a merchant on the reasonable assumption that the merchant would comply with the conditions imposed. What policies support this choice of legal rule, instead of allowing the original owner to recover?

C. Note on Certificate-of-Title Acts

As you will see reflected in the examples below, a significant number of cases arising under § 2-403 involve motor vehicles. As you may also know, if you have ever owned, bought, or sold a motor vehicle, there are state laws that govern obtaining and transferring title to vehicles, often including not only cars and trucks but also boats, trailers, off-road vehicles, and similar items. Such "certificate of title" acts (CTAs) help ensure orderly, traceable, non-fraudulent transfer of such particularly mobile goods, but each state has its own version, so in practice you will have to be alert to the existence and contents of any relevant CTA. Many of the CTAs contain a rule specifying when title has transferred from seller to buyer, at which time the state will issue the certificate of title. The CTA rule may differ from the rule in § 2-401, and the CTA rules may also affect or supersede conclusions about proper commercial practices for the purposes of analyzing whether a party is a good faith purchaser or a buyer in the ordinary course of business under § 2-403. Such differences have resulted in a muddled set of cases about whether the CTA rule prevails over §§ 2-401 and 2-403, or vice versa.[7] Thus, if the goods involved in the dispute are motor vehicles covered by a certificate of title, be sure to ascertain the result under the applicable CTA, as well as the applicable case law about which body of law governs the dispute in the event of a conflict between the UCC and the CTA.

EXAMPLES AND ANALYSIS

As noted in the introduction to this Assignment, the circumstances that lead to questions under 2-403 often involve goods being passed hand-to-hand through a series of transactions. We recommend that as you read through and analyze both the Examples and the Problems below, you create a diagram of the parties

---

[7] *See* Christina L. Kunz, Motor Vehicle Ownership Disputes Involving Certificate-of-Title Acts and Article Two of the U.C.C., 39 Bus. Law. 1599 (1984).

involved and the nature of the goods transfers involved at each stage. In addition to answering the questions posed, you should identify any issues that cannot be resolved without knowing more facts, and how those additional facts would affect the outcome.

Example H: *Bauer v. Curran*[8]

In the spring of 1979, Carl Davidson, a farmer, leased approximately 100 head of pregnant stock cows from Matthew Bauer. The cows calved in the spring of 1979 and again in the spring of 1980. In the fall of 1980, Davidson sold 16 cow-calf pairs to R.D. Curran. Curran made no attempt to find out whether Davidson actually owned the cattle.

Bauer brought a conversion action against Curran. Curran claimed ownership pursuant to 2-403(2): Bauer entrusted the cows to Davidson, Davidson is a merchant who deals in cattle, and Curran bought the cows from Davidson in the ordinary course of business.

Bauer claimed that Davidson was not a merchant, so under 2-403(1), Bauer retained title. Bauer testified that, although he had engaged in a large number of transactions in buying and selling cattle in the area, he had never seen or met Davidson before entering into the lease with him. Other testimony showed that, prior to the sale from Davidson to Curran, Davidson had leased approximately 20 head of cattle from another individual and entered into a lease-purchase agreement with a Clearview Cattle Company, and that he occasionally had sold cattle to cull his herd. He had also sold some of the other cattle leased from Bauer, but had done so under Bauer's name and at his direction.

The trial court submitted a special interrogatory to the jury, which found that Davidson was not a merchant, making 2-403(2) inapplicable. On appeal, Bauer argued that Davidson was a merchant as a matter of law, so the question should not have been submitted to the jury.

Analysis: The Iowa Supreme Court affirmed, holding that whether Davidson is a merchant was a question of fact and reasonable minds could disagree about the result. Do you agree with that judgment? If the jury had found Davidson to be a merchant for the purposes of 2-403(2), who would own the cattle?

---

[8]   360 N.W.2d 88 (Iowa 1984).

Example 1: *Robison v. Gerber Products Co.*[9]

Barbara Robison and her husband are co-owners of a piece of land in South Carolina used by J.B. Robison Farms, Inc. as a peach orchard. Robison Farms is a corporation operated by Robison's husband and his family. During the 1981 peach harvest, Gerber purchased the entire peach crop pursuant to a written contract with Robison Farms, as it had done regularly since 1970. Barbara Robison never received her share of the contract proceeds and sued Gerber for trespass and conversion.

In defense, Gerber claimed protection under 2-403(2). In response, Robison argued that (1) the peaches were not entrusted to Robison Farms and (2) Gerber was not a buyer in the ordinary course of business because one of Gerber's agents had been informed that Barbara Robison and her husband were having domestic problems, which led to the failure of Robison Farms to pay her share of the proceeds.

Analysis: The trial court held, and the court of appeals affirmed, that the peaches were entrusted to Robison Farms. Barbara Robison had allowed Robison Farms to retain possession and control over her portion of the peach crop for more than ten years, with the proceeds always going to Robison Farms, conduct that "falls squarely within the definition of entrusting."

The court also affirmed that Gerber was a buyer in the ordinary course of business (buying "in good faith" and "without knowledge that the sale violates the rights of another person in the goods"). Good faith requires "honesty in fact"[10] and there was no evidence it had acted otherwise. And although Gerber may have known that Robison and her husband had marital problems, Gerber was dealing with the corporation, not with the Robisons as individuals, and Gerber had no reason to question the corporation's right to sell the peaches and no duty to inspect title to the real estate on which the peaches were grown. In reaching its determination, the court described the rationale behind 2-403(2):

> The appellant seeks to impose on a commercial purchaser from a corporate seller the duty to be informed regarding the assets and the domestic tranquility of the shareholders and, should any hint of marital discord reach its agents, the duty to investigate what effect such disturbance might have

---

9   765 F.2d 431 (4th Cir. 1985).

10   Recall from Assignment 6 the varying definitions of "good faith," depending on which version of Article 1 is or was in effect at the time. In 1985 in South Carolina, the definition was as quoted in the text.

on the commercial transaction in which it is involved. Such a duty offends the very purpose of the Uniform Commercial Code in promoting greater negotiability of goods and in affording certain protection to participants in the commercial marketplace.

Do you agree with the outcome and rationale? If you had been representing Barbara Robison, what action might you have urged to better protect her interests in the proceeds of the sale of the peach crop?

Example J: *Met-Al, Inc. v. Hansen Storage Co.*[11]

Met-Al, Inc. is a manufacturer and seller of aluminum ingots. Metal Brokers International, Inc. (MBI) represented itself to Met-Al as a broker for certain buyers and arranged for shipment of aluminum by Met-Al to the buyers using a carrier, with bills of lading correctly issued naming Met-Al as the shipper. The carrier delivered the aluminum to a warehouse to await the time for delivery, a common practice in the industry. But MBI was not, in fact, a representative of the buyers, and it convinced the carrier to issue new bills of lading naming new consignees (recipients of delivery) for the shipments; MBI then sold the aluminum to new buyers and paid Met-Al some, but not all, owed under the fake orders from the original buyers. Eventually the scheme collapsed, and Met-Al sued the trucking and storage companies for its losses, claiming violation of the Federal Bill of Lading Act. In order to determine liability under the Act, the court considered the application of 2-403(1) to the transaction.

The court first considered whether MBI had voidable title, in order to apply the second sentence ("A person with voidable title has power to transfer a good title to a good faith purchaser for value."). The court then considered whether MBI had received the aluminum in a transaction of purchase in order to apply the third sentence ("When goods have been delivered in a transaction of purchase the purchaser has [the power to transfer good title] even though . . . .").

Analysis: The court determined that MBI did not have voidable title because Met-Al never intended to sell the aluminum to MBI; MBI acted solely as a broker

---

11   844 F. Supp. 485 (E.D. Wis. 1994).

in the transaction. Nor did MBI take the goods in a transaction of purchase. Purchase is the "taking by sale, discount, negotiation, mortgage, pledge, lien, issue or reissue, gift or any other voluntary transaction creating an interest in property" but that was not the case here. MBI was never intended to become the owner or to take any other property interest in the goods. Consequently, MBI did not have the power to transfer good title to the aluminum.

Example K: *Rudiger Charolais Ranches v. Van de Graaf Ranches*[12]

Rudiger Charolais Ranches (the "Gang Ranch") is a Canadian cow-calf operation that sells calves to cattle buyers. In February 1989, the Gang Ranch agreed to sell 306 head of cattle to Ernest Etherton, who falsely represented himself as a licensed and bonded cattle buyer. Payment for the cattle was to be made on the same day as the cattle passed customs, but when delivery was delayed until a Saturday, the wire transfer of the purchase price could not be made until the following Monday. The Gang Ranch transferred the cattle to Etherton on Saturday, without being paid, and Etherton was given the required shipping documents for each load. He was not given a bill of sale or a brand release (necessary to show true ownership if cattle are branded with the mark of someone other than the transferor), either of which would have made him the owner of the cattle.

Etherton entered an agreement to sell the cattle to Van de Graaf Ranches for about $40,000 less than Etherton was to pay the Gang Ranch. Van de Graaf Ranches accepted the cattle with copies (not the required originals) of only two of the thirty documents (a brand inspection certificate and a veterinarian's certificate) the Gang Ranch had provided to Etherton. Van de Graaf Ranches wired Etherton the contract price on the first business day after the cattle arrived but did not attempt to obtain other documentation or verify Etherton's ownership until two business days later.

Etherton later pled guilty to a criminal charge in connection with the cattle deal. The Gang Ranch recovered some of the purchase price from Etherton and sued Van de Graaf Ranches to recover the $107,817.12 shortfall.

With respect to the commercial standards of the beef cattle trade, the manager of the Gang Ranch testified that in the 100 to 200 cattle sale transactions in which he participated over 23 years, bills of sale had been

---

[12]   994 F.2d 670 (9th Cir. 1993).

used in only 10 to 20 transactions. Van de Graaf introduced testimony that it does not withhold payment until paperwork arrives because the federal Packers and Stockyard Act requires a dealer buying cattle to pay for it within 24 hours; that if cattle arrive without complete documentation, the seller normally mails any missing documents to the buyer; and that the transfer of possession customarily takes the place of a bill of sale. An accountant for Van de Graaf testified that bills of sale were used "very infrequently" and that brand inspection certificates were often obtained from the seller long after delivery of the cattle and usually by an inspector for the state Department of Agriculture for the purpose of auditing the ranch.

An applicable state statute requires that someone possessing livestock marked with the brand or tattoo of another must also have a certificate or permit from the owner of the brand or a brand inspection certificate or a bill of sale, unless the cattle also have on their bodies a healed brand mark that matches the possessor's recorded brand. It was conceded that Van de Graaf had none of the required documentation for four of the five loads of cattle delivered by Etherton.

The trial court granted a directed verdict to Van de Graaf. The Gang Ranch appealed the verdict; the issue presented on appeal was whether Van de Graaf held good title to the cattle under 2-403. The court considered (1) whether Etherton got void or voidable title to the cattle and (2) whether Van de Graaf Ranches was a "good faith purchaser for value."

Analysis: The Gang Ranch argued that Etherton's title was void because he was a thief, but the court held that he received voidable title because the seller had turned over possession to Etherton voluntarily. The court held that Van de Graaf purchased the cattle for value but was not a "good faith purchaser for value" because the violation of the state statute meant that, as a matter of law, the sale did not "comport with the usual or customary practices in the kind of business in which the seller is engaged," even though many transactions were conducted without compliance with that statute.

Do you agree with the court's judgment on both issues? What facts, arguments, and Code or Comment language support the court's judgment? What would support a different outcome?

APPLYING THE CODE

Problem 21-1.

Adeorike Ogunsanya Duros Inmi-Etti, a native and resident of Nigeria, came to the United States in June 1981 to visit her sister. While there, she decided to purchase a car and have it shipped back to Nigeria. An acquaintance of her family, David Butler, offered to assist her with the purchase. With his aid, she placed an order for a new 1981 Honda Prelude on June 15, 1981, with Wilson Pontiac putting down a $200 deposit. The purchase price was $8500, with the remaining funds due when the car was delivered. Inmi-Etti returned to Nigeria, leaving the cash balance of the purchase price with her sister. On June 24, 1981, the transaction was completed, and the car was delivered to Inmi-Etti's sister, who was accompanied by Butler. Butler drove the car to the sister's home. A certificate of title was delivered to Butler, naming Inmi-Etti as the owner.

On August 18, 1981, Butler drove the automobile from the sister's home to a location in Marlow Heights, Maryland. When Inmi-Etti informed her sister that the car's removal was not authorized, her sister applied for an arrest warrant charging Butler with theft, but the warrant was quashed before execution. Meanwhile, Butler arranged to sell the vehicle to Pohanka Oldsmobile-GMC, a car dealer, for $7200. Butler represented to Pohanka that he owned the vehicle, but did not produce a certificate of title. Pohanka paid Butler $2000 and agreed to pay the balance when he produced a certificate of title. Butler than applied for and received a certificate of title from the Motor Vehicle Administration by misrepresenting facts in a sworn affidavit, and Pohanka paid Butler the remaining $5200 on the purchase price.

Inmi-Etti sued Butler and Pohanka for conversion ("the wrongful possession or disposition of another's property as if it were one's own"). Pohanka's liability to Inmi-Etti turned on whether Pohanka received good title of the vehicle under the provisions of 2-403. How should the court rule?

Problem 21-2.

On August 2, 2006, Jane and Robert Powell executed a retail installment contract with Mercedes-Benz Financial (MB Financial) to finance a 2007 Mercedez-Benz S550V purchased for $97,647.20. The Michigan Department of State issued a certificate of title for the vehicle that displayed MB Financial as lien holder and the Powells as owners. In 2007 or 2008, the Powells made an agreement to sell the vehicle to Aaron Jacobs. Jacobs was to make payments to the Powells and the Powells were to forward the payments to MB Financial. Jacobs failed to make the payments, and the Powells defaulted on their contract with MB Financial. On July 3, 2008, the Powells filed for bankruptcy and informed MB Financial of their intent to surrender the vehicle, and of its sale to Jacobs. However, MB Financial did not locate or repossess the vehicle.

There was evidence at trial that a letter dated June 28, 2010, was sent to the Powells' address, falsely claiming that the debt owed to MB Financial had been satisfied and the lien released. The letter was signed "Lender Agent Brad Killinger." Killenger was unknown to the Powells or to MB Financial. On June 30, 2010, a duplicate Certificate of Title was issued by the Michigan Department of State showing a release of plaintiff's lien. The duplicate title read that DC FIN SVCS AMER LLC (under which name MB Financial did business) had released its lien on the vehicle. The signature of the agent purportedly authorizing release was again that of the unknown Brad Killinger. Jacobs signed the duplicate title as purchaser under the "title assignment by seller" section and Jacobs received a new certificate of title stating "No Secured Interest on Record."

Marvin Dabish, the owner of Motor City Automotive and Collision and an authorized agent for a dealership called Zak's Auto, purchased the vehicle from Jacobs on behalf of Zak's Auto, remitting a cashier's check to Jacobs in the amount of $25,000 on July 31, 2010. A Certificate of Title was never issued in Dabish's name. Later, Dabish allegedly sold the vehicle to Erick Ellis for $20,000 (though Dabish denied receiving the $20,000 that Ellis claimed to have paid). On September 29, 2010, another transfer of title application was filed that listed Jacobs as the seller, Ellis as the purchaser, and the sale price as $20,000. By the time Ellis purchased the vehicle, the wheel rims were bent and it needed approximately $4,000 worth of repair work. On September 30, 2010, the Michigan Department of State issued Ellis a purportedly lien-free or "clean" Certificate of Title.

MB Financial filed a complaint against Ellis on June 7, 2011, seeking recovery of the car. Both parties have moved for summary judgment. Is MB Financial or Ellis entitled to summary judgment based on 2-403? If so, on what basis? If not, what issues of fact remain for decision in order to render judgment for or against MB Financial?

Problem 21-3.

On December 6, 1986, Mercedes-Benz Credit of Canada entered into a car lease of a 1987 Mercedes-Benz 560 SEL with Robert Barnabe of Quebec, Canada. In his credit application, Barnabe represented that he owned a home with considerable equity and was the president of several companies, including Rallye Motors Ltd. of Quebec, Canada. Barnabe entered into the lease in his individual capacity for a five-year term with monthly payments of $1717.02. Barnabe made timely lease payments until January 1989. Thereafter, his lease payments were often late. In September 1989, Barnabe ceased making lease payments to Mercedes-Benz.

Although Barnabe continued to make lease payments for almost three years after the purchase, he did not have possession of the car for much of that time period. On December 9, 1986, Barnabe unlawfully obtained a Canadian Certificate of Registration for the car in the name of Rallye Motors, an unregistered Canadian Honda dealership. On December 16, 1986, he entered into a contract for sale of the Mercedes-Benz to Gran Prix Auto Wholesalers, Inc., a New York corporation, for $51,500. Since its incorporation in 1974, Gran Prix had purchased and sold more than 78,000 vehicles. When Barnabe contacted Gran Prix about a possible sale, he represented that he was a Honda dealer. The president of Gran Prix telephoned Honda of North America to inquire whether Rallye Motors was an authorized Honda dealership, and he was informed that it was, though he acknowledged that contacting a manufacturer does not disclose whether the dealer's license has been revoked. The purchase from Barnabe was Gran Prix's first transaction with Barnabe and one of the few times that Gran Prix had purchased a car from Canada; the president of Gran Prix testified that he was unfamiliar with the documentation necessary to obtain registration or title for a Canadian vehicle. Unlike the 50 U.S. states, Canada is not a certificate-of-title jurisdiction.

Upon delivery to Gran Prix, Barnabe delivered the Canadian title document he had received, which was sufficient for Gran Prix to obtain title in New Jersey and New York. After purchasing the car, Gran Prix sold it to Ray Catena Motor Corp. for $53,650; thereafter, Catena transferred the car to its wholly-owned subsidiary and leasing agent, Touch of Class Leasing. Touch of Class leased the car to Dr. Ralph Del Priore. On March 23, 1990, the New Jersey State Police impounded the car while it was in Dr. Del Priore's possession. Meanwhile, Barnabe was arrested and sentenced to jail in Canada as a result of his "sale" of numerous cars in a manner similar to the transaction described in this case.

Touch of Class and Ray Catena instituted suit against Mercedes-Benz, claiming that title resided in Touch of Class. Mercedes-Benz moved for summary judgment, declaring that it had title to and ownership of the car and seeking an order requiring the State Police to deliver the car to its authorized agent. The plaintiffs filed cross-motions for summary judgment.

Are any of the parties entitled to summary judgment? If so, under which part of 2-403? If not, what issues of fact remain to be resolved, and what arguments will each party make to the fact-finder supporting its claim for relief?

Chapter 9

Remedies

Key Concepts

- Remedies available to an aggrieved buyer due to a seller's failure to deliver goods or delivery of defective goods
- Remedies available to an aggrieved seller due to a buyer's failure to take or pay for goods
- Ability of the parties to limit remedies for breach
- Statute of limitations applicable to Article 2 disputes

This Chapter consists of four Assignments covering the remedy provisions for both buyer and seller, which appear in Part 7 of Article 2. Assignment 22 covers the final set of buyer's remedies (you have already studied the buyer's rights to reject or revoke acceptance appearing in Part 6). Assignment 23 covers seller's remedies. Assignment 24 covers agreed-upon remedy limitations and exclusions. Finally, Assignment 25 covers the statute of limitations.

Before launching into the nuts and bolts of the remedies provisions in the next several assignments, it is worth looking first at the general policies of the Code related to remedies, as those underlie the interpretation and application of the remedies provisions.

Reading the Code:
§ 1-305

Read 1-305 and its Comments.

Question 1. What general policies with respect to remedies are articulated in 1-305? What policy or policies are added in the Comments?

Question 2. Which of the following common law remedies principles are reflected in 1-305 and its Comments? Where do you find them?

- Preventing double recovery by the aggrieved party

- Avoiding a forfeiture or a windfall

- Requiring reasonable certainty in damage amounts

- Preventing the aggrieved party from recovering damages that it could have avoided (mitigated)

- Preferring the interests of the aggrieved party over those of the breaching party, when both parties' interests cannot be accommodated

Assignment 22
Buyer's Remedies for Seller's Breach
§§ 2-502, 2-711 through 2-717, 2-723

Assignments 17 and 18 covered the first of two groups of buyer's remedies for seller's failure to perform according to the contract: buyer's rights under Part 6 of Article 2 to reject or revoke acceptance of the goods. This Assignment covers an aggrieved buyer's additional remedies in Part 7 of Article 2, including damages and specific performance. The availability of many of these remedies depends on whether buyer kept the goods (usually by accepting them) or does not have the goods (because buyer either never received the goods or gave them back to the seller after rejection or revocation). Most of buyer's remedies appear in §§ 2-711 through 2-717.

LEARNING OUTCOMES AND OBJECTIVES

At the completion of this Assignment, you should be able to

- identify and compare the remedies available to the buyer in the event of the seller's breach and the limitations placed on a buyer's recovery;
- determine what recovery is available for unaccepted goods and under what circumstances the buyer may be entitled to recover goods from the seller;
- determine and compare a buyer's cover and market damages;
- account for expenses saved and incidental and consequential damages in determining damages;
- determine a buyer's remedy for accepted goods;
- evaluate the efficacy of an agreed-to liquidated damages clause;
- determine the effect that the economic loss doctrine has on the ability of a buyer to bring a tort claim for the breach of a sales contract; and
- apply the relevant portions of Article 2 to determine what remedy a buyer is entitled to in a given set of facts in the event of the seller's breach.

As you explore buyer's remedies in this Assignment, keep in mind that the seller may have breached the contract in any of the following ways repudiating (antici-patorily or otherwise), failing to give the buyer notice of shipment, not delivering, delivering late, delivering nonconforming goods, not tendering required documents, tendering defective documents, making a carrier contract inappropriate to the nature of the goods (temperature control, length of trip, packing and cushioning, etc.), or wrongfully requiring the buyer to pay before inspection. Keep this range of possible breaches in mind as you complete the problems.

Article 2 provides two distinct remedial paths for an aggrieved buyer depending on whether the buyer has accepted the goods despite their nonconformity or has not accepted the goods (sometimes because they were not delivered). We will start with the latter path.

A. Buyer's Remedies for Unaccepted Goods

Section 2-711 provides a starting place for determining remedies for aggrieved buyers who have not accepted the goods and a roadmap to other sections providing more detail about the remedies. Section 2-711 encompasses circumstances where the buyer has refused to take or keep the goods because they were non-conforming and circumstances where the buyer does not have the goods because the seller did not deliver them. Under these widely varying situations, the buyer may sometimes want only damages for the seller's breach and may sometimes want to get the unde-livered goods from the seller. Both kinds of relief are identified in § 2-711. If the buyer chooses the damages-only path, § 2-711 offers the aggrieved buyer the right to cancel the contract, to recover the amount already paid (a considerable concern if the buyer has made a substantial down-payment for the goods), and to collect damages for the lost opportunity to buy based either on "cover" (buyer purchases substitute goods) or on market-based measures. Finally, if the buyer has rejected or justifiably revoked acceptance of the goods but still has them in its possession, § 2-711 recognizes that the buyer may have a security interest in the goods to help satisfy its damage claim against the seller.

Reading the Code: § 2-711

Read 2-711.

Question 1. Which buyer's remedies does 2-711 list for each type of breach? Place a check in a box if the remedy in the left column is at least sometimes available for the breach specified in the top row.

	Seller fails to deliver	Seller repudiates	Buyer rightfully rejects goods	Buyer justifiably revokes acceptance
2-711: Cancel contract				
2-711: Recover price paid				
2-712: Cover damages				
2-713: Market damages*				
2-502: Recovery of identified goods				
2-716: Specific performance or replevin				
2-711(3): Security interest in goods; resale				

*Although 2-711 refers to "damages for non-delivery as provided in . . . 2-713," the damages in 2-713 are commonly referred to as market damages.

Question 2. In your answers to Question 1, do your blank squares make sense? That is, why would that remedy not be available for that category of breach?

Question 3. Why does 2-711 provide for "cancellation" rather than "termination"? *See* 2-106.

1. Buyer's Recovery of the Goods from the Seller

Consider the plight of the aggrieved buyer who did not receive the goods (because seller repudiated or failed to deliver), but who still would like to get the goods from the seller, perhaps because the goods are scarce in the market or because the seller's skill makes the goods especially desirable. The Code allows the buyer to recover the goods upon seller's insolvency (§ 2-502), to obtain specific performance (§ 2-716(1), (2)), or to replevy the goods (§ 2-716(3)). These remedies overlap to some extent, but they address somewhat different fact situations.

**Reading the Code:
§§ 2-502, 2-716**

Read 2-502 and 2-716 and the accompanying Comments.

Question 4. Identify the prerequisites for the buyer to have the right to obtain the goods from the seller under 2-502.

Question 5. Identify the prerequisites for the buyer to have the right to obtain specific performance from the seller under 2-716(1).

Question 6. Identify the prerequisites for the buyer to have the right to obtain replevin of the goods from the seller under 2-716(3). Recall that the buyer "effects cover" by buying substitute goods in the market. In answering, consider only the first two sentences of Comment 3 to 2-716(3). The remainder of Comment 3 pertains to a security interest issue under Article 9.

Question 7. Why are there three different mechanisms that enable the buyer to get the goods back?

Example A: *Groeb Farms, Inc. v. Alfred L. Wolff, Inc.*[1]

Groeb Farms, Inc. (the buyer) entered into a contract with Alfred L. Wolff, Inc. (the seller) for a large amount of Korean honey and another contract for Indian honey. When the seller tried to deliver Chinese honey instead, the Department of Homeland Security refused to allow the importation of the honey due to anti-dumping restrictions. The buyer requested specific performance of the seller's promise to sell Indian and Korean honey. The buyer claimed that it could not obtain honey in the market in the quantities and prices set forth in the contract. The seller moved to dismiss the buyer's claim.

Analysis: The court denied the seller's motion to dismiss, noting that "uniqueness" under 2-716 can arise from market conditions. The court explained that the inability to cover could provide grounds for specific performance, particularly since the seller's inability to deliver the honey may have arisen from its attempt to deliver Chinese honey subject to anti-dumping restrictions, rather than supplying the Indian and Korean honey the buyer had ordered.

How does the rule of 2-716 on specific performance differ from that at common law? Do you agree that ordinary goods like honey can be unique in some circumstances? Would the buyer be able to obtain specific performance if Indian and Korean honey were readily available in the marketplace, but at a higher cost?

2. Buyer's Cover and Market Damages

Consider the situation of the aggrieved buyer who does not have the goods and does not want to (or does not have the right to) obtain the goods from the seller. The buyer's expectation interest—getting the benefit of the bargain—may not be satisfied by simply recovering the price already paid, since the buyer will be left without the goods in what may be a rising market. To recover the loss incurred, the buyer may claim money damages, choosing between measuring it by cover (the buyer's purchase of replacement goods, under §§ 2-711(1)(a) and 2-712) or by

---

[1] 68 U.C.C. Rep. Serv. 2d 539 (E.D. Mich. 2009). Note that this case was also discussed in Assignment 6, Example A.

using the market price for the goods (§§ 2-711(1)(b) and 2-713). We will return to consider the relationship between the cover and market measures after first exploring the nature of each of these remedies.

Reading the Code:
§§ 2-712 and 2-713

Read 2-712(2) and 2-713(1).

Question 8. Write out the mathematical formula for "cover damages" (2-712) and "market damages" (2-713), side by side. Use the following components: incidental damages, consequential damages, market price, cost of cover, expenses saved because of breach, and contract price. Use "+" and "−" as needed. You need not use all of the components. When you are done, consider whether each formula makes sense (that is, does each formula accurately measure the injury to the buyer?).

Question 9. What is the key difference between the formulas for the two types of damages in Question 8? Is one of the two formulas a better measure of injury to the buyer than the other formula? Why would Article 2 include both measures?

Question 10. What are the requirements for a buyer to effect a valid "cover"? Do the cover goods have to be identical to the contracted-for goods? See 2-712 Comment 2.

Read 2-713(2).

Question 11. The market price of goods may differ in different parts of the country or the world. What geographical market is used for establishing the market price under 2-713?

Section 2-713(1) says market price should be measured "at the time when the buyer learned of the breach." If the breach is a defect in the goods or a missed delivery date, the time when the buyer learned of the breach is easy to determine. But what if the breach is an anticipatory repudiation by the seller? The courts have split three ways on the question of what "learned of the breach" means when the seller anticipatorily repudiates its performance under the contract, concluding it might mean:

- *When buyer receives notice of seller's repudiation:* This timing makes sense because the buyer learns of the breach when the buyer hears of seller's repudiation so the market price at that time arguably best measures the market that the buyer could have used to make a substitute purchase. A possible second rationale is that § 2-723 uses this moment to measure the market if the case comes to trial before the time for performance.

- *A commercially reasonable time after buyer receives notice of seller's repudiation:* This timing makes sense because, under § 2-610, the buyer is allowed to wait a reasonable period after the seller announces repudiation before treating the repudiation as a breach, and as long as the buyer has not treated the repudiation as a breach, the seller may be able to retract under § 2-611. In addition, a buyer who obtains cover has a reasonable time in which to do so. Most courts apply this measure.

- *When seller's performance would have been due:* This timing makes sense because it is arguable that the actual "breach" is not certain to occur until the performance time is due; before that, seller's actions are a repudiation which buyer may react to as though it is a breach, but not really a breach.

If you were a judge, which of the three measures would you adopt? Why?

**Reading the Code:
§§ 2-712, 2-713,
and 2-715**

Read § 2-712(3) and Comment 3 and 2-713 Comment 5.

Question 12. May the buyer elect to receive damages under 2-713, even though the buyer has made a proper cover purchase?

Question 13. Must buyer effectuate cover, if cover is possible?

Question 14. If buyer does not cover, what effect does that have on damages under 2-715?

Question 15. Can a buyer ever recover under both 2-712 and 2-713?

EXAMPLES AND ANALYSIS

Example B: *Man Industries (India), Ltd. v. Midcontinent Express Pipeline, LLC*[2]

Midcontinent Express Pipeline, LLC (Midcontinent) contracted to buy pipe from Man Industries (India), Ltd. (Man). After Man fell behind on the delivery of the pipe, Midcontinent refused Man's request to extend the time for performance by one month. Midcontinent contracted with another supplier for cover of 10% of the pipe at the cost of the least expensive pipe that could be delivered by the contract deadline (a total of $3,720,800.66 above contract price). After Man missed another delivery deadline, Midcontinent purchased another 10% of the pipe from another supplier, again at fair market price (a total of $17,090,745.67 above contract price). Man did not meet other delivery requirements. Midcontinent brought suit for breach of contract and other claims. Man argued that Midcontinent could not collect its cover damages because, even though Midcontinent paid a fair market price for the replacement pipe, Midcontinent's decision to cover was not reasonable or in good faith because Midcontinent could have waived strict compliance with the production deadline without delaying its pipeline project.

Analysis: The Texas Court of Appeals affirmed the lower court's award of cover damages to Midcontinent under 2-712. The court rejected Man's argument that Midcontinent was not entitled to cover damages because it could have waived strict compliance with the production schedule. The court found that the contract contained a delivery schedule and that Midcontinent insisted that "time was of the essence." The court held that the obligation of good faith in obtaining cover

---

2   407 S.W.3d 342 (Tex. Ct. App. 2013).

did not require Midcontinent to extend the delivery deadline for Man or risk delay in project completion.

What part of the text of 2-712 would Man argue favors denying cover damages? Why did the court disagree? The court found that Midcontinent satisfied the requirements of 2-712(1) and so was entitled to obtain cover damages. Why? Should an aggrieved buyer have to accommodate the breaching seller if it can before covering?

Example C: *Allegheny Energy Supply Co. v. Wolf Run Mining Co.*[3]

Allegheny Energy Supply Co. contracted to buy all coal reserves at the Sycamore No. 2 Mine owned by Wolf Run Mining Co. The contract included a force majeure clause that would excuse some nonperformance by Wolf Run. In the second year of the agreement, Wolf Run experienced problems at the mine and informed Allegheny Energy that it would not be able to meet its obligations under the agreement. That same month, Wolf Run sent Allegheny Energy a formal force majeure notice, claiming that problems at the mine were beyond its control. Allegheny Energy bought coal elsewhere and sued Wolf Run for breach of contract for both its cover damages and future damages as a result of the mine's repudiation of future deliveries. At trial, Allegheny Energy put on evidence of cover damages of approximately $84,163,895. Wolf Run put forth its own damage estimates for Allegheny Energy based upon market price, finding damages amounted to only $11,304,332.

Analysis: The trial court rejected Wolf Run's arguments for force majeure, finding underperformance of the mine was not covered by that contract clause. The court also rejected the proof of cover damages put forth by Allegheny Energy, awarding market-based damages in accord with Wolf Run's calculations. With respect to future damages, the trial court awarded damages calculated from the time of trial.

The appellate court agreed with the award of market-based damages, but reversed the future damages. The court held that Allegheny Energy "learned of

---

[3] 53 A.3d 53 (Pa. Super. Ct. 2012).

the repudiation" not at the time of trial, but rather, when Wolf Run informed it of the repudiation by providing the formal force majeure notice, so that was the appropriate time for the determination of the market price under 2-713 with respect to future damages.

Do you agree with the trial court or with the appellate court? Explain how the timing issue relates to the amount of damages awardable. Should a buyer that fails to establish its cover damages still be entitled to market-based damages? What provision of the Code supports your position?

3. Expenses Saved as a Result of Breach

Damage calculations for both cover damages and market damages include deduction for "expenses saved in consequence of the seller's breach."

EXAMPLES AND ANALYSIS

Example D. A farmer purchases a tractor from the seller. Farmer uses the tractor for one month for fall harvest and is able to get the produce to market but ultimately revokes acceptance of the tractor because of substantial defects. In an action brought by the farmer against the seller, the seller claims the farmer saved some expenses by having the benefit of the use of the tractor for the buyer's harvest for the month.

Example E. A farmer contracts to purchase corn from the seller, but has not yet paid for the corn. After the seller fails to deliver the corn, the farmer is able to purchase corn locally and save transportation costs on delivery. In an action brought by the farmer against the seller, the seller claims the farmer saved the transportation expense by purchasing locally.

Analysis: In both Examples D and E the seller could reasonably argue for a reduction of the buyer's recovery for an expense saved. Of course, the breaching seller would have to prove that the use of the defective goods amounted to a savings to the farmer in Example D and that the farmer would have paid transportation costs in the original contract in Example E.

B. Buyer's Remedies for Accepted Goods

Recall that § 2-711 lists buyer's remedies only for unaccepted goods. If a buyer has accepted (and not revoked acceptance of) the goods, buyer's remedies are specified in § 2-714. In contrast to the computation specified in §§ 2-712 and 2-713, § 2-714 provides an open-ended general measure of damages (subsection (1)) and a somewhat more specific definition of damages for breach of warranty (subsection (2)).

EXAMPLES AND ANALYSIS

Example F: *KSW Mechanical Services v. Johnson Controls, Inc.*[4]

KSW Mechanical Services, Inc. (KSW) contracted to buy air handling units from Johnson Controls, Inc. (JCI). The agreement of the parties expressly excluded recovery of consequential damages. After the parties were unable to resolve a dispute over the amount of pre-assembly done by JCI prior to delivery, KSW brought suit for breach of contract, and JCI counterclaimed for the unpaid price. JCI moved for summary judgment, asserting that KSW could state only a claim for consequential damages, which the agreement expressly precluded. Accordingly, JCI argued that the remedies in 2-714 were not available to KSW.

Analysis: The court disagreed with JCI. Denying the seller's motion for summary judgment, the court held that 2-714(1) allows for recovery of "direct" damages (those that directly, immediately, and naturally flow from the breach of a contract) calculated "in any manner which is reasonable," including damages for "any failure of the seller to perform according to his obligations under the contract." 2-714 Comment 2. While 2-714(3) permits the recovery of incidental and consequential damages, the "precise demarcation between direct and consequential damages is a question of fact . . . ." *KSW Mech. Serv.* at 146 (quoting *Am. Elec. Power Co., Inc. v. Westinghouse Elec. Corp.*, 418 F. Supp 435, 459-60 (S.D.N.Y. 1976).

---

[4]   992 F. Supp. 2d 135 (E.D.N.Y. 2014).

Rejecting a "broad" view of consequential damages that would undercut direct damages, the court explained:

> KSW enumerates what it purports to be direct costs incurred by JCI's supplying non-conforming goods that were not pre-assembled, including assembly costs, costs for the rigger to lift additional crates, costs to construct and design supports, costs for the use of a crane, and a 15% markup for KSW's additional overhead and diminished profits. The Court does not, at this time, address the reasonableness of KSW's alleged damages. Concerning simply whether or not is possible for KSW to state a claim for such damages under the UCC and the terms of the contract, this Court cannot find as a matter of law that KSW's damages are precluded consequential or incidental damages. If direct damages are "what it would take to put the non-breaching party in the same position that it would be in had the breaching party performed as promised under the contract," KSW's enumerated costs might well fall within that definition. [Other] [c]ases . . . provide examples of analogous damages that those courts determined to be direct damages.

Do you agree with the court's reading of 2-714? Must all direct damages be measurable by the primary formula under 2-714(2)?

**Reading the Code:
§ 2-714**

Read 2-714.

Question 16. Which of the following are available as 2-714 damages? For those that are, specify the applicable portion of 2-714:

   (a) Cost of repairing the defect.

   (b) Market price of conforming goods, minus the resale price of the goods delivered.

   (c) Rental value of goods during repair.

(d) The value of the defect, based on an appraiser's testimony.

(e) Contract price of goods minus appraiser's valuation of goods delivered.

Question 17. In calculating breach-of-warranty damages under 2-714(2), at what place and what time are the values of the goods determined?

1. Measuring the Recovery for Breach of Warranty

In a suit that claims damages under section 2-714(2), two amounts must be compared: (i) the value of the goods accepted and (ii) the value the goods would have had if they had been as warranted. There is no single recognized way for measuring the value of goods either as accepted or as warranted. The purchase price is often an appropriate measure of the value of the goods *if they had been as warranted*, but this might not be the case if, for example, the buyer obtained the goods at a discount below the market value or paid above market rate. The value of goods *as accepted* is determined at the time and place of acceptance. Fair market value is a measure frequently used, but it may be difficult to determine the market value of defective goods. Courts often take into account the cost to repair as equivalent to the difference in value; the repair cost may be the discount the market would demand for defective goods, to permit them to be restored to the full value of conforming goods. When litigating damage claims, the buyer must use ingenuity and resourcefulness to identify persuasive arguments regarding measurement of both values.

EXAMPLES AND ANALYSIS

Example G: *O'Rourke v. American Kennels*[5]

O'Rourke purchased a puppy warranted to be the breed "Teacup Maltese." A year later, based on the animal's growth and weight gain, it became obvious that the animal was in fact not a "Teacup." The buyer did not wish to return the dog, but sued for damages under the Code for breach of warranty.

---

[5]   2005 WL 1026955 (N.Y. Civ. Ct. 2005).

Analysis: For value of the goods as warranted, the court accepted the contract price of $2,500 as the value of a Teacup Maltese. The court also held that the market price for a non-Teacup-bred Maltese was $1,500—the price for a non-teacup Maltese puppy from the seller on the date of the original purchase.

Example H: *Canterbury Apartment Homes LLC v. Louisiana Pacific Corp.*[6]

Canterbury Apartment Homes LLC (Canterbury) purchased siding for its apartment complex from Louisiana Pacific Corporation (LP). The siding came with a 25-year written warranty against defects. Pieces of the siding fell off the apartment building, mushrooms grew out of the siding, and the siding did not retain its shape. Canterbury requested that LP replace the siding. After Canterbury did not hear from LP, it sent a letter to LP informing LP that Canterbury would replace the siding. After seeking bids from several companies, Canterbury selected the lowest bidder and replaced the siding at a cost of $817,584.44 plus $105,439.34 to paint the new siding and $16,893.11 for building permits related to the installation of the replacement siding. After LP offered Canterbury $8363 as compensation for the damaged siding, Canterbury brought a claim for breach of warranty and other claims. The jury found for Canterbury in the amount of $755,314.17 and LP appealed, claiming, among other things, that the jury's award of damages that took into account replacement costs was not consistent with 2-714.

Analysis: The appellate court disagreed with LP and affirmed the jury award. The court found that both repair and replacement costs can be a proper measure of damages under 2-714(2). The court concluded that, because it was not possible to repair the defective siding, replacement cost was a proper measure of the difference between the goods as warranted and the goods as delivered.

Based on the facts you know in this case, what amount would you claim as damages on behalf of Canterbury? How might the jury have come to award the amount it did? Is replacement cost justified as a measure of damages under

---

[6]   84 UCC Rep. Serv. 2d 185 (Ct. App. Wa. 2014).

2-714(1) or (2)? At what point is a buyer permitted to claim replacement damages? Must the goods be completely unrepairable?

2. Amounts Owed to the Seller

An aggrieved buyer who has accepted defective goods or who has other claims of injury remains liable for the price of the accepted goods. Unlike § 2-711 (damages for unaccepted goods), § 2-714 does not give buyer the right to cancel or get back money already paid. But the buyer may not want to pay some or all of the price still due, given the injury it has suffered. What should the aggrieved buyer do?

Reading the Code:
§ 2-717

Read 2-717.

Question 18. What does 2-717 say about the dilemma described above? Does this section apply to cover damages (2-712)? To market damages (2-713)? To damages to accepted goods (2-714)? If you're stumped, consider when buyer is obligated to pay the contract price. What section imposes that obligation?

Question 19. If the buyer accepts goods that are defective and has not yet paid any portion of the contract price, what is the formula governing how much buyer has to pay seller?

EXAMPLES AND ANALYSIS

Example I: *KSW Mechanical Services v. Johnson Controls, Inc.*[7]

KSW Mechanical Services, Inc. (KSW) contracted to buy air handling units from Johnson Controls, Inc. (JCI). After the parties were unable to resolve a dispute over the amount of pre-assembly done by JCI prior to delivery, KSW brought suit for breach of contract and JCI counterclaimed for the unpaid price. KSW asserted that, notwithstanding its acceptance of the non-conforming goods, 2-714 and 2-717 permitted it to withhold partial payment on the contract to remedy JCI's alleged breach. JCI moved for summary judgment claiming that because KSW retained the goods, it was bound to pay the full price.

Analysis: The court agreed with KSW. Denying the seller's motion for summary judgment, the court held that even though JCI could prevail in an action for the price under 2-709, KSW might be able to deduct damages from any price due under 2-717. The court rejected JCI's argument that it was entitled to summary judgment because KSW's acceptance of the units precluded its action for damages. Summary judgment was not appropriate where a fact issue remained as to the amount of KSW's damages and whether they directly resulted from "the ordinary course of business from the seller's breach."

Do you agree with the court's reading of 2-714 and 2-717? Is 2-717 limited to breaches involving the non-delivery of goods? Can a buyer take advantage of both 2-714 and 2-717 simultaneously? What form must the buyer's notice to the seller take, as to the buyer's intention to exercise its rights under 2-717 ? *See* Comment 2. If representing KSW, what would you have advised it with respect to notice regarding nonpayment of the invoice for the price?

C. Incidental and Consequential Damages

Whether the buyer has accepted defective goods, rejected them, or revoked acceptance, damages to the buyer may include consequential and incidental damages. Under the common law, incidental damages have often been associated with the expenses of "mopping up the breach," that is, the expenses associated with mitigating or avoiding additional losses by the aggrieved party. They do not include

---

[7]   2 F. Supp. 2d 135 (E.D.N.Y. 2014). Note that this case was also discussed in Example F above.

lost profits or injuries resulting indirectly from the breaching party's defective performance. Those items are instead consequential damages. As explained in Example F above, courts sometimes struggle over which losses suffered by a party are direct damages and which are incidental or consequential damages, leaving the issue for the factfinder.

EXAMPLES AND ANALYSIS

Example J: *Barko Hydraulics, LLC v. Shepherd*[8]

Michael Shepherd purchased a knuckle boom loader from Barko Hydraulics, LLC or $202,274. The loader came with a warranty. Shepherd was initially pleased with the loader, but began having problems after about four months. Barko made a number of repairs during the warranty period but refused to make additional repairs after the warranty term expired. Shepherd brought suit for breach of warranty, claiming compensatory damages for lost profits, mental anguish, and punitive damages. Shepherd alleged that he lost his business because of the problems with the loader and that the loss of his logging business caused his divorce, resulting in his spending less time with his daughter. After a jury trial, the trial court confirmed a verdict in favor of Shepherd in the amount of $450,000. Barko appealed, claiming that damages should be limited to the cost to repair the Loader and should not have included any damages for mental anguish.

Analysis: The Supreme Court of Alabama held that damages under 2-714(2) would include the difference between the actual value of the loader and its value if it had been as warranted, along with incidental and consequential damages under 2-715. The court rejected recovery for mental anguish. While the court did not exclude the possibility of mental anguish damages in a proper case, in order to recover for such an injury as consequential damages, the contractual duty must be "'so coupled with matters of mental concern or solicitude . . . that a breach of that duty will necessarily or reasonably result in mental anguish or suffering.' . . . There must be some nexus between the mental-anguish damages and the intention and contemplation of the parties at the time the contract was made." The court found no such nexus. Because the jury had returned only a

---

8   84 UCC Rep. Serv. 2d 728 (Ala. 2014).

general verdict, the court could not determine the amount the jury awarded for each type of damages, some of which were properly awardable and some of which were not. The court therefore reversed the judgment in its entirety and remanded for a new trial.

Example K: *Packgen v. Berry Plastics Corp.*[9]

Packgen is in the business of manufacturing and selling catalyst containers, including foil-laminated intermediate bulk containers used by petroleum refineries for transportation and storage of fresh and spent catalyst , referred to as "Cougars." Berry Plastics Corporation (Berry) supplied Packgen with foil-laminated material (woven polypropylene fabric that was chemically bonded to a layer of aluminum foil) in a series of transactions. The laminated material was subsequently used in the production of Cougars. One of these Cougars, sold to one of Packgen's largest customers, failed. Packgen brought suit for damages arising from breach of contract, including lost profits. Packgen claimed that "[a]s a result of the failure of the Cougars at [the customer's] facility, Packgen lost sales of Cougars that the thirty-seven refineries would have placed. Packgen's lost profits arise out of allegedly lost sales to [the customer] and anticipated sales to thirty-seven refineries with which Packgen had no previous customer relationship." In its motion for summary judgment, Berry argued that these damages were not recoverable because they were not foreseeable and were disproportionate to the value of the contract. Packgen argued that, because the UCC defines consequential damages as "any loss," it was entitled "to recover all losses even if they are large in comparison to the contract price." Moreover, Packgen also argued that Berry "knew of Packgen's requirements and needs, knew about Packgen's business relationship with [the customer] and anticipated business relationships with the refineries, and had reason to know that Packgen would suffer lost profits if the Cougars failed and that these damages would be substantial" at the time of contracting.

Analysis: The court denied summary judgment to Berry. The court noted that, "to recover lost profit damages, a plaintiff must establish causation, foreseeability,

---

9   2015 WL 3868965 (D. Me. 2015).

reasonable certainty as to amount, and that lost profits are not barred by applicable mitigation doctrines." There is no requirement that the damages be proportionate to the value of the goods. Why was summary judgment not appropriate here? Are lost profits incidental or consequential damages under 2-715? What parts of 2-715 will Berry want to argue preclude Packgen's claim for consequential damages?

D. Liquidated Damages

As at common law, Article 2 permits parties to fashion their own remedies by agreement. A liquidated damage clause sets out an agreed-upon measure of damages in the event of a particular type of breach or a particular type of injury resulting from a breach. It may take the place of direct, consequential, or incidental damages. Such clauses, like other parts of an agreement, are subject to scrutiny for unconscionability. As at common law, the Code imposes important limitations on the ability of a parties to use liquidated damages clauses, aimed toward avoiding the imposition of any penalties.

Reading the Code:
§ 2-718

Read 2-718(1).

Question 20. The traditional common law rule is that the reasonableness of the amount of liquidated damages is judged at the time of contract formation. How does the UCC rule differ? What might be the logic for the UCC rule?

EXAMPLES AND ANALYSIS

Example L: *Garden Ridge, L.P. v. Advance Int'l, Inc.*[10]

Garden Ridge, L.P., a houseware and home décor store, contracted to purchase eight- and nine-foot-tall waving inflatable snowmen from Advance International, Inc. for $49,176 and $29,178, respectively. When the first order of snowmen arrived at Garden Ridge's store, the style of the eight-foot-tall snowmen was incorrect, as they did not wave, but held a banner instead. The style of the nine-foot-tall snowmen was correct—they did wave. Garden Ridge sold both types of snowmen at its Thanksgiving Shop-a-Thon sale and made a $113,000 profit selling the snowmen (the same profit Garden Ridge would have made if the snowmen had all waved). The Garden Ridge vendor compliance manual, which was incorporated in the contract, contained a liquidated damages provision that permitted Garden Ridge to "charge back" the entire cost of noncompliance to a seller. Relying on this provision, Garden Ridge did not pay the invoice for either the eight- or nine-foot-tall snowmen. Advance demanded payment for the snowmen and staged protests at Garden Ridge. Garden Ridge sued Advance for breach of contract and a declaratory judgment that it had complied with the contract. Advance counterclaimed for breach of contract, arguing that the "chargeback" provision was unreasonable and therefore unenforceable as a penalty under 2-718. Garden Ridge claimed that its actual damages were not relevant where the chargeback provision was created because damages from noncompliance violations are difficult to calculate.

Analysis: The jury awarded Advance the amounts due for the snowmen. The appellate court affirmed, rejecting Garden Ridge's argument that the trial court erred by considering the actual harm done from the breach in determining reasonableness of the liquidated damages clause. The court noted that 2-718 specifically provides that reasonableness is judged taking into account "the anticipated or *actual* harm caused by the breach." Accordingly, it is proper for courts to consider both values when evaluating a liquidated damages clause for reasonableness. The court agreed that Advance met its burden of proving the chargeback provision was a "disproportionate estimation" of actual damages and was void as a penalty where Garden Ridge suffered no actual damages. Moreover, the court found that the chargeback provision was also unreasonable in light of

---

[10]   403 S.W.3d 432 (Tex. Ct. App. 2013).

the anticipated harm, as it imposed damages of 100% of the cost of merchandise for all noncompliance, even if minor or trivial, allowing Garden Ridge to keep the merchandise (conforming and non-conforming) without paying.

Do you agree with the court's analysis here? Why or why not? Could Advance prevail if it only proved that Garden Ridge had no actual damages, but put forth no proof with respect to anticipated damages? Is there an argument to be made on behalf of Garden Ridge in favor of 100% harm for trivial defects? Under the "chargeback" provision, could Garden Ridge claim it did not have to pay for the snowmen if the contract described the snowmen as having red buttons, but instead, when they arrived, the buttons were green?

E. Economic Loss Doctrine

Litigants often have alternative bases for claiming relief, but the juxtaposition of Article 2 and tort claims presents special difficulties. Buyers or others who suffer losses caused by defects in purchased goods may seek to hold the seller liable for those losses not only by claiming breach of obligation under Article 2, but also by alleging that the seller was negligent or is strictly liable for distributing a defective and unsafe product. If a contract contains effective disclaimers of warranty liability or exclusions of consequential damages, should the buyer be permitted to bypass the contractual restrictions by seeking damages in tort? If Article 2 relief is barred because the statute of limitations has run under § 2-725, should a buyer be able to seek tort recovery, which may not be barred because the statute of limitations for tort claims began to run when the injury occurred rather than when the goods were tendered?

Article 2 itself says nothing about how such alternative claims for relief should be handled, so the courts address the problem as a matter of common law. The rule that has been adopted by many courts—commonly called the "economic loss doctrine"—establishes restrictions on the damages that will be recoverable in tort for defects in goods when Article 2 also applies to the transaction. *See East River S.S. Corp. v. Transamerica Delaval*, Inc., 476 U.S. 858 (1986), in which the Supreme Court adopted the economic loss doctrine in admiralty law to bar a tort cause of action arising from a breach of warranty. The "economic loss doctrine" is generally understood as follows: If injury results from defects in goods bought and sold, negligence or strict liability claims are available only for personal injury and for injury to real or personal property other than the goods themselves. Other forms of injury (e.g., damage to the purchased goods, lost profits, expenses incurred as a result of the breach) are called "economic loss"[11] and are governed only by Article 2.

EXAMPLES AND ANALYSIS

Example M: *Wade v. Tiffin Motorhomes, Inc.*[12]

Dennis and Denise Wade purchased a recreational vehicle (RV) designed and manufactured by Tiffin Motorhomes, Inc., a Texas company. Two years later, while traveling from Vermont to their home in Ohio, the Wades were at a campground in New York when a fire broke out in the RV, destroying both the RV and the Wades' belongings that were inside. The cause of the fire appeared to be due to a faulty propane system in the RV. The Wades had not made any substantial alterations to the RV since its purchase. The Wades brought claims for the damage to the RV and to their personal property inside the RV, which was destroyed in the fire, claiming strict product liability, negligence, and breach of warranty. The manufacturer moved for summary judgment on the tort claims.

Analysis: The court recognized that the economic loss doctrine limits the recovery by an owner of a product who suffers purely monetary harm to the product itself, consigning the owner to contract rather than tort damages for that injury. The owner may still have tort claims against a manufacturer for personal injuries caused by a defect in the product. The rationale behind the rule is to preserve the distinction between warranty and strict product liability. A less settled area, however, is when a plaintiff, like the Wades, suffers damage to "other property" in addition to the product itself.

Applying the economic loss rule, the court granted summary judgment against the Wades on their tort claim for damage to the RV itself but denied summary judgment with respect to the Wades' tort claim for damage to the contents of the RV. Finding that the Wades' personal property stored inside the RV was a classic

---

[11] The terminology is a bit confusing, because damage to the person and to other property also represents a form of economic loss, but it is not within the definition of "economic loss" as used in the cases.

[12] 686 F. Supp. 2d 174 (N.D.N.Y. 2009).

example of "other property," the court held that the economic loss doctrine did not operate as a bar to those claims. If the Wades had suffered any personal injuries arising from the incident, those would have been allowed to proceed as well.

Does the court's judgment on the Wades' tort claim for loss to the RV mean that the Wades have no recourse for that injury? More generally, should claimants have access to both contract and tort remedies for all injuries? Can you suggest an explanation for why courts have limited access to tort remedies for what is essentially an Article 2 claim?

Example N: *Giddings & Lewis, Inc. v. Industrial Risk Insurers*[13]

The buyer purchased a Diffuser Cell System, which consisted of a vertical turning lathe, two vertical machining centers, and a material handling system. After seven years of use, several parts of the lathe flew off and catapulted around the workspace. Though the flying parts weighed about 5200 pounds, no one was injured and damage to property beyond the Diffuser Cell System was minimal. The buyer brought claims for fraud and negligent misrepresentation against the seller.

Analysis: The Kentucky Supreme Court applied the economic loss doctrine to preclude the tort claims. The court relied on the classic position that economic losses (costs for repair or replacement of the product itself, lost profits and similar injuries) in essence deprive the purchaser of the benefit of his bargain and that such losses are best addressed by the parties' contract and relevant provisions of Article 2 :

> Today we hold that the economic loss doctrine applies to claims arising from a defective product sold in a commercial transaction, and that the relevant product is the entire item bargained for by the parties and placed in the stream of commerce by the manufacturer. Further, the economic loss rule applies regardless of whether the product fails over a period of time or destroys itself in a calamitous event, and the rule's application is not limited to negligence and strict liability claims, but also encompasses negligent misrepresentation claims.

---

[13]   348 S.W.3d 729 (Ky. 2011).

As reflected in its focus on the "relevant product" that was "placed in the stream of commerce by the manufacturer," the court rejected the buyer's argument that the components purchased with the lathe were "other property" for purposes of the economic loss rule, finding the components to be an integrated system. The court noted that even though some buyers purchase the components separately, courts must focus on the transaction that actually took place, which, in this instance, was the purchase of a complete Diffuser Cell System, of which the lathe was a part. The economic loss doctrine thus precluded tort claims that were related to the system as a whole and not just those related to the lathe. The court's ruling encompassed not only negligence and strict liability claims, but also claims of negligent misrepresentation, even where a seller allegedly made affirmative statements. And the court rejected decisions made in some jurisdictions to limit the economic loss rule by allowing tort claims related to "calamitous events." As a result, the only remedies available to the buyer were those under Article 2.

In light of the length of time here (seven years) before the lathe self-destructed, what impediments might the buyer face to bringing Article 2 claims? Do you agree with the characterization that the product here for purposes of the economic loss rule should be the entire Diffuser Cell System?

APPLYING THE CODE

Problem 22-1.

In each of the factual settings below, does the buyer save expenses because of the seller's breach?

(a) A buyer pays freight for the goods, per the contract. The buyer then rightfully rejects the goods and obtains cover in the seller's city, paying freight on the substitute goods.

(b) A buyer pays freight for the goods, per the contract. The buyer then rightfully rejects the goods and decides not to obtain cover, but instead to seek market damages.

(c) A seller repudiates the contract with the buyer, who was supposed to pay freight for the goods. The buyer obtains cover in the buyer's city. The buyer picks up the substitute goods with its own truck.

(d)   A seller repudiates the contract with the buyer, who was supposed to pay freight for the goods. The buyer then obtains cover in the seller's city, paying freight on the substitute goods.

(e)   A seller repudiates a contract with the buyer, who was supposed to pay freight for the goods under an F.O.B. shipment contract. The market price has risen, and the buyer decides not to obtain cover, but instead to seek market damages.

Problem 22-2.

Label the following buyer's damages as likely to be considered consequential (C), incidental (I), or neither (N):

(a)   Buyer's kitchen is damaged by fire when a defective coffee pot catches fire.

(b)   Buyer rejects a defective new car, but has paid for registration and towing the car.

(c)   Buyer requests punitive damages in action for breach against seller after seller represented that its mouthwash was safe for use for oral care.

(d)   Buyer is liable to its own customer for failure to timely deliver goods that buyer was to manufacture using seller's component goods, had buyer not rejected the seller's goods because they were defective. Seller was aware of that "downstream contract" during the parties' negotiations.

(e)   Buyer pulls its administrative staff off its usual duties and assigns them to phone suppliers to find "cover" goods.

(f)   Buyer's employee who was working as a pipe insulator is killed from severe burns received when a suction diffuser purchased from seller fractured, releasing 185 degree water.

(g)   Before opening her new store, Buyer pays a down-payment on the contract price for furniture, which arrives late, costing the buyer business. The buyer pays rent for her store, which sits empty with no furniture.

(h)   Buyer pays transportation costs for "cover" tires that are not available in the local market, where buyer would have otherwise obtained the tires if seller had not breached.

(i)   Buyer, a manufacturing company, loses $2555 in profits because it has to shut down a production line for two days to disentangle seller's defective goods from the machinery.

Problem 22-3.

Bennett and CMH Homes entered into a contract for purchase of a custom-built mobile home. Shortly after the purchase, the Bennetts found several defects in the mobile home including the following: "[All] three levels of the triple wide were not level; the floors were uneven; there were sunken areas; the marriage lines were different heights; there were structural defects in the drywall, ceiling and brick foundation; the carpet was wrinkled; part of the roof was warped due to improper installation; and the lights would go very dim when air or heat [was] used." CMH did not cure the defects, and, ultimately, the Bennetts revoked acceptance of the home after living there for 88 months and paying $123,200 toward the loan on the home. In an action for breach of contract, the Bennetts requested:

(a) $109,597 for the purchase price of the home;

(b) $80,000 in interest;

(c) $9600 in lost wages representing the value of six weeks of vacation time that Bennett used to attend to problems with the home;

(d) $4038 in appraisal and permit fees, television and phone jacks, flood lights, screen doors and shower heads for the mobile home;

(e) $15,200 for future expenses to rent a furnished apartment for ten months while they secure another custom-built mobile home;

(f) $10,000 for future expenses to move and store furniture for ten months while they secure another custom-built mobile home;

(g)   Punitive damages;

(h)   Mental anguish damages from having to live in the mobile home;

(i)   Prejudgment interest at 10%; and

(j)   Attorneys' fees.

Which of the requested items are recoverable? What arguments do you expect the parties to make regarding the claim?

Problem 22-4.

(a) Roy wants to protect himself and his family from natural or man-made calamities and so purchases an Earth-dome 60 survival shelter from Radius, Inc., at a cost of $1,800,000. The Earthcom Dome 60 is a fiberglass dome manufactured by Radius in pie-shaped sections that are shipped to the home site, where they are assembled and buried. After installation, there were cracks in and gaps between the sections, resulting in water leakage and mold. Roy hired a company to repair the Earthdome 60, but repairs were futile, and the Earthdome 60 is unsuitable as a survival shelter and cannot be used for any other purpose. In an action against Radius for breach of warranty, if Roy prevails, how much should he recover?

(b) Presume that at trial, Radius puts forth evidence that Roy could seal the inside of the dome with fiberglass and urethane foam at a cost of $35,000. If true, how would this affect Roy's claim for damages?

Problem 22-5.

Azin, an engineer, orders a scanner for her home computer from a mail-order company. As specified in the catalog, Seller ships it to her F.O.B. Azin's home, buyer to pay seller for shipping. Her credit-card authorization to the mail-order company includes $18.00 shipping (fairly standard price for the industry), in addition to the contract price. When the scanner arrives, the shipping box looks damaged and the plastic casing of the scanner is cracked, but the scanner works fine. In addition:

- Her mail-order price is $550 on August 28, an especially good deal on the scanner because the scanner is on sale at the beginning of the school year.

- She receives the mail-order scanner on August 30.

- The average mail-order price (without shipping) for the same model of scanner at five similar mail-order businesses is:

    $575 on August 28;

    $570 on August 30;

    $600 on September 4; and

    $620 on September 6.

- At six stores in Azin's area, the best price for the same model of scanner is

    $589 on August 28;

> $595 on August 30;
>
> $625 on September 4; and
>
> $640 on September 6.

- Round-trip driving expense to local store, Computer Centre, is $4.70.

Each set of facts below is independent of the other sets of facts. For each question below, first ascertain the formula for the specified remedy, then locate the dollar amount for each element in the formula. You do not need to perform the actual addition and subtraction. You might not use all of the above facts in the questions below.

(a) On August 30, Azin rightfully and effectively rejects the mail-order scanner by calling the company, describing the damage, saying that she does not want the scanner, and asking for instructions on how to reship it to the company. No instructions are forthcoming. She pays U.P.S. $22.50 to send the damaged scanner back to the mail-order company. Round-trip driving expense to U.P.S. is $9.10. Seller declines to cure.

Azin has a chance to do a quick job over the Labor Day weekend for a client, but she has to decline the job because she does not have a scanner at home. The job would have generated $85 in profit. The sale prices in the industry last only until Labor Day, when scanner prices go back up to normal levels. Between August 30 and September 6, Azin spends two hours on the phone getting prices from local and mail-order companies. Her net billing rate in her business is $45 per hour. On September 4, the day after Labor Day, Computer Centre has the best price in her city on the same model of scanner ($625). Even though the price is $15 more than the average mail-order price as of that date, she decides to buy the replacement scanner locally, to avoid the hassle of possibly receiving another damaged scanner by mail order. She decides to buy the replacement scanner immediately, to avoid any further increase in prices. On September 4, she buys from Computer Centre the same model scanner that she had originally ordered, paying by check. When her credit card bill arrives with the cost of the original scanner and shipping on it, she disputes and therefore does not pay that portion of her payment. Can she get cover damages? If so, how much can she recover?

(b)   On August 30, Azin rightfully and effectively rejects the mail-order scanner by calling the company, describing the damage, saying that she does not want the scanner, and asking for instructions on how to reship the scanner to the company. No instructions are forthcoming. She pays U.P.S. $22.50 to send the damaged scanner back to the mail-order company. Round-trip driving expense to U.P.S. is $9.10. Azin has already paid the mail-order company with a $568 check, and the check cleared before she could stop payment on it. Seller declines to cure. She pays her part-time administrative assistant $24 to phone around town to determine scanner prices at various stores, but then she decides not to buy a replacement, thinking she can get by using a friend's scanner. She uses the friend's scanner to complete a Labor Day job offered by a client. If she had used the same scanner at a nearby photocopy shop, it would have cost her $123. She pays her friend $40. How much can Azin recover from the seller by way of market and other damages?

(c)   Azin does not contact the mail-order company and does not send the damaged scanner back. She decides to have the scanner checked out by a nearby computer repair shop, to see if she can avoid the hassle of returning it. On August 30, she takes the damaged scanner to a repair shop and asks for an estimate of how much it will cost to replace the outside plastic casing and anything else that is broken. The shop calls her back on September 4 and tells her that the repair cost will be $125. She authorizes the repairs and picks up the repaired scanner on September 6. If Azin gives the mail-order company notice under 2-607(3)(a), how much does she owe the mail-order company, using 2-714 and 2-717? How much does she owe if she does not give 2-607(3)(a) notice? Assume that the credit card bill has not yet arrived and that she has not paid yet.

(d)   On August 30, Azin rightfully and effectively rejects the mail-order scanner by calling the company, describing the damage, saying that she does not want the scanner, and asking for instructions on how to reship the scanner to the company. The company asks her to ship it back via U.P.S., and says that the company will reimburse her. She does so. Her round-trip driving expense to U.P.S. is $9.10. The mail-order company replaces the cracked case and sends the scanner back to her, along with reimbursement for her shipping and driving expenses. Delighted, Azin pays the credit card bill for the scanner and uses it for a month before part of the motor overheats because a self-lubricating bearing in the scanner was damaged in the shipping accident but took a month to fail. The scanner motor is destroyed by the overheating, but the motor can be replaced. Otherwise, the scanner is fine. What are Azin's options, in terms of remedies? What is her best course of action?

Problem 22-6.

Sometimes the damages formula in a Code remedy must be adjusted in order to provide full compensation but not a windfall. Consider the following examples:

(a) What happens to your answer to Problem 22-5(a) if Azin obtains cover with a slightly better and more expensive model of scanner (perhaps because the model she is replacing is unavailable or because buyer's needs have changed)? How might you adjust the Code formula to fit the actual solution?

(b) What happens to your answer to Problem 22-5(c) if Azin is not able to get the scanner fully repaired but is able to make it functional, save one or two features that still do not work? How might you adjust the Code formula to fit the actual solution? Assume that Azin gave 2-607(3)(a) notice.

(c) Assume that when Azin purchases her scanner, the seller also agrees to install it into her existing computer network. If goods predominate over services in the purchase, what remedies are available to Azin if the seller fails to install the scanner or installs it defectively?

Problem 22-7.

For the following liquidated damage clause, what additional facts do you need to evaluate the clause's validity under 2-718(1)?

"If Seller does not deliver each weekly installment of goods by 8 p.m. Sunday to Buyer's manufacturing plant, Seller must pay Buyer the current FedEx price of shipping substitute goods overnight from Buyer's designated alternate supplier, as well as $600."

Problem 22-8.

Gage Farms (Gage) purchased a used John Deere combine from French Implement Company (FIC), with no warranty from the manufacturer, Deere & Company (Deere). Several months later, Gage purchased from FIC a used John Deere corn-head (the device that attaches to the front part of the combine to harvest corn from the field), again with no warranty from Deere. A couple of months later, the combine caught fire and was destroyed, with significant damage done also to the cornhead. How might the economic loss rule apply to limit Gage's damages? Is the cornhead "other property" for purposes of the economic loss rule? What arguments might you expect the parties to make? Does it matter that the buyer purchased the goods second hand?

Assignment 23
Seller's Remedies for Buyer's Breach

§§ 2-702 through 2-710, 2-718

In Assignment 22, we explored the buyer's remedies for seller's breaches. In this Assignment, we turn to a consideration of the remedies a seller has for buyer's breaches. Because the buyer's obligation is simply to accept the goods and to pay for them (§ 2-301), the buyer can breach in fewer ways than the seller might: repudiation (anticipatory or otherwise), wrongful rejection of the goods, unjustified revocation of acceptance, and failure to pay. Seller's remedies for buyer's breach appear primarily in §§ 2-702 through 2-710.

As you explore seller's remedies in this Assignment, keep in mind the range of possible buyer breaches to help you understand the structure and organization of the Code remedies.

LEARNING OUTCOMES AND OBJECTIVES

At the completion of this Assignment, you should be able to

- identify and compare the remedies available to the seller in the event of a buyer's breach;
- describe and apply the limitations placed on a seller's recovery;
- compare a seller's resale and market damages;
- account for expenses saved and incidental damages;
- determine when a breaching buyer is able to recover a prepayment from a seller;
- determine when a seller is entitled to collect the price;
- evaluate the efficacy of an agreed-to liquidated damages clause;
- evaluate whether a seller can reclaim or recover the goods; and
- apply the relevant portions of Article 2 to determine what remedy a seller is entitled to in a given set of facts in the event of a buyer's breach.

A. Overview of Seller's Remedies

Section 2-703 provides an overview of the remedies available to the aggrieved seller when the buyer breaches. Unlike § 2-711, which lists the buyer's remedies according to the type of seller's breach, § 2-703 makes a cumulative list of all of seller's remedies for any kind of buyer's breach.

Reading the Code:
§ 2-703

Read 2-703.

Question 1. Consider the language of 2-703 and use your common sense to determine which of the remedies are available to the seller for each type of buyer's breach. In the chart below, place a check in each applicable box if the remedy in the left column is at least sometimes available for the breach specified in the top row. (This chart omits the action for the price under 2-709 because that remedy applies only to a narrow set of facts.)

	Buyer repudiates	Buyer fails to make payment due on or before delivery	Buyer wrongfully rejects goods	Buyer wrongfully revokes acceptance of goods
2-703: Withhold delivery				
2-705: Stop delivery				

	Buyer repudiates	Buyer fails to make payment due on or before delivery	Buyer wrongfully rejects goods	Buyer wrongfully revokes acceptance of goods
2-704: Identify goods, resale/ completion option				
2-706: Resale and damages				
2-708: Damages for Non-acceptance				
2-703: Cancel contract				

Question 2. Read Comment 1 to 2-703, and note the lack of connecting conjunctions among the parts of 2-703. Recall 1-106(1) and the policies underlying contract remedies. Why is a seller not able to recover all provable remedies listed in 2-703 for any given breach by the buyer?

B. Seller's Resale and Market Damages

1. Comparing Resale and Market Damages

The Code makes clear that when there has been non-acceptance or repudiation by the buyer, the seller may either resell the goods and hold the buyer responsible for the difference between resale price and contract price (§ 2-706) or simply hold the buyer responsible for the difference between the market price and the contract price (§ 2-708(1)).

Reading the Code:
§§ 2-706(1), 2-708(1)

Read 2-706(1) and 2-708(1)

Question 3. Write out the mathematical formulas for "resale damages" (2-706) and "market damages" (2-708(1)), side by side. Use the following components: incidental damages, market price, resale price, expenses saved because of breach, and contract price. (Ignore the word "unpaid" used to describe "contract price" in 2-708(1); it probably was included in error.) Use "+" and "−" as needed. You need not use all of the components. When you are done, consider whether each formula makes sense (that is, does each formula accurately measure the injury to the seller?). What is the key difference between the formulas for the two types of damages?

Question 4. Look back at your answer to Question 8 from Assignment 22. Compare the formulas for buyer's and seller's market damages. Then compare the formulas for buyer's cover damages and seller's resale damages. Aside from the inclusion of consequential damages, the other key difference between the two buyer's formulas and the two seller's formulas is that the order of the two main components is reversed. That is, the contract price is the item subtracted in one formula, but it is the item subtracted-from in the other formula. Why does that difference make sense?

Question 5. What do 2-708(1) and 2-723(1) say about the time and place at which the market price is measured?

Question 6. Read 2-704 and Comments 1 and 2. What alternative courses of action may an aggrieved seller take under this section? How should the seller decide among these alternatives? Of what relevance are the market and resale measures of damage?

2. Requirements for Resales

Rather than market damages, an aggrieved seller who has possession of the goods may desire the more certain remedy of reselling them under § 2-706 and holding the breaching buyer liable for the difference between the resale price of the goods and the contract price. The seller's desire for resale damages, though, must be considered alongside the buyer's right to some measure of commercial reasonableness relative to such sales. To protect the buyer, the Code limits access to the resale remedy to those sellers who comply precisely with specific requirements. The seller loses the protection of the resale remedy if it does not comply with those requirements. In such cases, the Code "relegates him to that [remedy] provided in Section 2-708." *See* Comment 2.

**Reading the Code:
§ 2-706**

Read 2-706 and its Comments.

Question 7. Under 2-706(1) and (2), what are the requirements for a valid public (auction) or private resale?

Question 8. What function do 2-706(3) and (4) serve, relative to (1) and (2)?

EXAMPLES AND ANALYSIS

Example A: *Apex LLC v. Sharing World, Inc.*[1]

Between February 2008 and January 2009, a commodities merchandiser entered into 12 contracts to sell about 19,000 tons of cottonseed to the buyer, to be delivered between October 2008 and August 2009. The buyer failed to accept and pay for 14,000 tons of the goods. In August 2009, almost a year after the buyer first refused delivery of the cottonseed, the seller elected to "wash" the unaccepted cottonseed. ("Washing" a commodity means buying the goods back at the then-market price, which under industry rules is the equivalent of a market resale.) The seller sued and sought damages in the amount of the difference between the contract prices and the resale price (the market price at the time of the "wash"). The buyer objected, claiming that the sale in August 2009, in a depressed market almost a year after the buyer breached, was not commercially reasonable. The trial court denied the seller's recourse under 2-706 because the seller did not prove its cost basis in the cottonseed and had not conducted the "wash" in a commercially reasonable manner when it waited almost a year to do so and then did so in a depressed market. The seller appealed.

Analysis: The appellate court ruled that 2-706 does not require the seller to prove its cost basis in the cottonseed. The appellate court also rejected the trial court's finding that the sale was not commercially reasonable, noting that the seller engaged in extensive negotiations with the buyer to resolve the matter, repeatedly offered to rewrite the contracts, and several times offered to conduct a "wash" sale of the unaccepted cottonseed. The court particularly observed that while a resale should occur as soon as practicable after a buyer's breach, the reasonableness of a seller's delay is dependent upon the nature of the goods and the market. The court said that the trial court's blanket conclusion that the seller "intentionally and unreasonably" waited to conduct the "wash" sale was not a reasonable inference from the facts. It remanded the case back to the trial court to conduct the necessary contract-by-contract, shipment-by-shipment determination of whether the delay was unreasonable.

How does a court determine whether the seller has resold in a commercially reasonable manner? Why might the one-year delay in resale be commercially

[1]   142 Cal. Rptr. 3d 210 (Ct. App. 2012).

reasonable here? What arguments would you expect the buyer and seller to make on remand? What kinds of facts would be relevant to the court's determination?

Example B: *Fuji Photo Film USA, Inc. v. Zalmen Reiss & Associates, Inc.*[2]

A retail buyer of memory cards for use in digital cameras discovered that its seller's competitor was selling the cards at a lower wholesale price. When the buyer was unable to sell all the cards purchased from the seller at a profit, it returned the unsold cards to the seller and sought a credit from the seller for those cards, claiming an industry practice of "price protection." The contract price and the seller's list price was $19.49 each, but the seller resold the returned cards at a discount rate of $4.50 each in a single-lot sale to a reseller without notice to the buyer. The seller denied that the buyer was entitled to price protection and claimed damages under 2-706 for the resale of the cards. The buyer objected to the resale due to lack of notice.

Analysis: The trial court agreed that the contract and industry rules did not give the buyer any price protection, so the buyer breached when it returned unsold cards to the seller. However, the court rejected the seller's recourse to the resale remedy, finding that notice to the buyer is indispensable to recovery under 2-706. The court observed that "the resale of the returned merchandise, significantly below market value, to a single vendor selected by [the seller], was not conducted in a commercially reasonable manner." The court also rejected the seller's attempt to use the resale price as conclusive as to the market price under 2-708, as the burden is on the seller to "establish the applicable market price so as to demonstrate that the unnoticed private sale resulted in a fair price reflective of the actual value." The court rejected the seller's argument that the $4.50 resale price was indicative of the market price in light of the non-custom nature of the goods and continued listing of the cards for sale by the seller in its catalogue at the retail buyer's contract price. Because the seller did not adequately prove damages in the trial, the court dismissed the seller's complaint.

---

[2]   2011 WL 2327261 (N.Y. Sup. Ct. 2011).

When must a seller provide notice to a buyer of resale? Why was the resale price not indicative of market price here, as an alternative measure of damages? What should the seller have done at trial to avoid dismissal of its complaint?

3. Choosing between Resale and Market Damages

As you have seen, § 2-703 seems to give the seller a choice between § 2-706 resale damages and § 2-708(1) market damages. But may the seller freely choose between these two measures of damages?

To see the problem clearly, consider the following hypothetical: Suppose that the contract price is $1000. Buyer wrongfully repudiates. The market price at the time and place of the would-be tender is $800, but Seller resells for $900, complying in all respects with § 2-706. How could this be possible? Seller might have found a buyer willing to pay above market price for fast delivery or may simply have driven a hard bargain and done better than market value. Or perhaps the market price rose after the time of tender (which is the time at which § 2-708 damages are measured), allowing the seller to resell at the then market price, which is higher than the amount used for § 2-708(1).

Having resold at $900, $100 under the contract price, Seller could seek damages under § 2-706, recovering $100. However, Seller could get a larger recovery ($200) under § 2-708(1), because the resale brought a price higher than the market price at the time and place of tender. Is Seller permitted to choose § 2-708 damages, even though it resold the goods? Section 2-703 does not expressly preclude that choice, but some cases and commentators have argued that the Seller would be overcompensated for its injury if it could choose to recover under § 2-708. The case law on this issue is split.[3]

---

[3]   See, e.g., Coast Trading Co. v. Cudahy Co., 592 F.2d 1074 (9th Cir. 1979) (limiting seller's damages to actual loss if reselling the goods); Peace River Seed Coop, Ltd. v. Proseeds Mktg., Inc., 322 P.3d 531 (Or. 2014) (permitting seller recourse to market-based damages after favorable resale); Wendling v. Puls, 610 P.2d 580 (Kan. 1980) (allowing seller recourse to market-based damages, but without analysis); Eades Commodities, Co. v. Hoeper, 825 S.W.2d 34 (Mo. Ct. App. 1992) (implying a limitation on the seller's damages to no more than actual loss); Tesoro Petroleum Corp. v. Holborn Oil Co., 547 N.Y.S.2d 1012 (Sup. Ct. 1989) (limiting the seller's damages to the actual loss if reselling the goods).

Reading the Code:
§ 2-703, 706

Read 2-703 Comment 1 and 2-706 Comment 2.

Question 9. Must a seller attempt a resale, if it seems commercially feasible? If the seller does not attempt to resell when it is commercially feasible, does that choice bar some of the seller's damages? Should a seller be permitted to elect to recover under 2-708(1), even though a proper resale has occurred? Be prepared to argue, as appropriate, from the statute and its comments, from your answers to Question 12 from Assignment 22, and from public policy, including whether the buyer or the seller should reap the advantage of the market's fluctuations.

4. Expenses Saved as a Result of Breach

Like the remedies for aggrieved buyers seen in Assignment 22, damage calculations for both resale damages and market damages awardable to an aggrieved seller include a reduction for "expenses saved in consequence of the seller's breach." *See* §§ 2-706(1), 708(1). The types of expenses that sellers save are often the same types of expenses that buyers save, such as shipping and insurance costs. It is important to evaluate what contractual obligations the seller had in order to determine which might have been saved due to the buyer's breach.

EXAMPLES AND ANALYSIS

Example C. Return to the facts from Example B but with a few alterations. Assume for purposes of this example that the original contract required the seller to prepare and print marketing and instructional materials in Spanish for the memory cards, which the seller had not done before the buyer returned the cards. The seller resells the memory cards in a resale conforming with 2-706 to a buyer who does not need the Spanish language marketing and instructional materials.

Analysis: The seller here would appear to have saved expenses because the resale did not require the seller to prepare Spanish language materials. This expense saved would be subtracted from the amount recoverable by the aggrieved seller. Why does subtracting that amount result in appropriate compensation for the seller?

5. Incidental and Consequential Damages

Recall that § 2-715 defines consequential damages for the buyer, and §§ 2-712 and 2-713 accord buyer the right to receive incidental and consequential damages in an appropriate case. In contrast, notice that § 2-710 does not mention consequential damages, nor does any remedy section provide seller a right to receive consequential damages. Recall, too, that under § 1-106(1), consequential damages are recoverable only as "specifically provided by this Act or by other rule of law." As a result, seller is not entitled to consequential damages upon a buyer's breach.

**Reading the Code:
§ 2-710**

Read 2-710.

Question 10. Compare the definition of seller's incidental damages in 2-710 with the definition of buyer's incidental damages in 2-715. To what extent are they the same? Different? Why do the two definitions make sense?

Question 11. What kind of consequential injury might a seller suffer if the buyer breaches? (Hint: Consider that a buyer typically breaches by failing to take the goods or to pay for them in a timely fashion.) Why do you think the Code drafters might have chosen not to include consequential damages for sellers, even though there is no absolute bar to such damages under the common law or in Restatement of Contracts 2d § 351?

C. Recovery of Prepayment by a Breaching Buyer

Recall that § 2-711(3) allows an aggrieved buyer who has not accepted the goods to recover any price already paid as part of damages. A breaching buyer who has paid more to the seller than the amount of damages owed to the seller may also have a right to recover part or all of the price already paid, which will affect the amount of damages the seller will recover.

Reading the Code:
§ 2-718

Read 2-718(2), (3) and Comment 2.

Question 12. What part of the buyer's prepayment is an aggrieved seller allowed to keep under (2)? Explain why 2-718(2)(b) might be called a "statutory liquidated damages" provision.

Question 13. What effect does (3) have on the amount the aggrieved seller is allowed to keep under (2)?

EXAMPLES AND ANALYSIS

Example D: *Santos v. DeBellis*[4]

Santos contracted with DeBellis to purchase a mobile home located in Ft. Pierce, Florida, paying a $6000 deposit. Santos never paid the remaining $27,000 due for the mobile home and brought an action to recover her deposit.

Analysis: The trial court dismissed her action after trial. Reversing, the appellate court applied 2-718(2) to hold Santos was entitled to return of all but $500 of the

---

[4]   72 UCC Rep. Serv. 2d 308 (N.Y. Sup. Ct. 2010).

deposit. DeBellis had not shown any damages from the breach or demonstrated any benefits received by Santos.

Why does the seller here get to keep $500? Would the answer change if DeBellis later resold the mobile home in accordance with 2-706 and suffered a loss of $1000 on the resale? What if DeBellis suffered a loss of only $300?

D. Action for the Price

A seller's first preference is to be able to recover the full contract price, rather than the usually smaller amount available under §§ 2-706 and 2-708(1). Section 2-703(e) says that an aggrieved seller may recover the price only "in a proper case," however. That "proper case" is identified in § 2-709, which reflects the fact that a seller who receives the full purchase price as a remedy has in essence forced the buyer to complete the contracted-for purchase. As reflected in the terms of § 2-709, such a"forced sale" is inappropriate if the seller retains the goods and can still resell them. A seller who is unable to prevail in an action for the price may still be awarded damages under § 2-706 (with a proper resale) or § 2-708.

Reading the Code: § 2-709

Read 2-709.

Question 14. Under 2-709(1), under what three sets of circumstances may a seller recover the contract price? Why would each of those sets of circumstances be appropriate occasions for the seller to receive the purchase price?

Question 15. What restriction does the opening clause of 2-709(1) place on the seller's right to receive the contract price? Consider that phrase in light of 2-507(1).

Question 16. What restrictions or requirements does 2-709(2) place on the seller?

Question 17. Why is a seller's right to recover the price limited to the circumstances described in 2-709? Why doesn't a seller always get the price instead of damages? Think back to the policies underlying common law contract remedies, which are listed at the beginning of Chapter 9.

1. Goods Accepted or Lost or Damaged

Under § 2-709(1)(a), the seller obtains the right to the price with respect to "goods accepted." A seller who believes she is entitled to the price may face arguments from the buyer that the buyer has not "accepted" the goods under the provisions of § 2-606.

EXAMPLES AND ANALYSIS

Example E: *American Seating Co. v. Archer Plastics Inc.*[5]

American Seating Co. (American) contracted to sell used stadium seats to Archer Plastics Inc. (Archer), who contracted to purchase and remove the seats from Camden Yards Baseball Stadium in Baltimore, Maryland and Foley Field at University of Georgia. The seats were to be removed in two phases, so as not to interfere with the baseball season. While Archer removed and paid for approximately 17,000 seats in the first phase, it took no action to remove or pay for the rest after its market for resale deteriorated. American removed and sold the remaining seats for salvage value and sued Archer for the price.

On motion for summary judgment, the court held that all of the seats in the stadium constituted one commercial unit, so when Archer paid for the first 17,000 seats, it accepted the entire commercial unit under 2-606(2). Accordingly, American argued it was due the unpaid price for all the seats. Archer claimed that American did not hold the seats for it and failed to mitigate damages by reselling the remaining stadium seats at salvage value rather than paying to store the seats, so that American should not collect the price.

---

[5]   84 UCC Rep. Serv. 2d 746 (D.N.J. 2014).

Analysis: The court agreed with American that it was due the price under 2-709. American's resale at salvage price was not improper where the resale at salvage was commercially reasonable, as there was no market for the seats and the buyer itself had been unable to sell them. American was not required to hold the goods for Archer where it would be fruitless to do so. The court explained that the seller was not required to mitigate by storing the seats and attempting a later resale where the space and cost considerations made the option not viable. Accordingly, the court awarded the seller its contract price less payments and resale credits.

What part of 2-709 supports American's argument? What part supports Archer? When might a seller be obliged to "hold" the goods for the breaching buyer? At whose cost and for how long?

2. Goods Identified to the Contract but Unsellable

An action for the price arises under § 2-709(1)(b) if the goods are identified to the contract, but the seller has been unable to resell them or resale appears not to be feasible. The issues in these § 2-709 cases tend to turn on whether the seller made sufficient efforts to resell and whether additional effort might have produced a reasonable resale.

EXAMPLES AND ANALYSIS

Example F: *Grandoe Corp. v. Gander Mountain Co.*[6]

Grandoe Corp. (Grandoe) manufactured and sold winter gloves to Gander Mountain Co. (Gander), pursuant to ongoing oral commitments. Grandoe and Gander orally negotiated a $3.05 million deal for gloves based upon spreadsheet projections of sales. After Grandoe manufactured most of the gloves with the Gander Mountain logo, Gander purchased only $940,000 of gloves and subsequently ceased doing business with Grandoe entirely. Grandoe did not resell the already-manufactured gloves and brought an action for the price.

---

[6]   761 F.3d 876 (8th Cir. 2014).

Analysis: The jury awarded the price to Grandoe under 2-709(1)(b), finding no obligation to resell the gloves where resale was unlikely due to the presence of the Gander logo on the gloves. The Eighth Circuit affirmed. How does a court decide whether goods are resalable? Must the goods be generic in nature?

E. Seller's Alternative to Market and Resale Damages

A seller may receive § 2-706 resale damages in a proper case and alternatively may receive § 2-708(1) market price damages. You may recall that a seller's recovery under § 2-708(1) is "subject to subsection (2)." Section 2-708(2) contains an alternative measure of damages when the damages in § 2-708(1) would not fulfill a seller's expectation interest (are "inadequate to put the seller in as good a position as performance would have done"). Case law and commentators agree that § 2-708(2) damages are available only if § 2-706 also is inadequate to fulfill the seller's expectation interest. Furthermore, a seller who is able to recover the price and accompanying damages under § 2-709 will be made whole under that section and will not instead choose to seek the lesser damages under § 2-708(2).

The remainder of this section explores how to measure § 2-708(2) damages and the circumstances that trigger use of the damages defined there.

Reading the Code:
§ 2-708(2)

Read 2-708(2) and Comment 2.

Question 18. Write out the mathematical formula for the damages in 2-708(2), using "+" and "−" as needed.

---

1. Lost-Volume Sellers

Damages under § 2-708(2) are sometimes used to compensate a "lost-volume seller"—a seller who would have made an "extra" sale if the contract had not been breached. A seller who is left with the goods and resells them to a customer who would have bought from the seller anyway will "use up" a future customer, thereby losing the extra profit on the additional sale that is no longer possible. Similarly, a seller who operates as an intermediary (buying and reselling on demand) would have made two sales rather than one if the buyer had not breached. The formula in § 2-708(2) is designed to provide the seller with the profit that would have been earned on the lost sale.

Case law has furnished criteria for judging whether a seller is a lost-volume seller and therefore entitled to § 2-708(2) damages. For instance, some courts have required the seller to prove that it would have solicited another buyer had there been no breach, that such a solicitation would have been successful, and that the seller could have performed the additional contract. Other courts have considered whether a seller could have recovered its lost profit on the original sale (and mitigated its damages) by reselling to a substitute purchaser offered by the breaching buyer.

EXAMPLES AND ANALYSIS

Example G: *Jewish Federation of Greater Des Moines v. Cedar Forest Products Company*[7]

The Jewish Federation of Greater Des Moines (Jewish Federation) contracted with Cedar Forest Products Company (Cedar) for the manufacture of a pre-cut building package. The Jewish Federation paid for the package, but ultimately rescinded the contract and requested return of all monies paid. Cedar returned all monies, but retained $53,887.46 as lost profit. The Jewish Federation brought suit for return of the remaining money. Cedar claimed it was a lost-volume seller and was entitled to the lost profit. The District Court found that Cedar was a lost-volume seller but awarded only incidental damages of $13,470.17. Cedar appealed.

Analysis: The appellate court agreed that Cedar was a lost-volume seller and awarded profits. The court rejected the Jewish Federation's argument that Cedar was not entitled to its lost profits because it had not begun to assemble the building package at the time of breach. The court held that lost profits are awardable even where the goods are not yet manufactured. The court explained:

---

7   2003 WL 23008855 (Iowa Ct. App. 2003).

The rationale for these holdings appears to be that a lost volume seller can handle a certain number of sales during the year and when one negotiated sale is lost, the seller simply cannot recoup that anticipated profit. Instead, the seller is one sale short of normal capacity. *See R.E. Davis Chem. Corp.*, 826 F.2d at 683 (defining a lost volume seller as "one that has a predictable and finite number of customers and that has the capacity either to sell to all new buyers or to make the one additional sale represented by the resale after the breach"). So to put the seller in the position he would have been but for the breach, the Illinois statute provides the seller a remedy which includes the anticipated profit as well as incidental expenses and costs incurred. Therefore, the district court erred in its application of Illinois law. As a lost volume seller, CFP is entitled to its lost profits of $53,887.46 . . . .

Who has the burden of proving that lost-volume damages are warranted? What evidence do you think the court would find adequate to meet that burden in a case like this one? Why did the buyer receive incidental damages?

Example H: *Distribu-Dor, Inc. v. Karadanis*[8]

Distribu-Dor, an intermediary distributor, contracted with Karadanis to supply custom mirrors and tub and shower enclosures for the Tahoe Inn under construction by Karadanis. Distribu-Dor visited the Tahoe Inn, measured the walls, and ordered the mirrors. Karadanis decided to purchase the supplies from another company. Distribu-Dor re-edged the mirrors and sold them to another buyer. Distribu-Dor then brought suit for breach of contract, claiming damages under 2-708(2).

Analysis: The court awarded Distribu-Dor damages under 2-708(2) as a "middle-man." The court explained, "in cases involving a sale to a buyer by an intermediate dealer whose relationship with a producer enables him to supply all obtainable customers, the buyer's breach does not make possible a new sale in which the profit lost by the breach would be replaced but, rather, results in an irreplaceable loss of profits because every new sale by such seller would bring in a new profit.'"

---

[8]   11 Cal.App.3d 463 (1970).

Why are regular damages under (1) inadequate for intermediary sellers, warranting recovery under (2)? Would it make a difference if Distribu-Dor had agreed to sell the Tahoe Inn mirrors that it already had in stock for another sale that did not come to fruition?

2. Goods without Scrap or Salvage Value

Consider the situation of a seller who is specially manufacturing goods that are suited solely to the needs of its buyer, where the buyer repudiates before or after the goods have been completed. If the goods are completed and can be resold, even for scrap, the seller can be compensated by damages under § 2-706. But if the goods cannot be resold for scrap or salvage value, then the seller cannot be fully compensated by § 2-706. Nor will there be a market price for these goods, so § 2-708(1) will not apply. Moreover, the buyer's repudiation will prevent the seller from being able to recover the price under § 2-709 because the requirements of that rule will not have been met.

If the specially manufactured goods are not yet completed at the time of the breach, the seller must exercise reasonable commercial judgment about whether to complete the goods under § 2-704(2) and Comments 1 and 2. Since the finished goods likely could not be resold when completed, the seller will likely decide not to complete the manufacture of the goods. If the unfinished goods can be sold for scrap or salvage, once again § 2-706 can provide adequate damages, but if no such sale is possible, neither § 2-706 nor § 2-708 can provide adequate relief.

Under both sets of circumstances, as well as any other time the seller is left with goods that have no scrap or salvage value, § 2-708(2) provides an alternative measure of damages.

Reading the Code:
§ 2-708(2)

Re-read 2-708(2).

Question 19. Write the formula for 2-708(2) damages as it would apply to the scenario of specially or partially manufactured goods that cannot be resold for scrap or salvage. Will those damages meet the requirement of 1-106 by putting the manufacturer in as good a position as performance would have? Leaving aside the issue of overhead, for the moment, what facts would you need to calculate seller's profit?

EXAMPLES AND ANALYSIS

Example I: *In re S.N.A. Nut Co.*[9]

A Chapter 11 debtor, S.N.A. Nut Co. (SNA) brought an action against one of its creditors, Häagen-Dazs Co. for breach of an installment contract for the supply of almonds, walnuts, coated macadamia brittle, coated macadamia brittle fines, and coated macadamia nut brittle for mini-cups. SNA specially manufactured the nuts to HD specifications and using its recipes. The nuts were not generally resalable and prone to rapid spoilage. After HD refused to take the nuts, SNA personnel contacted every SNA customer in an attempt to sell the finished and unfinished HD- specification nuts. SNA contacted companies that were not HD customers and enlisted outside brokers and distributors. SNA sold a small quantity of the nuts to other ice cream companies. As the products became too old for human consumption, SNA sold some of the nuts to animal feed manufacturers. Ultimately, SNA destroyed the goods it could not sell once they became rancid. At trial, SNA asserted damages under 2-708(2) and HD asserted defenses, including failure to mitigate.

---

[9]   2000 WL 351421 (N.D. Ill. 2000).

Analysis: The court agreed that 2-708(2) was the appropriate measure of damages for the nuts not resold because the goods were specially manufactured goods for which there was no market. The court found SNA was entitled to the profits it would have earned if HD had not breached, including overhead, plus incidental damages and costs. The court awarded SNA the difference between the contract price and the resale price with respect to the nuts it was able to resell. The court rejected HD's argument that SNA failed to hold the nuts for it, noting that 2-708(2) does not have the 2-709(2) requirement that the seller hold goods for the buyer and that requiring a seller to hold rotten goods would be "ridiculous."

Why does a seller like SNA choose 2-708(2) rather than 2-708(1)? How does a court determine if 2-708(2) is appropriate to measure the damages? Why did the goods qualify in this case?

3. Cost of Overhead

Accountants have spent many hours on the witness stand analyzing what constitutes "overhead" under § 2-708(2). White and Summers sum up the debate with the following advice:

> Presumably the Code gives the seller net profit after taxes plus that part of his fixed costs which he would have satisfied out of the proceeds from this contract. Courts should not be hesitant to award more than the plaintiff's net profit; a contract with a theoretical net profit of zero may nevertheless carry a substantial economic benefit to the contracting party. . . . [I]t is logical and also consistent with the policy of 1-106 to award the seller not only its net profit but also that pro rata share of its fixed costs which the broken contract would have satisfied.[10]

When you try to determine the appropriate amount of overhead to include in the formula, you should, as always, apply the general principle that the aim is to fully compensate the injured party for the breach without overcompensating.

---

[10] James J. White et. al, Uniform Commercial Code § 7-13 (6th ed. 2012).

Reading the Code:
§ 2-708(2)

Question 20. What facts would you need to calculate the recoverable overhead of S.N.A. Nuts, the manufacturer described in Example I in the previous section?

F. Seller's Right to Stop Delivery

If, before delivery of the goods, circumstances arise that give the seller reason to doubt that the buyer will pay for the goods, what recourse does the seller have? If the goods are still in the seller's possession or are in transit in the seller's own vehicles, the seller can demand adequate assurances of performance (see Assignment 19) and, if warranted, withhold the goods from the buyer. But what if the goods have been shipped by carrier or are in the hands of a third-party bailee? Section 2-705 gives the seller some rights to stop delivery in those circumstances as well. Of course, an improper stoppage—one not justified by buyer's breach or seller's legitimate concerns about breach—will be a breach of contract by the seller, so a seller should be cautious about taking this step.

Reading the Code:
§ 2-705

Read 2-705 and its Comments.

Question 21. In what four situations may an aggrieved seller stop delivery of the goods? What is the difference between the first (stopping delivery for insolvency) and the others? Why should they be different?

Question 22. Does "insolvent" for the purposes of 2-705 mean the same thing as under the federal bankruptcy law?

Question 23. What is the common idea behind (a) through (d) of subsection (2)?

Question 24. For whose primary benefit is subsection (3)?

EXAMPLES AND ANALYSIS

Example J: *In re Trico Steel Co., LLC*[11]

Cargill Inc. entered into a contract to sell pig iron to Trico Steel Co. (Trico). To fulfill the contract, Cargill purchased iron from another company and arranged for carriers to ship and deliver the iron to New Orleans, where a barge company would provide transportation of the pig iron from New Orleans to the Trico facility in Decatur, Alabama. When the pig iron arrived in New Orleans, it was loaded onto barges for transport to Decatur. While the pig iron was in transit, Cargill learned that Trico was insolvent. Cargill notified the carrier that, due to the insolvency, it was exercising its right to stop the pig iron in transit . Shortly thereafter, Cargill filed an adversary action in bankruptcy court seeking a declaration that it was entitled to possession of the pig iron. Trico asserted that it had received the pig iron under 2-705(2) when the goods arrived in New Orleans and were unloaded by agents of Trico.

Analysis: The bankruptcy court agreed with Cargill, and the district court affirmed. First, the court concluded that the workers who unloaded the goods were not agents of the buyer, but rather intermediaries in transit. Moreover, New Orleans was not the final destination of the pig iron for the purpose of determining whether the buyer had received the goods. Decatur, Alabama was the destination for the pig iron, so Trico never came into possession of the goods. The court also concluded that 2-705(2)(c) did not apply where the barge carrier was not a "carrier by reshipment" or "carrier by warehouseman." Thus, Trico never received the goods so Cargill retained its right to stoppage under 2-705(2).

---

[11]   302 B.R. 489 (D. Del. 2003).

What part of 2-705 was helpful to Cargill? To Trico? Why is it important for a seller like Cargill to have a right to stop goods in transit? If Trico had cut off Cargill's right to stop delivery, what would Cargill's prospects be for getting paid?

G. Seller's Limited Right to Reclaim the Goods

The seller has some power and right to stop goods in transit if the buyer is insolvent or there are other reasons for the seller to doubt buyer will pay. What if those circumstances arise after the buyer is already in possession of the goods? Section 2-702 gives a seller a very limited right to reclaim the goods from the buyer, triggered only if the buyer is insolvent and certain other requirements are met.

Reading the Code:
§ 2-702(2), (3)

Read 2-702(2), (3).

Question 25. Under 2-702(2), what two facts must be present in order for the seller to be able to reclaim the goods from the buyer? How does the section say seller must exercise its rights?

Question 26. Does the seller have the right to reclaim the goods if the buyer has transferred them to someone else after delivery?

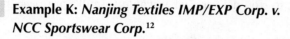

EXAMPLES AND ANALYSIS

Example K: *Nanjing Textiles IMP/EXP Corp. v.*
NCC Sportswear Corp.[12]

Nanjing Textiles IMP/EXP Corp. sold custom clothes to NCC Sportswear Corp. After NCC failed to pay for some of the clothes, Nanjing brought suit, including a claim to seize the apparel under 2-702(2). Nanjing claimed NCC misrepresented its solvency when it paid for the goods with three dishonored checks, signed invoices stating the goods were "received in good order," and promised to pay. NCC claimed it made no representations regarding solvency and had never transferred or dissipated assets to avoid claims of a creditor.

Analysis: The court agreed with NCC and denied the reclamation. First, the court found insufficient evidence that NCC was insolvent. Paying with dishonored checks was not enough to show insolvency, especially since NCC paid those obligations using wire transfers after the checks were dishonored. Second, because Nanjing did not demand the goods within ten days of delivery, it had to demonstrate that NCC misrepresented its solvency in writing, and it failed to do so.

When must a seller act in order to have its best chance to reclaim goods under 2-702? Why is presentation of dishonored checks not a mark of insolvency or a misrepresentation of solvency? What might a seller show in order to demonstrate insolvency?

H. Comparing Buyer's and Seller's Remedies

Many of buyer's and seller's remedies resemble each other or are the mirror image of each other. Fill in the chart below showing those relationships, creating a handy reference of the source of buyers' and sellers' remedies.

---

[12]   60 UCC Rep. Serv. 2d 709 (S.D.N.Y. 2006).

Buyer's remedy	Commonality	Seller's remedy
2-711	Overview list	2-703
	Market damages	
	Substitute performance and damages	
	B keeps goods	
	Specific performance	
2-711(3) (buyer's security interest)	Resale of goods in possession to mitigate damages	2-704(2) (Unfinished goods)
	Cancellation	
	Incidental damages	
	Consequential damages	(What is seller's closest equivalent?)
	Insolvency of other party	

APPLYING THE CODE

Problem 23-1.

In each of the factual settings below, did the seller save expenses because of the buyer's breach?

(a) A buyer repudiates the contract before shipment by the seller, who was contractually obligated to pay freight for the goods. The seller resells the goods in its own city to a buyer who picks up the goods with its own truck.

(b)   A seller pays freight for the goods, per the contract. The buyer then wrongfully rejects the goods, which the seller resells in the buyer's city with only a small additional shipment expense.

(c)   A seller is obligated by contract to pay for cold storage of the goods in a warehouse until the buyer picks them up some time during the specified three-month period. The buyer repudiates at the end of the first week of the three-month period, so seller resells the goods to another buyer a week later.

Problem 23-2.

Label the following seller's damages as likely to be considered consequential, incidental, or neither, keeping in mind that consequential damages are not recoverable by a seller in a contract for sale of goods:

(a)   Buyer repudiates, and the seller pays for freight, inspection, and certification in the course of reselling the goods.

(b)   Buyer wrongfully rejects the goods, which are perishable, and the seller pays for cold storage while looking for another buyer.

(c)   Buyer wrongfully revokes acceptance, and the seller pays commission to a broker, in order to find a new buyer.

(d)   Buyer repudiates, and the seller, who has not yet ordered the goods it intends to send to the buyer, loses its volume discount with its supplier. Seller then has to pay more for goods it is ordering for other buyers and so loses some profit on those sales.

(e)   Seller has to take out a loan in order to cover the buyer's late payment and has to pay interest on that loan until the buyer finally pays the contract price.

(f)   In the facts immediately above, the seller then pays off the principal due under the loan.

Problem 23-3.

Stalloy contracted to sell to Kennametal 120,000 pounds of scrap carbide at $12.25/pound for a total price of $1,470,000. Kennametal wrongfully rejected the scrap after the market price dropped precipitously, thereby breaching the parties' contract. Stalloy attempted to mitigate its damages by reselling the scrap at a private sale without notifying Kennametal. However, based on changed market conditions, Stalloy was forced to resell it at an average price of $7.124/pound totaling $854,880, for a loss of $615,120, for which it sought an award of damages. What damages is Stalloy entitled to and why? What would you advise Stalloy to do in the future to ensure that it can recover resale damages?

Problem 23-4.

Land O'Lakes sold 2400 weaned pigs to Jaeger every nine weeks for fourteen months. After the July shipment of pigs, the invoice for $93,112 remained unpaid. Jaeger offered to return the pigs, but Land O'Lakes did not take them back. Land O'Lakes files suit for the $93,112, but Jaeger claims Land O'Lakes must take the pigs back to reduce its damages. Who is correct?

Problem 23-5.

Nancy and Richard have long wished to have a log cabin by a lake. They contracted with Louisiana Log Homes (LLH) for a log-cabin kit costing $43,000 in order to save money on building the house. The contract required them to pay installments toward the kit. The sales agreement stated that "all monies paid on this contract are earnest monies and that no refund will be made if delivery is refused or if this contract is terminated by the purchaser without the mutual consent of the seller." After paying about $37,000 of the purchase price, Nancy and Richard could not afford to make the last payment and breached the contract. LLH diverted the log cabin kit, which was in transit to Nancy and Richard, to a warehouse and demanded payment. Nancy and Richard brought suit for return of their money. LLH resold nine of the twelve logs in the kit to another buyer for $24,000. LLH's profit on the log-cabin kit would have been $8000.

Does LLH owe Nancy and Richard any money? Do Nancy and Richard owe LLH any money? How would your answer change if the deposit paid by Nancy and Richard was only $4300?

Problem 23-6.

The Peterson Oil Refinery (POR), located in Minneapolis, MN, agreed to buy 10,000 barrels of crude oil a year for 5 years at $50.00 per barrel from Ropella's Drilling (RD), located in Fargo, ND. The contract provided for shipment of the oil to POR, F.O.B. Minneapolis, MN, with shipment no later than February 25 of each year, and delivery at the destination by March 1 of each year. The cost of shipping ($1 per barrel) was to be paid by RD. POR repudiated the deal on Feb. 10th of the third year, when crude oil was selling for $40 per barrel everywhere in the country. RD decided not to resell.

Following are the market prices for crude oil in Fargo and Minneapolis for the remaining years of the contract. Ignoring any possible incidental damages, and assuming there is no case for damages under 2-708(2) or 2-709, calculate:

(a) RD's damages if the case comes to trial during what would have been the fourth year of the contract; and

(b) RD's damages if the case comes to trial after the five-year term of the contract has passed.

Date	Market price of crude oil in Fargo, per barrel	Market price of oil in Minneapolis, per barrel
Feb. 25, year 3	$30.95	$30.90
March 1, year 3	$40.15	$40.10
Feb. 25, year 4	$30.85	$30.80
March 1, year 4	$40.25	$40.20
Feb. 25, year 5	$40.35	$40.30
March 1, year 5	$40.45	$40.40

Problem 23-7.

On February 23, the parties contract to have electrical motors shipped (F.O.B. seller's place of business) on March 6, to arrive at the buyer's factory on March 8, where the buyer is planning to install them immediately in its production line, as components in electric drills. The quantity is 1230 motors, and the buyer contracts to buy at $38 per motor. In addition:

• When bought in quantities similar to buyer's order, the price of this type of motor in buyer's city is

$37 on February 23;

$34 on March 3;

$33 on March 6;

$32 on March 8.

- When bought in quantities similar to buyer's order, the price of this type of motor in seller's city is

    $39 on February 23;

    $36 on March 3;

    $35 on March 6;

    $33 on March 8.

- When bought in quantities similar to buyer's order, seller's price for this type of motor is

    $38 on February 23;

    $35 on March 3;

    $34 on March 6;

    $32 on March 8.

- The contract calls for seller to pay freight. The freight cost is (or would be) $388.

- Seller's costs for materials and labor on each motor are $25.

- Seller's overhead expenses (taxes, building costs, administrative costs, etc.) included in the price of each motor are $2.

Each set of facts below is independent of the other sets of facts. Merely list the numbers to be added, subtracted, or multiplied; do not do the math.

(a) On March 3, the buyer repudiates the contract before the seller ships the electric motors to buyer. Between March 3 and 8, the seller does not find any buyers who need quantities similar to buyer's order, so the seller does not resell the motors until March 8, when seller's broker finds another buyer for the seller's price on that day (seller to pay $124 freight). The seller pays the broker $450. Assume that the seller gives the original buyer proper notice under 2-706(3) for a private sale. What are the seller's resale damages?

(b) On March 3, the buyer repudiates the contract before the seller ships the electric motors to buyer. What are the seller's market damages?

(c) Why can't the seller recover the price in (a) or (b)?

(d) On March 3, the buyer repudiates the contract before the seller ships the electric motors to buyer. The motors were specially manufactured for buyer, have no reliable market price, and are not easily resalable, except to just a few of seller's customers. Seller contacts those customers and finally, on March 8, finds a customer who was planning to buy motors in May but is willing to buy these 1230 motors now for $38 apiece (seller to pay $124 freight). Assume that the seller gave the original buyer proper notice under 2-706(3) for a private sale and that the resale is in good faith and is conducted in a commercially reasonable manner. What are the seller's damages under 2-708(2)?

Assignment 24
Modification or Limitation of Remedies
§§ 2-302, 2-719

In Assignments 22 and 23, we explored the buyer's and seller's remedies for breaches by the other. This Assignment considers how an agreement to modify or limit remedies impacts those remedies. As permitted by § 1-102(3), the buyer and seller are free to vary by agreement the default remedies in Parts 6 and 7 of Article 2 "except as otherwise provided in this Act." Section 2-719 expressly permits the parties to supplement, replace, or limit the default remedies, while also specifying constraints on contractual modification or limitation of remedies, as explored more fully below.

LEARNING OUTCOMES AND OBJECTIVES

At the completion of this Assignment, you should be able to

- identify a remedy limitation and distinguish it from a warranty disclaimer;
- evaluate whether a remedy limitation is exclusive and provides a minimum adequate remedy;
- describe what it means for a remedy limitation to fail its essential purpose;
- determine when the Magnuson-Moss Warranty Act restricts or precludes remedy limitations; and
- apply the relevant portions of Article 2 to determine whether an exclusive remedy limitation is enforceable.

A note of explanation on vocabulary: This Assignment refers to any agreed-to changes in the parties' remedies as "remedy limitations." A remedy after it has been altered by the remedy limitation is a "limited remedy."

A. Article 2 Remedy Limitations in General

Section 2-719 allows parties to contract for a remedy in addition to or in substitution for any remedy provided under the Code. It also allows them to agree that the stated remedy is the exclusive remedy for the buyer. The agreed-to limited remedy often takes the form of a promise to repair, replace, or refund the purchase price (often at seller's option). Whether a limited remedy will be appealing to a disappointed buyer will often depend on the particular loss suffered by the buyer and whether the seller honors its warranty commitment.

Disclaimer or Limitation?

Recall from Assignment 12 that contracting parties can disclaim warranties so long as the disclaimer satisfies the requirements of § 2-316. A warranty disclaimer limits or excludes the extent of a seller's responsibility with respect to the nature and quality of the goods. A remedy limitation is different—it modifies the nature and extent of the remedies otherwise available for a party's breach of whatever warranty or other contract obligation the party has taken on (affecting, e.g., damages, right to reject or revoke acceptance, specific performance).

Reading the Code: § 2-719

Read 2-719.

Question 1. What kinds of remedy limitations or exclusions are permitted by 2-719(1) and 2-719(3)? What kinds of limitations or exclusions are not permitted?

Question 2. Read Comment 3. Is a seller free to exclude all consequential damages under 2-719? Is a seller free to disclaim all warranties that could lead to consequential injury? How do you reconcile the answers to those two questions?

Question 3. If the contract explicitly identifies a remedy available to the buyer, does that remedy replace all the Code remedies otherwise available? *See* Comment 2.

1. Making Limited Remedies Exclusive

As you saw in answering Question 3, § 2-719(1) makes resort to a limited remedy optional unless the limited remedy is identified as "exclusive." An exclusive remedy can bar a party from accessing some or all of the Article 2 default remedial provisions.

EXAMPLES AND ANALYSIS

Example A: *Canterbury Apartment Homes LLC v. Louisiana Pacific Corp.*[1]

Canterbury Apartment Homes LLC purchased siding for its apartment complex from Louisiana Pacific Corporation (LP). The siding came with a 25-year written limited warranty against defects. The limited remedy provided that a disappointed buyer could receive up to twice the retail cost of the original siding, with the amount decreasing each year after the 6th year, until after 25 years "no warranty shall be applicable." At the end of the warranty and remedy description, the contract read: "Except for the express warranty and remedy set forth above, L-P disclaims all other warranties, express or implied, including the implied warranties of merchantability or fitness for a particular purpose."

Pieces of the siding fell off of the apartment building, mushrooms grew out of the siding, and the siding did not retain its shape. Canterbury requested that LP replace the siding. After Canterbury did not hear back from LP, it sent a letter to LP informing LP that Canterbury would replace the siding itself. After seeking bids from several companies, Canterbury selected the lowest bidder and replaced the siding at a cost of $817,584.44 plus $105,439.34 to paint the new siding and $16,893.11 for building permits related to the installation of the replacement siding. LP offered Canterbury $8363 for the damaged siding (based on the limited warranty and its estimate that only 11% of the siding was defective). Canterbury brought a claim for breach of warranty and other injury. LP argued that the remedy given in the contract was the "sole and exclusive remedy" for Canterbury.

---

[1] 84 UCC Rep. Serv. 2d 185 (Wash. Ct. App. 2014). Note that this case was also discussed in Assignment 22, Example H.

Analysis: The trial court instructed the jury that the limited remedy was not exclusive "because it did not contain unmistakable language that the stated remedy is the exclusive remedy." The court explained that LP had the ability to include the exclusive language, but did not. The appellate court affirmed. Canterbury could therefore pursue other remedies under the Code.

Example B: *Pine Tel. Co. v. Alcatel-Lucent USA, Inc.*[2]

Pine Telephone Co. and Alcatel-Lucent USA, Inc. contracted for Pine's purchase of telecommunications equipment from Alcatel. The agreement provided:

> If any of the equipment is not as warranted in this Article, then (a) Purchaser shall obtain from Alcatel a Material Return Authorization ("MRA") and return the Equipment and MRA to Alcatel's designated repair facility, and (b) Alcatel shall repair or replace the Equipment and return it to Purchaser's point of shipment. . . . If, after the exercise of commercially reasonable efforts by Alcatel to repair or replace any Equipment or correct any Software, Alcatel determines that the Product cannot be repaired, replaced or corrected, then Alcatel may, in its sole discretion, refund to Purchaser the Purchase Price of the Product, less a reasonable adjustment for beneficial use.
>
> . . . .
>
> NOTWITHSTANDING ANY PROVISION OF THIS AGREEMENT TO THE CONTRARY, THE PROVISIONS OF THIS ARTICLE CONSTITUTE PURCHASER'S SOLE REMEDY UNDER THIS AGREEMENT. . . .

Pine brought suit for breach of contract after the goods failed to perform and claimed $19,861,327 in damages. Alcatel moved for summary judgment based upon its limited warranty.

Analysis: The court agreed with Alcatel and held that the limited remedy was exclusive, noting the "sole remedy" language. Because Alcatel honored the limited warranty by taking a return of the equipment, the exclusive remedy controlled and was satisfied as a matter of law under the contract.

---

[2]   82 UCC Rep. Serv. 2d 569 (E.D. Okla. 2015).

2. Minimum Adequate Remedy and Unconscionable Limitations

While the Code permits parties to provide a limited remedy, it also directs that "at least minimum adequate remedies be available." § 2-719 Comment 1. One commentator noted:

> While this is easy to state, it is difficult to apply. An agreement to modify or limit remedies means that an aggrieved party may not recover its full expectancy-based damages for a breach of contract, as previously discussed. On the other hand, if the remedy is quantified with an exclusive limited remedy clause, presumably that fact is reflected in the parties' bargained exchange. For example, if the seller has warranted the goods to be free of defects and the limited remedy is repair or replacement of defective parts and an exclusion of all consequential and incidental damages, the buyer may have paid a lower price than if the seller had not limited the remedy and thus had liability for all the damages provided for in Section 2-711 when the goods are defective. If a limited or modified remedies clause does not provide a "fair quantum of remedy" for breach, it is unenforceable and the remedies as provided in Article 2 apply.[3]

Section 2-313 Comment 4 notes that parties are free to "make their own bargain as they wish," but "the probability is small that a real price is intended to be exchanged for a pseudo-obligation."

Section 2-719(3) and Comments 1 and 3 explicitly note that unconscionable restrictions on remedies are impermissible. Section 2-302 more generally bars contract clauses that a court finds were unconscionable when made, and § 2-302 Comment 1 illustrates the "underlying basis" for that section with cases refusing to enforce certain remedy restrictions. But courts applying the common law doctrine typically will not find unconscionability unless the claimant is disadvantaged by a gross disproportionality of bargaining power and has an absence of meaningful choice. Such elements are rarely present in contracts between merchants, so the requirement that a party (merchant or non-merchant) must have a minimum adequate remedy expands the law's protections against surprising terms.

We have seen that a seller may limit the remedy arising from express representations about the goods and may disclaim all implied warranties. However, whatever

---

[3]   William D. Hawkland & Linda J. Rusch, Uniform Commercial Code Series § 2-719:2 (2015).

warranties are made must be enforceable with at least minimum remedies designed to compensate in some fashion for the breach of the remaining obligations.

EXAMPLES AND ANALYSIS

Example C: *American Licorice Co. v. Total Sweeteners, Inc.*[4]

American Licorice Company (American Licorice) contracted to purchase molasses from Total Sweeteners, Inc. (Total). The contract stated:

> WARRANTY: SELLER expressly warrants that any goods contracted herein will be representative of the brand or grade specified herein to be sold, and will comply with all of the applicable provisions of the Federal Food, Drug and Cosmetic Act and of any applicable State Pure Food and Drug Act. Buyer hereby waives any claim or defense based on the quality of the commodities specified herein, unless . . . within forty-five (45) days after receipt of notice of arrival of said commodities at destination, BUYER sends SELLER at SELLER'S main office a letter by registered mail specifying the nature of the complaint; . . .

> Except as expressly set forth herein, SELLER states that no warranties, express or implied, contained in the uniform commercial code or otherwise (including, without limitation, the implied warranty of fitness for a particular purpose) shall apply to the products sold hereunder and BUYER acknowledges that except as expressly set forth in the first sentence of this section, it is purchasing the goods, "as is" and "where is" . . . . SELLER shall in no event be liable for consequential, special or punitive damages hereunder.

The California Department of Public Health (CDPH) determined that some of American Licorice's black licorice candy contained quantities of lead significantly in excess of permissible levels and ordered a recall. American Licorice later performed an investigation into the adulteration of its candy and concluded that the excess lead originated in molasses it purchased from Total. American Licorice brought suit for breach of contract against Total. Total moved for summary judgment claiming the contract barred the claims.

---

[4]   84 UCC Rep. Serv. 2d 1070 (N.D. Cal. 2014).

Analysis: The court first ruled that the disclaimer of implied warranties was ineffective due to the lack of conspicuousness. The court decided, though, that the consequential damages exclusion was valid and granted summary judgment to Total as to that issue. The court concluded that the exclusion was not unconscionable for purposes of 2-719(3). First, the court found that the exclusion was not procedurally unconscionable even though "hidden in a maze of fine print," where the first page of the contract brought attention to the terms and conditions on the reverse side and the parties had bought and sold molasses on at least 13 different occasions with the same or a similar contract. As to substantive unconscionability, the court found in favor of Total where the risk of adulterated ingredients is not unusual or unforeseeable. The court held that the consequential damages exclusion was not unconscionable and was enforceable.

Since the court ruled the exclusion of consequential damages valid, what damages would be recoverable in an action for breach of contract if American Licorice prevails? Would the outcome change here if the consequential damages exclusion was hidden in a maze of fine print, but there was no reference to the terms and conditions on the first page of the contract? Must a party prove both procedural and substantive unconscionability to strike down the consequential damages limitation?

Example D: *Bennett v. CMH Homes, Inc.*[5]

Bennett entered into a contract for the purchase of a mobile home from CMH Homes, Inc. (CMH). The contract provided that the buyer's damages were limited to the lesser of the cost of repairs or the market value of the home and that the buyer would not be entitled to incidental or consequential damages. Shortly after the purchase, Bennett found substantial defects in the home, including unlevel floors, sunken areas, marriage lines at different heights, structural defects, wrinkled carpeting, warped roofing, electrical issues, water leakage, and other major problems. Bennett brought suit for breach of contract and requested both revocation of acceptance and monetary damages. CMH asserted that the contract's limited remedy clause meant Bennett could not revoke acceptance and could not receive consequential damages.

---

5   79 UCC Rep. Serv. 2d 481 (M.D. Tenn. 2013). The facts of this case appeared in Assignment 22, Problem 22-3.

Analysis: The court agreed with Bennett, finding the limitation of damages clause unconscionable:

> Factors which go into the determination include "the attendant circumstances;" "weaknesses in the contracting process;" "whether the terms are unreasonably favorable to the drafter;" "whether the terms provide favorable default remedies to one party and deny them to the other;" and "whether the terms are so one-sided that 'no reasonable person would make them on the one hand, and no honest and fair person would accept them on the other.'"

The court found the clause both procedurally and substantively unconscionable where the buyer was unsophisticated in business, and the clause was one-sided and harsh, preventing damages "even if the home falls apart around the buyer's ears."

Do you agree with the court's ruling? Is it a sufficient response by the seller that a buyer could shop for a manufactured home elsewhere? What significance is there to the fact that sellers often use standard form contracts, leaving consumers with little choice as to the terms? Are all standard form contract limitations on remedy unconscionable? What makes the *Bennett* case different?

3. Failure of Essential Purpose

As seen earlier in this Assignment, the parties' remedy limitations are policed by the doctrine of unconscionability, by a requirement that exclusiveness of remedy be explicit, by the policy requiring a minimum adequate remedy, and by the provisions of Magnuson-Moss Warranty Act that will be discussed below. In addition to these protections, which apply to the agreement upon formation, another doctrine—failure of essential purpose—applies to the agreement during its performance and enforcement phase.

Reading the Code: § 2-719

Read 2-719(2) and the last sentence of Comment 1.

Question 4. When 2-719(2) refers to "its" intended purpose, is it the purpose of the (limited) remedy that matters? The purpose of the buyer in buying the goods? The purpose of the limitation on the remedy?

In order to determine whether circumstances have caused a limited remedy to fail of its essential purpose, one must first ascertain the purpose(s) of the limited remedy. By far, the most common limited remedy is a seller's promise to repair or replace the defective goods. A common back-up limited remedy is seller's refund of the price paid to date. Other limited remedies may be conditioned on a time limit on reporting defects, notice requirements for reporting defects, and buyer's obligation to transport the goods to a particular repair facility. These limited remedies serve a variety of purposes for the parties, depending on the parties' intent, the nature of the remedy limitation, and the circumstances of the contract. For instance:

- An exclusive remedy of repair or replacement makes the buyer whole by providing the buyer with the promised goods in a reasonably timely fashion, thereby fulfilling buyer's expectation. Repair or replacement also prevents or reduces buyer's consequential damages and keeps down the cost of the goods (because seller does not incur litigation costs, is not liable for consequential damages, and can furnish the repair or replacement cheaply).

- An exclusive remedy of a refund prevents seller's unjust enrichment by providing restitution to the buyer, giving back to the buyer the financial resources to obtain substitute goods, and keeping down the cost of the goods (because seller does not incur litigation costs and is not liable for consequential damages).

- Time limits on buyer's reporting of defects allow the seller to have "repose," i.e, knowing when no further claims on the goods can be made, while encouraging buyer to act promptly to find and report defects.

- Notice requirements for buyer's reporting of defects (e.g., specifications about addressee, format, and content) allow the seller to receive the notice with certainty, reduce administrative processing costs, and promptly receive the information necessary for seller to give buyer the needed relief.

The idea behind a limited remedy is to allocate the risks between the parties by limiting the relief available for the injured party if there is a breach. By definition, then, the limited remedy will prevent the injured party from being fully compensated. However, when circumstances cause "an apparently fair and reasonable" limited remedy to fail of its essential purpose—when the remedy does not operate as it was intended—the party whose remedies were limited (usually the buyer) then can avail itself of the full range of remedies in Article 2. Comment 1 explains that when a limited remedy clause "operates to deprive either party of the substantial value of the bargain," the limited remedy "must give way to the general remedy provisions" of Article 2. Some courts use Comment 1 as a rationale for ignoring a limited remedy if the injured party is left uncompensated for substantial costs or losses. The better analysis, though, is to ask whether the parties' bargain allocated risk of such costs or losses to that party (that is, whether the limited remedy operated as intended) or whether circumstances caused costs or losses not contemplated in the original bargain.

If the contract contains a remedy limitation *and* an exclusion of consequential damages, what happens to the exclusion if the remedy limitation "fails of its essential purpose"? Courts disagree about whether such an exclusion should be understood as a separate limitation that is valid unless unconscionable under § 2-719(3) or should instead be understood as part of the limited remedy that has "failed of its essential purpose," allowing the buyer to collect consequential damages under § 2-715. This issue is discussed in *Sheehan v. Monaco Coach Corporation* later in this Assignment.

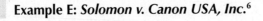

EXAMPLES AND ANALYSIS

Example E: *Solomon v. Canon USA, Inc.*[6]

Buyer purchased a camera and lenses manufactured by Canon, USA. Canon provided a one-year warranty and limited a buyer's remedies to

---

6   73 UCC Rep. Serv. 2d 162 (N.Y. App. Term 2010).

repair or replacement in the event of defects. Approximately three months after purchase of the camera, the buyer returned the camera to Canon after experiencing a problem with the lenses while on an overseas vacation. Canon repaired the camera, and it worked properly after the repair. The same problem reoccurred while the buyer was on a later vacation. Canon offered to repair the camera and lenses, but the buyer declined the offer and brought suit for breach of express and implied warranties. Canon moved for summary judgment.

Analysis: The court affirmed the grant of summary judgment to Canon. The court stressed that an exclusive remedy of repair or replacement is enforceable unless the remedy fails of its essential purpose. The court found that the remedy did not fail of its essential purpose where Canon repaired the camera successfully the first time and offered to repair the camera and lenses upon the second malfunction. The failure of the buyer to accept the second offer of repair precluded his argument that the limited remedy failed of its essential purpose.

Why does the court reject the buyer's claim that the remedy failed of its essential purpose? Might the case be different if Canon had repaired the camera twice and then it malfunctioned again on a later vacation? What if Canon repaired the camera and lenses on five different occasions?

Example F: *Kraft v. Staten Island Boat Sales, Inc.*[7]

Kraft purchased a Silverton recreational boat from Staten Island Boat Sales (Staten) in 2005. The purchase agreement disclaimed warranties by Staten, but Silverton provided a one- year limited remedy of repair or replacement. On the date of purchase, Kraft discovered oil and water leaking into bilge (the area between the deck and hull of the boat), which the Staten mechanic repaired. One month later, gasoline leaked into the bilge, which Staten attempted to repair. On several additional occasions, Kraft reported leaking water, and Staten promised to repair. In 2008, a different mechanic discovered the problem and corrected it, but black mold had developed in the hull. Repair of the black mold would cost $61,950. Kraft brought suit for claims including breach of warranty. The seller moved for summary judgment.

---

[7] 71 F. Supp. 2d 464 (S.D.N.Y. 2010).

Analysis: The court allowed the breach-of-warranty claims against Silverton to proceed, explaining:

> A limited remedy fails its essential purpose under section 2-719(2) if "the circumstances existing at the time of the agreement have changed so that enforcement of the limited remedy would essentially leave plaintiff with no remedy at all." *AT & T v. N.Y. City Human Res. Admin.*, 833 F. Supp. 962, 986 (S.D.N.Y.1993) . . . . A buyer is not required to show that the seller acted negligently or in bad faith to establish a failure of a limited warranty under 2-719. Rather, a buyer can lose a substantial benefit of the bargain where the warrantor is unable to repair the item or does not repair the defect within a reasonable time. Thus, whether the limited warranty failed in its essential purpose is a question of fact for the jury to determine based on circumstances transpiring after the contract was formed.

The court held that a material question of fact existed as to whether the remedy failed of its essential purpose where Kraft complained of leaking on many occasions and the problem was not fixed during the warranty period. Such a failure to repair would deprive Kraft of "a substantial benefit of the bargain," so Kraft was entitled to pursue other Article 2 remedies. The court, though, upheld the contract exclusion of consequential damages such that Kraft could only recover the cost of repairing the leak, about $115.

Why does the court uphold the buyer's claim that the remedy failed of its essential purpose? How does the exclusion of consequential damages affect Kraft's case? What might a buyer in Kraft's position do if a seller fails to repair?

Example G: *Holbrook v. Louisiana-Pacific Corp.*[8]

Holbrook contracted for purchase of a new home and his builder purchased and installed 1580 linear feet of Louisiana-Pacific Corp. (LP) TrimBoard. LP warranted the TrimBoard for ten years against defects, so long as properly installed and maintained. The LP warranty limited liability to the cost of repair or replacement, but not greater than twice the purchase price of the Trimboard. After Holbrook's TrimBoard deteriorated, he sought compensation from LP under its warranty. The purchase price of the TrimBoard

---

8   2015 WL 1291534 (N.D. Ohio 2015).

LP determined was damaged and compensable was approximately $585. LP offered Holbrook $4219.98, an amount substantially more than twice the purchase price. Holbrook claimed the actual replacement costs were between $30,000 and $32,000 and brought suit for breach of warranty. LP moved for summary judgment, claiming it had not breached its limited-remedy termbecause it had offered Holbrook more than the amount recoverable by him under the limited remedy.

Analysis: The court denied summary judgment to LP. The court determined that Holbrook was the intended beneficiary of the warranty in the contract between LP and the builder for purchase of the TrimBoard, so he could invoke the warranty in his lawsuit. The court also held that the limited- remedy provision was not unconscionable because the limitation was clear on the face of the contract and had been arranged between sophisticated commercial entities (LP and the builder). The court, concluded, however, that a jury could find that the remedyhad failed of its essential purpose. The court explained that "[a] limited remedy fails of its essential purpose when the aggrieved party cannot obtain the intended benefit of the remedy for which it bargained." This typically occurs when a seller is unable or unwilling to make repairs in a timely manner or a latent defect prevents or delays discovery of the breach so the repair-or-refund remedy does not work as intended. The court said failure of essential purpose may also occur where the warranty "covers only a fraction of [the buyer's] allegedly substantial—and foreseeable—economic hardship" because the limited remedy would not be adequate to cover the buyer's actual loss. Limiting Holbrook's recovery to twice the cost of the TrimBoard would not take into account the foreseeable and necessary cost of removing and installing the new trim, the court said, so the remedy might be found to have failed of its essential purpose.

Do you agree with the court's judgment and analysis? What was the purpose of the limited remedy? Did the limited remedy fail of its essential purpose? Did the limited remedy work precisely as intended by the parties to the sale? Is the problem that the remedy failed to provide a minimum adequate remedy to Holbrook? Do you think the result would be different if the builder rather than Holbrook had sued LP? Remember that many consumer products are not purchased from the manufacturer directly. Should a consumer be able to successfully argue unconscionability or failure of essential purpose even if the manufacturer and retailer engaged in arm's length negotiation of the limited remedy term?

B. Remedy Provisions of the Magnuson-Moss Warranty Act

As discussed in Assignment 12, the Magnuson-Moss Warranty Act applies if (either at the time of sale or within ninety days thereafter) a supplier gives a "written warranty" or enters into a "service contract" as to a "consumer product." Recall the following definitions, focusing on the italicized portions, which pertain to remedies:

- A "written warranty" is

    (1) a written affirmation of fact or promise (by a direct or indirect supplier to the buyer) that affirms or promises that the material or workmanship of the goods is defect-free or will meet a specified level of performance over a specified period of time, or

    (2) a supplier's written *undertaking to refund, repair, replace, or take other remedial action* as to the goods upon the failure of the goods to meet contract specifications,

    if the affirmation, promise, or undertaking becomes *part of the basis of the bargain* between the supplier and the buyer for purposes other than resale of the goods.[9]

- A "service contract" is a written *contract to perform maintenance or repair services* over a fixed period of time.

As also discussed in Assignment 12, Magnuson-Moss establishes a mandatory two-tier system of warranty labeling for "written warranties": Full Warranty or Limited Warranty. Recall that a warrantor[10] giving a Full Warranty cannot disclaim or limit any of the implied warranties. In addition, the warrantor giving a Full Warranty of a consumer product must abide by the following rules on remedies and remedy limitations:

- The warrantor cannot require the product owner to do more than notify the warrantor of the defect in order to be entitled to a remedy, unless the

---

9   Note that neither a written representation nor a supplier's written undertaking to refund, repair, replace, or take other remedial action is a "written warranty" under Magnuson-Moss unless it is part of the basis of the bargain. Recall from Assignment 11 that under Article 2, express warranties are effective only if they are part of the basis of the bargain, but Article 2 does not impose the same requirement on other terms of a sales contract, including remedial promises such as the promise to repair or replace.

10   Magnuson-Moss defines a "supplier" as a person in the business of making a consumer product directly or indirectly available to consumers. A "warrantor" is a supplier or any other person who makes (or offers to make) a "written warranty" or who is (or may be) obligated under an implied warranty.

warrantor can prove that the additional duty is reasonable. In particular, the warrantor cannot require the buyer to register its purchase or return a "warranty card" in order to receive the remedy.

- The warrantor must give the minimum adequate remedy of curing any breach of a written warranty within a reasonable time and without charge.

- After the warrantor has made a reasonable number of attempts to remedy defect(s), the warrantor must allow the consumer product owner to elect between refund and replacement (without charge).

- The warrantor cannot limit or exclude consequential damages for breach of a written or implied warranty, unless the limitation or exclusion is conspicuous and on the face of the warranty.

A warrantor giving a Limited Warranty has no additional restrictions, aside from those discussed in Assignment 12.

The Magnuson-Moss Warranty Act encourages consumers and warrantors to resolve their disputes without litigation by use of "informal dispute settlement mechanisms" that operate under standards set up by the Federal Trade Commission's rules. These informal dispute settlement mechanisms often involve mediation or arbitration in private forums set up by manufacturers, trade associations, or large vendors. If a warrantor sets up a dispute settlement mechanism that complies with the Magnuson-Moss regulations, the warrantor can contractually require the consumer product owner to resort to that mechanism *prior to* pursuing judicial remedies. The Federal Trade Commission, though, has long banned mandatory, binding arbitration provisions for warranty claims made under the MMWA. However,many courts have upheld binding arbitration of MMWA claims so long as the procedure complies with the MMWA requirements regarding the organization conducting the dispute settlement mechanism.[11]

In addition, the consumer product owner must allow the warrantor a reasonable opportunity to cure before bringing suit. Federal jurisdiction is available if the total amount in controversy is at least $50,000 and, if the dispute is a class action, if it consists of at least 100 plaintiffs, each with an individual claim of at least $25. Otherwise, the buyer can bring the suit in state court. If the consumer product owner prevails, the owner also can recover costs and attorneys' fees (based on actual time).

---

[11] See, e.g., Cunningham v. Fleetwood Homes of Georgia, Inc., 253 F.3d 611 (11th Cir. 2001); Borowiec v. Gateway 2000, Inc., 808 N.E.2d 957 (Ill. 2004).

Example H: *Miller v. Four Winds International Corp.*[12]

Miller bought a motor home that was protected by a limited warranty promising repair or replacement for defects. Miller alleges the motor home suffered from a variety of serious defects that were not remedied, despite Four Winds' attempts to repair. Miller sued under state UCC law and Magnuson-Moss and asked for return of the purchase price of the motor home.

Analysis: The court ruled that Magnuson-Moss does not require a manufacturer to refund the purchase price when the buyer receives a limited rather than a full warranty. Magnuson-Moss requires the seller to allow return of goods and to refund the purchase price only when there is a full warranty. Similarly, the UCC does not require the return of the purchase price. If the buyer could prove that the limited remedy failed of its essential purpose, buyer would be entitled to remedies under the Code, but because the buyer had accepted the motor home, the Code remedy was 2-714 damages for breach of warranty, not refund of the purchase price, unless the motor home was valueless. To be eligible for a refund, buyer would have to revoke acceptance, but that remedy was not available against the manufacturer, only against the immediate seller. The court awarded the seller partial summary judgment as to buyer's claim for refund.

Example I: *Ventura v. Ford Motor Co.*[13]

Ventura brought suit against the dealer and manufacturer for defects in the car he purchased. Dealer had disclaimed all warranties, express or implied, but had promised to "promptly perform and fulfill all terms and conditions of the owner service policy" based on warranties made by the manufacturer.

Analysis: The court held that that promise was a written warranty under Magnuson-Moss. Therefore, the dealer could not disclaim implied warranties Because New Jersey did away with the privity requirement for revocation of acceptance, Ventura was entitled under state law to a refund if he showed

---

[12]   827 F. Supp. 2d 1175 (D. Idaho 2011).
[13]   433 A.2d 801 (N.J. Super. 1981).

grounds for revocation under the Code. Ventura was also entitled to a judgment of rescission and refund against the dealer. Although Magnuson Moss itself was not grounds for rescission (because Ford gave a limited, not a full, warranty), rescission and refund was still possible under state law.

As might be apparent, a seller often desires to limit exposure on its goods through use of a written limited warranty that contains a limited remedy provision. Most commonly, such limited remedy provisions direct that the seller will repair or replace, or sometimes refund the purchase price, in the event the product is defective. Such a repair or replacement is often coupled with an exclusion of consequential damages. A difficulty sometimes arises when the seller is not readily able to accomplish the repair or replacement. In such cases, the buyer will want to claim that the limited remedy fails of its essential purpose, and the seller will want to enforce the limited remedy. Courts are often faced with troublesome questions about when a claim under the MMWA is permitted, when a seller's repair attempts that are unsuccessful amount to a failure of essential purpose for purposes of state law, and what remedy might be permitted if it does. The case below, *Sheehan v. Monaco Coach Corp.*, addresses those issues. As you read the case, consider these questions:

(1)   Why does the court conclude that Monarch did not have to provide the Sheehans a refund under the MMWA?

(2)   Can the Sheehans bring an MMWA action if Monarch did not violate the requirements of the MMWA?

(3)   Why does the Sheehans' claim for breach of implied warranty fail?

(4)   Does the court find that the limited remedy failed of its essential purpose?

(5)   When a limited remedy fails its essential purpose, what remedy is the buyer entitled to claim? What does the court say about the availability of consequential damages to the Sheehans?

SHEEHAN v. MONACO COACH CORP.

2006 WL 208689 (E.D. Wis. 2006)

CALLAHAN, MAGISTRATE JUDGE.

I. PROCEDURAL AND FACTUAL BACKGROUND

This action was commenced on June 21, 2004, when the plaintiffs, Raymond Sheehan and his wife, Lynn Sheehan, (the "Sheehans") filed a complaint in the Circuit Court for Kenosha County, Wisconsin alleging breach of express and implied warranties as well as a violation of Wisconsin's motor vehicle lemon law.

. . . .

The Sheehans are residents of Salem, Wisconsin. Monaco is a corporation with its principal offices located in Coburg, Oregon, and is in the business of manufacturing Beaver Contessa motor homes, which are distributed throughout the United States. The 2002 Monaco Beaver Contessa motor home ("2002 Beaver") . . . was manufactured by Monaco's Beaver Division.

On March 20, 2003, the Sheehans purchased the 2002 Beaver from Landry's Work'N Play in Fort Myers, Florida for the amount of $288,491.28. The Sheehans received a copy of the 2002 Beaver's limited twelve month/12,000 mile written warranty at or before the time of sale.

. . . .

The 2002 Beaver, while at Landry's Work'N Play in Florida, had problems that could not be fixed by Landry's and, therefore, an appointment was set up with the Monaco factory in Indiana for repair of the 2002 Beaver.

The Sheehans allege that the following is a nonexhaustive list of the multiple problems that were to be addressed by Monaco when the 2002 Beaver was at Monaco's Indiana factory:

- Living room on the motor home leaking water
- Ceiling stained from the water problems
- Woodwork being damaged in the vehicle
- The Galley slide-out moving out and sliding out of the motor home while vehicle is traveling

- The Galley slide-out leaks into the overhead cabinets when [it] is in and when it is out
- Bedroom slide-out making a lot of noise when operating sliding in and out
- Defrost Vent on the dash was broke
- Refrigerator door panel on the right side was water stained
- Rubber Mats coming off the steps to the vehicle
- Scratches on the dinette table
- Front security curtains are water stained
- Carpet under passenger seat coming up
- Second window from driver's seat on slide out needed blind to be replaced
- Scrape on sink on the top galley slide out
- Satellite will not stay on track
- Water comes out of ceiling speaker behind driver seat
- Value extensions missing on rear wheels
- Awning fabric on driver side on main slide out was mildewed
- Motor home would not stay level
- Freshwater dump switch inoperable
- Galley slide out awning was not hung straight
- Windshield leaked down the center post
- Paint peeling off the lower trim
- Repair side of Galley slide out as needed due to moving patio arm

The Sheehans further allege that after the 2002 Beaver was at the Monaco Indiana factory for repairs, the 2002 Beaver continued to have the water leaking problem, the slide-out problems, and the mold problems. The Sheehans also allege that the motor home's water leaking problem created a severe mold problem and that Raymond Sheehan developed medical problems while operating in the mold-contaminated vehicle.

. . . .

III. ANALYSIS

Monaco moves for summary judgment arguing that the Sheehans are not entitled to a refund under the Magnuson-Moss Warranty Act ("the Act") because the refund/replacement provision of the Act only applies to full warranties, not limited warranties. Monaco further argues that the Sheehans' claim for consequential damages must similarly fail because the 2002 Beaver's limited warranty conspicuously disclaims liability for consequential damages.

. . . The Act also provides that "[i]f the written warranty does not meet the federal minimum standards for warranty set forth in section 2304 . . . then it shall be conspicuously designated a 'limited warranty.'" 15 U.S.C. § 2303(a)(2).

In light of these statutory provisions, Monaco argues that limited warranties need not comply with the requirements of section 2304. The court agrees. A limited warranty is not subject to the requirements of section 2304 and thus, "not subject to the Act's substantive remedies, including a refund of the . . . purchase price." *Schimmer v. Jaguar Cars, Inc.,* 384 F.3d 402, 405 (7th Cir.2004). There can be little dispute that the written warranty given by Monaco with the purchase of its 2002 Beaver Contessa motor home is conspicuously designated as a limited warranty. Thus, because the 2002 Beaver Contessa warranty is a limited warranty, not a full warranty, Monaco need not comply with the refund/replacement remedy provided in section 2304(d). Yet, despite Monaco's argument that the court's inquiry regarding this issue should end here, it shall not.

Monaco argues that the Sheehans' claim for a refund/replacement must be dismissed in its entirety. This is because the Sheehans' only remaining claim is a violation of the Act, and as a matter of law, Monaco did not violate the Act by not complying with the requirements of section 2304. However, to prove a violation of the Act, a plaintiff need not prove a violation of the substantive provisions of the Act. Indeed, a plaintiff may prove a violation of the Act by pleading and proving a breach of a written or implied warranty. The Act states that "a consumer who is damaged by the failure of a supplier, warrantor or service contractor to comply with any obligation under [the Act] or under a written warranty, implied warranty or service contract, may bring suit for damages and other legal and equitable relief." 15 U.S.C. § 2310(a)(3), (d)(1) (emphasis added). Simply stated, the Act creates a federal private cause of action for individual consumers to sue for breach of written or implied warranties pertaining to consumer products.

In their amended complaint, the Sheehans allege the following: "Monaco has failed to conform Plaintiffs' motor home to its express written warranties and implied warranties, each of which violates the Magnuson-Moss Warranty Act." . . . Thus, the Sheehans have adequately alleged that Monaco has failed "to comply with [its] obligation[s] . . . under [its] written warranty, [and its] implied warranty."15 U.S.C. § 2310(a)(3), (d)(1).

. . . .

A. Breach of Implied Warranty

Under the Act, a consumer who is damaged by a warrantor's failure to comply with an implied warranty may file a claim in federal court. 15 U.S.C. § 2310(d). The Act defines "implied warranty" as "an implied warranty arising under state law . . . in connection with the sale by a supplier of a consumer product." 15 U.S.C. § 2301(7). The Court of Appeals for the Seventh Circuit has held that implied warranty claims asserted under the Act are interpreted solely under state law and thus, if state law requires privity of contract to establish a breach of an implied warranty, privity is also required under the Act. . . .

. . . It is undisputed that the parties are not in contractual privity because the Sheehans did not purchase the 2002 Beaver directly from Monaco. Nor can the Sheehans establish privity of contract based upon the written warranty Monaco extended to them. *Mesa,* 904 So.2d at 458; *see also Pack v. Damon Corp.,* 320 F. Supp. 2d 545, 561 (E.D.Mich.2004) ("[A]n express warranty running directly from a manufacturer to a buyer does not create contractual privity."). Thus, because the parties lack privity of contract, the Sheehans' breach of implied warranty claim under the Act fails as a matter of law.

B. Breach of Written Warranty Claim

Under the Act, a consumer who is damaged by a warrantor's failure to comply with a written warranty may file a claim in federal court. 15 U.S.C. § 2310(d)(1). The Sheehans claim that Monaco breached its written warranty by failing to repair the 2002 Beaver or replace its defective parts while it was at

Monaco's factory for fifty-seven days. The Sheehans also claim that the 2002 Beaver had more problems after it spent those fifty-seven days at Monaco's factory. However, while Monaco admits that the Sheehans requested repair of the 2002 Beaver, Monaco claims that the requested repairs were made in accordance with Monaco's limited written warranty. Accordingly, a genuine issue of material fact exists as to whether Monaco fulfilled its obligation to repair or replace defective parts under the limited written warranty. Thus, the Sheehans' breach of written warranty claim under the Act will survive summary judgment.

Although Monaco argues that the Sheehans cannot establish their breach of written warranty claim because the parties lack contractual privity, contractual privity is not required to bring a breach of written warranty claim under the Act. The Court of Appeals for the Second Circuit has stated that, under the Act, "it is clear that with regard to written warranties, full or limited, privity is not required [to bring a breach of written warranty claim]." *Abraham*, 795 F.2d at 248.

. . . .

Florida law provides that if a consumer establishes that a warranty's limited remedy failed of its essential purpose, then the consumer may seek all of the other remedies available under the Uniform Commercial Code (UCC), including revocation of acceptance. . . . Florida courts have recognized that if a plaintiff proves that an exclusive, limited remedy provided in a warranty fails of its "essential purpose," then the consumer may "resort . . . to the additional remedies of the UCC." *Tampa Farm Serv., Inc. v. Cargill, Inc.*, 356 So.2d 347, 350 (Fla.Dist.Ct.App.1978).

Thus, if the Sheehans establish that the limited remedy provided in the warranty failed of its essential purpose, they may then seek the additional remedies provided under Florida's codification of the UCC, including revocation of acceptance. However, it is worth noting that, to ultimately succeed in obtaining the remedy of revocation of acceptance, the Sheehans must also establish the requirements set forth in section 672.608, which include, inter alia, that the 2002 Beaver's "nonconformit[ies] substantially impair[ ] its value." Fla. Stat. 672.608(1). It is also worth noting that if the jury were to find that the Sheehans could revoke acceptance of the 2002 Beaver, Monaco would also be entitled to re-take possession of the motor home, and would be entitled to a credit for the value the Sheehans received from their use of the 2002 Beaver while it was in their possession. However, this court need not address the damages issue with any specificity at this point, because there is a genuine issue of material fact as to whether there was a breach of the limited written warranty, and also as to whether the limited remedy failed of its essential purpose.

C. Disclaimer of Consequential Damages

In their complaint, the Sheehans allege that Monaco's breach of its limited written warranty entitles them to receive "all out of pocket expenses related to the motor home . . . [and] recover loss of use damages measured by the cost to rent a like motor home for the periods during which the subject motor home has not conformed to the written or implied warranties." However, the 2002 Beaver's Limited Warranty, provided to the Sheehans at the time of sale, disclaims all consequential and incidental damages:

- DISCLAIMER OF CONSEQUENTIAL AND INCIDENTAL DAMAGES:

- THE ORIGINAL PURCHASER OF THE MOTORHOME AND ANY PERSON TO WHOM THE MOTORHOME IS TRANSFERRED, AND ANY PERSON WHO IS AN INTENDED OR UNINTENDED USER OR BENEFICIARY OF THE MOTORHOME, SHALL NOT BE ENTITLED TO RECOVER FROM WARRANTOR ANY CONSEQUENTIAL OR INCIDENTAL DAMAGES RESULTING FROM ANY DEFECT IN THE MOTORHOME. THE EXCLUSION OF CONSEQUENTIAL AND INCIDENTAL DAMAGES SHALL BE DEEMED INDEPENDENT OF, AND SHALL SURVIVE, ANY FAILURE OF THE ESSENTIAL PURPOSE OF ANY LIMITED REMEDY. Some states do not allow the exclusion or limitation of consequential or incidental damages, so the above exclusions may not apply to you.

The Act provides that warrantors offering a full warranty may not limit or exclude consequential damages unless the provision appears conspicuously on the face of the warranty. 15 U.S.C. 2304(a)(3) (emphasis added). This provision, however, does not require that any exclusion or limitation of consequential or incidental damages appear conspicuously on the face of a limited warranty. . . . Thus, because the Act does not address the exclusion or limitation of consequential damages in limited warranties, such exclusion or limitation is governed by state law.

. . . The Sheehans argue that the limited warranty is "adhesion in nature . . . [because the Sheehans] had no opportunity to negotiate its terms" and because they are not "sophisticated parties." Thus, the Sheehans appear to be arguing that the consequential damages disclaimer is unconscionable. Under Florida law, "[u]nconscionability has generally been recognized to include an absence of meaningful choice on the part of one of the parties together with contract terms which are unreasonably favorable to the other party. Whether a meaningful choice is present in a particular case can only be determined by consideration of all the circumstances surrounding the transaction. In many cases the meaningfulness of the choice is negated by a gross inequality of bargaining power. The manner in which the contract was entered is also relevant to this consideration. Did each party to the contract, considering his obvious education or lack of it, have a reasonable opportunity to understand the terms of the contract, or were the important terms hidden in a maze of fine print and minimized by deceptive sales practices? Ordinarily, one who signs an agreement without full knowledge of its terms might be held to assume the risk that he has entered a one-sided bargain. But when a party of little bargaining power, and hence little real choice, signs a commercially unreasonable contract with little or no knowledge of its terms, it is hardly likely that his consent, or even an objective manifestation of his consent, was ever given to all the terms. In such a case the usual rule that the terms of the agreement are not to be questioned should be abandoned and the court should consider whether the terms of the contract are so unfair that enforcement should be withheld." *Fotomat Corp. of Florida v. Chanda*, 464 So.2d 626, 628-29 (Fla.Dist.Ct.App.1985) (quoting *Williams v. Walker-Thomas Furniture Co.*, 350 F.2d 445, 449-50 (C.A.D.C.1965)).

. . . .

This court finds that the limited written warranty's consequential damages disclaimer is not procedurally unconscionable. While the Sheehans argue that they are not "sophisticated parties," in light of the fact the Sheehans were experienced motor home purchasers, the court does not find that argument persuasive. Indeed, the 2002 Beaver was the Sheehans' seventh motor home. Moreover, while whether Mr. Sheehan read the warranty at the time of sale is in dispute, it is undisputed that the Sheehans received a copy of the limited written warranty at the time of the sale. And, although the consequential damages disclaimer is not on the first page of the warranty, it is referenced on the first page, and it is indeed conspicuous, as it is set apart from the other provisions, is in all capital letters, and is in bold typeface.

It is true that the Sheehans were not given an opportunity to negotiate the terms of the limited written warranty. However, if the Sheehans would have read the warranty at or before the time of sale, and had decided that they did not approve of the consequential damages disclaimer, they could have looked into buying a different brand of motor home. Thus, this court finds that the evidence falls short of showing procedural unconscionability, and therefore, need not discuss substantive unconscionability.

Even in light of this court's finding that the disclaimer is enforceable, the Sheehans argue that if they can prove that Monaco's limited written warranty failed of its essential purpose, then the consequential damages disclaimer should be unenforceable. As aforementioned, if an exclusive or limited remedy fails of its essential purpose, then the aggrieved buyer is free to pursue all remedies set forth in Article 2 of the UCC, as though the limit had not appeared in the contract. Whether a buyer should be free to pursue incidental and consequential damages, even if they have been disclaimed, when a limited remedy has failed of its essential purpose has not been addressed by the Florida courts.

. . . .

In discussing the buyer's argument, that the failure of essential purpose of the original remedy also voids the restriction on consequential damages, White & Summers note that buyers typically rely upon Comment 1 to section 2-719, which states that a remedy that fails "must give way to the general remedy provisions of this Article." *Id.* However, according to White & Summers, courts that accept these buyers' arguments are mistaken. *Id.*

Rather, according to White & Summers, the correct approach under the Code, and the majority view (albeit a close majority) of the courts that have addressed this issue, is that expressed in *American Electric Power Co., Inc. v. Westinghouse Electric Corp.*, 418 F. Supp. 435 (S.D.N.Y.1976):

> [W]e favor the *American Electric Power* line of cases. Those cases are most true to the Code's general notion that the parties should be free to contract as they please. The text of the Code disfavors judges' and juries' rewriting contracts that allocate risks between the parties. UCC sections 1-102, 2-316, 2-719, and many other accord primacy to the terms of the contract over the general law of the Code. Indeed, as to remedies, 2-719(1)(a) and (b) provide that the parties may provide for

remedies "in substitution for those provided in the article" and that the parties may make such remedies "exclusive."

White & Summers, at § 12-10. This court believes that if this question was presented to the Florida Supreme Court, especially in light of the specific facts of this case, that court too would agree with the majority view as expressed in *American Electric Power* ("*AEP*").

In *AEP*, as in this case, the defendant argued that even if the plaintiff can show that the limited remedy failed of its essential purpose, the disclaimer of consequential damages stands independently of the remedy limitation and therefore, the plaintiff is still precluded from recovering consequential damages. Plaintiffs, however, argued that the court should read the limited remedy of repair or replacement and the limitation of liability clause as dependent provisions, such that if the exclusive remedy of repair and replacement fails, defendant would not be entitled to rely on the contractual exclusion of consequential damages. After reviewing the cases relied upon by the plaintiff and the defendant, the court held that the interpretation of section 2-719(2) of the UCC urged by the defendant was the more appropriate one.

. . . .

Similarly, in this case, one provision of the warranty provides the limited remedy of repair or replacement of defective parts, and a completely separate provision limits the defendant's liability such that incidental and consequential damages may not be recovered. Moreover, in this case, the consequential damages disclaimer contains a provision specifically stating that "[t]he exclusion of consequential and incidental damages shall be deemed independent of, and shall survive, any failure of the essential purpose of any limited remedy." Thus, it would appear that the two clauses are independent and that the parties intended the buyer to bear the burden of consequential and incidental damages if the limited remedy failed of its essential purpose (which, theoretically could have led to a much lower purchase price for the buyer). As the court found in *AEP*, when the provisions are independent of each other "there is no reason to disturb the consensual allocation of risk" agreed upon by the parties. 418 F. Supp. at 458.

Moreover, in *AEP*, the court relied heavily on the fact that even if the remedy failed of its essential purpose, the plaintiff would still be able to obtain a "minimum adequate remedy," an undetermined amount of damages, which simply would not include consequential damages. *Id.* . . . Similarly, in this case, in the event that the jury finds that "the defendant has totally failed to perform its warranty to repair or replace, damages [or any other remedy provided under the Code, except for consequential/incidental damages] . . . will be recoverable," and therefore, a minimum adequate remedy will be available to the Sheehans. *Am. Elec. Power*, 418 F. Supp. at 459. Thus, because this court believes that the Florida Supreme Court would follow the *AEP* line of cases, it finds that even if the Sheehans can show that the limited remedy failed of its essential purpose, they will still be precluded from recovering consequential damages. Accordingly, Monaco's motion for summary judgment precluding the Sheehans from recovering consequential damages will be granted.

C. The Relationship of §§ 2-718 and 2-719

As seen in Assignment 22, a liquidated damages term establishes an agreed-to amount that a party is to recover upon the occurrence of a particular kind of breach. The validity of liquidated damages terms is determined under the criteria in § 2-718(1).

Reading the Code:
§§ 2-718 and 2-719

Read 2-718 and 2-719.

Question 5. Can a liquidated damages term also be affected by the rules in 2-719? Must it be exclusive to be effective? Can it fail of its essential purpose? As you answer, consider the introductory clause in 2-719(1).

APPLYING THE CODE

Problem 24-1.

Which, if any, of the following clauses prevent buyer from collecting damages under the Article 2 remedy provisions?

(a) Seller may repair or replace any defective goods.

(b) Buyer's remedy for any defect in manufacture is refund or replacement, at seller's option.

(c) Buyer's sole and exclusive remedy shall be repair or replacement of defective parts, at seller's option.

Problem 24-2.

Which, if any, of the following remedies deprive buyer of a minimum adequate remedy or a fair quantum of remedy for breach? If you would need additional information to answer, indicate what you would need to know.

(a) Seller shall not in any circumstance be liable to buyer for consequential or incidental damages.

(b) Return for any reason within 30 days. Store credit only.

(c) Seller disclaims all implied warranties, including the warranty of merchantability and the warranty of fitness for a particular purpose.

(d) Seller's liability for any breach of warranty shall not in any event exceed the purchase price paid to date by the buyer. (Assume the buyer has paid only 10% of the purchase price by the time buyer rightfully rejects the goods for breach of warranty.)

(e) Upon breach, buyer may not recover any amount in excess of $500. (Assume the contract price was $759.)

(f) All claims of breach must be made in writing, within 24 hours of delivery.

Problem 24-3.

(a)   What effect do the provisions of Magnuson-Moss have on the following agreement term, assuming that the goods are a "consumer product?

Full Warranty for the Life of the Product

Paragon warrants this product, for its life, to be free from defects in materials and workmanship. If a defect is found, our entire liability and your exclusive remedy shall be, at our option, free repair or replacement or a full refund, provided that you return the goods to us, postage prepaid. Paragon has no liability for any incidental or consequential damages, such as data loss. Some states do not allow the exclusion or the limitation of incidental or consequential damages, so the above limitation or exclusion may not apply to you.

(b)   How does your answer to (a) change if the heading on the warranty is instead labeled "Warranty of Quality"?

Problem 24-4.

Buyer runs a game arcade in a shopping mall. He purchases a spacecraft-simulator game in which the customer sits in a chair and pilots a simulated spacecraft using hand and foot controls while watching the simulated flight on a screen of the scene outside of the craft. The contract states that "buyer's sole and exclusive remedy for defects in the simulator is to return the defective parts to the seller, at buyer's expense, for repair or replacement, seller's choice. Seller is not, in any event, responsible for any consequential damages." The simulator catches fire and is completely destroyed. The fire also damages four other games in Buyer's arcade. The fire was caused by a wiring defect in the simulator. Buyer has nothing but a few melted plastic pieces and some charred wires to return to Seller. Seller maintains that its sole responsibility under the contract is to replace the defective wiring, which it has offered to do. Is Seller correct? What if the fire occurred while Buyer was demonstrating the game to others and Buyer suffered burns requiring medical attention?

Problem 24-5.

TOK is in the business of sourcing, qualifying, mixing, manufacturing, selling, and delivering chemicals for use in the semiconductor manufacturing process. Huntsman makes and supplies certain chemicals. TOK purchased from Huntsman propylene glycol (PG), a chemical that TOK combined with other chemicals to create a mixture that TOK then sold to its semiconductor manufacturing customer (Customer). Customer was engaged in a pilot test to determine if it wished regularly to use the chemical mixture that included PG. TOK, prior to contracting to purchase PG from Huntsman, signed an application to purchase from Huntsman on credit that stated:

> LIMITATION OF LIABILITY. Seller's maximum liability for any breach of this Agreement, or any other claim related to the Product, shall be limited to the purchase price of the Product or portion thereof (as such price is set forth on the first page of Seller's invoice) to which such breach or claim pertains. IN NO EVENT SHALL SELLER BE LIABLE FOR ANY CONSEQUENTIAL, INCIDENTAL, SPECIAL OR PUNITIVE DAMAGES, INCLUDING BUT NOT LIMITED TO ANY DAMAGES FOR LOST PROFITS OR BUSINESS OPPORTUNITIES OR DAMAGE TO REPUTATION.

TOK believed this language related to the credit application, as it had not yet purchased any products. TOK purchased product from Huntsman two years later after extensive negotiations and test purchases. The parties also agreed to detailed product specifications that included a process change notification clause that required Huntsman to notify TOK in advance of implementing any change in the manufacturing process, as the Customer's needs were sensitive to changes in formulation. When the Customer had problems with the mixture, it was traced back to a PG change made by Huntsman without notification to TOK. If TOK brings suit, should the terms and conditions in the credit application operate as a limitation of remedies? Would such a clause fail of its essential purpose? Is it unconscionable? What arguments might you expect the parties to make?

Problem 24-6.

Seller is a manufacturer of nuts, bolts, and washers that hold together large items like planes, ships, trains, and buildings. Buyer is a manufacturer of construction cranes. Seller sells Buyer 150 27-inch bolts, which Buyer uses in its manufacture of construction cranes. The parties' written agreement contains the following clause:

> If the bolts do not conform to Buyer's specifications, Buyer's sole and exclusive remedy is to return the nonconforming bolts to Seller for repair or replacement, Seller's choice.

Buyer sells its cranes to various customers (downstream buyers); each of the agreements with those buyers contains the following clause: "Crane manufacturer promises to indemnify customer for all losses directly resulting from defects in parts or workmanship." One of Crane's customers suffers a $456,000 loss when two of the bolts sheer off, causing the crane to topple and resulting in damage to the crane and other property, but no personal injuries. No one disputes that the accident was caused by the two bolts, both of which were defective and did not meet the Buyer's specifications in the agreement with Seller.

Buyer pays its customer for the $456,000 loss under the indemnity clause and now maintains that Seller owes the same to Buyer, as consequential damages. Seller argues that the repair-or-replacement clause is valid and has offered to replace the two defective bolts, but refuses to pay any damages. What arguments would you expect from each party?

Assignment 25
Statute of Limitations
§ 2-725

Even if liability and a remedy would otherwise exist under Article 2, a party must file suit before the statute of limitations has expired in order to get relief. The limitations period for contracts for sales of goods is found in § 2-725.

LEARNING OUTCOMES AND OBJECTIVES

At the completion of this Assignment, you should be able to

- identify:
    - when the statute of limitations begins running;
    - the length of the limitations period; and
    - under what circumstances the limitations period will be extended beyond the length of time specified in the code; and
- apply the relevant portions of § 2-725 to determine whether a particular claim is time-barred or may proceed.

A. Triggering the Statute of Limitations

The statute of limitations plays a major role in sales litigation, particularly warranty litigation, potentially providing a seller-defendant with a relatively simple and absolute defense. The statute of limitations is particularly important in sales of goods because most warranties protect against future performance of the goods, and a buyer typically will not be able to determine whether the warranty has been complied with or breached until sometime after the goods are delivered. Even if the seller's promises are limited to describing the condition of the goods at delivery, the buyer may not discover latent defects until significantly after delivery. Moreover, where the agreement limits the buyer's remedy to repair or replacement, the buyer must first provide the seller an opportunity to repair or replace prior to bringing suit, thereby increasing the time during which the statute of limitations will be running.

In many instances, the statute of limitations will allow a defendant to defeat a claim as a matter of law early in the litigation, even where the claimant has an otherwise compelling case. Thus, knowing when and how the statute applies is extremely important to litigants as well as to contract drafters.

Reading the Code: § 2-725

Read 2-725 and its Comments.

Question 1. What triggers the running of the statute of limitations?

Question 2. Once the running of the statute of limitations is triggered, how long does the aggrieved party have to file suit?

Question 3. Complete the following chart, based on the three rules for when a cause of action accrues:

Nature of claim	When cause of action accrues
	When the breach is or should have been discovered
	When tender of delivery occurs
	When the breach occurs

Question 4. For violation of the implied warranties under 2-312, 2-314, or 2-315, does the cause of action ever accrue when the breach is or should have been discovered, rather than when tender of delivery occurs?

EXAMPLES AND ANALYSIS

Example A: *Woods v. Maytag Co.*[1]

Woods purchased a Maytag gas oven on July 21, 2005. On February 29, 2008, a malfunction caused the oven to explode. On December 10, 2009, Woods filed a class action alleging breach of contract and other claims against the sellers. The sellers moved for dismissal on the grounds that the statute of limitations had expired for the named plaintiff, making the claims untimely.

Analysis: The trial court agreed with the sellers. When did the statute of limitations expire for Woods' Maytag oven? Under which part of 2-725?

As reflected in your answers to the questions above, § 2-725 may be seen as establishing three general rules. First, "an action for breach of any contract for sale must be commenced within four years after the cause of action has accrued." Second, "a cause of action accrues when the breach occurs, regardless of the aggrieved party's lack of knowledge of the breach." Third, "a breach of warranty occurs when tender of delivery is made." As to the third rule, though, § 2-725(2) recognizes an exception: a warranty is not breached until the breach is or should have been discovered if the warranty "explicitly extends to future performance of the goods and discovery of the breach must await the time of such performance." That exception will be explored in Section F below.

Notwithstanding the establishment of a four-year limitations period, the Code makes clear that in their original agreement parties may reduce this time to not less than one year, but may not extend it (though they may later enter agreements to "toll" the statute—suspend its application—e.g., during negotiations to settle a dispute).

---

[1] 73 U.C.C. Rep. Serv. 2d 131 (E.D.N.Y. 2010).

EXAMPLES AND ANALYSIS

Example B: *SMD Investments Ltd. v. Raytheon Aircraft Co.*[2]

SMD Investments Limited (SMD) purchased an aircraft from Raytheon Aircraft Company (Raytheon) on November 3, 2003, for a purchase price of approximately $5.7 million. The purchase agreement specifically provided a limited warranty that stated that "any action by buyer for breach of this warranty by either Raytheon or seller must be commenced within one (1) year after the cause of action accrues." On April 7, 2004, during a landing, the aircraft hit an embankment and the wings detached, leaving the aircraft a total loss. The buyers claimed that defects in the aircraft caused the accident and brought suit for breach of contract on April 6, 2005. The sellers moved for summary judgment on the grounds that the statute of limitations had expired, making the claims untimely.

Analysis: The trial court agreed with the sellers in part. The buyers' cause of action for breach of express warranty accrued on the date of delivery of the aircraft and was subject to the reduced one year period of limitations. Because the express warranty claims were brought beyond one year after delivery of the aircraft, they were not timely. However, the court held that the reduction of the statute of limitations from four years to one year applied only to the express warranty given by the sellers, based upon an analysis of the language used in the warranty. The limitation to one year did not apply to or limit the statute of limitations for claims based on implied warranties. Accordingly, the implied warranty claims, which were brought within four years of the delivery of the aircraft, were not barred.

What part of 2-725 supports the argument of the buyers? What part of 2-725 supports the seller's argument that the express warranty claims were not timely? How could the sellers have drafted its warranty language in order to shorten both express and implied warranties limitations periods?

---

[2]   2006 WL 580968 (D. Kan. 2006).

B. Application to Mixed Transactions

Recall from Assignment 3 that a contract including both a sale of goods and a sale of services falls within the scope of Article 2 if the predominant purpose test is satisfied.

Reading the Code

Question 5. Assume a sales contract between a buyer and a seller contains both a sale of goods and a promise of services associated with installation of the goods. If the seller breaches its contract by failing to perform its installation services effectively, when does the statute of limitations begin to run for a claim regarding the installation?

EXAMPLES AND ANALYSIS

Example C: *Denson International Ltd. v. Liberty Diversified International, Inc.*[3]

In January 2013, Liberty Diversified International, Inc. (Liberty) designed and sold metal hand trucks. Under Liberty's contract with Denson International Limited (Denson), Denson coordinated with several factories in China to manufacture hand trucks to be sent to Liberty for resale. When hand trucks from one of these Chinese factories became subject to an anti-dumping duty rate of 383.6% on imports, Denson agreed to supply Liberty with hand trucks from another factory, subject to a lower antidumping rate of 26.49%. In February 2008, a shipment of hand trucks to Denson was rejected by the United States Customs and Border Protection (Customs) because the invoice did not certify that they were exempt from the higher antidumping duty. In February 2009, Liberty was informed by Customs that it was under investigation for failing to pay antidumping duties. The hand trucks Denson shipped in February 2008 were ultimately found

---

[3]   2014 WL 3361798 (D. Minn. 2014).

to have been manufactured by a factory subject to the higher antidumping rate, and Liberty was fined $1,242,045 by Customs. When Liberty sued Denson for breaching its contract, Denson moved for summary judgment, arguing that the breach-of-contract claim was subject to the four-year statute of limitations for sales of goods under 2-725. Liberty responded that the four-year statute of limitations did not apply because the contract at issue was not a contract for the sale of goods, but was rather a contract for serving as the liaison between Liberty and the manufacturing facilities.

Analysis: The court granted summary judgment to Denson, applying the predominant purpose test and concluding that the contract was for the sale of goods because 1) Liberty itself characterized the transaction as a purchase of hand trucks from Denson, 2) the purchase orders entered into by Liberty and Denson focused on goods rather than services, and 3) only the hand trucks—and no services—were listed on the invoices sent by Denson to Liberty. The court rejected Liberty's argument that, even if the four-year statute of limitations applied, its claim was still timely because the cause of action accrued when it discovered in February 2009 that it might have violated the anti-dumping regulations.

What part of § 2-725 supports Liberty's position? What part supports the court's decision? Was the claim timely on the given facts?

C. Extension of the Limitations Period

Notwithstanding the admonition in the Code that parties may not extend the period of limitation, there is one exception that permits actions to be brought after the four-year period ends.

Reading the Code:
§ 2-725(3)

_____

Read 2-725(3) and its Comments.

Question 6. Rephrase the rule in 2-725(3) using an if/then statement.

If_____ then _____.

D. Suit against a Remote Seller

As we have seen, applying the language of § 2-725 raises several critical issues of interpretation. Some of these questions cannot be settled solely by reference to the statutory language. For instance, under § 2-725(2), the cause of action for a breach of warranty accrues "when tender of delivery [of the goods] is made." But what does this mean if the goods have been sold (from manufacturer to retailer, for example) and then resold (from retailer to consumer)? Does the cause of action accrue for the consumer's suit against the manufacturer when the goods are tendered from the manufacturer to the retailer or when they are tendered from the retailer to the consumer?

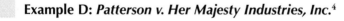

EXAMPLES AND ANALYSIS

Example D: *Patterson v. Her Majesty Industries, Inc.*[4]

On September 24, 1971, Patterson purchased a pair of pajamas from Lit Brothers for her daughter Kathleen, age 12. Her Majesty Industries, Inc. (Her Majesty) had manufactured the pajamas and sold them to Lit Brothers for resale. While Kathleen was wearing the pajamas on October 11, 1971, a spark from the household stove ignited the pajamas on fire and Kathleen was badly burned. Patterson brought suit on June 6, 1975, alleging a number of claims, including breach of warranty. Her Majesty

---

[4]   450 F. Supp. 425 (E.D. Pa. 1978).

moved for summary judgment on the warranty claims on the ground that the statute of limitations had run, arguing that the limitations period began on the date of sale by Her Majesty to Lit Brothers, rather than the date of sale to Patterson.

Analysis: The trial court concluded that the statute of limitations began to run from the retail sale date (the date the retailer sold the goods to the consumer). The court reasoned that the economic realities and marketing of goods in our society supports using the resale date because most products would be sold through resale channels. It would be inequitable to interpret the statute in a way that might bar a claim even before a consumer received the goods. Other decisions are in accord with the result in *Patterson*.

When did the statute of limitations expire for Patterson? Was the claim timely? What language supports the interpretation advanced by Her Majesty?

E. Suit for Indemnification

A seller who is found liable for a breach of warranty may have originally bought the goods from another seller. Such an "intermediate seller" may seek to recover what it owes to its own buyer by filing a claim against the "original seller." Although the claim by the intermediate seller against the original seller is based on a warranty breach, it is actually an indemnity claim, seeking reimbursement for a liability to a third party. How does § 2-725 apply to such a claim? As the following example illustrates, courts are split on this issue.

EXAMPLES AND ANALYSIS

Example E: *Electric Insurance Co. v. Freudenberg-NOK, General Partnership*[5]

General Electric Company (GE) purchased pump seal assemblies from Freudenberg-NOK, General Partnership (FNGP) beginning in 1994, for

---

[5]   487 F. Supp. 2d 894 (W.D. Ky. 2007).

use in GE dishwashers. The assemblies corroded, causing the dishwashers to leak and damage other property. GE's insurance company, Electric Insurance Company (EIC), paid homeowners over $8 million for property damage claims against GE, a portion of which was paid more than four years before the effective date of the lawsuit, under the parties' tolling agreement.[6] EIC's claim was partly a common law indemnity claim and partly a contractual indemnity claim; both arose from the contract between GE and FNGP, in which FNGP promised to hold GE harmless from failure of the assemblies. FNGP moved for dismissal on the grounds that the statute of limitations under 2-725 applied and it expired four years after the purchase of the goods, making the claims untimely. EIC denied that the Article 2 statute of limitations applied to its claim, relying instead on a 15-year statute of limitations applicable to general contracts claims.

Analysis: The trial court noted that a minority of courts apply 2-725 to indemnity actions on the grounds of "ensuring certainty and finality in commercial transactions," allowing buyers and sellers to "proceed with their affairs." The court chose to follow the majority rule, however, agreeing with EIC that 2-725 does not apply to indemnity claims. The court concluded that indemnity claims are separate equitable causes of action distinct from any Article 2 claim and that imposition of the four-year limitations period could have harsh results for commercial distributors and other intermediaries, who might become liable based on claims that might not even arise until more than four years after they distributed the goods to the ultimate seller. The court applied, instead, a five-year limitations period applicable to indemnity actions, with the limitations period beginning to run when the intermediary's liability arose, e.g., when EIC made payments on behalf of GE. The court explained:

> To be sure, the defendant has skillfully argued that a court's failure to consider the underlying contractual basis for an indemnity claim permits open-ended liability and also creates improper incentives for buyers of commercial products. As noted above, numerous courts and scholars have expressed concern that the majority rule leaves sellers of goods exposed to indemnity claims indefinitely, a result that is particularly troubling in light

---

[6] Recall that parties cannot agree to extend the statute of limitations period in their initial contract but they can agree to toll or delay the running of the statute of limitations to permit them to work towards settling rather than litigating a dispute. In this case, the parties agreed to toll the statute of limitations as of November 22, 2005 so that when the lawsuit was filed the following August, after settlement negotiations broke down, only claims barred by November 22, 2005, would be precluded.

of the UCC's goal of promoting certainty in commercial sales. A product manufacturer, however, not only owes a buyer the duty to perform under the contract but also may be liable to foreseeable users of its product in tort if that product causes damage or injury. Because the statute of limitations on a tort claim accrues at the time of injury, a manufacturer may be sued for personal injury or other tort damage long after the UCC statute of limitations has already run. *See Wilkinson, supra*, at 1446 ("With other causes of action involving the sale of goods, such as negligence and strict products liability, surviving well into the future, it is a foolish manufacturer who takes comfort from the possible repose of the breach of warranty action after four years."). It makes little sense to decry the potential open-ended liability to which the majority rule subjects sellers but allow such liability when an injured party is the plaintiff. Indeed, the minority rule leads to the incongruous result that a seller of a product could be held liable if sued directly by an individual harmed by its product while an intermediary buyer of its product could not recover if it was forced to pay the injured party and sought indemnity.

Accordingly, the court concluded that payments made more than five years before the effective date of the lawsuit were barred by the statute of limitations, but that payments made after that date were timely. Do you agree with the court's reasoning regarding application of a different limitations period for indemnity actions?

F. Remedial Promises and Warranting Future Performance

Section 2-725(2) specifies that "where a warranty explicitly extends to future performance of the goods," a cause of action for breach of warranty accrues not upon delivery (the general rule given in 2-725(1)) but rather when the breach is or should have been discovered. The critical task is thus identifying warranty language that fits this requirement.

APPLYING THE CODE

Problem 25-1.

Before learning how the courts have construed the 2-725 language, consider how you would interpret the requirement that would make the warranty "explicitly extend" to future performance of the goods? Which of the following clauses do you think satisfy that requirement?

(1)   Seller promises that the goods will perform as promised for 5 years.

(2)   Seller promises the goods are defect-free and will repair or replace items that fail within 5 years.

(3)   This product is sold with a 5-year warranty against defects.

EXAMPLES AND ANALYSIS

Example F: *Collins v. A-1 Auto Service, Inc.*[7]

Collins purchased a new 2006 Toyota Avalon from A-1 Auto Service, Inc. (A-1) on May 27, 2006. The manufacturer provided a warranty covering "repairs and adjustments" for 36 months or 36,000 miles. Collins also purchased an extended warranty from A-1 providing:

> EXTENDED WARRANTIES: A-1 Toyota/A-1 Scion will warranty your vehicle beyond the manufacturer's warranty of 3 years/36,000 miles to 42 months/42,000 miles on new vehicle purchases. Warranty work performed during the extended period must take place at A-1 Toyota/A-1 Scion as it is A-1 Toyota/A-1 Scion's warranty, not the manufacturer's.

Six months after purchase, Collins noticed a knocking sound in the engine and brought the vehicle to A-1 numerous times. A-1 claims the engine sound was normal. In July 2010, Collins took the vehicle to another Toyota dealership where the mechanic told him that the knocking sound was

---

[7]   2013 WL 541389 (Conn. Super. Ct. 2013).

caused by a valve problem arising from a defective oil hose that had been the subject of a recall. Collins brought suit on October 14, 2010 against A-1 for breach of contract. A-1 moved for summary judgment on the grounds that the complaint was barred by the statute of limitations. Collins claimed the warranty was one of future performance.

Analysis: The trial court agreed with the seller. The court explained that repair-or-replacement clauses do not normally constitute a warranty of future performance under 2-725. Rather, such clauses provide additional remedies to buyers for breach of the warranty given. Thus, repair-or-replace clauses, absent express language to the contrary, are not promises of future performance under the Code. The court explained: "The key distinction between these two kinds of warranties is that 'a repair or replacement warranty merely provides a remedy if the product becomes defective, while a warranty for future performance guarantees the performance of the product itself for a stated period of time.'"

What type of language might satisfy the court's reasoning in order to create a warranty of future performance? Should the use of the word "extended" in the A-1 extended warranty be considered to satisfy the explicit language requirement? Why or why not? Would it matter for statute of limitations purposes if A-1 provided Collins an extended warranty for a 10-year time period? Collins argument centered on the extended warranty provided by A-1. Could Collins assert an obligation of future performance arising from the breach of the implied warranty of merchantability?

The courts have reached inconsistent results in determining what contract language satisfies the requirement, but most construe the standard narrowly, often requiring an express statement referring to performance at a specific time in the future ("guaranteed to last for 10 years") rather than a general promise of performance that implicitly or generally includes the future ("promised to be durable") or a remedial promise to "repair or replace." What supports a narrow interpretation? What would support a broader rule?

Problem 25-2.

Consider the following phrases that might appear in a contract. Which of them appear to articulate a warranty that "explicitly extends to future performance of the goods"? Which do not? Be prepared to defend your conclusions or articulate arguments supporting one or the other result (or both). Also keep in mind the difference between a warranty and a remedy.

(a) Goods are warranted to be free from defects in material and work-manship for five years.

(b) We promise to repair the product if it malfunctions within the first five years.

(c) This boat is unsinkable.

(d) All parts of the Danze faucet are warranted to the original consumer purchaser to be free from defects in material and workmanship, for as long as the consumer purchaser owns it.

(e) Goods when purchased new are warranted to be free from substantial defects of material and workmanship under normal use and service for a period of 12 months from the date of delivery to the first retail purchaser.

(f) The sales clerk tells the buyer that "these hiking boots will survive even the toughest trail."

(g) Manufacturer warrants . . . that it will repair or replace . . . any load cell supplied with a motor truck scale which . . . is defective in material or workmanship for a period of two years from the date of the original shipment.

(h) If a defect in materials or workmanship . . . is brought to our atten-tion during the first 10 years from the date of sale, Pella Corporation will, at its option: (1) repair the product; (2) provide replacement part(s) or product(s); or (3) if we determine that repair or replace-ment is not practicable, we may elect to refund the original pur-chase price.

(i)   This service contract . . . provides full components and labor coverage for covered component failures due to defects in . . . materials or workmanship under normal use.

G. Tolling of the Statute of Limitations

Because § 2-725 "does not alter the law on tolling of the statute of limitations" (§ 2-725(4)), the usual common law principles and otherwise applicable state law provisions on equitable tolling apply. Under common law principles, the statute of limitations is generally tolled if the seller prevents the buyer from discovering a defect, if the seller engages in fraud or concealment of a defect, if and while the party seeking relief is a minor, or during the pendency of a prior suit between the parties on the same claim that was dismissed without prejudice. As previously noted, the statute of limitations may also be tolled by agreement of the parties to a dispute, to permit negotiations that might achieve a settlement, without risk the buyer may lose the right to sue if the negotiations are unsuccessful.

EXAMPLES AND ANALYSIS

Example G: *Patrickson v. Dole Food Co.*[8]

Six citizens of the countries of Costa Rica, Ecuador and Guatemala brought suit in 1997 against multiple sellers on a number of claims, including breach of implied warranty, against the sellers of a pesticide, dibromo-chloropropane (DBCP), which was used on farms from approximately the 1960s until the mid-1980s. Sellers withdrew DBCP from the market due to adverse health effects on users of the pesticide. The sellers moved for summary judgment on the grounds that the statute of limitations had expired, making the claims untimely because the last tender or delivery of DBCP was in the mid-1980s.

Analysis: The trial court agreed with the sellers, and the court of appeals affirmed. The users of the pesticide claimed a tolling of the statute based upon the sellers' alleged fraudulent concealment of the breach. The court explained:

---

[8]   330 P.3d 389 (Haw. 2014).

> To invoke the doctrine in the complaint, [plaintiffs] must plead with particularity the facts giving rise to the fraudulent concealment claim and must establish that they used due diligence in trying to uncover the facts. [Defendants'] silence or passive conduct does not constitute fraudulent concealment. Further, [plaintiffs'] mere ignorance of the cause of action does not, in itself, toll the statute.

The court held that allegations of conspiracy among the sellers to conceal information about the risks of DBCP were too general in nature and failed to satisfy the requirement to plead with particularly.

Which part of 2-725 supports the sellers? Does it matter whether the users of the pesticide had knowledge of the breach of the implied warranty? If a buyer must claim fraudulent concealment with particularity in order to toll the statute of limitations, how might a buyer obtain sufficient facts to sustain this burden?

The courts have disagreed regarding whether the statute of limitations is tolled when the seller attempts unsuccessfully to make repairs. Some courts have applied estoppel to toll the statute when evidence reveals that the seller attempted to repair the goods and made representations that the repairs would cure the defect, and the plaintiff relied upon the representations. Other courts have rejected this so-called "repair doctrine." For goods that are replaced rather than repaired, however, the statute of limitations begins to run anew when the replacement goods are delivered.

The following case, *Highway Sales, Inc. v. Blue Bird Corp.*, illustrates the effect of the statute of limitations on a buyer's ability to bring express and implied warranty claims against a seller. As you read the case, consider these questions:

(1) Why does the four-year statute of limitations under § 2-725 not apply here?

(2) Why doesn't the court dismiss the express warranty claim on the basis of the statute of limitations? When did the express warranty claim accrue?

(3) Why does the court dismiss the implied warranty claims on the basis of the statute of limitations? When did the implied warranty claim accrue?

(4)   Why does the court reject the buyer's attempt to argue equitable tolling?

(5)   In what ways does Judge Beam's concurring and dissenting opinion take issue with the majority opinion? How does Judge Beam view the application of the rule about tolling of the statute?

HIGHWAY SALES, INC. V. BLUE BIRD CORP.

559 F.3d 782 (8th Cir. 2009)

Riley, Circuit Judge.

Donald Oren (Oren) and Highway Sales, Inc. (Highway Sales) (collectively, plaintiffs), asserted claims against Blue Bird Corporation (Blue Bird) for (1) breach of express and implied warranties; (2) violation of the Magnuson-Moss Warranty Act, 15 U.S.C. § 2301-2312; (3) violation of Minnesota's Lemon Law, Minn.Stat. § 325F.665; and (4) revocation of acceptance under Minn.Stat. § 336.2-608.

. . . .

I. BACKGROUND

Plaintiffs' claims arose from their purchase of a defective recreational vehicle (RV) manufactured by Blue Bird. On July 31, 2003, Highway Sales purchased, for Oren's use, a Blue Bird Wanderlodge M380 RV from Shorewood RV, a Blue Bird authorized dealer. The purchase price was $337,244.

In the months following the sale, Oren discovered numerous defects, including failures of the RV's electrical system, batteries, seals, slides, gauges, compressor, monitor, and lighting. Oren returned the RV to Shorewood RV for repairs on a number of occasions, and Shorewood RV attempted to remedy the RV's various defects. Despite Shorewood RV's efforts, Oren continued experiencing problems with the RV.

On July 2, 2004, Oren delivered the RV to Shorewood RV's lot, giving the keys to Shorewood RV and removing his belongings. Oren informed Anthony Santarsiero (Santarsiero), a Shorewood RV employee, that Oren was returning the RV as of that day. Santarsiero gave Oren the name of Blue Bird's CEO and told Oren to call or write the CEO a letter to try to resolve the problem. On July 8, 2004, Oren wrote a letter to Blue Bird's CEO asking him to authorize repurchase of the RV at its original cost.

. . . .

On September 7, 2004, Blue Bird's Director of Customer Service formally rejected Oren's request for a refund, asserting, "[y]our electrical issue on your M380 has been repaired. . . . We do not refund purchases or buy units back. We are committed to working with our Dealers and Customers to resolve any service needs that may occur. I know you have had some battery issues with your unit, but I am confident that these issues have been resolved. You have a reliable unit that should give you the service and performance it is designed for."

. . . .

On November 19, 2004, Blue Bird's attorney responded [to Oren's letters] . . . stating, "Blue Bird and its distributor have worked on the motor home and believe that the cause of the battery problem you identified, as well as any other issues, have been remedied. Therefore, Blue Bird has fully complied with the requirements of its warranty and the Minnesota lemon law." This letter went on to reiterate Blue Bird's willingness to continue working with Oren and Shorewood RV "to assure [Oren] that the motor home conforms to the warranty."

. . . .

On July 15, 2005, plaintiffs filed suit in Minnesota state court against Blue Bird. Blue Bird removed the case to federal court based on diversity of citizenship. Plaintiffs later amended their complaint, adding Shorewood RV as a defendant.

. . . .

The district court concluded defendants were entitled to summary judgment on all of plaintiffs' claims, including the state law claim for breach of express warranty. The district court determined, as a matter of law, plaintiffs' breach of express warranty claim was untimely because the claim accrued no later than July 8, 2004, and plaintiffs filed suit more than one year later, on July 15, 2005. Plaintiffs now argue: (1) their breach of express warranty claim was timely; (2) Blue Bird's repeated promises to repair the RV tolled the limitations period on plaintiffs' breach of express and implied warranty claims; (3) plaintiffs' sale of the motor home did not bar their Minnesota

Lemon Law Claim; and (4) plaintiffs were entitled to pursue their claims for revocation of acceptance against Blue Bird and Shorewood RV.

II. DISCUSSION

. . . .

B. Breach of Warranty

1. Accrual of Breach of Express Warranty Claim

Plaintiffs argue the district court erred by finding their claim for breach of express warranty was barred by the one year limitations period contained in Blue Bird's Limited Warranty. The limited warranty guaranteed certain components of the RV would "be free from defects in material and workmanship" for specified periods of time. It also provided, "[a]ny suit alleging a breach of this limited warranty or any other alleged warranty must be filed within one year of breach."[FN4]

FN4. Minnesota law provides a four year statute of limitations "for breach of any contract for sale." Minn.Stat. § 336.2-725(1). However, the parties may agree to "reduce the period of limitation to not less than one year. . . ." *Id.*

Under Minnesota law, "[a] cause of action [for breach of warranty] accrues when the breach occurs, regardless of the aggrieved party's lack of knowledge of the breach." Minn.Stat. § 336.2-725(2). "A breach of warranty occurs when tender of delivery is made, except that where a warranty explicitly extends to future performance of the goods and discovery of the breach must await the time of such performance the cause of action accrues when the breach is or should have been discovered." *Id.* Thus, when a warranty extends to future performance, the cause of action accrues "when the plaintiff discovers or should have discovered the defendant's refusal or inability to maintain the goods as warranted in the contract."

The parties agree the limited warranty explicitly extends to future performance by guaranteeing certain components of the RV would "be free from defects in material and workmanship" for specified periods of time. Because the limited warranty extends to future performance, Oren's breach of warranty claim accrued on the date Oren "discover[ed] or should have discovered [Blue Bird]'s refusal or inability to maintain the [RV] as warranted in the contract."

The parties agree Blue Bird expressed a continued willingness to repair the RV long after July 8, 2004. Thus, our concern is not the date Blue Bird refused to maintain the RV, but the date Oren discovered Blue Bird's inability to maintain the RV as warranted. The parties dispute when this discovery occurred. Blue Bird argues, and the district court found, that by July 8, 2004, Oren firmly believed Blue Bird was unable to maintain the RV as warranted. The district court determined, as a matter of law, Oren's July 8, 2004 letter unequivocally demonstrated Oren's belief Blue Bird was unable to maintain the RV as warranted. We disagree.

Oren's July 8, 2004 letter stated, in relevant part:

> . . . After almost a year of continued problems with this motor home, I have come to three conclusions. First, the Model M380 was released before it had been properly designed, tested, and debugged. Second, Shorewood RV is a terrific dealer for you, but even they could not overcome the inherent problems in the M380. Third, I have run out of patience, confidence, and trust that the problems can be fixed in a reasonable time, and I request that you return my purchase price.

> . . . .

> On July 2, 2004, after the engine batteries once again died, I removed all my personal belongings and returned the coach to the dealer. This was the final event-the last straw.

> Suffice it to say that I am out of patience, and that both of our lives will be made easier if you will simply authorize a repurchase of the coach at its original cost. This coach simply needs to be permanently recalled until major corrections are made.

> . . . .

> . . . I'm not interested in further retrofits, patches, or excuses. I will never take this coach back.

Oren's July 8, 2004 letter certainly evidences Oren's high level of frustration and disgust with the need for repeated repairs on the RV. However, the district court erred by concluding as a matter of law that Oren believed the RV was beyond repair as of that date. Oren's statement he had "run out of patience, confidence, and trust that the problems can be fixed in a reasonable time" does not necessarily mean Oren, at that moment, believed the RV was beyond repair. A factfinder could just as reasonably conclude Oren was simply tired of dealing with the RV's defects. Saying "I am out of patience" or "I'm not interested in further retrofits, patches, or excuses" is not the same as saying, "I believe Blue Bird is incapable of maintaining this RV as warranted."

The fact Oren allowed additional repairs to be completed on July 31, August 19, September 28, and October 4, 2004, strongly suggests Oren continued to believe Blue Bird was capable of eventually repairing the RV. It was not until November 29, 2004, that Oren first informed Blue Bird he believed Blue Bird had failed "in meeting its obligations to conform the vehicle to the applicable express warranties." We conclude a genuine issue of material fact exists regarding the date Oren knew or should have known Blue Bird was unable to maintain the RV as warranted.

2. Accrual of Breach of Implied Warranty Claim

Unlike express warranties, under Minnesota law, "[i]mplied warranties cannot, by their very nature, explicitly extend to future performance."FN5 A breach of implied warranty occurs, and the claim accrues, "when tender of delivery is made. . . ." Minn.Stat. § 336.2-725(2). Thus, the fact Blue Bird expressly warranted various components of the RV would be free from defects for specified periods of time after tender of delivery does not extend the accrual date for a breach of implied warranty claim. The parties agree tender of delivery of the RV occurred on July 31, 2003. Plaintiffs filed suit almost two years later, on July 15, 2005. Plaintiffs' breach of implied warranty claim is therefore untimely, unless Blue Bird is equitably estopped from asserting the statute of limitations defense.FN6

FN5. Plaintiffs do not argue the implied warranty limitation is inconspicuous and do not assert implied warranties may extend to future performance under Minnesota law. Contrary to the dissent, we follow our general rule not to consider issues not raised by the parties or the district court, because such issues are waived.

FN6. In addition to their state law claims for breach of express and implied warranty, plaintiffs assert claims against Blue Bird for breach of express and implied warranty under the Magnuson-Moss Warranty Act, 15 U.S.C. §§ 2301-2312. The parties agree that, because the Magnuson-Moss Warranty Act contains no statute of limitations, plaintiffs' Magnuson-Moss claims are governed by the same limitations period as plaintiffs' state law breach of warranty claims.

3. Equitable Estoppel

Plaintiffs argue even if their breach of express warranty claim accrued on July 8, 2004, and their breach of implied warranty claim accrued on July 31, 2003, the limitations period was tolled until at least November 2004 because Blue Bird repeatedly promised to repair the RV and conform it to the limited warranty. Under the doctrine of equitable estoppel, if a buyer delays filing suit as a result of reasonable and detrimental reliance on a seller's assurances it will repair the defective goods, the limitations period is tolled during that period of delay.FN7

FN7. Plaintiffs do not argue or propose equitable tolling may exist from promises to repair alone without detrimental reliance by plaintiffs. Such arguments are now waived. Furthermore, the Minnesota Supreme Court has noted the "so called 'repair theory' has not been afforded universal acceptance." Hydra-Mac, Inc. v. Onan Corp., 450 N.W.2d 913, 919 n. 4 (Minn.1990) (emphasis added). Under Minnesota law, equitable tolling applies only with detrimental reliance. See Sohns v. Pederson, 354 N.W.2d 852, 855 (Minn. Ct.App.1984) ("Estoppel requires proof of three elements: 1) defendant made representations on which 2) plaintiff reasonably relied, and 3) plaintiff will be harmed if equitable estoppel is not invoked.").

There is ample evidence in the record from which a factfinder could conclude Blue Bird made ongoing assurances it would repair the RV. After Oren delivered the RV to Shorewood RV's lot on July 2, 2004, Blue Bird technicians attempted repairs on July 31, August 19, September 28, and October 4, 2004. On September 7, 2004, Blue Bird rejected Oren's request for a refund but maintained, "We are committed to working with our Dealers and Customers to resolve any service needs that may occur." As late as November 2004, Blue Bird asserted it had complied with Minnesota's Lemon Law and the requirements of its warranty, although reiterating its willingness to continue working with Oren and Shorewood RV to "assure [Oren] that the motor home conforms to the warranty."

The critical question, then, is whether plaintiffs delayed filing suit as a result of reasonable and detrimental reliance on Blue Bird's ongoing assurances to repair the RV, and, if so, on what date plaintiffs' reliance (and the tolling of the limitations period) ended. There is no evidence in the record from which a reasonable factfinder could conclude plaintiffs reasonably and detrimentally relied on Blue Bird's efforts or promises to repair the RV after Oren delivered the RV to Shorewood RV's lot on July 2, 2004. On the contrary, by July 2, 2004, Oren manifested no reliance on Blue Bird's or Shorewood RV's assurances the defective RV would soon be repaired.

Although plaintiffs insist Blue Bird "resorted to bald assertions that the motor home was not defective despite its continuing failures and need for repairs," plaintiffs do not claim Oren believed these assertions or that plaintiffs delayed filing suit as a result of detrimentally relying upon such assertions. Nowhere do plaintiffs maintain Blue Bird's assurances or repair attempts after July 2, 2004, caused any detrimental reliance, nor does the record support such an inference. The fact Oren may have believed Blue Bird was capable of eventually repairing the RV falls far short of establishing that Oren detrimentally relied upon Blue Bird's promises to repair the RV. On July 8, 2004, Oren wrote Blue Bird's CEO announcing the "last straw," and explaining Oren had run "out of patience . . . that the problems can be fixed in a reasonable time," and he was "not interested in further retrofits, patches, or excuses." Because plaintiffs have identified no action they took or failed to take after July 2, 2004, in reliance upon any statements or actions of Blue Bird, the district court did not err by determining, as a matter of law, plaintiffs were not entitled to equitable tolling.

. . . .

III. CONCLUSION

Genuine issues of material fact exist with respect to plaintiffs' breach of express warranty and Magnuson-Moss warranty claims against Blue Bird and plaintiffs' revocation of acceptance claim against Shorewood RV. We reverse the district court's grant of summary judgment on these claims. We affirm the district court's grant of summary judgment on (1) the equitable tolling issue, (2) plaintiffs' claim under the Minnesota Lemon Law, and (3) plaintiffs' revocation of acceptance claim against Blue Bird.

BEAM, Circuit Judge, concurring and dissenting.

. . . .

I.

As stated above, the UCC provides that breach of an implied warranty "must be commenced within four years" but the parties may reduce the period of limitation by agreement to not less than one year. Minn.Stat. Ann. § 336.2-725(1). Thus, by agreement, the UCC authorized Blue Bird to shorten the period to one year subject to restrictions set forth in section 336.2-316(2) above, that is that any modifications or exclusions be in writing, unambiguous, and mention the word "merchantability." . . . In this case, however, on the crucial issues of disclaiming implied warranties and reducing the litigation limitation period as authorized by Minn.Stat. Ann. § 336.2-725(1), we face very different facts. Oren makes no statement that he was asked to or did read the language outlining the reduced limitation period. And, as noted in Appendix A, the capitalized language dealt not with the lawsuit limitation period but rather created the overall length of the warranty period, including an implied warranty duration of two or three years, limited the nature of some recoverable damages, and specified which of Blue Bird's employees could make additional representations. It bears repeating that this capitalized portion of the contract did not at all deal with the period of time in which litigation could be commenced for breach of any of the warranties. Indeed, the statute of limitation reduction language is found in a wholly new paragraph presented in significantly smaller, uncapitalized type. The new paragraph totally deals with a different subject than the capitalized portions. Blue Bird slips the limitation language into the fourth and last sentence of the new paragraph, which sentence reads, in isolation both as to location and subject matter, as follows: "[a]ny suit alleging a breach of this limited warranty or any other alleged warranty must be filed within one year of breach." There is no mention of either "implied warranty" or "merchantability" within or near this supposedly limiting language.

. . . .

II.

Assuming, but purely for argument's sake, the validity of Blue Bird's claimed one-year statute of limitation, and its contention that the limitation period began to run at the time of the July 31, 2003, delivery, Oren's implied warranty of merchantability claim is still not barred. As an initial matter, Blue Bird's express warranties purport to be valid for either two or three years and the implied warranties "are limited to the warranty period of this written warranty." Giving Oren the benefit of these inconsistent terms, the warranty period for the implied warranties would be three years. Nonetheless, for our purposes, a two-year period is more than enough. . . . An implied warranty of merchantability was clearly imposed upon Blue Bird as a matter of law and public policy under Minn.Stat. Ann. § 336.2-31414 and such a warranty carries with it measures of liability and damages beyond those purportedly "excluded" or "modified" by Blue Bird's "limited warranty."

See Minn.Stat. Ann. § 336.2-316. Thus, the viability of the merchantability warranty is more than of academic interest to Oren.

. . . .

Accordingly, if you credit Blue Bird's one-year statute of limitation affirmative defense and attempt to square it with the court's conclusions in this appeal, the one-year lawsuit limitations period for the implied warranties "expired" well before Blue Bird gave up its right to cure the defects which would have made the RV comply with the requirements of the implied warranty. This result flies in the face of approximately fifty years of consumer equity policy imbedded within the enactment of the Uniform Commercial Code in, by now, all fifty states, some territories, and a commonwealth. Blue Bird's clever penmanship and paragraph positioning cannot be allowed to overrule the policy pronouncements of the Uniform Commercial Code.

III.

Even if you avoid the ambiguity, conspicuousness and public policy problems inherent in the facts at work in this case, a further, and perhaps more important, error lurks within the court's opinion. . . . At least three tolling theories serve to protect Oren's breach of implied warranty cause of action. They include the doctrines of equitable estoppel, estoppel through misrepresentation and estoppel by repair. While the court does recognize the applicability of equitable estoppel in this action and, indeed, incompletely applies it to this case, it incorrectly decides the issue as a question of law. . . .

Upon equivocal evidence, equitable estoppel, or not, is a question of fact for the jury. Of even more importance, Blue Bird's statute of limitations affirmative defense is also a question of fact for the jury. The court concedes that Blue Bird attempted, and Oren permitted, additional, but failed, repairs until at least October 4, 2004. Based upon this uncontradicted evidence, the court correctly states "Oren continued to believe Blue Bird was capable of eventually repairing the RV" and concluded that a genuine issue of fact existed as to "the date Oren knew or should have known Blue Bird was unable to maintain the RV as warranted"—i.e, the date that the defect could be cured by Blue Bird making the vehicle merchantable as impliedly warranted. This is, of course, the stuff of detrimental reliance, an important and likely controlling element of equitable estoppel. Yet for purposes of a statute of limitations calculation on Oren's implied warranty, the court adopts July 2, 2004, a date untethered to any legally significant event in this transaction. And, in doing so, without explanation, the court appears to lift Blue Bird's burden of proof on its affirmative limitations defense and effectively places it upon Oren. The court does this by requiring Oren to adduce direct (as opposed to circumstantial) evidence of his affirmative forbearance in commencing suit based upon Blue Bird's many failed efforts to make the RV merchantable.

Even so, and without regard to burdens of proof, factual questions abound on both issues—equitable estoppel and statute of limitations. For instance, as the court concedes, Oren permitted Blue Bird to complete additional repairs as late as October 4, 2004, which, according to the court "strongly suggest[ed] Oren continued to believe Blue Bird was capable of eventually repairing the RV." This is, of course, full-blown evidence of reliance by Oren on Blue Bird's assurances. If anything, equitable estoppel interrupting the running of the statute of limitations could have been determined as a matter of law on this evidence alone. But, in November 2004, Blue Bird twice wrote to Oren, representing that it would "stand behind our commitment to provide [Oren] the best possible service" and that it "remain[ed] willing to work with [Oren] directly or through our distributor to assure [Oren] that the motor home conform[ed] to the warranty." Thereafter, Oren alerted Blue Bird in a letter dated November 29, 2004, that the RV again would not start. Then, Blue Bird responded on December 1, 2004, finally stating there was nothing wrong with the motor home and that Blue Bird had lived up to its obligations. In response, on December 6, 2004, Oren, for the first time, raised the issue of litigation. Clearly then, until late into November 2004, there are enough disputed facts to require presentation of the issues of equitable estoppel and the limitation defense to a jury. Even the earlier October 4 estoppel date would have been less than ten months prior to the expiration of a twelve-month statute of limitations.

There are also other fact issues in play in this litigation, given Blue Bird's reservation of its right to cure defects for a two-year period. This raises the possibility of estoppel by misrepresentation. *Cf. Vesta State Bank v. Indep. State Bank of Minn.*, 518 N.W.2d 850, 855 & n. 7 (Minn.1994) (noting that statute of limitations begins to run only when the aggrieved party discovers the facts constituting fraud, and that this rule applies to causes of actions arising in transactions governed by the UCC due to the operation of § 336.2-725(4)).

Finally, the court does not address, and in fact, summarily rejects, Minnesota's estoppel-by-repair doctrine. I concede that the Minnesota Supreme Court has never held that promises by a seller to make repairs give rise to estoppel or a tolling of a statute of limitation. I predict, however, that available precedent establishes the viability of the doctrine in Minnesota.

. . . .

[The] Minnesota precedent convinces me that the estoppel-by-repair doctrine is alive and well in Minnesota in addition to the equitable estoppel doctrine already validated by the court. At the bottom line, estoppel, or not (under any of the three doctrines) presents a question of fact not susceptible to dismissal by the court as a matter of law through a motion for summary judgment.

CONCLUSION

For any and all of the above-stated reasons, the district court's grant of summary judgment dismissing Oren's implied warranty of merchantability claims should be reversed. From the court's contrary conclusion, I dissent.

APPENDIX A

. . .

ANY IMPLIED WARRANTIES, INCLUDING THOSE OF MERCHANTABILITY OR FITNESS, ARE LIMITED TO THE WARRANTY PERIOD OF THIS WRITTEN WARRANTY. WANDER LODGE SHALL NOT BE LIABLE FOR INCIDENTAL OR CONSEQUENTIAL DAMAGES RESULTING FROM BREACH OF THIS WRITTEN WARRANTY OR ANY IMPLIED WARRANTY. NO PERSON, INCLUDING SALESPEOPLE, DEALERS, SERVICE CENTERS OR FACTORY REPRESENTATIVES OF WANDER LODGE IS AUTHORIZED TO MAKE ANY REPRESENTATION OR WARRANTY CONCERNING WONDER LODGE PRODUCTS EXCEPT TO REFER TO THIS LIMITED WARRANTY.

Wander Lodge reserves the right to make changes in design and changes or improvements upon its products without imposing any obligation upon itself to install the same upon products therefore manufactured. Defects shall be repaired promptly after discovery of the defect and within the warranty period as stated herein. All claims for warranty adjustments must be received by Wander Lodge no later than 30 days after the repair date and shall be channeled through an authorized Wander Lodge dealer or factory representatives. Any suit alleging a breach of the limited warranty or any other alleged warranty must be filed within one year of breach.

APPLYING THE CODE

Problem 25-3.

Belsky purchased a new BMW from Field Imports on June 14, 2005. In 2009, she also purchased a service agreement covering many of the component parts. On October 1, 2012, the low oil warning light in Belsky's vehicle activated, and she brought the BMW to Fields for repair. The technicians replaced broken aluminum head bolts and performed related repairs at a cost of $1832. The service agreement did not cover this particular repair. Belsky brought suit for breach of contract based on defects in the car. Fields moves to dismiss the suit on the grounds of the statute of limitations. What arguments do you expect each party to make? How should the court rule in this case?

Problem 25-4.

Statler purchased five computers from Dell for his chiropractic business in 2003. Dell provided a five-year limited warranty, restricted to repair or replacement in the event of defects. Some time after the purchase, each of the computers manifested serious operational errors arising from faulty capacitors. Statler reported his problems to Dell customer service but Dell repair technicians were unable to satisfactorily repair the computers. In 2010, Statler read an article in the New York Times titled "Dell Won't Recall Defective Motherboards" that documented a 2007 lawsuit against Dell related to the same problems and Dell's awareness that faulty capacitors had made their way into the manufacturer supply chain. Statler brought a breach of contract action against Dell in 2010. What arguments would you expect Dell to make regarding the statute of limitations? Statler? How might the court rule in this case?

Problem 25-5.

Surplus.Com purchased "Dynamic Price Engine" computer software from Oracle on May 6, 2004, obtaining a software license, along with "maintenance and support." In order to make the software operational, Surplus.Com hired a separate company to develop and implement the software. Surplus.Com brought suit for breach of contract against Oracle on May 3, 2010. What argument would you expect Oracle to make regarding the statute of limitations? Surplus.Com? What will be important to the court in ruling on this issue?

Problem 25-6.

Aramark Sports and Entertainment Services, Inc. (Aramark) purchased 675-foot houseboats from Twin Anchors Marine, Ltd. (Twin Anchors) in 2006. In the "Warranties" section of the agreement, Twin Anchors warranted, among other things, that 1) "the Work shall be performed in accordance with the terms and conditions of this Agreement," 2) "the Houseboat shall be free from defects in design, workmanship and materials," and 3) "all Work will meet all applicable American Boat and Yacht Council standards as regulated and inspected by the National Marine Manufacturers Association, and the United States Coast Guard specifications and requirements applicable to houseboats." The agreement provided for a warranty for one year and contained an indemnity provision whereby Twin Anchors agreed to defend, indemnify and hold Aramark harmless from certain losses arising out of the purchase.

On June 21, 2008, Robert rented an Aramark houseboat for his family. Several family members became ill and one died due to a carbon monoxide leak aboard the houseboat. Aramark settled litigation brought by Robert and his family in November 2011 and brought an action against Twin Anchors on January 7, 2015, for indemnification under the agreement. Twin Anchors moved for dismissal on the grounds that the claim is not timely under the four-year limitations period of 2-725 applicable in Arizona. When did Aramark's cause of action accrue? If a four-year limitations period applies in Arizona, would Aramark's indemnification claim be timely? Why or why not?

Problem 25-7.

Axios provides payroll and human resources support for its clients. Thinkware represented to Axios that Thinkware's Darwin software would meet Axios's needs and was compatible with Axios's other software. Thinkware also represented that Darwin would enable Axios to provide its clients with web access to client and employee data. Thinkware provided demonstrations of Darwin software which seemed to confirm its compatibility with Axios's other software. Axios, however, had heard rumors of lawsuits against Thinkware concerning problems converting to Darwin software, but Thinkware denied that there were any legal actions pending against Thinkware. At the time, however, there were lawsuits pending against Thinkware in Texas and New Mexico concerning Darwin software.

Axios purchased Thinkware's "Darwin" human resources software on August 6, 2012, signing a license agreement and receiving installation on August 29, 2012. Axios experienced problems shortly after installation and by November 2012 the system was locking up. In January 2013, Axios and Thinkware had a conference call to discuss resolution of the problems Axios was having with the software. Based on Thinkware's representations during the conference call concerning Darwin's capabilities, Axios elected to proceed with Darwin rather than seek an alternative vendor. Nevertheless, the problems with the software persisted, and, as a result, Axios lost a major client in August 2013. After ongoing adjustments, the software was still not working in December 2013. Axios terminated the license agreement on December 29, 2014.

The license agreement contained several limitations on warranties and provided its own statute of limitations for bringing claims arising out of the agreement. Notably, the agreement provided an express warranty that the software would perform substantially as described for a period of 120 days from the effective date of the agreement. The agreement disclaimsed implied warranties of merchantability and fitness for a particular purpose. Finally, the agreement provided that "[a]ny lawsuit arising out or related to this Agreement must be brought no later than one (1) year after cause of action accrues or it shall be forever barred."

Axios filed its complaint against Thinkware on May 20, 2015. Thinkware moved to dismiss Axios's breach of contract and breach of warranty claims on grounds that they were barred by the one-year statute of limitations set forth in the license agreement. What arguments should each party make regarding when the claim accrued? How would a court evaluate the motion? What date would you argue the statute of limitations expired?

Chapter 10

Comparing UCC Article 2 to Article 2A and to the Convention on Contracts for the International Sale of Goods (CISG)

Key Concepts

- Key similarities and differences between UCC Articles 2 and 2A
- Key similarities and differences between UCC Article 2 and the UN Convention on Contracts for the International Sale of Goods (CISG)

The preceding Chapters have covered how contracts for sale of goods operate under UCC Article 2 and its accompanying case law. Chapter 10 draws heavily on that knowledge base as it introduces you to two bodies of law that are closely related to Article 2:

- UCC Article 2A, which governs contracts for leases of goods; and

- The United Nations Convention on Contracts for the International Sale of Goods (CISG), which governs potentially many international sale-of-goods contracts.

A comprehensive treatment of these bodies of law is beyond the scope of this book. Instead, this Chapter takes a comparative approach, focusing on identifying and analyzing key similarities and differences between UCC Article 2 and Article 2A (Assignment 26) and between UCC Article 2 and the CISG (Assignment 27).

The treatment of contracts for leases of goods in Article 2A is similar but not identical to the treatment of contracts for sales of goods in Article 2, as you might surmise from the use of "2A" in its title. Many but not all of the sections in Article 2A are modeled after Article 2. The differences reflect the crucial differences between leases and sales as transactions in goods.

The CISG governs some but not all international contracts for sale of goods. As a convention that was drafted by a body within the United Nations and then adopted by many countries across the world, it reflects an interesting set of compromises among civil law and common law legal systems. Some of its provisions will be familiar to you from your training in sales and contract law. Other provisions will be less familiar but will resemble legal concepts that you have learned. Still other provisions will introduce you to new ways of solving issues of contract and sales law.

In keeping with the comparative approach adopted, both assignments contain some problems that also appear in previous assignments, inviting you to analyze them anew under these alternative bodies of law so that you can easily compare the results in the context of UCC Article 2A or the CISG.

Assignment 26
UCC Article 2A:
Contracts for Leases of Goods

A. Introduction

UCC Article 2A governs contracts for leases of goods. Many of its provisions mirror those in Article 2, so you will be able to gain a basic familiarity with Article 2A fairly quickly, in a single assignment, by using a comparative approach—comparing provisions in Articles 2A and 2. This Assignment flags the differences and elucidates the new concepts and vocabulary associated with leases of goods.

LEARNING OUTCOMES AND OBJECTIVES

At the completion of this Assignment, you should be able to

- identify which contracts are governed by UCC Article 2A;
- determine whether a lease is a finance lease;
- identify which rules in Article 2A differ from those in UCC Article 2; and
- apply Article 2A to common fact situations.

After providing background on Article 2A as a whole (its organization and drafting history), this Assignment presents the topics treated in Article 2A in the same order they were treated in the earlier parts of this text with respect to Article 2:

Textbook Chapter	Topic	Assignment 26 Section
2	Scope	B
3	Contract Formation & Content	C
4	Statute of Frauds	D

Textbook Chapter	Topic	Assignment 26 Section
5	Warranties	E
7	Performance	F
8	Title & Priority Disputes	G
9	Remedies	H

1. Drafting History

UCC Article 2 was drafted in the 1940s, promulgated as part of the UCC in the 1950s, and enacted by nearly every state over the next few decades. During the 1960s and 1970s, some jurisdictions applied UCC Articles 2 and 9 by analogy to leases of goods. Meanwhile, the equipment that large companies formerly purchased outright increasingly came to be leased. "Equipment leasing grew at an estimated rate of [30% per year] during the 1950s and . . . exceeded the [30% per year] growth rate several times during the [period from the late 1960s to the late 1980s]."[1] By the late 1980s, "approximately 20% of all capital investment in the United States [was] directly attributable to equipment leasing with over $310 billion dollars in lease receivables [then] outstanding."[2] Consumer leasing of vehicles and other goods also increased greatly in the same period. This growth was driven by a complex mix of factors, including federal income tax rules and corporate accounting strategies. It generated legal issues that could not be answered (or were answered incorrectly) by mere analogies to Articles 2 and 9.

During the 1980s, a new UCC Article—2A—was drafted, drawing on both Article 2 (contracts for sale of goods) and Article 9 (secured transactions), to solve leasing and financing issues. The drafters did not always copy the language from Articles 2 and 9 exactly. Of course, words like "sale," "buyer," and "seller" needed to be changed to "lease," "lessee," and "lessor." And by then, the UCC had three decades of usage and case law, so it was possible to make the following improvements:

---

[1] Amelia Boss, The History of Article 2A: A Lesson for Practitioner and Scholar Alike, 39 Ala. L. Rev. 575 (1988).

[2] Id.

- Provide more descriptive and accurate subject headings,

- Reword troublesome provisions that had caused confusion,

- Add useful insights from case law and commentary,

- Streamline comments that had proved cumbersome, and

- Move provisions to more logical locations.

Nonetheless, you will see very close similarities between Article 2A and its source material in Articles 2 and 9.

Like other UCC articles, Article 2A is governed by the general provisions and definitions in Article 1. In addition, Article 2A contains its own definitions, most of which are centralized or listed in § 2A-103. That list in § 2A-103 also refers to eighteen definitions from Articles 2 and 9.

2. Organization of Article 2A

The organization of Article 2A sought to improve on the organization of Article 2, by putting sections into more logical locations in five Parts:

Article 2A		Article 2	
Part 1	General provisions (includes unconscionability)	**Part 1**	General construction and subject matter
Part 2	Formation and construction of lease contract (statute of frauds, parol evidence rule, formation, warranties, disclaimers, identification, risk of loss, casualty)	Part 2 §§ on statute of frauds, parol evidence rule, formation	
		Part 3 §§ on warranties and disclaimers	
		Part 5 §§ on identification, insurance, risk of loss, casualty	
Part 3	Effect of lease contract (rights of title, possession, alienability, lien priority, and creditors)	**Part 4**	Title, creditors, and good faith purchasers
Part 4	Performance of lease contract: repudiation, substituted performance, and excuse	Part 6 §§ on repudiation, retraction, substituted performance, excuse	

Part 5	Default (includes rejection, cure, acceptance, revocation, remedies)	Part 6 §§ on rejection, cure, acceptance, revocation
		Part 7 — Remedies

3. Consumer Leases

Section 2A-103(1)(e) defines a "consumer lease"[3] as involving the following parties:

- A lessor regularly engaged in the business of leasing or selling, and

- A lessee who is an individual and who takes under the lease primarily for a personal, family, or household purpose.

Note that the "personal, family, or household purpose" is narrower in this definition than in the Magnuson-Moss Warranty Act (MMWA). As you learned in Assignment 12, the scope of MMWA is determined in part by whether the *goods* are *usually* used for a personal, family, or household purpose. Here, the scope of a "consumer lease" is determined by the *actual* lessee and his or her *intended* use, at the time of contract formation.

Consumer leases are governed by special provisions on unconscionability, choice-of-law clauses, choice-of-forum clauses, and finance leases. Those provisions are covered later in this Assignment.[4]

B. Scope[5]

1. Comparing Leases and Sales

The table below sets out the scope provisions and accompanying definitions from Articles 2A and 2:

---

[3] The definition also includes an optional provision containing a dollar-amount cap, above which the transaction is not a consumer lease. If a state adopts this provision, it chooses the dollar amount.

[4] At the federal level, personal-property leasing to consumers is governed by the Consumer Leasing Act, which is implemented by Regulation M. The Act and the regulation require meaningful disclosures and accurate advertising; they also limit the size of balloon payments. See www.federalreserve.gov/bankinforeg/regmcg.htm.

[5] Chapter 2 of this text covers the scope provisions in Article 2.

	Article 2A		Article 2
Scope 2A-102	Article 2A "applies to any transaction, regardless of form, that creates a lease." (The limitation of scope to "goods" appears in the "lease" definition below.)	**Scope 2-102 2-106(1)**	"Unless the context otherwise requires, [Art. 2] applies to transactions in goods . . . ." "[U]nless the context otherwise requires[,] 'contract' and 'agreement' are limited to those related to the present or future sale of goods."
"Lease" 2A-103(1)(j)	"'Lease' means a transfer of the right to possession and use of goods for a term in return for consideration, but a sale, including a sale on approval or a sale or return, **or retention or creation of a security interest** is not a lease. Unless the context clearly indicates, the term includes a sublease."	**"Sale" 2-106(1)**	"A 'sale' consists in the passing of title from the seller to the buyer for a price (Section 2-401)."
"Goods" 2A-103(1)(h)	"'Goods' means all things that are movable at the time of identification to the lease contract, or are fixtures (Section 2A-309), but the term does not include money, documents, instruments, accounts, chattel paper, general intangibles, or minerals or the like, including oil and gas, before extraction. The term also includes the unborn young of animals."	**"Goods" 2-105(1)**	"'Goods' means all things (including specially manufactured goods) which are movable at the time of identification to the contract for sale other than the money in which the price is to be paid, investment securities (Article 8) and things in action. 'Goods' also includes the unborn young of animals and growing crops and other identified things attached to realty as described in the section on goods to be severed from realty (Section 2-107)."

The definition of "lease" excludes a "sale" (§ 2-106), including a "sale on approval" and a "sale or return" (defined in § 2-326, a section you may not have read before). A lease cannot be a sale because it gives the lessee (or sublessee) a temporary right to possess and use the goods, but the lessor retains title and the reversionary interests in possession and use. If the lessee defaults, the lessor can repossess the goods. It need not sell the goods and return any excess proceeds to buyer, because the lessor owns the residual interest.

 **Reading Article 2A:
Scope**

**Read the provisions listed in the table above, but ignore
the bolded phrase in the "lease" definition, until the
discussion following this Question.**

Question 1.

    (a) How do the provisions from Articles 2 and 2A differ substantively?

    (b) Notice that the Article 2A definition of "goods" includes "fixtures" and refers to 2A-309. Article 2 does not include fixtures in its definition of "goods," nor does it mention fixtures in 2-107(2). Cf. 2-107 Comment 2 ¶ 1. How do these differences affect the scope of Articles 2A and 2?

---

2. Comparing "True Leases" and Disguised Security Interests

The definition of "lease" excludes "retention or creation of a security interest." Under the scope provision in § 9-109(a), Article 9 governs security interests in goods, fixtures, and other personal property, but not real estate. (Article 9 also applies to some other types of transactions that are not important here.)

The most difficult issue concerning the scope of Article 2A is determining when a transaction that looks like a lease is in fact a security interest. If it is, it falls outside of Article 2A and is instead governed by Article 9. (A lease transaction can also include a security interest, but that is a different issue.)

a. A Brief Primer on Secured Transactions and UCC Article 9

To understand this issue, you need some basic knowledge about security interests, which are covered in detail in a course on Secured Transactions. A common transaction is a "purchase money security interest"—known colloquially as "seller financing." It involves a sale of goods, with the goods used as collateral for the purchase, tied into a secured transaction, as shown in the next diagram:

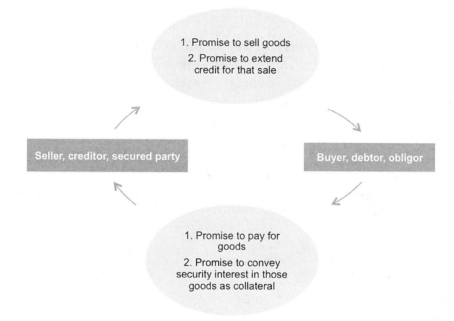

The promises marked "1" are the contract for sale of goods. The promises marked "2" are the secured transaction that is tied to the sale. The "security interest" that the buyer/debtor promises to convey is defined in § 1-201(b)(35) as

> an interest in personal property or fixtures which secures payment or performance of an obligation . . . .

A security interest gives the secured party the right to seize the collateral and sell it if the debtor/buyer does not perform its promise to pay according to the promised terms. For that reason, a secured party has a higher "priority" than an unsecured creditor if the debtor/buyer goes into bankruptcy. Article 9 sets out the rules for how to create, "attach," and "perfect" a security interest; which security interests have a higher priority; how a secured party seizes and sells the collateral upon default of the debtor/buyer; and many more matters.

In the transaction above, the security interest is called a "purchase money security interest." If the buyer/debtor defaults on its promise to pay, the seller/secured party can repossess the goods, sell them, and use the proceeds to satisfy the remaining debt and the seller's expenses associated with repossession and sale. The seller/secured party, though, must return the remainder of the sale proceeds to the buyer/debtor.

b. Distinguishing True Leases from "Disguised Security Interests"

As with other areas of commercial law, the parties' characterizations of their transactions are not always accurate. What matters is the economic reality of the transaction, *not* the parties' intent, at the time when the transaction was entered. That economic reality determines which body of law—here, which UCC article—governs the parties' rights and duties.

Because of considerations based on tax law, accounting, bankruptcy, and possibly even avoidance of the rules in Article 9, the parties sometimes try to camouflage the above-diagrammed "seller financing" transaction—a sale with a security interest[6]—as a lease:

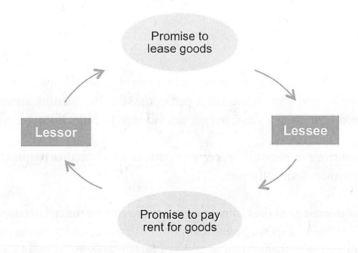

---

6   Although case law and commentators call this as a "disguised security interest," it really is a disguise that masks both a sale and a security interest.

Why does it matter whether a particular transaction is a lease or, instead, a sale with a security interest? It matters because of the differences between Article 2A (governing a lease) and Articles 2 and 9 (governing a sale with a security interest). Article 9 covers creation and attachment of a security interest to the collateral (including a special statute of frauds). It also contains detailed rules that determine the priorities among competing security interests in the same collateral—whether a financing statement needs to be timely filed, in order to "perfect" the security interest and thereby protect the secured creditor's rights in the collateral. In addition, Article 9 sets out detailed provisions governing the obligor/debtor's default and the secured party's enforcement of the security interest. If a so-called lessor actually has a security interest and does not file a financing statement to "perfect" that security interest, the so-called lessor might lose the goods to a secured party who is perfected in the same goods. (These matters are covered in a course on Secured Transactions and are too intricate for further coverage in this Assignment.)

The statutory test for whether a so-called lease is actually a sale with a security interest appears in § 1-203. Many courts and commentators call this test the "bright-line test,"[7] but it is hardly a bright line, because the section is very complicated. (Below, we have paraphrased the key part—subsection b.) The test seeks to determine whether the lessor's reversionary interest in the goods at the end of the lease is "economically meaningful." If the worth of that interest is zero or nearly so, the so-called lease is really a sale with a security interest. According to § 1-203(e), the test is applied to the facts existing at contract formation.

Under § 1-203(b), a transaction in the form of a lease cannot be a sale with a security interest if either or both of the following are true:

(1)   The lessee's duty to possess and pay rent for the goods does not stretch over the full term of the lease, or

(2)   The lessee has a right to terminate the lease before its full term.

In either of these instances, the lessor has a "meaningful reversionary interest," so the transaction is a true lease.

However, if the lessee has no right to terminate and its obligations of possession and payment run for the full term of the lease, the transaction is instead a sale with a security interest if at least one of the following is true:

---

7   Another term is the "per se test."

(1) The lease term equals or exceeds the life of the goods,

(2) The lessee has agreed to renew the lease until the end of the goods' life or has agreed to become the owner of the goods at some point in the lease,

(3) The lessee has an option to renew the lease until the end of the goods' life in return for nominal or no consideration, or

(4) The lessee has an option to own the goods in return for nominal or no consideration.

Under subsection (1), a sale with a security interest exists if the lease runs for the full life of the goods, so that the lessor gets back worthless goods at the end of the lease. That makes sense, when you remember that a true lease must have an economically meaningful reversionary interest. The same principle makes subsection (2) make sense: A sale with security interest exists if the lessor does not get goods back at the end of the lease because the lessee is bound to renew the lease until the end of the goods' life or because the lessee is bound to become the owner.

Subsection (3) addresses the situation when the parties attempt to disguise the security interest by giving the lessee a very cheap or free option to *renew* until the end of the goods' life, so that it does not make sense for the lessee to fail to exercise the option. Subsection (4) addresses the situation when the parties attempt to disguise the security interest by giving the lessee a very cheap or free option to *own* the goods, so that it does not make sense for the lessee to fail to exercise that option. In both cases, there is essentially no reversionary interest in the lessor, because it does not make economic sense for the lessee to return the goods to the lessor.

So, to paraphrase again the test in § 1-203, goods purportedly being "leased" are instead collateral for a security interest in a sales contract if

(1) The lessee's duties to possess the goods and pay rent for them run for the full term of the lease, and the lease contract is not terminable by the lessee; and

(2) Any of the following is true:

(a) The lease (or lessee's renewal or option to renew) runs for at least the life of the goods, with nominal or no consideration; or

(b) The lessee has agreed to become the owner of the goods (or has an option to do so) at the end of the lease, with nominal or no consideration.

"Nominal consideration" is defined briefly in § 1-203(d), which also furnishes two "safe harbors" by saying when additional consideration is *not* nominal. Section 1-203(c) lists facts that do not, by themselves, turn a lease into a secured transaction.

That completes our summary of the "bright-line test" in § 1-203. However, even if a lease survives the "bright-line" test in § 1-203(b), that does not end the issue. Section 1-203(b) says what happens if a lease fails the test (it *is* a security interest), but it does not say what happens if the lease *is not* a security interest under the "bright-line" statutory test. So case law steps in to determine whether the lease might still be found to be a sale with a security interest[8] under a common law "economic realities" test that looks at whether the lessor retains an "(economically) meaningful reversionary interest" in the goods at the end of the lease, as judged by the facts at contract formation.[9] Under this test, "if at the end of the lease term, the only economically sensible course for the lessee to take is to exercise the option to purchase the property, then the lease is a security agreement."[10] Some courts have articulated the following two factors for this test:

(1)   Whether the lease contains a purchase option that is nominal; and

(2)   Whether the lessee develops equity in the property, such that the only economically reasonable option for the lessee is to purchase the goods.[11]

To summarize, a "true lease" cannot be a security interest under the test in § 1-203, *and* it must satisfy the common law test for a lease—that the lessor retains an "(economically) meaningful reversionary interest" in the goods at the end of the lease.

---

[8]   Case law has been consistent in interpreting § 1-203(b), as well as its predecessor in § 1-201(37) (definition of "security interest") to leave open the possibility of adding a common law test of which transactions in actuality create a security interest. The result would have been different if § 1-203(b) had said that a lease is a sale with a security interest if and only if the stated test is met. That would have pre-empted any common law test.

[9]   See, e.g., Sunshine Heifers, LLC v. Citizens First Bank (In re Purdy), 763 F.3d 513, 520 (6th Cir. 2014); In re Ladieu, 2011 WL 748566, at *11 (Bankr. D. Vt.); In re Sankey, 307 B.R. 674, 680 (D. Alaska 2004).

[10]   In re Kentuckiana Medical Center LLC, 455 B.R. 694, 701 (Bankr. S.D. Ind. 2011).

[11]   Sunshine Heifers, LLC v. Citizens First Bank (In re Purdy), 763 F.3d 513, 520 (6th Cir. 2014).

EXAMPLES AND ANALYSIS

Example A: *In re Kentuckiana Medical Center LLC* [12]

The medical center leased equipment under three leases that were not terminable by the lessee and that required the lessee to pay rent for the terms of the leases. At the end of the leases, if the lessee was not in default, the lessee had three choices:

(1) Purchase Option: Pay a fair market value for the equipment that would not be less than 10% of the lessor's total acquisition cost.

(2) Renewal Option: Renew the lease for a renewal term of 1 month at a monthly rental payment of a certain amount, after which title to the equipment would transfer to the lessee by bill of sale.

(3) Return Option: Return all equipment to the lessor; pay any and all moving expenses, storage fees while the lessor found a buyer for the equipment (approximately 180 days under normal market conditions), sales commissions, and other selling expenses incurred by the lessor in the sale of the equipment; and guarantee to lessor a minimum resale equipment value equal to 10% of the lessor's total acquisition cost.

The medical center later went into bankruptcy and brought an action for declaratory judgment, asking the court to rule that the three leases were instead security interests.

Analysis: The court held that each purported lease was a sale with the retention of a security interest. It reasoned that the Purchase Option and Renewal Option resulted in the same payment obligations to the lessor, and both ultimately vested ownership in the medical center. The court held that the purchase option price was "nominal," because the reasonably predictable cost of returning the equipment exceeded the amount of the purchase option. The court reasoned "that the Leases were structured in such a way as to make [the medical center's] 'reasonably predictable cost' of returning the collateral exceed the cost of purchase. The . . . bright-line test of [1-203(b)(4)] is satisfied as well as the economic realities test otherwise known as the 'sensible person' test. After making almost $3 million in rental payments over a five year period, no sensible person would choose to incur significant additional expense to abandon equipment, essential

---

[12] 455 B.R. 694 (Bankr. S.D. Ind. 2011).

for ongoing operations, when it could purchase the equipment outright for an arguably nominal amount."[13] (Note that the court did not need to reach the common-law economic realities test once it found that the lease was a security interest under the bright-line test in 1-203.)

Example B. *In re Kinds*[14]

Lessees (husband and wife) entered into a 60-month lease agreement with lessor for a used mobile home, in return for monthly installment payments of $533.00, which included a monthly insurance premium of $36.00. The lessees also had to pay the personal property taxes each year on the mobile home. Lessees were given a $7,000 net allowance on the transaction (either the value of a trade-in or a cash down-payment). The lessees had the option of terminating the lease at any time. If the lessees elected to terminate, lessor could recover only the lease payments that were due prior to the date of the termination plus accrued collection charges, if any. The lessor was to retain ownership of the mobile home. Once the lease was signed, the lessor executed an Application for Certificate of Title which designated the lessees as owners of the mobile home, ostensibly to enable the lessees to acquire insurance and to facilitate the payment of the personal property taxes. The lessees filed for bankruptcy under Chapter 7 (liquidation) two days after the lease was signed.

Analysis: The court concluded that the agreement was a true lease and not a security agreement, even though it was a "close call." The court applied the predecessor to 1-203 (which has the same content) and was persuaded by the following facts:

(1) The lessees could terminate the agreement at any time after making the first monthly payment, and would be liable only for delinquent payments up to the date of termination, plus any accrued collection costs.

---

[13] *Id.* at 701-02.

[14] 2010 WL 4386929, at *2-3 (Bankr. N.D. Miss.).

(2) The lessees had no option to purchase the leased property for a nominal consideration at the conclusion of the lease term.

(3) The lease provided that lessor would retain ownership and title to the leased property. Even though lessor executed an Application for Certificate of Title in favor of the lessees, the lessees do not dispute that lessor remained the owner.

(4) The lease agreement provided that the lessees had no right to sell, transfer, assign, sublease, or in any way encumber the leased property. These rights were specifically reserved to lessor.

(5) Although the lessees were given a net allowance of $7,000, this is significantly offset by the lessees' failure to make lease payments and tax payments totaling $5,101.01. The lessees' past performance indicates that their future performance will likewise be unsatisfactory.

(6) Considering that the lease term is five years, the court concludes that the economic life of the mobile home exceeds the original term of the lease.

(7) Since the lessees can terminate the lease at any time, they are not required to renew the lease for the remaining economic life of the mobile home.

(8) On "Bankruptcy Schedule G—Executory Contracts and Unexpired Leases," the lessees listed the agreement as a residential lease. Lessor was not listed as a secured creditor.[15]

Some commentators have noted that the court did not address whether the lessees were less likely to terminate because the lessor would get to keep their $7000 down-payment (nearly 25% of the total amount due) if the lessees terminated the lease.[16] The court did not apply the common-law "economic realities" test, concluding that the agreement was a true lease based solely on the UCC test.

[15] This fact is probably irrelevant, because the parties' intent is not to be considered in making this determination. U.C.C § 1-203 cmt. 2 ¶ 6.

[16] Robert Downey, Barry A. Graynor, & Stephen T. Whelan, Leases in The Uniform Commercial Code Survey, 66 Bus. Law. 1101, 1104 (2011).

APPLYING ARTICLE 2A

Problem 26-1.

The lessee, a business, entered into a 42-month lease agreement for the rental of three trucks. The lease said that the lessee assumed the risk of loss or damage to the equipment, did not allow the lessee to terminate the agreement, and gave the lessee the option of purchasing the equipment at the end of the lease for $1.00. Is the lease a true lease or a disguised sale with retention of a security interest?

Problem 26-2.

A dairy farmer agreed to lease 435 dairy cattle from the lessor for 50 months and to make monthly rent payments. The lease did not give the farmer any option to purchase the cattle, and it forbade him from terminating the agreement. The practice in the cattle-leasing industry allows aging or ill cattle to be culled from the herd and replaced by the lessor, so that, at the end of the lease term, the herd of cattle contains most of the cattle originally leased, as well as some leased replacements. Thus, the economic life of these leased goods was greater than the lease term. Is the lease a true lease or a disguised sale with retention of a security interest?

C. Contract Formation and Content of the Contract[17]

Article 2A hews closely to many contract formation provisions in Article 2, as reflected in the text and questions below. Note that, in jurisdictions that have adopted new Article 1, course of performance, course of dealing, and usage of trade are all defined and their interpretational priority set in Article 1, so that they apply to Article 2A as they apply to every article of the UCC, as discussed in Assignment 6.

---

[17]   Chapter 3 of this text covers the Article 2 provisions on contract formation and the content of the contract.

Reading Article 2A:
Contract Formation and Content

Read the sections listed in the left-hand column. For each section, look at the "Uniform Statutory Source" listed in the Official Comment.

Question 2. The first two columns list Article 2A sections (and their subject headings) that resemble Article 2 sections. In the third and fourth columns, fill in the pertinent Article 2 sections and note the substantive differences. Note the interesting location of the provision on unconscionability. Why does this location make sense?

Article 2A section	Article 2A section heading	Article 2 section	How Art. 2A differs substantively, if at all
2A-108	Unconscionability		
2A-202	Final Written Expression: Parol or Extrinsic Evidence		
2A-204	Formation in General		
2A-205	Firm Offers		
2A-206	Offer and Acceptance in Formation of Lease Contract		
2A-208	Modification, Rescission, and Waiver		

Notice that Article 2A does not contain any analog to § 2-206(1)(b), on "prompt or current shipment" and "accommodation shipments." This omission seems to have been because the typical lease transaction is not initiated by the lessee placing an order for goods. Moreover, it is not ordinarily concluded by the lessor simply shipping the goods to the lessee.

Furthermore, Article 2A does not contain any analog to § 2-207, on the so-called "battle of forms." This omission seems to have been partially because of the continuing controversy and criticism of § 2-207, but much more because the typical lease contract does not involve a "battle of forms." Instead of an exchange of standard-form documents between lessor and lessee, either the lessor furnishes a standard-form lease contract (which may or may not be negotiable), or the parties negotiate a lease contract.

Reading Article 2A: No Analog to § 2-207

Reread 2A-204 and 2A-206.

Question 3. Considering the common patterns of how lease contracts are formed (see the preceding paragraph), how does the omission of an analog to 2-207 affect contract formation under Article 2A?

Article 2A also lacks many of the "gapfiller" provisions that appear in Article 2:

§ 2-304: Price Payable in Money, Goods, Realty, or Otherwise

§ 2-305: Open Price Terms

§ 2-306: Output, Requirements and Exclusive Dealings

§ 2-307: Delivery in Single Lot or Several Lots

§ 2-308: Absence of Specified Place for Delivery

§ 2-309: Absence of Specific Time Provisions; Notice of Termination

§ 2-310:   Open Time for Payment or Running of Credit: Authority to Ship under Reservation

§ 2-503:   Manner of Seller's Tender of Delivery

§ 2-504:   Shipment by Seller

§ 2-505:   Seller's Shipment under Reservation

Article 2A omits these gapfillers because they are not needed in typical lease contracts, which tend to be more negotiated and more complete. In addition, the leasing industry does not have universal or common choices for many of these gapfillers, so it did not make sense to codify default provisions that did not represent the usual leasing terms.

A few provisions protect consumer lessees entering into consumer leases. As you were reading § 2A-108 on unconscionability (see Question 2 above), you should have noticed that subsection (2) gives consumer leases additional protection, beyond the usual unconscionability in subsection (1) and in Article 2. In addition, § 2A-106 invalidates certain clauses on choice of law and choice of forum in a consumer lease.

Reading Article 2A:
Choice-of-Law and Choice-of-Forum
Clauses in Consumer Leases

Read 2A-106 and its Comments.

Question 4.

(a) What is the difference between a choice-of-law clause and choice-of-forum clause?

(b) What kind of choice-of-law clause is invalidated by this section? What public policy supports this rule for consumer leases?

(c) What kind of choice-of-forum clause is invalidated by this section? What public policy supports this rule for consumer leases?

D. Contract Enforceability: Statute of Frauds[18]

Reading Article 2A: Statute of Frauds

Read 2A-201 and its Comment, and 2-201.

Question 5. How do these sections differ? Aside from the obvious differences between leases and sales, how do these differences affect the application of the statute of frauds?

E. Warranties[19]

The general warranty provisions in Article 2A closely track the Article 2 provisions, except to the extent necessary to reflect leasing differences. However, Article 2A also contains some unique warranty provisions that apply to a three-party relationship called a "finance lease."

1. General Warranty Provisions

Reading Article 2A: Warranties

Read the sections listed in the left-hand column. For each section, look at the "Uniform Statutory Source" listed in the Official Comment.

Question 6. The first two columns list Article 2A sections (and their subject headings) that resemble Article 2 sections. In the third and fourth columns,

---

18 Chapter 4 of this text covers the statute of frauds in Article 2.
19 Chapter 5 of this text covers the warranties and disclaimers in Article 2.

fill in the pertinent Article 2 sections and note the substantive differences. For the time being, ignore any references to "finance leases."

Article 2A section	Article 2A section heading	Article 2 section	How Art. 2A differs substantively, if at all
2A-210	Express Warranties		
2A-211	Warranties Against Interference and Against Infringement; Lessee's Obligation Against Infringement		
2A-212	Implied Warranty of Merchantability		
2A-213	Implied Warranty of Fitness for Particular Purpose		
2A-214	Exclusion or Modification of Warranties		
2A-216	Third-Party Beneficiaries of Express and Implied Warranties		

2. Finance Leases and their Warranty Rules

Article 2A codified an existing commercial practice called "finance leasing." A finance lease is a three-party transaction whereby:

- The supplier has goods that the lessee wants to lease, not buy.
- The finance lessor buys the goods from the supplier (an Article 2 transaction), intending to lease them to the lessee.
- The lessee leases the goods from the finance lessor.

This arrangement saves the supplier from having to extend credit to the lessee (sometimes for many years) or having to manage the lease contract. It also saves the lessee from having to obtain credit to buy the goods. The lessor steps in, to finance the goods and manage the lease contract.

Section 2A-103(1)(g) provides a lengthy definition of "finance lease."

Reading Article 2A: Finance Lease

Read 2A-103(1)(g).

Question 7. What are the three requirements for a finance lease? What is the overarching purpose of the requirement in (iii)(A)-(D), even though it can be fulfilled in four ways? Why do each of the three requirements make sense? (Hint: Who specifies the type of goods that the lessor eventually purchases from the supplier?)

Question 8. Some or perhaps many finance leases are not really "leases," but are instead disguised sales with the retention of security interests ("disguised security interests") (see the Scope section at the beginning of this Assignment). Why are finance leases more likely than other leases to be "disguised security interests"?

Finance leases are governed by different warranty rules than are other leases. In the Article 2A warranty sections that you read for Question 6 above, three of the sections or subsections began with the phrase, "Except in a finance lease . . .":

- 2A-211(2): implied warranty of non-infringement, by merchant regularly dealing in goods of the kind

- 2A-212(1): implied warranty of merchantability, by merchant with respect to goods of that kind

- 2A-213: implied warranty of fitness for a particular purpose

Thus, a finance lease does not contain any implied warranties from the lessor, except the warranty against interference in § 2A-211(1). In addition, the typical finance lessor tries hard not to make any express warranties about the goods. In essence, the finance lessor is more like a lender than an owner-lessor. The finance lessor buys the goods in order to lease them, to get cash flow from the finance lessee (rent payments) in return.

The finance lessee, though, is not necessarily out of luck. Even though the supplier and the finance lessee are not in privity, § 2A-209 makes the lessee a third-party beneficiary of the sale-of-goods contract between the supplier (seller) and the finance lessor (buyer). As in the third-party beneficiary relationship in § 2-318, the finance lessee "stands in the shoes" of the buyer (finance lessor) and gets whatever warranties the finance lessor obtained from the supplier in the sale contract. These "pass-through warranties" also include any third-party warranties that the supplier obtained when it bought the goods. Thus, if the finance lessee has problems with the goods, it may be able to obtain relief from the supplier or its upstream seller(s). Recall the requirements for a finance lease in § 2-A103(1)(g)(iii) (Question 7, above). These pass-through warranties are part of the reason why that provision requires that the finance lessee be given advance notice of the proposed contract terms between the supplier and the finance lessor.

However, some situations will prevent certain warranties from arising and, therefore, from being passed through. Under § 2A-212 (similar to § 2-314), if the supplier is not a "merchant with respect to goods of that kind," then the finance lessor (and hence, the finance lessee) does not obtain an implied warranty of merchantability. Under § 2A-213 (similar to § 2-315), if the facts do not give rise to an implied warranty of fitness for a particular purpose, then the finance lessor (and hence, the finance lessee) does not obtain that warranty. Even more importantly, if the supplier validly disclaims or limits any warranties, those disclaimers and limitations against the finance lessor are valid against the finance lessee as well. Again, the finance lessee "stands in the shoes" of the finance lessor (as buyer), for better and for worse.

A finance lessee who is having problems with the leased goods is sometimes tempted to stop making rent payments to the finance lessor or to deduct its damages from the rent payment. This response will usually be a breach. Section 2A-407 codifies what is known commercially as a "hell or high water clause," so that it is implied into every finance lease except a consumer lease.[20] This provision means that the finance lessee's promises become irrevocable and independent of any defects in the goods. Thus, the finance lessee cannot cancel, terminate, modify, repudiate, or be excused from its promises under the lease contract, once the lessor tenders and

---

[20] See the discussion of "consumer leases" in the Introduction to this Assignment.

the lessee accepts the goods. The effect of the implied clause protects not only the finance lessor, but also its assignees and other third parties. The clause is subject to the lessee's right to revoke acceptance or raise any contract formation defenses and subject to the lessor's obligation of good faith.

If a finance lease turns out to be a "disguised security interest" (a sale with a security interest), it will be governed by Article 9, not Article 2A. Article 9 does not imply a "hell or high water" clause, so commercial parties routinely include an express "hell or high water" clause like the following one that appears in many leases:

> The lessee's obligation to pay lessor all amounts due hereunder is absolute and unconditional, and lessee shall not be entitled to any abatement, reduction, set-off, counter-claim, defense, or deduction with respect to any rent or other sum payable hereunder.

These express clauses guard against the possibility that the finance lease is not a true lease and therefore is governed by Article 9, rather than Article 2A. Comment 6 to § 2A-407 leaves open the question of whether an express "hell or high water clause" is enforceable in a consumer lease that is a finance lease, or in lease that is not a finance lease, but courts have routinely enforced these clauses, especially in the financial leasing context.[21]

APPLYING ARTICLE 2A

Problem 26-3.

A manufacturer of eyeglass lenses wanted to add to its assembly line a machine that safely packaged the lenses in custom-labeled cardboard boxes as they came off the assembly line, thereby reducing breakage and labor costs. The machine had a useful life of ten years. The cost of the machine was beyond the budget or credit-worthiness of the manufacturer, so its bank referred the manufacturer to a leasing company that said it was willing to purchase the needed machine and lease it to the manufacturer for an acceptable monthly rent payment. The manufacturer notified the leasing company of the machine's model number and desired additional features. The leasing company found a machine meeting the manufacturer's specifications, showed the sale contract to the manufacturer, and then bought the machine. Then

---

the manufacturer entered a 48-month lease contract with the leasing company; the lease did not contain an express "hell or high water" clause or any options to renew the lease or purchase or own the machine. The leasing company had the machine delivered to the manufacturer, which tested the machine for two weeks and then expressly accepted it. However, four months later, the machine's gaskets began to fail at an unusually high rate. The manufacturer notified the leasing company, which said that it had no remaining obligations as to the machine. The manufacturer also notified the company that sold the machine to the leasing company, but that company said that it had sold the machine to the leasing company "as is" and without any express warranties, so it had no warranty obligations to the manufacturer. The manufacturer checked the sale contract and found a large-print bolded "as is" clause; there were no express warranties except the description of the machine. Irritated at the lack of response by the leasing company and the company that sold the machine, the manufacturer now wants to know whether it can cease or decrease rent payments, return the machine, or get someone to fix it without charge.

(a) Is this a lease? If so, what kind of lease is it?

(b) Is the leasing company correct that it has no remaining obligations as to the machine?

(c) Can the manufacturer cease or decrease its rent payments?

(d) Is the seller of the machine correct that it has no warranty obligations to the manufacturer?

(e) Are there any other possibilities for the manufacturer getting someone to fix the machine without charge?

F. Performance Issues

Chapter 7 of this textbook covers the performance provisions in Article 2: identification, tender, delivery, risk of loss, title, inspection, rejection, cure, acceptance, revocation, insecurity, repudiation, retraction, and excuse. Those provisions appear in both Part 6 and Part 7 of Article 2.

Article 2A greatly improved upon the Article 2 organization by centralizing into Part 5 all of the parties' remedies and rights upon default. Thus, Part 5 includes a buyer's rejection, acceptance, revocation, and accompanying duties, as well as a seller's right to cure, both parties' damages, specific performance, and other remedies. The result is a much more cohesive section on remedies, because it recognizes that a buyer's rights to reject, accept, or revoke acceptance are indeed remedies for seller's default (breach).

Consistent with the Article 2A organization, this Assignment covers all the remedies topics in the upcoming section on Default (Section H). This Section of this Assignment covers the rest of the traditional Article 2 performance issues: identification, tender, delivery, risk of loss, title, inspection, insecurity, repudiation, retraction, and excuse.

Reading Article 2A: Performance Issues

Read the sections listed in the left-hand column. For each section, look at the "Uniform Statutory Source" listed in the Official Comment.

Question 9. The first two columns list Article 2A sections (and their subject headings) that resemble Article 2 sections. In the third and fourth columns, fill in the pertinent Article 2 sections and note the substantive differences.

Article 2A section	Article 2A section heading	Article 2 section	How Art. 2A differs substantively, if at all
2A-217	Identification		
2A-218	Insurance and Proceeds		
2A-219	Risk of Loss		
2A-220	Effect of Default on Risk of Loss		
2A-221	Casualty to Identified Goods		

Article 2A section	Article 2A section heading	Article 2 section	How Art. 2A differs substantively, if at all
2A-401	Insecurity: Adequate Assurance of Performance		
2A-402	Anticipatory Repudiation		
2A-403	Retraction of Anticipatory Repudiation		
2A-404	Substituted Performance		
2A-405	Excused Performance		
2A-406	Procedure on Excused Performance		

APPLYING ARTICLE 2A

Problem 26-4.

A manufacturer leased two industrial copiers to a lessee with a 60-month lease contract. It contained an express "hell or high water" clause, held the lessee "responsible for loss and damage to the copiers from any cause once the copiers are delivered," imposed on lessee the duty to repair or replace any damaged copier, and required the lessee to make monthly rent payments. The lessee accepted the copiers soon after delivery. Nineteen months later, Hurricane Sandy flooded the lessee's premises, giving new meaning to the term "hell or high water" and rendering the copiers unusable. The lessee ceased making payments, and the lessor repossessed the copiers, resold them to a buyer in the business of salvage goods, and sued for resale damages. The lessee claimed that the doctrines in Restatement (Second) of

Contracts §§ 261 (supervening impracticability) and 265 (frustration of purpose) permitted the lessee to cease payments. (Assume that both sections have been adopted by the courts in this jurisdiction.) The lessee also claimed that the lessor had the risk of loss for the copiers, which were uninsurable against a calamity like a hurricane. Finally, the lessee claimed that the lease was really a "disguised security interest," so the "hell or high water" clause was unenforceable.

(a) Is this a finance lease?

(b) Which party had the risk of loss at the time of the loss?

(c) Is the lessee entitled to excuse from performance?

G. Engaging with Third Parties in Complex Sales Transactions: Title and Priority Disputes

Title is sometimes analogized to a bundle of sticks, with each stick representing a particular kind of right to the property. In a sale of goods, full title (the entire bundle of sticks) passes from seller to buyer. However, in a lease of goods, only some of the sticks pass to the lessee, and they pass only temporarily, for the term of the lease. The typical lessee gets the temporary right to possess and use the goods, and sometimes has other temporary rights as well, such as the right to sublease the goods or (less commonly) to encumber them with liens or security interests.

In this textbook, Assignment 16 covers the passing of title to the goods from seller to buyer, and Assignment 21 covers the situations in which a good faith purchaser for value and a buyer in the ordinary course of business sometimes prevail over the title rights of the original owner. This Section of this Assignment summarizes the related provisions in Article 2A governing title rights and priority disputes. Part 3 of Article 2A (§§ 2A-301 to -311) contains the rules governing the priority rights of a lessor, a lessee, a sublessor, a sublessee, a sublessee in the ordinary course, a good faith sublessee or buyer, a lienholder, a creditor of lessee or sublessee, and many combinations of the above. Comments 3 and 4 to § 2A-301 provide a good primer on these rules, some of which resemble §§ 2-401 (title), 2-402 (creditor's rights), and 2-403 (good faith purchaser for value, buyer in the ordinary course of business).

Under §§ 2A-301 and 2A-302, a true lease that complies with the statute of frauds is effective between the parties and against third parties, unless another Article 2A section provides to the contrary. This is true even when a third party, not the lessor, has title, and even if a third party, not the lessee, has possession.

If the so-called lease is instead a disguised security interest,[22] then the security interest is governed instead by Article 9, including its requirements for creation, attachment, and perfection of a security interest. In many situations, the secured party will need to file a financing statement and comply with other requirements in order to gain priority over other creditors as to the goods. A true lease, however, is not subject to the requirements of Article 9.

Under § 2A-303, the lease contract cannot prohibit a transfer of a right to damages for default, or make such a transfer into a default. If a party transfers "the lease" or "all my rights under the lease" or the like, that transfer is usually construed as a delegation of duties by the transferor to the transferee. When the transferee accepts the transfer, that transfer creates a promise by the transferee to perform those duties.

Sections 2A-304 and 2A-305 deal with third parties who are good-faith transferees of the leased goods, as well as lessees in the ordinary course of business.[23] Under § 2A-304, if the lessor transfers any interest to a transferee, that transferee is considered to be a subsequent lessee. This section resolves the priority disputes that may then arise between the original lessee and the subsequent lessee. Under § 2A-305, if the lessee transfers any interest to a transferee, that transferee is considered to be a buyer or sublessee of the goods. This section resolves the priority disputes that may arise between the transferee and the original lessor (or third parties claiming through the lessor).

Section 2A-306 furnishes a rule governing priority disputes arising against the lessor or lessee by lien holders who have furnished services or materials for the leased goods. These liens arise under state laws. Section 2A-307 furnishes a rule for priority disputes between the lessor and creditors of the lessee, as well as disputes between the lessee and creditors of the lessor. These two sections are modeled on portions of Article 9.

Section 2A-308 provides a collection of rules governing allegedly fraudulent transfers and preferences, modeled after § 2-402.

Sections 2A-309 and 2A-310 provide the rules governing leased goods that are or become "fixtures" (defined in § 2A-309(1)(a)) or "accessions" (defined in § 2A-310(1)). Fixtures are goods that are so related to real estate that they are governed by real estate law. Accessions are goods that are affixed to or installed in other goods.

---

[22] See the previous discussion on "disguised security interests," in Section B on Scope.
[23] Sections 2A-304 and 2A-305 are close cousins of § 2-403, which is covered in Assignment 21.

Finally, § 2A-311 allows the parties to alter all of these priority provisions by agreement, so these rules are just default rules.

APPLYING ARTICLE 2A

Problem 26-5.

A dealership sold a vehicle to a buyer on credit; the buyer gave the dealership a security interest in the vehicle, to secure its monthly payments over three years. (This is a "purchase money security interest," in which the dealership is both the seller and the secured party.) The buyer took the vehicle home. A week later, the buyer leased custom wheels and tires from an automotive supply shop and had them installed, without telling the dealership. The shop put the original wheels and tires in the trunk. A few months later, the buyer defaulted on his payments on the vehicle, as well as his payments on the wheels and tires. The dealership repossessed the vehicle (complying with the repossession rules in Article 9) and refused to relinquish the wheels or tires to the buyer or the shop. The shop sued the dealership, to regain possession of the wheels and tires.

   (a) Which section governs this dispute between the dealership and the shop?

   (b) Which party prevails, as to the wheels and tires?

H. Default (Breach and Remedies)

1. Comparison of Article 2 and Article 2A Remedies

Chapter 9 of this text covers the remedies in Part 7 of Article 2. This Section of this Assignment focuses on Part 5 of Article 2A, which covers "default," including

- Breach (except repudiation, which appears in Part 4), and

- Remedies.

Like Part 7 in Article 2, Part 5 in Article 2A is divided into these subparts:

- General remedy provisions (consolidating some general provisions that were scattered in Article 2),

- Lessee's remedies (resembling buyer's remedies), and

- Lessor's remedies (resembling seller's remedies).

This Assignment follows that organization.

As mentioned in Section F of this Assignment, on Performance, Article 2A greatly improved upon the Article 2 organization by centralizing into Part 5 all of the parties' remedies and rights upon default. Thus, Part 5 includes a buyer's rejection, acceptance, revocation, and accompanying duties, as well as a seller's right to cure, both parties' damages, specific performance, and other remedies. The result is a much more cohesive section on remedies, because it recognizes that a buyer's rights to reject, accept, or revoke acceptance are indeed remedies for seller's default (breach). This Section on Default covers all of those topics, rather than splitting them between Performance and Default.

In this part of Article 2A, the drafters cleared up many drafting ambiguities left in Article 2:

- Definitions in substantive sections are moved to the definitional section in 2A-103.

- Missing or implied remedies are added into Article 2A.

- The text of Article 2A sections includes explicit cross-references to related sections, rather than just listing them after the section.

- Most Article 2 remedies are actually default provisions, but Article 2 does not emphasize the parties' right to "contract out" of these remedies. Article 2A emphasizes that right and the importance of agreed remedies.

- In Article 2, revocation gets less coverage than rejection. Article 2A remedies that deficiency.

- The same is true of installment contracts—they figure more prominently in the Article 2A remedies.

- And most importantly, related provisions are located near each other, rather than being stranded in separate Parts, as they are in Article 2.

2. General Remedy Provisions

The largest substantive differences between the remedies in Articles 2A and 2 appear in the general provisions.

Reading Article 2A:
Default—General Provisions

Read the sections listed in the left-hand column. For each section, look at the "Uniform Statutory Source" listed in the Official Comment.

Question 10. The first two columns list Article 2A sections (and their subject headings) that resemble Article 2 sections. In the third and fourth columns, fill in the pertinent Article 2 sections and note the substantive differences.

Article 2A section	Article 2A section heading	Article 2 section	How Article 2A differs substantively, if at all
2A-503	Modification or Impairment of Rights and Remedies		
2A-504	Liquidation of Damages		
2A-505	Cancellation and Termination* and Effect of Cancellation, Termination, Rescission, or Fraud on Rights and Remedies		
2A-506	Statute of Limitations		

*The definitions of cancellation and termination appear in 2-103(1)(b), (z).

> **Question 11.** Read the comment to 2A-504. Why does 2A-504(1) differ so much from 2-718(1)? What effect do these changes have upon leasing transactions, as compared with other kinds of contracts under Article 2 and the common law?

If you analyzed the substance of the above sections, rather than their exact wording, you might have correctly observed that the most notable differences between these provisions in Articles 2A and 2 are in the sections on liquidated damages and the statute of limitations. Liquidated damage clauses under Article 2A are frequently litigated, because they are a common part of many leases and because creative drafting practices are constantly pushing the edge of validity.

EXAMPLES AND ANALYSIS

Example A: *VFS Leasing Co. v. S.T.I., Inc.*[24]

The parties entered into two leases covering ten tractor trailer trucks. The court explained the leases as follows: "[I]n addition to the monthly rent, the parties also agreed that at the end of the lease term, [Lessees] would either buy the trucks from [Lessor] for a price equal to 25% of Lessor's Cost for the Equipment ("Purchase Price") or [Lessor] could try to sell the trucks. . . . [I]f the sales amount was less than 25% of the Lessor's Cost for the Equipment, [Lessees] would be obligated to make up the difference between the sales price and the Purchase Price [according to the liquidated damages clause]. However, if the sales price exceeded the Purchase Price, the difference would be paid to [Lessees]. In short, regardless of whether [Lessees] purchased the trucks or they were sold to a third party, at the end of the lease term, [Lessor] would receive a final payment in the amount of 25% of the Lessor's Cost for the Equipment." The leases also allowed the lessor, upon lessees' default, to accelerate all future unpaid rent. After the lessees defaulted on both leases, the lessor repossessed the trucks, sold them at a private sale after notice, and sued lessees for the deficiency under the liquidated damages clauses.

---

[24] 2013 WL 1352032 (N.D. Ala.). See also Robert Downey, Edward K. Gross, & Stephen T. Whelan, Leases, The Uniform Commercial Code Survey, 69 Bus. Law. 1169, 1179-80 (2014).

Analysis: The lessees argued that the liquidated damage clause was invalid because it was not reasonable under the then-anticipated-harm standard in 2A-504(1), so the reasonable measure of damages was instead the amount by which the accelerated, unpaid rent under each lease schedule exceeded the total sales proceeds of the leased trucks. The court reasoned that the lessees' proposed formula would cover the lessor's loss of future rent, but not the lessor's bargained-for residual value expectation of 25% of the original cost of the leased vehicles. The court found that the lessor's actual damages would be the remaining rent payments and the anticipated 25% residual amount. That sum was greater than the amount recoverable under the liquidated damage clauses, which the court upheld under the "anticipated harm" standard in 2A-504(1).

Example B: *CIT Group/Equipment Financing, Inc. v. Shapiro*[25]

The lease contained a clause allowing lessor to accelerate future rent payments upon lessees' default, a liquidated damage clause, and a severability clause. The lessees defaulted on a lease of a commercial scanner, and lessor sold the scanner. The lessor then sued the lessees to recover the accelerated rent payments, late charges, property taxes, and liquidated damages "representing the difference between the amount owed pursuant to a stipulated loss value schedule . . . and the stipulated-to proceeds of a commercially reasonable sale of the Equipment."

Analysis: The court stated, "This arrangement immediately triggers two alarms. . . . Given that contracts are ordinarily written with the expectation of complete performance, it would be very surprising if [Lessor] had not also accounted for capital depreciation in the rent payment. Damages comprising an independent sum for capital depreciation *and* future rent payments would impermissibly 'double-dip.'" In addition, the court found the acceleration clause and the liquidated damages to be "duplicative . . . . On the one hand, [Lessor] demands rent payments stretching in the future after the moment of breach. On the other hand, [Lessor] . . . . sells the machine at the moment of breach. And not only does [Lessor] get the proceeds of that sale, but [Lessor] also gets an additional amount reflecting the difference between those proceeds and the anticipated sale value at that moment . . . . So [Lessor] gets all future rent payments on the Equipment, all proceeds of a sale of the Equipment,

---

[25] 2013 WL 1285269 (S.D.N.Y.). See also Robert Downey, Edward K. Gross, & Stephen T. Whelan, Leases, The Uniform Commercial Code Survey, 69 Bus. Law. 1169, 1179-80 (2014).

and an amount designed to compensate [Lessor] for any drop in the value of the Equipment. Simply put, this is the very definition of an unconscionable arrangement." In addition to this substantive unconscionability, the court noted that there were "hints of procedural unconscionability in the bargaining process." The court used the severability clause to sever the Lessor's right to recover the accelerated rent payments, property taxes, and late charges on the already-sold equipment, all of which the court said were "manifestly unjust and therefore void as against public policy." The court enforced the liquidated damage clause, because it represented "the parties' best *ex ante* approximation of the sale value of the Equipment at the point of the breach."

3. Lessee's Remedies

Now we turn to lessee's remedies. In the chart below, the provisions mentioning the lessor sometimes also include the supplier, because, in a finance lease, the supplier sometimes "stands in" for actions that would otherwise be performed by the lessor.

Reading Article 2A: Lessee's Remedies (Default by Lessor)

Read the sections listed in the left-hand column. For each section, look at the "Uniform Statutory Source" listed in the Official Comment.

Question 12. The first two columns list Article 2A sections (and their subject headings) that resemble Article 2 sections. In the third and fourth columns, fill in the pertinent Article 2 sections and note the substantive differences. Skip the damages calculations in 2A-518(2) and 2A-519(1) until Question 13.

Article 2A section	Article 2A section heading	Article 2 section	How Art. 2A differs substantively, if at all
2A-508	Lessee's Remedies		

Article 2A section	Article 2A section heading	Article 2 section	How Art. 2A differs substantively, if at all
2A-509	Lessee's Rights on Improper Delivery; Rightful Rejection		
2A-510	Installment Lease Contracts: Rejection and Default		
2A-511	Merchant Lessee's Duties as to Rightfully Rejected Goods		
2A-512	Lessee's Duties as to Rightfully Rejected Goods		
2A-513	Cure by Lessor of Improper Tender or Delivery; Replacement		
2A-514	Waiver of Lessee's Objections		
2A-515	Acceptance of Goods		
2A-516	Effect of Acceptance of Goods; Notice of Default		
2A-517	Revocation of Acceptance of Goods		

Article 2A section	Article 2A section heading	Article 2 section	How Art. 2A differs substantively, if at all
2A-518	Cover; Substitute Goods		
2A-519	Lessee's Damages for Non-delivery, Repudiation, Default, and Breach of Warranty in Regard to Accepted Goods		
2A-520	Lessee's Incidental and Consequential Damages		
2A-521	Lessee's Right to Specific Performance or Replevin		
2A-522	Lessee's Right to Goods on Lessor's Insolvency		

If you analyzed the substance of the above sections rather than the exact wording, you should have concluded that the substantive differences between these remedies in Articles 2A and 2 are small and not very significant. In this portion of Article 2A, the drafters stayed very close to the substance of Article 2.

The thorniest comparisons lie in the following damages sections, where the language is particularly dense:

Reading Article 2A:
Lessee's Cover and Market Damages

Re-read 2A-518(2) and 2A-519(1), (2).

Question 13. In both sections, note the content of the introductory "except" clause and "if" clause. Then focus on the formula in the remainder of this very long sentence, and mark the word "minus." Note that both formulas share the same basic structure, for the lessee's damages:

- Present value,* as of a particular date, of
  - The rent for the remaining term of the original lease, calculated from
    - the replacement lease, or
    - its equivalent— "market rent,"
  - Minus the rent under the original lease, for the remaining term of that lease;
- Plus any incidental and consequential damages, less expenses saved in consequence of lessor's default.

(a) In the first bullet above, what is the particular date for the formula in 2A-518(2)? In 2A-519(1)? Why do these dates differ between these formulas?

(b) In the first bullet above, why do the items in the sub-bullets below it need to be converted to "present value"?

(c) What guidance does 2A-519 provide as to "market rent"? Recall from Article 2 that any market value needs a specified time and place.

(d) How are these two formulas similar to the analogous formulas in Article 2? Aside from the differences between leases and sales, are the differences significant?

---

* Defined in 2A-103(1)(u).

708 • Learning Sales Law •

APPLYING ARTICLE 2A

Problem 26-6.

A corporation leased a box-assembly machine from the manufacturer, in a lease contract that specified five testing procedures before lessee's acceptance of the machine. The three-year lease involved a machine with a useful life of five years and did not give the lessee any right or option to renew, purchase, or own the machine. The lessee notified the manufacturer that the machine had failed three of the five tests. The manufacturer sent a service representative to fix and adjust the machine. The machine then passed all but one of the tests. After two more attempts to fix and adjust the machine, the manufacturer said that it was done and that the corporation would have to live with the problem.

    (a) Is this a true lease or a disguised sale with a security interest?

    (b) Can and should the lessee reject the machine? If so, what steps must it take?

    (c) If the lessee rejects the machine, what remedy options does it have? Which option seems better?

Problem 26-7.

A manufacturer of copy machines leased a copy machine to a business customer. The lease contract included an express "hell or high water clause." Seven months later, the lessee sent an email notifying the lessor that the machine had started to have frequent paper jams and so was a breach of warranty of accepted goods. Two weeks later, the lessee ceased making payments. The lessor sued the lessee for the overdue rent payments, and the lessee counterclaimed for a refund of its rent payments made to date and damages for breach of warranty.

    (a) Is this a finance lease?[26] A consumer lease?[27]

    (b) Has the lessee accepted the goods? If so, why is revocation of acceptance unlikely to be available?

---

[26]   Finance leases are covered in Section E of this Assignment, on Warranties.

[27]   Consumer leases are covered in the Introduction to this Assignment.

(c) If the lessor has breached a warranty, what step must the lessee take, in order to not be barred from any remedy? Has the lessee satisfied this requirement?

(d) If the lessor has breached a warranty, what damages can the lessee obtain?

(e) What is the effect of the "hell or high water clause"?[28] Is the lessor entitled to the late payments? Is the lessee entitled to a refund of rent payments made to date?

(f) Could the lessee offset its breach-of-warranty damages against its future rent payments?

4. Lessor's Remedies

Now we turn to the lessor's remedies—a much shorter list than the lessee's remedies, because they do not include rejection, cure, acceptance, revocation, and the accompanying duties.

Reading Article 2A:
Lessor's Remedies (Default by Lessee)

Read the sections listed in the left-hand column. For each section, look at the "Uniform Statutory Source" listed in the Official Comment.

Question 14. The first two columns list Article 2A sections (and their subject headings) that resemble Article 2 sections. In the third and fourth columns, fill in the pertinent Article 2 sections and note the substantive differences. Skip the damages calculations in 2A-527(2), 2A-528(1), and 2A-529(1) until Question 16.

Article 2A section	Article 2A section heading	Article 2 section	How Art. 2A differs substantively, if at all
2A-523	Lessor's Remedies		

---

28 "Hell or high water" clauses are covered in Section E of this Assignment, on Warranties.

Article 2A section	Article 2A section heading	Article 2 section	How Art. 2A differs substantively, if at all
2A-524	Lessor's Right to Identify Goods to Lease Contract		
2A-525	Lessor's Right to Possession of Goods		
2A-526	Lessor's Stoppage of Delivery in Transit or Otherwise		
2A-527	Lessor's Rights to Dispose of Goods		
2A-528	Lessor's Damages for Non-acceptance, Failure to Pay, Repudiation, or Other Default		
2A-529	Lessor's Action for the Rent		
2A-530	Lessor's Incidental Damages		

Question 15. The lessor has an additional remedy in 2A-532, which has no analog in Article 2. Explain this section, in plain English.

If you analyzed the substance of the above sections rather than the exact wording, you should have concluded that the substantive differences between these remedies in Articles 2A and 2 are small and not very significant. As with lessee's remedies, in this portion of Article 2A, the drafters stayed very close to the source material in Article 2.

The thorniest comparisons lie in the following damages sections, where the language is particularly dense:

Reading Article 2A:
Lessor's Replacement-Lease Damages,
Market Damages, and Action
for the Rent

Re-read 2A-527(2), 2A-528(1), and 2A-529(1)(a), (b).

Question 16. In the first two sections, note the content of the introductory "except" clause and "if" clause. In the third section, note the content of the "after" clause and "if" clause. Then focus on the formula in the remainder of this very long sentence, and mark the word "minus." Note that all three formulas share the same basic structure, for the lessor's damages:

- Accrued and unpaid rent, as of a particular date;
- Present value, as of the same particular date, of
  - The rent under the original lease, for the remaining term of that lease,
  - Minus the rent for the remaining term of the original lease, calculated from
    - the replacement lease, or
    - its equivalent—"market rent," or
    - [nothing is subtracted],
- Plus any incidental damages, less expenses saved in consequence of lessee's default.

(a) Recall from Question 13 that the lessee's damages did not include the "accrued and unpaid rent," in the first bullet. Why do lessor's and lessee's damages differ in this respect? In other words, why does it make sense to award this item to the lessor?

(b) In the first and second bullets above, what is the particular date for the formula in 2A-527(2)? In 2A-528(1)? In 2A-529(1)(a)? In 2A-529(1)(b)? Why do these dates differ among these formulas?

(c) What guidance does 2A-528(1) provide as to "market rent"? Recall from Article 2 that any market value needs a specified time and place.

(d) In the 2A-529 formula for action for the rent, why does it make sense that nothing is subtracted from "the rent under the original lease, for the remaining term of that lease? If you are stumped, recall the analogous remedy for seller in 2-709 (action for the price).

(e) How are these three formulas similar to the analogous formulas in Article 2? Aside from the differences between leases and sales, are the differences significant?

APPLYING ARTICLE 2A

Problem 26-8.

(This Problem involves the same situation as in Problem 26-6, but with a default by the lessee, rather than the lessor.) A corporation leased a box-assembly machine from the manufacturer, in a lease contract that specified five testing procedures before lessee's acceptance of the machine. The three-year lease involved a machine with a useful life of five years and did not give the lessee any right or option to renew, purchase, or own the machine. The lessee falsely notified the manufacturer that the machine had failed three of the five tests. The manufacturer sent a service representative to test the machine and correctly concluded that the machine conformed to the lease agreement and that the lessee was trying to get out of the lease. The lessee notified the manufacturer that it was rejecting the machine.

(a) Is this a true lease or a disguised sale with a security interest?

(b) Does the manufacturer have the right to repossess the goods?

(c) If the manufacturer wants to lease the machine to another company, what requirements must it fulfill to recover damages, if the replacement lease is for a lesser amount than the original lease?

(d) If the manufacturer wants to resell the machine as a used machine, what kind of damages can the manufacturer recover?

(e) If the manufacturer is unable to enter into a replacement lease or resale of the machine for a reasonable price, what remedy can the manufacturer obtain?

I. Conclusion

During the drafting process, Article 2A borrowed heavily on Article 2 provisions, but also improved on portions of Article 2, in terms of both organization and substance. The result is a UCC article that is relatively easy to learn by comparison to Article 2. However, sales law is not identical to leasing law. Article 2A contains some tricky scope issues associated with security interests disguised as leases, warranty issues associated with finance leases, hell-or-high-water clauses, a few special rules for consumer leases, priority rules among various competing parties, and more intricate damages formulas.

Assignment 27

The Convention on Contracts for the International Sale of Goods (CISG)

LEARNING OUTCOMES AND OBJECTIVES

At the completion of this Assignment, you should be able to

- identify which contracts are governed by the CISG;
- determine which aspects of contract law are governed by the CISG and which aspects the CISG has left to be governed by other law;
- identify which CISG rules differ from those in UCC Article 2 and the United States' common law rules; and
- apply the CISG to common fact situations.

A. Introduction

Many international sale-of-goods contracts are governed by the United Nations Convention on Contracts for the International Sale of Goods (CISG), a convention issued by the UN Commission on International Trade Law (UNCITRAL). Some CISG provisions mirror those in Article 2, other provisions are similar in concept but not wording, and still other provisions present new concepts and vocabulary. Nonetheless, your familiarity with contract law and sales law will enable you to learn the basics of the CISG in a single assignment, by using a comparative approach—comparing provisions in the CISG and Article 2. More thorough coverage is available in a course on International Business Transactions or International Sales. This Assignment flags the differences and elucidates the new concepts and vocabulary associated with the CISG. After providing background on the CISG (drafting history, adoptions, research tools, and organization), this Assignment presents the CISG topics in the same order they were covered in the earlier Chapters of this text:

Textbook Chapter	Topic	Assignment 27 Section
2	Scope	B
3	Contract Formation & Content	C
4	Statute of Frauds	D
5	Warranties	E
7	Performance	F
9	Remedies	G

As in many areas of international law, the CISG drafters had to craft a path between common law and civil law rules, so that the final version of the treaty was consistent enough with both bodies of law to encourage countries from both legal traditions to adopt the treaty.[1] Sometimes, the solution was to draft a hybrid rule, with aspects of both common law and civil law. Sometimes, the solution was to trade off one common law rule against one civil law rule, so that each side "won one and lost one." Sometimes, the solution was to draft a brand new rule that broke away from both traditions. Rarely, where no compromise could be found, the solution was to let an adopting country opt out of a particular provision by "declaring a reservation" to that provision at the time of adoption.

Once the CISG was adopted[2] by 10 countries (called "Contracting States"), including the United States, it took effect on January 1, 1988. As of the end of 2015, the CISG was in effect in 83 Contracting States listed at http://www.uncitral.org/uncitral/en/uncitral_texts/sale_goods/1980CISG_status.html.[3] In some countries, the CISG has taken effect ("entered into force") fairly recently (for example, Japan and Lebanon, 2009; Turkey, 2011; and Brazil, 2014). Vietnam adopted the CISG in 2015, but the CISG will not take effect in Vietnam until the beginning of 2017. Adoption is not universal, of course. As of the end of 2015, the CISG had not been

---

[1]   For an interesting table of countries' legal systems, see the CIA World Factbook, at https://www.cia.gov/library/publications/the-world-factbook/geos/xx.html.

[2]   Various countries use different nouns for this process—adoption, ratification, accession, succession, and approval. This Assignment uses "adoption" to describe all of these alternatives.

[3]   This table also notes which countries have "declared a reservation" under Article 92, 95, or 96.

adopted by the United Kingdom, India, Thailand, and many African countries.[4] Thus, in the initial analysis of each fact situation, it is always wise to consult an up-to-date list of Contracting States in which the CISG has been adopted and has taken effect.

As a convention adopted by a Contracting State, the CISG becomes part of that country's domestic law. In the United States, that means that the CISG is federal law because it was adopted by Congress. Under the Supremacy Clause, the CISG prevails over conflicting state law, such as the UCC.

Abstracts of CISG cases can be found in an UNCITRAL database called "Case Law on UNCITRAL Texts" (CLOUT).[5] In addition, Pace University's Institute of International Commercial Law has long maintained a thorough "CISG Data-base" with a wider range of CISG research sources, including CLOUT.[6] These case abstracts are digested from their original opinions and written in one of the six official languages of the United Nations, translated into the other five languages as well, and then posted on the UNCITRAL website. The purpose is to promote greater awareness of other countries' decisions involving the CISG and to thereby encourage greater uniformity of decisions across countries and tribunals. Reading CLOUT case abstracts is a learned skill. The abstracts often lack the specificity of facts, authorities, and reasoning that appear in published cases, so they sometimes leave the reader wanting. On the other hand, they are much shorter and can be easier to read than full cases.

Additional CISG materials are available and searchable on the UNILEX data base, developed and maintained by the Centre for Comparative and Foreign Law Studies, in Rome.[7]

The CISG is divided into "articles," rather than sections. Unlike the UCC, the CISG contains no official comments and no sections devoted to definitions. The CISG articles lack subject headings, which makes it difficult to navigate the CISG and learn its provisions. The following table of contents for the CISG will give you an overview of the Convention and help you locate pertinent articles:

---

[4]   See the interactive world map at http://www.uncitral.org/uncitral/en/uncitral_texts/sale_goods/1980CISG_status_map.html.

[5]   http://www.uncitral.org/uncitral/en/case_law.html.

[6]   http://www.cisg.law.pace.edu.

[7]   http://www.unilex.info.

Becoming familiar with the provisions of the CISG is vital in the increasingly global world of commerce. In learning about this Convention, remember that the contractual parties are likely to be separated by large distances, cultural differences, and even communication difficulties. Many of the CISG rules are designed to bridge some of these challenges.

B. Scope[8]

In the CISG, Articles 1-3, 6, 10, and 95 determine which contracts are within the scope of the CISG, based on

- the subject matter of the contract and

- the respective places of business of the contract parties.

Some of these Articles use rules that resemble rules in UCC Art. 2, but others include rules unfamiliar to you. The next two Questions explore these CISG scope provisions.

Reading the CISG:
Scope—Contract Subject Matter

Read Articles 1, 2, and 3.

Question 1. These CISG scope provisions resemble parts of UCC 2-102 ("transactions in goods"), 2-105(1) (definition of "goods"), and 2-106(1) ("contract" and "agreement" usually mean "sale"), but some aspects differ. The first two columns contain the rules and provisions on the subject-matter scope of the CISG. How does that scope compare to the scope of Article 2? Fill in your conclusions in the third column. Also note the pertinent UCC section, or whether the result comes from case law.

CISG rule paraphrase	CISG provision	How similar is UCC Art. 2 and related common law?
The CISG applies to contracts for sale of goods . . .	**Art. 1**	Same (2-102, 2-106(1))
but not if the party furnishing the goods predominantly supplies services in the contract	**Art. 3(2)**	

---

[8]   Chapter 2 of this text covers the scope of UCC Article 2.

CISG rule paraphrase	CISG provision	How similar is UCC Art. 2 and related common law?
(goods that are manufactured or produced under the contract are "sales" (not services) unless the buyer is going to supply a substantial part of the raw materials)	Art. 3(1)	
The CISG does not apply to contracts for sales . . .	Art. 2	
of goods purchased for consumer use (unless the seller did not have actual or constructive knowledge of the consumer use by the time of contract formation)	Art. 2(a)	
of stocks, shares, investment securities, negotiable instruments, or money	Art. 2(d)	
of ships, vessels, hovercraft, or aircraft	Art. 2(e)	
of electricity	Art. 2(f)	Cases are in disagreement
by auction	Art. 2(b)	
by authority of law, such as "on execution"	Art. 2(c)	

The table above is a handy checklist for determining whether a particular dispute is within the subject-matter requirements for the scope of the CISG.

Based on the subject-matter scope provisions, CISG case law has excluded franchising contracts and distribution contracts from coverage,[9] because they usually set up a

---

9   See Joseph Lookofsky, Understanding the CISG in the USA § 2.5, at 18 (2d ed. 2004).

legal relationship that will give rise to contracts for sale of goods but rarely include any provision transferring title to specified goods. Software contracts have led to mixed and unpredictable results, depending on the court and the following facts:

- Whether the software is "materialized" in some tangible movable form (CD, external drive, etc.);

- Whether the software is to be "manufactured or produced" by the seller and therefore is within Article 3(1); and

- Whether the contract transfers ownership of the software, not just a license, to the buyer. [10]

APPLYING THE CISG

Problem 27-1.

Revisit the fact situation that appeared in Problems 2-7 and 3-2, but with a few twists to raise CISG issues: PerfectFit Tailors (a business in Singapore) agrees to make a custom-fitted suit for Hal (a German businessman visiting Singapore). (Both countries have adopted the CISG.) Is this contract within the subject matter of the CISG?

Problem 27-2.

A company in Belgium engages a company in France to apply two fabric finishes to 4000 yards of the Belgian company's fabric. (Both countries have adopted the CISG.) Is this contract within the subject matter of the CISG?

Problem 27-3.

A company in Italy enters into an agreement that makes a company in the U.S. the exclusive distributor of the Italian company's gelato in the U.S. The agreement does not specify any quantity of gelato or other goods to be purchased from the Italian company, nor does it set any time limit for the distributorship, other than specifying both parties' termination rights. (Both countries have adopted the CISG.) Is this contract within the subject matter of the CISG? (Hint: courts deciding this issue have often used Article 14 in their reasoning.)

---

[10]   See Peter Huber & Alastair Mullis, The CISG: A new textbook for students and practitioners § 3, at 43 (2007).

As noted at the beginning of this section, the CISG scope is determined not just by the subject matter of the contract, but also by the respective places of business of the contract parties.

Reading the CISG: Scope—Parties' Places of Business

Re-read Article 1, and read Articles 10 and 95.

Question 2. UCC Article 2 has no analog for the CISG scope provisions that look to the parties' places of business. In the right-hand column below, fill in which CISG provision contains the following rules on the scope of the CISG. Edit the rule paraphrase in the left-hand column as needed to reflect your understanding of the provisions.

CISG rule paraphrase	CISG provision (be specific!)
The CISG applies • if the parties' places of business are in different "Contracting States" (countries adopting the CISG)	
· (if a party has >1 place of business, use the one with the closest relationship to the contract)	
· (if a party has no place of business, look to his or her habitual residence)	
· (ignore any place-of-business facts not apparent by the time of contract formation)	
· (ignore the nationality of the parties, as well as their civil and commercial character)	
• OR if private international law rules apply the law of any Contracting State	
· unless that Contracting State "declared a reservation" to Article 1(1)(b), at the time of CISG adoption	

CISG Article 1 narrows the CISG scope to parties with their respective places of business in different countries, so the CISG cannot apply when the parties' respective places of business are in the same country. Article 1 does not look to the nationality of the persons involved in the contract and considers only the facts that are known or apparent by the time of contract formation. Article 10 furnishes supplementary rules to deal with issues of multiple places of business and with parties who have no place of business.

Once we know that the subject matter is within the CISG scope and that the parties' places of business are in different countries, we look to see if both countries are CISG Contracting States,[11] per Article 1(1)(a). If so, the CISG applies. If not, Article 1(1)(b) looks to whether private international law rules[12] (that is, the conflict-of-law rules applied by the court hearing the dispute) would apply the law of any Contracting State to the dispute. Since the Contracting State has adopted the CISG, applying its laws would mean applying the CISG. If the CISG does not apply under private international law rules, then some other law governs the contract—a topic outside of the scope of this Assignment.

However, Article 95 allows a Contracting State, at the time of adoption, to "declare a reservation" to Article 1(1)(b) and therefore not be bound by it. If a Contracting State has made an Article 95 declaration, a court in that State should not apply Article 1(1)(b) and should instead apply the Contracting State's choice-of-law doctrines to determine what law applies (probably the domestic sales of one of the parties, rather than the CISG). Once again, these other choice-of-law doctrines are outside of the scope of this Assignment.

Study this flow chart depicting the application of these scope rules regarding the parties' places of business:

---

[11]   See the UNCITRAL list at http://www.uncitral.org/uncitral/en/uncitral_texts/sale_goods/1980CISG_status.html.

[12]   "Private International law rules" are those rules that cover non-government entities (businesses and individuals) from different countries. The details of these rules are a large and complicated topic beyond the scope of this textbook.

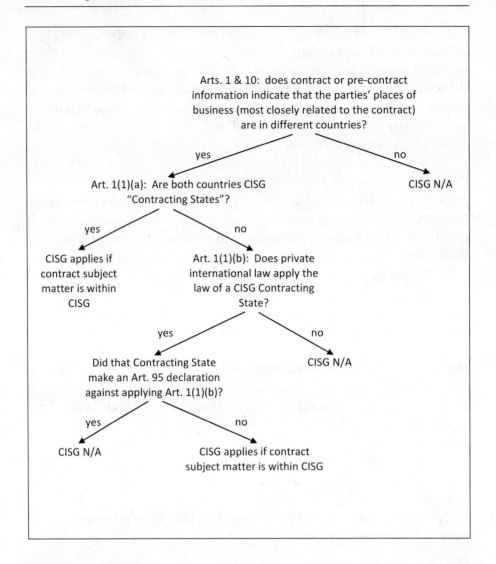

Arts. 1 & 10: does contract or pre-contract information indicate that the parties' places of business (most closely related to the contract) are in different countries?

yes → Art. 1(1)(a): Are both countries CISG "Contracting States"?

no → CISG N/A

Art. 1(1)(a): Are both countries CISG "Contracting States"?

yes → CISG applies if contract subject matter is within CISG

no → Art. 1(1)(b): Does private international law apply the law of a CISG Contracting State?

Art. 1(1)(b): Does private international law apply the law of a CISG Contracting State?

yes → Did that Contracting State make an Art. 95 declaration against applying Art. 1(1)(b)?

no → CISG N/A

Did that Contracting State make an Art. 95 declaration against applying Art. 1(1)(b)?

yes → CISG N/A

no → CISG applies if contract subject matter is within CISG

EXAMPLES AND ANALYSIS

Example A. The two parties to a contract have pertinent places of business in two different countries, only one of which is a "Contracting State." The contract contains a choice-of-law clause specifying the law of France, which is a Contracting State.

Analysis: Because one party is not in a Contracting State, the contract is not within the CISG under Article 1(1)(a), but Article 1(1)(b) might apply to the contract. Because France is a Contracting State and has not declared a reservation under Article 95, France is bound by Article 1(1)(b). If private international law rules affirm the parties' choice of French law, the contract will be governed by the CISG, based on its adoption in France (if the contract's subject matter is within the scope of the CISG).

Example B. The two parties to a contract have pertinent places of business in two different countries, one of which is not a "Contracting State." The contract contains a choice-of-law clause specifying the law of the United States, which is a Contracting State.

Analysis: Because one party is not in a Contracting State, the contract is not within the CISG under Article 1(1)(a), but Article 1(1)(b) might apply to the contract. According to the UNCITRAL Status list, the United States is a Contracting State, but it has declared a reservation under Article 95, so it is not bound by Article 1(1)(b). If private international law rules affirm the parties' choice of U.S. law, the contract will not be governed by the CISG, but instead will be governed by whichever U.S. law is chosen under U.S. choice-of-law principles (probably the UCC, if the contract's subject matter is within the scope of the UCC).

APPLYING THE CISG

Problem 27-4.

A business in Italy sells 5000 cans of cannellini to a business in New York. The U.S. business later claims damages from the delivery of the cannellini and brings suit in a federal court sitting in New York. Is the dispute governed by the CISG?

Problem 27-5.

A business in the United Kingdom orders 120 plaid wool blankets from a manufacturer in Canada. The manufacturer-seller accepts the order and ships the goods. The UK buyer later claims that the blankets do not conform to the contract and refuses to pay for them. Assume that private international law in the UK and Canada applies the law of the seller's country to this kind of dispute.

   (a) The manufacturer-seller brings suit in a Canadian court. Is the dispute governed by the CISG?

   (b) Would the result be different if suit were brought in the UK?

Reading the CISG: "Opting out" of the CISG

Read Article 6.

Question 3. Both the UCC and the CISG allow the parties to contract out of certain provisions, but they differ as to the scope of the variations allowed.

   (a) Consider CISG Article 6, but ignore the reference to Article 12, for the time being. How do the UCC and CISG differ?

   (b) Interestingly, Article 6 allows the parties to completely "opt out" of CISG coverage. Is it a good idea to let parties "opt out" of all CISG coverage? Why does the UCC not allow the parties to opt out of its coverage? Should it?

APPLYING THE CISG

Problem 27-6.

Have the parties successfully opted out of the CISG if they agree that the contract is governed by

   (a) "Pennsylvania law"?

   (b) "the law of Germany"?

Problem 27-7.

Draft "airtight" contract language that opts out of the CISG.

C. Contract Formation and Content[13]

The CISG sets out rules on contract formation, interpretation, and implied terms. It also lists some topics that are excluded from the CISG.

1. Contract Formation

The CISG's contract formation provisions appear in Part II (Articles 14-24). These provisions address more of the minutiae of the mutual assent process than does UCC Article 2, which leaves many of those issues to be resolved by the common law. Here, again, you can see the compromises between the civil law and the common law rules. Other compromises were motivated by the challenges of international trade (distance, cultural differences, and communication difficulties).

**Reading the CISG:
Mutual Assent Rules**

Read Articles 14 to 19 and 24.

Question 4. Compare the CISG provisions below with the rules in UCC Article 2 (or, if none, the common law).

CISG Art.	Subject	Significant differences
14(1)	Proposal addressed to specific person(s)	
14(2)	Proposal not addressed to specific person(s)	

---

13 Chapter 3 of this text covers the Article 2 provisions on contract formation and the content of the contract.

CISG Art.	Subject	Significant differences
15(1)	Timing of offer's effectiveness	
15(2)	Revocation overtaking offer	
16(1)	Revocation before acceptance dispatch	
16(2)	When offer is irrevocable	
17	Offer terminated by rejection	
18(1)	Defines acceptance	
18(2)	Timing of acceptance's effectiveness	
18(3)	Acceptance by performance	
19(1)	Rejection and counteroffer	
19(2)	Varying terms in reply to offer	
19(3)	Which varying terms materially alter	
24	When communication "reaches" addressee	

The CISG drafters declined to include a separate provision addressing "the battle of forms." The issue was then still unresolved in some countries, while other countries had reached differing solutions. Instead, the CISG contains a conservatively crafted exception to the mirror image rule.[14] Often, the result is essentially a "last

---

[14]   See John A. Spanogle & Peter Winship, International Sales Law: A Problem-Oriented Coursebook 135 (2d ed.

shot rule"—"the party who last made reference to his conditions will prevail if the other party indicates assent—or is supposed to—under Article 18(3)."[15]

If a Contracting State ratifies the CISG subject to a reservation under Article 92, the Contracting State is not bound by CISG Part II on contract formation (Articles 14-24). The Status table on the UNCITRAL website[16] notes which Contracting States made such declarations under Article 92. Four Scandinavian countries (Denmark, Finland, Norway, and Sweden) made Article 92 declarations, because their contract laws differ so much from the CISG provisions.[17]

Although Article 14 states that a valid offer must specify the price or a means of ascertaining it, Article 55 states that a valid contract without an express or implied price is deemed to include "the price generally charged at the time of the conclusion of the contract for such goods sold under comparable circumstances in the trade concerned" (a result very similar to the "reasonable price" in UCC § 2-305(1)(a)). This seeming contradiction between Articles 14 and 55 has generated considerable controversy and two solutions:

- Minority solution: Give Article 55 precedence over Article 14. Thus, in any case in which the parties clearly intended to form a valid contract without determining the price, Article 55's default rule can be applied to supply the price.

- Majority solution: Give Article 14 precedence over Article 55. Thus, Article 55 can be applied only in the limited circumstances under which Article 14 would not prevent the parties from having formed a valid contract without determining the price. Those situations include the following:

    · Contracts formed by complex clause-by-clause negotiations, without a generally applicable offer and acceptance of the entire contract, so that article 14 is inapplicable;

    · Contracts that the parties clearly intended to form without determining the price and thereby implicitly derogated from that part of article 14, using article 6; and

---

2012); Peter Huber & Alastair Mullis, The CISG: A new textbook for students and practitioners § 4, at 91 (2007); Joseph Lookofsky, Understanding the CISG in the USA § 3.8 (2d ed. 2004).

[15] See John A. Spanogle & Peter Winship, International Sales Law: A Problem-Oriented Coursebook 139 (2d ed. 2012) (quoting P. Schlechtriem, Uniform Sales Law: The Un-Convention on Contract for the International Sale of Goods 56–57 (1986)).

[16] http://www.uncitral.org/uncitral/en/uncitral_texts/sale_goods/1980CISG_status.html.

[17] Joseph Lookofsky, Understanding the CISG in the USA § 3.1, at 45 (2d ed. 2004).

> • Contracts not governed by articles 14-24 because of a contracting state's reservation under article 92, because of the parties' derogation from article 14 , using article 6, or because of a similar effect under usages or practices, under article 9.[18]

Below are three UNCITRAL CLOUT case abstracts[19] of cases illustrating judgments about contract formation issues. The first case deals with the conflict between Articles 14 and 55. In reading CLOUT Case 139, consider the following questions:

(1) Did the tribunal adopt the minority or majority solution above?

(2) What would the result have been, if these parties had implicitly agreed to derogate from Article 14 (see second sub-bullet above)? What kinds of facts might have indicated that agreement?

UNCITRAL CLOUT Case 139[20]

Tribunal of International Commercial Arbitration at the Russian Federation Chamber of Commerce
Mar. 3, 1995

An Austrian firm (claimant) brought a claim against a Ukrainian firm (respondent) for damages resulting from the latter's refusal to deliver a certain quantity of goods. The respondent denied liability on the grounds that no such agreement had been reached between itself and the claimant.

. . . [T]he tribunal noted that, under article 14 CISG, a proposal for concluding a contract should be sufficiently definite. It was considered to be such if it indicated the goods and expressly or implicitly fixed or made provisions for determining their quantity and price. A telex communication from the respondent regarding the delivery of the goods within a specified period indicated the nature of the goods and their quantity. However, it omitted to indicate the price of the goods or any means of determining their price. The indication in the telex that the price of the goods in question would be agreed ten days prior to the beginning of the new year could not be interpreted as making provisions for determining the price of the

---

[18] Peter Huber & Alastair Mullis, The CISG: A new textbook for students and practitioners § 4, at 76–77 (2007).

[19] See the Introduction to this Assignment for an explanation of CLOUT case abstracts. See also http://www.uncitral.org/uncitral/en/uncitral_texts/electronic_commerce/1996Model.html.

[20] Reproduced from the CLOUT project with the permission of UNCITRAL.

goods, but was merely an expression of consent to determine the price of the goods at a future date by agreement between the parties. The claimant, who confirmed the contents of the telex communication, thus expressed its consent to the price of the goods being made subject to further agreement between the parties.

The tribunal also noted that in this particular instance Article 55 CISG, allowing the price of goods to be determined where it was not expressly or implicitly fixed in a contract or where a contract made no provision for determining it, was not applicable since the parties had implicitly indicated the need to reach agreement on the price in future.

Agreement on the price had not subsequently been reached by the parties. The respondent indicated to the claimant that it was not possible to conclude a contract for the specified quantity of goods. Finding that no contract had been concluded between the parties, the tribunal dismissed the claim.

While reading CLOUT Case 445, consider the following questions:

(1) The Court says that it is applying Article 8, but the CLOUT abstract does not articulate the details. What role do you think Article 8 plays in the Court's analysis?

(2) What role does Article 7 play in the Court's analysis?

UNCITRAL CLOUT Case 445[21]

Germany: Bundesgerichtshof (Supreme Court)
Oct. 31, 2001

This decision by the Federal Supreme Court of Germany deals primarily with the incorporation by reference of standard terms into sales contracts under articles 8 and 14 CISG.

The defendant (seller), a German company, sold to the plaintiff (buyer), a Spanish corporation, a used gear-cutting machine for the price of DM

---

[21] Reproduced from the CLOUT project with the permission of UNCITRAL.

370,000. The written confirmation of the order by the seller contained a reference to its standard conditions of sale, which were not attached to the confirmation. These standard conditions of sale contained an exemption clause, which excluded any liability for defects of used equipment.

After delivery, the machine could only be rendered operational with the assistance of outside experts. In its claim against the seller, the buyer sought reimbursement for the costs involved.

In an appeal on questions of law, the main question before the Federal Supreme Court concerned the requirements for the incorporation by reference of standard conditions into international sales agreements. The court first observed that the CISG did not provide any specific rules on the incorporation of standard terms by reference. Thus, the general rules on contract formation, articles 14 and 18 CISG, were applicable. Whether the standard terms had become part of the offer had to be determined in accordance with article 8. The court stated that the recipient of an offer must be given a reasonable chance of considering the standard conditions, if these conditions are to become part of the offer. This requires that the recipient is made aware of the offeror's intention to include the standard terms. Moreover, it also requires that the offeree is sent the standard conditions or otherwise given the opportunity to read them.

The court noted that, due to the differences between the many legal systems and traditions worldwide, standard terms used in one particular country often differ considerably from those used in another. Therefore, knowledge of such terms is vital to the offeree. For a party wishing to rely on these terms it does not constitute any difficulty to attach them to the offer. If the recipient, on the other hand, had to inquire about the standard terms, this would often lead to delay in the formation of the contract, which would be unnecessary and unwelcome to both parties. The court thus concluded that it would contravene good faith in international trade, as embodied in article 7(1) CISG, as well as the parties' duty to cooperate, to request the offeree to inquire about standard conditions and to hold the offeree liable in case such an inquiry was not made. Therefore, standard conditions could only become part of the offer if they were attached to it or otherwise placed at the disposal of the offeree.

. . . .

While reading CLOUT Case 827, consider the following questions:

(1) When and how was the contract formed? Was the invoice part of that contract formation process?

(2) If this title-reservation clause had become part of the contract and had been governed by UCC Article 2, what would its effect have been? See UCC § 2-401 (title).

UNCITRAL CLOUT CASE 827[22]

Belgian company v. First Dutch company
The Netherlands: Court of Appeals of 's-Hertogenbosch
May 29, 2007

A Belgian company sold and delivered a machine to a Dutch company. The invoice sent by the seller indicated that "the goods remain our property until complete payment has been received." The seller utilized general conditions which also indicated that "delivered goods remain the property of the seller until full payment has been received, meaning in particular that the buyer cannot resell the goods or give them as collateral." The Dutch buyer, however, did not pay the entire purchase price and sold the machine to a third company, leasing the machine back from that company. The Belgian seller claimed that the Dutch buyer had acted tortiously towards it by selling the machine to a third party without first paying the entire purchasing price, thus violating the property reservation.

. . . .

The Court of Appeals determined that . . . the question whether the seller and the buyer had agreed on a reservation of property and/or whether the general terms and conditions of the Belgian company and therewith the reservation of property enshrined therein are applicable, must be answered by reference to article 14 and 19 CISG regarding offer and acceptance and to article 8 and 9 CISG regarding the interpretation of the Convention.

It was clear that both companies were in business with each other on a regular basis. It was also clear that the fronts of the invoices sent by the

---

[22] Reproduced from the CLOUT project with the permission of UNCITRAL.

Belgian company to the Dutch company had always indicated that sales were subject to a reservation of property subject to payment of the full purchase price. However, the purchasing contract nowhere indicated that the purchase was subject to such a reservation of property. Article 18(1) CISG provides that neither silence nor failure to respond to an offer constitutes an acceptance as such. The seller argued that the reservation of property was not agreed on silently, but was explicitly referred to on the invoices.

The question thus is whether the Belgian company can invoke the reservation of property against the buyer, despite article 18 CISG, on the basis that they have conducted business with each other multiple times before. In light of the provisions of the CISG, this question must be answered negatively.

Since there was no evidence that the reservation of property was an established practice or usage by which the Dutch company would be bound and since the Dutch company could only have become aware of the reservation of property after receiving the invoice (regardless of whether the reference to the reservation of property was made on the front or the back thereof), it cannot be held that under articles 18, 8 and 9 CISG the buyer had consented to and thus accepted the reservation of property. Therefore, it was never agreed that the machine would be delivered subject to a reservation of property by the seller, and there is no basis for the claim of the Belgian company that the Dutch company acted tortiously towards it. Neither the use of a sale-and-lease-back construction, which is not unusual, nor the refusal by the second company to use the money obtained from the third company to reimburse the first selling company can give rise to a tort. . . .

APPLYING THE CISG

Problem 27-8.

A business in Finland offers 300 smoked hams to a business in Virginia, at a very good price. Before the Virginia business can accept the offer, the Finnish seller revokes its offer. Claiming that the seller remains bound by the offer, the would-be buyer demands damages for breach. Does the CISG govern the issue of contract formation here?

Problem 27-9.

Revisit Problem 5-3(b), to see how it would be solved under the CISG: Sam (the owner of an ice cream shop in Vancouver, Canada) sends an e-mail to Matthew's Dairy (in the state of Washington) using Sam's standard purchase order form, requesting 500 gallons of cream, to be delivered the following Monday. Matthew's Dairy replies with an e-mailed acknowledgement of Sam's purchase order on its acknowledgement form, which includes the standard term, "Delivery due within 48 hours of sending of this acknowledgement form." Under the CISG:

(a) Is Sam's e-mail an offer?

(b) Assuming that Sam's e-mail is an offer, is it accepted by Matthew's Dairy?

(c) Assume that Matthew's Dairy accepts the offer and that the transaction is governed by the UNCITRAL Model Law on Electronic Commerce,[23] which matches the rules in UETA § 15 on this issue (see Assignment 14). Exactly when is the acceptance effective?

Problem 27-10.

Revisit Problem 7-9, but now from a CISG perspective. On July 11, 2013, Great Lakes (in Salt Lake City, Utah) received a catalog for J&J Tomato Farms (in Mexico), which contained a list of the various types of tomatoes sold, prices, and delivery information. Great Lakes completed the order form provided with the catalog and ordered a shipment of 1,800 boxes of grape tomatoes from J&J, submitting the form through the J&J website. J&J shipped the grape tomatoes ordered by Great Lakes

---

[23] http://www.uncitral.org/uncitral/en/uncitral_texts/electronic_commerce/1996Model.html.

on July 13, 2013, to the railroad yard closest to Great Lakes. Great Lakes sent one of its drivers to pick up the shipment. The driver signed a bill of lading for the shipment prepared by J&J, dated July 13, 2013. The bill of lading listed the quantity (1,800 total boxes) of bulk grape tomatoes but did not include a price per unit, and indicated the total amount due was $0.00. J&J also sent Great Lakes an invoice by mail dated July 15, 2013, for $28,710.00, which Great Lakes alleges arrived a week later on July 22, 2013. By the time the invoice arrived, Great Lakes had already received the shipment and distributed the tomatoes to its customers. Both the bill of lading and invoice included the following language, which was not on the order form or in the catalog:

> Interest shall accrue at 1.5% per month (18% per annum) on all unpaid invoices. The buyer agrees to pay all costs of collection, including attorney fees.

Upon receipt of the invoice, Great Lakes did not contact J&J to object to the contractual terms. Both Great Lakes and J&J use attorney fees provisions in their standard invoices, and such provisions are commonplace in the produce industry. This transaction was the first and only transaction between the parties because Great Lakes was not pleased with the quality of the grape tomatoes, having received several complaints from its own customers.

After Great Lakes failed to pay the invoice and J&J's collection efforts proved unsuccessful, J&J filed litigation in November 2014 for breach of contract.

(a) Was a contract formed in this scenario, and if so, how?

(b) Does the contract require Great Lakes to pay attorney fees?

2. Contract Interpretation and Implied Terms

Chapter II of the CISG governs matters of interpretation, as well as writing requirements. Some of these rules will sound familiar to you, but may not exactly match the UCC rules.

**Reading the CISG:
Contract Interpretation
and Implied Terms**

Read Articles 7, 8, and 9.

Question 5. In the table below, fill in the empty boxes. Edit the rule paraphrase in the left-hand column as needed to reflect your understanding of the provisions.

CISG rule paraphrase	CISG provision (be specific!)
Interpret the CISG to promote good faith, the CISG's uniformity, and its international character	
Otherwise, look to applicable general principles or, if none, rules of private international law	
The parties are bound by relevant usages of trade, courses of dealing, and courses of performance (even though the CISG does not use the latter two terms)	
	Article 8(1)
	Article 8(2)
	Article 8(3)

Some CISG articles contain "gapfillers" (default provisions) that closely resemble those in UCC §§ 2-305, 2-308, 2-309, and 2-310, which fill in the details of these obligations if the parties have not agreed otherwise. For instance, Articles 31 and 33 fill in the place, manner, and timing of seller's delivery obligations. Articles 57 and 58 fill in the location and timing of buyer's payment of the price.

3. Topics Excluded from the CISG

Reading the CISG:
Topics Excluded from the CISG

Read Articles 4 and 5.

Question 6. Recall that UCC Article 2 left some topics to be covered by common law—for instance, what constitutes consideration and many of the rules governing offer and acceptance. Similarly, the drafters of the CISG decided to cover only some topics of sale-of-goods contracts and to explicitly exclude some topics. According to Articles 4 and 5, which topics are excluded?

Other law besides the CISG (sometimes other treaties) would decide which country's law would govern these excluded topics.

Note that these excluded topics are distinct from the CISG's rules governing the subject-matter scope of the CISG. Those rules (in Articles 1, 2, and 3) dictate which contracts are completely in or out of the CISG's scope (if the parties' places of business meet the rule in Article 1(1)(a or b)). For any contract within the CISG's scope, you look to Articles 4 and 5 to see which aspects of the contract are not covered by the CISG.

APPLYING THE CISG

Problem 27-11.

A Danish businessman visiting New Orleans cracks two teeth on a pearl in a raw oyster, while eating in a restaurant. He sues the restaurant for breach of contract and accompanying warranties. Is this dispute governed by the CISG?

D. Statute of Frauds and other Writing Requirements[24]

The drafters of the CISG could not craft a unified solution on when to require a contract to be evidenced by a signed writing. As covered in Assignment 9, the statute of frauds for sales of goods originated in British law in the 1600s, but England repealed that statute of frauds in 1954, just as the UCC was being drafted to re-enshrine it in an updated sales law. Thus, even common law jurisdictions vary considerably on writing and signature requirements.

Reading the CISG:
Requirements of Writing and Form

Read Articles 11, 12, 29, and 96.

Question 7. Paraphrase Articles 11 and 29. Then explain how those two Articles are affected by Articles 12 and 96.

APPLYING THE CISG

Problem 27-12.

As you can see from the second sentence of Article 11, the CISG does not contain a parol evidence rule. Under what CISG authority might the contracting parties add such a rule to their contract? Draft specific language that would achieve this effect.

---

[24]   Chapter 4 (Assignment 9) of this text covers the statute of frauds in Article 2. Assignment 8 of this text covers the parol evidence rule in Article 2.

E. Warranties ("Conformity of the Goods")[25]

The CISG texts and many cases refer to this topic as "conformity of the goods" rather than as "warranties." These provisions contain some verbatim passages from the UCC Article 2 warranty rules, but other passages diverge from UCC Article 2.

Reading the CISG:
Warranties ("Conformity of the Goods")

Read Articles 35, 41, and 42.

Question 8. In the table below, fill in the empty boxes. Several of the boxes are already filled in for you.

CISG provision	Type of warranty	Analogous UCC (sub) section(s)	Significant differences
35(1)	Express, implied merchantability	2-313(1)(a), (b) (loosely); 2-314(1)(f)	Express: No requirement of "basis of bargain"; implied: not limited to merchant in goods of that kind
35(2)(a)	Implied fitness for ordinary purpose		Not limited to merchant in goods of that kind
35(2)(b)			
35(2)(c)	Sample or model		
35(2)(d)	Implied merchantability (packaging)		

---

[25] Chapter 5 of this text covers the warranties and disclaimers in Article 2.

CISG provision	Type of warranty	Analogous UCC (sub) section(s)	Significant differences
35(3)	Exclusion of quality warranty	2-316(3)(b)	Focuses on buyer's constructive awareness of any defects, rather than buyer's examination
41			Less detailed but same coverage
42			(1)(a) and (b), (2)(a) are unique to the CISG; not limited to merchant regularly dealing in goods of that kind

While reading CLOUT Case 720, consider the following questions:

(1) Why did the tribunal select the "merchantable quality" interpretation rather than the "reasonable quality" interpretation?[26]

(2) Why did the tribunal select the latter rather than the former interpretation?

(3) In what way did the tribunal end up applying the "merchantable quality" test?

---

[26] For more details about these three interpretations of Article 35(2), see Peter Huber & Alastair Mullis, The CISG: A new textbook for students and practitioners § 6, at 134 (2007).

UNCITRAL CLOUT Case 720[27]

Nederlands Arbitrage Instituut/Netherlands Arbitration Institute (NAI)
Oct. 15, 2002

The core part of the case concerns the interpretation of whether the goods conformed to the contract as being fit for the purposes for which goods of the same description would ordinarily be used. The Arbitral Tribunal also discussed the notice of non-conformity and its addressee and the possibility of refusal and suspension of delivery.

The claimants in this case, several Dutch companies, hereafter referred to as "the sellers," were active in the exploration of offshore gas fields in The Netherlands' continental shelf. The buyer, an English company, was a major international player in the field of exploration, production and refining of crude oil and distribution of oil products and gas. In 1993 and 1994, the parties concluded twelve contracts concerning condensate, a crude oil mix referred to as "Rijn[28] Blend." On June 11, 1998, the buyer informed the sellers that it would not accept the next delivery of Rijn Blend, because, due to high levels of mercury therein, further processing or sales were impossible. On June 16, 1998, the buyer notified the sellers that it would suspend taking delivery until a solution for the mercury problems was found. No solution was found however; therefore, the buyer let some contracts expire and terminated the other contracts. In the meanwhile, the sellers sold the Rijn Blend that was not taken by the buyer to third parties at an alleged loss compared to the contact price.

In May 2000, the sellers initiated arbitration proceedings against the buyer at the NAI (Netherlands Arbitration Institute). The sellers argued that the Rijn Blend, even with increased levels of mercury, was in conformity with the contract since no specific quality requirements were agreed upon. Thus the buyer breached the contract in not taking delivery and suspending its contractual obligations. The sellers claimed damages. The buyer on the other hand declined any liability and stated that the goods were not in conformity with the contract because the sellers knew or should have known that, since Rijn Blend is used in the refinery business, Rijn Blend with such high levels of mercury might cause damages downstream. Because of this non-conformity, the buyer maintained that it was entitled to refuse delivery and suspend its obligations under the contracts.

---

[27] Reproduced from the CLOUT project with the permission of UNCITRAL.

[28] Rhymes with "pine."

Because the contract contained no quality specifications, the Arbitral Tribunal found that the issue of conformity should be decided based on Article 35(2)(a) CISG, which requires that the goods are fit for the purposes for which goods of the same description would ordinarily be used. The Arbitral Tribunal explained that three possible interpretations in this respect exist. The first interpretation requires the goods to be of a merchantable quality. In this view, which is favoured[29] in English common law legal systems, goods are in conformity with the contract if a reasonable buyer would have concluded contracts for the goods at similar prices if the buyer had known the quality of the goods. A second line of thought, derived from civil law, calls for goods of average quality. A third interpretation rejects the merchantable and average quality standard, stating those do not fit in the CISG system, and suggests a reasonable quality criterion.

Interpretations based on the merchantable and average quality norms led to different conclusions in this case. Therefore, the Arbitral Tribunal decided that Article 35(2)(a) CISG should be interpreted according to the reasonable quality criterion. The Arbitral Tribunal found that . . . the reasonable quality test met the terms of Article 7(1) CISG since it did not rely immediately on domestic notions. It also was consistent with Article 7(2) CISG, allowing general principles of CISG as gap fillers. The reasonable quality standard furthermore was compatible with the preparatory works of CISG. Moreover, if Dutch law would be applied in this case, the reasonable quality interpretation would prevail.

The Arbitral Tribunal decided that the Rijn Blend did not meet the reasonable quality norm, because the price the parties agreed upon would not be paid for condensate with increased levels of mercury. Also, no quality issues occurred in the first years after the contracts were closed and buyer could therefore expect a constant quality level of Rijn Blend. Thus the Arbitral Tribunal found that the buyer was entitled to suspend future deliveries according to Article 73(1) CISG, since the contracts were instalment contracts.

However, the Arbitral Tribunal held that the buyer, concerning the June instalment, had not complied with Article 71(3) CISG, which requires an immediate notification of the suspension of delivery. The buyer had spoken to a third party about its intentions to suspend delivery, but this third party had solely been given authority in certain commercial matters. The third

---

[29] This CLOUT case abstract was written by an author who uses British spellings of words like "favoured" and "instalment."

party could not be considered an express nor implied agent of the sellers and therefore discussing the issue with this third party did not constitute a notice as required by Article 71(3) CISG. Consequently, the Arbitral Tribunal confirmed the annulment of the contract with regard to future deliveries, but awarded damages the sellers had sustained with respect to the June instalment.

APPLYING THE CISG

Problem 27-13.

A Swiss seller agreed to sell six machines to a French buyer, which intended to resell them. The machines, as delivered, did not contain labeling necessary for resale under French law, but Swiss law had no such requirements. The contract said nothing about labeling, and no usage of trade addressed the issue. Is the seller in breach of warranty?

Problem 27-14.

Two contracting parties wish to disclaim the CISG's implied warranties of quality. Can they? If so, what drafting language would accomplish that goal?

F. Performance[30]

After some general provisions, Part III of the CISG sets out the seller's performance obligations, followed by the buyer's performance obligations:

- Ch. II. Obligations of the Seller (Art. 30)
    - Sec. I. Delivery of the Goods and Handing Over of Documents (Arts. 31-34)
    - Sec. II. Conformity of the Goods and Third Party Claims (Arts. 35-44)

---

[30]   Chapter 7 of this text covers the performance provisions in Article 2.

The separation between the seller's and buyer's obligations is typical of civil law codifications of contract law. (Contrast it with UCC Art. 2, which unites the parties' performance rights and duties in the 2-300s, 2-400s, and 2-500s.) This Section of this Assignment focuses on the performance obligations, not the remedies.

Chapters II and III begin with overviews of the seller's and buyer's obligations, respectively, in Articles 30 and 53. No surprises here—seller must deliver the goods, hand over the required documents, and transfer the property in the goods; buyer must pay the price and take delivery of the goods.

1. Risk of Loss

The CISG contains default risk-of-loss provisions that resemble some but not all of the UCC provisions on risk of loss.

Reading the CISG:
Risk of Loss

Read Articles 67 to 70.

Question 9. Articles 67-70 set out risk of loss provisions that loosely track parts of UCC §§ 2-501, 2-509, and 2-510. In the table below, fill in the empty boxes. Several of the boxes are already filled in for you.

CISG provision	Analogous UCC (sub)section(s)	Significant differences
67(1), 1st sentence		

CISG provision	Analogous UCC (sub)section(s)	Significant differences
67(1), 2nd sentence		
67(2)	2-501, loosely	Although 2-501 deals with identification, no risk of loss for any of the goods in 2-509 can pass without them being identified
68	None	N/A
69(1)		
69(2)		
69(3)	2-501, loosely	Although 2-501 deals with identification, no risk of loss for any of the goods in 2-509 can pass without them being identified
70	2-510(1), loosely	No mention of insurance deficiency

As noted, the provisions outlined above are merely default provisions, from which the parties can agree to derogate, according to Article 6. What happens, then, if the parties include a shipping term like "CIF"? How will that be understood in a contract governed by the CISG?

Unlike Article 2, the CISG does not contain any shipping terms. Article 7(2) says that issues not expressly settled in the CISG or resolved by its general principles should be settled "in conformity with the law applicable by virtue of the rules of private international law." Article 9(2) incorporates into the contract usages of trade (the customary understandings for international contracts in the particular trade concerned). International shipments almost universally use "Incoterms," a set of shipping terms developed, defined, and periodically updated by the International Chamber of Commerce (ICC).[31] (Recall the discussion of the Incoterms shipping terms in Assignment 16, Section G.) The current version, "Incoterms 2010," includes eleven shipping terms, brief descriptions of which can be found at http://www.iccwbo.org/products-and-services/trade-facilitation/incoterms-2010/the-incoterms-rules/. The details of those terms are available in various ICC publications on the Incoterms. (Your law library may have a copy.) In addition, many international shipping organizations have posted online charts and diagrams depicting the differences among the Incoterms; locate them with a Google images search for diagrams depicting "Incoterms 2010."

So how does this answer the question about the meaning of the CIF shipping term? Recall that the UCC contains a C.I.F. shipping term in § 2-320. However, this term is intended for domestic shipments within the United States. International CIF shipments are likely governed by Incoterms 2010, which also contains a CIF shipping term, but its details differ from the UCC version. Using the provisions in Articles 7(2) and 9(2) discussed in the previous paragraph, courts have held that the CISG impliedly incorporates the Incoterms as a usage of trade.[32] Of course, the parties can expressly agree to a particular version of a shipping term, such as "C.I.F. (UCC)," which would trump any usage of trade. Or the parties can eliminate any ambiguity by agreeing to "CIF (Incoterms 2010)," as opposed to the earlier Incoterms version, which had thirteen terms and some differing details.

Whenever a contract is expressly or impliedly governed by any shipping term (Incoterm, UCC, or other) or agreed-to risk of loss, the CISG's default rules on risk of loss are trumped and do not apply. Nonetheless, you should still know the CISG's risk-of-loss provisions, which apply to contracts that fail to specify a shipping term or do not involve any shipment (such as goods stored in a warehouse and transferred by way of a warehouse receipt).

---

[31] See generally www.iccwbo.org.

[32] BP Oil Int'l v. Empresa Estatal Petroleos de Ecuador, http://cisgw3.law.pace.edu/cases/030611u1.html (5th Cir. 2003).

2. Inspection ("Examination"), Notice of Non-conformity, and Cure

Some CISG articles resemble portions of UCC Article 2 as to buyer's inspection and notice of non-conformity, and seller's cure:

- Art. 38: Buyer's "examination" (similar to inspection under UCC § 2-513)

- Art. 39: Buyer's notice of nature of non-conformity (similar to UCC §§ 2-602(1), 2-605)

- Art. 37: Seller's right to cure if delivery was made early (similar to UCC § 2-508(1))

- Art. 48: Seller's right to cure after the contractual delivery date (similar to UCC § 2-508(2))

Notice that the CISG does not use the concepts of rejection and revocation of acceptance. However, as we will see in the upcoming section on remedies, a buyer can "avoid" the contract in some circumstances and thereby accomplish the same effect—getting the seller to take back the goods, in return for a refund of the price.

APPLYING THE CISG

Problem 27-15.

Revisit Problem 7-1, with a few changes to demonstrate CISG issues. A purchasing clerk at Troy Industries, Inc. (in Detroit, Michigan) uses a standard company purchase order form to order business cards from Annie's Business Printing (in Windsor, Ontario, Canada). On the back of that standard form is a clause stating, "Purchaser has 90 days after receipt of goods to notify us of any lack of conformity." Annie's Business Printing responds with a "Purchase Acknowledgement" saying, "We accept your order, but only if you consent to the terms in our standard contract set forth on the back of this confirmation, by initialing this form and returning it to us." The preprinted terms on the back include one that says, "Notice of lack of conformity of goods must be made within 30 days of receipt." Troy Industries does not send back the Purchase Acknowledgement. It receives the business cards and pays for them. Assume that Troy's purchase order is an offer and that acceptance by shipping is an accepted trade usage.

(a) How long does Troy Industries have to give notice of lack of conformity if it finds an error on the business cards?

(b) If the cards contain an error and if Troy gives the proper notice of that error, does Annie's Business Printing have a right to cure? If so, within what constraints?

3. Excuse from Breach ("Exemption")

The common law doctrine of excuse is known as "exemption" in the CISG. Note that it applies to both buyer and seller.

Reading the CISG: Excuse ("Exemption")

Read Article 79.

Question 10. The CISG sometimes allows a breaching party to be exempted from liability.

(a) What elements must be satisfied in order for the CISG exemption to apply?

(b) Which common law excuse(s) does the CISG exemption most closely match?

(c) In what respects is the CISG exemption doctrine broader than the common law excuse, as applied in the United States?

G. Remedies for Breach[33]

The CISG remedy provisions are organized somewhat differently than the UCC remedy provisions:

- Articles 45-51: Aggrieved buyer's remedies

---

[33] Chapter 9 of this text covers the remedies in Article 2.

- Articles 61-65: Aggrieved seller's remedies

- Articles 71-77: Remedy provisions for any aggrieved party

Reading the CISG:
Articles 45 and 62

Read Articles 45, 62, and skim the Articles mentioned in those Articles.

Question 11. As is true of UCC Article 2, many of buyer's and seller's remedy provisions in the CISG are analogous or even identical to each other. The list of buyer's overall remedies appears in Article 45, and the list of seller's overall remedies appears in Article 61. In the table below, fill in the empty boxes. Some of the boxes are already filled in for you.

Remedies for aggrieved buyer	Analogous remedy provision	Remedies for aggrieved seller
Art. 45	List of remedies	Art. 61
Art. 46	Specific performance*	Art. 62
	Suspend performance	
	Set additional time for breaching party to perform ("Nachfrist notice")	
	Avoid the contract	
	Avoid an installment of a contract	
	Avoid the contract because of anticipatory repudiation	

	Expectation damages, generally	
	Damages from a substitute transaction (cover or resale)**	
	Market damages**	
	Mitigation of loss	

* Subject to the restriction in Article 28.
** If the contract has been avoided.

The CISG contains three remedies (not in the table above) that are available to only one party:

- Art. 50: The buyer can choose the remedy of paying a reduced price for non-conforming goods unless the seller has successfully cured the breach (or buyer has refused seller's offer to cure).

- Art. 51: If the seller makes only a partial delivery or if only part of the delivery conforms to the contract, the buyer has the right to specific performance, to set an additional time for seller's performance, to allow seller to cure, to avoid the contract (if a fundamental breach results), and to reduce the price.

- Art. 65: If the contract requires the buyer to "specify the form, measurement or other features of the goods" and buyer fails to do so, the seller may make the specification (as in UCC § 2-311(3)(b)), but the seller must inform the buyer and give the buyer a reasonable time to specify differently.

The CISG remedies reflect considerable influence from civil law remedies, resulting in some surprising rules for those of us from the common law tradition:

- Availability of specific performance to both buyer and seller (subject to the restriction in Article 28, as well the aggrieved party's duty to mitigate and act in good faith);

- Aggrieved party's right to set a new deadline for the breaching party's performance (known in case law as a "Nachfrist notice"); and

- Aggrieved party's right to "avoid" the breached contract.

The CISG has no analog to the UCC's "perfect tender rule" in § 2-601—the buyer's right to reject for "any defect."

The CISG remedy provisions can be depicted as follows:

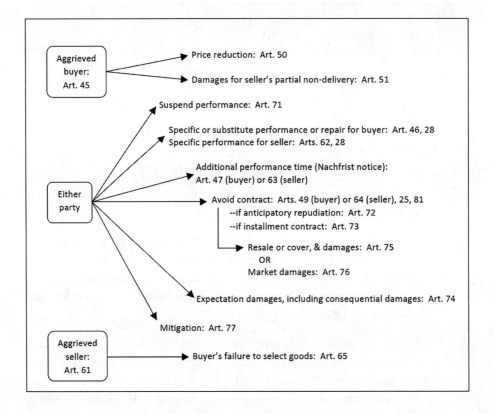

The following CLOUT case abstract illustrates how the CISG provisions on scope, contract formation, performance duties, default, and remedies mesh together. As you read CLOUT Case 480, consider the following questions:

(a) What kind of contract was this, in UCC parlance? Does an offer for this kind of contract satisfy the requirements of CISG Article 14? Does it need to?

(b) How did the court fill in the missing obligation to buy, by the defendant?

(c) Why was there no exemption under Article 79?

UNCITRAL CLOUT CASE 480[34]

Romay AG v. SARL Behr France
France: Cour d'appel—Colmar
June 12, 2001

A French manufacturer of air conditioners for the automobile industry (the defendant) concluded a "collaboration agreement" on 26 April 1991 with its supplier, a Swiss company (the plaintiff). The plaintiff undertook to deliver at least 20,000 crankcases over eight years according to the needs of the defendant's client, a truck manufacturer. The goods were described in a precise manner and the method of calculating the price was fixed for the entire duration of the contract initially envisaged by the parties. Following a sudden collapse in the automobile market, which caused the truck manufacturer to change its terms of purchase radically by imposing on the defendant a price for the air conditioners which was fifty per cent lower than the price of the incorporated components sold by the plaintiff, the defendant declared in a letter of 6 December 1993 its desire to stop using the crankcases manufactured by the plaintiff in the production of air conditioners. As of 31 December 1993, only 8,495 of the 20,000 casings had been delivered. On 19 June 1996 the plaintiff brought an action against the defendant before the Colmar District Court to obtain 3,071,962 Swiss francs in damages.

. . . .

The Court of Appeal . . . . found the CISG to be applicable to the "collaboration agreement." Despite the title of the agreement, the Court defined it as a sales contract under the terms of CISG. The Court stated that the important factor was to determine the actual content of the agreement and to verify whether the parties had entered into the obligations of a buyer

---

[34] Reproduced from the CLOUT project with the permission of UNCITRAL.

and a seller as defined in articles 30 and 53 CISG. The designation of the parties as manufacturer and buyer, the precise determination both of the goods to be delivered and of the method of calculating the price, and the fixing of a minimum quantity of 20,000 crankcases led to the conclusion that the agreement had all the characteristics of a sales contract. The Court recognized that the agreement did not contain any clause expressly imposing an obligation to buy on the defendant. However, "it follows from the general economic balance of the contract—and from the particular stipulation with regard to the obligation to build up inventory—that the delivery obligation expressly contracted by the [plaintiff] entails an implicit obligation on the [defendant] to buy the goods that the [plaintiff] undertook to deliver." Moreover, the court noted that "the obligation imposed on one party to deliver the goods—rather than merely to keep them available—implies the prior agreement of the counterparty to receive the goods at the agreed price and, therefore, the counterparty's undertaking to pay the price of the goods to be delivered."

The Court of Appeal then noted that the defendant had taken delivery of 8,495 crankcases at the time of termination of the contractual relationship. As the defendant had undertaken to receive and pay for 20,000 units, it had not performed its obligations. Pursuant to article 61 CISG, the plaintiff therefore had grounds for claiming damages unless the significant modification of the terms of purchase of the defendant's client could be found to constitute grounds for exemption under article 79 CISG. However, the Court emphasized that this modification, which made it very costly for the defendant to continue incorporating components produced by the plaintiff, was neither exceptional nor unforeseeable in a contract whose duration was fixed at eight years. The court observed that "it was up to the [defendant], a professional experienced in international market practice, to lay down guarantees of performance of obligations to the [plaintiff] or to stipulate arrangements for revising those obligations. As it failed to do so, it has to bear the risk associated with noncompliance."

The Court of Appeal thus concluded that the claim for compensation for the damage was in principle well-founded. However, the Court considered it necessary to carry out an expert evaluation before ruling on the amount of compensation. Article 77 CISG obliged the plaintiff to mitigate the loss. The Court noted that the damage alleged by the plaintiff—the loss of profit and the cost of the raw materials which became unusable—might not have been so great if the inventory had been resold and if the sum invested in the implementation of the agreement could have been amortized in a different way.

As you may have noticed, some CISG remedies apply only if the other party has committed a "fundamental breach," as described in Article 25. Those remedies include the following:

- Buyer's right to require re-delivery: Article 46(2)

- Buyer's right to avoid the contract: Article 49(1)(a)

- Seller's right to avoid the contract: Article 64(1)(a)

- Aggrieved party's right to avoid the contract for anticipatory repudiation: Article 72(1)

- Aggrieved party's right to avoid an installment or installment contract: Article 73(1, 2)

Reading the CISG: Fundamental Breach

Read Article 25 and the related Articles discussed below.

Question 12.

(a) Which common law concept most closely resembles the CISG's fundamental breach? How do these concepts differ, if at all?

(b) Why might the CISG have limited the remedies listed above to situations involving fundamental breach?

(c) Recall from your answers to Question 11 that Articles 47 and 63 allow the aggrieved party to set a new deadline for the breaching party to perform (what the courts and commentators call a "Nachfrist notice"). If the original breach was not a fundamental breach and

> if the breaching party fails to perform by this new deadline, what remedy does the aggrieved party gain, under Articles 49 and 64?

Two types of damages are available only if the contract has been avoided:

- Aggrieved party's right to substitute-transaction damages: Article 75

- Aggrieved party's right to market damages: Article 76

CISG Article 25's definition of fundamental breach has two features:

- A "substantial deprivation" test, and

- An exception for "lack of foreseeability."

The "substantial deprivation" test is usually met in the following situations:

- Delivered goods are so non-conforming that the buyer cannot use them or the goods are not fit for ordinary purposes;

- Seller delivers the goods so late that the buyer cannot use them or has to seek substitute goods before delivery; or

- Either party deprives the other party of the value of the contract by breaching an ancillary duty, such as a non-compete clause or a duty to obtain a letter of credit or bank guarantee.

However, even if the "substantial deprivation" test is met, there is no fundamental breach if the breaching party did not foresee the substantial deprivation that resulted from the breach and a reasonable person in the breaching party's shoes would not have foreseen that result. An easier way to understand this aspect of fundamental breach is to change the lack-of-foreseeability exception into a foreseeability element, so that a fundamental breach requires two elements (one of which is in the alternative):

- Aggrieved party has been substantially deprived of the expected benefit of the contract; and

- Either

    · Breaching party foresaw the result of such a breach; or

    · Reasonable person in the breaching party's shoes would have foreseen such a result.

In this phrasing, the second element is similar to the foreseeability test for common law consequential damages (*Hadley v. Baxendale*), except that it is part of the test for fundamental breach, not a particular kind of damages.

The three following UNCITRAL CLOUT case abstracts illustrate how tribunals apply the doctrines of fundamental breach, contract avoidance, and accompanying remedies. As you read CLOUT Case 282, consider the following questions:

(1)   What does this case add to your understanding of "fundamental breach"?

(2)   After reading this case, what advice would you give your clients who are buyers, if they are entering into contracts to which the CISG might apply?

UNCITRAL CLOUT Case 282[35]

Germany: Oberlandesgeright Koblenz
Jan. 31, 1997

A Dutch seller, plaintiff, delivered acrylic blankets to a German buyer, defendant. The buyer gave notification of the lack of quality of the goods and claimed that five reels of blankets were missing. The buyer also argued that the sale was conditional upon an exclusive distributorship agreement between the parties, which had been violated by the seller. The seller brought an action for the outstanding purchase price and the buyer claimed set-off.

The court held that the seller's claim was justified (article 53 CISG). Lack of conformity includes lack of both quality and quantity (article 35(1) CISG), but the buyer had lost its right to rely on the lack of conformity under the Convention. Although the buyer gave notice that five reels of blankets were missing, it did not specify of which design. As the seller had delivered blankets in different designs, the notice did not enable the seller to remedy

---

[35]   Reproduced from the CLOUT project with the permission of UNCITRAL.

the non-conformity. Therefore, the notification was said to lack sufficient specification (article 39(1) CISG).

As to the sale being conditional upon compliance with an exclusive distributorship agreement, the court stated that, if any such condition existed, which the buyer had failed to prove, the buyer had lost its right to declare the contract avoided as it failed to do so within a reasonable time (article 49(2)(b)(i) CISG). The period of time considered reasonable must be determined in the light of the seller's interest in certainty and whether the seller has to arrange for alternative use of the goods. Even taking into account the time required for consideration, to obtain legal advice, and for negotiations between the parties, eight weeks was held to be unreasonable. These considerations also would apply to the time period within which the buyer could declare the contract avoided due to the lack of conformity of the goods.

Moreover, since the seller had made an offer to deliver new goods, which was refused by the buyer, the lack of quality did not amount to a fundamental breach of contract (article 25 CISG). In considering a breach to be fundamental, account has to be taken not only of the gravity of the defect, but also of the willingness of the party in breach to provide substitute goods without causing unreasonable inconvenience to the other party (article 48(1) CISG). Thus, in the given case, even a serious lack of quality was said not to constitute a fundamental breach as the seller had offered to furnish additional blankets (article 49(1) CISG). Therefore, the buyer was not entitled to damages as it had rejected the seller's offer for new delivery without justification (article 80 CISG). It thereby also lost its right to reduce the price (article 50 (second clause) CISG). The seller was entitled to interest (article 78 CISG), determined according to Dutch law.

. . . .

As you read CLOUT Case 905, consider the following questions:

(1)   If this case were governed by U.S. domestic law, would it fall within the scope of UCC Article 2?

(2)   Which time limits for notice did the court hold that the buyer had met?

UNCITRAL CLOUT Case 905[36]

Switzerland: Cantonal Court of the Canton of Valais
Feb. 21, 2005

The judgement in question, given by default, dealt with the sale of a production plant by a German company (the defendant) to a limited company from Valais (the plaintiff). On delivery of the plant in October 2003, the plaintiff realized that the ordered goods were totally rusted. The defects were immediately reported to the defendant, even prior to assembly. After laying out the equipment and commencing assembly, the erectors discovered that that the plant was not in operating condition. The defendant was offered the possibility of carrying out the assembly itself, against the provision of a security. It did not take up that offer and thereafter gave no further news. In a letter dated 25 November 2003, the plaintiff invited the defendant to take back the plant by mid-December 2003.

The court held that the plaintiff, by its letter of 25 November, had declared the contract avoided within the meaning of article 49 CISG. It deemed the requirements for such avoidance to have been met. The fact that the plant was unfit for operation and the defendant, in violation of its obligations, had failed to put the plant into service constituted, in the court's view, a fundamental breach of contract within the meaning of articles 49(1)(a) and 25 CISG. The court deemed the declaration of avoidance to have been made in timely fashion with the meaning of article 49(2)(b)(i) CISG. It was admittedly difficult to determine the exact day in October when delivery had actually taken place but, given that the defendant had had the possibility of carrying out itself the assembly of the plant following discovery of the defects and that the plaintiff had had survey reports prepared by different persons prior to avoidance of the contract, that time limit had in any event been observed. By giving notice immediately following delivery, the plaintiff had also observed the time limit provided for in article 39(1) CISG.

Since the defendant, despite a further invitation, had never taken back the plant, the plaintiff requested, in addition to the court's cancellation of a bank guarantee in favour of the defendant, authorization to discard the plant. That second request was rejected by the court on the basis of article 81(2) CISG. The plaintiff had a duty to make restitution of the plant to the defendant but the defendant had an obligation to take back the plant at the principal place of business of the plaintiff.

---

[36] Reproduced from the CLOUT project with the permission of UNCITRAL.

A claim for damages by the plaintiff was also rejected since the plaintiff had not sufficiently detailed the loss.

As you read CLOUT Case 747, consider the following questions:

(1) The buyer in the previous case (905) was almost late in giving notice of avoidance. This buyer was too late. Without knowing the precise dates and usages of trade, what fact seemed to have persuaded the court that the buyer gave notice too late?

(2) Which buyer ultimately fared better—the buyer in Case 905 or this buyer?

UNCITRAL CLOUT CASE 747[37]

Austria: Oberster Gerichtshof (Supreme Court)
May 23, 2005

The seller sold coffee machines to the buyer, who resold it to its customers. The coffee machines were defective and several attempts to repair them were made in vain. The defects were so serious that the coffee machines had no commercial value at all. The buyer refused to pay the price, but it had lost the right to declare the contract avoided according to article 49 CISG, as it had not acted within reasonable time. Therefore, it argued that, pursuant to article 50 CISG, it was entitled to reduce the price to zero.

The Supreme Court ruled that article 50 CISG could be applied in cases where the buyer (in principle) could declare the contract avoided according to article 49 CISG and it allowed the buyer to reduce the price to zero if the goods had no value at all.

---

[37] Reproduced from the CLOUT project with the permission of UNCITRAL.

APPLYING THE CISG

Problem 27-16.

In December, Petersen Food Processors (PFP) (in Germany) entered into an agreement with Schwab's Farm (in the Netherlands) for the purchase of lettuce for the next twelve months, beginning in January. Under this agreement, Schwab's would deliver to PFP 15 loads of lettuce on the last day of each month, and PFP would pay Schwab's 4 cents per kilo for the lettuce. (Each load of lettuce consists of 2,200 kilos of lettuce.) PFP sold all of the lettuce it received from Schwab's to a lettuce broker named Seaborg Company, who in turn sold it to Sprain Suppliers, a company that chops and shreds lettuce for the fast food industry (specifically, Burger King, Taco Bell, and Pizza Hut). Schwab's had numerous lettuce customers other than PFP, including the McDonald's fast food chain. In September, when the price of lettuce went up dramatically, Schwab's refused to supply PFP with lettuce at the contract price; instead, it sold the lettuce to McDonald's, which was offering to pay 8 cents per kilo to keep up its supply, which was 2 cents higher than the market price on September 30. PFP entered into a contract with another lettuce supplier for the rest of the year, at a price of 6 cents per kilo. PFP had to pay a "rush delivery" fee of €150 for the month of September, as it had no lettuce, and a sales commission to another lettuce broker of €200 to make the new deal possible. Assuming there are no expenses saved as a result of the breach, what damages should PFP get for this breach?

Problem 27-17.

A South Korean seller contracted with a German buyer to manufacture 3000 photocopier motors for €150,000. After the seller shipped the motors by ocean carrier, the buyer ran into financial problems and apologized profusely but said it could not go through with the order. The seller avoided the contract under Article 64 and sued for damages. Similar motors sell for €60 each, and the seller has found another buyer who is willing to buy the entire shipment for €120,000. What should the seller do?

Problem 27-18.

A Canadian buyer contracted with a Chinese seller for the sale of 2000 tablet computers. The contract called for a 1-terabyte external hard drive with each tablet. The tablets arrived without the external hard drives. The buyer immediately informed the seller of this deficiency and sent the seller an e-mail that stated, "We must have the external hard drives for all of the tablets by no later than 31 May. We will not accept delivery after that date." The buyer can sell the tablets without the external hard drives without difficulty because most other tablets sold on the market do not have an external drive. The seller cannot deliver the external hard drives in time. What remedies does the buyer have?

H. Conclusion

As noted at the outset, this Assignment provides only a brief comparative overview of the CISG, to introduce you to the CISG, its scope, and how it compares with UCC Article 2 and accompanying case law. As you can see from the Problems in this Chapter, some of your commercial law clients will have contracts that are governed by the CISG, and that number is likely to increase in the future. For a more thorough understanding of the CISG and its relationship to other aspects of international commerce, consider taking a course on International Sales or International Business Transactions.

Index

Note on use of the index: This index contains references to pages on which the indicated terms are explicitly mentioned or discussed. Because many concepts appear in the answers to questions and problems, and sometimes not in the related text in the book, the index cannot be used to find every page in the book on which a concept is raised. To identify all the pages on which any given issue appears, the reader of this book should use a combination of the index, the table of contents, and the table of statutory authorities.